NATIONAL UNDER

a division of ALM Global, LLC

THE FUNDAMENTALS OF WRITING A FINANCIAL PLAN, SECOND EDITION

John E. Grable, Ph.D., CFP®
Michelle E. Kruger, Ph.D., CFP®
Megan R. Ford, M.S., CFT-I™

Fundamentals of Writing a Financial Plan, Second Edition provides a totally revised and unique approach to helping aspiring financial planners write a comprehensive financial plan. The book outlines how the CFP Board of Standards, Inc. 7-step systematic financial planning process can be applied when writing a comprehensive financial plan for an individual or family.

The book not only highlights various elements involved in comprehensive financial planning, including estate, tax, cash flow, education planning, and much more—but also introduces important behavioral perspectives and communication techniques. As a way to synthesize these pieces and learn how the plan writing process unfolds, students follow a running case—the Hubble family.

The text features:

- A thorough review of the new 7-step systematic financial planning process.

- A description of the regulatory environment in which every financial planner operates.

- An in-depth discussion of client communication and counseling techniques.

- Financial planning approaches that can be applied to a variety of clients and client circumstances.

- A chapter-by-chapter focus on analytical tools and techniques that can be used to evaluate client data.

- An example of a complete written financial plan with explanations about how analyses lead to the recommendations.

- Chapter-based learning aids, including access to a fully integrated Financial Planning Analysis Excel™ package and other online support materials, including video examples of client communication and counseling strategies.

- Instructions on how to do calculations essential to creating a financial plan.

- Numerous self-test questions to test comprehension of material.

Related titles also available:

- *The Case Approach to Financial Planning: Bridging the Gap Between Theory and Practice*

- *Financial Planning for Senior Clients*

- *Introduction to Investment Planning*

- *Principles of Estate Planning*

- *The Psychology of Financial Planning*

- *The Tools and Techniques of Estate Planning*

For customer service questions or to place orders for any of our products, please call 1-800-543-0874 or mail CustomerService@nuco.com.

The Fundamentals of Writing a Financial Plan

Second Edition

John E. Grable, Ph.D., CFP®

Michelle E. Kruger, Ph.D., CFP®

Megan R. Ford, M.S., CFT-I™

National Underwriter Academic Series

ISBN 978-1-954096-57-8

This publication is designed to provide accurate and authoritative information in regard to the subject matter covered. It is sold with the understanding that the publisher is not engaged in rendering legal, accounting, or other professional service. If legal advice or other expert assistance is required, the services of a competent professional person should be sought. – From a Declaration of Principles jointly adapted by a Committee of The American Bar Association and a Committee of Publishers and Associations.

THE NATIONAL UNDERWRITER COMPANY

Copyright © 2022
The National Underwriter Company
a division of ALM
5081 Olympic Blvd.
Erlanger, KY 41018

Second Edition

Printed in the United States of America

DEDICATION

This book is dedicated to every aspiring financial planner who wishes to increase their professional competencies and skills, particularly when writing and presenting a financial plan to a client.

We also wish to dedicate this book to:

Emily, with love, John

Joey, with love for you and gratitude for the coffee, Michelle

Craig and my family, for all the support, encouragement, and sacrifice. All my love, Megan

TABLE OF CONTENTS

ABOUT THE AUTHORS

JOHN E. GRABLE, PH.D., CFP®

Professor and Athletic Association Endowed Professor of Financial Planning, University of Georgia

Professor John Grable teaches and conducts research in the Certified Financial Planner™ Board of Standards Inc. undergraduate and graduate programs at the University of Georgia where he holds an Athletic Association Endowed Professorship. Prior to entering the academic profession, he worked as a pension/benefits administrator and later as a Registered Investment Adviser in an asset management firm. Dr. Grable has served the financial planning profession as the founding editor of the *Journal of Personal Finance* and co-founding editor of the *Journal of Financial Therapy* and *Financial Planning Review*. He is best known for his work in the areas of financial literacy and education, financial risk-tolerance assessment, behavioral financial planning, and evidence-based financial planning. He has been the recipient of numerous research and publication awards and grants and is active in promoting the link between research and financial planning practice where he has published over 150 refereed papers, co-authored several textbooks, co-authored a financial planning communication book, and co-edited a financial planning and counseling scales book and a graduate-level personal finance book. Since earning his Ph.D., Dr. Grable has served on the Board of Directors of the International Association of Registered Financial Consultants (IARFC), as Treasurer and President for the American Council on Consumer Interests (ACCI), and as Treasurer and board member for the Financial Therapy Association. He has received numerous awards, including the prestigious Cato Award for Distinguished Journalism in the Field of Financial Services, the IARFC Founders Award, the Dawley-Scholer Award for Faculty Excellence in Student Development, and the ACCI Mid-Career Award. He currently writes an economics and investing column for the *Journal of Financial Service Professionals* and provides research and consulting services through the Financial Planning Performance Lab.

MICHELLE E. KRUGER, PH.D., CFP®

Private Practice, Athens Georgia

Michelle Kruger earned her Ph.D. in Financial Planning at the University of Georgia (UGA). She graduated magna cum laude with a B.B.A. in Finance from the Terry College of Business at UGA. After serving as an Assistant Professor of Finance at Loras College, Michelle pivoted to an industry role. She is currently a Senior Financial Planner at Elwood & Goetz Wealth Advisory Group, a fee-only, comprehensive financial planning firm located in Athens, Georgia. Michelle has taught classes in computer applications in financial planning, as well as advanced financial planning seminar courses. Her research interests include financial planning interventions, risk tolerance assessment, and behaviors associated with building wealth. Dr. Kruger also conducts research through the Financial Planning Performance Lab, the nation's only applied clinical facility designed to obtain evidence about the effectiveness of the financial planning process. She also has served as a financial counselor at the Aspire Clinic, an interdisciplinary teaching and research institution, applying marriage and family therapy theories and techniques to her work with financial clients.

MEGAN R. FORD, M.S., CFT-I™

Clinic Coordinator at The University of Georgia

Megan Ford has served as the ASPIRE Clinic Coordinator at the University of Georgia since 2011. ASPIRE is a unit of the College of Family and Consumer Sciences (FACS) and a first-of-its-kind interprofessional training, research, and service center joining together the disciplines of therapy, financial planning, nutritional sciences, and law. Megan leads an unparalleled experiential learning opportunity at ASPIRE for both graduate and undergraduate students through direct service learning and research endeavors, helping the local community and those across the state of Georgia access low- to no-cost services. For her work and leadership, Megan was named one of the College's 100 Centennial Honorees in acknowledgement of her commitment to the ideals of FACS and instrumental impact on student experiential learning. Megan earned her doctorate in Financial Planning, Housing and Consumer Economics from the University of Georgia. Prior to, she completed a Master's degree in Family Studies and Humans Services with an emphasis in Marriage and Family Therapy from Kansas State University. With a unique blend of education, research, and practice experience in therapy and financial planning, Megan has become an emerging leader in the financial therapy field. Her research interests center on couple relationships and money, as well as holistic intervention. She served as President of the Financial Therapy Association's (FTA) board of directors from 2016-2018 and was integral in the development of the Certified Financial Therapist(TM) designation. Serving as a member of the FTA Certification Committee, she continues these efforts of education and training in financial therapy.

ACKNOWLEDGMENTS

The idea for this book came about during a financial planning academic conference. During an informal meeting at the conference, several financial planning students were joined by faculty members from a variety of colleges and universities and a few practitioners. The group met to discuss what resources are needed to help financial planning grow as a profession. An almost unanimous conclusion vocalized by the group was the need for a resource showing how someone new to the financial planning profession can (or should) go about writing a financial plan in a way that aligns with the Certified Financial Planner Board of Standards, Inc. seven-step financial planning process. As academics involved in teaching financial planning classes, we were surprised that no one had written such a resource. We looked at each other and said, "We can do that."

As a team, we have a unique perspective in terms of financial plan writing. One of us is a long-time financial planning university instructor and researcher. Another is a practitioner-scholar who blends experience from practice with an intimate knowledge of the needs and concerns of those learning about the financial planning process. The third team member is a counseling and communication expert who understands how intimidating the writing and presentation process can be. Our objective when drafting chapters has been singularly focused on helping readers understand the essential steps needed to write a comprehensive financial plan. The process that is described in this book is based on the Certified Financial Planner Board of Standards, Inc. seven-step financial planning process. Our experience indicates that the process, while very useful, is often thought of as being too conceptual. We wrote this book with the hope of showing how the seven-step financial planning process can be so much more. In fact, as illustrated throughout this book, the process can be used as a guide when writing a comprehensive financial plan.

Moving from a discussion at a conference to a finished product has been a challenging process. Numerous individuals have been instrumental in keeping us on track, particularly with this revision. First and foremost, we wish to thank our spouses and partners for being patient and supportive during the writing and editing process. We are also grateful for the work and support of our editor at The National Underwriter Company—Susan Gruesser (and our former editor Jason Gilbert). Susan has been nothing but encouraging as we have undertaken this revision to the book, even during periods when we had our doubts. Gratitude also goes to Jay Caslow for encouraging us to revise the book and for Danielle Tralongo for keeping us on schedule. We want to acknowledge and extend thanks to all of the anonymous reviewers who spent countless hours evaluating chapters prior to publication. We are particularly grateful to Sherman Hanna, Michael Halvorsen, David Nanigian, Carolynn Tomin, Joanne Snider, Luke Dean, Ann Woodyard, Kenneth White, Sarah Fallaw, Sarah Asebedo, Stu Heckman, Wookjae Heo, Ruth Lytton, Abed Rabbani, Jorge Ruiz-Menjivar, Joseph Goetz, Amy Hubble, Jerry Gale, Lance Palmer, Swarn Chatterjee, Jamie Lynn Byram, and Kristy Archuleta for their review of chapter materials over the past several years.

Additionally, we are very grateful to our colleagues and their students around the country (and world) who have adopted this book and helped make this project possible, including those at: Angelo State University, Ball State University, Bentley College, Biola

University, Boston University, California Lutheran University, Columbia University, Creighton University, Davenport University, Fairleigh Dickinson University, Florida Atlantic University, Florida State University, Fort Hays University, Franklin University, George Fox University, Golden Gate University, Illinois State University, Immaculata University, Indiana University, Indiana State University, Iowa State University, Kansas State University, Liberty University, Loras College, Metro College, Michigan State University, Montana State University, University of Nebraska, Nevada State College, Nichols College, Old Dominion University, Olivet College, Robert Morris University, San Diego State University, Shepherd University, Suffolk University, Texas Tech University, Transylvania University, University of California Los Angeles, University of Akron, University of Alabama, University of Central Oklahoma, University of Cincinnati, University of Colorado, University of Georgia, University of Houston, University of Missouri, University of North Florida, University of Redlands, University of South Florida, University of Kentucky, University of Wisconsin, University of Minnesota, Duluth, University of North Florida, University of the Incarnate Word, Vancouver University, Virginia Tech, and Western Kentucky University.

Also, we are very appreciative for all the help Ed Morrow of Financial Planning Consultants in Middletown, Ohio has provided over the years, particularly for allowing us to include some PracticeBuilder™ forms and client letters in this book. Similarly, we are indebted to the CFP Board of Standards, Inc. for allowing us to include excerpts from the *Code of Ethics and Professional Standards*.

We are honored to be a part of your learning experience. We sincerely hope that you find the material in this book a benefit to your academic and professional career.

John Grable

Michelle Kruger

Megan Ford

PREFACE

The likely reason you are reading this book is because you are enrolled in an academic financial planning program that is registered with the Certified Financial Planner Board of Standards, Inc. (CFP Board). You may be an undergraduate student, a student studying advanced financial planning concepts in a graduate program, a career changer enrolled in a certificate program, or a currently practicing financial planner who wants to advance professionally by obtaining a nationally recognized certification. You may also be reading this book to learn more about how to write a financial plan to meet the requirements of another certification organization or to gain skills to write your own financial plan. Regardless of your reason for using this book, our hope is that you learn more about applying the financial planning process in your life and the lives of others. Ultimately, our goal is to help you write a well-thought out and defensible financial plan.

The Fundamentals of Writing a Financial Plan, Second Edition came about for two reasons. First, several years ago the Certified Financial Planner Board of Standards, Inc. made a significant change to the educational requirements needed to become a Certified Financial Planner® certificant. CFP Board introduced what is now known as the Financial Plan Development Course requirement. This requirement mandates that anyone wishing to sit for the national CFP® examination must "demonstrate the ability to integrate and apply their knowledge of financial planning topics, as received through the curricula taught by CFP Board-Registered Programs."[1] This led to the requirement that all CFP® candidates complete a Financial Plan Development Course—sometimes called a capstone class. This course, found in all CFP Board registered academic and certificate programs, is designed to be competency-based, which means that "instruction and experiences consist of a body of related skills and knowledge that affect a significant portion of one's performance in a given profession. Through the use of competency-based learning objectives, learner achievement can be quantified against universally accepted performance standards."[2] According to CFP Board:[3]

> The Board's adoption of this new course requirement is recognition of the increasing importance for the educational requirements for CFP® certification to prepare students not only with technical financial planning knowledge, but also the skills to integrate, apply, and communicate this knowledge to their clients. Through this course requirement, future CFP® professionals will have proven their ability to apply the financial planning process to real-life situations, as well as their ability to communicate their planning recommendations to a client.

Being involved in teaching the capstone class, we searched for an appropriate text that would illustrate to students how to write a financial plan in a way that corresponds to CFP Board's mandate. We were disappointed in our search, so we decided to write something that would meet our needs and hopefully the needs of our colleagues who were tasked with teaching a capstone course.

The second reason that prompted us to write this book is that over the course of our academic careers, whenever we have asked a student to write a financial plan, the typical response has been one of reluctance. Few students have ever seen a financial plan, let alone drafted one using Word™ and Excel™. So, imagine how students (and those who teach financial planning classes) often feel when they must write a plan in order to sit for a certification examination, to meet the requirements of a professional organization, or to graduate from college. The situation is even worse for those who are trying to draft a financial plan for their own use or to begin writing financial plans within the context of providing professional financial planning services.

Given the importance of writing financial plans, one would assume that numerous books and manuals exist to help guide a student through the writing process. Unfortunately, this is an incorrect assumption. There are, in fact, few resources someone can turn to that can be used as a guide to writing a financial plan. This books fills this needed gap in the academic landscape. *The purpose of this book is to help readers apply the seven-step financial planning process when writing a comprehensive financial plan.*

This book was written to specifically meet the following learning outcomes that are associated with CFP Board's Financial Plan Development Course requirements:[4]

1. *Demonstrate a comprehensive understanding of the content found within the Financial Planning curriculum and effectively apply and integrate this information in the formulation of a financial plan.*

2. *Effectively communicate the financial plan, both orally and in writing, including information based on research, peer, colleague, or simulated client interaction and/or results emanating from synthesis of material.*

3. *Collect all necessary and relevant qualitative and quantitative information required to develop a financial plan.*

4. *Analyze personal financial situations, evaluating clients' objectives, needs, and values to develop an appropriate strategy within the financial plan.*

5. *Demonstrate logic and reasoning to identify the strengths and weaknesses of various approaches to a specific problem.*

6. *Evaluate the impact of economic, political, and regulatory issues with regard to the financial plan.*

7. *Apply the CFP Board Financial Planning Practice Standards to the financial planning process.*

As noted in the title to the book—*The Fundamentals of Writing a Financial Plan*—each chapter provides a step-by-step guide showing how the financial planning process[5] can be used to obtain needed client data, analyze a client's situation, conceptualize strategies, present and implement recommendations, and monitor outcomes, with the ultimate outcome being a written financial plan.

The chapters in this book are built around the seven-step financial planning process. In order to bring the process to life, each of the core chapters illustrates how a financial plan can be written for a hypothetical client family – the Hubbles. The core financial planning content areas[6] for the Hubble family are examined in this book. Each chapter follows the Hubble family by illustrating the way a client case can be analyzed, evaluated, and assessed with the goal of writing a financial plan. Each of the core chapters follows the same outline:

- Learning Objectives: Student learning outcomes for the chapter.

- The Process of Financial Planning: A step-by-step review of the financial planning process as it relates to a chapter topic.

  o Understand the client's personal and financial circumstances. This discussion provides a summary of important issues a financial planner should examine at the first step of the financial planning process.

  o Identify and select goals. This section provides guidance on ways a financial planner can assess, shape, and select a client's financial goals.

  o Analyze the client's current course of action and potential alternate course(s) of action. This discussion reviews essential analytical tools, models, and procedures a financial planner can use when evaluating a client's current financial situation.

  o Develop financial planning recommendations. This section provides an overview of fundamental financial planning skills and techniques that can be used when developing client-specific recommendations.

  o Present the financial planning recommendations. This section offers insight into ways recommendations can be communicated to clients, both in writing within a financial plan and orally, when discussing financial planning alternatives with a client. Instructors and students can find videos showing how financial planning recommendations can be presented to clients on the book's accompanying website.

  o Implement the financial planning recommendations. This section illustrates the way a financial planning recommendation can be presented to a client that will maximize the probability of recommendation implementation. Strategies within each chapter are presented in a way that will allow a client to understand the "who, what, when, where, why how, how much, and effect on cash flow" for each recommendation.

  o Monitor program and update. This discussion provides guidelines that can be used to help facilitate ongoing monitoring of a client's financial plan and previously made recommendations.

- Comprehensive Hubble Case: For most students, this comprises the outcome focus of each chapter. The case narrative represents what is actually provided to a client as a section or chapter in a financial plan.[7]

- Chapter Equations: This section provides a summary of the formulas one should be familiar with given the chapter topic.

- Self-Test Questions: Five end-of-chapter self-assessment questions are provided in each chapter.

- Self-Test Answers: Answers to the multiple choice end-of-chapter questions are provided in this section.

- Chapter Resources: This section includes materials that a reader may find useful related to the chapter topic.

Four features make this book unique:

1. A running case that flows throughout the book, with solutions illustrated as a written financial plan presented in each chapter.

   A unique and significant feature of this book is the inclusion of the *Chandler and Rachel Hubble comprehensive case*. This case was written to illustrate how the process of financial planning can be followed when developing and presenting a comprehensive financial plan. An example of a written section of a financial plan is presented at the end of each chapter.

   Two objectives guided the development of the Hubble case narrative. The first was to be as comprehensive as possible, meaning that it is difficult, if not impossible, to develop client alternatives for one section of the case without impacting other case sections. Second, the narrative was developed to support both simple and complex strategies and recommendations. This aspect of the case enables students and case study instructors to formulate strategies that encompass the spectrum of available recommendations. The plan illustrations provided in each chapter represent one way (but not the only way) the case can be solved.

   At a minimum, this feature of the book fills a gap in the pedagogical application of the financial planning process. Specifically, the chapter illustrations provide a guide for those who have never seen, yet along written, a financial plan.

2. Forms and spreadsheets that can be accessed through the book's accompanying website.

   The financial planning process promotes the repeated use of financial planning forms and procedures to guide and document the financial planning process. Some financial planners, instructors, and students find the repeated use of tools and techniques useful for framing a protocol to address client issues and questions. Nearly all the forms presented in the book are available on the book's accompanying website as fillable forms for students and instructors to download and complete.

   In addition, a completely new Financial Planning Analysis Excel™ package is available with the purchase of this book. Examples from the Excel™ package are presented whenever the Hubble case is discussed.

3. Video content.

   Numerous videos supplement the book. Practical examples of communication and counseling techniques are available on the book's accompanying website. Each of the core chapters also contain at least one video showing how financial planning recommendations can be presented to clients.

4. Instructor resources.

A number of resources are available on the book's companion website for instructors. PowerPoint presentations are provided for each chapter, as are test bank questions.

It is worth noting another exciting aspect of this text. This book is closely aligned with *A Case Approach to Financial Planning: Bridging the Gap between Theory and Practice, Fifth Edition* (coauthored by John Grable, Ron Sages, and Michelle Kruger). The material presented in this book complements what readers will find in the *A Case Approach to Financial Planning: Bridging the Gap between Theory and Practice, Fifth Edition*. Readers who wish to test their financial planning skills through the case study approach will find *A Case Approach to Financial Planning: Bridging the Gap between Theory and Practice, Fifth Edition* to be a valuable resource. Not only does the companion book apply the seven-step financial planning process to case scenarios, the Financial Planning Analysis Excel™ package is fully integrated into each chapter. Both books are published by National Underwriter.

Our wish, as authors, is that you find the material presented in this book to be interesting, stimulating, and useful. We believe that this text provides everything you need to apply the seven-step financial planning process when writing a financial plan. We wish you great success as your use this book as a starting point in your financial planning career.

John Grable

Michelle Kruger

Megan Ford

Endnotes

1. CFP Board: https://www.cfp.net/for-education-partners/college-degree-certificate-programs/resources-for-registered-programs/capstone-course/criteria-for-the-financial-plan-development-course

2. *Ibid.*

3. *Ibid.*

4. Even though the book matches CFP Board requirements, the concepts, tools, and techniques work presented throughout the text work equally well for other designations, certifications, and regulatory purposes.

5. As will be discussed in more detail later in the book, CFP Board describes the financial planning process as follows:
   1. Understanding the client's personal and financial circumstances;
   2. Identifying and selecting goals;
   3. Analyzing the client's current course of action and potential alternate course(s) of action;
   4. Developing the financial planning recommendations(s);
   5. Presenting the financial planning recommendations;
   6. Implementing the financial planning recommendations; and
   7. Monitoring progress and updating.

6. Core content areas include cash flow and net worth planning, tax planning, life insurance planning, health insurance planning, disability insurance planning, long-term care insurance planning, property insurance planning, investment planning, education planning, retirement planning, and estate planning.

7. The written sections presented throughout the plan provide an example of how a student can use a case narrative when writing a comprehensive financial plan. Each core chapter highlights the type of information needed to conduct an analysis that leads to the development of client-specific recommendations. It is important to note that the example is not necessarily the solution. Different financial planners, using varied experiences, knowledge, and preferences, could realistically provide the Hubble family with different, yet distinct and accurate, recommendations.

ABBREVIATIONS COMMONLY USED IN FINANCIAL PLANNING

Accredited Investment Fiduciary®—AIF®

Alternative Minimum Tax—AMT

American Institute of Certified Public Accounts—AICPA

Assets under management—AUM

Central Registration Depository—CRD®

Certificate of deposit—CD

Certified Financial Planner Board of Standards, Inc.—CFP Board

Certified Financial Planner® Certification Examination—CFP® exam

Certified Financial Planner—CFP®

Certified investment management analyst—CIMA

Certified investment management consultant— CIMC (No longer awarded)

Charitable remainder annuity trust—CRAT

Charitable remainder unitrust—CRUT

Chartered financial analyst—CFA

Chartered financial consultant—ChFC

Chartered investment counselor—CIC

Chartered life underwriter—CLU

Chief compliance officer—CCO

Consolidated Omnibus Budget Reconciliation Act—COBRA

Continuing education—CE

Coverdell education savings account—Coverdell ESA or CESA

Discretionary cash flow—DCF

Employee Retirement Income Security Act of 1974—ERISA

Enrolled agent—EA

Errors and omissions insurance—E&O insurance

Exchange traded fund—ETF

Federal Deposit Insurance Corporation—FDIC

Federal Trade Commission—FTC

Financial Industry Regulatory Authority—FINRA

Financial Planning Association—FPA

Flexible spending account—FSA

Government Accountability Office—GAO

Gramm-Leach-Bliley Act—GLBA

Grantor retained annuity trust—GRAT

Grantor retained unitrust—GRUT

Guaranteed auto protection insurance—GAP insurance

Health Insurance Portability and Accountability Act of 1996—HIPAA

Health savings account—HSA

High-deductible health plan—HDHP

Homeowners policy—HO policy

Incentive stock option—ISO

Individual retirement arrangement—IRA

Investment adviser public disclosure—IAPD

Investment advisor representative—IAR

Investment Advisor Registration Depository—IARD

Investment policy statement—IPS

Internal Revenue Code—IRC

Internal Revenue Code § 529—§ 529 plan

Internal Revenue Service—IRS

Irrevocable life insurance trust—ILIT

Joint tenancy with right of survivorship—JTWROS

Long-term care—LTC

Million Dollar Round Table—MDRT

Minimum required distribution—MRD

Municipal Securities Rulemaking Board—MSRB

National Association of Insurance Commissioners—NAIC

National Association of Personal Financial Advisors—NAPFA

National Association of Securities Dealers—NASD

Nonqualified stock option—NQSO

North American Securities Administrators Association—NASAA

Payable on death—POD

Personal automobile policy—PAP

Personal financial specialist—PFS

Qualified personal residence trust—QPRT

Qualified terminable interest property trust—QTIP trust

Real estate investment trust—REIT

Registered investment advisor—RIA

Required minimum distribution—RMD

Securities and Exchange Commission—SEC

Securities Industry and Financial Markets Association—SIFMA

Securities Investor Protection Corporation—SIPC

Self-regulatory organization—SRO

Spousal lifetime access trust—SLAT

Tenancy/tenants by the entirety—TBE

Tenancy/tenants in common—TIC

Transferable on death—TOD

Uniform Gift to Minors Act account—UGMA account

Uniform Prudent Investor Act—UPIA

Uniform Transfers to Minors Act account—UTMA account

Variable universal life—VUL

Chapter 1

A Review of the Financial Planning Process

Learning Objectives

- Learning Objective 1: Describe how the financial planning process, as established by the Certified Financial Planner Board of Standards, Inc. (CFP Board), serves as a framework for guiding financial planners when working with clients.

- Learning Objective 2: Describe the benefits of utilizing a consistent financial planning process when writing comprehensive financial plans.

- Learning Objective 3: Summarize and explain the steps of the financial planning process.

- Learning Objective 4: Identify what client data is needed to provide financial planning services and explain how the data are collected.

1.1 AN INTRODUCTION TO THE FINANCIAL PLANNING PROCESS

Financial planning is a recognized profession and an important force for positive change in the lives of individuals and families. Starting with fewer than fifty Certified Financial Planner (CFP®) professionals in the early 1970s, the number of CFP® certificants has grown both nationally and internationally. As the profession has evolved, the number of students studying financial planning has also grown.

Professional organizations and leading members of the financial planning community have defined financial planning in a variety of ways. The most recognized definition, offered by the **Certified Financial Planner Board of Standards, Inc. (CFP Board)**, describes **financial planning** as:

> "The collaborative process that helps maximize a client's potential for meeting life goals through financial advice that integrates relevant elements of the client's personal and financial circumstances." [1]

Traditionally, the practice of financial planning has followed what is generally referred to as the financial planning process. As shown in Figure 1.1, in its *Standards of Professional Conduct*, CFP Board describes the **financial planning process** as involving seven steps:

Figure 1.1. The Financial Planning Process.

1. Understand the Client's Personal and Financial Circumstances
   - Obtain qualitative and quantitative information
   - Analyze information
   - Address incomplete information

2. Identify and Select Goals
   - Identify potential goals
   - Select and prioritize goals

3. Analyze the Client's Current Course of Action and Potential Alternative Course(s) of Action
   - Analyze current course of action
   - Analyze potential alternative courses of action

4. Develop the Financial Planning Recommendation(s)
   - Consider assumptions and estimates
   - Consider how recommendation(s) will help the client reach their goal(s)
   - Consider the time and priority of recommendation(s)
   - Consider the degree to which a recommendation integrates with other recommendations

5. Present the Financial Planning Recommendation(s)
   - Exercise professional judgment in determining the best way to present recommendation(s)

6. Implement the Financial Planning Recommendation(s)
   - Address implementation responsibilities
   - Identify, analyze, and select actions, product, and services
   - Recommend actions, products, and services
   - Select and implement actions, products, or services

7. Monitor Progress and Update
    *   Monitor and update responsibilities
    *   Monitor the client's progress
    *   Obtain current qualitative and quantitative information
    *   Update goals, recommendations, or implementation decisions

Financial planners are encouraged to take a comprehensive approach when working with clients. The major subject areas typically included in a financial plan are: financial statement preparation and analysis (including cash flow and net worth management and budgeting), insurance planning and risk management, employee benefits planning, investment planning, income tax planning, retirement planning, and estate planning. When working through the financial planning process, financial planners are expected to follow a consistent, well-defined approach. The following discussion explores each step in the financial planning process and the type of expectations regulators and certification organizations consider when evaluating the quality of financial planning services..

1.2 ESTABLISH AND DEFINE THE CLIENT THE RELATIONSHIP[2]

Although not specifically included in CFP Board's definition, the financial planning process always begins by establishing and defining the scope of the engagement. Engaging with a client is complicated by the need to combine professional, disclosure, and contractual responsibilities with the necessity of developing rapport, or trust, with a new client. When engaging with a client, a financial planner should discuss potential products and services and formalize the scope of the client-financial planner engagement. The relationship usually begins by outlining the responsibilities of both the financial planner and client and the extent of the contractual arrangement. This is known as the engagement. Specifically, conflicts of interest, compensation arrangements, the length of the agreement period, and the products or services to be provided should be fully disclosed and agreed upon. Client engagement activities encompass regulatory, contractual, and professional expectations.

Professional practice expectations and regulatory agencies often dictate how a client-financial planner engagement moves forward. For example, the **Securities and Exchange Commission (SEC)** and state regulatory agencies require that a registered investment advisor (RIA) distribute Part Two of Form ADV—the Uniform Application for Investment Advisor Registration—to prospective clients before, or at the time, an agreement is executed. Similarly, a privacy statement and opt-out procedures for sharing information with nonaffiliated third parties must be provided before an agreement is executed. A privacy statement must be provided annually, and clients must be informed of material changes in ADV Part Two and offered a copy annually.

Once the client-financial planner relationship has been established, a financial planner can then begin the process of financial planning. The steps of the financial planning process are examined in more detail below.

1.3 STEP 1: UNDERSTAND THE CLIENT'S PERSONAL AND FINANCIAL CIRCUMSTANCES

At this step in the process, a financial planner is obligated to obtain appropriate qualitative and quantitative information from a client. Appropriate data is determined by the scope of the client-financial planner engagement. While there are no best practice standards regarding the best way to collect data from a client, many financial planners request that their clients provide copies of source documents that the financial planner can then use to evaluate the client's financial situation. Examples of source documents include current check stubs, savings account statements; prior year tax returns; investment and retirement account statements; life insurance policies; copies of wills, trusts, and other estate planning forms; employee benefit plan booklets; credit card statements; loan information; and insurance policies. Other financial planners ask clients to provide detailed financial information on a client data-intake form prior to meeting with the financial planner. A sample client data-intake form is shown in Appendix 1A.

A financial planner must possess the professional competence to analyze qualitative and quantitative client data, as well as anticipate what additional information will be needed from a client.

Qualitative (subjectively evaluated) client data include:

- Health Status

- Family Situation

- Life Expectancy

- Family Values, Expectations, and Attitudes

- Risk Tolerance

- Risk Capacity

- Wishes and Wants

- Goals

- Goal Priorities

Quantitative (objectively evaluated) client data include:

- Age

- Cash Flow Situation

- Value of Assets and Liabilities

- Current and Future Income

- Current and Projected Tax Liability

- Use of Government Benefits

- Sources of Liquidity

- Availability of Financial and Social and Community Resources

- Insurance Coverages

- Estate Planning Documentation

- Education and Special Needs Documentation

- Retirement Plan Documentation

- Current Financial Plan

1.4 STEP 2: IDENTIFY AND SELECT GOALS

[A] Goals and Objectives

Identifying client goals and objectives requires a financial planner, in consultation with their client, to pinpoint outcomes or accomplishments that should flow from the planning process. Broadly defined, **goals** should give meaning to a client's life and motivate the client to pursue implementation of financial planning recommendations. Depending on the issue considered, a goal can range from the abstract to the concrete. A goal can be thought of as a global statement of a client's intended personal or financial outcome, while an **objective** is a more discrete financial target that supports a goal. The most useful financial planning goals are specific and time-bound, typically consisting of a dollar amount and a time horizon. For example, a client may set a goal of a "comfortable retirement," but only through further discussions and clarification can a financial planner discern a definite objective, based on the client's proposed retirement lifestyle, of accumulating, say, $2.65 million by age fifty-five.

Planning Reminder

Recording a client's goals and objectives is a good way to develop a checklist for further discussion. Furthermore, realistically framing, articulating, and ranking goals can occur only as the client's "dreams" are brought into perspective by the data-gathering and analytical skills of the financial planner. A thoughtful and honest interchange between client and financial planner is necessary to arrive at final goals for the plan—and all parties must realize that goals and the plan are subject to changing circumstances and the vagaries of the future.

Although a client's goals can be framed or defined in limitless ways, goals basically emanate from:

- Wants and needs

- Life-cycle events

- Life transitions

Wants and needs are differentiated by their significance in sustaining life. A need encompasses something one must possess in order to survive (e.g., food, water, shelter), while a want is something desired, but not necessary for basic survival. Though seemingly simple by definition, in practice financial planners may find that clients' perceptions of needs versus wants are less clear cut. For instance, what constitutes acceptable shelter might vary widely from one client to another - one might perceive that simply a roof overhead and four walls is "needed" shelter, whereas another may consider a home with a list of comforts to be a need.

Life-cycle events represent biological, socioeconomic, or sociocultural events that occur over a lifetime. Life-cycle events can guide the establishment of goals, and in some cases, be influenced by the completion of goals. Life transitions are also associated with the process of identifying new goals, modifying existing goals, or changing the hierarchy of goals. Mitch Anthony, a financial planning thought leader, defines a **life transition** as a change in a client's life that is occurring in the present or expected to occur in the near future.[3] Perceived wants and needs, life-cycle events, and life transitions are not mutually exclusive and each, individually or jointly, can play a role in the way goals are established and managed.

The communication skills required to fully identify and frame goals can sometimes be challenging. Financial planners play an important role in their clients' lives by helping clients identify nuances and subtle priorities among goals. Recognizing and examining relationships among goals and objectives provides a deeper understanding of a client's situation. Reviewing goals also ensures that what a client would like to accomplish is, in fact, feasible and actionable. It is worth remembering that many times, a goal may be easily defined even when the means to achieve the goal are not available. In these situations, such a goal can be classified as a 'future' goal.

Financial planners and clients should view goals holistically. Goals can be independent, interrelated, or interdependent. The best solution for one goal may have a deleterious effect on achieving another goal. For interrelated goals, the first goal might have to be fulfilled as a prerequisite to fulfilling the second goal. As an example, a client may need to accomplish securing a down payment of $35,000 (goal 1) and a mortgage loan (goal 2) before actually purchasing a home (goal 3).

Goals are typically categorized by a **time horizon** for accomplishment:

- **Short-term** goals can be accomplished in less than two years.

- **Intermediate-term** goals may require two to ten years to accomplish.

- **Long-term** goals, such as preparing for retirement, take more than ten years and can require effort over several decades.

The use of a **personal goal hierarchy** or ranking system is a best practice. Some clients can easily prioritize their goals. Others find prioritization difficult. In cases where a client has several equally important but somewhat conflicting goals, ranking becomes significantly more problematic. Of course, the ranking of goals may not be an issue if sufficient funding is available; however, this is rarely the case. Just because goals can be ranked does not necessarily mean that the highest-ranking goal should be dealt with first. Client goals, and the corresponding recommendations developed to help a client reach their goals, can be moderated by a financial planner's professional judgment and knowledge of their client's unique situation.

[B] Determine What Client Data are Collected

Financial planners are regularly challenged to gain enough information in order to develop a full picture of a client's personal and financial situation, to assess the client's situation, to generate a workable plan of action that is acceptable to the client, and to do so effectively and efficiently. As if this is not sufficiently challenging, it is important to remember that many people find talking about money to be difficult or uncomfortable, which can create additional challenges during data collection.

There are four client-specific factors that characterize clients. Each one can influence a client's relationship with their money. Three of the factors also characterize financial planners—as both individuals and professionals. These factors are:

1. *Temperament and Personality.* **Temperament** is commonly explained by inherited cross-cultural traits that characterize mood or disposition. Behavioral, emotional, and attitudinal tendencies comprise **personality**. Together, these dimensions provide a profile of individuals and offer insights into a client's relationships with others and money. For example, an extroverted client who is talkative, free-spirited, and spontaneous will likely have a very different view of retirement than an introvert who is organized, disciplined, and enjoys a quiet home life. An anxious client who lacks organization and tends to avoid financial decisions might be easily distracted from focusing on financial goal achievement. Clients who exhibit less organization and focus may require more financial planner and staff time to collect needed data. These clients might also require more external motivation to implement recommendations.

2. *Attitudes, Beliefs, Values, and Behaviors.* Attitudes, beliefs, values, and behaviors are interrelated concepts in that attitudes and beliefs are thought to affect behavior. **Attitudes** reflect an individual's views, opinions, desires, choices, purposes, and values. Although the concept of belief prompts different meanings, **beliefs** are recognized as a type of attitude because a belief reflects an interpretation, expectation, or claim about some aspect of life. Beliefs indicate an individual's perception of what is right or desirable. **Values** reflect an individual's fundamental meaning or interpretation of life, and as such are a noteworthy influence on client goals and choices. Gaining an understanding of a client's values and beliefs about money is essential to building trust and outlining relevant financial recommendations. It is also worth noting that attitudes, beliefs, and values are not set in stone. Rather, engaging in the financial planning process may invite shifts in the client's perspectives and behaviors. Therefore, continuing to be mindful of this factor, particularly in long-term financial planning engagements, is key to financial planning outcome success.

All individuals are impacted by their relationship with money, whether a client or a financial planner. With this in mind, financial planners are encouraged to consider how their own attitudes, beliefs, values, and behaviors might influence the recommendations they make to clients. It is impossible to remain "neutral," as money is so often intertwined with one's thoughts, daily habits, and even someone's identity. However, maintaining an awareness of one's own relationship with money and the effect of this relationship on the financial planning process is important.

Financial planners also need to develop mechanisms for the purposes of learning more about client attitudes. This is typically accomplished through assessments. Though various attitudes related to financial well-being, economic trends, or market returns can be assessed, a client's financial risk tolerance is one attitude frequently assessed. In fact, it is a required assessment from which to base investment recommendations. **Financial risk tolerance** is defined as the maximum amount of risk a client is willing to take when faced with a choice that is uncertain and entails the possibility of a financial loss. Appendix 1B shows the types of questions that can be asked when evaluating a client's risk tolerance.

Financial risk tolerance influences a wide range of financial decisions beyond the obvious application to investments where questions of client **best interest** and **suitability** are typical and assessment of risk tolerance is required by regulators. To assess risk tolerance, some financial planners use scales included in financial planning software or tools provided by their broker-dealer or custodian. Other financial planners purchase tests from independent firms or rely on publicly available risk scales, such as the popular Grable and Lytton Risk-Tolerance Scale.[4]

Considered in the context of portfolio management, risk tolerance centers on a client's reactions to, or level of comfort with, losses in investment value. A client's risk tolerance can also influence decisions concerning mortgages, debt levels, emergency funds, choices of insurance coverage, tax preparation approaches, and/or estate planning tools. A client who exhibits a high risk tolerance can be expected to take greater risks and act with less information than someone with less risk tolerance. Those who are risk averse often require more certainty before making financial decisions.

3. *Financial Knowledge and Experience.* Within a client-financial planner relationship, **financial knowledge** and **financial experience** can be quite different between client and financial planner. Both parties bring varying levels of knowledge and experience to the planning engagement. Some clients lack knowledge, while others may have the knowledge, but lack confidence, and want a financial planner to confirm that their "financial situation is okay". Professional responsibility constrains financial planners to offer services within the purview of their acknowledged expertise. Not only must a financial planner stay within their scope of expertise, but they must also provide guidance that is suitable and based on a client's knowledge, experience, and **risk capacity** (i.e., the financial ability of a client to withstand a potential financial loss). Some recommendations will almost certainly include products or services about

which a client lacks experience or knowledge. In such cases, it becomes even more important to educate clients about the risks and benefits of such products and services.

4. *Socioeconomic Descriptors.* Socioeconomic descriptors represent a broad range of factual or quantitative characteristics that can be used to describe a client. Categories of information include the **demographic profile** of a client's household, including relevant medical history or other factors that can influence client goals, financial data (e.g., income, assets, liabilities, insurance coverage, etc.), and a description of a client's lifestyle. **Lifestyle factors** can include travel expenditures, hobbies, collectible interests, leisure activities, personal property preferences, and/or real estate that supports the client's lifestyle.

Gathering client data needed for a thorough and defensible evaluation of a client's situation—whether for a single-issue analysis, to support a product sale, or to complete a comprehensive plan—may appear intrusive, but in practice, these data provide a necessary foundation for future steps in the financial planning process.

[C] Limitations Associated with the Data Collection Process

Clients and financial planners enter a financial planning engagement with unique temperament, personality, attitude, belief, financial knowledge, and experience characteristics. These factors shape how a financial planner works through the financial planning process. Without specific training, or involvement by a psychologist or a financial therapist as a part of the planning team, a financial planner's experience may be the best guide when working with the range of temperaments, personalities, attitudes, values, knowledge, and experience that clients bring with them. The more a financial planner knows about a client, the greater the likelihood of developing a plan that will accommodate the client's unique situation. A financial planner's role is to collect and objectively evaluate client data. However, three limitations must be acknowledged.

Limitation 1. First, regardless of all efforts to function as objective and independent professionals, financial planners are constrained by their own personal temperament, personality, attitudes, beliefs, values, financial knowledge, and experience. These personal attributes often act as lenses, directly and indirectly influencing the way a financial planner views and works with clients. As such, care must be taken to minimize the impact of personal feelings, interpretative judgments, subjective inferences, blind spots, and opinions. Rather than taking steps based on one or more assumptions, all interpretations should be confirmed with the client.

Limitation 2. A financial planner is privy only to the information that a client is willing to share. Clients may knowingly withhold information from lack of trust or unknowingly because the information is thought to be irrelevant or overlooked. Without a client's full disclosure, a financial planner will be constrained when making recommendations. It is incumbent on financial planners to make every attempt to encourage clients to share as much relevant information during the financial planning engagement as possible.

Limitation 3. As professionals, financial planners must fully acknowledge their own expertise limitations, **conflicts of interest**, and threats to professional judgment. Steps should be taken to mitigate such issues in the professional engagement. Typically, providing services as a **fiduciary**—someone who places a client's needs above their own at all times—and providing full disclosure of conflicts of interests provides a way to deal with potential conflicts.

[D] Procedures for Collecting Data

Several methods can be used to collect client data. Accuracy and security are primary concerns. As noted earlier, financial planners must strive for professional objectivity and maximum accuracy when collecting and recording client data (either in the form of a data gathering questionnaire or directly from source documents). Care also must be taken to ensure, to a reasonable extent, that the client is candid and forthright when disclosing appropriate data. This points again to the importance and development of planner-client trust. The most effective financial planners develop secure systems for collecting, organizing, and managing data throughout the financial planning process, as well as safeguarding these data for the future. Three data collection approaches are considered below:

1. *Supporting Documents.* Original **source documents** can be used to acquire and to verify information provided by the client. Clients can also authorize a financial planner to obtain data from other financial service professionals. For example, it may be appropriate to request tax forms from a client's CPA or legal documents from a client's attorney. Such requests generally must be made in writing. Care must be taken to safeguard all documents, and the client's privacy, and to return original documents quickly after electronic scanning or copying. Customer Relationship Manager (CRM) software can be very helpful in tracking when documents were received, assigning activities to use the documents as needed, and reminding financial planner staff to return these documents in a timely manner.

2. *Client Data-Intake Form.* Although not all financial planners use a formalized **client data-intake form** or **data collection questionnaire**, such forms provide several benefits. First, because data gathering can be somewhat subjective, it is a good policy to complete an objective data collection questionnaire with every client. To the extent a questionnaire is completed with accuracy and candor, a well-designed form or questionnaire can capture a client's quantitative and, to a more limited extent, qualitative information. Second, a form can reduce professional liability claims from clients, family members, or legal entities. Financial planners who document client responses objectively and definitively are usually better prepared to defend themselves against claims of professional misconduct. Third, the consistent use of a standard form can help a financial planner pinpoint a client's financial strengths and weaknesses, as well as attitudes or expectations that can affect the client-financial planner relationship. When utilized appropriately, the use of a client data-collection questionnaire provides a framework for summarizing a client's goals, attitudes, and financial profile, all of which are needed to write and communicate a comprehensive financial plan.

A client data-intake form can be completed in a number of different ways. A data-intake form may be provided to a client either as a hard copy or in electronic format. Software has been created to assist financial planners with collecting data in an efficient and systematic manner. Some software programs even allow financial planners to make customized data-intake forms that clients complete online. Once the client has completed the requested information, the financial planner can have the information transferred to a financial planning software platform or CRM software, shortening data entry time and decreasing the risk of data entry mistakes.

3. *Guided Client-Financial Planner Interviews.* The purpose of a client data-intake form is to facilitate the collection of accurate quantitative and qualitative client data. Often, however, these forms lack the flexibility to document a client's goals, attitudes, values, dreams, concerns, fears surrounding money, or the role of money in a client's life. This is the reason why nearly every financial planner incorporates interviews into the data gathering process. A **focused interview** is an excellent way to explore a client's feelings, experiences, perceptions, attitudes, and knowledge. The concept of a focused interview is borrowed from social science research, where a set of questions guides the interview, but the order of the questions, their wording, and the follow-up probes and interviewer responses can be adapted by the interviewer. The interview is focused on learning about the client's **experiential map**, as defined by their feelings, experiences, views, or knowledge, whereas a standardized interview tends to be formally structured, like the client data-intake form, to collect specific quantitative data.

1.5 STEP 3: ANALYZE THE CLIENT'S CURRENT COURSE OF ACTION AND POTENTIAL ALTERNATIVE COURSE(S) OF ACTION

The third step in the financial planning process involves analyzing and evaluating a client's current situation and course of action. The analysis should begin by determining whether a client is on course to meet their financial goal(s) without additional financial planning.

One way to visualize this step in the process is to imagine that a client has engaged the services of a financial planner by the hour to complete a cash flow and net worth statement. The client may need these documents as evidence for a loan or simply to determine how they are doing in relation to making progress towards a particular financial objective. To attend to step three in this example, a financial planner would use client-provided data, without projections of future income, expenses, assets, or liabilities, to complete a cash flow and net worth statement. These documents would then represent the client's current situation. The analysis could also include documenting how the client's goals align with their current financial situation, noting any possible threats or opportunities.

Many financial planning practitioners view the step of analyzing and evaluating a client's financial situation as the essence of financial planning. The realities of a client's income and expenses, net worth, financial products owned, and financial strategies employed to date are examined during the third and fourth steps of the financial planning process. From the narrowest viewpoint, these steps tend to be fact based and solution oriented. But central to the evaluation of a client's situation is the need to understand how client-specific characteristics shape the evaluation process.

It can take years of study and practice to fully comprehend the nuances and complexities of conducting a thorough analysis and evaluation of a client's situation. Mastering this skill is a financial planning challenge built upon known facts about a client, inferences gleaned from the client-financial planner relationship, and assumptions that should be mutually agreed upon by a financial planner and client. Too often, a "solution-focused" financial planner overemphasizes quantitative analyses. A best practice is to use a client's goals and related planning assumptions to guide an evaluation. By knowing a client's specific goals and using the assumptions agreed on with the client, a financial planner can better anticipate, determine, and quantify planning needs. Then, in conjunction with the client, a course of action offering the best risk-adjusted probability of success can be identified.

The analysis of a client's current financial situation requires a financial planner to review and distill all the information collected about a client's situation in the context of the tax, economic, political, and legal or regulatory environment. A current situation analysis is designed to answer four questions in the context of each core financial planning content area:

1. *What is the client's financial planning need?* Financial planning needs can range from a discrete financial question or issue involving one core content planning area to an extensive review of all a client's financial matters. The determination, or identification, of a planning need is typically based on a financial planner's professional judgment and familiarity with a client's situation in consultation with the client. Both quantitative and qualitative data are considered to identify both known and unknown needs. For example, currently known or identified financial needs might cross several different core content planning areas. The review can also reveal other unknown or unrecognized needs that could affect the client presently or in the future. For example, a forty-five-year-old client might be strongly committed to purchasing a long-term care insurance policy—now or in the future—because of a foreseen need created by a family history of Alzheimer's disease.

2. *What assumptions are relevant to the client's financial planning need?* **Assumptions** are inferences based on premises, reasoned conclusions, facts, or circumstantial evidence that affect a client's planning need and the quantification of that need. For example, historical stock market returns, recent inflationary increases in the cost of higher education, and average skilled nursing home costs are supported by factual data and can be included in the quantification of a client's needs. These assumptions, and many others, reflect current or projected data related to tax, economic, political, and regulatory environments. Other assumptions reflect a client's personal situation (e.g., the assumed need for long-term care insurance, the likelihood of a child receiving college scholarships or fellowships, or life span projections). Assumptions must be fully disclosed, mutually agreed upon, and realistic.

3. *Can the client's financial planning need be quantified?* Technical expertise, computations, and other analytical tools should be used (where applicable) to objectively analyze and quantify a client's financial need. For some core content planning areas, such as estimating life insurance needs, several recognized approaches are available and supported by software applications. The quantification of other needs (e.g., the need for long-term care insurance protection) can be more difficult to calculate and defend because of multiple seemingly unrelated factors, such as the client's projected net worth or the daily benefit amount for future medical care.

4. *How is the financial planning need currently being met?* A financial planner must document planning efforts currently in place to meet identified needs or the absence of any efforts on the part of a client to address needs. This should be followed by a thorough and objective assessment of the products and strategies currently in use to meet current and future needs. Results of this evaluation can reveal needed changes or validate a client's approach and show that no changes are warranted.

Client data should provide the following insights whenever a client's current situation is evaluated:

- An awareness of a client's temperament, personality, motivations, risk tolerance, financial knowledge, experience, and perceived level of current financial success. Based on this information, a financial planner can begin to develop recommendations by focusing on strategy, recommendation, and implementation questions that relate to *who* and *why*, as well as *for whom, what,* and *how*.

- Clarification on mutually agreed-upon definitions of client goals, planning objectives, and desired outcomes from the financial planning process. A financial planner can begin to answer recommendation and implementation questions associated with *why, what, when,* and *for whom*.

- For each of the core content planning areas—cash flow and net worth management, income taxes, risk management (e.g., life, health, disability, long-term care, property, and liability), investments, education or other special needs planning, retirement planning, and estate planning—a financial planner can begin to answer other recommendation and implementation questions: *why, what, when, where, how,* and *how much*.

Once the client's current financial situation has been documented, a financial planner should identify strengths and weaknesses associated with the client's situation. Once these have been identified, a financial planner—working at this step of the financial planning process—should begin to consider appropriate potential recommendations. The purpose of preliminarily developing recommendations is to identify strategies that will help the client maximize goal achievement.

1.6 STEP 4: DEVELOP THE FINANCIAL PLANNING RECOMMENDATION(S)

The fourth step in the financial planning process involves selecting and formalizing the strategies that will be recommended to a client. Once an analysis of a client's financial situation has been completed in the context of the economic environment, a financial planner should possess a clear understanding of the issues to be addressed, and thus be ready to proceed to recommendation development. The process of analyzing a client's situation focuses on the identification of possible strategies or alternatives available to meet a client's needs and goals. With the results of a quantitative and qualitative analysis complete, a financial planner can begin to fully answer the strategy, recommendation, and implementation questions of *why, when, where, how much, how,* and *by whom.*

Strategies reflect the universe of solutions that can apply to a client's situation. Strategies represent a financial planner's array of tools, techniques, solutions, and answers that can be applied to help a client reach their financial goal(s). Strategies can be categorized as either product or procedural. A **product strategy** reflects the use of a specific type of product or product feature to meet a financial planning goal or need. A **procedural strategy** emphasizes a process, service, or type of ownership, rather than a product. Product and procedural strategies should be identified for each of the core content planning areas.

With strategies identified, a financial planner can more easily match recommendations to a client's need(s). It is worth noting that client-centered recommendations often need to be altered or combined as a financial planner weighs the advantages and disadvantages of each potential recommendation while considering the probable outcomes and effects on a client's situation. As a financial planner attempts to align recommendations with a client's goal(s), the total cost of the recommendations must be compared to the available cash flow or other assets available to fund the recommendations. A fundamental rule of financial planning is never recommend a strategy that cannot be funded or has a high probability of becoming underfunded in the future.

The process of separating, distilling, and integrating client characteristics, financial planner preferences, and strategies often results in the development of one or more client-centered recommendations that defines the scope of the financial planning engagement. This is true whether a financial planner is developing a comprehensive plan or a financial plan that targets a single issue. Recommendations should offer the client cost-effective, adaptable alternatives. Contingent on the scope of the engagement, and the degree of specificity implied in the arrangement, recommendations should address the following implementation questions:

- Who should implement the recommendation?

- What should be done?

- When should the recommendation be implemented?

- Where should the client (or other party) implement the recommendation?

- Why should the recommendation be implemented? Why is it important to the client's financial future?

- How should implementation take place?

- How much should be purchased, saved, or invested to implement the recommendation? Specifically, what is the cost of the recommendation?

These questions may seem overly simplistic to be meaningful. Answering all seven may seem unnecessary. However, the systematic use of these questions is known to be an effective way to frame recommendations. The use of these questions, as a recommendation development rubric, can be a powerful tool for two reasons. First, careful consideration of these questions helps a financial planner reconsider the logic of each recommendation and its consistency with a client's goals and situation. Second, the rubric helps financial planners meticulously consider and articulate funding and other implementation issues critical to sound plan development and motivated client action.

Figure 1.2 shows a **Planning Recommendation Form**. This form can help financial planners focus on the essential issues to include in an actionable recommendation. This useful planning tool summarizes the answers to the seven critical recommendation questions of *who, what, when, where, why, how*, and *how much* into one document. When initially identifying possible recommendations, the form is useful for summarizing and projecting the costs and benefits of recommendations. As a plan develops, it may be necessary to combine, sort, and rank recommendations from other core content planning areas. The forms can quickly be revised for each recommendation. Once finalized, the forms can be used to document information for financial planning staff or to communicate information to a client. Possibly one of the most beneficial uses of the form is to document the titling of assets and beneficiary designations.

Figure 1.2. Planning Recommendation Form.

Financial Planning Content Area				
Client Goal				
Recommendation No.		**Priority (1–6) lowest to highest:**		
Projected/Target Value ($)				
Product Profile				
Type				
Duration				
Provider				
Funding Cost per Period ($)				
Maintenance Cost per Period ($)				
Current Income Tax Status	Tax-qualified		Taxable	
Projected Rate of Return				
Major Policy Provisions				

Procedural Factors				
Implementation by Whom	Planner		Client	
Implementation Date or Time Frame				
Implementation Procedure				
Ownership Factors				
Owner(s)				
Form of Ownership				
Insured(s)				
Custodial Account	Yes		No	
Custodian				
In Trust For (ITF)	Yes		No	
Transfer on Death (TOD)	Yes		No	
Beneficiary(ies)				
Contingent Beneficiary(ies)				
Proposed Benefit				

To summarize, a recommendation may be as simple as suggesting that a client continue their current course of action. More often, however, recommendations will involve having a client do something new. Recommendations should include the following elements:

1. A summary of the assumptions and inputs used to arrive at the strategy.

2. How the recommendation will help the client meet their goal(s).

3. How implementation of the recommendation will materially influence the client's financial and personal circumstances.

4. How the recommendation integrates with other elements of the client's financial plan.

5. A review of the timing and priority of a recommendation.

6. A description of the way in which the recommendation should be implemented.

1.7 STEP 5: PRESENT THE FINANCIAL PLANNING RECOMMENDATION(S)

The fifth step in the financial planning process involves communicating the advantages and disadvantages of each recommendation to the client. This step in the financial planning process should be focused on describing why one or more recommendations is appropriate in helping a client reach their goal(s). Any conflicts of interest, actual or perceived, should be reviewed with the client at this point.

1.8 STEP 6: IMPLEMENT THE FINANCIAL PLANNING RECOMMENDATION(S)

Although each step of the financial planning process is important, the sixth step is of primary consequence. Without client engagement and recommendation implementation, each of the previous steps in the financial planning process add up to wasted effort. Four elements should accompany an implementation plan:

1. Defining who is responsible for implementation.

2. Identifying and selecting appropriate actions, products, and/or services.

3. Describing the process of implementation in a specific and actionable manner.

4. Describing any real or potential conflicts of interest.

Generally, three implementation options exist. First, a client may be tasked with implementation. Second, a financial planner may be the person to implement a recommendation, or third, an outside party may be called upon to help a client implement a recommendation. Regardless of the method of implementation, a financial plan should not be communicated in a way that limits recommendation implementation solely to the financial planner or a third party. Although it is unlikely that a client will implement recommendations on their own, recommendations should be presented in a way which enables most clients to implement them independently.

1.9 STEP 7: MONITOR PROGRESS AND UPDATING

The last step in the financial planning process focuses on determining who and how implemented recommendations will be monitored and updated. Generally, a financial planner will be responsible for ongoing monitoring unless a client or outside party takes on this responsibility explicitly within the client-financial planner engagement, or unless the monitoring activity is outside a financial planner's scope of practice. Five factors should be determined, discussed, and agreed upon with a client:

1. Which actions, services, and/or products will be or will not be reviewed by the financial planner.

2. How often ongoing monitoring and updating will occur.

3. The client's responsibility in informing and updating the financial planner about new qualitative and quantitative data.

4. The financial planner's legal and professional responsibility to inform the client of necessary information.

5. How often financial planning recommendations will be updated.

As generally understood, a financial planner is under a professional obligation to search for and evaluate new client-specific data, both qualitative and quantitative, as well as review and anticipate changes in environmental factors, including inflation, rates of return, and tax rates, when conducting ongoing recommendation and plan monitoring. The ultimate objective, at this stage of the financial planning process, is to ensure that a client is progressing toward goal achievement. If goal achievement appears problematic, appropriate action must be taken.

Figure 1.3 illustrates how the financial planning process is circular in nature, with ongoing monitoring continually informing the type of information a financial planner must obtain to ensure that a client is moving toward goal achievement.

Figure 1.3. The Circular Nature of the Financial Planning Process.

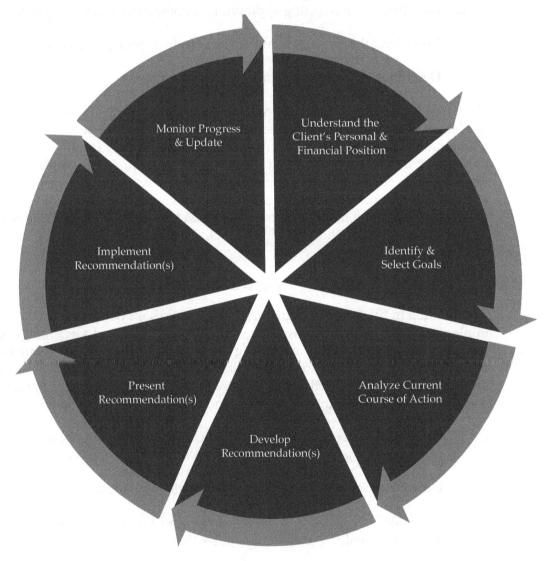

1.10 PRACTICE STANDARDS AND ETHICS

Financial planning professionals who are CFP® certificants must follow practice standards developed and promulgated by CFP Board. These standards are described in CFP Board's *Standards of Professional Conduct*—all of which have evolved within the profession to guide professional actions and benefit consumers. The CFP Board *Practice Standards and Code of Ethics* are intended to:

- Assure that the practice of financial planning by CFP® professionals is based on established norms of practice;

- Advance professionalism in financial planning; and

- Enhance the value of the financial planning process.

All CFP® professionals must adhere to the following Code of Ethics:

1. Act with honesty, integrity, competence, and diligence;

2. Act in the client's best interests;

3. Exercise due care;

4. Avoid or disclose and manage conflicts of interest;

5. Maintain the confidentiality and protect the privacy of client information;

6. Act in a manner that reflects positively on the financial planning profession and CFP® certification.

CFP Board's *Standards of Conduct* provide specific guidance to CFP® professionals when working with clients within the scope of the Code of Ethics. There are fifteen actions that comprise a financial planner's duties when conducting financial planning:

1. Fiduciary duty;

2. Integrity;

3. Competence;

4. Diligence;

5. Disclose and manage conflicts of interest;

6. Sound and objective professional judgment;

7. Professionalism;

8. Comply with the law;

9. Confidentiality and privacy;

10. Provide information to a client;

11. Duties when communicating with a client;

12. Duties when representing compensation method;

13. Duties when recommending, engaging, and working with additional persons;

14. Duties when selecting, recommending, and using technology; and

15. Refrain from borrowing or lending money and commingling financial assets.

CFP Board also provides guidance on the ways a CFP® professional must act when applying the financial planning process and when dealing directly with CFP Board.

"Among the factors that CFP Board will weigh in determining whether a CFP® professional has agreed to provide or provided financial advice that requires financial planning are:

a. The number of relevant elements of the client's personal and financial circumstances the financial advice affects;

b. The portion and amount of the client's financial assets the financial advice may affect;

c. The length of time the client's personal and financial circumstances may be affected by the financial advice;

d. The effect of the client's overall exposure to risk if the client implements the financial advice; and

e. The barriers to implementing the financial advice."

A key takeaway from this statement is that a financial planner must act in the best interest of their client at all times when delivering financial advice. For the purposes of the Practice Standards, a **client** is defined as:

"Any person, including a natural person, business organization, or legal entity, to whom the CFP® professional renders professional services pursuant to an engagement."

Within this definition, an **engagement** is defined as:

"A written or oral agreement, arrangement, or understanding."

The Practice Standards apply to the delivery of **financial advice**, which is defined as:

"A communication that, based on its content, context, and presentation, would reasonably be viewed as a suggestion that the client take or refrain from taking a particular course of action with respect to:

1. The development or implementation of a financial plan addressing goals, budgeting, risk, health considerations, educational needs, financial security, wealth, taxes, retirement, philanthropy, estate, legacy, or other relevant elements of a client's personal or financial circumstances;

2. The value of or the advisability of investing in, purchasing, holding, or selling financial assets;

3. Investment policies or strategies, portfolio composition, the management of financial assets, or other financial matters;

4. The selection and retention of other persons to provide financial or professional services to the client; or

5. The exercise of discretionary authority over the financial assets of a client."

When determining whether financial advice has been provided to someone, CFP Board looks at the level of communication specificity. For example, if advice is customized and communicated to an individual client, the advice will likely be considered financial advice. On the other hand, general education communications will not be viewed as financial advice.

It is important to remember that the preceding discussion relates only to CFP Board. Other certification organizations, regulatory authorities, and policy organizations follow different rules, procedures, and definitional frameworks.

1.11 OTHER CONSIDERATIONS

[A] Professional Judgment

Financial planning can be challenging for those who prefer problems with one answer. In practice, there may be multiple solutions that enable a client to reach a goal. Stated another way, client situations can be addressed in multiple ways by different financial planners. While one financial planner may dismiss a recommendation as ill-conceived, another financial planner may view the same recommendation as worthwhile. The difference in opinion often comes down to a financial planner's experience, knowledge, and expectations. These financial planner attributes contribute to what is known as **professional judgment**.

One way to expand and refine professional judgment is to develop financial planning skills and apply accumulated skills in a systematic manner. Successful financial planners use a consistent, well-defined approach when working with clients. This approach employs the use of financial planning forms and protocols to guide and document actions taken at each step of the planning process. A systematic, methodical, and organized approach can help a financial planner:

- Consolidate what may initially appear to be an overwhelming mass of data and analysis into a manageable format;

- Focus attention on critical planning needs;

- Focus attention on problems or issues that might require research or consultation with other professionals;

- Focus attention on issues or questions that require additional input from the client;

- Recognize the need for creative alternatives to meet a client's goals; and

- Feel confident that relevant issues have not been overlooked.

Planning Reminder

Whether a CFP® professional (1) produces a comprehensive plan, (2) works on a per-project basis focusing on analysis and advice, (3) writes a targeted or modular plan, (4) provides financial planning analysis—but no plan—as a means to provide products, or (5) develops a plan as a means to establish product needs, a financial planner is expected to follow the financial planning process.

Use of the financial planning process not only helps guide the analytic work of a financial planner, but the process also helps define the presentation, implementation, and monitoring of a financial plan.

It is worth remembering that the conceptualization of the financial process as distinct and sequential steps is a conceptual representation of the reality of financial planning. In actual client work—and when done in the context of different business planning models—some activities might not occur exactly as described in the process. Because of the circular nature of the financial planning process, several steps can be ongoing and overlapping as a client progresses through the process when attempting to meet different goals and objectives.

With this in mind, it is important to exhibit certain financial planning skills before engaging with a client in the financial planning process. The following discussion highlights some of the most important financial planning skills and considerations needed to ensure success.

[B] Gather and Frame Client Goals and Objectives

Collecting information and data from a client and identifying client goals is an almost daily financial planning task. Client information can be obtained in numerous ways. One approach consists of having the client complete a **data collection questionnaire** or client **data-intake form** (completed by the client independently or in conjunction with the financial planner). Another approach involves having the client supply source documents, including past tax returns, pay stubs, insurance documents, and similar records. Regardless of the method(s) utilized, the primary objective is for the financial planner to gather vital financial and personal information—quantitative and qualitative—that encourages an open dialogue with the client. A financial planning best practice suggests that clients should be encouraged to complete basic data forms and attitudinal assessments (e.g., a risk-tolerance questionnaire) independently, via hard copy or via secure encrypted electronic access, whenever possible. This frees up client-financial planner meeting time to review **quantitative data** and information as a precursor to exploring a client's values, goals, dreams, attitudes, and beliefs.

Planning Reminder

The most recent copy of an investment adviser's Form ADV can be accessed at the Investment Advisor Public Disclosure Website (typically referred to as the *IAPD Website*), for either state- or SEC-registered financial planners.

Data collection is usually termed **discovery**. There are two important outcomes associated with discovery meetings: (1) the establishment of trust between a client and financial planner, and (2) the collection and exploration of information to help a financial planner better understand a client personally, as well as financially. Given the significance of the discovery process, and the variety of approaches utilized to gather data in practice, every financial planner should ask the following questions when beginning work with a new client:

1. What client data should be collected?

2. How does the financial planner use the data?

3. How should the data be collected?

4. What does it mean to frame goals and objectives?

[C] Economic Concepts and the Financial Planning Process

Financial planners, by the very nature of their training and education, tend to bring a multidisciplinary perspective to their practice. This is one reason why financial planners need to understand and eventually master economic concepts as an element of the financial planning process. Issues related to macroeconomic events, the money supply, and interest rates all play an important role in shaping the types of strategies and recommendations used to help clients reach their financial goals. This brief discussion highlights some of the most important economic concepts underlying many financial planning strategies.

[1] Microeconomic Concepts

One of the building blocks of economic theory is the **law of supply and demand**. This law states that there is a direct positive relationship between prices and supply and an inverse relationship between demand and prices. Application of this law can be seen in the marketplace when prices increase for a product or service. Demand usually drops with other products and services acting as a **substitute good** for the original item. For example, as fees on mutual funds increased from the 1970s through the 1990s, investors substituted other products with lower fees, such as exchange traded funds. This had an overall effect of decreasing fees across all investment products. Sometimes an item acts as a **complementary good**. This can be seen in the life insurance marketplace. The demand for life insurance generally increases as wealth increases, even though the effect should be the other way around.

The law of supply and demand helped introduce the notion of **opportunity costs**, which are the explicit or implicit costs associated with forgoing one choice in favor of another option. For instance, assume a client elects to save for college expenses using a Section 529 plan. There is an opportunity cost associated with this choice; namely, the forgone opportunity to save for retirement or another goal using a different product. Another important microeconomic concept is the degree to which products and services exhibit **price elasticity**. Price elasticity refers to the degree demand for a product or service drops as the result of a price increase. Something is considered to be relatively **price inelastic** if demand drops slightly or not at all when prices move up. Some have argued that financial planning services are relatively price inelastic; however, the introduction of **robo-advisory services** is putting this assertion to the test. Robo-advisors provide automated financial planning services at a very low cost. If the concept proves successful, robo-advisory firms should grow as more consumers shift from higher priced traditional firms to these lower cost service providers.

[2] Macroeconomic Concepts

Fiscal policy tends to be a topic of great importance among financial planners. **Fiscal policy** refers to the government's tax and spending policies. As one of the four components of **gross domestic product (GDP)**, **government spending**—a direct element of fiscal policy—plays a role in shaping economic growth and **inflation** (i.e., a phenomenon marked by generally increasing prices).

The financial planning community also pays close attention to actions taken and forecasts to be taken by the **Federal Reserve (Fed)** through **monetary policy**. Monetary policy encompasses the Fed's control of the **credit markets** and establishment of **reserve requirements**. Historically, the Fed, as an independent federal agency, has been tasked with the dual objective of maintaining high national employment and relatively low inflation. The Fed attempts to meet these seemingly contradictory objectives by establishing the **discount rate** at which the Fed charges depository institutions, such as banks and credit unions, for short-term loans. If the Fed is attempting to increase employment, the Fed will decrease the discount rate to spur lending.

The Fed also intervenes in the bond market via the **Federal Open Market Committee (FOMC)**. The FOMC is based out of the Federal Reserve Bank of New York. The purpose of the FOMC is to engage in open market buying and selling of U.S. Treasury securities. The FOMC can increase **liquidity** in the markets—thus stimulating demand and increasing inflation and GDP—by purchasing and selling Treasury Securities. Although not used often, the Fed can also change reserve requirements for depository institutions. Since the global financial crisis, reserve requirements—the percent of total deposits a depository institution must keep in reserve—have been near historically low levels. The Fed has other tools, but these are typically used infrequently (e.g., *term auction facilities, money market investor funding facilities, commercial paper funding facilities*, etc.).

Financial planners also spend time tracking the overall health of the economy. This fascination with the macro economy stems from the need to project current events into planning assumptions for future analyses. For example, a financial planner might reasonably ask if they should continue to project very low interest rates into long-term retirement distribution scenarios. One way to answer this question involves tracking **economic indicators**. Some of the most important indicators include:

- **Consumer Price Index (CPI)**: This measure of inflation represents a market basket of household goods. An alternative is the **CPI-U**, which represents inflation in urban markets.

- **Producer Price Index (PPI)**: Producer prices tend to be a leading indicator—a precursor to something that will happen in the future—of inflation. This measure is watched by those in the financial planning community to anticipate future changes in the price of goods and services.

- **Gross Domestic Product (GDP)**: The state of the economic environment can be measured by GDP, which is comprised of government spending, business investment, consumer expenditures (consumption), and net exports.

- **Business Cycle**: A country's stage of growth can be defined by the business cycle, which itself is an indication of GDP. Figure 1.4 illustrates the two stages of the business cycle: contraction and recovery/expansion. As shown, the contraction phase is marked by a peak and decline in GDP to a trough, whereas the expansion phase is represented by an increase in GDP from trough to peak.

Figure 1.4. The Business Cycle.

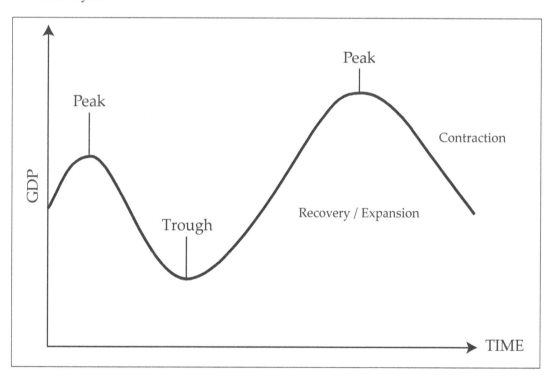

In addition to these economic indicators, financial planners often classify economic data as a leading, coincident, or lagging indicator. The following economic data points are considered to be **leading economic indicators** of future expansion or contraction: unemployment claims, manufacturing new orders, product delivery times, new orders for capital (non-defense) goods, building permits, stock prices, money supply growth, the spread between the **federal funds rate** (i.e., the rate at which depository institutions lend money to other depository institutions) and ten-year U.S. Treasury bonds, and consumer expectations. Four indicators are thought to be indicative of current market conditions or **coincident economic indicators**: industrial production, personal income less transfer payments (e.g., Social Security), manufacturing sales, and nonagricultural payrolls. The following indicators are considered to be **lagging economic indicators** of economic growth: loans outstanding, duration of unemployment, change in labor cost per unit of output, the level of installment credit to personal income, the ratio of inventories to sales, the prime interest rate, and the CPI for services.

Financial planners also place a great deal of emphasis on tracking and predicting the **yield curve**. The yield curve shows the relationship between bond yields and bond durations. The yield curve can be used to describe and predict the business cycle and inflation. Figure 1.5 illustrates a typical positively sloping yield curve where rates increase as maturity increases. In this illustration, investors expect inflation to increase over time, and as such, they expect to receive a higher **yield to maturity (YTM)** on their fixed-income investments. Further, because the risks associated with longer maturity bonds tend to be higher than short maturity bonds due to liquidity, reinvestment, and default risks, investors typically expect to receive a higher return on their investment. Sometimes the yield curve will invert, with yields on short-term bonds higher than long-term bond yields. This is generally an indication of an economic slowdown. In this situation, investors believe that the economy is near a peak, which should prompt an increase in interest rates. When and if an interest rate increase occurs, bond values will fall, with the longest maturity bonds dropping by the greatest percentage. In preparation for this potentiality, investors flock to short-term bonds, which inverts the yield curve.

Figure 1.5. A Positive Sloping Yield Curve.

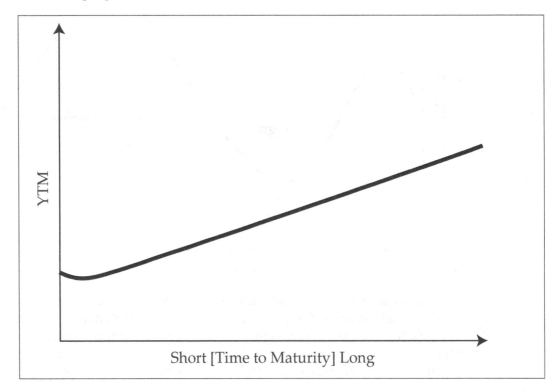

[D] Develop a Cash Flow Tracking System

As noted previously, the implementation phase of the financial planning process is, for many financial planners, the most enjoyable aspect of being a financial planner. It is at this point in the financial planning process where the work of analysis and recommendation development comes together to help a client meet objectives and goals. In the context of writing a comprehensive financial plan, however, the implementation of recommendations places a burden on a financial planner. It is essential that a financial planner ensure that all recommendations can realistically be implemented within the context of the financial plan. In order to do this, a financial planner must have a systematic way to track the impact of recommendations throughout the financial plan.

This can be accomplished by using a cash flow and asset tracking form or system. The success of a financial plan is contingent on the availability of discretionary cash flow, savings, and other available assets to fund recommendations. This statement really cannot be over-emphasized. It is important to justify the choice of each recommendation thoroughly and objectively in a client's financial plan. A key element associated with this justification involves providing proof that a client can afford to implement a given recommendation. If a client has $3,000 in available cash flow, but a recommendation requires a $6,000 annual investment, the recommendation—even one that is technically sound—is not realistic. Stated another way, the client must have the financial capacity to fund all recommendations made in a financial plan. It is up to the client's financial planner (as the author of the financial plan) to document the affordability of recommendations. A **cash flow and other assets tracking form** will be discussed in more detail in Chapter 2.

1.6 SUMMARY

This chapter described the financial planning process as conceptualized by the CFP Board of Standards, Inc. The process, as outlined in this chapter, can be used as a framework for guiding the work financial planners do on a day-to-day basis when working with clients. The process can also serve as a roadmap for those who write comprehensive financial plans. Following the financial planning process ensures that a systematic approach is used consistently when working with clients. When applied across client scenarios, the financial planning process enhances client outcomes, which serves as a building block for establishing and maintaining strong financial planner-client relationships.

1.7 SELF-TEST

[A] Questions

Self-Test 1

Lanny is an accomplished golfer. He intends to join the professional senior golf tour when he retires from his position as an executive with a large firm. He tells his financial planner that he would like to have a home in Florida, California, and Wisconsin so that he has a "home base" while playing golf around the country. Lanny's desire can best be described as a:

(a) Need

(b) Want

(c) Necessity

(d) Goal Hierarchy

Self-Test 2

A client's willingness to engage in a risky behavior in which the possibility of financial loss exists is known as a client's:

(a) Risk Capacity

(b) Risk Tolerance

(c) Risk Perception

(d) Risk Desire

Self-Test 3

Lionel is preparing for a meeting with a prospective client. Under Securities and Exchange Commission and CFP Board rules, all the following must be disclosed to the client, except:

(a) Lionel's marital status.

(b) Lionel's fee schedule.

(c) Any conflicts of interest.

(d) b and c.

Self-Test 4

All the following are assumptions, except:

(a) The annualized rate of return that can be earned on retirement assets.

(b) The life expectancy of a client.

(c) The future cost of living in a large city.

(d) The date when a client may claim Medicare.

Self-Test 5

Tabatha inherited a 20-year A+ rated bond from her uncle two years ago. Yesterday she found out the Fed has raised interest rates. She does not know whether to be happy or sad about this event. What will happen to the value of Tabatha's bond now that rates have increased?

(a) Nothing, the bond value will remain unchanged.

(b) The value of the bond will increase.

(c) The value of the bond will decrease.

(d) The value of the bond will first increase, then decrease, and finally emerge unchanged.

Self-Test 6

Which of the following recommendations is closest to being an actionable recommendation?

(a) Refinance your mortgage as soon as possible.

(b) Purchase a stock mutual fund in the next 30 days.

(c) Save $300 per month into EE Savings Bonds using Treasury Direct.

(d) All of the above.

Self-Test 7

John is a stamp collector. He really enjoys finding, sorting, and pricing stamps. He spends several thousand dollars each year on his hobby. His financial planner thinks buying stamps is a bad investment. The financial planner recently pointed out that John's rate of return on his stamp purchases is about three percent, whereas the stock market, during the same time period, has returned nine percent. The six percent difference is known as John's:

(a) Substitution effect cost.

(b) Opportunity cost.

(c) Complementary good cost.

(d) Discount rate.

Self-Test 8

The Fed controls:

(a) The federal funds rate.

(b) The Consumer Price Index (CPI).

(c) The discount rate.

(d) All the above.

[B] Answers

Question 1: b

Question 2: b

Question 3: a

Question 4: d

Question 5: c

Question 6: c

Question 7: b

Question 8: c

CHAPTER RESOURCES

Anthony, M. Your Clients for Life: The Definitive Guide to Becoming a Successful Financial Planner. Chicago, IL: Dearborn Financial Publishing, 2002.

Assessing a Client's Financial Risk Tolerance: http://pfp.missouri.edu/research_IRTA.html

Certified Financial Planner Board of Standards, Inc. (www.cfp.net).

DataPoints™ (www.datapoints.com).

Diliberto, R. T. Financial Planning—The Next Step: A Practical Approach to Merging Your Clients' Money with Their Lives. Denver, CO: FPA Press, 2006.

Financial Industry Regulatory Authority (FINRA) (www.finra.org).

Financial Planning Performance Lab (www.fpplab.com).

FinaMetrica® (www.finametrica.com).

Investment Adviser Registration Depository (www.iard.com/).

Investment Financial Planner Public Disclosure Website: www.adviserinfo.sec.gov/ (S(l2wrhvakmfteghqc1qtt0v5m))/IAPD/Content/IapdMain/iapd_SiteMap.aspx

Kinder, G., and S. Galvan. Lighting the Torch: The Kinder Method™ of Life Planning. Denver, CO: FPA Press, 2006.

Klontz, B., R. Kahler, and T. Klontz. Facilitating Financial Health: Tools for Financial Planners, Coaches, and Therapists; Second Edition). Cincinnati, OH: National Underwriter Company, 2015.

Klontz, B., and T. Klontz. Mind over Money: Overcoming the Money Disorders That Threaten Our Financial Health. New York: Crown Business, 2009.

Lytton, R., J. Grable, and Klock, D. The Process of Financial Planning: Developing a Financial Plan, 2nd Ed. Erlanger, KY: National Underwriter, 2012.

Money Quotient® Putting Money in the Context of Life™ (moneyquotient.org/).

The Kinder Institute of Life Planning (www.kinderinstitute.com).

U.S. Securities and Exchange Commission (www.sec.gov).

CHAPTER ENDNOTES

1. Certified Financial Planner Board of Standards, Inc., *The 7 Step Financial Planning Process*. Available at https://www.cfp.net/ethics/compliance-resources/2018/11/focus-on-ethics---the-7-step-financial-planning-process .

2. Elements of this discussion were adapted with publisher permission from R Lytton, J Grable, & D Klock, *The Process of Financial Planning: Developing a Financial Plan* (Cincinnati, OH: National Underwriter, 2012).

3. See: https://www.mitchanthony.com/planning-for-the-unplanned-transitions/.

4. Available at: http://pfp.missouri.edu/research_IRTA.html.

5. CFP Board: https://www.cfp.net/for-cfp-professionals/professional-standards-enforcement/code-and-standards

6. Details about each standard of conduct can be found at: https://www.cfp.net/ethics/compliance-resources/2018/09/highlights-of-cfp-boards-new-code-of-ethics-and-standards-of-conduct.

7. See: https://www.cfp.net/ethics/enforcement.

8. See: https://www.cfp.net/ethics/code-of-ethics-and-standards-of-conduct.

9. *Ibid*.

Sample Client Data Intake Form

Thank you for taking the time to complete this confidential client questionnaire. We realize it takes time and effort to retrieve the information requested. However, we are available to assist where needed and welcome your calls or emails. Please do not hesitate to contact us, or if it is easier for you, simply collect the insurance policies, financial statements, or other documents and return them with this form. Collecting this information is an important first step in our collaboration to develop a financial plan based on your financial and life goals. This is the *only* reason for asking for so much information. We look forward to learning more about your situation and working with you.

Section 1: Confidential Client Data

Personal Information

Client 1		Client 2	
Name		Name	
DOB		DOB	
SSN		SSN	

Contact Information

Client 1		Client 2	
Home phone		Home phone	
Mobile phone		Mobile phone	
Email		Email	
Home address		Home address	

Children (or Other Financial Dependents) Information

Name		DOB		Relationship		At home?	
Name		DOB		Relationship		At home?	
Name		DOB		Relationship		At home?	
Name		DOB		Relationship		At home?	
Name		DOB		Relationship		At home?	
Name		DOB		Relationship		At home?	

Section 2: Please tell us about your family. This information will give us a better understanding of who is affected by your financial decisions. (Please consider children and other financial dependents, including immediate and/or extended family.)

Are there any special considerations that relate to the future of your children—perhaps their future education or living conditions? *(Exceptionally bright? Special talents? Disabilities or special need? Prior marriages?)*

_____

_____

_____

_____

_____

_____

Is there anyone you are supporting now, or will be supporting in the future, whom you want to consider in your planning? If yes, please list below:

_____

_____

_____

_____

_____

_____

Are there any rare aspects of your family situation that warrant additional consideration or special planning? If yes, please explain below:

_____

_____

_____

_____

_____

_____

Section 3: If you are currently employed, please tell us about your job below: (If retired, skip to Section 3a)

Employment Information

	Client 1	Client 2
Employer		
Occupation		
Work phone		
Work address		
Number of years employed		
Position		
Annual salary		
Annual bonuses/commissions		
Other earned income		
Do you anticipate employment changes?		
If so, when (date)?		
At what age do you plan to retire?		

If you were going to retire today, approximately how much annual after-tax income would you need to live comfortably? _____

Do you feel that you are on track to have enough income-generating assets to live comfortably in retirement?   *(Circle)* Yes   No

If no, please explain. _____

_____

Section 3a: If you are currently retired, please tell us about your current situation below:

Retirement Information

	Client 1	Client 2
Number of years retired		
Annual Social Security income		
Annual pension income		
Annual income from annuities		
Annual income from investments		
Other annual income		

	Client 1	Client 2
Do you feel that your current income is sufficient to meet your needs?	*(Circle)* Yes No	*(Circle)* Yes No

If no, please explain. _____

_____

_____

	Client 1	Client 2
Do you anticipate working again?	*(Circle)* Yes No	*(Circle)* Yes No

If **yes**, please explain. _____

_____

_____

Section 4: Leisure activities are important to consider when planning your financial future. Please help us identify the activities that you enjoy by answering the questions below:

How do you use your leisure time? *(Outside organizations, activities, clubs, etc.)*

_____

_____

_____

_____

_____

_____

What other activities do you enjoy? *(Skydiving, long/short vacations, bridge, etc.)*

_____

_____

_____

_____

_____

_____

What activities would you like to begin in the future? *(Traveling, volunteering, etc.)*

_____

_____

_____

_____

_____

_____

Section 5: Please tell us what you consider to be your primary goals and objectives for the future.

Rank your goals/objectives using the following scale and time horizons. It is recommended that you complete this individually as well as jointly. Please do not discuss your responses together until each client has been able to individually complete the form.

Importance Scale		Time Horizon
0 – Not applicable at this time	3 – Important	S/T – 1–2 Years
1 – Not important	4 – Very important	I/T – 2–10 Years
2 – Somewhat important	5 – Crucial	L/T – 10+ Years

The generic goals provided below are typical examples for people throughout the lifecycle and are meant to assist us with goal setting.

Client 1 Goals / Objectives	Importance Level (0–5)	Time Horizon to Begin	Time Horizon to Complete
Personal			
Becoming more financially knowledgeable			
Improving recordkeeping methods			
Starting a family			
Advancing in current career			
Changing careers			
Returning to college			
Caring for parents			
Retiring early			
Traveling in retirement			
Other:			
Other:			
Other:			
Other:			
Financial			
Reducing revolving debt			
Increasing periodic savings			
Reducing taxes			
Evaluating insurance needs			
Increasing investment diversification			
Increasing investment returns			
Starting a small business			

Saving for children's education			
Purchasing a vehicle			
Saving for the down payment on a home			
Purchasing a home			
Investing an inheritance			
Saving for retirement			
Giving to charity			
Transferring estate assets			
Other:			
Other:			
Other:			

Client 2 Goals /Objectives	Importance Level (0–5)	Time Horizon to Begin	Time Horizon to Complete
Personal			
Becoming more financially knowledgeable			
Improving recordkeeping methods			
Starting a family			
Advancing in current career			
Changing careers			
Returning to college			
Caring for parents			
Retiring early			
Traveling in retirement			
Other:			
Other:			
Other:			
Other:			
Financial			
Reducing revolving debt			
Increasing periodic savings			
Reducing taxes			
Evaluating insurance needs			
Increasing investment diversification			
Increasing investment returns			
Starting a small business			

Saving for children's education			
Purchasing a vehicle			
Saving for the down payment on a home			
Purchasing a home			
Investing an inheritance			
Saving for retirement			
Giving to charity			
Transferring estate assets			
Other:			
Other:			
Other:			

Section 6: It is important to know the exact amount of your current insurance coverage to fully evaluate whether you are over-, under-, or adequately insured. Please provide the following information:

Life Insurance Information	Policy 1	Policy 2	Policy 3	Policy 4
Insurance company				
Policy owner				
Insured				
Beneficiary(ies), primary				
Beneficiary(ies), contingent				
Face value				
Group or individual policy				
Total annual premium cost				
Premiums paid (self or employer)				
Pretax or post-tax dollars				
Term or cash value policy				
If term, years remaining				
Policy Provisions				
Renewability[a]				
Inflation protection				
Declining value (term)				
If you have a cash value policy, please also provide the following information:				
Cash value				
Tax-equivalent rate of return				
Current dividend (if applicable)				
Current death benefit/face value				

[a] Renewability options include: annually renewable, guaranteed renewable, non-cancellable.

	Client 1	Client 2
Have you ever been turned down for life insurance?	*(Circle)* Yes No	*(Circle)* Yes No

If yes, what was the reason? _____

Disability Insurance Information	Policy 1	Policy 2	Policy 3	Policy 4
Insurance company				
Policy owner				
Insured				
Group or individual policy?				
Cost per year				
Premiums paid (self or employer)				
Pretax or post-tax dollars?				
Policy Provisions				
Type (short-term or long-term?)				
Disability definition[a]				
Waiting period (days)				
Benefit period (years)				
Total annual benefit				
Total benefit (life of policy)				

[a] Disability definitions include: any occupation, similar occupation, own occupation.

	Client 1	**Client 2**
Have you ever been turned down for disability insurance?	*(Circle)* Yes No	*(Circle)* Yes No

If yes, what was the reason? _____
_____
_____

Do you anticipate any changes in the coverage or need for coverage for any of the policies listed above? _____
_____

Do you anticipate making changes to any of these policies that would alter any planning recommendation based on the preceding information?_____
_____

Health Insurance Information	Policy 1	Policy 2	Policy 3	Policy 4
Insurance company				
Policy owner				
Primary insured				
Group or individual policy?				
Cost per year				
Premiums paid (self or employer)				
Pretax or post-tax dollars?				
Policy Provisions				
Individual or family policy?				
Annual deductible amount				
Annual stop-loss limit ($)				
Lifetime maximum benefit				

Client 1   **Client 2**

Have you ever been turned down for health insurance?   *(Circle)* Yes No   *(Circle)* Yes No

If yes, what was the reason? _____
_____
_____

Do you anticipate any changes in the coverage or need for coverage for any of the policies listed above? _____
_____

Do you anticipate making changes to any of these policies that would alter any planning recommendation based on the preceding information? _____
_____

Long-term Care Insurance Information	Policy 1	Policy 2	Policy 3	Policy 4
Insurance company				
Policy owner				
Primary insured				
Group or individual policy				
Cost per year				
Premiums paid (self or employer)				
Pretax or post-tax dollars?				
Policy Provisions				
Individual or joint policy?				
Elimination period				
Eligibility (number lost ADLs)				
Per-day benefit amount				
Lifetime maximum benefit				
Single or shared benefit pool				
Inflation rider (fixed or variable?)				
Inflation rider (simple or compound?)				

	Client 1	Client 2
Have you ever been turned down for long-term care insurance?	*(Circle)* Yes No	*(Circle)* Yes No

If yes, what was the reason? _____
_____

Do you anticipate any changes in the coverage or need for coverage for any of the policies listed above? _____
_____

Do you anticipate making changes to any of these policies that would alter any planning recommendation based on the preceding information? _____

Personal Automobile Insurance Information	Policy 1 / Vehicle 1	Policy 2 / Vehicle 2	Policy 3 / Vehicle 3	Policy 4 / Vehicle 4
Insurance company				
Policy owner				
Primary insured				
Other insured(s)				
Cost per year				
Liability Coverage				
Coverage per person				
Coverage per accident				
Property damage coverage				
Coverage per person (Uninsured/underinsured)				
Coverage Per Accident (Uninsured/underinsured)				
Property Damage Coverage (Uninsured/underinsured)				
Medical coverage per person				
Comprehensive and Collision Coverage				
Collision deductible				
Comprehensive deductible				
Uninsured/underinsured deductible				
Additional Coverage				
Towing/labor				
Rental reimbursement				

Homeowners/Renters Insurance Information	Policy 1	Policy 2	Policy 3	Policy 4
Insurance company				
Policy owner				
Property insured				
Cost per year				
Amount of dwelling coverage				
Deductible				
Amount of liability coverage				
Deductible/co-payment				
Special property endorsements				
Inflation rider				

	Client 1	Client 2
Have you ever been turned down for either homeowners or auto insurance?	(Circle) Yes No	(Circle) Yes No

If yes, what was the reason? _____

_____

_____

_____

_____

_____

_____

	Client 1	Client 2
Have you ever been turned down for auto insurance or had a policy cancelled?	(Circle) Yes No	(Circle) Yes No

If yes, what was the reason? _____

_____

_____

_____

_____

_____

Do you anticipate any changes in the coverage or need for coverage for any of the policies listed above? _____

_____

_____

_____

_____

_____

Do you anticipate making changes to any of these policies, or the property covered, that would alter any recommendations? _____

_____

_____

_____

_____

_____

Do you own a watercraft, motorcycle, RV, ATV, or other off-road vehicle?

(Circle) Yes   No

If yes, do you have coverage for the watercraft, motorcycle, RV, ATV, or other off-road vehicle?

(Circle) Yes   No

Additional Insurance:

	Client 1		Client 2	
	Coverage/Cost	Group or Individual?	Coverage/Cost	Group or Individual?
Umbrella liability	——————	——————	——————	——————
Professional liability	——————	——————	——————	——————
Errors & omissions	——————	——————	——————	——————

Is your primary residence currently covered by a state homestead exemption?   *(Circle)* Yes No Unknown

Have you ever been turned down for any other insurance product?   *(Circle)* Yes No

If yes, what was the reason? _____
_____
_____
_____
_____
_____

Section 7: To better understand your current financial position, we need to review your available assets. Please tell us about your taxable and tax deferred assets.

Taxable Investment Assets*:	Ownership (Name or "Joint")	Current Value ($)	Cost Basis ($)	Current Annual Contribution ($) (if applicable)	Current Total Return (%)	Current Annual Yield (%)	Use Cash to Settle Estate? (Y/N)
		$	$	$			
		$	$	$			
		$	$	$			
		$	$	$			
		$	$	$			
		$	$	$			
		$	$	$			
		$	$	$			
		$	$	$			
		$	$	$			
		$	$	$			
		$	$	$			

* Taxable account examples include: checking, savings, certificates of deposit (CDs), money market mutual funds, money market deposit accounts, U.S. Savings Bonds, stocks, bonds, mutual funds, ETFs, direct or indirect real estate, precious metals, and other.

Taxable Investment Assets* (cont'd):

Ownership (Name or "Joint")	Current Value ($)	Cost Basis ($)	Current Annual Contribution ($) (if applicable)	Current Total Return (%)	Current Annual Yield (%)	Use Cash to Settle Estate? (Y/N)
	$	$	$			
	$	$	$			
	$	$	$			
	$	$	$			
	$	$	$			
	$	$	$			
	$	$	$			
	$	$	$			
	$	$	$			
	$	$	$			
	$	$	$			
	$	$	$			
	$	$	$			
	$	$	$			

* Taxable account examples include: checking, savings, certificates of deposit (CDs), money market mutual funds, money market deposit accounts, U.S. Savings Bonds, stocks, bonds, mutual funds, ETFs, direct or indirect real estate, precious metal, and other.

Tax-deferred Investment Assets*:

	Ownership	Current Value ($)	Cost Basis ($)	Current Annual Contribution ($) (if applicable)	Current Total Return (%)	Current Annual Yield (%)	Use Cash to Settle Estate? (Y/N)
		$	$	$			
		$	$	$			
		$	$	$			
		$	$	$			
		$	$	$			
		$	$	$			
		$	$	$			
		$	$	$			
		$	$	$			
		$	$	$			
		$	$	$			
		$	$	$			
		$	$	$			
		$	$	$			

* Examples of tax-deferred accounts include: 401(k), 403(b), 457, profit sharing, Keogh, Simple, SEP, traditional IRA, Roth IRA, 529 plans, Coverdell Education Savings Accounts (ESAs), fixed annuities, variable annuities, whole life, variable life, universal life, and variable universal life.

Tax-deferred Investment Assets* (cont'd):

Ownership	Current Value ($)	Cost Basis ($)	Current Annual Contribution ($) (if applicable)	Current Total Return (%)	Current Annual Yield (%)	Use Cash to Settle Estate? (Y/N)
	$	$	$			
	$	$	$			
	$	$	$			
	$	$	$			
	$	$	$			
	$	$	$			
	$	$	$			
	$	$	$			
	$	$	$			
	$	$	$			
	$	$	$			
	$	$	$			
	$	$	$			
	$	$	$			

* Examples of tax-deferred accounts include: 401(k), 403(b), 457, profit sharing, Keogh, Simple, SEP, traditional IRA, Roth IRA, 529 plans, Coverdell Education Savings Accounts (ESAs), fixed annuities, variable annuities, whole life, variable life, universal life, and variable universal life.

Investment Asset Allocation (%): Client 1

Optional, if this information is available.

(Please list accounts in same order as above.)

	Total Value ($)	Large-Cap	Mid-Cap	Small-Cap	Intl. Stock	Corp. Bonds	Govt. Bonds	High-Yield Bonds	Real Estate	Gold	Cash
Taxable	$										
	$										
	$										
	$										
	$										
	$										
	$										
	$										
	$										
	$										
	$										
Tax-deferred	$										
	$										
	$										
	$										
	$										

Investment Asset Allocation (%):
Client 2
Optional, if this information is available.

(Please list accounts in same order as above.)

	Total Value ($)	Large-Cap	Mid-Cap	Small-Cap	Intl. Stock	Corp. Bonds	Govt. Bonds	High-Yield Bonds	Real Estate	Gold	Cash
Taxable	$										
	$										
	$										
	$										
	$										
	$										
	$										
	$										
	$										
	$										
Tax-deferred	$										
	$										
	$										
	$										
	$										
	$										

Section 8: We also need to learn about the types of personal assets you own. Use the following form to record your asset information:

Personal/Business Assets*	Ownership (Name or "Joint")	Purchase Price	Current Value	Appreciation Rate (if applicable)	Use Cash to Settle Estate? (Y/N)
		$	$		
		$	$		
		$	$		
		$	$		
		$	$		
		$	$		
		$	$		
		$	$		
		$	$		
		$	$		
		$	$		
		$	$		

* Suggestions for personal/business asset descriptions include: primary residence; secondary residence; vacation home; automobile, boat, motorcycle, ATV, or RV; land; passive business interests; active business interests; and other.

Section 9: Now we would like to review your debts and liabilities. Use the following form to identify your financial liabilities:

Personal/Business Liabilities*	Person Liable (Name or "Joint")	Current Amount Owed ($)	Monthly Payment ($)**	Interest Rate (%)	Fixed or Variable	Origination Date	Maturity Date	To be Paid-off at Client's Death?
		$	$					
		$	$					
		$	$					
		$	$					
		$	$					
		$	$					
		$	$					
		$	$					
		$	$					
		$	$					
		$	$					
		$	$					

*Suggestions for personal/business liability descriptions include: primary residence; secondary residence; vacation home; automobile, boat, motorcycle, ATV, or RV; other consumer credit (e.g., credit cards, gas cards, store credit cards, etc.); student loans; land; passive business interests; active business interests; and other.

**For credit card, gas card, or department store accounts, please indicate whether the monthly payment is the minimum monthly payment, an amount paid each month to reduce the balance, or the typical payment to pay the balance off in full each month.

> **Section 10:** Please indicate how much you spend on the following items on a monthly basis. If you are spending money on something not indicated, please add that item.

Housing

Mortgage/rent	$
Property taxes	$
Home repairs	$
Home insurance	$
Utilities	$
Telephone/Internet/Cable	$

Transportation

Auto payment	$
Auto insurance	$
Fuel	$
Maintenance	$
License	$
Parking/tolls	$
Bus/train	$

Taxes and Withholding

Federal income taxes	$
State & local taxes	$
FICA taxes	$
Other withholdings	$

Other Items

After-tax retirement	$
Other	$
Other	$
Other	$

Household/Personal

Groceries	$
Personal care	$
Clothing	$
Domestic help	$
Dependent care	$
Professional dues	$
Education	$
Allowances	$
Child care	$

Personal Insurance

Health insurance	$
Life insurance	$
Disability insurance	$
Long-term care	$
Medical/dental	$
Prescription drugs	$
Other	$

Savings

Pretax retirement	$
Roth IRA	$
Traditional IRA	$
Other savings	$
Emergency fund	$
Interest & dividends	$
Capital gains	$

Loan Payments

Credit card	$
Credit card	$
Installment loan	$
Installment loan	$
Other payment	$
Other payment	$

Alimony and Child Support

Alimony	$
Child support	$

Variable/Discretionary Expenses

Dining out	$
Bank charges	$
Recreation	$
Dues	$
Movies	$
Events	$
Hobbies	$
Vacation/travel	$
Gifts	$
Charitable giving	$
Laundry/dry cleaning	$
Other	$
Other	$
Miscellaneous	$
Miscellaneous	$

Section 11: Understanding your feelings toward investments can help us guide you when making investment choices. Please provide a response to each statement below that best matches your opinion today:

Client 1	Strongly Disagree	Disagree	Neutral	Agree	Strongly Agree
1. Keeping pace with inflation is important to me.					
2. I am comfortable borrowing money to make a financial investment.					
3. Diversification is important to investment success.					
4. The return I am making on my current investments is acceptable.					
5. I need to earn more spendable income from my investments.					
6. I am comfortable with the volatility I experience with my portfolio.					
7. Reducing the amount of taxes paid on my investments is a top priority.					
8. I am willing to risk being audited by the IRS in return for higher returns.					
9. I am willing to risk being audited by the IRS in return for paying less tax.					
10. My friends would tell you that I am a real risk taker.					

Client 2	Strongly Disagree	Disagree	Neutral	Agree	Strongly Agree
1. Keeping pace with inflation is important to me.					
2. I am comfortable borrowing money to make a financial investment.					
3. Diversification is important to investment success.					
4. The return I am making on my current investments is acceptable.					
5. I need to earn more spendable income from my investments.					
6. I am comfortable with the volatility I experience with my portfolio.					
7. Reducing the amount of taxes paid on my investments is a top priority.					
8. I am willing to risk being audited by the IRS in return for higher returns.					
9. I am willing to risk being audited by the IRS in return for paying less tax.					
10. My friends would tell you that I am a real risk taker.					

Section 12: We would also like to learn about your expectations regarding the future.

Client 1: Please provide your opinion of the following statements:

1. *Over the next five years, do you expect the U.S. economy, as a whole, to perform better, worse, or about the same as it has over the past five years?*

1	2	3	4	5	6	7	8	9	10
Perform worse				Perform about the same					Perform better

2. *How satisfied are you with your current level of income?*

1	2	3	4	5	6	7	8	9	10
Not satisfied									Very satisfied

3. *How satisfied are you with your present overall financial situation?*

1	2	3	4	5	6	7	8	9	10
Not satisfied									Very satisfied

4. *Overall, how satisfied are you with your current job or position?*

1	2	3	4	5	6	7	8	9	10
Not satisfied									Very satisfied

5. *Rate yourself on your level of knowledge about personal finance issues and investing.*

1	2	3	4	5	6	7	8	9	10
Lowest Level									Highest Level

Client 2: Please provide your opinion of the following statements:

1. *Over the next five years, do you expect the U.S. economy, as a whole, to perform better, worse, or about the same as it has over the past five years?*

1	2	3	4	5	6	7	8	9	10
Perform worse				Perform about the same					Perform better

2. *How satisfied are you with your current level of income?*

1	2	3	4	5	6	7	8	9	10
Not satisfied									Very satisfied

3. *How satisfied are you with your present overall financial situation?*

1	2	3	4	5	6	7	8	9	10
Not satisfied									Very satisfied

4. *Overall, how satisfied are you with your current job or position?*

1	2	3	4	5	6	7	8	9	10
Not satisfied									Very satisfied

5. *Rate yourself on your level of knowledge about personal finance issues and investing.*

1	2	3	4	5	6	7	8	9	10
Lowest Level									Highest Level

Section 13: One way that we can help you is by identifying specific areas in your financial life that need immediate attention. Take a few minutes to answer the following questions about retirement and estate planning.

Estate Planning Document Information	Client 1	Client 2
Do you have a will?		
If so, was it drafted more than five years ago?		
Do you have a living trust? If so, please list revocable or irrevocable.		
Do you have a living will?		
Do you have an advance medical directive (AMD)?		
Do you have a durable power of attorney? If so, please list by name.		
Have you named a health care proxy? If so, please list by name.		
Are you or your spouse/partner named as the beneficiary of a trust?		
If so, from whom or where?		

Estate Planning Valuation Information	Client 1	Client 2
Do you or your partner expect to receive an inheritance?		
If so, when?		
Approximate value?		
Have you made any gifts to relatives?		
Have you received any gifts from relatives?		
Have you made substantial gifts to charities?		
Do you plan to make substantial gifts to charities in the future?		
If you or your spouse/partner were to die, would you pay off your mortgage?		
If you or your spouse/partner were to die, would you pay off your nonmortgage debt?		
If you or your spouse/partner were to die, would you fund your child's education goal?		
If you or your spouse/partner were to die, would you fund your retirement goal?		
Do you or your spouse/partner own real estate in a state other than your primary domicile?		

Section 14: It is possible that you either have worked with or are currently working with someone in the financial services profession. Please inform us of your existing advisors so that we may coordinate advice when appropriate:

Do you have a CPA, accountant, enrolled agent, or tax preparer?   *(Circle)* Yes No

    If yes, who? _____

    How long have you worked with this person? _____

    Would you recommend this person to others? _____

    May we contact this person or firm directly on your behalf? _____

    If yes, an additional form must be signed granting this authorization.

Do you have an attorney or other person you depend on for legal advice?   *(Circle)* Yes No

    If yes, who? _____

    How long have you worked with this person? _____

    Would you recommend this person to others? _____

    May we contact this person or firm directly on your behalf? _____

    If yes, an additional form must be signed granting this authorization.

Do you have any other financial advisors?   *(Circle)* Yes No

    If yes, who? _____

    How long have you worked with this person? _____

    Would you recommend this person to others? _____

    May we contact this person or firm directly on your behalf? _____

    If yes, an additional form must be signed granting this authorization.

Are there any other financial professionals of whom we should be aware?   *(Circle)* Yes No

    If yes, who? _____

    How long have you worked with this person? _____

    Would you recommend this person to others? _____

    May we contact this person or firm directly on your behalf? _____

    If yes, an additional form must be signed granting this authorization.

Section 15: Summary

Is there any other information that you would like to share with us regarding your personal or financial situation?_____

_____

_____

_____

_____

_____

_____

_____

What is the primary outcome that you expect when hiring us as your financial planner/financial planning firm? What is the most important objective(s) that you wish to accomplish? _____

_____

_____

_____

_____

_____

_____

_____

_____

Again, thank you for taking the time to complete this confidential client questionnaire.

Welcome to our financial planning family!

We look forward to working with you.

Chapter 2

Writing a Financial Plan

Learning Objectives

- Learning Objective 1: Describe the benefits of following the financial planning process when drafting a financial plan.

- Learning Objective 2: Describe the elements of a comprehensive financial plan.

- Learning Objective 3: Explain how recommendations and implementation procedures can be described in a written document.

- Learning Objective 4: Discuss the role plan presentation plays in shaping client expectations.

- Learning Objective 5: Identify and discuss the questions that guide the presentation of planning recommendations within a comprehensive financial plan.

2.1 WRITING A COMPREHENSIVE OR MODULAR FINANCIAL PLAN

The financial planning process, as described by CFP Board and other organizations, provides a proven and consistent method for practicing financial planning. Through uniform practice of the financial planning process, it is possible to develop the professional judgment necessary to conduct analyses, interpret the results in the context of a client's goals, develop recommendations, and create implementation strategies.

There are numerous outcomes associated with the practice of financial planning. Financial planners provide services, deliver products, provide advice and counsel, and occasionally offer therapeutic interventions. One thing sets financial planning apart from services provided by other advisors: the delivery of a financial plan. A **financial plan** is a detailed written document that describes the processes and procedures a client should follow to reach their financial goals.

A financial plan synthesizes recommendations into a document that serves as a roadmap for current and future action. A financial plan can be targeted, modular, or comprehensive as described below:

- A **targeted financial plan** tends to be brief, with recommendations focused on one or two financial planning topic areas.

- A **modular financial plan** encompasses more financial planning topic areas, but like a targeted financial plan, tends to be narrow in its coverage.

- A **comprehensive financial plan**, as the name implies, provides detailed observations and recommendations across a broad set of financial planning target areas.

Whereas a comprehensive financial plan can be as long as two-hundred pages, a targeted financial plan can be as short as five or ten pages. A modular financial plan's length will fall between these two extremes. The actual document, regardless of the approach taken, can be written and bound in a binder, presented electronically, or shown as an online interactive document.

Planning Reminder

While the focus of this book deals with writing and presenting a comprehensive financial plan, a growing trend in the financial planning community involves drafting targeted or modular financial plans that explore one, two, or three client questions. Although shorter than a comprehensive financial plan, these targeted plans can still benefit from following the financial planning process.

The focus of this book is on the preparation of a comprehensive financial plan. The concepts and skills described here can easily be adapted to the writing of either a targeted or modular financial plan. Several features can be used to describe a well-written financial plan:

- The plan describes in detail a client's financial goal(s).

- The plan is written in an accessible way, with definitions of unfamiliar concepts provided.

- Analyses within the plan are complete, with key assumptions highlighted and explained.

- Clear observations of a client's current financial situation are provided for each financial planning topic included in the financial plan.

- Recommendations within the financial plan represent strategies that are suitable and in the best interest of the client.

- Alternative recommendations are provided when appropriate.

- Recommendations are fundable through the use of client cash flow, debt financing, and/or client assets.

- Clear implementation procedures are provided.

- The plan meets legal requirements.

In practice, financial planners often use a software program as a tool to consolidate analyses and recommendations into a document, whereas other financial planners draft financial plans using a combination of Excel™ and Word™ or similar programs. The discussion that follows focuses on methods a financial planner who drafts their own documents can use to maintain consistency within a financial plan.

2.2 WRITING STYLE GUIDELINES

Every financial planner has a preferred writing style. Some financial planners prefer a very formal approach when referring to a client. For example, when discussing the output of an analysis, a financial planner may state:

"Mrs. Smith, you are currently spending more than you earn."

Other financial planners use a more intimate style, such as:

"You are currently spending more than you earn."

Typically, the use of singular first or second person pronouns (e.g., I, you, my) work to make a financial plan more accessible to a client. The use of *we* should be used with caution. It is appropriate to use 'we' in the context of describing a financial planner's firm, such as:

"Our team met, and we noted that you are underinsured."

The use of 'we' to describe a client's actions should be avoided. Consider the following statement:

"Our recommendation is to purchase more coverage. Doing so will decrease cash flow, but *we* will see an immediate increase in risk capacity."

In this example, the interpretation of 'we' is difficult. Is it the client or the financial planner, or both, that will see an increase in risk capacity? It would be better to write directly, such as:

> "Our recommendation is to purchase more coverage. Doing so will decrease your cash flow, but *you* will see an immediate increase in risk capacity."

It also is worth noting that the use of *I* can sometimes be misinterpreted by clients. The purpose of a financial plan is to help a client reach their goal(s). As such, the presentation of the plan should focus on the client, rather than the financial planner. The use of *I* too often changes the focus from the client back to the financial planner.

Lastly, a financial plan is an action document. The writing within the plan should encourage implementation on the part of the client. The use of an active voice is generally appropriate. Consider these two examples:

> "I believe that you should purchase additional insurance coverage."

> "Our team's recommendation is for you to purchase additional insurance coverage."

Although the difference between these two sentences is subtle, there are distinctions. The first sentence is passive. The second sentence implies action, which is generally preferable.

2.3 PLAN FORMAT GUIDELINES

Regardless of the stylistic approach taken, it is important for the final financial plan to be written in a consistent manner. Each element within a financial plan should look and read like other sections in the plan. Consistency should also exist across financial plans presented to different clients. The following outline can be used to guide the development of a financial plan. Important aspects of the outline are discussed in more detail below:

1. Plan Cover Page

2. Table of Contents

3. Letter to Client

4. Client Engagement Letter

5. Introductory Materials

    a.   Mission and/or Vision Statement

    b.   Ethics Statement or Policy

    c.   Privacy Statement

    d.   Other Firm Specific Documentation

       e.   Summary of Client Goals

       f.   Summary of Planning Assumptions

6. Executive Summary

7. Review of Financial Planning Topic Areas

8. Plan Summary

       a.   Implementation and Monitoring Procedures

       b.   Documentation of Goal Achievement

9. Client Acceptance Letter

10. Appendices

       a.   Documentation of Calculations (if not included in the review of financial planning topic areas)

       b.   Copies of Client Intake Materials

       c.   Other Documentation (as needed)

[A] Cover Page

The cover page should include information about the financial planner's firm, including address and contact information. The cover page should also be customized to include the client's name. A cover page should be visually interesting. Consider including a unique company logo. The logo can then be incorporated into the header or footer of the planning document.

[B] Table of Contents

Although sometimes overlooked, a table of contents is an essential element within a comprehensive financial plan. A table of contents helps organize the topics within a financial plan, while also serving as a guide for clients.

[C] Letter to Client

A client letter describes the purpose of the financial plan, as well as information that has important implications when interpreting plan results. For example, the client letter can include legal disclosures, firm policies, and performance disclaimers, such as "Projections made in this plan are forward looking and based on information provided by the client." An example of a client letter is provided in Appendix 2A.

[D] Client Engagement Letter

The client engagement letter, which is typically signed early in the financial planning engagement process, should be included in the financial plan. The client engagement letter represents the contract between the client and financial planner and/or the financial planner's firm. Issues related to timing, products, services, and costs should be outlined in the letter. An example of a client engagement letter is shown in Appendix 2B.

Planning Reminder

Some financial planners also include a client's investment policy statement in a financial plan's introductory materials. It is more common, however, for an investment policy statement to be included in the investment section of a financial plan.

[E] Introductory Materials

Mission and/or Vision Statement. Although primarily used as a marketing piece within a financial plan, the inclusion of a mission and/or vision statement can signal financial planner competence. A mission statement summarizes a financial planner's or financial planner's firm's core strengths. A vision statement tends to be more aspirational. The following is the mission statement for the National Association of Personal Financial Advisers (NAPFA):[1]

> "We provide networking opportunities, education, business development, and advocacy to promote the professional success of fee-only, comprehensive financial advisors."

A vision statement could be written as:

> "We strive to increase access to financial planning services to all through the application of fee-only comprehensive financial planning."

Ethics Statement or Policy. Nearly all professional organizations require their affiliates to abide by specific practice standards and a code of ethics. It is appropriate to include a restatement of these statements/policies in a written financial plan. Doing so confirms a financial planner's commitment to provide services and recommendations that are in the best interest of the client. A fee-only financial planner could, for example, include the following code of ethics from NAPFA:[2]

- Objectivity: NAPFA members strive to be as unbiased as possible in providing advice to clients, and NAPFA members practice on a Fee-Only basis.

- Confidentiality: NAPFA members shall keep all client data private unless authorization is received from the client to share it. NAPFA members shall treat all documents with care and take care when disposing of them. Relations with clients shall be kept private.

- Competence: NAPFA members shall strive to maintain a high level of knowledge and ability. Members shall attain continuing education at least at the minimum level required by NAPFA. Members shall not provide advice in areas where they are not capable.

- Fairness & Suitability: Dealings and recommendation with clients will always be in the client's best interest. NAPFA members put their clients first.

- Integrity & Honesty: NAPFA members will endeavor to always take the high road and to be ever mindful of the potential for misunderstanding that can accrue in normal human interactions. NAPFA members will be diligent to keep actions and reactions so far aboveboard that a thinking client or other professional would not doubt intentions. In all actions, NAPFA members should be mindful that in addition to serving our clients, we are about the business of building a profession, and our actions should reflect this.

- Regulatory Compliance: NAPFA members will strive to maintain conformity with legal regulations.

- Full Disclosure: NAPFA members shall fully describe method of compensation and potential conflicts of interest to clients and also specify the total cost of investments.

- Professionalism: NAPFA members shall conduct themselves in a way that would be a credit to NAPFA at all times. NAPFA membership involves integrity, honest treatment of clients, and treating people with respect.

Privacy Statement. The Gramm-Leach-Bliley Act of 1999 requires that financial services firms, banks, credit unions, and other organizations that maintain confidential financial records inform clients of firm-specific privacy policies. Financial planners must also follow the Act. An example of a privacy statement is provided in Appendix 2C.

Summary of Client Goals. This section within a financial plan's introductory materials should provide a review of the financial goals that will be addressed in the core topic analysis and recommendation elements on the financial plan.

Summary of Planning Assumptions. A list of assumptions used when (1) identifying client goals, (2) documenting a client's current situation, and (3) developing recommendations should be provided. Essentially, the summary of assumptions should include enough detail so that another financial planner, working independently with data presented in the financial plan, could replicate results. The documentation process is important because significantly different results can occur if and when assumptions are altered. Being clear regarding the assumptions used during the financial planning process can preempt second guessing on the part of a client and/or other advisors.

[F] Executive Summary

An executive summary, as the name implies, summarizes the most important recommendations made in the financial plan. The executive summary tends to be the last plan element written by a financial planner. An executive summary should:

- Sum up each recommendation made in a financial plan, showing:

  o The final recommendation, and

  o A review of the recommendation implementation plan.

A snapshot of a larger executive summary is included in Appendix 2D.

2.4 REVIEW OF FINANCIAL PLANNING TOPIC AREAS

A comprehensive financial plan can include, at minimum, each of the following topic areas (sometimes referred to as chapters or elements within a financial plan):

- Financial statement preparation and analysis (including cash flow and net worth management and budgeting)

- Tax planning

- Insurance, risk management, and employee benefits planning

- Investment planning

- Retirement planning

- Estate planning

- Special needs planning

These topic areas comprise the core elements of a financial plan. It is in these sections that the steps of the financial planning process are followed. As noted previously, standardization and consistency within a financial plan is an indication of quality. The following outline provides a writing scheme that can be used to standardize how material within each topic area is presented to a client.

[A] Overview of Topic

This section offers a brief summary of the purpose underlying the analysis. It should also include a definition of important terms.

[B] Summary of Assumptions Used in Topic

This section reviews the assumptions utilized when client data was analyzed and when recommendations were formulated.

[C] Analysis of Client's Current Situation

This is the principal focus of each topic in a financial plan. The analysis should focus on describing a client's current financial situation in relation to goal achievement. This section may include a screenshot of the Excel™ or software analysis output, although some financial planners prefer to include supporting documentation in a plan appendix. At a minimum, the current situation analysis should include both:

- A narrative description of the findings, and

- A graphical representation of findings when appropriate.

[D] Observation of Client's Current Situation

Whereas the analysis of a client's current situation is fact based—a presentation of data—this section of a financial planning topic area should provide an interpretation of the current situation. A financial planner should attempt to answer the following questions:

"What does the data mean?"

"Will the client's current course of action lead to goal achievement?"

Answers to these questions can be presented in a narrative format, as bullet points, or as a combination of approaches. Keep in mind that a best practice involves presenting at least one positive observation per section. Presenting both strengths and limitations of a client's current planning efforts help ensure that the tone of a financial plan remains positive and action-oriented.

[E] Presentation of Recommendations

Every topic section in a comprehensive financial plan should include client-centered recommendations that move the client towards goal achievement. Recommendations can be very simple, such as stating that no action is needed. Recommendations in most situations, however, necessitate more detail. Keep in mind that recommendations should be written in a way that promotes implementation.

[F] Benefits Associated with Implementation of Recommendations

While this section within each topic area can be short, the inclusion of a discussion about how the implementation of a recommendation will benefit the client is important. Say, for example, a client is faced with a negative cash flow situation. One logical recommendation may be to refinance a current mortgage as a way to reduce monthly expenses, which should increase cash flow. It is important for a financial planner to describe how implementation of the recommendation will improve the client's cash flow situation. For example, a financial planner could write the following: "Refinancing your home mortgage will increase cash flow by reducing the monthly mortgage payment by approximately $300." In this example, it is important to point out that it may take weeks for a client to be approved for a new mortgage; as such, the recommendation and justification should avoid implying a guaranteed reduction in monthly payments.

[G] Presentation of Alterative Recommendations

A truism in financial planning is that there are typically multiple solutions that can be recommended to help a client deal with a financial issue. It is important that the final recommendation represent the strategy that is in the best interest of the client, based on the financial planner's professional judgment. The financial plan writing approach outlined in this book is premised on the assumption that a financial planner can identify a preferred recommendation. The presented recommendation is the one that best matches the needs of a client.

There are times, however, when a financial planner's recommendation may conflict with a client's values, goals, or preferences. This is the reason why alternative recommendations should be presented when appropriate. Keep in mind that the alternative(s) should still be suitable and in the best interest of the client.

[H] Recommendation Implementation Strategies

When developing and presenting recommendations, it is important to address the following seven implementation questions:

1. *Who* should implement the recommendation?

2. *What* should be done?

3. *When* should the recommendation be implemented?

4. *Where* should implementation take place?

5. *Why* should the client implement the recommendation?

6. *How* should implementation occur?

7. *How much* is needed and/or how much will implementation cost?

The implementation procedure should be precise and clear enough that a client, working independently, could implement each presented recommendation without the direct help of the financial planner. For this reason, detailed documentation is of critical importance when presenting a financial plan.

[I] Plan Summary: Summary of Action Items

Implementation and Monitoring Procedures. The amount of detail presented in a comprehensive financial plan can quickly become overwhelming for clients. To combat detail fatigue, it is valuable to include a plan summary within a written plan. The plan summary can resemble an executive summary, or it may be a compilation of all implementation strategies presented in each of the topic areas. An implementation checklist will be presented later in this chapter which can be used to help organize a plan summary. Some financial planners include a checklist in each topic area and then combine these to create a summary of action document.

Documentation of Goal Achievement. One point of confusion is common among those who have never written a comprehensive financial plan: determining how to integrate recommendations. Strategies to deal with this complication are presented later in the chapter, but for now, it is important to remember that at the end of the financial planning process, two outcomes should be apparent to a client:

1. When possible, documentation of goal achievement, and

2. Evidence that each recommendation, individually and when grouped together with other recommendations, is realistic.

This means that a financial planner should provide evidence that sufficient cash flow and/or assets are available to implement recommendations.

[J] Client Acceptance Letter

A client acceptance letter should be included in the written financial plan. The purpose of this letter is to document that a client received the plan and has had a chance to ask questions and discuss additional information. In situations where recommendations need to be implemented by the financial planner, a client acceptance letter can be used as authorization to begin implementation. An example of a client acceptance letter is presented in Appendix 2E.

2.5 OTHER CONSIDERATIONS[3]

The presentation of a financial plan is a primary outcome associated with the financial planning process. The presentation of a financial plan should educate a client, motivate client action, and objectively project potential outcomes for a client. Several issues guide the development of a financial plan. At its core, a financial plan provides documentation of a financial planner's attempts to balance planning for what a client values with the client's ability and capacity to fund financial goals. These two factors are not mutually exclusive, nor are they always compatible. Three issues guide the development of a financial plan:

1. whether all necessary recommendations have been identified,

2. whether the consequences of recommendations have been identified, and

3. whether the recommendations are actionable (i.e., affordable).

The first two issues align with a client's goal orientation, whereas the third issue, as well as identification of alternative funding options, corresponds to the cash flow and net worth positions of a client.

A financial planner who sets out to write a comprehensive financial plan for a client needs to account for a variety of input and output considerations. The following discussion provides insights into some of the most important financial planning issues that shape how a plan is written and presented. The discussion provides a summary of the tools and techniques that can be used to make the financial planning documentation and writing process easier.

[A] Resolving Recommendation Conflicts

Developing appropriate client-centered recommendations is of primary importance for those following the financial planning process when writing and presenting a financial plan. Resolving the multiple issues inherent in even a simple comprehensive case involves the development and integration of recommendations from multiple strategies that originate from the core topic areas. As illustrated in Figure 2.1, nearly all clients face a dilemma: they have limited resources and almost unlimited needs and wants. A financial plan must balance on the axis between a client's **goal orientation** and **cash flow orientation**, both of which ground the financial planning process within a client's situation. In other words, the plan must balance equally the commitment to achieving a client's goals with the reality of the assets, or cash flow, available to fund those goals.

Figure 2.1. Balancing Client Goals with Cash Flow and Asset Limitations.

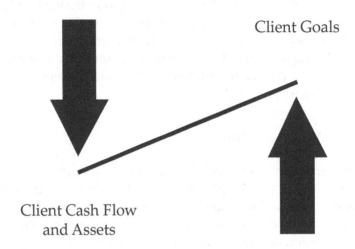

Financial planners should pay close attention to a client's cash flow position (which can include discretionary cash flow as well as other available assets) so that each recommendation presented in a plan is realistic and affordable, both in the current planning period and when projected into the future. Matching a financial plan's content to a client's goal orientation ensures that the plan aligns with the client's values, needs, and desires. Careful tracking of cash flow, assets, and liabilities is important to ensure that funding one goal does not expose the client to unwarranted risk or leave them unprepared for unexpected negative financial consequences.

[B] Important Questions to Consider When Writing a Financial Plan

The constantly evolving relationship between a financial planner and client helps shape the financial planning process and plan development. Mutually agreed-on goals and client characteristics serve as the foundation of core topic area analyses and the identification of possible strategies. When thinking about the writing process and recommendation development, it is helpful to consider the following three questions:

1. Given a client's financial planning needs, have all recommendations been identified and a preliminary implementation priority assigned?

2. Given a client's financial planning needs, what are the impacts or consequences, beneficial and detrimental, that can result from implementing all the proposed recommendations?

3. Given a client's financial planning needs, are all proposed recommendations affordable? Those recommendations that may not be affordable at the current time can be labelled as "recommendations for future implementation."

Answering these questions with confidence is a complex and intellectually challenging exercise that truly represents a financial planner's professional judgment. Repeated use of forms and checklists provides a method for building the expertise to manage this dynamic aspect of financial planning.

[C] Identifying and Prioritizing Recommendations

A **Recommendation Form** (Figure 2.2) can be used to summarize each recommendation developed in a financial plan. The form can be used to answer the seven questions of implementation (i.e., who, what, when, where, why, how, and how much).

Figure 2.2. A Recommendation Form Showing a Life Insurance Recommendation.

Planning Recommendation Form				
Financial Planning Content Area	Life insurance and investments			
Client Goal	Maximize tax-qualified investment opportunities			
Recommendation No.:	**1**	**Priority (1–6) lowest to highest:**		5
Projected/Target Value ($)	$500,000 (face value)			
Product Profile				
Type	Variable universal life policy			
Duration	Lifetime			
Provider	Northern Nevada Insurance Company			
Funding Cost per Period ($)	$6,000 annually			
Maintenance Cost per Period ($)	$0			
Current Income Tax Status	Tax-qualified	X	Taxable	
Projected Rate of Return	7% (with a guaranteed minimum of 1.5% on fixed-asset account)			
Major Policy Provisions	1. Loan provision 2. Automatic premium loans 3. Waiver of premium for periods of disability (restrictions apply)			
Procedural Factors				
Implement by Whom	Planner		Client	X
Implementation Date or Time Frame	Immediate			
Implementation Procedure	Contact Northern Nevada Life Company			
Ownership Factors				
Owner(s)	Mary E. Lamares			
Form of Ownership	Sole			
Insured(s)	John D. Lamares			
Custodial Account	Yes		No	X
Custodian	NA			
In Trust For (ITF)	Yes		No	X
Transfer on Death (TOD)	Yes	X	No	

	Beneficiary(ies)	Mary E. Lamares, spouse (100%)
	Contingent Beneficiary(ies)	William I. and Sarah B. Lamares, children (50% each)
	Proposed Benefit	Immediate life insurance protection with the added benefit of accumulating tax-advantaged assets for use during retirement

The use of a Recommendation Form can help a financial planner quickly identify the cost and priority of each recommendation. It is helpful to have this information accessible when comparing competing recommendations across the core financial planning topic areas. During the development of a comprehensive financial plan, it is common for recommendations from one topic area (e.g., life insurance) to compete against recommendations from another topic content area (e.g., education planning). Assuming there is insufficient funding for all recommendations, as is often the case, a Recommendation Form can provide guidance on which recommendation should be prioritized.

[D] Formalizing the Plan Development Process Using a Comprehensive Planning Checklist

Another form that can be used to streamline the financial plan development process is a **Comprehensive Planning Checklist**. This checklist encourages financial planners to carefully consider important questions related to each of the core financial planning areas. The checklist, shown in Appendix 2F, helps answer the broader question, "Has anything in the financial plan been overlooked?"

[E] Identifying the Consequences of Implementing Proposed Recommendations

Just as financial planning recommendations are not made in a vacuum, neither do the projected consequences of implementing recommendations occur independently. Implementing one recommendation tends to cause a ripple effect throughout a client's financial plan. This can be seen in Figure 2.3. The figure summarizes common results, or financial interactions, associated with implementing the most basic types of financial planning recommendations.

A review of impacts caused by recommendation implementation can suggest additional strategies for consideration in meeting a client's financial goals and objectives. Consider, for example, the relatively simple recommendation to purchase additional life insurance. If the insurance is owned by the insured who is also the client, or if the beneficiary is the estate of the insured, the insurance will be included in the client's gross estate. If the amount of the insurance is substantial, this inclusion could trigger an estate tax liability. In practice, this type of **cross-impact analysis** might prompt a client to reconsider ownership and titling of the insurance and/or to take steps to reposition assets to reduce potential estate tax liabilities.

Figure 2.3. Common Financial Interaction Examples that Have Multiple Impacts on a Client's Financial Situation.

Recommendation	*Potential Result*
Refinance mortgage (results will vary depending on whether closing costs are/ are not included or if cash is/ is not taken)	1. Change cash flow 2. Change net worth[a] 3. Change tax liability
Restructure debt	1. Change cash flow 2. Change net worth 3. Change tax liability
Change federal tax withholding	1. Change cash flow
Change state tax withholding	1. Change cash flow
Reallocate non-qualified portfolio assets	1. Change cash flow (only if earnings are not reinvested) 2. Change net worth[b] 3. Change tax liability
Liquidate non-qualified portfolio assets	1. Change cash flow (only if earnings are not reinvested) 2. Possible change in net worth depending on how the assets are used[b] 3. Change tax liability
Increase retirement savings	1. Change cash flow 2. Change net worth 3. Change tax liability 4. Change estate tax situation
Purchase additional life insurance	1. Change cash flow 2. Possible change in net worth depending on type of insurance 3. Change estate tax situation
Retitle assets	1. Change cash flow 2. Change net worth 3. Change tax liability 4. Change estate tax situation
Begin gift strategies	1. Change cash flow 2. Change net worth 3. Change tax liability 4. Change estate tax situation

[a] Assume closing costs are paid from assets rather than current income.
[b] Transaction costs or sales charges may apply.

[F] Identifying the Impact of Recommendations Using a Recommendation Impact Form

The use of a **Recommendation Impact Form** (Figure 2.4) provides a way to systematically verify that any potential interactions among recommendations have been uncovered. This form should be completed for each recommendation and then revised, if necessary, as final recommendations are determined. Should cash flow or other assets be insufficient to fund all financial planning recommendations, completing the Recommendation Impact Form can help a financial planner identify mutually exclusive recommendations that can be integrated and achieved by another multipurpose planning product or procedure.

Figure 2.4. Recommendation Impact Form.

Recommendation Impact Form						
Recommendation:						
Recommendation No.						
Planner Decision	Accept		Reject		Modify	
Client Decision	Accept		Reject		Modify	
Financial Impact						
Annual impact on cash-flow ($)						
Immediate impact on net worth ($)						
Planning Issue	**Degree of Significance**				**Notes**	
Major		Modest	Minor	None		
Financial situation—cash management						
Tax planning						
Life insurance planning						
Health insurance planning						
Disability insurance planning						
LTC insurance planning						
Property and liability insurance planning						
Investment planning						
Education or other special needs planning						
Retirement planning						
Estate planning						
Other planning need						
Other planning need						

By seriously considering the impact each recommendation may have on the other core topic areas, a financial planner can gain new insights into a client's unique situation. Likewise, if a financial planner cannot reasonably and knowledgeably assess the impact of recommendations, more research or consultation with other professionals may be warranted.

[G] Determining if Proposed Recommendations are Affordable When Developing Strategies in Cases Where Tradeoffs Must be Made

In addition to the impact of recommendations, funding recommendations is another critical issue that must be resolved before a financial plan can be finalized. Developing a financial plan involves allocating available cash flow, assets, and other resources towards goal achievement. Although creative options may be available, generally financial planners and clients are limited to considering one or more of the following recommendation alternatives, which are summarized below:

- Fully fund the most important recommendation in support of the goal determined by the financial planner and client; then prioritize other recommendations and corresponding goals or planning needs and apply the remaining resources.

- Agree to fund all recommendations, but stagger implementation over a reasonable period of time to avoid adversely affecting the client's financial situation. This approach assumes that additional cash flow, assets, or other resources will become available to facilitate future goal funding, thus freeing up money to be redirected to another goal(s).

- Reconsider recommendations and "downsize" or reduce one or more of the suggested funding alternatives so that all recommendations receive some funding.

- Review mutually exclusive recommendations that might be integrated and achieved through a different multipurpose planning product or procedure (e.g., a Roth IRA or life insurance).

- Prioritize recommendations and goals, fund those that are most important, and eliminate or postpone other recommendations.

- Increase available funding for all, or some, recommendations. This might be accomplished by reducing spending (for goods, services, or debt) or by increasing personal income, liquidating assets, or reallocating other assets for higher earnings.

The priority for funding usually centers on recommendations that most closely match a client's goals or that provide protection from the greatest perceived risk of loss. Complementary recommendations that can be used to meet more than one goal are sometimes the best choice. For instance, recommending that a client fund a Roth IRA can serve the dual goals of saving for retirement and a child's college expenses.

Although comprehensive plans are more complex, the synthesis of goals and funding strategies applies to both comprehensive and targeted (or modular) plans. The same is true in relation to product sales, because a client must be convinced that a product will fulfill a recognized need or goal and is worthy of funding. If funding is insufficient, a financial planner, using professional judgment, should conduct a cost-benefit analysis to determine the best use of available funds relative to the proposed recommendations.

[H] Tracking Cash Flow and Net Worth Before and After Making a Recommendation

Not only is it good practice to consider the impact of recommendations and funding alternatives, it is also a financial planner's responsibility to diligently track the financial impact of proposed recommendations. This can be accomplished by systematically tracking changes in cash flow and net worth before and after making a recommendation.

The success of a financial plan is contingent on the availability of discretionary cash flow, savings, and other available assets to fund recommendations. This implies that financial planners should thoroughly and objectively justify the choice of recommendations in a client's financial plan. This involves clearly explaining to the client how costs associated with the plan can be funded. One way to ensure that all recommendations can be implemented is to track cash flow and asset changes at the same time recommendations are determined.

An effective way to monitor funding is to use a **Cash Flow and Other Assets Tracking Form**, which can be easily developed using Excel™. A completed form, shown in Figure 2.5, illustrates how it can be used to document the effects of each recommendation on cash flow and net worth. The tracking form's principal purpose is to help a financial planner document that sufficient cash flow, savings, and assets are available to implement recommendations.

Figure 2.5. Cash Flow and Other Assets Tracking Form.

Annual Cash Flow Tracker							
					Running Balances		
		Frequency (single/annual)	Discretionary Cash Flow	Monetary Assets	Other Assets	Liabilities	Net Worth
Recommendation	(Cost)/ Benefit		($1,300)	$9,500	$42,000	$12,000	$39,500
Payment savings from mortgage refinance	$2,800	A	$2,800	$0	$0	$0	$0
			$1,500	$9,500	$42,000	$12,000	$39,500
Pay mortgage closing costs	($1,300)	S	$0	$0	($1,300)	$0	($1,300)
			$1,500	$9,500	$40,700	$12,000	$38,200
Pay-off credit card debt	($12,000)	S	$0	$0	($12,000)	($12,000)	$0
			$1,500	$9,500	$28,700	$0	$38,200

	$5,900	A	$5,900	$0	$0	$0	$0
Payment savings from paying off credit card debt			$7,400	$9,500	$28,700	$0	$38,200
Purchase life insurance	($1,000)	A	($1,000)	$0	$0	$0	$0
			$6,400	$9,500	$28,700	$0	$38,200
Increase education funding	($4,400)	A	($4,400)	$0	$4,400	$0	$4,400
			$2,000	$9,500	$33,100	$0	$42,600
Take $2,000 out of savings and contribute to an IRA	($2,000)	S	$0	($2,000)	$2,000	$0	$0
			$2,000	$7,500	$35,100	$0	$42,600
Final Balance			**$2,000**	**$7,500**	**$35,100**	**$0**	**$42,600**
Aggregate Change			**$3,300**	**($2,000)**	**($6,900)**	**($12,000)**	**$3,100**

In this example, the client begins the financial planning process with discretionary cash flow equal to –$1,300. In other words, the client is "short" more than $100 per month, which has probably contributed to the credit card debt of $12,000. The client has "unallocated" savings equal to $3,000 and another $42,000 in unallocated assets in a money market account and miscellaneous investments. **Unallocated assets** are those not specifically designated for goal accomplishment, other than for an emergency fund or other savings.

Initially, the financial planner in this example recommends that the client refinance their mortgage. This will result in a $2,800 per year decrease in expenses (ignoring any income tax changes and assuming that the refinancing will not subject the client to the Alternative Minimum Tax). The decrease in annual expenses flows directly to the client's discretionary cash flow, which is now a positive $1,500 (–$1,300 + $2,800).

However, refinancing the mortgage also results in $1,300 in closing costs, which is shown to be paid from unallocated assets. This reduces the assets available for other purposes to $40,700. Implementing an immediate payoff of the credit cards further reduces unallocated assets by $12,000 to $28,700. Implementation of this recommendation results in a $5,900 increase in discretionary cash flow because the client will no longer be making monthly credit card payments. This brings the available discretionary cash flow balance to $7,400.

Purchasing life insurance at an annual cost of $1,000 and saving $4,000 annually for a college fund reduces available cash flow to $2,000. Implementing a recommendation to reallocate $2,000 of unallocated savings toward retirement reduces the account from $3,000 to $1,000. The client now has enough cash flow, savings, and assets to implement all recommendations, but doing so will utilize $2,000 of unallocated savings and more than $13,000 in unallocated assets. Projected final balances equal $2,000 for available annual cash flow, $1,000 of unallocated savings, and a remaining balance of $28,700, ignoring any applicable taxes or transaction costs.

[I] Documenting an Implementation Procedure for Plan Recommendations

An effective way to motivate a client to act involves systematically summarizing recommendations so that implementation does not seem overwhelming. An **Implementation Checklist** can be used to summarize information needed to describe and implement each recommendation made in a financial plan.

An Implementation Checklist that summarizes all recommendations is a useful tool in both modular and comprehensive plans. Checklists can also be completed for each core topic planning area or for specific segments of time. For example, a client with staggered goals or goals with spread out or changing funding schedules might best be served by having one checklist for each of several six-month periods. In some instances, one comprehensive checklist may suffice, contingent on the complexity of the financial plan or a client's role in implementing one or more recommendations. An Implementation Checklist for Jamal and Haley is shown in Figure 2.6. The checklist summarizes five recommendations for Jamal and Haley using the framework of the seven questions of implementation to guide recommendations. Changes to Jamal and Haley's cash flow and net worth situation are also explained. As this example illustrates, a realistic and defensible summary of projected results can motivate and sustain client action and provide a valuable foundation for writing a plan.

Figure 2.6. Implementation Checklist for Jamal & Haley Clarke.

Implementation Checklist for Jamal & Haley Clarke							
Recommendation	Who	When	Where	Why	How	Cash Flow Impact	Net Worth Impact
The "What" Answer						(How Much)	
Refinance your home mortgage at 5.875 percent for 25 years.	Jamal and Haley	Start the process this week; interest rates are volatile.	First National Bank offers this loan with no points and $1,300 in closing costs.	Refinancing your mortgage will increase your monthly/yearly cash flow.	Meet with Lance Chatterjee to complete the mortgage application or use the online application portal. Sell $1,300 of XYX Mutual Fund. No taxes will be paid because of carry-over losses.	+ $2,800	–$1,300

Pay off all credit card balances.	Jamal and Haley	Within the month	Discover and Best Buy	This will eliminate high-interest debt by using liquid, low-earning assets to increase your cash flow.	Sell $12,000 of XYX Mutual Fund to pay the balances on your Discover and Best Buy cards. No taxes will be paid because of carry-over losses. Pay any outstanding balances each month.	+ $5,900	None
Purchase a $75,000 whole life insurance policy for Jamal.	Jamal and Haley	Within the next 6 weeks	With the Cia and Associates Insurance Brokerage	This will provide permanent life insurance in response to Jamal's concerns over family health history and financial risk.	Meet with an insurance professional at Cia & Associates Insurance Brokerage to complete the application.	($1,000)	None
Increase your quarterly contribution by an additional $1,100.	Jamal and Haley	Time of the next quarterly payment	With the existing Anystate 529 Savings Plan	This will allow you to meet your goal of having $50,000 saved for Freddy's education.	Increase the amount of your quarterly check or electronic payment to $2,500.	($4,400)	+$4,400
Total Impact of Recommendations on Cash Flow and Net Worth						**+$3,300**	**+$3,100**
Discretionary Cash Flow after Implementing Recommendations						**$2,000**	
Net Worth after Implementing Recommendations						**$42,600**	

[J] Incorporating Disclaimers into the Writing Process

During the writing process, it is important that any projections made in a financial plan include appropriate **disclaimers**, such as:

- "Past performance is no guarantee of future returns;"

- "All projections are based on historical data, which may not be reflected in future returns;" and

- "Projections are hypothetical."

Disclaimers remind clients that a financial plan is a living document subject to change across time. Other disclaimers and client reminders include:

- "This plan is based on data provided by the client as of [specified date];" and

- "Please consult your tax or legal professional for assistance in reviewing and implementing these recommendations."

[K] Developing a Method for Presenting Financial Plans to Clients

Although financial planning advocates have worked hard to distance **financial planning** from **selling**, in practice, sales and **marketing skills** are integral to a financial planner's success. A financial planner is always selling something, either explicitly or implicitly. The sale can be something obvious like financial advice, products, or services, or something subtler such as client education or a behavioral modification suggestion. Regardless of a financial planner's business model, the presentation of a financial plan can be framed as a marketing effort. A well-designed financial plan is the foundation that serves as the basis for current and future client action. As such, a best practice is to use a financial plan as mechanism to promote client well-being through the implementation of plan recommendations. This requires a skill set that includes presentation and sales proficiency. An effective presentation that results in client action is the result of practiced communication skills, thorough preparation, and genuine concern for a client.

[L] Providing Referral Guidance to Clients

Once a financial planner and client agree on a plan of action, implementation begins. A recommendation is only as good as a financial planner's, client's, or other professional's ability—working together or independently—to effectively implement it. Differences in implementation depend on a financial planner's business model and the products or services offered. Some financial planners will take most, if not all, of the responsibility for carrying out various aspects of a financial plan and ask little of the client (assuming such authority is granted). Other financial planners will inform or assist the client in implementing recommendations.

Financial planners often consider themselves the hub of a wheel as they facilitate plan implementation in collaboration with a client and other professionals (e.g., the client's accountant, attorney, trust administrator, or personal assistant). Some recommendations might require clients to work with professionals with whom they have an existing relationship (e.g., an insurance agent, broker, or banker), while other recommendations will require creating new relationships. Providing clients with a **professional referral** is one method to help a client move from recognition that action needs to be taken to recommendation implementation. If referrals are made, clients should be notified if fees are shared between the referring financial planner and consulting professional(s).

[M] Focusing on the Timing of Plan Implementation

Regardless of the range of a financial planner's products or services, or whether a client is solely or partly responsible for implementing recommendations, the actual implementation decision always rests with the client. Although it is often assumed that clients acting in their own best interest will put plans into action, this is not always the case. Regardless of the reason for inaction, lack of implementation is the single greatest deterrent to meeting financial goals. Therefore, it is imperative that a financial planner take steps to examine—and in some cases oversee or facilitate—the timeliness and effectiveness of client implementation, if such responsibilities are part of the engagement agreed to with the client.

Just because a client pays for a plan does not mean that they will necessarily be motivated to act on plan advice. It may be necessary to remind the client that, without proper implementation, their ability to reach long-term financial goals will likely be compromised. Other clients may know logically why they should implement recommendations, but emotional or other barriers (e.g., fear, lack of time or knowledge, or avoidance of tough decisions) can be significant deterrents to *when* implementation takes place.

Keeping clients motivated to take action in the short term and over longer periods of time is a financial planning skill that separates the best financial planners from the rest. It takes careful attention to detail to keep an implementation plan on track. The implementation of a recommendation and the fulfillment of a goal may occur in different time frames as highlighted in the following examples:

- Immediate implementation and immediate completion (e.g., filing a change-of-beneficiary form for a retirement account).

- Immediate implementation and delayed completion (e.g., opening a §529 plan and contributing $500 per month for the next five years to fund a client's education goal).

- Delayed implementation and immediate completion (e.g., opening a flexible spending account and changing a health insurance plan during the next open enrollment six months in the future).

- Delayed implementation and delayed completion (e.g., increasing retirement savings by $500 per month in five years once §529 funding is completed).

The meaning of immediate implementation or delayed implementation is fairly obvious, but the meaning of "immediate or delayed completion" is not as obvious. A goal that is completed immediately, such as paying off credit card debt, suggests that there is very little or no continuous action needed to achieve the desired result. However, if the results require periodic or continuous action and/or ongoing plan monitoring, then the goal should be categorized as a delayed-completion goal. Typically, this type of goal requires more commitment and effort by the client and financial planner to see the action through to fruition.

[N] Managing Client Expectations During the Implementation Process

A client may be apprehensive about their level of financial knowledge, experience, or capacity to implement recommendations. A client's fears or attitudes about money can be a source of anxiety. What a financial planner might interpret as reluctance to implement can actually be a client's lack of **confidence**. Managing **client expectations** is an important financial planner skill. Too often, clients assume that if a financial plan is executed perfectly, a financial planner's recommendations will seamlessly result in the projected outcome—with no deviations. The client may not fully understand that a financial planner (1) built the recommendation on the best (but imperfect) information available at the time; (2) used professional judgment to determine the best (but not foolproof) course of action; and (3) framed both the action and the expected outcome based on mutually agreed-upon assumptions (some of which can ultimately prove invalid). Managing client expectations when implementing and monitoring a plan hinges on three important concepts:

1. The client needs to acknowledge that the plan is based on information provided to the financial planner; consequently, withholding relevant information, giving "socially acceptable" answers, or otherwise knowingly or unknowingly misleading the financial planner will result in problematic outcomes.

2. The client should be fully informed of the function and formulation of hypothetical projections in the financial planning process.

3. The client must be educated about financial trends and economic issues as a pathway to providing a valid and reliable context for gauging plan results. This can be accomplished through pre-planned client-financial planner discussions, periodic monitoring meetings, workshops/webinars, newsletters, and website postings, social media, or blogs.

[O] Developing and Using an Ongoing Financial Plan Monitoring Process

The reason clients need a comprehensive financial plan is to ensure that their short-, intermediate-, and long-term financial goals are met. Only by looking at how all components of the client's financial life fit together can a full picture of financial threats and opportunities be drawn. Likewise, whether a client is on target to meet goals can be determined only by tracking and monitoring client outcomes.

Monitoring a client's situation enables a financial planner to determine a client's progress toward goal achievement, as well as a client's response to other economic or personal/life event changes. Continued monitoring also affords an opportunity for financial planners to add value to the client-financial planner relationship by helping them respond to unexpected situations, reduce anxiety, and feel more in control of and confident about their financial situation. Monitoring a financial plan entails the periodic evaluation of:

*   the effectiveness of the financial plan as a comprehensive tool for use in helping a client meet their needs in the current regulatory, economic, tax, and market environments;

*   the implementation of recommendations made to date;

*   the viability of the products and services incorporated into the financial plan and their continued usefulness to meet a client's needs; and

- the outcomes associated with recommendations and a client's overall progress toward goal achievement.

The extent of these monitoring activities—whether periodic or ongoing—varies with a financial planner's business model and agreed-on engagement with the client. However monitoring is conducted, monitoring—as the last step in the financial planning process—is important for the following reasons:

1. Monitoring compels a financial planner to stay in touch with a client to assess how well the financial plan is meeting the client's life and financial goals and objectives.

2. Periodic monitoring of a client's situation ensures that previously made recommendations, products, and services are still appropriate and useful given the client's current situation.

3. Monitoring keeps a financial planner and client on track when (a) making time-sensitive changes in response to the client's need or changes in the economy, the stock market, or taxes; (b) determining how implemented recommendations, and affiliated products, are or have influenced other areas of the client's financial plan; and/or (c) implementing recommendations that were not initially implemented. In this respect, monitoring involves assessing the cross-impact of one recommendation on other areas of the client's financial situation after implementation.

4. Monitoring provides an opportunity for a financial planner and client to celebrate what has been accomplished.

[P] Developing Strategies to Deal with Client and Plan Changes

Ongoing financial plan monitoring is multifaceted and integrative. Few aspects of a financial plan can be evaluated in isolation, even when a core topic planning area is the central focus. Significant changes to a financial plan may entail a reevaluation of a client's planning needs or priorities, including analysis of the client's situation, identification of prospective strategies, and development and presentation of recommendations. Depending on the extent of the changes, new recommendations may be needed for an isolated goal or core topic planning area, or for several goals integrated across multiple areas of a financial plan. Without consistent monitoring, a client's financial plan can inadvertently become obsolete.

Monitoring can be the responsibility of:

- the client;

- the financial planner, or the financial planner in coordination with other product or service professionals;

- a variety of product or service professionals with no coordination; or

- no one.

A financial planner's business model and scope of the established client-financial planner engagement generally set the parameters for monitoring, which can vary widely. Some aspects of monitoring pertain only to financial planners who are soliciting an ongoing relationship (i.e., for services, products, or servicing products) with their clients. Some financial planners are consistently involved with their clients, offering counsel on how to achieve financial and life goals. For financial planners who conduct their practices akin to a medical model (i.e., with a treat-as-needed approach), or for those who create modular plans (e.g., a plan focused on a single problem, issue, or core topic planning area), monitoring may be beyond the scope of the client-financial planner engagement. A financial planner may not have the opportunity to follow up with a client because implementation and monitoring are the client's responsibility, and/or the client may not re-engage the financial planner to review and evaluate progress. In more sales-based or product-delivery type models, services may not include monitoring of the situation once a product is sold to meet a specific need. Monitoring may be limited to a periodic review of a client's progress on a multiple-year schedule.

A financial plan must be responsive to change. A well thought out financial plan should evolve along with the client and their life-cycle progression, just as it should be responsive to unforeseen events, or the need for assorted products or services in the future. Failure to monitor plan implementation and outcomes is inconsistent with the intent of the financial planning process. Unfortunately, though, that is sometimes the case and may ultimately affect the client's goal attainment.. A financial planner can truly demonstrate their value added through monitoring activities.

2.6 SUMMARY

As discussed in this chapter, writing and presenting a client's financial plan is an important milestone for a financial planner. A financial plan includes numerous elements that should be standardized across a financial planner's practice. Every financial planner needs to find their own "voice" when drafting a financial plan. Some financial planners prefer a formal approach, whereas others favor an informal voice when writing. Regardless of style, there are minimum elements that should be included in a financial plan, including a client engagement letter, introductory materials, an executive summary, a review of financial planning topic areas, a plan summary, and relevant appendices. An important aspect of any well-written financial plan is a focus on documenting a client's current situation, providing an assessment of the situation, offering realistic recommendations, and illustrating an appropriate implementation procedure for each recommendation made in the financial plan.

2.7 SELF-TEST

[A] Questions

Self-Test 1

Farrell would like to retire in 9 years. His retirement income goal will require accumulating $7.5 million on the first day of retirement. He currently has $2 million saved. If Farrell is risk averse, which of the following would be an appropriate financial planning recommendation?

(a) Increase the risk of his portfolio in order to generate a 16 percent annualized return.

(b) Counsel Farrell to reevaluate his income need in retirement.

(c) Suggest that Farrell postpone retirement as a way to increase his savings.

(d) Both b and c are appropriate.

Self-Test 2

Nelda recommended that her client pay off high interest credit card debt using money from the client's money market account. Which of the following will likely occur when this recommendation is implemented?

(a) The client's level of discretionary cash flow will decrease.

(b) The client's net worth will increase.

(c) The client's net worth will decrease.

(d) The client's level of discretionary cash flow will increase.

Self-Test 3

George is a sole practitioner with a successful financial planning practice. When he meets with a prospective client, he makes it clear that he will only work with the person if he can conduct a review and provide recommendations on the following content topics: (a) cash flow/net worth, (b) taxes, (c) insurance, (d) retirement, (e) investments, and (f) estate. Given George's requirements, you can classify him as engaging in:

(a) Targeted Financial Planning.

(b) Modular Financial Planning.

(c) Comprehensive Financial Planning.

(d) Both a and b.

Self-Test 4

Which of the following professionals might a comprehensive financial planner refer her client to implement a plan recommendation?

(a) A stock broker to obtain a portfolio review.

(b) Property and casualty insurance agent to purchase homeowner's coverage.

(c) Accountant to conduct an estate tax evaluation.

(d) All the above.

Self-Test 5

Successful financial planners must possess which of the following skills?

(a) Sales Aptitude.

(b) Marketing Knowledge.

(c) Presentation Knowhow.

(d) All the above.

Self-Test 6

All the following are acceptable reasons to conduct an ongoing review of a client's situation except:

(a) To encourage client implementation of plan recommendations.

(b) To strengthen the planner-client relationship.

(c) To sell additional products, such as life insurance or annuities.

(d) To anticipate the changing needs of a client.

Self-Test 7

Who is the least likely to engage in ongoing plan monitoring?

(a) A financial planner who works on an hourly fee basis.

(b) A financial planner who writes comprehensive financial plans.

(c) A financial planner who meets with clients quarterly.

(d) Both b and c.

[B] Answers

Question 1: d

Question 2: d

Question 3: c

Question 4: d

Question 5: d

Question 6: c

Question 7: a

CHAPTER RESOURCES

A.M. Best Company (www.ambest.com).

Certified Financial Planner Board of Standards, Inc. (www.cfp.net).

Fitch Ratings (http://www.fitchratings.com/).

Insurance company ratings can be monitored at: www.ambest.com; www.fitchratings.com; www.moodys.com; www.standardandpoors.com; and www.demotech.com.

Lytton, R., Grable, J., and Klock, D. *The Process of Financial Planning: Developing a Financial Plan*, 2nd Ed. Erlanger, KY: National Underwriter, 2012.

Moody's Investor Service (http://www.moodys.com/cust/default.asp).

CHAPTER ENDNOTES

1. See: https://www.napfa.org/mission-and-fiduciary-oath.
2. *Ibid.*
3. Elements of this chapter were adapted by publisher permission from R. Lytton, J. Grable, and D. Klock, *The Process of Financial Planning: Developing a Financial Plan* (Cincinnati, OH: National Underwriter, 2006, 2012).

Sample Letter to Client

Mr. Lamar and Mrs. Emily Sample
2018 Lumpkin Street
Watkinsville, GA 30677

Dear Mr. and Mrs. Sample:

It was a pleasure to visit with you at my office on June 23rd. I truly appreciate your candor in sharing personal financial information with me, along with expressing both your present and long-term financial concerns and goals. This type of open dialogue and exchange of information and ideas is an essential element in the process of financial planning.

I understand from my time as a financial planning practitioner that client trust is earned across time. You should always feel free to ask questions about any recommendation I may make or course of action I suggest. Furthermore, you should also know I will hold your interests above my own during our professional engagement. I will treat your financial information as confidential, unless you expressly authorize me to share or discuss information with other third-party professionals (i.e., CPA, Attorney, Insurance representative, etc.) or family members. Following our review of the accompanying financial plan, we should discuss how you wish to be involved in the implementation and ongoing monitoring of your financial plan.

It is important, from a professional ethics and best practices perspective, to discuss any foreseeable conflicts of interest at the outset of an engagement or at the point in time either I or my staff becomes aware of the conflict or potential conflict. This is why I want to bring this matter to your attention now. I welcome your active participation in the financial planning process.

With this background, I will focus the remainder of this letter on the financial planning objectives we discussed during our meeting. Specifically, you requested that I undertake a comprehensive review of your current financial situation to include (1) whether you are on track as a couple to reach stated retirement goals, (2) a replacement income and financial security analysis in the event Lamar were to become disabled or to die prematurely, (3) an analysis of income and expenses (personal and business) and the corresponding impact on household cash flow. Focusing on these three core areas, I have developed a financial plan which presents an objective view of your current financial situation and provides personal and business considerations, alternative strategies for meeting objectives, and preliminary recommendations for you to consider as part of a long-term financial planning relationship and process. I look forward to working with you.

Sincerely,
Gregory Planner, Principal

Sample Client Engagement Letter[1]

Mr. Lamar and Mrs. Emily Sample
2018 Lumpkin Street
Watkinsville, GA 30677

Dear Lamar and Emily:

Re: Financial Planning Engagement

This letter confirms the terms of the financial services we will provide, per our recent conversation. As agreed upon, you will furnish complete and up-to-date information on your personal circumstances and financial and investment objectives. We will make this task easier by providing data intake and information forms for you to complete, which will be reviewed during an in-person meeting.

Once all your information has been assembled, we will analyze your present financial situation. This analysis will include a review of your assets and liabilities, current and projected income, current insurance program, retirement plan, education funding, estate documents, and investment plan.

We will provide written analyses and recommendations in the form of a financial plan. Your written financial plan will refer to such things as holding or selling securities and other assets, your projected income, cash flow, tax projections, and retirement, estate, and insurance planning.

Our recommendations will be based on the written data you provide and will include considerations of your stated personal, financial, and investment objectives and goals, so please use care when providing the data.

All information provided to us, and all recommendations and advice that we furnish you, will be kept confidential and will not be disclosed to anyone, except as we may agree in writing or be required by law. You may later request that a copy of our plan be delivered to another professional advisor.

When you receive your written financial plan, it will be your decision alone whether to implement the recommendations, either completely or in part. So there will be no future misunderstanding, you will pay a fee under this agreement for the written financial review alone, and this plan shall contain all our financial planning recommendations to you through the date of the plan delivery.

---

1. Adapted from *PracticeBuilder Financial*, Financial Planning Consultants, Inc., 2507 N. Verity Parkway, P.O. Box 430, Middletown, OH 45042-0430, www.FinancialSoftware.com. Used with permission.

After you have evaluated your financial plan, there are three aspects of follow-through:

1. Service Assistance

This involves delivery of documents to, and conferences with, your other advisors, as well as attention to the completion of forms and agreements to accomplish your objectives. There is no additional fee for this service.

2. Product Sales

This involves your voluntary acquisition of investment, real estate, or insurance products to accomplish your objectives. This agreement and fee do not provide for any product-related activity.

3. Plan Implementation Assistance

Implementation of any aspect of your plan via product acquisition is entirely at your discretion. We recognize that in many areas you will already have satisfactory business relationships, and we will assist you with them. However, if you request our assistance in making any financial acquisitions directly and decide to make purchases through us or our associates, we will receive commissions where commissions are due.

We emphasize that you are not obligated to make any purchases through our firm or associates. You are free to select any brokerage firm, insurance, or real estate agent(s), or other vendor(s) that you desire for the implementation of product recommendations.

We are not authorized or qualified to give you legal advice or to prepare legal documents for you. You should consult your own attorney for these services.

We are not authorized or qualified to prepare or amend the filing of personal income, gift, or estate tax returns for you. You should consult your own accountant for these services.

We are not authorized or qualified to act as trustee, and acting upon the advice of your attorney, you should select appropriate individuals or trust companies to provide this service.

We regard the responsibility of preparing your written financial plan as a very important personal relationship with you. So that you feel informed about working with us, we want you to have our brochure and a disclosure statement that describes our firm, its history, and our key personnel. Execution of this engagement letter acknowledges your receipt of this material.

Although we do not expect to ask anyone else to fulfill any of our responsibilities under this agreement, it may become necessary to do so. If such a situation should arise, we will obtain your prior written consent. Assignment will cancel this engagement.

If at any time you are dissatisfied with this agreement, you may cancel it. If you do so within five days of acceptance, you will receive a full refund. Thereafter, any fees that you have paid in advance will be charged for the time and effort we have devoted up until then, and the balance will be refunded.

Furthermore, you agree (as do we) that all controversies between us concerning any transaction or the construction, performance, or breach of this or any agreement between us, whether entered prior to, on, or after this date, shall be determined by arbitration as permitted by law. Such arbitration shall be conducted in accordance with the Commercial Arbitration Rules of the American Arbitration Association then applicable. The award of the arbitrators or their majority shall be final and binding and not subject to review or appeal.

Because of changes in the tax laws or in your personal financial situation, you may wish to receive an annual update of your written financial plan or a more frequent periodic review. These are available as a separate service of our firm. We feel that continued monitoring is essential to accomplish all your objectives.

Our practice for this continued service is to charge 60% of the initial planning fee, commencing the first quarter of the next calendar year. Should you request our continued service and updated financial plan, we will bill you 15% of this year's fee on a quarterly basis commencing next January. In future years, this amount may be adjusted to meet changing circumstances.

Our fee for preparing your financial review is determined based on the anticipated work to be done. We appreciate that our clients wish to know the exact amount of the fee before retaining us. Because we cannot accurately determine that amount until learning about family and financial circumstances, it is our practice to establish the fee after an initial, no-obligation session.

One half of the fee is payable after the information-gathering interview and the remainder upon receipt of your financial review. The total fee for your financial review is $_____.

If you understand the preceding terms and agree to them, please sign both copies of this letter and return one copy to us. You may include, or forward later, your deposit of one half of the initial fee.

We look forward to working with you for the achievement of your financial goals.

Understood and Agreed to by: _____

This _____, _____.

Sample Privacy Statement

Privacy Statement

Our Promise to You

As a client of ABC Financial Planning, you will be requested to share personal and financial information with us from time to time. Your privacy is important to us, and we are dedicated to safeguarding your personal and financial information.

Information Provided by Clients

In the normal course of doing business, we typically obtain the following non-public personal information about our clients' identity:

- Name, address, and Social Security number.

- Information regarding securities and other transactions effected by us.

- Client financial information such as net worth, assets, income, bank account information, and account balances.

- Financial planning related information including: personal information necessary as inputs for all aspects of financial planning, including risk management/insurance, retirement, taxes, estate planning, and investing; and information on others such as your dependents relevant to your financial well-being.

- Information about you from third parties, such as your agents or consumer reporting agencies.

We use this information as part of the financial planning process and to help you meet your personal financial goals.

How We Manage and Protect Your Personal Information

- ABC Financial Planning will not provide your personal information to mailing list vendors or solicitors.

- ABC Financial Planning will not share nonpublic personal information about clients or consumers with third parties not affiliated with ABC Financial Planning, except as noted below.

- With your permission, as reflected in our engagement agreement, ABC Financial Planning may share nonpublic personal information as necessary:

  - To complete transactions or account changes as authorized by the client.

  - To maintain or service a client's account with contracted service providers or other professionals such as attorneys, accountants, consultants, employees, insurance agents providing or supporting development and implementation of financial planning and or analysis services, recommendation implementation, asset management, and or administrative functions for ABC Financial Planning or on your behalf.

  - If ABC Financial Planning is required or permitted by law or regulatory authorities with jurisdiction over the firm.

We seek confidentiality in our agreements with unaffiliated third parties that require access to your personal information. You may opt out from our sharing information with any of these nonaffiliated third parties by notifying us at any time by telephone, mail, fax, email, or in person. We maintain physical, electronic, and procedural safeguards to protect your personal information. This includes maintaining appropriate security measures for computer and information systems, including the use of passwords, firewalls, and other internet security systems. Personally identifiable information about you will be maintained while you are a client, and for at least the required period thereafter that records are required to be maintained by federal and state securities laws. After that time, information may be destroyed.

Client Notifications

We are required by law to annually provide a notice describing our privacy policy. In addition, we will inform you promptly if there are changes to our policy. Please do not hesitate to contact us with questions about this notice.

Sample Executive Summary

The purpose of this comprehensive financial plan is to provide a framework for helping you reach your financial goals and objectives. The plan consists of a section for each of the following financial planning topic areas: cash flow and net worth situation; tax planning; insurance planning; retirement planning; education planning; and estate planning. A comprehensive review of your financial situation was conducted using information you provided to our firm. The plan was written to address three issues: (1) whether you are on track as a couple to reach stated retirement goals, (2) a replacement income and financial security analysis in the event Lamar were to become disabled or to die prematurely, (3) an analysis of income and expenses (personal and business) and the corresponding impact on household cash flow. Several financial strengths were identified during the analysis. It was determined that your net worth is excellent given your age and household income level. You are currently contributing to a company 401(k), and your household has both employment and self-employment income.

Our analysis also indicated that five specific areas need attention.

- First, Lamar will need to purchase an additional $2.6 million in life insurance coverage.

- Second, to achieve retirement at age sixty-five, you will need to save an additional $84,845 per year in a combination of tax-deferred and taxable accounts.

- Third, given the relative high interest rate on your home equity line of credit (in addition to no longer being able to deduct the interest) and credit cards, you should use monetary assets to pay these liabilities.

- Fourth, you should establish a life insurance and personal residence trust.

- Fifth, you should refinance the mortgage on your Florida home.

The following actions are recommended (additional details are provided in the financial plan).

- Purchase an additional $2.6 million in life insurance coverage.

  - Date to be completed: Immediately.

- Save an additional $84,845 per year in a combination of investment accounts. Invest all proceeds in stock growth portfolio.

  - Date to be completed: Yearly for next fifteen years.

- By the end of the year, pay off all credit cards and the home equity line of credit.

  o   Date to be completed: By the end of the year.

- Establish a Life Insurance and Personal Residence Trust.

  o   Date to be completed: Within twelve months.

- Refinance Florida home with new twenty-year 5 percent mortgage, using monetary assets for closing costs.

  o   Date to be completed: Within thirty days.

Sample Client Acceptance Letter

Mr. Lamar and Mrs. Emily Sample[1]
2018 Lumpkin Street
Watkinsville, GA 30677

Dear Lamar and Emily:

Re: Acceptance of Your Financial Analysis

The planning process is an evolution that started with gathering information, comparing your planning assumptions and objectives, analyzing where you are headed, and defining the major problems or obstacles you currently face and might face in the future.

Your written financial plan contains recommendations for your consideration, as well as a recommended implementation checklist.

However, at some point it may be necessary to "freeze" the current plan and proceed with implementation follow-through.

If you are satisfied with the written financial plan, please sign below and return a copy for our files. You might also call to schedule a session to begin plan implementation.

Plan accepted by: _____   Date: _____

---

1   Adapted from *PracticeBuilder Financial*, Financial Planning Consultants, Inc., 2507 N. Verity Parkway, P.O. Box 430, Middletown, OH 45042-0430. Used with permission.

Comprehensive Planning Checklist

Comprehensive Planning Checklist for _____				
Cash Flow Analysis to Maximize Client's Discretionary Cash Flow			Recommendation Needed?	
1. Has planner reviewed financial ratios and compared them to benchmarks?	Yes	No	Yes	No
2. Have steps been taken to designate savings or other assets for use as an emergency fund or source of emergency income?	Yes	No	Yes	No
3. Has planner reviewed client budget or income and expense statement for possible expense reductions?	Yes	No	Yes	No
4. Has planner verified that the client is able and willing to proactively save money on a regular basis?	Yes	No	Yes	No
5. Have debt reduction or debt restructuring alternatives been reviewed?	Yes	No	Yes	No
6. Have mortgage refinancing alternatives been reviewed?	Yes	No	Yes	No
7. Are there other client-specific cash management issues to consider?	Yes	No	Yes	No
Tax Analysis to Minimize Taxes and Maximize Client's Discretionary Cash Flow			Recommendation Needed?	
8. Have tax projections for 1, 3, or 5 years been done to guide the planning process?	Yes	No	Yes	No
9. Has client income tax withholding been matched to tax liability?	Yes	No	Yes	No
10. Has client FICA withholding been matched to FICA liabilities?	Yes	No	Yes	No
11. Has planner reviewed client's tax situation to ensure that other tax-reduction opportunities have not been overlooked?	Yes	No	Yes	No
12. Is the client currently subject to the AMT? Have projections been made for the next 1, 3, or 5 years?	Yes	No	Yes	No
13. Has planner checked to determine whether client is maximizing tax-reducing insurance alternatives? a. Health flexible spending account? b. Dependent care flexible spending account? c. Employer provided life, health, disability, or LTC benefits? d. Any other § 125 cafeteria plan benefits?	 Yes Yes Yes Yes	 No No No No	 Yes Yes Yes Yes	 No No No No

14. Are there other client-specific tax management issues to consider?	Yes	No	Yes	No

Insurance Analysis to Limit Client's Household Risk Exposures			**Recommendation Needed?**	
15. Has a life insurance analysis been conducted?	Yes	No	Yes	No
16. Has a disability insurance analysis been conducted?	Yes	No	Yes	No
17. Has a long-term care (LTC) insurance analysis been conducted?	Yes	No	Yes	No
18. Has a health insurance analysis been conducted?	Yes	No	Yes	No
19. Has a property, casualty, and liability insurance analysis been conducted?	Yes	No	Yes	No
20. Are there other client-specific risk management issues to consider?	Yes	No	Yes	No

Investment Planning Analysis to Maximize Client's Return			**Recommendation Needed?**	
21. Has an investment funding goal been identified?	Yes	No	Yes	No
22. Is the client on track to meet the targeted amount and date?	Yes	No	Yes	No
23. Are asset allocation and investments in the best interest of the client given the client's time horizon, risk tolerance, and other assumptions?	Yes	No	Yes	No
24. Is the client fully benefitting from tax-advantaged investments?	Yes	No	Yes	No
25. Are there other client-specific investment planning issues to consider?	Yes	No	Yes	No

Education or Special Needs Planning Analysis to Maximize Client's Return			**Recommendation Needed?**	
26. Has an education funding goal been identified?	Yes	No	Yes	No
27. Is the client on track to meet the targeted amount and date?	Yes	No	Yes	No
28. Are asset allocation and investments in the best interest of the client given the client's time horizon, risk tolerance, and other assumptions?	Yes	No	Yes	No
29. Is the client fully benefitting from tax-advantaged accounts?	Yes	No	Yes	No
30. Are there other client-specific education planning issues to consider?	Yes	No	Yes	No
31. Has a special needs funding goal(s) been identified? Is the client on track to meet the targeted amount(s) and date(s)?	Yes	No	Yes	No
32. Are there other client-specific special needs planning issues to consider?	Yes	No	Yes	No

Retirement Planning Analysis to Maximize Client's Return			Recommendation Needed?	
33. Has a retirement funding goal been identified?	Yes	No	Yes	No
34. Is the client on track to meet the targeted amount and date?	Yes	No	Yes	No
35. Are asset allocation and investments in the best interest of the client given the client's time horizon, risk tolerance, and other assumptions?	Yes	No	Yes	No
36. Is the client fully benefitting from any available match?	Yes	No	Yes	No
37. Is the client fully benefitting from tax-advantaged accounts?				
38. Are other retirement funds available?	Yes	No	Yes	No
39. Are there other client-specific retirement planning issues to consider?	Yes	No	Yes	No

Estate Planning Analysis to Minimize Estate Taxes and Ensure Client's Final Wishes			Recommendation Needed?	
40. Has the client begun giving assets to dependents, other family members, or charity?	Yes	No	Yes	No
41. Are documents in place to distribute property and provide for dependents, heirs, or charities?	Yes	No	Yes	No
42. Have steps been taken to minimize probate, estate, or inheritance taxes?	Yes	No	Yes	No
43. Have steps been taken to minimize settlement costs, including legal and accounting fees?	Yes	No	Yes	No
44. Are funds available, or plans in place, for the payment of estate taxes and settlement expenses?	Yes	No	Yes	No
45. Are documents in place to guide incapacitation or other end-of-life decisions?	Yes	No	Yes	No
46. Are documents in place to care for, or name guardians for, children or other financial dependents?	Yes	No	Yes	No
47. Are documents in place to care for a pet, if applicable?	Yes	No	Yes	No
48. Has a letter of last instructions been prepared to provide for the distribution of personal and digital assets (i.e., accounts, music, pictures, etc.) as well as other final wishes?	Yes	No	Yes	No
49. Are there other client-specific estate planning issues to consider?	Yes	No	Yes	No

Cross-planning Analysis: Have the Following Interactions Been Considered?			Recommendation Needed?	
50. Net worth ↔ insurance?	Yes	No	Yes	No
51. Income taxes ↔ insurance?				
a. Health flexible spending accounts?	Yes	No	Yes	No
b. Dependent care flexible spending accounts?	Yes	No	Yes	No
c. Employer-provided life, health, disability, and LTC benefits?	Yes	No	Yes	No

52. Income taxes ↔ mortgage refinance?	Yes	No	Yes	No
53. Life insurance ↔ estate planning?	Yes	No	Yes	No
54. Life/LTC hybrid ↔ life insurance?	Yes	No	Yes	No
55. LTC ↔ estate planning?	Yes	No	Yes	No
56. Education funding ↔ estate planning?	Yes	No	Yes	No
57. Education funding ↔ income tax planning?	Yes	No	Yes	No
58. Investment planning ↔ income tax planning?	Yes	No	Yes	No
59. Retirement planning ↔ income tax planning?	Yes	No	Yes	No

Chapter 3

Laws, Regulations, and Ethics: Standards Guiding the Financial Planning Process

Learning Objectives

- Learning Objective 1: Explain the intent underlying financial planning policies, rules, and regulations.

- Learning Objective 2: Describe the multiple ways financial planners are regulated in the marketplace.

- Learning Objective 3: Explain the role of the SEC, NASAA, NAIC, state regulators, self-regulatory organizations, and certification bodies in establishing and enforcing regulations and practice standards.

- Learning Objective 4: Describe the difference between the best interest and fiduciary standard of care.

- Learning Objective 5: Understand the requirements associated with registering as an investment adviser.

- Learning Objective 6: Understand the requirements associated with selling insurance.

- Learning Objective 7: Describe situations in which a financial planner must make disclosures.

3.1 THE FINANCIAL PLANNING REGULATORY ENVIRONMENT

Financial planners work in a highly regulated marketplace. Over the past one hundred years, laws and related regulations have been passed at the state and federal levels in an attempt to protect the consumer interest. In addition to state and federal rules, as shown in Figure 3.1, financial planners must often follow prescribed procedures and practice standards issued by industry regulators and certification boards. Given the importance of laws, regulations, and rules in shaping the way in which a financial planner provides services, it is important for financial planners to have a working knowledge of the ethical boundaries and practice standards that must be followed. This chapter summarizes some of the most important of these laws, regulations, and practice standards.

Figure 3.1. The Regulatory Environment for Financial Planning.

A working assumption among financial planning regulators is that a financial planner will follow the highest ethical standards when working with clients. **Ethics** represents doing what is right in terms of behavior when interacting with others. Rather than relying on a financial planner to derive their own set of ethical standards, regulators and certification boards typically outline minimally accepted standards of ethical behavior. Enforcement of financial planning laws, regulations, and practice standards follows a policy of absolutism rather than relativism. Among legal authorities, rules based on absolutism aligns with a **deontological ethical perspective**. This means that when a judge or arbitrator hears a dispute, their decision must follow the letter of the law. This contrasts with a **teleological** view of ethics where rulings are made taking into context the intentions and consequences of behavior.

The type of laws, regulations, and practice standards a financial planner must follow depend, to a great extent, on a financial planner's practice model and scope of practice.

As illustrated in Figure 3.2, the types of products and services provided, and the ways in which a financial planner is compensated, determine which state, federal, organizational, and certification board regulations must be followed. It is important to note that there almost always will be overlap among the categories shown in Figure 3.2. For example, a financial planner who earns commissions from the sale of products, while also providing services on a fee basis, must follow multiple laws, regulations, and practice standards.

Figure 3.2. Determination of the Regulatory Oversight of Financial Planners.

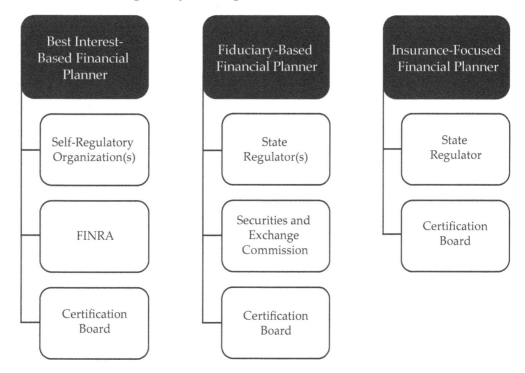

3.2 SELF-REGULATORY ORGANIZATION RULES

A **self-regulatory organization** (SRO) is a federally recognized entity that is tasked with certain responsibilities, including market surveillance, trade practice surveillance, audits, examinations of member firms, and oversight of firm employee compliance to rules developed by the SRO. SROs are also engaged in the licensing of firm representatives and ensuring that advisor interactions with clients are conducted with financial integrity, appropriate sales practices, and in compliance with recordkeeping requirements.

Planning Reminder

Financial planners who work for broker-dealer firms are known as brokers. Brokers generally must hold a Series 7 license. Brokers are also known as registered representatives, wire house representatives, and financial advisors.

SROs came into existence with the passage of the **Maloney Act of 1938**. This Act amended the **1934 Securities Exchange Act**—the federal law that established the

Securities and Exchange Commission (SEC)—by allowing registered securities associations to develop policies of self-regulation of securities firms and employees. In 1939, the National Association of Securities Dealers (NASD) became the first SRO. In 2007, NASD became the **Financial Industry Regulatory Authority (FINRA)**.

Someone who wishes to enter the securities industry to sell a broad range of products must pass two examinations. The first is the **Securities Industry Essential (SIE) examination**. The SIE is an entry-level test that must be passed prior to sitting for other FINRA examinations (e.g., Series 6, Series 7, Series 79, or Series 99). The SIE exam does not require a sponsor or registration as an investment advisor. The second is the FINRA **Series 7 examination**, which is also known as the *General Securities Representative Examination*. Financial planners who pass the Series 7 examination are eligible to register to trade a wide variety of securities products, including corporate securities, municipal bond securities, options, direct participation programs, investment company products, and variable contracts. Some fee-only financial planners may be required to pass the Series 7 exam as well. The exam consists of 125 questions. Test takers have 225 minutes to complete the exam.

Figure 3.3 shows other FINRA licenses that require an examination. Four are particularly relevant to the practice of financial planning:

- **Series 6**: Investment Company Products/Variable Contracts Representative Exam—this exam qualifies someone to sell mutual funds, variable annuities, and variable life insurance held within life insurance contracts.

- **Series 63**: Uniform Securities Agent State Law Exam—this exam qualifies someone to sell securities across state lines (sometimes referred to as the Blue Sky law).

- **Series 65**: Uniform Investor Adviser Law Exam—this exam qualifies a firm representative to act as an investment adviser and receive a fee for services.

- **Series 66**: Uniform Combined State Law Exam—this exam qualifies someone to be dually registered as an investment adviser (i.e., to receive a fee) and an agent of a broker-dealer (i.e., to receive a commission).

Figure 3.3. FINRA Licensing Examinations.

	Exam Duration (minutes)	Questions	Cost
Series 3 - National Commodities Futures Examination	150	120	$130
Series 4 - Registered Options Principal Exam (OP)	195	125	$105
Series 6 - Investment Company and Variable Contracts Products Representative Exam (IR)	135	100	$100

Series 7 - General Securities Representative Exam (GS)	360	250	$305
Series 9 and 10 - General Securities Sales Supervisor Examination	S9: 90 S10: 240	S9: 55 S10:145	S9: $80 S10: $125
Series 11 - Assistant Representative - Order Processing Exam (AR)	60	50	$80
Series 14 - Compliance Official Exam (CO)	180	110	$350
Series 16 - Supervisory Analysts Exam (SA)	Part 1: 90 Part 2: 120	Part 1: 50 Part 2: 50	$240
Series 17 - United Kingdom Securities Representative Exam (IE)	150	100	$80
Series 22 - Direct Participation Programs Representative Exam (DR)	150	100	$100
Series 23 - General Securities Principal Exam - Sales Supervisor (GP)	150	100	$100
Series 24 - General Securities Principal Exam (GP)	225	150	$120
Series 26 - Investment Company and Variable Contracts Products Principal Exam (IP)	165	110	$100
Series 27 - Financial and Operations Principal Exam (FN)	225	145	$120
Series 28 - Introducing Broker-Dealer Financial and Operations Principal Exam (FI)	120	95	$100
Series 30 - NFA Branch Manager Examination (formerly, Branch Managers Examination – Futures)	60	50	$85
Series 31 - Futures Managed Funds Examination	60	45	$85
Series 32 - Limited Futures Examination - Regulations	45	35	$85
Series 34 - Retail Off-Exchange Forex Examination	60	40	$85
Series 37 - Canada Securities Representative Exam - With Options (CD)	150	90	$185
Series 38 - Canada Securities Representative Exam - No Options (CN)	75	45	$185

Series 39 - Direct Participation Programs Principal Exam (DP)	135	100	$95
Series 42 - Registered Options Representative Exam (OR)	90	50	$75
Series 50 - Municipal Advisor Representative Examination	180	100	$265
Series 51 - Municipal Fund Securities Limited Principal Examination	90	60	$255
Series 52 - Municipal Securities Representative Examination (MR)	210	115	$280
Series 53 - Municipal Securities Principal Examination (MP)	180	100	$265
Series 57 - Securities Trader Representative Exam (TD)	225	125	$120
Series 62 - Corporate Securities Representative Exam (CS)	150	115	$95
Series 63 - Uniform Securities Agent State Law Examination	75	60	$135
Series 65 - Uniform Investment Adviser Law Examination	180	130	$175
Series 66 - Uniform Combined State Law Examination	150	100	$165
Series 72 - Government Securities Representative Exam (RG)	180	100	$110
Series 79 - Investment Banking Representative Exam (IB)	300	175	$305
Series 82 - Private Securities Offerings Representative Exam (PR)	150	100	$95
Series 86 and 87 - Research Analyst Examination (RS)	S86: 270 S87: 105	S86: 100 S87: 50	S86: $185 S87: $130
Series 99 - Operations Professional Exam (OS)	150	100	$130
Source: FINRA Qualification Exams: http://www.finra.org/industry/qualification-exams.			

A financial planner who is engaged in providing advice related to commodities and selling commodities, futures, options, and/or other products may be required to obtain additional licenses. Figure 3.4 shows some of the other large SROs operating in the U.S. securities markets in which a financial planner may acquire a license or have dealings.

Figure 3.4. Other Self-Regulatory Organizations.

Organization	Acronym	Members
Chicago Board Options Exchange	CBOE	Options trading firms
Municipal Securities Rulemaking Board	MSRB	Municipal bond dealers
National Futures Association	NFA	Derivative trading firms
New York Stock Exchange	NYSE	Securities firms
Options Clearing Corporation	OCC	Options trading firms

3.3 INVESTMENT ADVISER RULES

While the majority of financial planners working today earn some or all their annual income from the sale of products and services, a growing number earn a significant portion of their revenue from fees. A financial planner (who is also engaged in providing investment advice), who generates any income from a fee source (e.g., a fee for managing a client's portfolio and providing advice on investing in stocks, bonds, mutual funds, or exchange traded funds) must register as an investment adviser either in the state in which that financial planner does business or with the SEC. The **Investment Advisers Act of 1940** provides specific guidance on investment adviser registration requirements.

Investment adviser rules are strictly enforced. However, there are several exclusions from the investment adviser definition:[1]

- **Banks and Bank Holding Companies**. This exclusion is generally limited to U.S. banks and bank holding companies.

- **Lawyers, Accountants, Engineers, and Teachers**. This professional exclusion is available only to those professionals listed, and only if the investment advice given is incidental to the practice of their profession. Factors considered by the SEC to evaluate whether advice is incidental to a profession are: (a) whether the professional holds themselves out as an investment adviser; (b) whether the advice is reasonably related to the professional services provided; and (c) whether the charge for advisory services is based on the same factors used to determine the professional's usual charge.

- **Brokers and Dealers.** A broker-dealer that is registered with the SEC under the Securities Exchange Act of 1934 ("Exchange Act") is excluded from the Act if the advice given is: (a) solely incidental to the conduct of its business as broker-dealer and (b) the broker-dealer does not receive any special compensation for providing investment advice.

> *Planning Reminder*
>
> It is important to remember that regulators differentiate between the terms *adviser* and *advisor*.
>
> - An investment adviser is an individual or a firm that is in the business of providing advice about securities to clients for a fee.
>
> - An investment advisor is an individual or firm that provides investment counsel, guidance, or advice for a commission or other non-fee form of compensation.

- **Broker-Dealer Agents.** The SEC will exempt agents of a broker-dealer if the person is (a) providing advice within the scope of their employment with the broker-dealer; (b) the advice is incidental to their employer's brokerage activities; and (c) they receive no special compensation for their advice.

- **Publishers.** Publishers are excluded from registration, but only if a publication: (a) provides only impersonal advice (i.e., advice not tailored to the individual needs of a specific client); (b) is "bona fide," (containing disinterested commentary and analysis rather than promotional material disseminated by someone touting particular securities); and (c) is of general and regular circulation (rather than issued from time to time in response to episodic market activity).

- **Government Securities Advisers.** This exclusion is available to persons and firms whose advice is limited to certain securities issued by or guaranteed by the U.S. government.

- **Credit Rating Agencies.** This exclusion is available to any rating agency regulated under the Securities Exchange Act as a nationally recognized statistical rating organization.

- **Family Offices.** A family office that manages the wealth and financial affairs of a single family is excluded from the investment adviser definition if the office: (a) provides investment advice only to family clients; (b) is wholly owned by family clients and exclusively controlled by family members and/or certain family entities; and (c) does not hold itself out to the public as an investment adviser.

- **Governments and Political Subdivisions.** Registration requirements do not apply to the U.S. government, state governments and their political subdivisions, and their agencies or instrumentalities, including their officers, agents, or employees acting in their official capacities.

Dodd-Frank Act and SEC rules dictate which and where a financial planner or financial planning firm *must* register with the SEC as an investment adviser. Investment advisers must register with the SEC or at the state level. The thresholds and requirements for registration with the SEC are as follows:[2]

- A small adviser with less than $25 million of assets under management (AUM) is prohibited from SEC registration if its principal office and place of business is in a state that regulates investment advisers (currently all states except Wyoming).

- A mid-sized investment adviser with AUM between $25 million and $100 million of AUM:

  o Is required to register with the SEC if its principal office and place of business is in New York or Wyoming, unless a registration exemption is available.

  o Is prohibited from SEC registration if its principal office and place of business is in any state except New York or Wyoming, and the mid-sized investment adviser is required to be registered in that state. If the mid-sized adviser is not required to be registered in that state, then the investment adviser must register with the SEC, unless a registration exemption is available.

- An investment adviser approaching $100 million of AUM may rely on a registration "buffer" that ranges from $90 million to $110 million of AUM. The investment adviser:

  o May register with the SEC when it acquires $100 million of AUM;

  o Must register with the SEC once it reaches $110 million of AUM, unless a registration exemption is available; and

  o Once registered with the SEC, is not required to withdraw from SEC registration and register with the states until the investment adviser has less than $90 million of AUM.

- A large adviser with at least $110 million of AUM is required to register with the SEC, unless a registration exemption is available.

Confusion over who must register with the SEC (or appropriate state regulator) is complicated by the fact that often two entities are represented by the same person. If a financial planner is operating as an investment adviser, they must register as such. However, if a financial planner is working for an investment adviser firm, the financial planner generally must register as an **investment adviser representative** (IAR). At the state level, firms and IARs may be required to register if the firm or IAR provides services to five or more clients within a state.[3] A firm that is solely registered with the SEC need only file a notice with states where services are provided to five or more clients.

3.4 CERTIFICATION ORGANIZATIONS

[A] Certification Organizations in General

With over eighty thousand U.S. based financial planners holding the CFP® certification, the voice of the Certified Financial Planner Board of Standards, Inc. is important in shaping laws, regulations, and practice standards at the state and federal level. Before moving forward, it should be noted that CFP Board is not the only certification organization operating in the United States. The American College of Financial Services sponsors multiple designations and certifications, two of which are highly regarded in the financial planning community: Chartered Financial Consultant (ChFC™) and Chartered Life Underwriter (CLU™). Among financial planners who specialize in investment management, the CFA Institute's Chartered Financial Analyst certification (CFA™) is the best known. Other organizations, such as the International Association of Registered Financial Consultants (IARFC), the Association for Financial Counseling and Planning Education (AFCPE), the Financial Therapy Association (FTA), and the Investment Management Consultants Organization (IMCO) provide specialized training and certification for financial planners who have an interest in insurance, financial counseling, financial therapy, and investing, respectively. Other prominent certification organizations include the College for Financial Planning, American Institute of Certified Public Accountants, International Foundation for Retirement Education, and Money Quotient, with the list of other organizations numbering in the hundreds.

Each of the primary certification boards (and nearly all membership organizations within the profession) promulgate and regulate codes of ethics and practice standards. Among the most codified rules are CFP Board's *Code of Ethics and Standards of Conduct*. CFP Board undertook a significant revision of these rules in 2019. Given the role CFP Board's rules and standards play in shaping policy across the financial planning field, it is important for financial planners—even those who are not CFP® certificants or CFP® candidates—to understand what some consider to be fundamental practice standards. The following summarizes some of the key elements associated with CFP Board's practice standards.[4]

[B] CFP Board's Code and Standards

A financial planner who holds the CFP® marks is required to uphold CFP Board's *Code of Ethics and Standards of Conduct*. CFP Board's guidelines were drafted to benefit and protect the public when working with financial planners. The guidelines provide financial planners with specific standards for delivering financial planning services. As noted by CFP Board, "compliance with the Code and Standards is a requirement of CFP® certification that is critical to the integrity of the CFP® marks. Violations of the Code and Standards may subject a CFP® professional to discipline."[5] CFP Board's Code of Ethics states that a CFP® professional must:

1.   Act with honesty, integrity, competence, and diligence.

2. Act in the client's best interests.

3. Exercise due care.

4. Avoid or disclose and manage conflicts of interest.

5. Maintain the confidentiality and protect the privacy of client information.

6. Act in a manner that reflects positively on the financial planning profession and CFP® certification.

Practice standards described within the *Code of Ethics* are guided by CFP Board's *Standards of Conduct*. Detailed information about rules and applications of standards to particular situations can be found at www.cfp.net. Figure 3.5 provides an overview of the *Standards of Conduct*:

Figure 3.5. Overview of CFP Board's Standards of Conduct.

When providing financial advice, a CFP® professional must ...	
Act using Fiduciary Care	Duty of Loyalty Duty of Care Duty to Follow Client Instructions
Act with Integrity	
Act with Competence	
Act using Diligence	
Disclose and Manage Conflicts of Interest	Disclose Conflicts Manage Conflicts
Use Sound and Objective Professional Judgement	
Act with Professionalism	
Comply with the Law	
Act with Confidentiality and Privacy	
Provide Information to a Client	

Provide Accurate Information when Communicating with a Client	
Not Make False or Misleading Representations Regarding Compensation	Specific Representations: Sales-Related Compensation Related Party Connection with any Professional Services Safe Harbor for Related Parties Misrepresentations by a CFP(r) Professional's Firm Fee-Only and Fee-Based
Use Care when Recommending, Engaging, and Working with Additional Persons	
Use Care when Selecting, Using, and Recommending Technology	
Refrain from Borrowing or Lending Money and Commingling Financial Assets with Clients	

CFP Board's *Standards of Conduct* also provide specific guidance regarding the duties of a CFP® professional to their firm, subordinates, the CFP Board, and the profession. Figure 3.6 provides a summary of these standards. A more complete overview of CFP Board's Code of Ethics and Standards of Conduct can be found in Appendix 3B.

Figure 3.6. Summary of CFP Board's Professional Conduct Standards.

A CFP® professional must ...	
1. Use Reasonable Care When Supervising	
2. Comply with Lawful Objectives of CFP® Professional's Firm	
3. Provide Notice of Public Discipline	A CFP® professional must promptly advise the CFP® Professional's Firm, in writing, of any public discipline imposed by CFP Board.

4. Refrain from Adverse Conduct	A CFP® professional may not engage in conduct that reflects adversely on their integrity or fitness as a CFP® professional, upon the CFP® marks, or upon the profession. Such conduct includes, but is not limited to, conduct that results in:
	• a Felony or Relevant Misdemeanor conviction, or admission into a program that defers or withholds the entry of a judgment of conviction for a Felony or Relevant Misdemeanor;
	• a Finding in a Regulatory Action or a Civil Action that the CFP® professional engaged in fraud, theft, misrepresentation, or other dishonest conduct;
	• a personal bankruptcy or business bankruptcy filing or adjudication where the CFP® professional was a Control Person of the business, unless the CFP® professional can rebut the presumption that the bankruptcy demonstrates an inability to manage responsibly the CFP® professional's or the business's financial affairs;
	• the assessment of a federal tax lien on property owned by the CFP® professional, unless the CFP® professional can rebut the presumption that the federal tax lien demonstrates an inability to manage the CFP® professional's financial affairs responsibly; or
	• a non-federal tax lien, judgment lien, or civil judgment that has not been satisfied within a reasonable amount of time.
5. Provide written notice to CFP Board within 30 calendar days after the CFP® professional, or an entity over which the CFP® professional was a Control Person, has:	Been charged with, convicted of, or admitted into a program that defers or withholds the entry of a judgment or conviction for, a Felony or Relevant Misdemeanor;
	Been named as a subject of, or whose conduct is mentioned adversely in, a Regulatory Investigation or Regulatory Action alleging failure to comply with the laws, rules, or regulations governing Professional Services;
	Had conduct mentioned adversely in a Finding in a Regulatory Action involving failure to comply with the laws, rules, or regulations governing Professional Services, other than a Regulatory Action involving a Minor Rule Violation in a Regulatory Action brought by a self-regulatory organization;
	Had conduct mentioned adversely in a Civil Action alleging failure to comply with the laws, rules, or regulations governing Professional Services;
	Become aware of an adverse arbitration award or civil judgment, or a settlement agreement, in a Civil Action alleging failure to comply with the laws, rules, or regulations governing Professional Services, where the conduct of the CFP® professional, or an entity over which the CFP® professional was a Control Person, was mentioned adversely, other than a settlement for an amount less than $15,000;

		Had conduct mentioned adversely in a Civil Action alleging fraud, theft, misrepresentation, or other dishonest conduct;
		Been the subject of a Finding of fraud, theft, misrepresentation, or other dishonest conduct in a Regulatory Action or Civil Action;
		Become aware of an adverse arbitration award or civil judgment, or a settlement agreement in a Civil Action alleging fraud, theft, misrepresentation, or other dishonest conduct, where the conduct of the CFP® professional, or an entity over which the CFP® professional was a Control Person, was mentioned adversely;
		Had a professional license, certification, or membership suspended, revoked, or materially restricted because of a violation of rules or standards of conduct;
		Been terminated for cause from employment or permitted to resign in lieu of termination when the cause of the termination or resignation involved allegations of dishonesty, unethical conduct, or compliance failures;
		Been named as the subject of, or been identified as the broker/adviser of record in, any written, customer-initiated complaint that alleged the CFP® professional was involved in: • forgery, theft, misappropriation, or conversion of Financial Assets; • sales practice violations and contained a claim for compensation of $5,000 or more; or • sales practice violations and settled for an amount of $15,000 or more.
		Filed for or been the subject of a personal bankruptcy or business bankruptcy where the CFP® professional was a Control Person;
		Received notice of a federal tax lien on property owned by the CFP® professional; or
		Failed to satisfy a non-federal tax lien, judgment lien, or civil judgment within one year of its date of entry, unless payment arrangements have been agreed upon by all parties.
6.	Provide a Narrative Statement	The written notice must include a narrative statement that accurately and completely describes the material facts and the outcome or status of the reportable matter.
7.	Cooperate	A CFP® professional may not make false or misleading representations to CFP Board or obstruct CFP Board in the performance of its duties. A CFP® professional must cooperate fully with CFP Board's requests, investigations, disciplinary proceedings, and disciplinary decisions.
		Comply with Terms and Conditions of Certification and License. A CFP® professional must comply with the Terms and Conditions of Certification and License.

8. Prohibition on Circumvention	A CFP® professional may not do indirectly, or through or by another person, any act or thing that the Code and Standards prohibit the CFP® professional from doing directly.

3.5 STATE REGULATIONS AND RULES

Broker-dealer and investment adviser oversight is conducted at the federal, SRO, and state level. Standardization of state laws, rules, and procedures falls under the guidance of the **North American Securities Administrators Association** (NASAA). Founded in 1919, NASAA is the oldest international organization devoted to investor protection. NASAA is a voluntary association whose membership consists of 67 state, provincial, and territorial securities administrators in the 50 states, the District of Columbia, Puerto Rico, the U.S. Virgin Islands, Canada, and Mexico.[6] NASAA provides state regulators uniform procedures for:

- licensing investment adviser firms, investment adviser representatives, and stockbrokers;

- registering securities offered to investors at the state level;

- investigating consumer complaints;

- investigating investment fraud;

- examining firms and individuals to ensure compliance with state laws; and

- enforcing state securities and registration laws.

While regulation of investment advisers is fragmented between state and federal oversight, states play a more distinct role in the regulation of insurance firms and products and insurance salespeople. Whereas each state writes and passes unique insurance laws and regulations, the **National Association of Insurance Commissioners** (NAIC) provides guidance to ensure that laws are consistent across states and jurisdictions. The NAIC is the standard-setting and regulatory support organization created and governed by the chief insurance regulators from the 50 states, the District of Columbia, and five U.S. territories. According to the NAIC, state insurance regulators establish standards and best practices, conduct peer reviews, and coordinate regulatory oversight. NAIC staff supports these efforts and represents the collective views of state regulators domestically and internationally. NAIC members, together with the central resources of the NAIC, form the national system of state-based insurance regulation in the United States.[7]

Financial planners who sell insurance must generally obtain a state license. To obtain a license, a financial planner must:

- be eighteen years of age or older;

- apply to their state insurance regulator;

- submit an application fee;

- pass a licensing examination;

- provide proof of holding a FINRA Series 7 or Series 6 license if selling variable annuity contacts;

- obtain an insurance company certification; and

- meet continuing education requirements.

Figure 3.7 provides a summary of the types of insurance that require a state insurance license.

Figure 3.7. Categories of Insurance Licenses.

Type of Insurance	Required License
Property and Casualty	Crop Hail & Multi-peril Crop
	Customer Representative
	General Lines
	General Lines (Temporary)
	Industrial Fire or Burglary
	Industrial Fire or Burglary (Temporary)
	Personal Lines
	Surplus Lines
	Surplus Lines (Temporary)
Health and Life Insurance (including Annuities and Variable Contracts)	Debit Life and Health (Temporary)
	Health
	Health & Life (Including Annuities & Variable Contracts)
	Life (Foreign/Military)
	Life (Including Annuities & Variable Contracts)
	Life (Temporary)
	Variable Contracts

Title	Title Agent
Warranty	Home Warranty Sales Representative
	Motor Vehicle Service Agreement Salesperson
	Service Warranty Sales Representative
Bail Bond	Limited Surety (Temporary)
	Limited Surety
	Professional Bail Bond
Other	Portable Electronics Insurance - Lead
	Credit
	In-Transit & Storage Personal Property
	Legal Expense
	Managing General Agent
	Mediator
	Motor Vehicle Rental
	Neutral Evaluator
	Reinsurance Intermediary Brokers
	Reinsurance Intermediary Managers
	Service Representative
	Travel Agent

3.6 OTHER CONSIDERATIONS

Laws, regulations, and practice standards provide a foundation for every aspect of work a financial planner undertakes on a day-to-day basis. Financial planners who write and present financial plans must understand how laws, regulations, and practice standards influence how data are collected and managed, how recommendations and implementation suggestions are made, and how monitoring practices should be followed. As such, it is important for a financial planner to exhibit legal environment awareness when practicing financial planning. The following discussion provides insights into some of the legal and regulatory aspects of financial planning that form the basis of professional practice.

[A] The Best Interest and Fiduciary Standards of Care

Financial planners, regardless of their practice approach, play a vital role in helping consumers accumulate and manage household assets with the objective of reaching financial goals. According to reports published by the Securities and Exchange Commission,[8] when federal securities laws were enacted, Congress drew a distinction between broker-dealers, who are regulated as salespeople under the Securities Exchange Act of 1934, and investment advisers, who are regulated as advisers under the Investment Advisers Act of 1940. Over time, however, the roles of some broker-dealers and investment advisers converged. It is common for broker-dealers and investment advisers today to offer essentially the same services. Even the names used to describe functions are similar, which causes confusion in the marketplace.

As noted above, broker-dealers and investment advisers are subject to different legal standards when offering services. Broker-dealers are subject to a best interest standard, whereas investment advisers must always follow a fiduciary standard. Best interest and fiduciary duties provide distinct levels of protection for consumers. For example, a financial planner working under the **fiduciary standard** must act in the best interests of their clients and appropriately manage and fully disclose conflicts of interest that could bias recommendations. Financial planners who follow the **best interest standard** need only recommend products and services that the financial planner reasonably believes will meet a client's needs, given the client's income and net worth situation, investment objectives, and risk tolerance, in the context of the client's other security holdings.[9]

[B] The Fiduciary Standard

Standards of *fiduciary care* have been in existence for more than a century. Fiduciary laws are structured around the notion of "prudent person rules," which state that a trustee must observe standards of conduct that ensure trust assets are invested and managed in a prudent manner, with "prudent" indicating how someone would manage their own property. The **Uniform Prudent Investor Act of 1994** codified the way executors, conservators, and guardians of property must act in relation to trusts, estates, and similar holdings. The SEC adopted the fiduciary standard in relation to the regulation of investment advisers. Under SEC rules, investment advisers:[10]

- Have a fundamental obligation to act in the best interests of clients and to provide investment advice in a client's best interests.

- Owe clients a duty of undivided loyalty and utmost good faith.

- Should not engage in any activity in conflict with the interests of any client, and should take steps reasonably necessary to fulfill obligations.

- Must employ reasonable care to avoid misleading clients and must provide full and fair disclosure of all material facts to clients and prospective clients.

- Must eliminate, or at least disclose, all conflicts of interest that might incline the adviser—consciously or unconsciously—to render advice that is not disinterested.

- If the adviser does not avoid a conflict of interest that could impact the impartiality of advice, the adviser must make a full and frank disclosure of the conflict.

- Cannot use a client's assets for the adviser's own benefit or the benefit of other clients, without client consent.

The penalty for departing from this fiduciary standard can be severe. The SEC may claim, for example, that an investment adviser has committed fraud, which is punishable by fine and possible imprisonment.

[C] The CFP Board's Fiduciary Standard

Standards of care are relatively clear under SEC rules. It is important to note, however, that certification boards often require certificants to follow other standards.[11] Consider the fiduciary rule that all CFP® professionals and CFP® candidates must follow. Under the fiduciary duty practice standard, a CFP® professional must act as a fiduciary when providing financial advice to a client. This means acting in the best interest of a client. Under the rule, a CFP® professional must:[12]

1. "place the interests of the client above the interests of the CFP® professional and the CFP® professional's firm;

2. seek to avoid conflicts of interest, or fully disclose material conflicts of interest to the client, obtain the client's informed consent, and properly manage the conflict; and

3. act without regard to the financial or other interests of the CFP® professional, the CFP® professional's firm, or any individual or entity other than the client, which means that a CFP® professional acting under a conflict of interest continues to have a duty to act in the best interest of the client and place the client's interest above the CFP® professional's."

Planning Reminder

Prior to 2018, CFP Board defined a fiduciary as "one who acts in utmost good faith, in a manner he or she reasonably believes to be in the best interest of the client." Within this definition, when a CFP® professional provided financial planning or material elements of financial planning, the professional owed to the client the duty of care of a fiduciary as defined by CFP Board.

Under older CFP Board rules, it is worth noting that the fiduciary standard did not apply, using this definition, when advice was provided outside the scope of financial planning. Because the standard was confusing, CFP Board has since adopted the fiduciary definition described in the text.

Additionally, CFP Board rules state that "A CFP® professional must act with the care, skill, prudence, and diligence that a prudent professional would exercise in light of the client's goals, risk tolerance, objectives, and financial and personal circumstances."[13] Keep in mind that the only financial planners who are required to follow this particular fiduciary rule are CFP® professionals. Other organizations and governing boards have similar, and sometimes more stringent rules. For example, the National Association of Personal Financial Advisors (NAPFA) requires members to adhere to a stricter fiduciary standard even when providing non-specific financial advice. Similarly, the Financial Therapy Association (FTA) and the Association for Financial Counseling and Planning Education (AFCPE) require certificants to abide by a strict fiduciary standard.

[D] Registering as an Investment Adviser or Investment Adviser Representative

Nearly all financial planners who provide investment advice as an element of their practice are required to register as an investment adviser firm (this is also true if the financial planner is a sole proprietor) or as an investment adviser representative (IAR). Providing investment advice entails:[14]

1. making any recommendation or otherwise rendering advice regarding securities if the financial planner has direct advisory client contact;

2. managing accounts or portfolios of clients;

3. determining recommendations or advice regarding securities;

4. soliciting, offering, or negotiating the sale of or selling investment advisory services; or

5. directly supervising any investment adviser representative or the supervisors of those investment adviser representatives.

An IAR is a person, including but not limited to a partner, officer, or director, or a person occupying a similar status or performing similar functions, or other individual, except clerical or ministerial personnel, who is employed by or associated with an investment adviser registered at the federal or state level. As described previously, those who provide financial planning services who strictly do financial planning or that have less than $100 million under continuous and regular supervision or management are prohibited from registering with the SEC and instead must register at the state level.[15]

A key step in the registration process is passing the FINRA Series 7 examination, which is the same exam a registered representative must pass to work for a broker-dealer. Generally, a financial planner must be associated with or employed by a FINRA member firm to take a FINRA examination. An exemption to this rule exists. A financial planner may take the Series 63, 65, or 66 examinations without being affiliated with a FINRA member firm (those who have an application pending with a state that requires a particular exam are also exempt).

The first step in the firm registration process involves creating an **Investment Adviser Registration Depository** (IARD) account.[16] An applicant must first complete forms in the State Registration Entitlement Packet within the IARD. The IARD is a national computer database operated by FINRA. The IARD is used by the SEC and state regulators for registration and applicant tracking purposes. The second step involves submitting Form ADV (Parts I and II) for firm registration, or for those wishing to become an IAR, **Form U4**. Both forms are available online at the FINRA website. Fees must generally be paid as well. In most states, an applicant will partially file electronically through the IARD system and partially file on paper with the state securities division or regulator.

Several states also require applicants to file the following documents:[17]

- A financial statement accompanied by a notarized certification attesting to the accuracy of the information contained in the financial statement.

- A sample investment advisory contract.

- A sample business card, letterhead, brochure, circular, advisory newsletter, form letter, advertisement, and sales literature intended for distribution to prospective clients.

Next, sole proprietors and IAR applicants must submit documentation of passing qualifying examinations and/or holding specific professional certifications or designations. The qualifying examinations are:

- Series 65.

- Series 7 and 66.

Approved certifications and designations, in most states, include:

- Certified Financial Planner (CFP®).

- Chartered Financial Consultant (ChFC®).

- Personal Financial Specialist (PFS®).

- Chartered Financial Analyst (CFA®).

- Chartered Investment Counselor (CIC®).

Planning Reminder

Some states require investment advisers to hold errors and omission (E&O) insurance. Keep in mind that E&O insurance will not cover the actions of an investment adviser or financial planner who engages in purposeful neglect or misbehavior. Investment advisers who hold custody of client assets must also generally be bonded.

These rules and procedures only apply to investment advisers and IARs who are required to register at the state level. Under the federal **Investment Advisers Supervision Coordination Act of 1997**, SEC registered investment advisers need only notify the states in which they provide services if the firm provides services above the de minimis exemption (i.e., no place of business in the state and five or fewer in a 12-month period). Keep in mind, however, that an IAR of a firm that has a place of business in a state must register with the state.

[E] Compensation Issues

The way a financial planner is compensated is directly associated with the financial planner's classification as someone who follows a best interest or fiduciary standard of care. As shown in Figure 3.8, there are four widely used compensation methods within the profession. Two dominate:

1. Commissions, in which a financial planner earns a percentage of the value of the sale.

2. Fees, in which a predetermined fee is charged for services provided; the most common fee is a charge for managing assets. A typical fee is one percent of assets under management.

Figure 3.8. Financial Planner Compensation Methods.

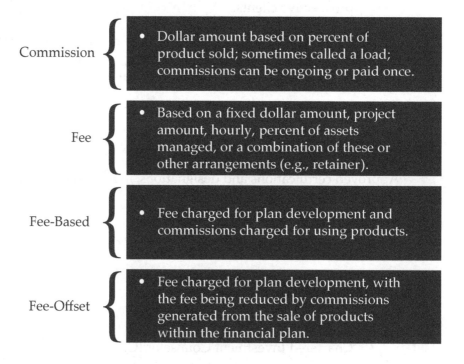

Commission	• Dollar amount based on percent of product sold; sometimes called a load; commissions can be ongoing or paid once.
Fee	• Based on a fixed dollar amount, project amount, hourly, percent of assets managed, or a combination of these or other arrangements (e.g., retainer).
Fee-Based	• Fee charged for plan development and commissions charged for using products.
Fee-Offset	• Fee charged for plan development, with the fee being reduced by commissions generated from the sale of products within the financial plan.

[F] Laws and Regulations

Numerous laws and regulations have been enacted since the Great Depression in the early 1930s to provide greater investor protection. The following discussion highlights the most important laws related to the practice of financial planning.[18]

[1] Securities Act of 1933

Often referred to as the "truth in securities" law, the Securities Act of 1933 had two objectives. First, to ensure that investors receive financial and other information concerning securities being offered for public sale, and second, to prohibit deceit, misrepresentations, and other fraud in the sale of securities. As a part of the Act, nearly all securities sold in the United States must be registered. The registration calls for:

• a description of a company's properties and business;

- a description of the security to be offered for sale;

- information about the management of the company; and

- financial statements certified by independent accountants.

Some exemptions from the registration requirement include:

- private offerings to a limited number of persons or institutions;

- offerings of limited size;

- intrastate offerings; and

- securities of municipal, state, and federal governments.

[2] Securities Exchange Act of 1934

The Securities Exchange Act created the Securities and Exchange Commission (SEC). The Act empowered the SEC with broad authority over all aspects of the securities industry, including oversight of brokerage firms, transfer agents, and clearing agencies, as well as SROs. The Act was important in curbing fraudulent activities of any kind in connection with the offer, purchase, or sale of securities. The Act also required a variety of market participants to register with the SEC, including exchanges, brokers and dealers, transfer agents, and clearing agencies.

[3] Trust Indenture Act of 1939

The Trust Indenture Act applies to debt securities such as bonds, debentures, and notes that are offered for public sale. Even though such securities may be registered under the Securities Act, they may not be offered for sale to the public unless a formal agreement between the issuer of bonds and the bondholder, known as the trust indenture, conforms to the standards of this Act.

[4] Investment Company Act of 1940

The Investment Company Act formalized the regulation of investment companies, including mutual funds, that engage primarily in investing, reinvesting, and trading in securities, and whose own securities are offered to the investing public. The regulation was designed to minimize conflicts of interest between clients and investment firms. The Act requires companies to disclose their financial condition and investment policies to investors. The focus of the Act is on disclosure to the investing public of information about the fund and the fund's investment objectives.

[5] Investment Advisers Act of 1940

Investment Advisers Act has the most direct impact on the practice of financial planning. The law instituted regulation of investment advisers. With certain exceptions, the Act requires that firms or sole practitioners compensated for advising others about securities and investments must register with the SEC and conform to regulations designed to protect investors. Since the Act was amended in 1996 and 2010, generally only advisers who have at least $100 million of assets under management or advise a registered investment company must register with the SEC.

[6] Sarbanes-Oxley Act of 2002

On July 30, 2002, President Bush signed into law the Sarbanes-Oxley Act of 2002. The Act mandated several reforms to enhance corporate responsibility, enhance financial disclosures, and combat corporate and accounting fraud. The Act also created the Public Company Accounting Oversight Board to oversee the activities of the auditing profession.

[7] Dodd-Frank Wall Street Reform and Consumer Protection Act of 2010

The Dodd-Frank Wall Street Reform and Consumer Protection Act was signed into law on July 21, 2010 by President Obama. The legislation set out to reshape the U.S. regulatory system in relation to consumer protection, trading restrictions, credit ratings, regulation of financial products, corporate governance and disclosure, and transparency.

[8] Jumpstart Our Business Startups Act of 2012

The Jumpstart Our Business Startups Act (the "JOBS Act") was enacted on April 5, 2012. The JOBS Act was designed to help businesses raise funds in public capital markets by minimizing regulatory requirements.

[G] Compliance Procedures

Financial planners who provide services under the Investment Advisers Act of 1940 are required to adopt and implement written policies and procedures that are reasonably designed to prevent violations of the Advisers Act.[19] While the SEC does not prescribe the exact policies and procedures a firm or financial planner must adopt, the SEC expects policies and procedures, at a minimum, to address the following issues:

Planning Reminder

All SEC registered investment advisers and SEC registered broker-dealers are required to deliver to retail investors a client relationship summary (CRS) that provides information about the firm. The CRS form is designed to help retail investors with the process of deciding whether to (1) establish an investment advisory or brokerage relationship, (2) engage a particular firm or financial professional, or (3) terminate or switch a relationship or specific service. The CRS requirements are in addition to all current disclosure and reporting requirements for broker-dealers and investment advisers.

- Portfolio management processes, including allocation of investment opportunities among clients and consistency of portfolios with clients' investment objectives, disclosures to clients, and applicable regulatory restrictions.

- The accuracy of disclosures made to investors, clients, and regulators, including account statements and advertisements.

- Proprietary trading by staff and personal trading activities.

- Safeguarding of client assets from conversion or inappropriate use by staff.

- The accurate creation of required records and their maintenance in a manner that secures them from unauthorized alteration or use and protects them from untimely destruction.

- Safeguards for the privacy protection of client records and information.

- Trading practices, including procedures by which staff satisfy best execution obligations, use client brokerage to obtain research and other services (referred to as "soft dollar arrangements"), and allocate aggregated trades among clients.

- Marketing advisory services, including the use of solicitors.

- Processes to value client holdings and assess fees based on those valuations.

- Business continuity plans.

[H] Form ADV

According to the SEC,[20] **Form ADV** has three parts. Financial planners registering or those that are registered with the SEC are required to complete Part IA, Part II, and Part III (most states require the same filing documentation). Form ADV is available electronically through the IARD. Exempt reporting advisers are required to only complete certain items in Part 1A. The three elements of Form ADV are:

- **Part I.** This section asks for information about an investment adviser's business, the persons who own or control the adviser, and whether the adviser or certain members of its staff have been sanctioned for violating securities or other laws.

- **Part II.** This section is a written disclosure statement (**brochure**) that provides information about business practices, fees, and conflicts of interest the adviser may have with its clients. The Part II brochure is a disclosure statement that an adviser must use to provide information to clients and potential clients. Rule 204-3 under the Investment Advisers Act of 1940 describes an investment adviser's legal obligations as follows:

  (1) to deliver a copy of the Part II brochure to prospective clients,

(2) to deliver a current brochure or a summary of material changes to clients annually, and

(3) to deliver a current brochure supplement to the client for each supervised person that provides advisory services to the client.

Financial advisers must keep Part II current, maintain a copy in the firm's files (as well as file it electronically through IARD, and make it available to SEC staff upon request).

- **Part III.** Part III of Form ADV provides a brief summary of the types of clients a financial adviser typically works with and the manner in which services are provided. Any firm, financial adviser, or financial planner that is required to deliver a relationship summary to clients (typically retail investors) must provide clients with Part III of Form ADV. Specifically, Part III of Form ADV provides disclosure about the relationships and services offered by the adviser, the costs and fees associated with services, conflicts of interest, standards of conduct followed when providing services, all past regulatory and disciplinary history, and how to obtain additional information about the financial adviser's firm.

An example of Form ADV can be found at: https://www.sec.gov/about/forms/formadv.pdf.

[I] Written Disclosure Statements and Documentation

Planning Reminder

CFP Board requires CFP® certificants to disclose conflicts of interest and other information to clients. Pre-formatted forms are available at: https://www.cfp.net/for-cfp-professionals/professional-standards-enforcement/compliance-resources/sample-disclosure-forms

According to the SEC,[21] registered investment advisers are required to provide their advisory and prospective clients with a written **disclosure document** (see Rule 204-3 under the Investment Advisers Act of 1940). This can be accomplished by providing current and prospective clients with Part II of Form ADV or through the delivery of a brochure that meets SEC requirements. An example of a brochure document is shown in Appendix 3A. This written disclosure document should be delivered to prospective clients before or at the time a client enters into an advisory contract.

Clients must receive Form ADV Part II or a summary of material changes each year. Delivery of the disclosure must be documented, reflecting the date on which such disclosure was given, or offered to be given, to any client or prospective client who subsequently became a client. Figure 3.9 shows a brief brochure receipt form.

Figure 3.9. Brochure Receipt Form.

ACKNOWLEDGEMENT OF RECEIPT OF FORM ADV PART II DISCLOSURE BROCHURE
I/We acknowledge receipt of John Grable and Associates, Inc.'s Form ADV, Part II Brochure. I/We have been advised that this document contains important information about John Grable and Associates, Inc., as well as the Firm's fee structure.
_____   _____ Client Name   Client Signature Date   _____   _____ Client Name   Client Signature Date
Please sign and return this form to John Grable and Associates, Inc., either by mail to the address below or at our Introductory Meeting.

[J] SEC Advertising Rules and Requirements

The SEC prohibits certain types of advertising practices by investment advisers. According to the SEC,[22] an **advertisement** includes any communication addressed to more than one person that offers any investment advisory service with regard to securities. An advertisement can be a written publication, website, newsletter, or marketing brochure, as well as an oral communication (including an announcement made on the radio or television).

Advertising must not be false or misleading and must not contain any untrue statement of a material fact. The SEC prohibits the following:

- testimonials;

- the use of past specific recommendations that were profitable, unless the adviser includes a list of all recommendations made during the past year;

- a representation that any graph, chart, or formula can in and of itself be used to determine which securities to buy or sell; and

- advertisements stating that any report, analysis, or service is free, unless it really is free.

If past investment performance is advertised, all material facts necessary to avoid any unwarranted inferences about performance must be disclosed. The SEC has indicated that performance data may be deemed misleading if the advertisement:

- does not disclose prominently that the results portrayed relate only to a select group of the adviser's clients, the basis on which the selection was made, and the effect of this practice on the results portrayed, if material;

- does not disclose the effect of material market or economic conditions on the results portrayed (e.g., an advertisement stating that the accounts of the adviser's clients appreciated in value 25 percent without disclosing that the market generally appreciated 40 percent during the same period);

- does not reflect the deduction of advisory fees, brokerage or other commissions, and any other expenses that accounts would have or actually paid;

- does not disclose whether and to what extent the results portrayed reflect the reinvestment of dividends and other earnings;

- suggests or makes claims about the potential for profit without also disclosing the possibility of loss;

- compares model or actual results to an index without disclosing all material facts relevant to the comparison (e.g., an advertisement that compares model results to an index without disclosing that the volatility of the index is materially different from that of the model portfolio); and

- does not disclose any material conditions, objectives, or investment strategies used to obtain the results portrayed (e.g., the model portfolio contains equity stocks that are managed with a view towards capital appreciation).

Planning Reminder

The SEC prohibits an investment adviser from using the term "RIA" after a person's name because using initials after a name usually indicates a degree or a licensed professional position for which there are certain qualifications.

Finally, an investment adviser may not imply that the SEC or another agency has sponsored, recommended, or approved the adviser. This means an investment adviser should not imply that being registered relates to a specific level of professional competence, education, or special training.

[K] SEC Books and Records Requirements

The SEC requires investment advisers to "make and keep true, accurate, and current certain books and records relating to your investment advisory business."[23] The books and records that must be made and kept are as follows:

- Advisory business financial and accounting records, including: cash receipts and disbursements journals; income and expense account ledgers; checkbooks; bank account statements; advisory business bills; and financial statements.

- Records that pertain to providing investment advice and transactions in client accounts with respect to such advice, including: orders to trade in client accounts (referred to as "order memoranda"); trade confirmation statements received from broker-dealers; documentation of proxy vote decisions; written requests for withdrawals or documentation of deposits received from clients;

and written correspondence you sent to or received from clients or potential clients discussing your recommendations or suggestions.

- Records that document an adviser's authority to conduct business in client accounts, including: a list of accounts in which you have discretionary authority; documentation granting you discretionary authority; and written agreements with clients, such as advisory contracts.

- Advertising and performance records, including: newsletters; articles; and computational worksheets demonstrating performance returns.

- Records related to the *Code of Ethics Rule*, including those addressing personal securities transaction reporting by access persons.

- Records regarding the maintenance and delivery of an adviser's written disclosure document and disclosure documents provided by certain solicitors who seek clients on an adviser's behalf.

- Policies and procedures adopted and implemented under the Compliance Rule, including any documentation prepared in the course of an adviser's annual review.

Planning Reminder

Generally, most books and records must be kept for *five* years from the last day of the fiscal year in which the last entry was made on the document or the document was disseminated. An investment adviser may be required to keep certain records for longer periods, such as records that support performance calculations used in advertisements.

Records must be kept in an easily accessible location. In addition, for the first two of these years, adviser records must be kept in the adviser's office(s). If records are maintained elsewhere, this information must be disclosed on Form ADV.

Original books and records may be stored in hard copy or using micrographic or electronic media (including microfilm, electronic text, digital images, proprietary and off-the-shelf software, and email). If an investment adviser uses email or instant messaging to make and keep records that are required under SEC rules, the email must be maintained (including all attachments). An investment adviser must take precautions to ensure electronic documents are secure from unauthorized access, theft, or unintended destruction.

[L] Consumer Protection Laws that Guide the Practice of Financial Planning

Financial planners deal with SEC, state, SRO, and certification board rules, regulations, and policies on a day-to-day basis. These are not, however, the only rule making entities that shape the financial planning environment. Congress, through its law making authority, has traditionally been deeply involved in protecting consumer rights. The laws shown in Figure 3.10 represent some of the most important regulations that influence the practice of financial planning outside of the legislative Acts already discussed.

According to the Federal Reserve Board,[24] these laws govern financial institutions and protect individuals in their financial dealings with financial professionals.

Figure 3.10. Important Consumer Protection Laws Related to the Practice of Financial Planning.

Community Reinvestment Act of 1977 Encourages financial institutions to help meet the credit needs of those living in communities, particularly low- and moderate-income neighborhoods.
Consumer Leasing Act of 1976 Requires that institutions disclose the cost and terms of consumer leases, such as automobile leases.
Electronic Fund Transfer Act (1978) Establishes the basic rights, liabilities, and responsibilities of (a) consumers who use electronic fund transfer services and (b) financial institutions that offer these services. Covers transactions conducted at ATMs, at point-of-sale terminals in stores, and through telephone-bill-payment plans and preauthorized transfers to and from a customer's account, such as direct deposit of salary or Social Security payments.
Equal Credit Opportunity Act (1974) Prohibits discrimination in credit transactions on many grounds, including sex, marital status, age, race, religion, color, national origin, the receipt of public assistance funds, or the exercise of any right under the Consumer Credit Protection Act. Requires creditors to grant credit to qualified individuals without requiring co-signature by spouses, inform unsuccessful applicants in writing of the reasons credit was denied, and allow married individuals to have credit histories on jointly held accounts maintained in the names of both spouses. Also entitles a borrower to a copy of an appraisal report.
Expedited Funds Availability Act (1987) Specifies when depository institutions must make funds deposited by consumers available. Requires institutions to disclose to customers their policies on funds availability.
Fair and Accurate Credit Transaction Act of 2003 Enhances a consumer's ability to combat identity theft, increases the accuracy of consumer reports, allows consumers to exercise greater control over the type and amount of marketing solicitations they receive, restricts the use and disclosure of sensitive medical information, and establishes uniform national standards in the regulation of consumer reporting. Amended the Fair Credit Reporting Act.
Fair Credit and Charge Card Disclosure Act of 1988 Requires that applications for credit cards that are sent through the mail, solicited by telephone, or made available to the public (for example, at counters in retail stores or through catalogs) contain information about key terms of the account. Amended the Truth in Lending Act.
Fair Credit Billing Act (1974) Specifies how creditors must respond to billing complaints from consumers; imposes requirements to ensure that creditors handle accounts fairly and promptly. Applies primarily to revolving and credit card accounts (for example, store card and bank card accounts). Amended the Truth in Lending Act.

Fair Credit Reporting Act (1970)
Protects consumers against inaccurate or misleading information in credit files maintained by credit reporting agencies; requires credit reporting agencies to allow credit applicants to correct erroneous reports.

Fair Debt Collection Practices Act (1977)
Prohibits abusive debt-collection practices. Applies to banks that function as debt collectors for other entities.

Fair Housing Act (1968)
Prohibits discrimination in the extension of housing credit on the basis of race, color, religion, national origin, sex, disability, or family status.

Federal Trade Commission Improvement Act (1980)
Authorizes the Federal Reserve to identify unfair or deceptive acts or practices by banks and to issue regulations to prohibit them. Using this authority, the Federal Reserve has adopted rules substantially similar to those adopted by the FTC that restrict certain practices in the collection of delinquent consumer debt (for example, practices related to late charges, responsibilities of cosigners, and wage assignments).

Flood Disaster Protection Act of 1973
Requires flood insurance on property in a flood hazard area that falls under the National Flood Insurance Program.

Gramm-Leach-Bliley Act (1999)
Regulation P: Privacy of Consumer Financial Information. Describes the conditions under which financial institutions may disclose nonpublic personal information about consumers to nonaffiliated third parties, provides a method for consumers to opt out of information sharing with nonaffiliated third parties, and requires financial institutions to notify consumers about their privacy policies and practices.
Regulation H: Consumer Protection in Sales of Insurance. Describes conditions for retail sales, solicitations, advertising, or offers of insurance products or annuities by state member banks or by others at an office of a bank. Prohibits coercion and misrepresentations and requires disclosures in connection with the initial purchase of an insurance product or annuity.

Home Equity Loan Consumer Protection Act of 1988
Requires creditors to provide consumers with detailed information about open-end credit plans secured by the consumer's dwelling, including a brochure describing home equity loans in general. Also regulates advertising of home equity loans and restricts the terms of home equity loan plans.

Home Mortgage Disclosure Act of 1975
Requires mortgage lenders to annually disclose to the public data about the geographic distribution of their applications, originations, and acquisitions of home-purchase and home-improvement loans and refinancing operations. Requires lenders to report data on the ethnicity, race, sex, and income of applicants and borrowers, as well as pricing data on certain loans. Also directs the Federal Financial Institutions Examination Council, of which the Federal Reserve is a member, to make summaries of the data available to the public.

Home Ownership and Equity Protection Act of 1994
Provides additional disclosure requirements and substantive limitations on home-equity loans with rates or fees above a certain percentage or amount. Amended the Truth in Lending Act.

Homeowners Protection Act of 1998
Establishes rules for automatic termination and borrower cancellation of private mortgage insurance (PMI) on home mortgages.

Real Estate Settlement Procedures Act of 1974
Requires that the nature and costs of real estate settlements be disclosed to borrowers. Also protects borrowers against abusive practices, such as kickbacks, and limits the use of escrow accounts.

Right to Financial Privacy Act of 1978
Protects bank customers from the unlawful scrutiny of their financial records by federal agencies and specifies procedures that government authorities must follow when they seek information about a customer's records from a financial institution.

Truth in Lending Act (1968)
Requires uniform methods for computing the cost of credit and for disclosing credit terms. Gives borrowers the right to cancel, within three days, certain loans secured by their residences. Prohibits the unsolicited issuance of credit cards and limits cardholder liability for unauthorized use. Also imposes limitations on home equity loans with rates or fees above a specified threshold.

Truth in Savings Act (1991)
Requires that depository institutions disclose certain information to depositors about their accounts—including the annual percentage yield, which must be calculated in a uniform manner—and prohibits certain methods of calculating interest. Regulates advertising of savings accounts.

Women's Business Ownership Act of 1988
Extends to applicants for business credit certain protections afforded consumer credit applicants, such as the right to an explanation for credit denial. Amended the Equal Credit Opportunity Act.

Congress, in an attempt to protect consumers and investors from losses resulting from the bankruptcy or failure of financial institutions that hold consumer accounts, created three quasi-governmental agencies to provide insurance coverage:

- **Securities Investor Protection Corporation**

When a brokerage firm that is a member of the Securities Investor Protection Corporation (SIPC) goes out of business, cash and securities held by customers is protected up to $500,000, which includes a $250,000 limit for cash. SIPC covers most types of securities, such as stocks, bonds, and mutual funds. It is important to remember, however, that SIPC does **not** protect against losses caused by a decline in the market value of securities, nor does SIPC provide protection for investment contracts not registered with the SEC.

- **Federal Deposit Insurance Corporation**

Depositors at banks receive up to $250,000 in Federal Deposit Insurance Corporation (FDIC) coverage for money held in deposit products, such as checking, savings and money market deposit accounts, and certificates of deposit. Coverage is based on each depositor. Non-bank products are generally not insured.

- **National Credit Union Share Insurance Fund**

Managed by the National Credit Union Association, the National Credit Union Share Insurance Fund (NCUSIF) provides an insurance amount of $250,000 per share owner (depositor), per insured credit union, for each account ownership category. The $250,000 standard share insurance account became permanent through the Dodd-Frank Wall Street Reform and Consumer Protection Act of 2010.

3.7 SUMMARY

As the discussion and examples in this chapter highlight, financial planners work in a highly regulated environment. Financial planners must understand and abide by state, federal, SRO, and certification board laws, regulations, and practice standards. As a profession, financial planners serve the needs of consumers best when they use high ethical standards to guide their practice. Given the importance of regulation in the financial planning marketplace, it is important for financial planners to understand the similarities and differences between and among the SEC, NASAA, NAIC, FINRA, and other regulatory organizations. Of particular importance to those either currently certified or hoping to be certified by the Certified Financial Planner Board of Standards, Inc. are CFP Board's *Code of Ethics and Standards of Conduct* and disciplinary procedures.

3.8 SELF-TEST

[A] Questions

Self-Test 1

The FINRA exam that qualifies a firm representative to act as an investment adviser and receive a fee for services is called a:

(a) Series 7.

(b) Series 63.

(c) Series 65.

(d) Series 66.

Self-Test 2

Abed is a sole proprietor working as an investment adviser/financial planner in Colorado. He currently manages $85 million in client assets. He must register his firm with:

(a) The SEC because he is a sole-proprietor.

(b) Colorado (the state where he does business).

(c) Both the SEC and Colorado (the state where he does business).

(d) Either the SEC or Colorado (the state where he does business).

Self-Test 3

Which of the following is not a certification board?

(a) FINRA.

(b) FTA.

(c) CFP Board.

(d) Both (b) and (c).

Self-Test 4

Micala works as an agent for a large insurance company. Her specialty is the sale of variable annuities. Of the licenses listed below, Micala must hold which license?

(a) A Series 63 license.

(b) A Series 65 license.

(c) A Series 7 license.

(d) A federal life insurance license.

Self-Test 5

Brackley is new to the financial planning profession. She holds no designations or certifications. In order to register as an investment adviser representative, Brackley must:

(a) Pass the Series 7 exam.

(b) Pass the Series 63 exam.

(c) Pass the Series 66 exam.

(d) Pass both the Series 7 and 66 exams.

Self-Test 6

The SEC was formed with the passage of the:

(a) Securities Act of 1933.

(b) Securities Exchange Act of 1934.

(c) Investment Company Act of 1940.

(d) Investment Adviser's Act of 1940.

Self-Test 7

Lamar, a SEC registered investment adviser, has asked his friend and client to do a commercial praising Lamar's financial planning firm. Lamar's friend is a famous actor and former baseball player. Under SEC rules, Lamar:

(a) Must disclose that his friend is a paid spokesperson.

(b) May not run this advertisement because it is a testimonial.

(c) Must obtain an endorsement from his state's securities regulator prior to running the advertisement.

(d) Must appear in the advertisement.

[B] Answers

Question 1: c

Question 2: b

Question 3: a

Question 4: c

Question 5: d

Question 6: b

Question 7: b

3.9 CHAPTER RESOURCES

Association for Financial Counseling and Planning Education (afcpe.org).

Certified Financial Planner Board of Standards, Inc. (www.cfp.net).

CFA Institute (www.cfainstitute.org).

Federal Reserve Board of Governors (www.federalreserve.gov).

Financial Industry Regulatory Authority (finra.org).

Financial Therapy Association (financialtherapyassociation.org).

International Association of Registered Financial Consultants (www.iarfc.org).

National Association of Insurance Commissioners (naic.org).

National Association of Personal Financial Advisors (napfa.org).

North American Securities Administrators Association (nasaa.org).

Securities and Exchange Commission (sec.gov).

The American College (www.theamericancollege.edu).

CHAPTER ENDNOTES

1. Securities and Exchange Commission: https://www.sec.gov/about/offices/oia/oia_investman/rplaze-042012.pdf.
2. Securities and Exchange Commission: https://www.investor.gov/additional-resources/news-alerts/alerts-bulletins/transition-mid-sized-investment-advisers-federal.
3. Nebraska, New Hampshire, Louisiana, and Texas are exceptions to this rule.
4. Certified Financial Planner Board of Standards, Inc.: https://www.cfp.net/ethics/code-of-ethics-and-standards-of-conduct
5. *Ibid.*
6. The North American Securities Administrators Association: http://www.nasaa.org.
7. The National Association of Insurance Commissioners: http://naic.org/index_about.htm.
8. Securities and Exchange Commission: https://www.sec.gov/spotlight/investor-advisory-committee-2012/fiduciary-duty-recommendation.pdf.
9. Securities and Exchange Commission: https://www.sec.gov/fast-answers/answerssuitabilityhtm.html.

10. Securities and Exchange Commission: https://www.sec.gov/divisions/investment/advoverview.htm.

11. Federal law always preempts certification body rules.

12. Certified Financial Planner Board of Standards, Inc.: https://www.cfp.net/docs/default-source/for-cfp-pros---professional-standards-enforcement/2017-proposed-standards/CFPBoard_Revised_Proposed_Standards.

13. *Ibid.*

14. Securities and Exchange Commission: https://www.sec.gov/divisions/investment/iaregulation/memoia.htm.

15. *Ibid.*

16. Information about the IARD can be obtained at the following website: http://www.iard.com.

17. State regulators also typically conduct a criminal background check of all applicants.

18. Securities and Exchange Commission: https://www.sec.gov/answers/about-lawsshtml.html.

19. *Ibid.*

20. Securities and Exchange Commission: https://www.sec.gov/divisions/investment/iard/register.shtml.

21. Securities and Exchange Commission: https://www.sec.gov/answers/about-lawsshtml.html.

22. *Ibid.*

23. *Ibid.*

24. Federal Reserve Board: https://www.federalreserve.gov/pubs/complaints/laws.htm.

Sample Brochure Document[1]

John Grable & Associates, Inc.

510 Sanford Drive

Athens, GA 30602

(706) 555-1212

www.jga.net

July 1, 20XX

This Brochure provides information about the qualifications and business practices of John Grable & Associates, Inc. (JGA). If you have any questions about the contents of this Brochure, please contact us at (706) 555-1212. The information in this Brochure has not been approved or verified by the United States Securities and Exchange Commission or by any state securities authority.

John Grable & Associates, Inc. is a registered investment adviser. Registration of an Investment Adviser does not imply any level of skill or training. The oral and written communications of an Investment Adviser provide you with information about which you determine to hire or retain an Adviser. Additional information about John Grable & Associates, Inc. also is available on the SEC's website at www.adviserinfo.sec.gov.

Material Changes

Pursuant to SEC Rules, we will ensure that you receive a summary of any material changes to this and subsequent Brochures within 120 days of the close of our business' fiscal year. We may further provide other ongoing disclosure information about material changes as necessary. We will further provide you with a new Brochure as necessary based on changes or new information, at any time, without charge.

Currently, our Brochure may be requested by contacting Michelle Kruger, Marketing Assistant, at (706) 555-3456. Our Brochure is also available on our web site www.JGA. net, also free of charge.

Additional information about JGA is available via the SEC's web site www.adviserinfo. sec.gov. The SEC's web site provides information about any persons affiliated with JGA who are registered, or are required to be registered, as investment adviser representatives of JGA.

Advisory Business

John Grable & Associates, Inc. (JGA) is a comprehensive financial planning firm offering to its clients discretionary investment advice and financial planning services regarding all aspects of their financial affairs. JGA was founded in 1992 by John Grable. The principal owners of JGA still remain John and Lynn Grable. Financial planning activities constitute approximately 80% of the services offered by JGA. Investment management services are provided on a discretionary basis through customized programs. Clients receive investment advice on equity securities, warrants, corporate bonds, municipal bonds, convertible bonds, variable rate bonds, foreign currency bonds, commercial paper, bank CD's, mutual fund shares, exchange-traded funds, executive stock options, government securities and partnerships investing in real estate and oil and gas interests. With the prior consent of the client, JGA furnishes discretionary investment management services defined as the authority to determine, without obtaining the specific client consent, the securities to be bought or sold, the amount of the securities to be bought and sold and the commission rates to be paid. Investment advice is also furnished through consultation.

JGA manages conservative, balanced, and aggressive portfolios based on the personal objectives of clients. A portfolio can consist of one or more of several types of accounts, established in the client's name. JGA works with clients to establish a risk tolerance profile that serves as a guide for investing. This risk segmentation profile is developed based on the clients overall financial goals, risk tolerance, risk capacity, risk preferences, other investments, and investment preferences. We do have processes in place to allow clients to impose restrictions on investing in certain securities or types of securities.

As of July 1, 20XX, JGA had over $900,000,000 in assets under management. As of that date, JGA managed $800,000,000 on a discretionary basis and $100,000,000 on a nondiscretionary basis. In addition, JGA manages approximately $8,000,000 in proprietary and employee assets. JGA manages accounts for 1,200 clients.

Fees and Compensation

The specific way fees are charged by JGA is established in a client's written engagement with JGA. The management fee structure is as follows:

- First $1,000,000 2% of Net Assets under management (with a $5,000 minimum).

- Plus 1 3/4% of the second million of Net Assets under management.

- Plus 1 1/2% of the third million of Net Assets under management.

- Plus 1 1/4% of the fourth million of Net Assets under management.

- Plus 1 1/8% of the fifth million of Net Assets under management.

- Plus 1% of Net Assets between five million and twelve million under management with a maximum annual fee, for the first twelve million of Net Assets under management, of one hundred twenty thousand dollars in any contract year.

For assets managed by John Grable & Associates, Inc. in excess of twelve million, the following fee schedule shall apply:

- 0.76% of the next three million of Net Assets under management.

- Plus 0.68% of the next five million of Net Assets under management.

- Plus 0.60% of the next five million of Net Assets under management.

- Plus 0.55% of Net Assets over twenty-five million.

The minimum fee and rate may be reduced for nonprofit organizations or other special situations. There are additional disclosures for ERISA Bonded accounts. The management fee is payable at the commencement of the contract year. Fees from capital additions in excess of the $250,000 minimum account size are billed on deposit at a prorated fee for the remainder of the contract year.

The appointment of JGA as investment manager is automatically renewed upon the contract date for subsequent one-year periods. The investment management contract may be canceled by a client upon providing at least sixty days written notice. The unearned portion of the management fee is reimbursed to clients; however, the initial year management fees shall in no event be less than $5,000 which is meant to compensate JGA for start-up expenses and analysis of a client's financial situation. John Grable & Associates, Inc. generally charges its fee for service on an annual basis in advance. Clients shall receive prior notification of the anticipated fee. Clients may elect to be billed directly for fees or to authorize JGA to directly debit fees from client accounts.

JGA's fees are exclusive of brokerage commissions, transaction fees, and other related costs and expenses which shall be incurred by the client. Clients may incur certain charges imposed by custodians, brokers, third party investment and other third parties such as fees charged by managers, custodial fees, deferred sales charges, odd-lot differentials, transfer taxes, wire transfer and electronic fund fees, and other fees and taxes on brokerage accounts and securities transactions. Mutual funds and exchange traded funds also charge internal management fees, which are disclosed in a fund's prospectus. Such charges, fees and commissions are exclusive of and in addition to JGA's fee, and JGA shall not receive any portion of these commissions, fees, and costs.

Performance-Based Fees and Side-By-Side Management

JGA does not charge any performance-based fees (fees based on a share of capital gains on or capital appreciation of the assets of a client).

Types of Clients

JGA provides portfolio management services to individuals, high net worth individuals, pension and profit-sharing plans, charitable institutions, foundations, endowments, trusts, and U.S. corporations.

John Grable & Associates, Inc. generally seeks clients with net assets for management in excess of $250,000.

Methods of Analysis, Investment Strategies, and Risk of Loss

JGA recommends securities based on fundamental and technical analysis methods. To identify undervalued securities, JGA uses a fundamental value technique that includes the evaluation of financial position, product and market factors, and management. In its analysis, JGA relies strictly on public information including research materials, corporate rating services, annual reports, prospectuses, filings with the Securities and Exchange Commission, company press releases, newspapers and magazines, and inspections of corporate activities. JGA has contractual relationships with members of the New York Stock Exchange (broker-dealers) to provide institutional research for the benefit of all clients.

JGA's approach combines strategic asset allocation, including preferred investment sectors, with some individual security selection. Value Based analyses are emphasized for most equity security decisions. Accounts are managed primarily at the client level, rather than an individual account level. Accounts are balanced with limitations placed on the level of high quality and aggressive equity investments based on individual risk segmentations.

Investing in securities involves risk of loss that clients should be prepared to bear. JGA emphasizes low to moderate risk investments. The use of balanced allocations (including fixed income securities) and equity diversification are critical elements to JGA's portfolio management process. The company does not trade short nor does it trade in options or commodities. JGA does not maintain margin accounts. Securities are usually purchased with the intent of holding them for at least one year; however, trading may occur more frequently. As part of our approach, security price points are key contributors to our buy and sell decisions. Investment and trading decisions are made on an ongoing basis.

Disciplinary Information

Registered investment advisers are required to disclose all material facts regarding any legal or disciplinary events that would be material to your evaluation of JGA or the integrity of JGA's management. JGA has no information applicable to this item.

Other Financial Industry Activities and Affiliations

JGA engages the services of Megan Ford as an Account Executive. Megan Ford, in her role as an independent financial planner, may also represent other investment advisers. JGA supervises and controls only the advisement of JGA clients by Ms. Megan Ford. JGA has no arrangements or understandings with any other investment advisors represented by Ms. Ford.

Code of Ethics

JGA has adopted a Code of Ethics for all supervised persons of the firm. The Code describes the firm's high standard of business conduct, and fiduciary duty to clients. The Code of Ethics includes provisions relating to the confidentiality of client information, a prohibition on insider trading, restrictions on the acceptance of significant gifts and the reporting of certain gifts and business entertainment items, and personal securities trading procedures, among other things. All supervised persons at JGA must acknowledge the terms of the Code of Ethics annually, or as amended.

JGA anticipates that, in appropriate circumstances, consistent with clients' investment objectives, it will cause accounts over which JGA has management authority to effect and will recommend to investment advisory clients or prospective clients, the purchase or sale of securities in which JGA, its affiliates and/or clients, directly or indirectly, have a position of interest. JGA's employees and persons associated with JGA are required to follow JGA's Code of Ethics. Subject to satisfying this policy and applicable laws, officers, directors, and employees of JGA and its affiliates may trade for their own accounts in securities which are recommended to and/or purchased for JGA's clients. The Code of Ethics is designed to assure that the personal securities transactions, activities and interests of the employees of JGA will not interfere with (a) making decisions in the best interest of advisory clients and (b) implementing such decisions while, at the same time, allowing employees to invest for their own accounts. Under the Code, certain classes of securities have been designated as exempt transactions, based upon a determination that these would materially not interfere with the best interest of JGA's clients. In addition, the Code requires pre-clearance of many transactions, and restricts trading in close proximity to client trading activity. Nonetheless, because the Code of Ethics in some circumstances permits employees to invest in the same securities as clients, there is a possibility that employees might benefit from market activity by a client in a security held by an employee. Employee trading is monitored under the Code of Ethics to reasonably prevent conflicts of interest between JGA and its clients.

Certain affiliated accounts may trade in the same securities with client accounts on an aggregated basis when consistent with JGA's obligation of best execution. In such circumstances, the affiliated and client accounts will share commission costs equally and receive securities at a total average price. JGA will retain records of the trade order (specifying each participating account) and its allocation, which will be completed prior to the entry of the aggregated order. Completed orders will be allocated as specified in the initial trade order. Partially filled orders will be allocated on a pro rata basis. Any exceptions will be explained on the order.

JGA's clients or prospective clients may request a copy of the firm's Code of Ethics by contacting Michelle Kruger.

It is JGA's policy that the firm will not affect any principal or agency cross securities transactions for client accounts. Principal transactions are generally defined as transactions where an adviser, acting as principal for its own account or the account of an affiliated broker-dealer, buys from or sells any security to any advisory client. A principal transaction may also be deemed to have occurred if a security is crossed between an affiliated hedge fund and another client account. An agency cross transaction is defined as a transaction where a person acts as an investment adviser in relation to a transaction in which the investment adviser, or any person controlled by or under common control with the investment adviser, acts as broker for both the advisory client and for another person on the other side of the transaction. Agency cross transactions may arise where an adviser is dually registered as a broker-dealer or has an affiliated broker-dealer.

Brokerage Practices

The policy of John Grable & Associates, Inc. is to utilize and maintain client accounts at unaffiliated third-party broker-dealers. Clients receive transaction confirmations as well as account statements directly from the unaffiliated third-party broker. Clients determine where to maintain their accounts from an approved broker list provided by JGA. Each broker-dealer has a set commission schedule and clients may receive lower commission rates based on household size and statement preferences. JGA typically utilizes the following criteria to review third-party broker selections:

- Strong structure and reputation to earn confidence and trust with a long-term relationship objective.

- Ready access to a large volume of fixed income securities and access to a wide range of investment vehicles coupled with broad capabilities.

- Attractive financial terms for individual client accounts that provide value to the clients.

- Strong technology and available account information to facilitate trading.

- Dedicated relationship managers associated with all aspects of client service.

It is common for John Grable & Associates, Inc. to purchase and sell securities for its clients under a method of block trade orders, which with certain broker-dealers provides efficiencies of scale. This practice of combining many client trades into one large trade improves JGA's ability to execute trades at favorable price levels. The average price per share of a block trade is allocated to each account that participates. Accounts that participate in the same block trade are charged transaction costs and commissions in accordance with their individual client agreements. Transactions in over-the-counter securities are implemented on an agency basis, for JGA to obtain the best possible price for clients, within the offering and bid price. Relative to such transactions, clients pay commissions to the broker-dealers either on a gross or net basis; if on a net basis, the difference in price is generally disclosed on the confirmation and generally results in a better total price for clients.

In certain situations, JGA allows clients to open an account with a broker-dealer that is not on the approved list. In such situations, it is possible that JGA may be unable to achieve the most favorable execution of client transactions. Directing brokerage in this manner may cost clients more money. For example, clients directing brokerage may also incur other transaction costs, greater spreads, or receive less favorable net prices on transactions for their accounts.

Some of the custodians utilized provide JGA with certain brokerage and research products and services that qualify as "brokerage or research services" under Section 28(e) of the Securities Exchange Act of 1934 ("Exchange Act"). We may also receive additional benefits (also known as "non-cash" compensation) as a result of our relationships with our custodians. These resources are also referred to as "Other Economic Benefits". Examples include:

- Receipt of duplicate client confirmations.

- Receipt of electronic duplicate account statements.

- Access to block trading which provides the ability to aggregate securities transactions and then allocate the appropriate shares to client accounts.

- Access to electronic communication networks for client order entry and account information.

- Access to the investment advisor portion of their web sites (this may include practice management articles, compliance updates, and other financial planning related information and research materials).

- Access to other vendors on a discounted fee basis through discounts arranged by the custodians.

JGA does not currently have any commitments in place to invest any specific amount or percentage of client assets with any specific broker-dealer or in any specific securities or other investment products as a result of the above arrangements.

Review of Accounts

Each account is internally reviewed by a member of the JGA Investment Committee at least quarterly. When new cash is added to the account it is reviewed more frequently as the account is invested. Portfolio adjustments will be made as changes in the client's financial circumstances warrant. Reports of portfolio holdings are issued quarterly; performance reports are prepared semiannually and are generally included with reports of portfolio holdings. Clients can elect to receive quarterly reports either via a paper copy or via an electronic copy accessed via a secure client portal. Clients also receive monthly or quarterly statements directly from the third-party broker who custodies their assets.

The investment committee that determines general investment management strategies consists of John Grable, Megan Ford, Kimberly Watkins, Ryan Turner, Narang Park, and Michell Kruger. The persons responsible for the primary quarterly account reviews are the President, the Director of Trading, and the Portfolio Manager. Other financial advisory and planning services are conducted by Account Executives. Account Executives who have direct responsibility for investment advisory services of JGA must have academic background and experience in the investment management field.

Client Referrals and Other Compensation

JGA may engage the services of an unaffiliated third-party as an Investment Adviser Solicitor. Solicitors will be identified and compensated in accordance with the terms disclosed in a separate written solicitor's agreement. Such terms and agreement will be provided to clients by the Solicitor at the time of solicitation. In addition, John Grable & Associates, Inc. may also provide employees with additional cash or non-cash compensation for client referrals. Referral fees will not increase the management fees paid by clients.

Custody

Clients will receive at least quarterly statements from the broker-dealer, bank, or other qualified custodian that holds and maintains a client's investment assets. JGA urges clients to carefully review such statements and compare official custodial records to the account statements provided by JGA. Our statements may vary from custodial statements based on accounting procedures, reporting dates, or valuation methodologies of certain securities.

In certain limited circumstances, employees of John Grable & Associates, Inc. may be appointed to a fiduciary capacity, such as trustee or executor, on behalf of a client. In those circumstances, John Grable & Associates, Inc. shall ensure that third party broker statements are provided to an unaffiliated interested person.

Investment Discretion

JGA usually receives discretionary authority from a client at the outset of an advisory relationship. The agreement allows JGA to select the identity and amount of securities to be bought or sold. In all cases, however, such discretion is to be exercised in a manner consistent with the stated investment objectives for a particular client account.

When selecting securities and determining amounts, JGA observes the investment policies, limitations, and restrictions of the clients for which it advises. Investment guidelines and restrictions must be provided to JGA in writing. Prior to JGA exercising any discretionary authority over an account, JGA requires a signed and properly executed contract between JGA and the client(s). In addition, all proper account paperwork needs to be on file and accepted by the third-party broker who maintains the investment assets.

Voting Client Securities

As a matter of firm policy and practice, JGA does not have any authority to and does not vote proxies on behalf of advisory clients. Clients retain the responsibility for receiving and voting proxies for any and all securities maintained in client portfolios. JGA may provide advice to clients regarding the clients' voting of proxies.

Financial Information

Registered investment advisers are required to provide clients with certain financial information or disclosures about JGA's financial condition. JGA has no financial commitment that impairs its ability to meet contractual and fiduciary commitments to clients, and has not been the subject of a bankruptcy proceeding. Please refer to our Condensed Statement of Financial condition below:

JUNE 30, 20XX JOHN GRABLE & ASSOCIATES, INC. INFORMATION DERIVED FROM AUDITED FINANCIAL STATEMENTS CONDENSED STATEMENT OF FINANCIAL CONDITION AS OF June 30, 20XX	
ASSETS	
Cash and equivalents	$ 7,328,288
Accrued interest & receivables/prepaid expenses & taxes	166,690
TOTAL CURRENT ASSETS	7,494,978
TOTAL FIXED ASSETS	2,427,945
TOTAL INVESTED ASSETS (SECURITIES @ FAIR MARKET VALUE)	46,311,239
TOTAL ASSETS	$ 56,234,162
LIABILITIES AND STOCKHOLDERS' EQUITY	
Accounts payable/accrued expenses	$ 3,222,028
Deferred shareholder distributions	3,452,829
Unearned investment management fees	8,854,280
TOTAL LIABILITIES	15,529,137
DEFERRED COMPENSATION	154,000
TOTAL STOCKHOLDERS' EQUITY	40,551,025
TOTAL LIABILITIES AND STOCKHOLDERS' EQUITY	$ 56,234,162
Notes: Accounting Principles	

This condensed Statement of Financial Condition was derived from the consolidating financial statements which were prepared in accordance with generally accepted accounting principles and audited by an independent public accounting firm.
Unearned Investment Management Fees
The Company receives management fees in advance for investment management and certain other client services. As services are provided, the fees are proportionally recognized as income.

CHAPTER ENDNOTE

1. This brochure was adapted from public records available at: https://adviserinfo.sec.gov/IAPD. The firm described in this sample document is fictional.

Summary of CFP Board's Code of Ethics and Standards of Conduct

As noted earlier in Chapter 3, in 2019, CFP Board made significant revisions to the organization's *Code of Ethics and Standards of Conduct*. Applying the rules and standards appropriately is of importance to those who hold the CFP® marks. The following discussion highlights some additional aspects of the revised *Code of Ethics and Standards of Conduct*.[1]

- At all times when providing *financial advice* to a *client*, a CFP® professional must act as a fiduciary, and therefore, act in the best interests of the client. The Fiduciary Duty includes a Duty to Loyalty, a Duty to Care, and Duty to Follow Client Instructions.

   o Six definitions are of particularly importance in relation to the Fiduciary Duty:

   ◆ A *client* is any person to whom a CFP® provides or agrees to provide professional services pursuant to an engagement.

   ◆ An *engagement* is an oral or written agreement, arrangement, or understanding.

   ◆ *Financial advice* includes communications that, based on their content, context, and presentation, would reasonably be viewed as a recommendation to take or refrain from taking a particular course of action with respect to the advisability of investing in, purchasing, holding, gifting, or selling financial assets.

      ▪ The more individually tailored the communication is to the client, the more likely the communication will be viewed as financial advice.

- General financial education materials, or general financial communications that a reasonable CFP® professional would not view as a financial advice, does not constitute financial advice.

♦ *Duty of Loyalty*: requires a CFP® professional to place the interests of the client above the interests of the CFP® professional and the CFP® professional's firm.

- A CFP® professional also must avoid conflicts of interest, or fully disclose material conflicts of interest to the client, obtain the client's informed consent, and manage the conflict.

♦ *Duty to Care*: requires a CFP® professional to act with care, skill, prudence, and diligence that a prudent professional would exercise in light of the client's goals, risk tolerance, objectives, and financial personal circumstances.

♦ *Duty to Follow Client Instructions*: requires a CFP® professional to comply with all objectives, policies, restrictions, and other terms of the engagement and all reasonable and lawful directions of the client.

- A CFP® professional must make full disclosure of all material conflicts of interest with the CFP® professional's client that could affect the professional relationship.

  o This standard requires a CFP® professional to provide the client with sufficiently specific facts so that a reasonable client would be able to understand the material conflicts of interest and the business practice that give rise to the conflicts, and give informed consent to such conflicts or reject them (Duty to Disclose and Manage Conflicts).

    ♦ A conflict of interest exists whenever a CFP® professional's interests are adverse to the CFP® professional's duties to a client.

  o A CFP® professional has a duty to adopt and follow business practices reasonably designed to prevent material conflicts of interest from compromising the CFP® professional's ability to act in the client's best interests.

    ♦ Material information is information that a reasonable client (or prospective client) would consider important when making a decision.

  o CFP Board's Duty to Disclose does not require written disclosure; evidence of oral disclosure of a conflict is given equal weight. However, CFP Board recommends that conflicts of interest be documented in writing before or when providing financial advice.

- When a CFP® professional works as part of a team to provide financial advice to a client, the Duty of Care requires the CFP® professional to communicate with the other members of the team about the scope of their respective services and the allocation of responsibility between them.

o   This rule may be satisfied by a firm policy or protocol that clarifies team member roles.

- When providing financial planning, a CFP® professional is required to follow the Practice Standards for the Financial Planning Process (essentially the seven-step financial planning process).

   o   A CFP® professional must comply with the Practice Standards of the Financial Planning Process, and therefore, provide financial planning, when:

      ◆   The CFP® professional agrees to provide or provides:

         ▪   Financial planning; or

         ▪   Financial advice that requires integration of relevant elements of the client's personal and/or financial circumstances in order to act in the client's best interests; or

      ◆   The client has a reasonable basis to believe the CFP® professional will provide or has provided financial planning.

   o   CFP Board has established the following integration factors that CFP Board will weigh in determining whether a CFP® professional has agreed to provide or provided *financial advice that requires financial planning*:

      ◆   The number of relevant elements of the client's personal and financial circumstances that the financial advice may affect;

      ◆   The portion and amount of the client's financial assets that the financial advice may affect;

      ◆   The length of time the client's personal and financial circumstances may be affected by the financial advice;

      ◆   The effect on the client's overall exposure to risk if the client implements the financial advice; and

      ◆   The barriers to modifying the actions taken to implement the financial advice.

   o   If a CFP® professional otherwise must comply with the Practice Standards, but the client does not agree to engage the CFP® professional to provide financial planning, the CFP® professional must either:

      ◆   Not enter into the agreement;

- ◆ Limit the scope of the engagement to services that do not require application of the Practice Standards, and describe to the client the services that the client requests that the CFP® professional will not be performing;

- ◆ Provide the requested services after informing the client how financial planning would benefit the client and how the decision to engage the CFP® professional to provide financial planning may limit the CFP® professional's financial advice, in which case the CFP® professional is not required to comply with the Practice Standards; or

- ◆ Terminate the agreement.

- When recommending the retention of additional persons to provide financial advice or professional services for a client, a CFP® professional must (1) have a reasonable basis for the recommendation based on the person's reputation, experience, and qualifications; and (2) disclose to the client, at the time of the recommendation, any arrangement by which someone who is not the client will compensate or provide some other material economic benefit to the CFP® professional, the CFP® professional's firm, or a related party for the recommendation.

  - o A CFP® professional may rely on the CFP® professional's firm's list of approved firms if the CFP® professional understands the process the CFP® professional's firm used to develop the list and determines that it is reasonably designed and implemented.

- The following information must be provided to a client prior to or at the time of the engagement:

  - o A description of the services and products to be provided;

  - o How the client pays for the products and services, and a description of the additional types of costs that the client may incur;

  - o How the CFP® professional, the CFP® professional's firm, and any related party are compensated for providing the products and services;

  - o The existence of any public discipline and bankruptcy, and the locations of the webpages of certain public websites that sets forth the CFP® professional's published disciplinary history or any personal or business bankruptcy when the CFP® professional was a control person;

  - o Full disclosure of all material conflicts of interest with the CFP® professional's client that could affect the professional relationship, including sufficiently specific facts so that a reasonable client would be able to understand the CFP® professional's material conflicts of interest and the business practices that give rise to the conflicts, and give informed consent to such conflicts or reject them;

o A written notice at the time of the engagement identifying policies regarding the protection, handling, and sharing of a client's non-public personal information that were adopted and implemented by the CFP® professional's firm, and thereafter not less than annually except under certain circumstances;

o Any arrangement by which someone who is not the client will compensate or provide some other material economic benefit to the CFP® professional, the CFP® professional's firm, or a related party for engaging or recommending the selection or retention of additional persons to provide financial or professional services for client; and

o Any other information about the CFP® professional or the CFP® professional's firm that is material to a client's decision to engage or continue to engage the CFP® professional or the CFP® professional's firm.

- A CFP® professional must not make false or misleading representations regarding the CFP® professional's or the CFP® professional's firm's method(s) of compensation. A CFP® professional may represent their or the CFP® professional's firm's compensation method as "fee-only" if:

o The CFP® professional and the CFP® professional's firm receive no sales-related compensation; and

o Related parties receive no sales-related compensation in connection with any professional services the CFP® professional or the CFP® professional's firm provides to clients.

♦ Sales-related compensation is defined as more than a de minimis economic benefit including any bonus or portion of compensation, resulting from a client purchasing or selling financial assets, from a client holding financial assets for purposes other than receiving financial advice, or from the referral of a client to any personal entity other than the CFP® professional's firm.

CHAPTER ENDNOTE

1. Material in this review was adapted from: https://www.cfp.net/for-cfp-professionals/professional-standards-enforcement/code-and-standards/case-studies-applying-the-new-code-and-standards?_zs=Bh8ce1&_zl=kxNK6.

Chapter 4

Fundamentals of Communication and Counseling in Financial Planning

Learning Objectives

- Learning Objective 1: Explain the importance of communication in financial planning.

- Learning Objective 2: Understand how effective communication can enhance the financial planning experience.

- Learning Objective 3: Explore verbal and non-verbal aspects of communication, as well as paralanguage cues in communication.

- Learning Objective 4: Identify the information processing and learning styles that may impact communication with clients.

- Learning Objective 5: Explain how to professionally present a written financial plan to a client.

4.1 THE IMPORTANCE OF COMMUNICATION AND COUNSELING COMPETENCE IN FINANCIAL PLANNING

Financial planning, as a field of study and professional occupation, is an activity that requires sound technical knowledge, quantitative and analytical skills, and an ability to communicate ideas and strategies as a way to move clients towards recommendation implementation. Yet financial planners must not forget that at the center of this technical work is a client. While the steps of the financial planning process, and ultimately the finished product—the financial plan—are important, the focus of all financial planning activities should be client-centered.

Most, if not all, of the steps in the financial planning process require the effective application of communication and counseling skills. Communication is the central mechanism for various aspects of the financial planning process. It is of paramount importance when developing the client relationship, identifying a client's financial objectives, as well as learning about their future hopes and dreams. Communication also facilitates the discovery of client attitudes, feelings, and experiences related to money, which helps the financial planner to better understand a client's financial beliefs and behaviors. In this regard, it is important for financial planners to recognize their own money attitudes and history, as these factors can easily influence the way financial planning is conducted with clients.

A financial planner must be ready to use communication and counseling skills as a means for gaining necessary client information and grasping the intricacies of the client's situation. It is worth emphasizing that communicating is not synonymous with communicating *well*. Becoming a great communicator is a continuous pursuit.

To illustrate this point, picture the following scenario:

> Sam, a financial planner in a mid-sized firm, begins working with a new client in order to help them develop a plan for retirement. During the initial meeting, Sam initiates the first step in the financial planning process and begins discussing the types of detailed data needed from the client. Sam works hard to convince the new client that the firm's team has the skills and resources necessary to help them. At the end of the meeting, Sam walks away from the interaction feeling generally positive. However, upon further reflection, Sam realizes that they dominated much of the conversation. They did not allow for much, if any, open conversation or collaborative goal-setting. After asking a few broad questions, Sam made assumptions and filled in a lot of the blanks. They wonder how their approach might impact future work with this client.

> Several weeks pass, and the client has not returned emails or phone calls to set up a second meeting. After one last attempt to call and get back on-track, Sam finally reaches the client, who tells Sam that they have chosen to work with another firm. Sam asks the client for feedback as to why they ultimately decided not to return. The client, somewhat hesitantly, shares that they were confident in Sam's technical

knowledge and capacity to build a solid plan for their retirement, but did not feel that Sam "heard" them during the initial meeting.

The takeaway here is that, ultimately, the client wanted more than technical answers to their questions. They wanted a partnership with their financial planner, one in which the client's needs, wants, desires, wishes, concerns, and questions would be listened to, honored, and discussed.

This scenario is not necessarily uncommon and is one that can lead to problematic outcomes, including the loss of a client. Worse still, if the communication and counseling techniques used by the financial planner in this example were to become habitual, the financial planner's reputation and livelihood could easily be compromised. Beyond the obligation some financial planners have to act as a fiduciary, this consequence may be one the best arguments for the importance of learning and applying better communication and counseling skills.

Communication skills can ultimately separate a good planner from a great one. As Grable and Goetz[1] highlighted in their work on communication skills, it takes more than formulas, numbers, and technical knowledge to be a successful financial planner.

Empirical research shows the importance of communication as well. Consider the results from one particularly compelling study. Researchers asked consumers to identify the most desired traits in a financial planner. A list of the top traits (see Figure 4.1) revealed a preference for not only technical competence, but also characteristics that one might find in a counselor or therapist. Clients found high intelligence important, in addition to qualities that are more established in the counseling domain, including:

- Empathy

- Understanding

- Warmth

- Sensitivity

This study, and others, indicate that clients prefer solving their concerns in collaboration *with* financial planners, rather than having a financial planner solve a problem *for* them. Financial planners can use communication and counseling techniques to help clients change, adapt, modify, and/or manage behavior affecting the financial planning process.

Figure 4.1. Preferred Financial Planner Communication Traits.

Trait	Example
Regards clients as persons of worth	Unconditional acceptance of the client and the client's past actions.
Nonpossessive warmth	Reflects genuine concern for the client with overtones of personal caring while at the same time fostering client independence and professional boundaries.
Competence and confidence	Presents an image that highlights personal strengths and professionalism through appearance and communication methods.
Sincerity and openness	Displays sincere openness and respect for the client as an individual.
Empathy and understanding	Strives to fully understand and respect the client's paradigms and share the client's concerns.
Sensitivity	Acknowledges the importance of the client's emotional and financial needs and respects personal values, morals, and ethics.
Objectivity	Provides neutral, suitable advice in the best interest of the client.
Flexibility	Is willing to explore new planning strategies and to adapt previous recommendations to new client, market, or economic situations.
High intelligence	Values the role of continuing professional education and lifelong learning.
Absence of emotional disturbance or instability	Avoids biases or moods that might distort or disrupt the client-financial planner relationship or the client's financial situation.
Personal style	Uses body language, humor, stories, and emotion comfortably when working with clients.
Miscellaneous aspects	Presents a congruent message consistent with age, gender, appearance, and habits.

Information in this figure is based on Geis, H.J. (1973). "Toward a Comprehensive Framework Unifying All systems of Counseling." In John Vriend (ed.). Counseling Effectively in Groups. Englewood Cliffs, NJ: Educational Technology Publications. Page 10-31.

4.2 THE MANY LAYERS OF COMMUNICATION

Most often, when someone thinks of the term "communication," verbal exchanges between one person and another come to mind. While this is certainly one element of communication, this tells only part of the story. In fact, communication is much more nuanced and multifaceted. It is important, for many of the reasons already discussed, that financial planners understand the various aspects of communication.

As a result of its complexity, defining communication succinctly is a difficult task. In reality, there are hundreds of definitions that exist. **Communication**, most broadly, is an exchange of information between two or more entities or persons. Contributing most foundationally to communication are *verbal* and *nonverbal* elements. Additionally, *paralanguage* cues like rate of verbalization, tone, and volume of speech are embedded within the building blocks of communication. Accurate interpretation of a client's message will often require attunement to all three.

With this in mind, communication experts emphasize a focus on nonverbal communication (e.g., body language, appearance, personal space, etc.) and **paralanguage** (e.g., loudness of speech, tempo of delivery, quality of voice, etc.) cues. Why? Research suggests that less than 10 percent of interpersonal communication is reflected in verbal messages. Simply focusing on what is said, or the **content** of a conversation, can lead to incorrect assumptions or incomplete exchanges. Therefore, it is important for financial planners not to rely solely on the content aspect of messages from clients.

Of course, this is not to suggest that content does not matter—it does. Perhaps you have heard the phrase, "It's not *what* you say, it's *how* you say it." Financial planners need to be aware of communication content, but can also learn a great deal from the **process** which encompasses the action happening, or the "how you say it." The process part of communication involves how content is conveyed within communication, as well as the subtext or someone's unspoken thoughts and motivations. While words do matter, it should be emphasized that what is often more important are the process-oriented underpinnings of communication. Interpreting the way in which words are delivered by a client is an essential financial planning skill. This is particularly true for financial planners who want to better identify and interpret client emotions and feelings as a way to enrich the financial planning process.

Navigating paralanguage and other nonverbal communication successfully is also crucial. For example, a client might say, "This is unbelievable." However, to fully understand the message, a financial planner needs to be attuned to the client's paralanguage. If the phrase is expressed quietly with a disconcerted look, the meaning should be interpreted differently than if the client exclaims the phrase loudly with a big smile.

Expanding on the difference between process and content, there is also the matter of congruence within communication. **Congruence** refers to the consistency between how something is said and what is said.

> Consider this example. Imagine a client says, "I think this could be the answer," as a way to share their uncertainty with the potential effectiveness of a strategy the

financial planner is suggesting. On the other hand, the client could use the exact same words, but be expressing genuine excitement about the fact that the financial planner provided a strategy of value.

Here, a client's tone of voice, syllable emphasis, paralanguage, and other nonverbal cues provide clarity about the client's state of mind. When the financial planner does not see congruency between what is being verbalized and what is not, they can assume that the nonverbal message is the most accurate. Incongruence should not be ignored. Rather, when things do not match, it should be explored further to understand what the financial planner may be missing. It is important to act with sensitivity and avoid projecting anything that could be interpreted by the client as frustration or blame. After all, when miscommunications and inconsistencies arise, it may be frustrating for the financial planner and the client.

One way to begin exploring inconsistencies is to make a simple observation, such as: "I feel like I could be missing something. Your words say this will work, but I notice that you do not seem fully convinced."

Noticing and addressing inconsistencies with a non-blaming and open stance, as well as more tentative language (i.e., less presumptive words such as could, may, perhaps, etc.) is important not only for goal discovery and plan development, but also in the context of developing a foundational level of trust with a client.

4.3 BODY LANGUAGE IN THE CONTEXT OF CLIENT COMMUNICATION

A primary way to recognize client emotions or feelings is through a client's **body language**. Body language can include:

- facial expressions,

- gestures or movements, and

- body positioning (i.e., the proximity, or space, observed between individuals).

Understanding and attending to body language offers the financial planner insight into a client's state of mind, comfort level, and feelings. Elements of body language include:

- posture,

- what the client is doing with their body (e.g., hands and feet), and

- facial expressions.

Planning Reminder

As practice, consider what you have been told by others about your body language. What communication skills do you think you should practice and improve?

Again, consider the meeting described earlier between Sam and the prospective client. During the meeting, as Sam dominates the conversation, the client looks away during discussions, frowns, and leans slightly back with arms folded across their chest. Without the client saying a single word, the body language clearly communicates a mood of disengagement, boredom, and/or annoyance.

Now consider another meeting after Sam has received some coaching on communication. As Sam engages with the client, they are nodding, smiling, sitting up straight, and leaning in. This client is sending another message, one of interest, connection, and engagement.

As these examples illustrate, an awareness of how body language can be perceived as negative or positive is important, as this can either enhance communication or detract from successful messaging. For instance, crossed arms, slouching, frowning, furrowed brows, looking at a device or phone during a conversation, or sitting too closely or too far away can be perceived as negative. Some body language, on the other hand, enhances the communication process, including upright posture, leaning forward when listening, showing active engagement with the other person, eye contact, relaxed facial expressions, and minimal anxious or distracting mannerisms.

4.4 THE IMPORTANCE OF CULTURAL DIFFERENCES IN THE COMMUNICATION PROCESS

Cultural differences can also play a role in both the projection and interpretation of communication cues. It is very important for financial planners to observe a comfortable **space** between themselves and clients. In terms of closeness or proximity, most North Americans in professional and formal social settings prefer to maintain a distance between each other of approximately one arm's length (three to four feet) while engaging in conversation. Sitting too closely while seated can make some clients uncomfortable. Similarly, when engaging with a client or learning more about them, sitting too far away may be equally counterproductive. Financial planners should be aware that personal touch (e.g., touching a shoulder or arm) can sometimes feel too intrusive or intimate. In the United States and Canada, it is common to provide others with sufficient personal space, sometimes referred to as "a bubble." This may not be the case in other countries where closer proximity is commonplace.

Planning Reflection

Think about times you may have misinterpreted communication signs or signals. Reflecting back now, how was culture, ethnicity, or gender a factor?

Eye contact is an important aspect of nonverbal messaging. Financial planners should be aware that client eye contact preferences may be rooted in their cultural background. As with all of the information that follows concerning culture, it is important to acknowledge that the cultural norms described are generalizations and can vary greatly person to person. Based on research by Sommers-Flanagan and Sommers-Flanagan:[2] Non-Hispanic Whites show a preference for engaging in and maintaining more eye contact and it is often socially expected. However, Indigenous Peoples or individuals from American Indian[3] cultures, as well as those from African American and Asian cultures, may favor less eye contact during meetings and interviews.[4]

Generally, Western norms suggest that a financial planner maintain eye contact when listening to clients as a way to show attention, but lessen eye contact when speaking. In the United States and Canada, steady eye contact communicates respect, attention, authenticity, confidence, and cordiality. Less eye contact may suggest a lack of self-assurance, indifference, aloofness, or anxiousness. Overall, it is important to strike a balance.

Cultural differences can also be observed on a smaller, regional level. Consider the verbal communication styles exhibited by those found in different areas of the United States. Differences observed in volume and tone during conversation may reflect the norms within a regional location. For instance, those who reside in the Northeast United States are often inclined to speak faster, louder, and even more pointedly than those from the Southern United States. The failure to acknowledge and appreciate cultural variations occurring within communication can lead to unintended missteps, which can hurt the financial planner-client relationship. Therefore, it is crucial to be aware and observant of cultural differences within verbal and nonverbal communication.

4.5 THE IMPORTANCE OF GENDER DIFFERENCES IN THE COMMUNICATION PROCESS

In many countries, women and men tend to be socialized differently, which may result in observed differences in communication preferences and tendencies. Women typically integrate more nonverbal cues and signals when engaged in active communication compared to men. This is seen specifically in women's' level of engagement with a speaker during conversation. Women tend to use affirmation or supportive statements more often than men. Women are also more likely to be attuned to someone who is speaking, and show signs that the speaker is being heard and understood more so than men.

Planning Reminder

As practice, put together a group of three other classmates or colleagues: Each person will take a turn role-playing (1) the financial planner, (2) the client, and (3) the observer. The "financial planner" should ask the person playing the "client" a simple prompt or a series of questions, such as "What brings you in for services?" or "Tell me more about your short-term and long-term goals." The "client" should feel free to make up responses that are typical of a financial planning scenario. While the "client" is talking, the financial planner should practice attending behavior. The observer should then watch the interaction and provide feedback to the financial planner about what was witnessed. Each person should rotate roles.

Further, men and women tend to use tone, vocalizations, and volume (i.e., paralanguage) differently. Women may utilize more tentative language, while men may be more inclined to speak with more certainty. Depending on the context and setting, women and men may be more or less dominant in conversation. As the examples above illustrate, cultural and gender differences vary widely and are important factors to attend to within professional communication efforts. Financial planners should also be careful not to over-rely on these descriptions or overgeneralize, as there are sure to be variations and distinctions within individuals, families, generations, and regions.

4.6 THE IMPORTANCE OF A CLIENT'S LEARNING AND INFORMATION PROCESSING STYLE

When a financial planner effectively aligns their communication style with the verbal, nonverbal, and paralanguage preferences of a client, it becomes easier to discern ways to help the client change behavior and move towards recommendation implementation. Another helpful consideration is how clients process information.

Everyone has a preferred information processing and learning style. Extensive counseling and psychological research has identified three primary modes used for learning and communication—*visual, auditory,* and *kinesthetic.* Once a client's preferred style is established through observation and additional conversation, a financial planner should attempt to augment general communication techniques, as well as the presentation of information, in a way that appropriately complements the client's communication style preference. While all three learning styles can be present simultaneously, research also suggests that the majority of people show a preference for one.

Visual processors favor using their eyes to read, gather information, and watch others complete a task or skill. Visual aids such as graphs and charts, videos, and visual presentation tools (e.g., PowerPoint slides, Prezi, etc.) can be very effective tools when working with visual learners.

Those with a visual processing preference favor the presentation of information in an organized, more sequenced manner. Oftentimes, visual learners like to process information by reading and taking notes (although note taking aligns closely with a kinesthetic learning style as well). Clients who prefer visual processing and communication generally want to read and make notes when reviewing a financial plan, prospectus, or annual report. Financial planners may notice in meetings that visually oriented clients appear quiet during formal discussions and presentations, likely due to observing carefully and reading along.

Planning Reminder

As you practice, consider your personal learning and information processing style. Reflect on how this style impacts your work as a financial planner and your communication with clients.

Unlike visual processors, an **auditory processor** relies less on visual displays or watching the completion of a skill or task. Instead, those with an auditory preference often anchor to what they hear. Auditory processors appreciate a back and forth dialogue. This means that auditory learners can be quite talkative during financial planner-client interactions. While those fitting this profile tend not to rely much on note taking or visual aids, they do favor question and answer opportunities and discussion. Financial planners should be aware that auditory focused clients generally want to talk about a strategy, technique, or plan with a financial planner, rather than read a planning document. Building in time for questions is a best practice when working with auditory processors.

A **kinesthetic processor** learns through tactile and physical involvement where the person is touching, feeling, or manipulating something. Kinesthetic learners prefer to engage in an experience of the skill or task. Beyond the physical aspect, those who exhibit this information processing style sometimes prefer engagements that include affective, or emotional, learning. Preferred communication techniques that appeal to kinesthetic processors include playing games, drawing pictures, and engaging in interactive or imagery exercises. Communication techniques like these can be used by financial planners to more fully engage clients who are kinesthetic learners.

Financial planners should also know what clients find less helpful based on their information processing style. As an example, insisting that a client read through a financial plan very meticulously or sit through a long planning meeting where the client is only observing or listening can be counterproductive for a kinesthetic learner. What is more appealing to a kinesthetic learner might be engaging with computer or tablet, an internet or software application, or a white board.

Of course, it is worth mentioning that the three learning and processing styles are generalizations. Most people can move across styles without prompting. Financial planners should be careful not to categorize someone as disinterested or disengaged until a review of learning style preferences has been conducted. What seems to be disinterest could actually be an indication the financial planner is not sufficiently accommodating the client's learning style. Figure 4.2 compares and contrasts the three learning and processing styles.

Figure 4.2. Information Processing and Communication Style Comparisons.

Learning and Processing Style	Visual	Auditory	Kinesthetic
Learns by listening		√	
Learns by watching others	√		
Learns by reading	√		
Learns by writing or recording notes	√		
Learns by doing or experiencing			√
Makes decisions after reading, reviewing, or conducting thorough research	√		
Makes decisions after hearing a proposal or engaging in an informative conversation		√	
Makes decisions based on lived experiences			√

Adapted from R. Lytton, J. Grable, & D. Klock. *The Process of Financial Planning*, 2nd ed. (Kentucky: National Underwriter, 2013).

Though most clients have a preferred learning or communication style, this may not be true for all. In the end, most clients find multiple ways to process information due to the circumstance or situation. A client who is predominantly an auditory processor may feel connected by a verbal engagement with a financial planner, but to fully grasp the recommendations presented, the same client may need to "see" data and outcomes presented visually. If a client appears confused or anxious after the presentation of a recommendation, it is a good idea to adapt and try another "channel" if one communication style does not seem to be connecting. Figure 4.3 includes phrases a financial planner can use to more readily identify a client's preferred communication style.[5]

Figure 4.3. Phrases Associated with Communication Styles.

Word or Phrase Reflecting Communication Style	Example	Visual	Auditory	Kinesthetic
Show	Show me what you mean.	√		
See	I see what you are saying.	√		
Look	Let me take a better look.	√		
Perspective	I hadn't viewed it from that perspective.	√		
Note	I need to make a note of that.	√		
Study	It would help me to study those documents further.	√		
Hear	I hear what you are saying.		√	
Sounds	It sounds like we are on the same page.		√	
Say	It says to me you understand.		√	
Touch base	Let's touch base in a few weeks.			√

Feel	I feel very positive about this direction.			√
Handle	Would you be willing to handle implementation?			√
Tie, found, follow	That certainly helps to tie things together. I found the explanation hard to follow.			√

Adapted from R. Lytton, J. Grable, & D. Klock. *The Process of Financial Planning*, 2nd ed. (Kentucky: National Underwriter, 2013).

Armed with a more complete overview of the foundational layers and complexities of basic communication and learning styles, financial planners stand to gain a richer understanding of a client's individuality: the unique experiences, emotions, and ideas influencing their financial decision-making and actions. This information is undoubtedly valuable to financial planners, but it may be even more valuable to clients. Clients often need a deeper level of understanding or discovery of their money management preferences, tendencies, and behaviors to ultimately be most effective in meeting personal goals and/or implementing recommendations within a financial plan. Using enhanced communication strategies, financial planners can begin to help clients explore, and understand their deeply held money beliefs and mental shortcuts. We will now explore an array of communication and counseling tools designed to help financial planners better understand and empower their clients.

4.7 THE ROLE OF COMMUNICATION AND COUNSELING TECHNIQUES IN THE FINANCIAL PLANNING PROCESS

The integration of counseling-based techniques is a new and evolving aspect of the financial planning process. Several foundational techniques including active listening, attending, clarifying, questioning, normalizing, reframing, affirming, empathizing, and self-disclosure are discussed below and help to deepen client engagement, trust, and rapport.

4.7.1 Active Listening

As it is a part of nearly every interaction with others, we can take listening for granted. Listening well takes a great deal of effort, especially when first attempting this technique. Often when we listen, we are already splitting our attention by beginning to construct a response to the information we are receiving. Listening well, in a focused and engaged way, involves the whole body, the mind, and the heart, is called **active listening**.

When engaged in active listening, the financial planner will listen beyond a client's words for what lies beneath: meaning, (in)congruency, and unspoken messages. Because of the concentration inherent in this communication technique, practice is necessary. When practicing, the listener should say very little, but still be able to convey interest. The active listening skill is very much built upon a foundation of patience, self-restraint, and, to a degree, selflessness. The listener must practice full focus and learn to ignore mental chatter in order to be completely engaged with the speaker.

Active listening does not necessarily equal agreement with the client; however, through facial expressions and body language, the financial planner can demonstrate interest and understanding. During active listening, a financial planner will engage in much less talking, although they will exhibit physical manifestations of engagement involving the face and body, showing the client that they are heard. Also, while engaging in active listening, a financial planner should try to avoid interrupting, overinterpreting, or prejudging the client.

To be clear, active listening does not involve inserting opinions or finishing a client's sentences. Active listening is very much meant to help engage both the financial planner and client more fully in communication. By working to be more engaged with a client through active listening, the financial planner is better able to incorporate additional communication strategies.

By involving the heart in listening, a financial planner will be in a better position to feel more empathy for clients. Again, even if a financial planner's own viewpoints or values are not aligned perfectly with a client's, listening with the heart does not require agreement or fully shouldering a client's perspective. Empathy, more than anything, requires trying to understand something from the client's perspective and connecting more fully to a client's point of view.

For example, what might make a client with a well-paying job and significant savings state strongly that they will not contribute to a college education fund for their child? This stance could be surprising to some financial planners. The client's statement may go very much against the financial planner's own stance on the matter. The client has asserted a value, one that is not congruent with the financial planner's point of view. However, it is not the financial planner's place to agree or disagree, or to alter the client's attitudes and feelings. Rather, the financial planner's role involves using active listening skills and other communication and counseling techniques to examine any issues that concern or inform the financial planning process.

It is also worth remembering that not every interaction will involve deep active listening. Much of what is discussed in financial planning meetings involves more straightforward or technical exchanges about "facts" (e.g., a client's family structure, health, employment, or financial status). These topics often unfold without emotions attached, but still call for sensitivity and awareness of verbal and nonverbal cues. Quantitative topics may not lead into deep emotional territory. Yet, the discussion of personal or "qualitative" issues (e.g., a client's relationships, family, and social dimensions, including their goals, interests, attitudes, and values) will likely require the financial planner to apply active listening.

4.7.2 Questioning

Financial planners engage in a back-and-forth dialogue from the first step in the financial planning process to the last step. A key component to dialogue with clients is the formulation and delivery of questions. Questions may seem simple enough, as they are integral to conversation and daily exchanges with others. However, formulating clear, effective questions requires practice. With much of the work of financial planners focused on the understanding of goals and objectives and eliciting the necessary information to make sound recommendations, both formulating and posing questions successfully are central to this objective.

Successful questions are thoughtful, intentional, and well-timed. The tone and timing of questions is also very important. Questions posed in different tones or at different points in a conversation can lead to very different outcomes. Keep in mind some questions regarding a client's financial life may also incite socially acceptable answers and may not truly reflect accurate feelings or behaviors. Cultural and societal expectations surrounding money and its use can affect the way clients choose to answer questions. Along with an awareness of paralanguage and context, financial planners must not discount the importance of trust, as a stronger alliance with the client can affect their level of transparency and honesty.

There is often a balance between posing too many questions or decidedly too few. Both can impact the working relationship between a financial planner and a client. An overabundance of questions might result in:

- the client feeling bombarded or interrogated, and

- the financial planner being perceived as overbearing or nosy.

Too few questions, on the other hand, is not optimal either. Asking a client too few questions might result in:

- the client feeling unimportant or ignored,

- the client perceiving the advice or solutions offered are not customized or tailored specifically to their needs, or the financial planner being perceived as detached, disinterested.

Questions can also be formulated in an open or closed manner. The former is encouraged during the financial planning process, as open-ended questions elicit more information and allow clients to explain their thoughts and feelings. Though open questions are typically preferred, both question types can be used effectively depending on the scenario.

- **Open-ended questions** typically begin with "what" and "how," or phrases like, "I'm wondering..." or "Tell me about...". The objective is to encourage a client to share information, feelings, perceptions, and observations. Follow-up questions and verbal or nonverbal reinforcements can be integrated to encourage further dialogue. Open-ended questions also tend to be more objective and less leading than closed-ended questions.

Closed-ended questions are typically used to elicit a brief, less explanatory answer (e.g., yes/no) or reply based on data and facts. Questions beginning with "do," "did," "when," and "where" are likely closed-ended. While closed-ended questions are most helpful for data gathering or confirming information, the use of this technique is less so when trying to better understand a client's beliefs, attitudes, and motives.

4.7.3 Attending

Another important skill is **attending**. Attending weaves together verbal and nonverbal aspects of communication to show the financial planner is "tracking" along with the client. Nonverbally, this technique looks like maintaining comfortable eye contact, keeping appropriate distance between parties, and demonstrating calm, but confident, body language—all in ways that are respectful to any cultural, gender, and personal differences. Attending techniques in financial planning may also involve the use of verbal responses that are congruent with the client's, including mirroring their tone and volume of voice, as well as the intentional repeating of key words and phrases the client has used.

Effective verbal attending ensures that a client feels seen and heard. In order to do this, a financial planner should adapt their approach by asking questions and making observations that align with the client's message or the topic being discussed. They can also use short phrases, such as "Okay," "I see what you mean," "I'm following you," or "I understand."

When attending is displayed through body language, the financial planner should orient themselves physically toward the client, using steady eye contact, nodding, and leaning forward to show engagement. These actions demonstrate not only an acknowledgement of the client's presence, but also that they have the financial planner's full, undivided attention. Attending techniques can help the client to feel validated and better understood by increasing the belief they, as well as the topic they are discussing, is important. Effective attending certainly can deepen the working relationship and enhance the financial planning process. Attending reinforces, supports, and encourages the client to continue talking about ideas, experiences, and/or emotions.

On the other hand, the overuse of attending techniques can quickly become less effective. Financial planners are cautioned that some clients may find the overuse of attending behavior as irritating, or worse, as intimidating or manipulative. Each of the following actions can become problematic:

- Overly energetic body language and vigorous head nods,

- Too much eye contact (i.e., staring too intensely without relief),

- Overuse of "filler words," such as "uh huh" or "mmhmm,"

- Conveying "I understand" in response to a client's highly individualized experiences,

- Overly precise mirroring of a client's gestures or body language (e.g., mimicking or copying too exactly), and

- Verbal summaries which duplicate a client's own words too exactly (e.g., parroting).

The following behaviors should be avoided when attempting to incorporate attending techniques.

- interrupting a client,

- abruptly moving to a new subject or topic,

- making additional interpretations of statements, and

- overanalyzing or investigating client statements.

4.7.4 Clarifying Techniques

Errors in communication occur when a speaker and listener encounter mutual misinterpretation and misunderstanding. A speaker may say something that a listener interprets differently than intended. Realistically, communication errors are inevitable and expected, but the danger is that missteps can eventually become destructive when left unchecked and unattended to.

For the purposes of financial planning, this means that when something is not understood or clear, make sure an effort is made to clarify. If clarification attempts are not made, financial planners may risk missing crucial information, or are left to fill in the blanks themselves—and incorrect conclusions or unsuitable recommendations potentially follow. The process of clarification, sometimes referred to as "checking in" with a client, is yet another pillar of effective communication. Clarification strategies ensure a financial planner is accurately understanding the client, as well as their goals and wishes. Clarification also demonstrates interest and engagement. A few specific techniques for clarification include *restating, paraphrasing, summarizing, and reflecting.*

Restating, sometimes referred to as rephrasing, involves repeating a client's communication back for accuracy. Through restating, the main idea is repeated or presented in an abbreviated manner. Restating also usually involves repeating some of the exact words used by the client. Financial planners are, however, cautioned not to view restating as a direct mimic or echo of a client. For this reason, restating is best used intermittently and not in repetition. This is also not a strategy meant to involve interpretation or looking for further meaning.

For instance, while discussing goals, a client might state: *"I want to save money for retirement, but I would also like to assist my children with their college expenses – I don't see how I can do both at the same time."*

If a financial planner were to incorporate restating here, they might say: *"You would like to save for both education and retirement, but you are unsure about meeting these goals at the same time."*

Paraphrasing, which goes a step further, involves rewording a client's core message using a concise summary statement. When paraphrasing, the financial planner uses more of their own words as a way to clarify a client's comment or concern. Paraphrasing can draw attention to a particular idea or issue and helps to enhance understanding for the client and for the financial planner.

For example, imagine a client says: *"I'm just not sure what to do. I know that investing more aggressively when you're young is common, but it doesn't sit well with me."*

Using paraphrasing to clarify, a financial planner might reply: *"I'm hearing concern with the amount of investment risk you're personally comfortable taking as compared with others who may be a similar age."*

After using any technique involving an element of interpretation, like paraphrasing, the financial planner should consistently observe nonverbal or verbal cues from their client to confirm whether the interpretation and "rewording" was successful. If the paraphrase is accurate, a range of indications might include:

- A nod in agreement,

- Positive facial expressions or smiling,

- Open body posture and leaning forward, and

- Confirmatory phrases:

  o "Mmhmm,"

  o "Yes,"

  o "Correct,"

  o "That's exactly what I think (or how I feel)"

Paraphrasing can also be useful when the financial planner notices a discrepancy or a mixed message from the client. Say a client is sending a mixed message, indicating a desire to increase savings, but during the same conversation, they also indicate a tentativeness to change excess spending patterns—a necessary step for meeting the savings goal. Here, a paraphrased statement offers an opportunity to highlight the discrepancy, initiate additional clarification efforts, and better gauge a client's responses.

A financial planner might say to the client: *"From what I've heard you say, both increased savings and the freedom to spend are important to you. Can you help clarify how you might see those goals working together?"*

In other situations, the financial planner may want to incorporate summarizing as a clarification strategy. **Summarizing** involves briefly highlighting the main points within a segment of conversation or after an extended discussion, such as longer remarks, stories, or comments which are somewhat off-track or unrelated. Summarizing may have various uses in communication, but typically emphasizes main ideas and also packages the dialogue into a more cohesive reflection. This clarification technique enables progression of a discussion, whether from one topic to another, or more broadly from one meeting to another. Summarizing is useful throughout client discussions and can be incorporated at the end of a meeting as a way to refocus and "close the loop" on questions or outstanding items. Summarizing can also be used to begin concurrent client meetings in order to establish completed tasks and future directions. In the latter case, a financial planner can utilize summarizing as a way to bridge a previous meeting to a current meeting, as well as highlight actions or results that have occurred since.

> For instance, a financial planner at the outset of a meeting might state: *"During our last meeting, we discussed several goals including finding a more appropriate life insurance policy as well as finding an attorney who can assist you with legal documents related to your estate plan. We had agreed you were going to do some research on your current assets and personal property in order to have a clear idea of what you may want to distribute to any beneficiaries or heirs. I'd like to begin our meeting with your findings, then we'll plan to discuss our recommendations for a new life insurance policy towards the second half of the meeting today."*

A summary at the end of a client meeting may involve one or more of the following:

- Revisiting the key points discussed,

- Highlighting potential answers and solutions,

- Summarizing any recommendations,

- Establishing tasks or responsibilities (e.g., "next steps") to be completed by the financial planner or the client, and

- Reminding the client of unfinished business or unresolved dilemmas that need further attention, consideration, or discussion with others.

At other times, a financial planner may find **reflecting** a useful clarification skill, as reflecting involves the restating back of both the words and emotions expressed within a message. Reflecting allows a client to hear "a playback" of thoughts and feelings and demonstrates that the financial planner understands more completely the client's experience, further solidifying trust and rapport. Reflecting can be a very effective communication and counseling technique, and it is also more advanced due to the acknowledgement and interpretation of client feelings. Practice is typically needed.

Regardless of the amount of practice, it can still be difficult to accurately assess the feelings of another individual. The majority of people are equipped to identify basic emotions we display like sadness, happiness, anger, fear, and surprise. Yet individual variability affects how these feelings are displayed. Fear can be clearly shown on an expressive face, but might also manifest as disinterest or argumentativeness in other clients. Even the most recognizable emotions can be misinterpreted without context, investigation, or clarification. A financial planner may interpret the argumentativeness in a client as an unwillingness to follow recommendations, when actually a client is feeling fearful of the advice or strategy presented. Reflection techniques serve to uncover more of what a client is experiencing at a deeper level.

A common hesitation with the reflecting technique is, "What if I'm wrong?" The idea that the financial planner may offend their client by venturing into emotional territory remains a primary reason most steer away from reflection statements. While sensitivity and care must be taken when approaching feelings, it is not about perfect interpretation or getting it "right". Reflecting is more about conveying a genuine desire to understand the client's perspective and experience. Reflecting techniques can still be useful without 100 percent accuracy, as a client can be invited to correct the reflection. Prefacing a reflection statement with the following can reduce some of the risk surrounding "getting it wrong":

- "Please let me know if this doesn't reflect your feelings…"

- "Feel free to adjust my words if they don't fit…"

- "I am using my words now, and if these words don't feel accurate, I invite you to help me…"

- "I may not have interpreted this correctly, so if not, please say so…"

Normalizing is a foundational technique used to "depathologize" concerns. Normalizing is used to suggest that an issue or experience is common or expected. Normalizing helps a client to re-conceptualize the concern as something many experience, rather than an issue only weighing on them. Normalizing is intended to help a client feel less alone or isolated and to reduce negative self-perception.

When a person is experiencing a problem or facing a difficult situation, it can feel isolating. People may forget that many personal problems are universal and human experiences are not necessarily unique. This is not to downplay individualized experience, but rather to point out the universality in which clients encounter life's bumps and hurdles. This is particularly true for clients' financial lives. Though the majority of clients, if not all, encounter financial challenges or concerns across the lifespan, feelings of isolation and shame are often very prominent when facing money concerns. One technique financial planners can use to reduce feelings of embarrassment, guilt, or shame is normalizing.

> An example of an effective normalizing phrase for a client who experiences embarrassment about their perceived low level of retirement savings may be: *"I am hearing that this is not the amount of savings you wanted to have, and I also want to assure you this experience is pretty normal. I see quite a few clients who are experiencing similar concerns."*

Financial planners are cautioned that the normalizing technique can be interpreted as trivializing if used ineffectively. When normalizing, a best practice is to avoid language or phrases that reduce or demean a client's unique experience. Financial planners should not overuse normalizing techniques, as this can be read as disingenuous or dismissive.

Reframing is a technique that helps to create a shift in the way people see things and also invites alternative ways of viewing ideas, events, situations, or experiences, typically bringing the interpretation from more negative to positive. Essentially, reframing is like putting a different "frame" around experiences or life events in order to paint a different, usually more optimal or preferred, picture.[6] Reframing demonstrates acceptance of a client's feelings and does not attempt to diminish or change feelings directly.

As an example, reframing for a client who has a negative view of investment risk might be: *"You're correct, investments are not without risk. The good news is quite a bit of risk can be mediated through appropriate diversification strategies. Keep in mind that risk and return go hand in hand, so taking on some risk can also help you to yield better returns."*

Another example of reframing with a client who feels a great amount of stress and shame over student loan debt is: *"You've shared that student loan debt causes stress for you, and in many ways, these loans have also helped to get you through your education and into what you described as your dream job. I wonder if this helps the debt look any differently?"*

Encouragement and acknowledgement can be great motivators for clients. For this reason, financial planners may want to use an affirming strategy as a way to show a client they are seen, appreciated, and valued. **Affirming** is the process of extending a thoughtful, genuine statement, usually as a means to encourage, motivate, or feel more positive. Affirming validates a client in some way, whether it be to support or reinforce a specific positive financial behavior or to recognize a more personal, inherent strength the financial planner observes or admires in their client.

For example, affirming a client may involve saying something like: *"I appreciate the work that it took to prepare for our meeting, so I want to thank you. Your efforts will assist us with the development of our recommendations."*

Another example is: *"I value your thoughts and input as we finalize your financial plan. You are the expert on your life and your goals, so I appreciate how active you have been throughout this process."*

Clients seek to feel understood and accepted. Though a client may be seeking financial advice, feeling like a financial planner understands their concerns and needs is important for clients, whether or not this is expressed outwardly and directly. To ensure a client feels accepted, the financial planner should try to demonstrate empathy when possible. **Empathizing** is a technique used to better understand concerns, thoughts, and emotions from a client's perspective. Empathizing involves putting oneself in "someone else's shoes" as a means to more fully appreciate how they might think or feel. As the two are often confused, it is important to note that empathy is distinct from sympathy. **Sympathy** does not necessarily involve appreciation or understanding; rather, to sympathize is to express pity or sorrow for someone's circumstances or experience. To empathize, it is not required that a financial planner share the exact same, or even similar experiences. Rather, the financial planner must convey, in a caring and considerate manner, they can imagine and appreciate the impact of the experience. The most important element of an empathizing statement is genuineness and tone. A client should not be made to feel patronized by an empathizing statement.

An empathizing statement, for example, could be: *"Though I have not been through a situation like losing my business, I can try to appreciate how incredibly difficult that was for you at the time."*

One of the most powerful tools a financial planner has is the "self." That is, their personal characteristics, perspectives, and experiences which can serve to elevate the financial planning experience and increase the financial planner-client connection. **Self-disclosure** is the conscious (and at times subconscious) act of revealing information about oneself to others. Self-disclosure may include sharing thoughts, feelings, aspirations, experiences, goals, failures, successes, and fears, as well as one's likes and dislikes. In some instances, a financial planner might utilize self-disclosure to help a client know them better, to appear more personable, or to enhance a client's sense of comfort. This technique needs careful consideration in professional environments, as self-disclosure can be well-intentioned, but may also be interpreted as "over-sharing". Financial planners need to think carefully before revealing personal experiences or stories and consider the purpose of the disclosure. Unconsciously, the financial planner could potentially use self-disclosure as a way to deal with personal insecurities or feelings. This is considered an inappropriate use of "self," as it can create discomfort for the client, situate the client to feel responsible for "taking care" or remedying, or burden the client with a financial planner's problem. A few questions can help to clarify whether self-disclosure is appropriate:

- What is the purpose of the self-disclosure?

- How might the self-disclosure help the client?

- How will this sharing affect the client?

- What does the financial planner gain from the disclosure?

- Can the self-disclosure statement be perceived as burdensome or unprofessional in any way?

To briefly summarize, the communication and counseling techniques discussed within this chapter are meant to aid the development of trust and rapport between the financial planner and their clients. Use of these techniques can contribute to:

- The financial planner's understanding of the client's feelings, beliefs, values, and choices;

- The financial planner's capacity for attentiveness and connection within the client relationship;

- Meaningful exploration of any client issues or experiences which may inform or impact the financial planning process; and

- Increasing trust and collaboration, which are key for the outlining of goals and objectives, understanding client decision-making, and for selecting and implementing recommendations within a financial plan;

It is also worth noting if a financial planner identifies concerns that extend beyond their own scope of practice, it is advised they help the client to seek out referrals or supplemental services, which could involve a mental health professional, a financial therapist, a financial coach, or a financial counselor.

4.8 THE IMPORTANCE OF WRITTEN COMMUNICATION

The chapter thus far has put a great deal of emphasis on verbal aspects of communication. However, financial planners also must rely on written communication, as it is central to nearly all aspects of the financial planning process, from an initial email exchange with a prospective client to the writing of the financial plan itself. Written communication is important for not only conveying instructions and directives within the financial plan, but it is also a demonstration of professionalism and competence. Further, from a legal and ethical standpoint, clearly documented written communication is invaluable. It may be the only thing that you have to verify an interaction occurred or a financial recommendation was given. For this reason, written communications can be indispensable to financial planners.

As discussed, verbal communication and paralanguage centers on the tone, pacing, and body language between a speaker and listener. Written communication, though, involves key aspects like semantics, punctuation, and grammar. Writing is a different communication mechanism which often needs honing and continuous monitoring. It is worth remembering that written communication that is thoughtful and clear facilitates the building and maintaining of trust between the financial planner and the client.

Financial planners should consider the following points regarding written communication and financial plan writing:

- Consider and develop a consistent writing style, whether more or less formal.

- Be clear and as concise as possible; avoid overly wordy descriptions and frivolous details.

- Attend to the fundamentals of good written communication, including proper grammar and spelling, as well as appropriate punctuation.

- Take care to thoroughly proofread electronic communication and financial planning documents.

- Consider an active voice which conveys action, especially when communicating financial planning recommendations.

4.9 SUMMARY

This chapter described the essential elements associated with client communication and counseling within the context of the financial planning process. As noted in this chapter, a financial planner must be able to do more than analyze data, recommend strategies, and implement recommendations. A competent financial planner needs to possess skills related to understanding a client's emotions, biases, and values and to utilize communication techniques when presenting financial planning concepts and recommendations to clients. The role of communication and counseling is embedded throughout each step of the financial planning process. Developing and expanding communication and counseling skills should be a high priority task for financial planners who want to truly master writing and delivering comprehensive financial plans.

Self-Test Questions

Self-Test 1

A financial planner who understands and respects their client's paradigms and demonstrates appreciation for their client's concerns is exhibiting:

(a) Openness

(b) Empathy

(c) Flexibility

(d) Objectivity

Self-Test 2

At a recent meeting, a client stated, "That makes a lot of sense. I can see that happening in reality." What type of information processing style was this person using?

(a) Visual

(b) Kinesthetic

(c) Auditory

(d) Experiential

Self-Test 3

A financial planner who extends a thoughtful, genuine statement to a client is using what type of communication technique?

(a) Normalizing

(b) Reframing

(c) Affirming

(d) Empathizing

Self-Test 4

Which aspects of culture should financial planners attend to?

(a) a client's preferences for where to bank

(b) their gender and ethnic background

(c) eye contact, space, and touch

(d) b & c only

Self-Test 5

When considering written communication, financial planners should:

(a) use text messaging with clients as much as possible

(b) be formal with their writing style

(c) proofread all messages and documents

(d) incorporate a passive voice

Self-Test Answers

Question 1: b

Question 2: a

Question 3: c

Question 4: d

Question 5: c

CHAPTER RESOURCES

The Financial Life Planning Institute (http://www.flpinc.com/).

Kay, M. F. The Business of Life: *An "Inside-Out" Approach to Building a More Successful Financial Planning Practice*. Sunnyvale, CA: PlannerPress, 2010.

Kinder, G. *Seven Stages of Money Maturity: Understanding the Spirit and Value of Money in your Life*. New York: Dell Publishing, 2000.

Kinder, G., and S. Galvan. *Lighting the Torch: The Kinder Method™ of Life Planning*. Denver, CO: FPA Press, 2006.

The Kinder Institute of Life Planning (http://www.kinderinstitute.com/index.html).

Klontz, B., Kahler, R., and Klontz, T. *Facilitating Financial Health: Tools for Financial Planners, Coaches, and Therapists*. Cincinnati, OH: National Underwriter Company, 2008.

Money Quotient® Putting Money in the Context of Life™ (http://moneyquotient.org/).

Parisse, A., and Richman, D. *Questions Great Financial Planners Ask…and Investors Need to Know.* Chicago, Kaplan Publishing, 2006.

West, S., and Anthony, M. *Your Client's Story: Know Your Clients and the Rest Will Follow.* Chicago, Kaplan Publishing, 2005.

CHAPTER ENDNOTES

1. J. Grable and J. Goetz, *Communication Essentials for Financial Planners: Strategies and Techniques* (Hoboken, NJ: Wiley, 2017).

2. R. Sommers-Flanagan and J. Sommers-Flanagan, *Clinical Interviewing*, 4th ed. (New York: Wiley, 2009).

3. "American Indian" is not necessarily representative or preferred. There are various terms used to describe Tribal nomenclature and these unique identities, including Indigenous Peoples, First Nations, Native American, or Indian.

4. *Ibid*.

5. See: R. Lytton, J. Grable, & D. Klock (2013). *The Process of Financial Planning,* 2nd ed., Erlinger, KY: National Underwriter.

6. C. Pulvino, & C. Pulvino. (2010). *Financial Counseling: A Strategic Approach* (5th ed.) Sarasota, FL: Instructional Enterprises.

Chapter 5

Meet Your Clients

Learning Objectives

- Learning Objective 1: Use the financial planning process when drafting a financial plan.

- Learning Objective 2: Use client data in the development of a comprehensive financial plan.

- Learning Objective 3: Show how recommendations and implementation procedures can be described in a written document.

- Learning Objective 4: Provide actionable recommendations for financial plan implementation.

5.1 INTRODUCING THE COMPREHENSIVE CASE: CHANDLER AND RACHEL HUBBLE

A running case is provided in each of the remaining chapters in this book. The case features Chandler and Rachel Hubble and Phoebe, their daughter. The Hubble family, a hypothetical household, are meant to represent the type of client that might seek the help of a financial planner during the early- to mid-stage of the financial planner's career. Chandler and Rachel earn more income than the average American family and significantly more than the typical family living in Springfield, Missouri, where they reside.

Some may ask, "Does the fact that Chandler and Rachel earn more than other young families make the case too easy?" Having high relative income does not necessarily make the case any easier—it merely provides different planning strategies and alternatives for use by those working on the case. Additionally, having more income to work with provides greater opportunities to meet a client's long-term goals by allowing the development of more creative solutions. As a client's income increases, so does the range and complexity of solutions. This means that in terms of pure simplicity, it can sometimes be easier to work with clients who are aspiring to wealth because suggestions and alternatives tend, by default, to be constrained by available cash flow. Because higher-income clients may not be as income constrained, potential solutions are often riddled with the complexities inherent in multiple, interrelated options.

Furthermore, income and lifestyle are relative measures. Certainly, Chandler and Rachel earn a respectable amount of money for a young couple living in southwest Missouri. On the other hand, their income may be quite modest in relation to the cost of living and different lifestyle demands of a similar household in cities like Los Angeles, San Francisco, New York, Washington, or Boston. But the fact that a client earns a relatively high income in no way means that all goals and objectives can be met. Clients tend to "live up" to their level of income regardless of how much they earn. In other words, high-income clients tend to spend much of their income, just as moderate-income clients tend to spend most of their income.

The Hubble case narrative was developed with two aims in mind. One goal was to make the case as comprehensive as possible, meaning that it is impossible to resolve issues in one core content planning area without influencing the Hubbles' other issues and goals. When faced with developing strategies and recommendations, financial planners will encounter several interrelated issues and constraints, all of which influence each other. These interacting issues make the case relatively difficult to analyze, yet not too difficult to develop a plan to improve the Hubbles' financial situation—both now and for the future. The second goal was to allow the Hubbles' needs to be resolved using both simple and complex solutions. This aspect of the case approach provides greater opportunities to offer unique client proposals that may vary by financial planner but still offer a viable option for meeting the Hubbles' goals and objectives.

5.2 INTRODUCING CHANDLER AND RACHEL HUBBLE

The purpose of this narrative is to provide you with the information needed to write a comprehensive financial plan for your clients, Chandler and Rachel Hubble. By studying this case, you should have a relatively solid understanding of the types of personal and financial information that a planner needs to write a comprehensive financial plan. It will become increasingly important for you to have a clear understanding of the case facts.

As you read through the case, you should make a concerted effort to highlight and note any special assumptions presented. Strive to be inquisitive and to anticipate how certain case facts and assumptions might influence your choice of strategies, the development of interrelated recommendations, the implementation of recommendations, and future monitoring actions. Train yourself to identify the client's financial strengths and weaknesses. This list will help ensure that the Hubbles' stated— and even unrecognized—financial goals and objectives have been addressed.

By the end of the planning process, you should be able to collaborate with Chandler and Rachel to prioritize their goals and objectives, determine the net impact of strategies on cash flow and net worth, and develop a clearly delineated implementation plan that will enable Chandler and Rachel to accomplish their primary financial aspirations. In doing so, you will chart a course that could change the Hubbles' financial lives and establish the foundation of a long-term client-planner relationship.

[A] The Hubble Family Profile

Recently, Chandler and Rachel Hubble took time to start thinking about financial planning issues. They were prompted to do so by two events. First, Rachel's close high school friend Brenda died of a heart attack. Brenda left a grieving husband and three children. She had no life insurance, and from what Rachel could learn, Brenda's husband was having a hard time financially. This event was followed by an advertisement by a major financial planning firm that caught their attention. The advertisement encouraged viewers to start planning today for the future.

Both events started Chandler and Rachel thinking about the need for financial planning. As a result, they made a new year's resolution to seek the counsel and advice of a competent financial planner in January.

Today is the day Chandler and Rachel have come to see you, armed with a large amount of financial and personal information. Figure 5.1 provides demographic data about the Hubble family. The narrative that follows provides more detail about the Hubbles' financial life.

Figure 5.1. Personal and Family Information.

Chandler Hubble	Rachel Hubble
Age: 42	Age: 42
State of residence: Missouri	State of residence: Missouri
Citizen: U.S.	Citizen: U.S.
Health status: No known health issues	Health status: No known health issues
SS#: 555-55-5555	SS#: 555-55-4444
Dependent Children	
Phoebe Hubble	
Age: 5	
Health status: No known health issues	
Home Address	
727 Success Lane	
Springfield, MO	
Employment	
Chandler:	Rachel:
Golden Tee Golf Association, Inc.	The Family and Career Institute
6282 Star Drive	5600 Cedar Lane Road, Suite #150
Springfield, MO	Springfield, MO
Occupation: Sales consultant	Occupation: Career counselor
Years employed: 12	Years employed: 3

[B] Overview of Family History

Chandler and Rachel Hubble met during their undergraduate days at the University of Nevada in Reno. After graduation, they were married at a Lake Tahoe chapel. Shortly thereafter, they moved to Springfield, Missouri, so that Chandler could begin his career as a golf course sales consultant. Chandler and Rachel love Springfield and have no plans to leave the area.

This is Chandler and Rachel's first marriage and, from what you've learned, they are happily married. Their first child, Phoebe, was born five years ago. At this point, they do not anticipate having any more children.

Phoebe is a bright and enthusiastic child. She is actively involved in sports. She particularly likes youth basketball and soccer. She and her mom are taking golf lessons together. She is also currently taking piano lessons. Phoebe's future is an additional reason Chandler and Rachel decided to seek your financial advice. By talking with friends and co-workers, they have learned that college can be expensive.

Because one of their goals is to fund as much of Phoebe's college education as possible, they thought now could be the time to work through some college funding numbers with a professional. The good news is that Chandler and Rachel have already investigated some college costs. They have determined that four years of in-state tuition to a good public university today would cost about $10,000 per semester, including room and board.

Rachel is the youngest child of a very large family. She has four brothers and three sisters. Her mother Jenny passed away when Rachel was age 30. Her father Terrance passed away three years later. Both died of cancer. Rachel's parents donated the majority of their estate to a church in California. Rachel received a few items from the estate, including a gold nugget ring, three signed collector paintings, an antique china cabinet with a full eight-piece set of collector's china, and her mother's harp.

Chandler's life growing up was significantly different from Rachel's. Chandler is the only child in his family. His parents, both age sixty-five, are healthy and living in Springfield. His parents' wills currently list him as the sole beneficiary of their combined assets. However, Chandler and Rachel are not expecting an inheritance anytime soon, and they do not want to plan on receiving assets from Chandler's parents.

Neither Chandler nor Rachel has had much experience working with other professional advisors. They have used the services of an enrolled agent at tax time. They are pleased with the service provided. They do not have a relationship with an attorney or any other financial planning professional. Until this point, they have relied on advice from friends and family regarding their financial situation.

5.3 CASH FLOW PLANNING

[A] Income Discussion

Rachel enjoys her job as a career counselor. She received her undergraduate degree in Family Studies, but because she was unable to find a job right after college, she decided to pursue a graduate degree in Family Counseling. Her first job as a counselor was with a small private practice in Springfield. She worked for the practice for four years before resigning to spend time with Phoebe.

When Phoebe was older, Rachel took a part-time job with her current employer, The Family and Career Institute of Missouri. She is paid a monthly salary and anticipates receiving a 3.0 percent salary increase each year in the future.

Currently, Phoebe is enrolled in kindergarten on a half-day basis. Chandler's mother picks her up from school and takes care of Phoebe until the early afternoon. They have no regular childcare expenses. As soon as Phoebe begins school, Rachel plans to devote more time to volunteer activities in the community.

Chandler is highly valued by his employer. He has a degree in golf course management and a Master's in Business Administration. Chandler works for Golden Tee Golf Association, Inc., a relatively small (29 employees) golf course management consulting firm.

Chandler's job requires him to travel monthly to golf courses associated with his firm and conduct onsite management and consulting services. He is also responsible for soliciting new golf course management contracts. He is very successful in his career and plans to stay with his current employer until he retires.

Chandler is currently paid a salary and bonus. He conservatively estimates that his salary will increase by 3.0 percent each year. His bonus—50 percent of his salary paid out semiannually—is very generous, and also very consistent.

Before meeting with you, Chandler and Rachel summarized their current yearly income situation in Figure 5.2.

Figure 5.2. Income (Gross).

	Client	Amount	Frequency
Salary	Chandler	$2,633.33	Biweekly
Salary	Rachel	$2,708.00	Monthly
Bonus	Chandler	$17,116.65	Semiannually

[B] Expense Summary

Unlike many clients, Chandler and Rachel have always kept a close eye on household income and expenses. The majority of household annual expenses are detailed in Figures 5.3 through 5.6.

Figure 5.3. Income and Payroll Taxes.

	Amount	Frequency
Chandler		
Federal income tax withholding	$ 600.00	Biweekly
State and local income tax withholding	$ 187.00	Biweekly
FICA (Social Security and Medicare) tax withholding	$ 300.00	Biweekly
Rachel		
Federal income tax withholding	$ 292.50	Monthly
State and local income tax withholding	$117.00	Monthly
FICA (Social Security and Medicare) tax withholding	$207.17	Monthly
Note: Late last year, the Golden Tee Golf Association, Inc. had a computer payroll problem. The firm responsible for tracking FICA withholding miscalculated the maximum cap on the Social Security portion of FICA. Chandler believes that the amount withheld for FICA may be incorrect.		

Both Chandler and Rachel are allowed to invest in a limited number of mutual funds within their 401(k) plans. These mutual funds are the same ones that your financial planning firm tracks on a regular basis. For a complete list of the funds, refer to the rates-of-return section presented later in the case. Figure 5.4 lists the funds that Chandler and Rachel are currently using to fund their retirement objectives.

Figure 5.4. Retirement Plan Contributions.

	Contribution Amount	Notes	Employer Contribution
Chandler's Investment Choices			
Consumer Fund	3% of base salary	401(k) plan deductions are not taken from bonus payments (the employer does not match bonus payments)	0%
Graham Fund	3% of base salary		3% (100% match on the first 3%)
Rachel's Investment Choices			
Rocket Fund	10% of salary	For future planning, 401(k) plan deductions are not taken from bonus payments (the employer does not match bonus payments)	3% (50% match on the first 6%)

Chandler and Rachel are diligent savers. Figure 5.5 shows how much they save each month. Note that at the current time, only annuity and money market account savings are allocated to a goal. Additional regular expenses are shown in Figure 5.6.

Figure 5.5. Systematic Savings Outside of Qualified Retirement Plans.

Description	Amount	Frequency	Savings Purpose
Sagebrush Fund	$250	Monthly	Any purpose
Haley G&I Fund	$250	Monthly	Any purpose
Ruth Fund	$250	Monthly	Any purpose
Individual conservative fixed-annuity contract	$250	Monthly	Rachel's retirement
Money market account	$150	Monthly	Cash reserves

Figure 5.6. Household Expenses.

Housing	Periodic Amount	Frequency
Real estate taxes	$1,675	Annually
Homeowners insurance	$700	Annually
Utilities (e.g., electric, fuel, water, sewer)	$400	Monthly
Other household (e.g., yard service, trash)	$100	Quarterly
Food/Clothing/Transportation		
Food/groceries	$475	Monthly
Clothing	$700	Quarterly
Auto maintenance (e.g., oil, fuel)	$125	Monthly
Auto insurance premiums	$1,014	Semiannually
Missouri vehicle plate/tag tax	$450	Annually
Loan Payments		
Mortgage loan payments	$1,088	Monthly
Auto loan payments	$451	Monthly
Charge account and credit card payments	$425	Monthly
Other Committed Expenses		
Medical costs (copay)	$20	Monthly
Prescriptions	$30	Monthly
Dental and eye care expenses	$50	Monthly
Life insurance premiums	$172	Monthly
Medical (health) insurance premiums (pretax through a Section 125 plan)	$375	Monthly
Umbrella insurance premiums	$175	Annually
Disability insurance premiums	$25	Monthly

Other misc. insurance premiums	$25	Monthly
Telephone (land line and cell)	$125	Monthly
Bank charges	$10	Monthly
Personal care (e.g., grooming, dry cleaning)	$100	Monthly
Discretionary Expenses		
Entertainment (e.g., movies, plays, shows)	$225	Monthly
Satellite TV	$50	Monthly
Dining out	$275	Monthly
Recreation (e.g., boating, hiking)	$225	Monthly
Travel (e.g., trips to Branson)	$3,000	Annually
Savings for art and art gallery	$150	Monthly
Gifts to charities:		
University alumni fund	$1,000	Annually
Church	$350	Monthly
United Way	$50	Monthly
Holiday giving	$2,500	Annually
Home improvements	$150	Monthly
Dues (e.g., organizations, golf course, health clubs)	$200	Monthly
Subscriptions (e.g., *Time, Money*)	$80	Monthly
Housekeeping service	$80	Monthly
Pet care expenses	$75	Monthly
Tax preparation fees	$400	Annually

Note: Some expenses may not be accounted for in this table.

[C] Asset and Liability Summary

The Hubble family lives in a split-level, 2,250-square-foot home on a ¾-acre lot. It has a brick veneer on the first level and vinyl siding over the upper floor. It has a formal living room, dining room, and kitchen on the main floor; three bedrooms and two full baths on the upper floor; and a family room, laundry area, and a half-bath on the ground floor along with a two-car attached garage. The Hubbles' home features a gas fireplace, a vaulted ceiling in the living and dining rooms, and a standing-seam metal roof. The metal roof is fairly new and was recommended to them because of the wind associated with violent spring thunderstorms that frequently develop tornadoes.

Chandler and Rachel have also provided you with a list of household assets and liabilities, with current market values. They have attempted to calculate all liabilities, but in a few cases, they were unable to determine a pay-off value. They are hoping you can help them determine some of these key account balances. Assets and liabilities are shown in Figures 5.7 through 5.11.

Figure 5.7. Personal and Real Assets.

Description	Owner/Title	Current Value
Home	Joint	$250,000
Furnishings	Joint	$45,000
Four-door sedan (3 years old, Ford Taurus)	Joint	$20,000
Minivan (5 years old, Nissan Quest)	Joint	$15,500
Yard equipment (John Deere x500, plus other small equipment)	Joint	$8,000
Jewelry and collectibles (Rachel's ring, paintings, china cabinet w/china, and harp)	Joint	$10,000
Phil Mickelson-signed Callaway Driver golf club	Joint	$5,000
Golf clubs/other sporting equipment	Joint	$2,500
Golf artwork (Linda Hartough reproductions, set of 5 lithographs)	Joint	$5,000
Aluminum boat (2004 Alumacraft V16 Lunker LTD; w/ 50hp Mercury motor)	Joint	$5,800

Figure 5.8. Monetary Assets.

Description / Purpose	Owner	Market Value	Current Yield
Savings account (cash reserve)	Joint	$10,000	3.00%
Checking account I (cash reserve)	Joint	$3,500	0.00%
Money market account (cash reserve)	Joint	$10,000	3.00%
Checking account II (savings: art gallery/collection)	Joint	$5,000	0.00%

Figure 5.9. Investment Assets (Nonretirement).

Description	Owner	Market Value	Current Yield
Miscellaneous EE bonds*	Joint	$25,000	3.50% Deferred
Haley G&I Fund**	Joint	$19,000	3.20%
Konza Fund**	Joint	$13,000	1.75%
Ruth Fund**	Joint	$13,000	4.00%
Sagebrush Fund**	Joint	$8,000	0.50%

* The EE bonds were purchased twelve years ago by Chandler's parents as a gift for Chandler and Rachel. The bonds will earn interest for the next eighteen years and reach the $30,000 face value in another five years, as guaranteed by the U.S. Treasury.

**The Hubbles' basis in these assets is equal to 50 percent of the assets' value. *Note that the Hubbles' received an unexpected dividend this year in the Haley G&I mutual fund of $2,125.50.This dividend is above and beyond the yield earned by the Haley G&I fund.*

Figure 5.10. Retirement Assets.

Description	Owner	Market Value	Rate of Return
Chandler's 401(k) Consumer Fund Graham Fund	Chandler	$69,000 $134,000	8.75% 4.10%
Chandler's Traditional IRA certificate of deposit	Chandler	$52,000	3.50%
Rachel's 401(k) Rocket Fund	Rachel	$15,250	14.00%
Rachel's Rollover IRA Ruth Fund	Rachel	$32,500	4.80%
Rachel's Traditional IRA certificate of deposit	Rachel	$52,000	3.50%
Conservative annuity Potsdam Fixed Annuity	Rachel	$125,000	5.00%

Figure 5.11. Other Liabilities.

	Liability 1	Liability 2	Liability 3	Liability 4
Description	Mortgage	Sedan car loan	Visa credit card	MasterCard credit card
Loan detail	Nixa National Bank (joint liability)	Ford Motor credit (joint liability)	Nixa National Bank (joint liability)	University Bank (joint liability)
Loan type	Installment	Installment	Revolving	Revolving
Interest rate (APR)	7.875%	3.90%	18.25%	16.75%
Minimum payment calculation	Amortization	Amortization	Greater of 4% of monthly balance or $50	Greater of monthly interest charge + 1.5% of balance or $50
Minimum payment	$1,088.00 (rounded)	$451.00 (rounded)	$140.00 (rounded)	$60.00 (rounded)
Payment frequency	Monthly	Monthly	Monthly	Monthly
Original balance	$150,000* *Chandler and Rachel purchased this home with a special 100% financing loan option.	$24,549	$3,500 (current balance)	$2,000 (current balance)
Number of payments made	124	36	NA	NA
Original term (months)	360	60	NA	NA

5.4 INSURANCE PLANNING ISSUES

Chandler and Rachel are also concerned about the negative outcomes associated with dramatic events like death or disability. Over the past several years, they have taken steps to purchase insurance to meet different life, health, and property contingencies. Chandler and Rachel are still uncertain whether these policies are best suited to their needs. Details about the insurance policies are presented below.

[A] Health Insurance Policies

Health insurance is provided for the entire family by a group health insurance policy offered through Chandler's employer. The health provider, Peacock & Peacock, is a health maintenance organization. Chandler pays $375 per month in premiums for this coverage through his company's Section 125 plan. The plan allows for pretax premium payments.

The policy has an annual deductible of $450 and a stop-loss of $3,000. Under the policy, doctors' visits cost $20 per appointment to the primary care physician and $40 per visit to specialists, and for emergency treatment a $100 copayment is required. Monthly prescriptions are $10 for generic brands and $25 for other brands. There is no copayment for hospitalization in semiprivate accommodations, and private rooms are provided when medically necessary. The original lifetime ceiling for services, per family member, was $2 million; however, with the passage of the Patient Protection and Affordable Care Act, limits have been removed.

Over the past several years Chandler and Rachel have averaged about $50 per month in dental and eye care expenses, which they pay out of discretionary cash flow. A flexible spending account for health costs is available through Chandler's employer. They have not funded this account in the past because of uncertainty related to "use it or lose it" rules.

[B] Disability Policies

Chandler and Rachel are automatically covered for disability by employer-provided plans. Rachel also pays for additional long-term disability coverage through her employer. Information about each policy is presented in Figure 5.12.

Figure 5.12. Disability Policies.

	Policy 1	Policy 2	Policy 3	Policy 4
Type of Policy	Group	Group	Group	Group
Insurance company	Mid-America Disability Assurance Corporation	All-World Life and Disability Company	Mid-America Disability Assurance Corporation	All-World Life and Disability Company
Rating	A.M. Best: A	A.M. Best: A	A.M. Best: A	A.M. Best: A-
Person insured	Chandler	Rachel	Chandler	Rachel
Wait periods (days)	0 days	0 days	90 days	90 days
Benefit period	90 days	90 days	To age 65	To age 65
Disability benefit	100% of salary and bonus	100% of salary and bonus	60% of salary and bonus	70% of salary and bonus
Definition	Own occupation	Own occupation	Own occupation	Modified own occupation
Benefit frequency	Biweekly	Monthly	Biweekly	Monthly
Premium amount	Company paid	Company paid	Company paid	$25 monthly (purchased through employer with pretax dollars)
Premium payment frequency	NA	NA	NA	Monthly

[C] Life Insurance Policies

Chandler and Rachel currently have life insurance through their employers and through private policies. Their private policies were purchased several years ago from a friend who was selling life insurance. Information about the insurance policies is shown in Figure 5.13.

Figure 5.13. Life Insurance Policies.

	Policy 1	Policy 2	Policy 3	Policy 4
Type of policy	Whole-life*	Whole-life*	Group term	Group term
Insurance company	Manhattan Insurance Company	Manhattan Insurance Company	Great Plains Assurance and Protection Corporation	Virginia Highland Life Insurance Company
Rating	A.M. Best: A	A.M. Best: A	A.M. Best: A	A.M. Best: A
Equivalent after-tax rate of return	5.50%	5.50%	0%	0%
Death benefit	$100,000	$100,000	1 x salary (not including bonus)	4 x salary (not including bonus)
Person insured	Chandler	Rachel	Chandler	Rachel
Owner	Chandler	Rachel	Chandler	Rachel
Beneficiary	Rachel	Chandler	Rachel	Chandler
Cash value	$8,750	$8,350	$0	$0
Premium amount	$92	$80	Company paid	Company paid
Payment frequency	Monthly	Monthly	NA	NA

*At the beginning of last year, the cash value of the whole-life policies equaled $7,850 for Chandler and $7,500 for Rachel. They both received a dividend in the policy equal to $250.

[D] Automobile Insurance

Chandler and Rachel have split-limit coverage of 100/300/50 on both of the vehicles, in addition to $100,000 of uninsured/underinsured motorist coverage. Automobile insurance is provided by Missouri Valley Insurance Corporation (A.M. Best Rating: A). Deductibles are $500 for comprehensive coverage and $500 for collision coverage. This insurance includes medical payments, car rental coverage, and towing. Boats, RVs, and motorcycles are specifically excluded.

[E] Homeowner's Insurance

Chandler and Rachel currently have an HO-3 policy with a $100,000 liability limit that provides replacement value on contents through an endorsement underwritten by Missouri National Insurance (A.M. Best rating: A). The Hubbles' home is currently insured for $225,000. They do not know if the policy has an inflation endorsement. The deductible is $500. The premium is $700 per year.

Three years ago, their insurance agent recommended that they purchase a $500,000 umbrella insurance policy. The premium for the policy is $175 per year.

5.5 INVESTMENT PLANNING ISSUES

Before meeting with you, Chandler and Rachel completed a confidential risk tolerance questionnaire downloaded from an Internet website. The results from the risk quiz suggested that both Chandler and Rachel have a moderate to lower level of financial risk tolerance.

Chandler and Rachel are interested in ideas that could improve current returns without taking excessive risk. However, Chandler has made it very clear that he is extremely apprehensive about investing and feels that he tends to be risk averse. Rachel, on the other hand, feels comfortable taking additional risks if she is confident that she can earn higher returns.

5.6 RETIREMENT PLANNING ISSUES

Chandler and Rachel have expressed a strong desire to retire at age sixty-two. They both have other hobbies, talents, and dreams that they would like to pursue during retirement. Chandler loves golfing, gardening, and traveling. His dream is to teach aspiring young golfers on a volunteer basis during retirement.

Rachel loves to paint, attend art shows, and occasionally golf. With the demands of her job, motherhood, and volunteer activities, she has had little time for any of these activities. Her plan in retirement is to build a small addition to their home and fill it with art. If built today, the addition would cost $20,000.

Rachel would then like to open a small art gallery in downtown Nixa (a neighboring community). She estimates that the cost of the gallery would be $80,000 if opened today. If she is successful as an art gallery owner, she plans to donate any net revenue from the art gallery to local youth groups to enhance creative learning.

In addition, Rachel would like to improve her golf game so that Chandler would enjoy playing more golf with her.

Neither Chandler nor Rachel has a strong desire to travel in retirement. Chandler travels enough now, and he would prefer to enjoy life in southwest Missouri during retirement. They do, however, plan on taking an occasional trip, especially to go and see Phoebe if she is not living in the Springfield area.

Chandler and Rachel feel that with these occasional trips, they will need approximately 85 percent of current earned before-tax income (in today's dollars) when they retire. They believe they will receive Social Security benefits, and they want to take benefits at the earliest opportunity. Also, they have a strong desire to leave an estate as large as possible for Phoebe's benefit at their death. Therefore, Chandler and Rachel would very much like to minimize the depletion of retirement assets. Chandler and Rachel are willing to assume that the taxes they will need to pay in retirement are accounted for in the rates of return provided in the case.

5.7 ESTATE PLANNING ISSUES

Chandler and Rachel have wills that they created when Phoebe was two years old. They used a will kit purchased at an office supply store because they did not have much time—they were about to begin a 14-day vacation in Europe when it occurred to them that they should have a will. They have not looked at their wills since.

In their wills, Rachel's oldest sister Barbara—who is single and living in Oregon—was named Phoebe's guardian. The Hubbles' wills leave all assets to each other in case of death.

Chandler and Rachel want to make sure they do not pay unnecessary estate taxes. They have also been reading magazine articles about probate. Rachel is particularly concerned about maintaining privacy and making Phoebe's life less complicated in the event that she or Chandler was to die.

5.8 ADDITIONAL INFORMATION AND ASSUMPTIONS

[A] Rate of Return Assumptions

Your firm has established expected rate-of-return and portfolio risk objectives for all investment portfolios and has concluded that these rate-of-return expectations (shown in Figure 5.14) represent the maximum returns that should be used in financial planning models.

Figure 5.14. Expected Rates of Return.

	Expected After-tax Total Rate of Return*	Maximum Portfolio Risk	
		Beta (indexed to S&P 500)	Standard Deviation
Conservative	5.25%	< 0.40	< 7.0
Moderately conservative	7.75%	< 0.80	< 9.0
Moderately aggressive	10.00%	0.80 < 1.00	< 13.0
Aggressive	12.14%	> 1.00	> 13.0

*Note that these returns include capital appreciation, dividends, and interest received.
**Assumes a combined federal and state tax rate of 30 percent.

Your financial planning firm uses a screening technique to select and track mutual funds that can be used in client portfolios. Your firm currently uses eleven equity funds, six bond funds, one money market fund, and one variable-annuity product. Chandler and Rachel, after consulting with you, have agreed to use these investments, as you recommend, to meet their financial planning goals and objectives. These are the same investments available in the employer-sponsored 401(k) plans; the investments are also similar to options available in Traditional and Roth IRAs. Detailed information on each investment product is presented in Figures 5.15 and 5.16.

Figure 5.15. Equity Funds.

Fund	Investment Style	Before-tax Rate of Return	Standard Deviation	Correlation with Equity Market	Yield
Value Fund	Large cap	9.00%	12.00%	0.95	3.00%
Growth Fund	Large cap	10.20%	15.00%	0.90	2.00%
Eastside Fund	Mid-cap	8.40%	10.00%	0.92	2.00%
Konza Fund	Mid-cap	9.20%	13.00%	0.91	1.75%
Sagebrush Fund	Small cap	11.20%	21.00%	0.80	0.50%
Rocket Fund	Small cap	14.00%	22.00%	0.75	0.00%
Consumer Fund	Small cap	8.75%	11.00%	0.99	2.50%
Acquisitions Fund	Mid-cap	7.50%	5.20%	0.20	4.00%
International Fund	International (EAFE Index)	10.00%	11.20%	0.50	2.00%
Haley G&I Fund	Large cap	8.00%	10.00%	0.90	3.20%
Graham Fund	Real Estate and Precious Metals	4.10%	12.00%	0.10	2.00%

Figure 5.16. Bond Funds.

Fund	Investment Style	Before-tax Rate of Return	Standard Deviation	Correlation with Bond Market	Yield
Ruth Fund	Government bond	4.80%	4.90%	0.85	4.00%
Cardinal Fund	Corporate bond	5.20%	5.10%	0.90	4.80%
Clock Fund	Corporate bond	6.00%	6.20%	0.98	5.40%
Ely Fund	Government bond	6.10%	6.05%	0.92	6.00%
Companion Fund	High yield	7.00%	13.00%	0.80	6.10%
States Fund	Government bond	5.70%	6.00%	0.75	4.00%
Barrister Fund	Money market	3.00%	0.00%	0.00	3.00%

Other investments available for use when working with Chandler and Rachel include:

- The Potsdam Fixed Annuity (current guaranteed yield of 5.0 percent). Contract was purchased eight years ago for $90,000. The guaranteed yield period will expire in two years.

- The Bostonian Variable Annuity includes a guaranteed investment contract that currently yields 5.0 percent and allows investments in all of the funds listed in the preceding Figures. The cash and cash equivalent assets listed in the following Figure are also available.

Additionally, your financial planning firm finds it useful to create custom benchmarks by which to measure the performance of each client's portfolio. General information about the various segments of the market are shown in Figures 5.17 and 5.18.

Figure 5.17. Market Indexes.

Index	Before-Tax Rate of Return	Standard Deviation	Yield
T-Bills	4.00%	2.00%	4.00%
Equity Market	8.80%	11.00%	2.50%
Bond Market	6.10%	6.50%	6.10%
Other Indexes			
Treasury coupon bonds	5.00%	6.00%	5.50%
Treasury zero-coupon bond "strips"	6.00%	6.50%	0.00%
Investment-grade corporate coupon bonds	7.00%	7.00%	7.00%
Investment-grade corp. zero-coupon bonds	7.50%	8.00%	0.00%
High-yield corporate bonds	9.00%	12.00%	9.00%
International bonds	10.00%	15.00%	10.00%
U.S. large-cap equity	10.00%	18.00%	2.25%
U.S. small-cap equity	12.00%	+20.00%	<1.00%
Developed international equity	15.00%	+25.00%	≈0.00%
*RoR and Yields may not reflect current market conditions.			

Figure 5.18. Cash and Cash Equivalents.

Asset	Yield*
Savings accounts	2.00%
Money market accounts	3.00%
Money market mutual funds	3.00%
Missouri municipal money market account	2.30%
One-year certificates of deposit	3.50%
*More representative of long-term averages than current market conditions.	

[B] Universal Assumptions

- The universal inflation rate is expected to average 3.0 percent per annum.

- The prime interest rate is currently 3.25 percent, but is expected to increase in the future.

- Life expectancy for Chandler and Rachel is age ninety-five.

- They would like to assume a 30.0 percent combined state and federal tax bracket until retirement and a 25.0 percent combined state and federal marginal tax bracket during retirement.

5.9 SPECIFIC GOALS AND OBJECTIVES

Chandler and Rachel's primary goal is to live life with a relatively high level of financial satisfaction. Chandler and Rachel want to be self-sufficient in retirement. As such, the Hubbles' primary objective is to retire at age sixty-two, if possible. Their secondary objective is to fund 100 percent of Phoebe's college education.

As suggested earlier, Rachel would like to turn her love of collecting art into a small business during retirement by renting a retail outlet and selling art supplies and collectibles. They are also interested in maintaining the privacy of their financial affairs. Finally, they would like to ensure Phoebe's financial welfare if they die.

[A] Cash Reserve Issues

- The Hubbles' cash reserve goal is six months of total dedicated and discretionary expenses, not including taxes paid. In case of an emergency, Rachel is willing to use her accumulated art gallery savings as long as the money remains in a bank, checking, or money market account. They would like to achieve this goal within two years.

- Chandler and Rachel are comfortable assuming a yield of 3.0 percent before taxes on savings and money market accounts. The checking accounts do not earn interest.

- Chandler and Rachel are comfortable assuming that the EE savings bonds will grow at a 3.50 percent tax-deferred rate and not mature for at least another ten years.

- For simplified tax-planning purposes, dividends are considered nonqualified and do not qualify for reduced tax rates.

- Chandler and Rachel do not want to pay off the car loan at this time, but Chandler and Rachel will consider pay off strategies. They anticipate always having some form of auto loan in the future.

- Any mortgage refinancing will incur 3.0 percent of the mortgage as a closing cost. Chandler and Rachel would like to see an analysis showing the impact of both including closing costs in the mortgage and paying closing costs from assets.

- Current mortgage rates in the Springfield marketplace average:

  15-year fixed   6.0 percent

  20-year fixed   6.25 percent

  30-year fixed   6.5 percent

- Their home is expected to appreciate by approximately 4.0 percent annually over the long-term.

- Chandler and Rachel would also like to assume that any interest earned from savings is reinvested rather than spent on household expenses, and that all dividends and capital gains from other investment assets are also reinvested.

[B] Tax Planning Issues

- Chandler and Rachel spent several hours the previous day calculating their state income tax liability. They believe that the amount of state tax withholding closely matches the estimated state tax due for the year, but Chandler and Rachel would like you to double-check their figures.

- For the purposes of this case, Chandler and Rachel are in the 5.0 percent Missouri tax bracket; they qualify for one state deduction worth $1,000 and two state exemptions valued at $900 each. The state calculation is based on federal adjusted gross income.

- The Hubble family did not receive a federal or state income tax refund for the previous tax year.

[C] Disability Insurance Coverage Issues

After careful thought, Chandler and Rachel are willing to assume the following:

- They will receive no Social Security disability benefits.

- They plan to continue to save for other financial planning goals in the event of a disability.

- Any cash settlements received will be invested using a moderately conservative asset allocation approach.

- They will need a 70 percent income replacement ratio.

- The applicable before-tax investment return is 7.75 percent.

[D] Long-term Care Issues

The following assumptions should be used only to address long-term care insurance planning issues.

- For planning purposes, Chandler and Rachel would like to assume that annual nursing home expenses in in the Springfield area are currently $49,000.

- The average age for entering as assisted living facility is seventy-five, with an assumed average length of stay of 2.5 years.

- The average age for those entering a nursing home is eighty-three, with an assumed average stay of 1.5 years.

- They would like to cover six years of total expenses in the event either were to enter a facility.

- Long-term care expenses have been increasing at 5.0 percent per year.

- In the event either Rachel or Chandler enters a nursing home, they are willing to allocate $200,000 from net worth (today's dollars) to help pay for LTC expenses.

- Assets for use in funding long-term care expenses will grow at a modest 5.5 percent after-tax rate of return.

[E] Asset Management Issues

- Rachel's annuity is invested 100 percent in the Potsdam Fixed Annuity earning 5 percent (no other investment alternatives are available within the annuity). She originally purchased the annuity when she was thirty-four years of age. The annuity has a seven-year declining withdrawal penalty.

- Both traditional IRAs are in one-year certificates of deposit maturing in a few months. The CDs yield 3.50 percent annually. The renewable rate is also 3.50 percent.

- Rachel's rollover IRA is currently invested in the Ruth Fund.

- Chandler's 401(k) has a 100 percent employer match, up to 3 percent of the amount he contributes. The entire match is going to the Graham fund.

- Rachel is contributing 10 percent to the Rocket Fund in her 401(k) plan. Her employer is matching 50 percent of her contributions, up to 6 percent of contributions.

- In the event that an investment asset is sold, Chandler and Rachel would prefer to assume (for tax purposes) that the basis in all after-tax investments is equal to 50 percent of the fair market value of these assets, and that all investment gains are subject to capital gains tax rates.

- Chandler and Rachel would also like to assume that any interest earned from savings is reinvested rather than spent on household expenses, and that all dividends and capital gains from other investment assets are also reinvested.

[F] Education Issues

The following assumptions should be used only to address education planning issues.

- In-state tuition at a good private university for four years will cost $10,000 per semester, including room and board (in today's dollars).

- Tuition costs are increasing at 5.0 percent per year.

- Chandler and Rachel are willing to invest in a moderately aggressive portfolio for this goal, before Phoebe begins college and during her college years.

- Chandler and Rachel want all college savings to be accumulated before Phoebe begins college and therefore plan to stop saving for college expenses once Phoebe begins college.

- No assets are currently targeted for college savings needs.

- They would prefer to invest in a tax-advantaged investment to pay for college, if possible.

[G] Premature Death Issues

The following assumptions should be used only to address life insurance planning issues.

- Assets available at Chandler's death include his IRA and 401(k) plan.

- Assets available at Rachel's death include her IRA, her 401(k) plan, the annuity, and her IRA rollover account.

- The clients will need $115,000 in before-tax yearly income to fund total household expenses at the death of either Chandler or Rachel.

- Chandler and Rachel are willing to allocate $100,000 of nonretirement investment assets toward survivor needs.

- In case of death, the surviving spouse will invest any cash settlements in a moderately conservative portfolio before and after retirement; Chandler and Rachel want this assumption to supersede all other rate-of-return assumptions used in other calculations.

- Chandler and Rachel would like to prefund their retirement and education objectives, even if one of them dies.

- Assume the expense reduction ratio will be 100 percent, as they do not expect household expense needs to decrease from $115,000 during any stage.

- For insurance planning purposes, the surviving spouse will need approximately $115,000 per year (in today's dollars) when the spouse retires.

- Chandler and Rachel feel that the following allocations will meet their final expense needs: $20,000 for final debts (e.g., credit card, auto loans, etc., but not the mortgage); $1,500 for final illness costs; $9,000 for funerals; $13,500 for estate administration costs; $10,000 for other short-term needs; and $25,000 for a spousal adjustment period.

- In the event that either Chandler or Rachel dies prematurely, each would like all liabilities, including the home mortgage, to be paid off.

- Social Security benefits, in the event of Chandler's death, are as follows:

  ○ $23,448 yearly to Rachel after age sixty-seven

  ○ $17,580 additional yearly to Rachel until Phoebe turns age eighteen

  ○ $17,580 yearly to Phoebe until age eighteen

  ○ $16,765 yearly to Rachel from age sixty to age sixty-seven (this is a 28.5 percent reduction in benefits based on age sixty-seven survivor benefits)

- Social Security benefits, in the event of Rachel's death, are as follows:

  ○ $26,400 yearly to Chandler after age sixty-seven

  ○ $9,552 additional yearly to Chandler until Phoebe turns age eighteen

  ○ $9,552 yearly to Phoebe until age eighteen

  ○ $0 to Chandler from age sixty to sixty-seven

- In the event of either spouse's death, the other spouse plans to stop working at age sixty and begin taking early retirement survivor benefits (if available).

- For conservative planning purposes, Chandler and Rachel do not plan to use interest or dividends as an income source when planning insurance needs.

- The capital retention replacement ratio is assumed to be 100 percent.

[H] Retirement Issues

The following assumptions should be used only to address retirement planning issues.

- Rachel would like to build a small addition to their home and fill it with art. If built today, the addition would cost $20,000.

- Rachel would then also like to open a small art gallery. She estimates the cost of the gallery would be $80,000 if opened today.

- Chandler and Rachel are willing to invest in a moderately aggressive portfolio to fund the art gallery and house addition. Currently, assets and savings for these goals are invested very conservatively in a bank account.

- They will need approximately 85 percent of current earned before-tax income (in today's dollars) when they retire.

- They are willing to reallocate retirement assets and savings to earn a moderately conservative rate of return prior to retirement. Chandler and Rachel are willing to increase their rate of return through a reallocation of retirement assets to meet these return assumptions. At the current time, however, Chandler and Rachel are earning less, given the allocation of their current portfolio.

- Once retired, Chandler and Rachel would like to assume a conservative rate of return.

- Chandler and Rachel would like to assume a 25 percent federal marginal tax bracket while in retirement.

- Normal retirement age is age sixty-seven for Chandler and Rachel.

- Chandler and Rachel want to retire at age sixty-two, but it is more important that they do not deplete their assets over their lifetime.

- They are unwilling to reduce their projected life expectancy unless absolutely required to achieve their age-at-retirement objective.

- They are willing to reallocate assets and savings to meet their retirement objective.

- They believe that their incomes will increase at the rate of inflation into the future.

- Chandler and Rachel plan to increase contributions to their retirement accounts by 3.0 percent each year.

- The primary insurance amount in today's dollars at age sixty-seven for Chandler is $2,200 and $1,300 for Rachel.

[I] Estate Planning Issues

The following assumptions should be used only to address estate planning issues.

- The assumed appreciation rate on their gross estate, debt, loans, and other financial position items is 4.0 percent.

- Funeral and administration expenses are assumed to be $9,000 for each person. These expenses will grow 4.0 percent annually. Executor fees are anticipated to be approximately $13,500 each.

5.10 THE NEXT STEP: TAKING ACTION

The Hubble case is an integral part of learning and applying the financial planning process when writing a financial plan. This case represents a real-life situation that a financial planner might face. Chandler and Rachel are meant to help you confront—but also confine—the complexity and ambiguity of the practical world by focusing on the questions to ask, the assumptions to use, and the calculations to complete when analyzing a client's situation.

There is a logical progression from the analysis of each of the core content areas to the identification of strategies consistent with the Hubbles' characteristics. Through an integrative analysis of the Hubbles' situation and identification of potential strategies, client-specific recommendations will emerge that can then form the basis of a written financial plan. The identification of implementation and monitoring plans completes the financial planning process. The following actions will help you get started in the writing process:

1. Complete a Client Intake Form for Chandler and Rachel Hubble. For any client information that is not provided in the case narrative, make a defensible assumption to guide the financial planning process. For information that is unavailable, note how data could have been collected from Chandler and Rachel.

2. Develop a thorough but brief description of the financial planning process to help Chandler and Rachel understand the services to be provided by you and your firm. Prepare this description for inclusion in the financial plan *or* for presentation to the client, with or without the aid of PowerPoint slides or handouts.

3. Make a note of documents that should be presented to Chandler and Rachel. Why are these documents needed? What purpose do the documents serve?

4. Develop a preliminary list of five to ten financial strengths, weaknesses, opportunities, and threats (typically referred to as a SWOT analysis) for the Hubble household. During which step(s) of the financial planning process might these SWOT factors be identified?

5. Why is a goal stated as "to live life with a relatively high level of financial satisfaction" not very useful in terms of a practical financial planning analysis? How might Chandler and Rachel be more specific when stating this and other goals?

6. List and prioritize the Hubbles' financial goals. Classify each as emanating from needs or wants, a life cycle event, or a life transition event. Classify each goal as short-, intermediate-, or long-term.

7. What needs, wants, life cycle events, or life transitions might influence the Hubbles' financial plans over the next five, ten, or fifteen years? Why is it important to consider these issues, either independently as a financial planner or in discussion with Chandler and Rachel?

8. What other information would be helpful to obtain from Chandler and Rachel as you move forward with developing a comprehensive financial plan?

9. Make a list of additional information or original source documents that you would request from Chandler and Rachel. Be sure to review the Client Intake Form for ideas. What explanation might you provide regarding why the documents are needed?

10. Prepare and organize a list of general or critical core content financial planning assumptions for use when working on the case.

11. Given the initial review of the Hubbles' situation, what other professionals might be needed to help you as a financial planner develop the Hubbles' plan? How are these decisions guided by CFP Board's practice standards?

12. If you were to rewrite the case narrative, given the current state of the economy, how would you change the rate-of-return assumptions presented in the case? What other assumptions should be changed or updated?

13. Draft the introductory section of the financial plan, including cover page, client letter(s), vision/mission statement, privacy statement, and other documentation.

5.11 COMPREHENSIVE HUBBLE CASE

Each of the following chapters will provide an example of how the financial plan for Chandler and Rachel Hubble can be written and presented. The following narrative is an example of how the introductory elements of a comprehensive financial plan can be written.

XYZ

Financial Planning

Confidential Comprehensive Financial Plan

Prepared for
Chandler & Rachel Hubble

January 1, 20XX

Prepared by

Trevor Sand, CFP®

XYZ Financial Planning
1234 Sanford Drive
Springfield, Missouri

Disclosures: The projections in this plan are based on historical information. The projections may not reflect actual investment results. Asset or portfolio earnings and/or returns shown, or used in this plan, are not intended to predict nor guarantee the actual results of any investment products or particular investment style. All information in this plan is confidential.

LETTER TO CLIENT

January 1, 20XX

Dear Chandler and Rachel,

The purpose of this letter is to reiterate our commitment to helping you meet your goals and to outline my firm's professional relationship with you.

Our Financial Planning Process

Based on the information you have provided to me and the firm, my team has prepared a comprehensive financial plan for you. As part of the financial planning process, my team and I gathered information about your current financial situation and your goals. These data inputs were used to analyze and evaluate your financial status. Based on the analysis, our team has developed financial planning recommendations that we believe, when implemented, will lead you to goal achievement. Once the recommendations have been presented, and if both parties agree to continue the working relationship, our team will assist in implementing the financial planning recommendations and/or providing referrals to other professionals who can assist with implementation. After recommendations have been implemented, we will continually monitor your progress towards goal achievement.

Monitoring Your Financial Plan

As your circumstances and goals change, this written financial plan will need to be reviewed and updated. You should consider this plan a "living document,"
meaning my team and I will work to update recommendations and implementation strategies on an ongoing basis. You should plan to meet with me annually to review your goals and financial plan; however, my team is happy to meet with you more frequently if you prefer. Please keep me informed of changes to your financial situation and/or goals. Over time, my team and I may request additional documentation, including paystubs, tax returns, and legal forms. Typically, my team and I will request documentation at least two weeks prior to a scheduled review meeting.

The Ongoing Relationship

My team and I will provide you with quarterly reports showing portfolio performance. Quarterly reports will be uploaded electronically to your secure client vault. Performance reports are also available upon request by calling or emailing the office. I will also share an annual newsletter providing updates on market performance and any changes that have occurred over the past year that might impact your financial plan. At any time, if you have any questions or concerns, please do not hesitate to call or email our office.

Warmest regards,

Trevor Sand

Trevor Sand, CFP®

CLIENT ENGAGEMENT LETTER

January 1, 20XX

Trevor Sand, CFP®
XYZ Financial Planning
1234 Sanford Drive
Springfield, Missouri

Chandler and Rachel Hubble
727 Success Lane
Springfield, MO

Dear Mr. and Mrs. Hubble,

Thank you for the opportunity to meet with you. I welcome the opportunity to work with you as your financial planner. This engagement letter outlines the specific terms of the financial planning engagement between:

Trevor Sand, CFP® and Chandler and Rachel Hubble.

If the scope or terms of the financial planning engagement change, changes should be documented in writing and mutually agreed upon by all parties to the engagement.

Please be assured that all information that you provide will be kept strictly confidential. During the financial planning engagement, my team and I may, on occasion, be required to consult with other third-party professionals, at which time we will obtain your written permission to disclose your personal information.

As discussed during the introductory meeting, this engagement includes all services required to develop a comprehensive financial plan. These services will specifically include:

- Reviewing and prioritizing your goals and objectives.

- Developing a summary of your current financial situation, including a net worth statement, cash flow summary, and insurance analyses.

- Reviewing your current investment portfolio and developing an asset management strategy.

- Developing a financial management strategy, including financial projections and analysis.

- Completing a retirement planning assessment, including financial projections of assets required at estimated retirement date.

- Assessing estate net worth and liquidity.

- Identifying tax planning strategies to optimize your financial position.

- Developing education funding recommendations.

- Presenting a written financial plan that will be reviewed in detail with you. The plan will contain recommendations designed to meet your stated goals and objectives, supported by relevant financial summaries.

- Developing an action plan to implement the agreed upon recommendations.

- Referring to other professionals, as required, to assist with implementation of the action plan.

- Assisting you with the implementation of the financial plan as needed or required.

- Determining the necessity of financial plan revisions.

This will be an on-going professional relationship. At a minimum, I will meet with you (as a couple) on an annual basis to ensure the financial plan is still appropriate for you. Either party may terminate this agreement at any time by notifying the other in writing. Any fees incurred prior to the date of termination will be payable in full.

My firm's services will be charged on an assets-under-management (AUM) basis with a minimum fee of $250 per month. My firm will charge the greater of a 1 percent of AUM annual fee or $3,000 per year, which will be billed on a monthly basis from your investment accounts under my team's direct management. The fee includes development and delivery of your financial plan, unlimited email communication, and review meetings.

Please be advised that my team and I do not receive referral fees from, nor do we pay referral fees to, any other professionals to whom my team and I may refer you.

In order to ensure that this financial plan contains sound and appropriate recommendations, it is your responsibility to provide complete and accurate information regarding pertinent aspects of your personal and financial situation, including objectives and goals, needs and values, investment statements, tax returns, copies of wills, powers of attorney, insurance policies, employment benefits, retirement benefits, and relevant legal agreements. This list is not all-inclusive and any other relevant information should be disclosed in a timely manner. It is your responsibility to ensure that any material changes to the above noted circumstances are disclosed to me and/or my team on a timely basis, since changes can impact the financial planning recommendations.

My team and I have no known conflicts of interest in the acceptance of this engagement. I commit that I will advise you of any conflicts of interest, in writing, if they should arise.

My team and I adhere to CFP Board's *Code of Ethics and Standards of Professional Conduct*, as well as all applicable federal and state rules and regulations. At all times during this engagement, my team and I shall place your interests ahead of our own when providing professional services.

I look forward to working with you and helping you reach your financial goals.

Sincerely,

Trevor Sand

Trevor Sand, CFP®

Trevor Sand: Chandler and Rachel Hubble:

I accept the terms of this engagement letter.   We accept the terms of this engagement letter.

_____   _____ & _____

FINANCIAL PLAN TABLE OF CONTENTS

- Letter to Client ....
- Client Engagement Letter ....
  - Firm Mission and Vision Statement ....
  - Ethics Statement ....
  - Privacy Statement..
  - Client Profile..
  - Summary of Goals..
  - Executive Summary ....
- Core Content Planning Sections ....
  - Cash Flow and Net Worth Analysis..
    - Emergency fund needs..
  - Tax Analysis..
  - Insurance/ Risk Management Analysis...
    - Life insurance ....
    - Health and disability insurance...
    - Long-term care insurance ....
    - Property and liability insurance ....
  - Investment Analysis...
    - Investment Policy Statement..
  - Retirement Analysis ....
  - Education Funding Analysis ....
  - Estate Planning Analysis..
- Appendices ....

FIRM MISSION STATEMENT

XYZ Financial Planning's mission is to provide world-class financial planning client service through education, analysis, and client interactions that lead to client goal achievement. The staff members working at XYZ Financial Planning share a goal of helping each client attain financial freedom through comprehensive financial planning.

FIRM VISION STATEMENT

Every staff member working at XYZ Financial Planning strives to earn the title of "most trusted adviser" in the life of a client by providing world-class fiduciary advice. Staff members attend to the details of every client's financial life. This involves learning about clients as people rather than numbers.

Those working at XYZ Financial Planning also share a common vision of giving back to the Springfield community by offering financial planning to those less fortunate in the community through pro-bono efforts. XYZ Financial Planning works daily to make the community in which clients and staff members live and work a better place.

ETHICS STATEMENT

In addition to adhering to a strict fiduciary standard when working with clients, each staff member at XYZ Financial Planning follows a strict Code of Ethics while adhering to Standards of Professional Responsibility. By working with XYZ Financial Planning, a client can be assured that advice is provided with integrity, objectivity, competence, fairness, confidentiality, professionalism, and diligence as outlined below:

Integrity

Trust is central to a successful financial planning relationship. Clients can rely on our honesty, professionalism, and abilities.

Objectivity

Your needs will be at the heart of all recommendations. Staff members have an ethical obligation to act in your best interest when providing financial planning advice. Staff members pledge to use experience and judgement to carefully consider each client's situation when providing client-specific advice and counsel.

Competence

Staff members who hold the CFP® marks have demonstrated an appropriate level of knowledge to offer financial planning advice. The CFP® certification provides confidence that staff members have completed rigorous education and experience requirements, including continuing education coursework designed to ensure competence in financial planning.

Fairness

Staff members will clearly state what services will be provided and at what cost. Staff members will also explain the risks associated with all financial recommendations, along with any potential conflicts of interest.

Confidentiality

As noted in the privacy statement, staff members follow a very strict confidentiality standard.

Professionalism

Staff members will not provide investment advice or financial planning services unless the staff member is properly qualified and licensed to do so, as required by state or federal law. If a client's situation falls outside a staff member's scope of practice, a referral will be made.

Diligence

Before engaging someone as a client, staff members will discuss that individual's goals and objectives and explain what can be expected from a relationship with the firm. Staff members pledge to ensure that all products or services recommended are both suitable and most appropriate for each client.

Source: https://www.cfp.net/ethics/code-of-ethics-and-standards-of-conduct

XYZ FINANCIAL PLANNING
PRIVACY POLICY

Investment advisers are required by law to inform their clients of their policies regarding privacy of client information. My team and I are bound by professional standards of confidentiality that are even more stringent than those required by law.

Federal law gives the client (you) the right to limit some but not all sharing of personal information. The law also requires us to tell you how my team and I collect, share, and protect your personal information.

TYPES OF NONPUBLIC PERSONAL INFORMATION (NPI) COLLECTED

My team and I collect nonpublic personal information about you that is either provided to us by you or obtained by us with your authorization. This can include but is not limited to your Social Security Number, Date of Birth, Banking Information, Financial Account Numbers and/or Balances, Sources of Income, Credit Card Numbers, and/or Other Information. If there comes a time when you are no longer our client, my team and I may continue to share your information only as described in this notice.

PARTIES TO WHOM INFORMATION IS DISCLOSED

As an investment firm, my team and I may need to share your personal information with others during the course of everyday business. In the section below, the reasons that my team and I may share your personal information are listed:

- For everyday business purposes, such as to process your transactions, maintain your account(s), respond to court orders and legal investigations, or report to credit bureaus;

- For our marketing, to offer our products and services to you;

- For joint marketing with other financial companies;

- For our affiliates' everyday business purposes, such as information about your transactions and experiences; or

- For non-affiliates to market to you.

Clients may opt out of sharing information for joint marketing to other financial companies, to our affiliates, and to non-affiliates. If you are a new client, my team and I may begin sharing your information on the day you sign the agreement. When you are no longer a client, my team and I may continue to share your information as described in this notice. However, you may contact us at any time to limit sharing of information.

PROTECTING THE CONFIDENTIALITY OF CURRENT AND FORMER CLIENT INFORMATION

To protect your personal information from unauthorized access and use, my team and I use security measures that comply with federal law, including computer safeguards and secured files and building.

FEDERAL LAW GIVES YOU THE RIGHT TO LIMIT SHARING—OPTING OUT

Federal law allows you the right to limit the sharing of your NPI by "opting-out" of the following: sharing for non-affiliates' everyday business purposes, including information about your creditworthiness and sharing with non-affiliates who use your information to market to you. State laws and individual companies may give you additional rights to limit sharing. Please notify us immediately if you choose to opt out of these types of sharing.

DEFINITIONS: <u>Affiliates</u>: companies related by common ownership or control. Affiliates can be financial and non-financial companies; <u>Non-affiliates</u>: companies not related by common ownership or control. Non-affiliates can be financial and non-financial companies; <u>Joint marketing</u>: a formal agreement between non-affiliated financial companies that together market financial products or services to you.

Please call me or my team if you have any questions. Your privacy, our professional ethics, and the ability to provide you with quality financial services are very important to us.

CLIENT PROFILE

Chandler Hubble	Rachel Hubble
Age: 42	Age: 42
State of residence: Missouri	State of residence: Missouri
Citizen: U.S.	Citizen: U.S.
Health status: No known health issues	Health status: No known health issues
SS#: 555-55-5555	SS#: 555-55-4444

Dependent Children

Phoebe Hubble
Age: 5
Health status: No known health issues

Home Address

727 Success Lane
Springfield, MO

Employment

Chandler:	Rachel:
Golden Tee Golf Association, Inc.	The Family and Career Institute
6282 Star Drive	5600 Cedar Lane Road, Suite #150
Springfield, MO	Springfield, MO
Occupation: Sales consultant	Occupation: Career counselor
Years employed: 12	Years employed: 3

Client Goals

- Chandler and Rachel, your primary goal is to live life with a relatively high level of financial satisfaction.

- Chandler and Rachel, you want to be self-sufficient in retirement.

  o   As such, your primary objective is to retire at age sixty-two, if possible.

- A secondary objective is to provide 100 percent of Phoebe's college education.

- Rachel, you would like to turn your love of collecting art into a small business during retirement by renting a retail outlet and selling art supplies and collectibles.

- Chandler and Rachel, you are also interested in maintaining the privacy of your financial affairs.

- You would like to ensure Phoebe's financial welfare in the case of death.

SUMMARY OF GOALS

Cash Flow and Net Worth

- Live a financially satisfying life.

- Increase discretionary cash flow to fund other goals.

- Establish an emergency fund of six months of total dedicated and discretionary expenses (not including taxes paid). You would like to achieve this goal within two years.

- Continue to increase assets and reduce debt.

Taxation

- Reduce tax withholdings to increase monthly discretionary cash flow.

- Maximize deductible expenses.

- Maximize the use of tax-advantaged investments.

- Monitor the impact of other planning recommendations on the tax situation.

Life Insurance

- Determine whether a need exists for additional life insurance.

- Evaluate current policies to ensure that each policy is appropriately priced.

- Confirm that survivors will be protected financially in the event either Chandler or Rachel was to prematurely pass.

Health Insurance

- Maintain appropriate health insurance coverage through Chandler's employer.

- Take advantage of any tax-advantaged plans that may be available through Chandler's or Rachel's employer, or through a private provider.

- Continue to ensure that any health coverage is appropriate in terms of costs and coverage.

Disability Insurance

- Determine whether your disability insurance policies are best suited to your needs and whether additional coverage is necessary.

Long-Term Care Insurance

- Ensure you can meet future long-term care needs through a combination of insurance and savings.

Property and Liability Insurance

- Minimize personal liability exposures.

- Minimize liability exposures resulting from the use of personal property.

- Maintain appropriate property and casualty insurance coverage on a year-to-year basis.

- Obtain replacement cost coverage for property that may be currently underinsured.

- Purchase additional coverage to ensure that family asset and liability exposures are adequately covered in the case of property loss or liability claim.

- Continue to ensure that any property, casualty, and liability coverage is appropriate in terms of costs.

Investments

- Develop an investment plan for Phoebe's education fund.

- Evaluate tax-advantaged investing alternatives.

- Develop and manage household portfolios to match the time horizon, risk capacity, and risk tolerance of Chandler and Rachel for (1) retirement, (2) special situation needs, and (3) an emergency fund.

Education

- Provide 100 percent of Phoebe's college education costs.

- Choose appropriate education saving vehicles to meet educational funding need (you prefer to invest in tax-advantaged investments to pay for college, if possible).

Retirement

- As a family, you would like to retire at age sixty-two.

- You want to be self-sufficient in retirement (you will need 85 percent of your current earned before-tax income in today's dollars when you retire; you do not wish to deplete your assets over your lifetime).

- Rachel would like to turn her love of collecting art into a small business.

- Rachel would also like to build a small addition to your home and fill it with art.

- You want to plan on taking occasional trips during retirement.

- You would like to begin receiving Social Security benefits as soon as possible.

Estate

- Prepare for future events, such as incapacity or death, which can impact your financial situation.

- Adequately provide for Phoebe in the event of Chandler and Rachel's death.

- Minimize estate settlement costs, such as probate, inheritance, and estate taxes.

- Avoid probate and maintain privacy of your financial affairs.

- Ensure that your end-of-life wishes, both to protect your family and your financial situation, are known and planned for to the greatest extent possible.

EXECUTIVE SUMMARY

The purpose of this comprehensive financial plan is to provide a comprehensive and integrated set of strategies that you can follow to achieve your financial goals and objectives. Our firm has conducted an extensive analysis of each of the following financial planning topic areas: cash flow and net worth management; tax planning; insurance planning; retirement planning; education planning; and estate planning. Our analysis was based on the information that you provided to our firm. The results of the data analysis are presented throughout this plan.

Chandler and Rachel, your net worth and diligent saving behavior have placed you in an excellent position as you begin to prepare to meet upcoming financial objectives, including paying for Phoebe's college education costs, funding retirement, and putting your estate plan in order. What follows is a summary of some of the key findings from the analysis plus a review of some of the most important recommendations from the financial plan.

Based on the analysis, the following items need specific and timely attention:

- First, given the high interest rates on your credit cards, you should use funds from your savings account to pay off all credit card liabilities.

- Second, you should refinance the mortgage on your primary residence.

- Third, you need to continue to increase your emergency savings fund and establish a home equity line of credit for emergency needs.

- Fourth, you need to reduce the amount of tax being withheld from your pay.

- Fifth, Chandler you need to purchase an additional $1.25 million in life insurance coverage, whereas Rachel, you need an additional $400,000 in life insurance coverage.

- Sixth, you need to begin contributing to a Flexible Spending Account (FSA) to help pay for unreimbursed medical expenses.

- Seventh, you both need to purchase additional long-term disability insurance coverage.

- Eighth, although not recommended at this time, you should continue to review your need for long-term care insurance coverage.

- Ninth, you should purchase additional excess liability coverage to maximize home and auto protection.

- Tenth, you should allocate $26,100 of investment assets to help fund Phoebe's future college costs and begin saving $1,800 into an education fund annually until she begins college.

- Eleventh, to achieve retirement at age sixty-two, you will need to save an additional $27,000 per year in a combination of tax-deferred and tax-free accounts.

- Twelfth, you need to reallocate investment assets to achieve your goal of opening an art gallery and adding an addition to your home.

- Thirteenth, you should establish a living trust to hold assets as a way to make the management of household assets more efficient.

- Fourteenth, you should have an estate attorney draft new estate planning documents.

Details regarding each of these needs is provided in the separate sections of this financial plan. The following actions are recommended (additional details are provided in the financial plan):

✓ Pay off your $5,500 of credit card debt with money from your savings account.

   o   Date to be completed: Before your next credit card payment date.

✓ Refinance your primary residence with a fifteen-year, 6 percent mortgage, using monetary assets to pay the closing costs.

   o   Date to be completed: Within thirty to forty-five days.

✓ Build an emergency fund of $40,060. Use your savings, life insurance cash value, and open a $7,000 home equity line of credit to meet this need.

   o   Date to be completed: Within two years.

✓ Decrease income tax withholdings and ensure withholdings for Social Security and Medicare are correct.

   o   Date to be completed: Within thirty to forty-five days.

✓ Purchase an additional $1.25 million in term life insurance coverage with Chandler as the insured. Purchase an additional $400,000 in term life insurance coverage with Rachel as the insured.

   o   Date to be completed: Within thirty to forty-five days.

✓ Fund a Flexible Spending Account (FSA) with an amount equal to your annual non-reimbursed medical expenses.

   o   Date to be completed: Prior to your employer's open enrollment due date.

✓ Obtain quotes and purchase a private supplemental long-term disability policy for the maximum permissible income replacement percentage.

   o   Date to be completed: Within thirty to forty-five days.

✓ Consider the purchase of a long-term care policy with a ninety-day elimination period and a six-year benefit period.

   o   Date to be completed: When you reach age fifty-five.

✓ Increase your liability insurance coverage by purchasing a $1 million umbrella policy. Increase the deductible and the liability coverage on your homeowner's insurance policy to $300,000 and add an inflation endorsement.

    o   Date to be completed: Within thirty to forty-five days.

✓ Contribute $26,100 of your current savings to a Section 529 plan for education funding and contribute $1,800 to the account each year. Invest contributions in a moderately aggressive portfolio.

    o   Date to be completed: Annually until Phoebe begins college (at age eighteen).

✓ Save an additional $11,000 per year using Roth IRAs and an additional $16,000 per year using your employer-provided 401(k) plans. Invest contributions in a moderately conservative portfolio.

    o   Date to be completed: Annually for the next twenty years.

✓ Allocate $37,350 held in mutual funds to the Art Gallery goal, and allocate $9,335 held in mutual funds to the Home Addition goal. Invest these assets in a moderately aggressive portfolio.

    o   Date to be completed: Within thirty days.

✓ Establish a living trust.

    o   Date to be completed: Within thirty to forty-five days.

✓ Hire an estate attorney to draft new wills, advance medical directives, durable powers of attorney for health care, and durable powers of attorney for finances. Write letters of last instruction to ensure your wishes are known at death.

    o   Date to be completed: Within thirty to forty-five days.

Chapter 6

Cash Flow and Net Worth Planning

Learning Objectives

- Learning Objective 1: Develop cash flow and net worth statements.

- Learning Objective 2: Estimate a client's cash flow and net worth position.

- Learning Objective 3: Describe appropriate funding techniques for an emergency fund.

- Learning Objective 4: Analyze a client's mortgage and refinancing situation.

- Learning Objective 5: Evaluate a client's financial capacity using financial ratios.

6.1 THE PROCESS OF CASH FLOW AND NET WORTH PLANNING

Cash flow and net worth planning serves as the foundation of the financial planning process. The cash flow and net worth planning process provides a window into a client's current and potential financial situation. Calculation of the cash flow and the net worth statement provide insights into a client's efforts to manage income in support of short-, intermediate-, and long-term financial goals. These analysis efforts, in combination with a review of a client's current financial position, are integral to the financial planning process, as they lead to the identification of strategies that can improve household financial management, increase cash flow, and/or reduce the cost of debt. The following discussion highlights how the financial planning process can be used when conducting a cash flow and net worth analysis.

Step 1: Understand The Client's Personal and Financial Circumstances

At Step One of the financial planning process, it is important to remember that a client's temperament, personality, attitudes, beliefs, financial knowledge, and experience help shape their current financial position. A client's financial statements can be used to assess their financial circumstances. For example, a client's values and attitudes can often be identified by reviewing spending patterns, whereas risk tolerance, financial knowledge, and experience can sometimes be inferred from a client's net worth statement—a risk averse client will likely hold lower risk assets. A client's emotional reaction to spending patterns or other financial decisions can offer additional useful insights during the client data-intake process. Before beginning a cash flow and net worth analysis, it is important to explore qualitative personal characteristics as a way to better understand a client's unique financial planning intentions. Spending time to understand a client's personal and household characteristics can also provide necessary insights to help facilitate future financial planning recommendations.

Figure 6.1 provides a review of the Hubbles' personal and financial circumstances. The information in Figure 6.1 is typical of what a financial planner would likely evaluate at the first step of the financial planning process.

Figure 6.1. The Hubbles' Personal and Financial Circumstances.

During your initial meeting with Chandler and Rachel you learned the following information that may impact cash flow and net worth planning issues:	
Chandler Hubble	Rachel Hubble
Age: 42	Age: 42
State of residence: Missouri	State of residence: Missouri
Citizen: U.S.	Citizen: U.S.
Life status: No known life issues	Life status: No known life issues
Income: $2,633.33 biweekly	Income: $2,708.00 monthly
Bonus: $17,116.65 semiannually	
Other important client characteristics and factors include:	

- Rachel enjoys her job as a career counselor. She works for The Family and Career Institute of Missouri. She is paid a monthly salary and anticipates receiving a 3.0 percent salary increase each year in the future.

- Currently, Phoebe is enrolled in kindergarten on a half-day basis. Her grandmother picks her up from school and takes care of Phoebe until the early afternoon. Chandler and Rachel have no regular childcare expenses. As soon as Phoebe begins school, Rachel plans to devote more time to volunteer activities in the community.

- Chandler is highly valued by his employer. He has a degree in golf course management and a MBA. Chandler works for Golden Tee Golf Association, Inc., a relatively small (29 employees) golf course management consulting firm. Chandler's job requires him to travel monthly to golf courses associated with his firm and conduct onsite management and consulting services. He is very successful in his career and plans to stay with his current employer until he retires.

- Chandler is currently paid a salary and bonus. He conservatively estimates that his salary will increase by 3.0 percent each year. His bonus—50 percent of his salary paid out semiannually—is very generous, and also very consistent.

- The Hubble family lives in a split-level, 2,250-square-foot home on a ¾-acre lot. Chandler and Rachel do not anticipate moving in the near future.

- Chandler and Rachel are motivated to create a financial plan.

- The Hubbles' employment situation is stable, and Chandler and Rachel enjoy their jobs.

- Chandler and Rachel are already saving money on a regular basis.

- Chandler and Rachel have substantial equity in their home.

- The Hubble family has come to rely on Chandler's yearly bonus.

- An economic downturn could adversely affect Chandler's ability to reach his bonus benchmark.

- With slight modifications in spending, Chandler and Rachel may be able to save more to meet their goals.

Step 2: Identify and Select Goals

Financial planning, fundamentally, is about helping clients prepare for what is sometimes referred to as the **certainty of uncertainty**. This goes beyond managing risk and applying the law of large numbers. A significant outcome associated with financial planning involves helping clients measure and evaluate needs, wants, life cycle events, and life transitions that can have immediate and long-term impacts on a client's financial situation. In this way, a financial planner, and their client, can gain a better perspective on current needs, resources to meet needs, and the client's willingness to engage in behavioral change.

Care must be taken at this step in the financial planning process to identify and rank a client's relevant financial goals thoroughly and accurately. The reason this is so important is that most clients have limited resources (e.g., cash flow and assets) but nearly unlimited wants and needs. If goals remain too flexible or unidentified, a client runs the risk of underfunding one or more needs in pursuit of attaining unrealistic or lower priority objectives. Identifying goals is especially important in relation to cash flow and net worth planning. Measures of cash flow and net worth position can provide insights into whether a client is over committing income to savings, debt repayment, or spending, as well as showing the degree of financial flexibility the client has in terms of available cash flow and unallocated assets. Figure 6.2 provides an overview of the Hubble family's cash flow and net worth goals.

Figure 6.2. The Hubbles' Cash Flow and Net Worth Goals.

During the initial client data gathering phase of the financial planning process, Chandler and Rachel were able to identify several specific financial planning goals, many of which have an association with Hubble family's cash flow and net worth situation. Specifically, Chandler and Rachel have the following cash flow and net worth goals:

- Live a financially satisfying life.
  - o This is a long-term goal, based on both a want and need.
- Increase discretionary cash flow to fund other goals.
- Establish an emergency source of income.
  - o The Hubbles' cash reserve goal is six months of total dedicated and discretionary expenses (not including taxes paid). In the case of an emergency, Rachel is willing to use her accumulated art gallery savings for an emergency as long as the money remains in a bank, checking, or money market account.
  - o Chandler and Rachel are comfortable assuming a yield of 3.0 percent before taxes on savings and money market accounts; the Hubbles' checking accounts do not earn interest.
  - o Chandler and Rachel would like to achieve this goal within two years.
- Continue to increase assets and reduce debt.

Step 3: Analyze The Client's Current Course Of Action and Potential Alternative Course(s) Of Action

Helping a client achieve their financial goals starts with an assessment of the client's current financial situation. The calculation of a client's annual cash flow and current net worth situation, coupled with diagnostic financial ratios, provides the foundation for evaluating a client's financial strengths and weaknesses. The process of evaluation begins with an analysis of a client's income and expense position, which can then be used to estimate a cash flow statement. The following discussion highlights key terms and concepts related to this step in the financial planning process.

Income is typically divided in one of two ways:

(1) based on source—earned or unearned (passive), or

(2) based on tax consequence—taxable or nontaxable.

Expenses, on the other hand, can be divided many ways, including:

(1) fixed or non-discretionary versus variable or discretionary,

(2) short-term versus long-term, and

(3) one-time versus recurring.

Although terms and definitions used by financial planners differ, the following terminology will be used to describe expenses throughout this book: dedicated and discretionary.

Dedicated expenses are cash flows required by contract or other similarly binding agreement. It is important to remember that such a narrow definition may not be appropriate all the time. A more flexible definition for this category of expenses includes additional client-defined life and goal "essential" items (e.g., insurance and savings). Dedicated expenses can also be viewed as fixed expenses that generally must be paid regardless of a client's current or future financial position.

Discretionary expenses, on the other hand, are cash flows that a client controls and can change as necessary to meet other objectives. Discretionary expenses tend to be more variable.

The eventual outcome associated with a cash flow analysis is the identification of a client's **discretionary cash flow** (DCF) position. DCF measures how much income remains at the end of a period after accounting for all expenses. DCF is defined as follows:

Discretionary Cash Flow = Total Income – Dedicated Expenses – Discretionary Expenses

A negative DCF indicates that a client is spending more than is being earned on a periodic basis. A positive DCF suggests that a client has unallocated income that can be used to meet other goals and objectives. Without positive cash flow, or the potential to generate positive cash flow—possibly via reductions in dedicated expenses or reallocation of discretionary expenses—it becomes difficult for clients to fund their financial goals.

Planning Reminder

Keep in mind that discretionary cash flow differs from savings, because discretionary cash flow can be reduced when a client allocates income to a fixed saving goal or towards investments. Many clients save some or all cash flow remaining at the end of a period, while other clients spend their discretionary cash flow either through planned or unplanned expenditures.

A thorough cash flow and net worth analysis should be conducted for every client seeking comprehensive financial planning services. Goals cannot be achieved unless a client has the capacity to fund most of, or at least the most important of, a financial planner's recommendations. Although reducing spending, increasing saving, or restructuring liabilities can sometimes be effective in helping a client meet some needs, nearly all long-term financial goals tend to be met through the planned allocation of DCF and savings, a reallocation of other assets, or a reduction in liabilities.

This last statement is not without debate. The approach taken in this book is cash flow focused. Some financial planners use another planning technique: **asset focused planning**. An asset focused approach places an emphasis on allocating client assets in a way that maximizes returns to meet objectives and goals. This approach works particularly well for high net worth clients, and those who are no longer working, who have sufficient assets to dedicate to specific goal achievement. The cash flow approach to financial planning, on the other hand, tends to be more effective for clients who are currently working and accumulating assets.

Within the cash flow focused financial planning approach, the process begins with the identification of a client's income and expense situation. This is done using an **income and expense statement** or what is called a **cash flow statement** in this text. A cash flow statement differs from a budget or spending plan. A **budget** is a written projection of how much a client thinks they will earn and spend in any given period, whereas a cash flow statement reflects actual consumption. Although it is important for most clients to have a budget, for the purposes of developing the financial plan, a detailed cash flow statement should be used to evaluate a client's situation. The amount of detail in the cash flow statement can vary with the financial complexity of a client's situation.

It is equally important to understand the balance of assets owned and debt owed because these factors play a role in increasing or decreasing a client's annual cash flow. A **net worth statement**, also commonly referred to as a **balance sheet**, provides a snapshot of a client's asset (i.e., what a client owns) and liability situation (what a client owes) in a current moment. A balance sheet provides an estimate of a client's cumulative financial progress. As shown in the following formula, the result of subtracting liabilities from assets is **net worth** or **wealth**.

Net Worth = Total Assets – Total Liabilities

Before beginning the analysis of a client's financial situation, a financial planner must determine a starting and ending date for the data collection period. An **annual cash flow statement** is typically recommended because annualized statements limit confusion about the timing of income and expenses. If a **monthly cash flow statement** is used, for example, it becomes difficult to account for income earned on a biweekly basis or expenses incurred on a non-monthly basis. Using income and expenses from the prior month or two, and then extrapolating to an annual basis, is a viable alternative, but this technique can lead to serious inaccuracies, depending on a client's recordkeeping. Annualized statements, on the other hand, provide a broad view of a client's asset and liability situation, which can be used to determine a client's financial position.

In general, one of two annual statement alternatives can be used.

- First, and perhaps the easiest, is to reproduce a calendar year twelve-month period. In this case, the cash flow and net worth statement would show a start date of January 1 and an end date of December 31.

- A second method is to reflect the twelve months preceding the month closest to the date of a client engagement. If a client were to engage financial planning services on May 8th, for example, the easiest approach would be to develop the cash flow statement from May 1st of the previous year through April 30th of the current year.

The important thing to remember is that accuracy and consistency matter more than the dates chosen for a statement. Finally, because the net worth statement reflects a point in time, and not a period of time, a financial planner has greater flexibility in choosing any reasonable date close to the initiation of the financial planning process.

6.2 DEVELOPING A CASH FLOW STATEMENT

Developing a cash flow statement for a client is a relatively straightforward process. As shown in Figure 6.3, an annual cash flow statement provides a summary of a client's earned, unearned, and nontaxable income. Income should be reported on a before-tax basis. Total taxable **income** includes all sources of income that could be subject to federal and state taxation (e.g., wages, salaries, tips, bonuses, group benefit income, interest, dividends, tax refunds, and pensions). It is also important to include all sources of **nontaxable income** (e.g., gifts, child support, qualified distributions from a Roth plan) to provide a complete accounting of all income sources available to the household.

Planning Reminder

The approach presented here is both mechanically and philosophically unique in that *cash flows committed to client goals are considered to be dedicated expenses.* Consider a client who is saving $1,000 each month into a 401(k) plan. The $1,000 is considered to be a dedicated expense in the cash flow statement. While this client does have the flexibility to stop the payment at any time, given that it is a fixed regular contribution, the payment is defined as a dedicated expense.

The term **dedicated expense** refers to everyday expenditures that a client has little control over, either because of a contractual commitment or a dedicated personal commitment to fund a goal. Primary categories of expenses include *income tax, debt service, insurance premiums,* and *savings and investments.* Note also that total taxable income is reduced by pre-tax employer deductions, such as employer-sponsored health and disability insurance, as well as deductions for other pre-tax benefits and funded retirement plans. Care should be taken to determine whether disability insurance is, in fact, a pre-tax deduction; if so, any benefits subsequently received are then taxable. Mortgage, auto, and education **loan payments** as well as **retirement contributions** generally occur on a regular basis. Often, an employer or creditor may deduct these obligations electronically.

Discretionary expenses are those that a client can control more directly, either by the choice to spend or the amount to spend. Major categories of expenses include *communication, entertainment, education, food, housing operation, household and personal care, medical, transportation, banking and investment,* and *miscellaneous.* Discretionary, or daily living, expenses tend to be flexible, and as such, can vary month-to-month and year-to-year. Unlike a mortgage payment, for instance, expenses such as entertainment, dining, and vacations tend to fluctuate from one period to the next. Separating dedicated expenses from discretionary expenses is necessary to better understand where a client's income is being spent.

The term *discretionary expense* is interchangeable with **variable expense**, which is an expression used to describe everyday living expenses that clients can more easily control. It is important to note that not everyone will agree with the expense categories shown in Figure 6.3. The statement is designed to be flexible. What is discretionary for one client may be a dedicated expense for another client. In many respects, the choice to call an expense *dedicated* (fixed) or *discretionary* (variable) is something a financial planner must make in consultation with the client to best represent the client's perception of the individual expense. For example, tuition expenses for a child to attend a private or parochial school may be considered discretionary by a client who is equally likely to send their child to a public school. The same expense may be deemed dedicated by a client who, for whatever personal reason, would not consider sending their child to a public school.

Figure 6.3. Annual Cash Flow Statement.

Yearly Income	Current
Salary Client One	
Salary Client Two	
Qualified Cash Dividends	
Taxable Interest Received	
Tax-Free Interest Received	
Short-Term Capital Gains	
Long-Term Capital Gains	
Client One Business Income	
Client Two Business Income	
LLC Rental Business	
Client One Bonus Income	
Client Two Bonus Income	
Pension Income	
Social Security Income	
Group Benefit Income (Sec 79)	
Other Income	
Total Income $	**-**

Dedicated Yearly Expenses	Current
Mortgage Payment	
Automobile Payment(s)	
Home Equity Loan	
Student Loan(s)	
Credit Cards	
Loan Payment Total $	**-**
Life Insurance	
Disability Insurance	
Medical Insurance	
Long-Term Care Insurance	
Homeowner's Insurance	
Automobile Insurance	
Group Benefit Insurance	
Condo Fees	
Umbrella Liability Insurance	

Insurance Total	**$**	**-**	
Federal Income Taxes Paid			
State Income Taxes Paid			
FICA Paid			
Real Estate Taxes Paid			
Personal Property Taxes Paid			
Other Taxes Paid			
Tax Total	**$**	**-**	
Regular/Allocated Savings			
Unallocated Savings			
Reinvested Div/CG/Interest			
Retirement Plan Contributions			
After-Tax Retirement Savings			
Savings Total	**$**	**-**	

Discretionary Yearly Expenses	**Current**
Electricity/Utilities	
Other Household Utilities	
Telephone	
Cable/ TV	
Other	
Other	
Utility Total $ -	
Home Maintenance & Repair	
Home Improvements	
Other Home Expenses	
Home Expense Total $ -	
Food at Home	
Clothing	
Laundry	
Child Care	
Personal Care	
Automobile Gas & Oil	
Automobile Repairs	

Daily Living Expense Total	$	-
Non-Auto Transportation		
Bank Charges		
Entertainment & Dining		
Recreation & Travel		
Club Fees & Dues		
Hobbies		
Gifts & Donations		
Other Expense Total	**$**	**-**
Unreimbursed Medical Expenses		
Miscellaneous Expenses		
Miscellaneous Expense Total	**$**	**-**
		Current
Total Income	$	-
Total Dedicated Expenses	$	-
Total Discretionary Expenses	$	-
Discretionary Cash Flow	**$**	**-**

When calculating a client's current cash flow position, it is important to account for **imputed**—taxable, but not spendable—income. **Internal Revenue Code §79 income** is an often overlooked, but commonly available, source of unearned income.

Certain employer-provided benefits, such as **group term life insurance** plans, can cause gross taxable income to be greater than salary or wages. Employer related term insurance plans are sometimes known as **§79 plans**. The first $50,000 in employer-funded group term life insurance coverage is generally tax free to all participants. Premiums paid by the employer for the benefit of the employee on amounts over $50,000 are subject to federal income tax (note that a key employee in a discriminatory plan cannot exclude the first $50,000 of coverage and is required to use the actual cost if it is higher than the imputed income based on Figure 6.4.) The taxable amount of the premium is calculated based on each participant's age and amount of insurance above $50,000 (if excludible) as shown in Figure 6.4. The numbers in Figure 6.4 are used to calculate the amount of taxable income that must be added to income and reported on a Form W-2.

Figure 6.4. IRS Ages and Costs Used to Determine the Taxable Fringe Benefit Amount.

Age	Cost per Month per $1,000 of Term Insurance Coverage	Cost per Year per $1,000 of Term Insurance Coverage
Under 25	$0.05	$0.60
25–29	$0.06	$0.72
30–34	$0.08	$0.96
35–39	$0.09	$1.08
40–44	$0.10	$1.20
45–49	$0.15	$1.80
50–54	$0.23	$2.76
55–59	$0.43	$5.16
60–64	$0.66	$7.92
65–69	$1.27	$15.24
70 and above	$2.06	$24.72

Source: IRS Employer's Tax Guide to Fringe Benefits, Publication 15-B, p. 14. Available at http://www.irs.gov/pub/irs-pdf/p15b.pdf.

Example. Assume that a client, age forty-two, earns $80,000 per year, and is insured for twice their annual salary ($80,000 × 2 = $160,000). The client may receive $50,000 in coverage tax free, but premiums paid by the employer for the remaining $110,000 of the policy are subject to tax. Therefore, the client's reported taxable income will increase by $132 for the year, as shown below.

$$Taxable\ Income = \frac{Insurance\ in\ Excess\ of\ \$50,000}{\$1,000} \times Table\ Factor \times 12$$

$$Taxable\ Income = \frac{\$160,000 - \$50,000}{\$1,000} \times 0.10 \times 12 = \$132.00$$

Planning Reminder

To accurately calculate discretionary cash flow, all §79 income should also be shown as an expense on the Dedicated Expense sheet. If this offsetting expense is not recorded, discretionary cash flow will be overestimated. §79 imputed income, although taxable, is not available for clients to spend.

6.3 DEVELOPING A NET WORTH STATEMENT

A client's net worth situation is calculated by subtracting liabilities from assets. Data for the calculation comes from a client's balance sheet (Figure 6.5). Assets are typically recorded on a balance sheet in a hierarchical manner based on liquidity. There are two broad asset categories: financial assets and use assets.

- **Financial assets** can be spent or invested.

- **Use assets** support a client's lifestyle and could necessitate property or liability insurance protection.

Although exceptions occur when a use asset might also be a financial asset (e.g., artwork, collectibles), these terms provide an easy preliminary method for categorization. Aside from these conventions, the categorization of assets may vary, but generally, assets fall into the following categories:

Monetary assets. Assets such as cash, checking accounts, money market mutual funds, and short-term certificates of deposit are summed to calculate total **monetary assets**— defined as financial assets that can be easily and quickly converted to cash.

Investment assets. While **investment assets** can include some of the same financial products as monetary assets, investments are generally designated for longer-term goals, rather than the day-to-day operation of the household. Common investment assets include stocks, bonds, mutual funds, and exchange traded funds. Typically, investment assets are held outside of tax-deferred retirement and/or insurance plans.

Retirement assets. **Retirement assets**, which are typically delineated by special tax or ownership status, can include both monetary and investment assets. The difference is that retirement assets are most often held in tax-deferred accounts, although taxable accounts and assets (e.g., rental real estate) can also be designated for retirement purposes.

Special needs assets. Another category of assets includes tax-advantaged savings for education, such as **§529 Plan accounts**, **Coverdell savings accounts**, and other assets specifically devoted to funding education expenses. In cases where a client has special goals (e.g., funding a house addition or improvement, funding a vacation) or special needs (e.g., accumulating funds for long-term support of a dependent with special needs), these assets should be clearly identified. Other special needs assets might include annuities or legal settlements. Because of special tax treatment and government regulations, **life insurance cash value** is also included as a separate category.

Primary residence. A client's **primary residence** is an example of a **real asset**, which is defined as a **physical asset**, as compared to a financial asset. Other real assets include a second home, ownership interests in vacation property, and other direct real estate holdings.

Personal property. If a client owns collectibles, art, antiques, or other assets, these should be classified as **personal property**. Examples include vehicles, motorcycles, boats, art, and collections (which are subject to personal property tax in many states).

Use assets. Furniture, appliances, electronics, and all other assets that support daily life can be listed as **use assets** or **lifestyle assets**. Carefully listing use assets can help a financial planner identify property and liability insurance needs that may be necessary to fully protect the client. A classification system that is systematically used can also help reduce the work associated with calculating a client's estate tax liability.

Liabilities, or **debts**, should be listed in hierarchal order on a balance sheet. **Current liabilities** include debts due within the month or other accounts that can be paid in full within the next twelve months. Although **credit card debt** is technically a liability, given the nature of revolving credit, credit cards may or may not be considered **current bills**. Clients who pay their credit card bills in full every month will have no outstanding credit card liability. This is true even if the bill has not been paid because the actual expenses (e.g., restaurant bills, shopping charges, entertainment expenses) shown on the credit card statement will have already been accounted for on the cash flow statement as routine expenses. If the bill is, or will be, paid monthly, there is no need to count the expenses as debt. In these cases, the credit card is simply used as a cash management tool for ease of payment.

Once all current debts and liabilities have been recorded, **long-term liabilities** must be identified. Examples include *mortgage debt, home equity debt, automobile loans, boat and recreational vehicle debt, education loans, life insurance loans, retirement plan loans,* and other types of *installment loans* with durations of more than one year.

When calculating a client's net worth situation, it is important to use the **fair market value** of each asset and the full, or outstanding, **balance due** for each liability. The subtraction of total liabilities from total assets yields net worth.

Figure 6.5. Balance Sheet.

Assets	Current
Cash	
Checking Accounts	
Savings Accounts	
Certificates of Deposit	
Money Market Funds	
Other Monetary Assets	
Monetary Asset Total $	**-**
EE/I Bonds	
Stocks	
Bonds	
Mutual Funds	
Brokerage Account Investments	
Investment Real Estate	
Other Investments	
Life Insurance Cash Value	
Investment Asset Total $	**-**
Primary Residence	
Second Home	
Third Home	
Other Housing	

Housing Asset Total	$	-
Vehicle One		
Vehicle Two		
Vehicle Three		
Other Automobiles		
Vehicle Asset Total	$	-
Artwork		
Collectibles		
Books		
Furniture and Household Goods		
Sporting Equipment		
Boat		
Other Personal Property		
Personal Property Asset Total	$	-
Client 401(k)		
Spouse 401(k)		
Client IRA		
Spouse IRA		
Other Retirement Assets		
Retirement Asset Total	$	-
Loans and Money Owed		
Market Value of Business		
Business Assets		
Other Asset Total	$	-
Liabilities and Debts		**Current**
Current Bills		
Other Short-Term Amounts Due		
Current Liability Total	$	-
Visa Credit Card(s)		
MasterCard Credit Card(s)		
Discover Credit Card(s)		
Other Credit Card(s)		
Credit Card Liability Total	$	-
First Mortgage		
Home Equity Loan		
LLC Rental Mortgages		

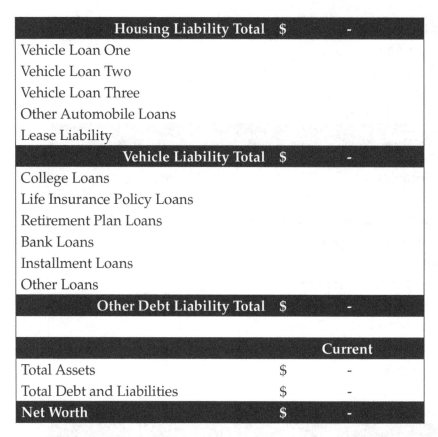

Housing Liability Total	$	-
Vehicle Loan One		
Vehicle Loan Two		
Vehicle Loan Three		
Other Automobile Loans		
Lease Liability		
Vehicle Liability Total	$	-
College Loans		
Life Insurance Policy Loans		
Retirement Plan Loans		
Bank Loans		
Installment Loans		
Other Loans		
Other Debt Liability Total	$	-
		Current
Total Assets	$	-
Total Debt and Liabilities	$	-
Net Worth	$	-

The following example shows how an analysis of the Hubble family's current cash flow and net worth situation can be used to shape financial management recommendations. Figure 6.6 provides a summary of the Hubbles' current cash flow and net worth choices. This is followed by a review of commonly used financial ratios and a refinancing analysis. Potential recommendations based on this information are then provided.

Figure 6.6. The Hubbles' Current Cash Flow and Net Worth Choices.

Statements of the Hubble family's cash flow and net worth positions are shown below:

DISCRETIONARY CASH FLOW WORKSHEET	
Yearly Income	**Current**
Salary Client One	$68,466.58
Salary Client Two	$32,496.00
Qualified Cash Dividends	$1,395.50
Taxable Interest Received	$600.00
Tax-Free Interest Received	
Short-Term Capital Gains	
Long-Term Capital Gains	
Client One Business Income	
Client Two Business Income	
LLC Rental Business	
Client One Bonus Income	$34,233.30
Client Two Bonus Income	$0.00
Pension Income	
Social Security Income	
Group Benefit Income (Sec 79)	$118.00
Other Income	
Total Income	**$137,309.38**
Dedicated Yearly Expenses	**Current**
Mortgage Payment	$13,051.25
Automobile Payment(s)	$5,412.00
Home Equity Loan	
Student Loan(s)	
Credit Cards	$5,100.00
Loan Payment Total	**$23,563.25**
Life Insurance	$2,064.00
Disability Insurance*	$300.00
Medical Insurance*	$4,500.00
Long-Term Care Insurance	
Homeowner's Insurance	$700.00
Automobile Insurance	$2,028.00
Group Benefit Insurance	$118.00
Condo Fees	$300.00
Umbrella Liability Insurance	$175.00

Insurance Total	$10,185.00
Federal Income Taxes Paid	$19,110.00
State Income Taxes Paid	$6,266.00
FICA Paid	$10,286.00
Real Estate Taxes Paid	$1,675.00
Personal Property Taxes Paid	
Other Taxes Paid	$450.00
Tax Total	$37,787.00
Regular/Allocated Savings	$3,600.00
Unallocated Savings	$9,000.00
Reinvested Div/CG/Interest	$1,995.50
Retirement Plan Contributions*	$7,357.59
After-Tax Retirement Savings	$3,000.00
Savings Total	$24,953.09
*Pre-Tax Expenses	
Discretionary Yearly Expenses	**Current**
Electricity/Utilities	$4,800.00
Other Household Utilities	
Telephone	$1,500.00
Cable/Satellite TV	$600.00
Other	$400.00
Other	
Utility Total	$7,300.00
Home Maintenance & Repair	
Home Improvements	$1,800.00
Other Home Expenses	$960.00
Home Expense Total	$2,760.00
Food at Home	$5,700.00
Clothing	$2,800.00
Laundry	
Child Care	
Personal Care	$1,200.00
Automobile Gas & Oil	$1,500.00
Automobile Repairs	

Daily Living Expense Total	$11,200.00
Non-Auto Transportation	
Bank Charges	$520.00
Entertainment & Dining	$6,000.00
Recreation & Travel	$5,700.00
Club Fees & Dues	$2,400.00
Hobbies	
Gifts & Donations	$8,300.00
Other Expense Total	$22,920.00
Unreimbursed Medical Expenses	$1,200.00
Miscellaneous Expenses	$1,860.00
Miscellaneous Expense Total	$3,060.00

Discretionary Cash Flow	Current
Total Income	$137,309.38
Total Dedicated Expenses	$96,488.34
Total Discretionary Expenses	$47,240.00
Discretionary Cash Flow	–$6,418.96
DCF + Unallocated Savings	$2,581.04

BALANCE SHEET WORKSHEET	
Assets	Current
Cash	
Checking Accounts	$8,500.00
Savings Accounts	$10,000.00
Certificates of Deposit	
Money Market Funds	$10,000.00
Other Monetary Assets	
Monetary Asset Total	$28,500.00
EE/I Bonds	$25,000.00
Stocks	
Bonds	
Mutual Funds	$53,000.00
Brokerage Account Investments	
Investment Real Estate	
Other Investments	
Life Insurance Cash Value	$17,100.00

Investment Asset Total	**$95,100.00**
Primary Residence	$250,000.00
Second Home	
Third Home	
Other Housing	
Housing Asset Total	**$250,000.00**
Vehicle One	$20,000.00
Vehicle Two	$15,500.00
Vehicle Three	
Other Automobiles	
Vehicle Asset Total	**$35,500.00**
Artwork	$5,000.00
Collectibles	$17,500.00
Books	
Furniture and Household Goods	$45,000.00
Sporting Equipment	
Boat	$5,800.00
Other Personal Property	$8,000.00
Personal Property Asset Total	**$81,300.00**
Client 401(k)	$203,000.00
Spouse 401(k)	$15,250.00
Client IRA	$52,000.00
Spouse IRA	$84,500.00
Other Retirement Assets	$125,000.00
Retirement Asset Total	**$479,750.00**
Loans and Money Owed	
Market Value of Business	
Business Assets	
Other Asset Total	**$0.00**
Liabilities and Debts	**Current**
Current Bills	
Other Short-Term Amounts Due	
Current Liability Total	**$0.00**
Visa Credit Card(s)	$3,500.00
MasterCard Credit Card(s)	$2,000.00
Discover Credit Card(s)	
Other Credit Card(s)	

Credit Card Liability Total	$5,500.00
First Mortgage	$130,332.00
Home Equity Loan	
LLC Rental Mortgages	
Housing Liability Total	$130,332.00
Vehicle Loan One	$10,396.00
Vehicle Loan Two	
Vehicle Loan Three	
Other Automobile Loans	
Lease Liability	
Vehicle Liability Total	$10,396.00
College Loans	
Life Insurance Policy Loans	
Retirement Plan Loans	
Bank Loans	
Installment Loans	
Other Loans	
Other Debt Liability Total	$0.00

Net Worth Calculation	Current
Total Assets	$970,150.00
Total Debt and Liabilities	$146,228.00
Net Worth	$823,922.00

Before formulating specific recommendations for Chandler and Rachel, the information shown in Figure 6.6 should be assessed using financial ratios. Merely looking at the numbers on a cash flow or net worth statement generally tells a limited story. **Financial ratios** can be used to help a financial planner better understand a client's current financial position by providing a quantitative measure of financial health that can be compared to a **financial benchmark**. As such, financial ratios can be used to diagnose problems or identify issues not immediately evident from a basic review of financial statements.

Financial ratios have long been used as measures of financial health in corporate finance, and although the earliest household applications of ratios reference the 1960s, it was not until the 1980s and 1990s when efforts were applied to studying the applicability of financial ratios at the household level. Although there is still some disagreement about which are the most reliable ratios to be used when evaluating current and future financial well-being, it has become commonplace to apply a variety of ratios dealing with **liquidity** (having adequate income to cover expenses) and **solvency** (having adequate assets to cover liabilities) to household finance issues.[1]

Several financial ratios are commonly used by financial planners when establishing baseline information about clients. Care should be taken to interpret ratios within the broader context of a client's financial situation and not in isolation. These ratios are summarized in Figure 6.7.

Figure 6.7. Commonly Used Financial Ratios.

Ratio	Formula	Benchmark
Current ratio	Monetary assets/Current liabilities	> 1
Emergency fund ratio	Monetary assets/Monthly living expenses	3–6 months
Savings ratio	Personal savings and employer contributions/Annual gross income	> 10%
Debt ratio	Total liabilities/Total assets	< 40%
Long-term debt coverage ratio	Annual gross income/Total annual long-term debt payments	> 2.5
Debt-to-income ratio	Annual consumer credit payment/Annual after-tax income	< 15%
Credit usage ratio	Total credit used/Total credit available	< 30%
"Front-end" mortgage qualification ratio	Annual mortgage (PITI) payment/Annual gross income	< 28%
"Back-end" mortgage qualification ratio	Annual mortgage (PITI) and credit payment/Annual gross income	< 36%
Rental expense ratio	Annual rent and renter's insurance premium/Annual gross income	< 25%

The **current ratio** is a measure of client liquidity. This ratio indicates whether sufficient current monetary assets are available to pay off all outstanding short-term debts. The recommended benchmark for the current ratio is a number greater than one, which means that if all current liabilities were paid, the client would still retain some monetary assets.

The **emergency fund ratio**, sometimes called the **month's living expenses covered ratio,** is very important because it indicates how long a client could live in a crisis situation without liquidating non-monetary assets or being forced into an unfavorable employment situation. A benchmark of three to six months of expenses is often recommended. The rationale for having a range rather than a single value is based on a number of factors. In addition to general economic conditions, including job and income stability, the number of household earners and the relative economic contribution of each, types and amount of available credit, the current credit usage ratio, and the current savings ratio, all play a role in shaping the appropriate dollar amount.

An alternative approach for calculating the emergency fund ratio uses monetary assets divided by monthly **emergency fund expenses**, rather than **monthly living expenses**. Defining emergency fund expenses tends to be more precise. For example, this number can be computed by taking gross living expenses and subtracting federal, state, and FICA taxes paid, dedicated savings, and other expenses that are not essential to the maintenance of a household, assuming that the emergency is caused by loss of employment, disability, or a similar event.

Another approach focuses on **fundamental living expenses** that clients must continue to pay regardless of employment status, such as auto and home loans, insurance premiums, utilities, and other variable expenses (e.g., grocery costs, utilities, home repairs). Regardless of what is or is not included, emergency fund expenses represent the bare minimum level of expense a household must pay in case of a financial crisis.

One of the most important questions clients ask financial planners is, "Am I saving as much as I should?" The **savings ratio** can be used to answer this question. This ratio sums a client's personal savings and employer contributions to retirement plans and divides this amount by the client's annual gross income. A benchmark of 10 percent or more is recommended. In other words, at least 10 percent of *gross* earnings should be saved annually. (Note: This ratio is very subjective and should not be blindly applied; rather, great care should be taken to match a client's total savings need to their total goal-funding need.)

Clients sometimes wonder whether they are carrying too much debt. The **debt ratio** provides a guideline to help answer this question. This ratio shows the percentage of total assets financed by borrowing. A benchmark of 40 percent is typically used for this ratio. That is, the typical client should strive to have no more than four dollars in liabilities for every ten dollars in assets.

As is the case with most financial ratios, the interpretation of this benchmark needs to be flexible, depending on a client's unique circumstances and stage in the life cycle. For example, clients in the early stage of their careers may not have much choice except to exceed the optimal percentage because of car loans, education loans, revolving credit accounts (for furniture and appliance purchases), and other household formation costs. Older clients, and those with few debts, may easily meet the ratio benchmark.

The **long-term debt coverage ratio** tells how many times a client can make debt payments, based on current income. This formula can be calculated in several ways. A common method involves dividing annual gross income by total annual **long-term debt payments**. Another method uses after-tax income as the numerator.

Examples of long-term debt payments include *mortgage payments, automobile loan payments, student loan payments,* and other debts that take more than one year to repay. If a client's monthly *credit card payment* is large enough that servicing the debt could take more than one year, this amount can also be included in the denominator of the formula.

A long-term debt coverage ratio of at least 2.5 is recommended. The inverse of this formula tells an interesting story. The inverse of a long-term debt coverage ratio of 2.5 is 0.40. This can be interpreted to mean that a client should allocate no more than 40 percent of income to cover long-term debt payments.

Related to the long-term debt coverage ratio is the **debt-to-income ratio,** which measures the percentage of take-home pay committed to consumer credit payments, defined as all revolving and installment non-mortgage debts. A ratio of less than

10 percent of take-home, or disposable, income is optimal, although up to 15 percent is considered safe. Between 15 percent and 20 percent is considered a questionable practice, while consumer debt repayments in excess of 20 percent of take-home pay are usually considered a serious problem. Because automatic payments, optional salary deferral retirement plans, and other employee benefits can further reduce after-tax income, it is important that a financial planner use care when calculating this ratio. However, the interpretation is rather clear: when clients commit 15 percent to 20 percent (or more) of disposable, or take-home, pay to consumer debt repayments, usually little is left for meeting all other financial obligations.

The **credit usage ratio** is not only a factor used to determine the adequacy of the emergency fund ratio, but it is also one of the key factors in determining a **credit score**. High credit usage, such as balances above 50 percent of a credit limit, is usually considered negative. This is because creditors may think more credit is being used than can be repaid. (Note: For clients with very high credit scores, as little as 20 percent credit usage can have a minor negative impact on a credit score.)

Lenders also use mortgage qualification ratios to measure repayment ability for mortgage qualification. Variations of debt-to-income ratios, in this case referred to as **mortgage qualification ratios,** are used to determine how much of a client's annual income can be used to pay for proposed monthly mortgage and existing non-mortgage, or consumer, debt payments. Two **debt limit ratios** are widely used.

The first is called the **28 Percent Rule**, or what some refer to as the **front-end mortgage qualification ratio** or the **mortgage debt service ratio**. This ratio results from a comparison of the projected total mortgage payment for principal, interest, taxes, and insurance (**PITI**) to gross household income. To pass this ratio, PITI generally cannot exceed 28 percent of gross annual income.

The second qualification ratio is called the **36 Percent Rule**, the **back-end mortgage qualification ratio**, or the **debt repayment ratio**. This rule states that a client should pay no more than 36 percent of gross income on the projected mortgage PITI plus other regular monthly consumer debt payments (e.g., credit card, student loan, auto loan).

These qualification ratios are currently applied throughout the mortgage industry for conventional loans, although the range may vary slightly by lender. Special loan programs or government-subsidized loan programs allow for more relaxed qualification ratios. Clients whose ratios exceed these benchmarks may not qualify for a mortgage or refinance option. If allowed, a lender may require a higher rate of interest or suggest using other available assets to reduce debt. One final but important note: for a client to qualify for a maximum mortgage, these two ratios implicitly limit other consumer debt payments to 8 percent of gross income. This corresponds closely to the original debt-to-income ratio that recommends a consumer credit payment limit of 10 percent of take-home income.

The **rental expense ratio** compares the cost of rent and renter's insurance to annual income. Renter expenses are not too different from homeowner expenses in that the rental income likely subsidizes principal, interest, taxes, and property insurance for the landlord, who also benefits from equity appreciation in the property. Given this analogy to PITI, it is prudent to apply a slightly stricter benchmark to the rental expense ratio (< 25 percent to < 28 percent of gross income) similar to the front-end mortgage ratio. Although the cost of rent in major urban areas could make this benchmark unachievable, offsetting reductions in other expenses that are not part of the urban lifestyle can balance the increased housing costs.

Figure 6.8 summarizes the financial ratio estimates for the Hubble family.

Figure 6.8. Financial Ratio Analysis for the Hubble Family.

• The current ratio.
$Current\ Ratio = \dfrac{\$23,500}{\$5,500} = 4.27$
4.27 > 1.00 benchmark
The ratio improves slightly if the $5,000 held in the checking account, which is earmarked for college savings, is included as a monetary asset.
$Current\ Ratio = \dfrac{\$28,500}{\$5,500} = 5.18$
5.18 > 1.00 benchmark
• The emergency fund ratio.
Living expenses = (Dedicated + Discretionary) – Savings
Living expenses = ($98,614 + $47,240) – $24,953
Living expenses = $120,901 / 12 = $10,075 per month
$Emergency\ Fund\ Ratio = \dfrac{\$28,500}{\$10,075} = 2.8\ months$
The emergency fund ratio of 2.8 falls slightly below the typically recommended three to six months of expense benchmark, and below the six-month level the Chandler and Rachel wish to obtain. Excluding the $5,000 earmarked for college savings reduce the ratio slightly.
• The savings ratio.
$Savings\ Ratio = \dfrac{\$24,953}{\$139,435} = 17.90\ percent$
The savings ratio exceeds the 10 percent recommended benchmark amount. The savings ratio increases if the savings amount includes the 401(k) matching of $2,054 for Chandler and $975 for Rachel:
$Savings\ Ratio = \dfrac{\$27,982}{\$139,435} = 20.07\ percent$
• The debt ratio.
$Debt\ Ratio = \dfrac{\$146,228}{\$970,150} = 15.07\ percent$

The resulting debt ratio of 15.07 percent is acceptable, falling below the maximum 40 percent benchmark amount.

- The long-term debt coverage ratio.

$$\textit{Long-Term Debt Coverage Ratio} = \frac{\$139{,}435}{(\$13{,}051 + \$5{,}412)} = 7.55$$

The long-term debt coverage ratio of 7.55 exceeds the 2.50 benchmark level.

Keep in mind that long-term debt payments include the mortgage and car loan, although an argument could be made to include the credit card balances. A reason to include the credit card balance is that with the current payments, and any new charges, it could take more than one year to repay the debt, thus qualifying the credit card debt as long-term debt; however, in practice, credit card debt is almost always considered to be short term in nature. Even if the credit card balances are included, the ratio exceeds the benchmark:

$$\textit{Long-Term Debt Coverage Ratio} = \frac{\$139{,}435}{(\$13{,}051 + \$5{,}412 + \$5{,}100)} = 5.92$$

Calculating the inverse of long-term debt coverage ratio offers another perspective: 17 percent of the Hubbles' gross income is committed to debt repayments, which is significantly less than 40 percent (the typical maximum benchmark amount).

- The debt-to-income ratio.

$$\textit{Debt-to-Income Ratio} = \frac{\$10{,}512}{\$99{,}534} = 10.56 \text{ percent}$$

The debt-to-income ratio of 10.56 percent exceeds the 15 percent benchmark level (note: the denominator represents net income [\$135,195 − \$19,110 − \$6,266 − \$10,286]).

- The credit usage ratio.

There is not enough information to estimate this ratio; however, given the facts of the case, it is likely that the Hubble family is utilizing less than 30 percent of total credit available. Based on the available information, the credit usage ratio is 14.10 percent assuming a credit limit of \$24,000 for the Visa card and \$15,000 for the MasterCard credit limit:

$$\textit{Credit Usage Ratio} = \frac{\$5{,}500}{\$39{,}000} = 14.10 \text{ percent}$$

- The front-end mortgage qualification ratio.

$$\textit{Front-End Ratio} = \frac{\$15{,}426}{\$135{,}196} = 11.41 \text{ percent}$$

Based on PI of \$13,051 + T of \$1,675 + I of \$700 = \$15,426, the ratio falls well below the maximum PITI benchmark level of 28 percent (maximum PITI: \$139,435 × .28 = \$39,042). Had a more conservative approach based on Wages, Tips, and Compensation been used, the ratio would still have exceeded the maximum benchmark (\$135,196 × .28 = \$37,855).

- The back-end mortgage qualification ratio.

$$Back\text{-}End\ Ratio = \frac{(\$15,426 + \$5,100 + \$5,412)}{\$135,196} = 19.19\ percent$$

The numerator for this calculation includes PITI + Other Debt Payments (PITI of $15,426 + $5,100 credit card + $5,412 auto payment = $25,938). The ratio of 19.19 percent falls below the maximum benchmark level ($139,435 × .36 = $50,197)

- Refinancing Alternatives:

The Hubble family may benefit from refinancing their current home mortgage. Numerous refinancing options are available. The estimates for two options are shown below:

Option 1

Step One: Calculate the payment on the present value of 30-year fixed annuity:

Input: PV = $130,331.61; FV = $0; N = 30*; I/Y = 6.50

Solve for PMT = –$823.78

*Because this is a monthly payment annuity, the calculator payment per year function should be set to 12 payments by pressing the [2nd],[I/Y],[12],[ENTER],[2nd], [CPT].

The algebraic equation, using the EPR is:

$$\$130,331.61 = \frac{PMT}{0.0054} \times \left(1 - \frac{1}{1.0054^{12 \times 30}}\right)$$

Option 2

Step One: Calculate the payment on the present value of 30-year fixed annuity:

Input: PV = $134,241.56; FV = $0; N = 30*; I/Y = 6.50

Solve for PMT = –$848.50

*Because this is a monthly payment annuity, the calculator payment per year function should be set to 12 payments by pressing the [2nd],[I/Y],[12],[ENTER],[2nd], [CPT].

The algebraic equation, using the EPR is:

$$\$134,241.56 = \frac{PMT}{0.0054} \times \left(1 - \frac{1}{1.0054^{12 \times 30}}\right)$$

It is also important to perform a mortgage refinance analysis for clients who own a home with a mortgage. Refinancing alternatives for the Hubble family are shown in Figure 6.9.

Figure 6.9. Refinancing Alternatives.

REFINANCE ALTERNATIVES						
Closing Cost Scenario	*Paid in Cash*	*Rolled into Loan*	*Paid in Cash*	*Rolled into Loan*	*Paid in Cash*	*Rolled into Loan*
Current Balance of Mortgage	$130,331.67	$130,331.67	$130,331.67	$130,331.67	$130,331.67	$130,331.67
Term (Years)	30	30	20	20	15	15
Rate	6.50%	6.50%	6.25%	6.25%	6.00%	6.00%
Closing Costs	$3,909.95	$3,909.95	$3,909.95	$3,909.95	$3,909.95	$3,909.95
Amount Financed	$130,331.67	$134,241.62	$130,331.67	$134,241.62	$130,331.67	$134,241.62
New Payment	$823.78	$848.50	$952.63	$981.21	$1,099.81	$1,132.81
Old Payment	$1,087.60	$1,087.60	$1,087.60	$1,087.60	$1,087.60	$1,087.60
Monthly Savings vs. Current Payment	$263.82	$239.10	$134.97	$106.39	($12.21)	($45.21)
Annual Savings	$3,165.78	$2,869.22	$1,619.63	$1,276.68	($146.55)	($542.48)
Breakeven (in Months)	15	16	29	37	Cannot Compute	Cannot Compute
Total Costs (Value of Payments + Closing Costs)	$300,472.48	$309,369.36	$232,541.37	$239,400.32	$201,876.24	$207,815.22

Based on the preceding analyses, the following potential recommendations are worth considering as a way to increase discretionary cash flow (DCF) and strengthen the Hubble's net worth situation:

- Use cash from the checking or savings account to pay down short-term debt.
- Refinance the home mortgage and roll the closing costs into the new mortgage.
- Refinance the home mortgage and pay closing costs with cash.
- Establish a home equity line of credit as a source of emergency income.
- Use life insurance cash values as a source of emergency income.
- Consider reducing some discretionary expenses and reallocating resources to fund defined financial planning goals.

Step 4: Develop the Financial Planning Recommendation(s)

The development of cash flow and net worth statements provides insight into the client's current financial position, as well as the client's potential ability to implement financial planning recommendations. After all, a client needs current cash flow, or the potential to generate positive DCF, in addition to investable assets, to gain the full value from a financial planning engagement. The next step in the cash flow and net worth planning process involves evaluating the accumulated data from Step Three, and then using accumulated insights to develop client-specific recommendations.

Keep in mind that all the data used to create a cash flow and net worth statement come from clients. A best practice is to confirm, rather than unquestionably accept, the information provided by a client. It is common, for example, for clients to occasionally forget to report income and expenses. These omissions can lead to inaccurate and/or inappropriate conclusions on the part of a financial planner.

As described previously, once client reported data has been confirmed, an analysis of a client's cash flow and net worth position can be undertaken. Financial planners commonly use benchmarks, usually developed in-house by a financial planner using regional or national spending data, to identify client financial strengths and weaknesses. Benchmarks can be used to engage clients in lifestyle and spending discussions. Depending on the client-financial planner relationship, and the amounts of income and DCF available, these types of discussions may or may not be necessary.

For clients with sufficient income to fund living expenses and identified goals, discussions about where resources are being spent or allocated may not be necessary. Other clients, again regardless of the amount of income or net worth, may spend beyond their means and be resistant to a financial planner's efforts to address the topic. Even so, it is worth the time and effort to review client spending, even if it results in creating stress within the client-financial planner working relationship. It is not uncommon for clients to be ambivalent about making changes, and therefore these conversations may be met with resistance. On the other hand, engaging a client in spending and saving discussions is often necessary for clients to seriously review and weigh the benefits of their current lifestyle against the benefits of accomplishing other short-, intermediate-, and long-term goals.

Whether a financial planner chooses to engage or avoid the conversation of a client's spending patterns, the information gained from a thorough review of a client's supporting financial documents can offer valuable insights that can be used when crafting financial planning recommendations. Increased DCF is most often the first goal to be achieved at the early stage of the financial planning process. Any information gained while reviewing a client's cash flow and net worth position can serve as a foundation in helping the client meet their financial goals and objectives.

Developing debt management recommendations is also important. One of the best places to look to increase a client's level of DCF is on the liability side of the net worth statement. A review of a client's type of debt, as well as the available and outstanding balances, may reveal the need for better debt management. Two options for restructuring consumer credit to optimize cash flow include:

(1) paying off **unsecured debt** with assets paying little or no after-tax return and

(2) replacing **unsecured non-tax-deductible debt** with **tax-efficient debt**.

Planning Reminder

While it is generally a good idea to recommend paying down credit card debt with monetary assets, this strategy only works when a client also agrees to stop revolving debt month-to-month. Stated another way, debt repayment strategies only work if a client willingly agrees to maintain an average zero balance month-to-month.

In almost all cases, efforts should be made to pay off high interest non-tax-deductible debt using monetary assets earning low rates of return. The interest rate paid on credit card or other unsecured debt almost always exceeds interest earned on monetary assets. If a' client still has short-term debt after reducing the balance with monetary assets, other short-term investment assets should be considered. The choice of which asset to use is contingent on the rate of return generated, although client preferences also must be considered. An EE Savings Bond, for instance, earning less than 3 percent compounded semiannually, may be an appropriate asset to pay off a credit card charging 15 percent compounded monthly. The cost of the high interest debt, compared to the after-tax rate of interest earned, offsets the advantage of holding monetary assets.

When viewed from a strict financial ratio perspective, liquidating assets can, on occasion, cause a client to fall below emergency fund benchmark levels. However, paying off short-term debt leads to an instant increase in monthly DCF that can be used to fund other goals or to rebuild monetary assets, assuming a client makes a commitment to avoid incurring revolving debt.

In some instances, restructuring assets and liabilities is not feasible or possible. Some monetary or investment assets can have particular significance or family value that excludes an asset from consideration in cash flow management planning. The client might prefer another alternative, regardless of the mathematical rationale. For clients who are unable to manage cash flow so as to pay off credit cards in full monthly, it may be necessary to consider other remedial debt management strategies.

While it is true that clients might experience a marginal loss of income from reduced interest on investment earnings when assets are used to pay down debt, the trade-off is often an attractive one. Consider the example in Figure 6.10. In this example, there is no change in net worth when the debt is paid down, although assets were used, because there was an offsetting reduction in the liability, leaving a net zero net worth change. Better yet, net income changed from negative to zero. In summary, using low-yielding assets to repay debt can have a major impact on a client's financial situation, countered by a modest impact on a client's tax plan.

Figure 6.10. The Zero Net Result of Using Assets to Pay Down Debt.

	Current Situation	Situation After Recommendation
Debt	$50,000	$0
Interest at 8 Percent (APR)	$4,000	$0
Asset	$50,000	$0
Earnings at 4 Percent (APY)	$2,000	$0
Net Worth	$0	$0
Net Income	–$2,000	$0

Planning Reminder

Interest on home equity debt generally cannot be deducted as an itemized expense. Prior to 2018, interest paid on home equity loans and lines of credit up to $100,000 was potentially deductible. Current tax law makes the use of home equity loans less attractive as a debt management strategy.

The costs and benefits associated with liquidating longer-term investment assets to pay off non-tax-deductible debt must be carefully considered. This strategy subjects a client to the verities of market conditions. A client who sells an investment at a depressed price may be less satisfied than a client who uses monetary assets, if available. A break-even sale, or one with a gain, can offer a client monetary benefits as well as psychological advantages from the elimination of the debt.

However, it is important to consider how implementation will potentially impact other goals, as well as the after-tax return on the assets compared to the interest rate on the non-tax-deductible debt. Selling an investment to pay off debt can trigger an unexpected tax liability, as well as commissions. However, liquidating an investment asset to pay off debt may be prudent when the sale can generate a needed capital loss.

It can be worthwhile for a client to finance certain purchases (e.g., furniture, appliances, automobiles) using manufacturer low- or zero-percent financing. Although the interest may not be tax deductible, the after-tax cost of the loan may be lower than that offered by a home equity line of credit or other traditional loan. Using multiple sources of credit also help to increase a client's **credit score**, which can reduce interest rates on all types of borrowing.

6.4 APPLICATIONS TO THE HUBBLE CASE

Generally, only modest changes will need to be made to the initial recommendations developed at Step Three of the financial planning process, although it is possible that new client information or data may necessitate a reevaluation. Figure 6.11 provides a summary of the final cash flow and net worth planning recommendations based on the Hubble family's financial goals.

Figure 6.11. Cash Flow and Net Worth Recommendations for Chandler and Rachel.

> *The final cash flow and net worth recommendations developed for the Hubble family match the preliminary recommendations identified at Step Three of the financial planning process. Specifically, Chandler and Rachel should:*

- Use $5,500 of current $10,000 savings or $10,000 from the money market account designated for cash reserves to pay off all credit card debt. This will eliminate high interest debt and increase discretionary cash flow by $5,100 annually (the amount allocated to credit card payments). The return on the use of the funds to eliminate the debt will far exceed the current earnings. Chandler and Rachel also need to limit future charges to an amount that can be paid off on a monthly basis.

- Refinance the home mortgage. Rather than extend the mortgage to increase cash flow, this recommendation involves refinancing the mortgage to a fifteen-year term at a 6 percent interest rate. The refinance costs are estimated to be $3,910 (3 percent multiplied by the current mortgage balance of $130,332). Chandler and Rachel should pay closing costs and other loan origination fees from the money market account to keep the new monthly payment as low as possible. The monthly payment will increase from $1,088 to $1,100. The $12 higher payment each month will enable the Hubble family to pay off the mortgage fifty-six months (almost five years) earlier.

- Open a home equity line of credit. The line of credit can be used as an emergency source of income. Implementing this recommendation will allow Chandler and Rachel to use monetary assets for other financial goals and objectives. Note also that Chandler and Rachel may use the cash value within their whole life insurance policies as a source of emergency funds, assuming that the policies are not exchanged or terminated.

- Consider discretionary expenses that Chandler and Rachel can agree to reduce without significantly compromising the family's lifestyle. Even small reductions can increase cash flow for meeting other goals or planning needs that will be identified as the analysis of their financial situation continues.

Step 5: Present the Financial Planning Recommendation(s)

Presenting cash flow and net worth planning recommendations can be both a rewarding experience and one that generates client questions, concerns, and worries. In most cases, recommendations require that a client change current and future behavior. This can be as simple as reallocating savings from one goal to another, to something more challenging, such as requiring a client to alter their spending behaviors. In general, recommendations to cut spending should be presented after other cash flow and net worth recommendations. The reason is that clients often view a recommendation to reduce spending on leisure activities, vacations, eating out, gifts, and charitable donations as a severe restriction that can be interpreted as a punishment for past behavior. Few people react well if they perceive a task as punishment. With that in mind, reasonable steps should be taken to help a client increase DCF and reduce debt with actionable activities that cause the least distribution to a client's current lifestyle. A best practice is to recommend that a client reduce expenses, in most cases, only after other recommendations have been made and when a client needs to increase DCF even further to meet client-defined goals.

Figure 6.12 summarizes some of the most important issues to consider when presenting cash flow and net worth recommendations to Chandler and Rachel Hubble.

Figure 6.12. Factors to Consider When Presenting Cash Flow and Net Worth Recommendations.

An important consideration when presenting the cash flow and net worth recommendations to Chandler and Rachel is that the Hubbles' net worth will initially decrease after the planning recommendations are implemented. Given that the Hubbles stated a goal of growing their assets, it is important to explain why recommendations that initially decrease net worth and discretionary cash flow are being made, why the recommendations are important to implement, and how the Hubbles will benefit in the short- and long-term by implementing the recommendations.

The Hubbles have provided very detailed information regarding their current income and expense items. This is ideal for a financial planner, as it allows financial statements and recommendations to be developed with a high level of detail; however, it is possible that Chandler and Rachel may become overwhelmed by the number of figures and calculations that are (and will continue to be) needed to analyze their personal and financial circumstances and develop recommendations. It is important to stay grounded as a financial planner. What is second-nature to most financial planners can be alarming and complex to clients. Be mindful of how Chandler and Rachel may process the information in this section of the financial plan as they see data and figures for the first time. It is a good idea to be strategic in choosing what calculations and figures to highlight throughout a meeting. This approach will help minimize the too common occurrence of a client getting lost in the numbers and ending up more confused about what should happen next.

At this point in the financial planning process, it is worth noting that the Hubbles' cash flow and net worth situation will be influenced by recommendations made in almost every other section of the financial plan. As the cash flow and net worth section is typically the first "chapter" in a financial plan, the Hubbles will not have seen any other elements of the plan when they read the cash flow and net worth section. Some financial planners find it helpful to show a client a summary of all recommendations in the cash flow and net worth section. This approach provides insights into how multiple recommendations blend together into a cohesive whole, which often eases a client's concerns.

Step 6: Implement the Financial Planning Recommendation(s)

There are numerous strategies that can be used to enhance a client's financial situation. Although recommendations will differ based on each client's unique situation, the fundamentals of cash flow and net worth planning apply to all clients. As such, a thorough analysis of client specific qualitative and quantitative characteristics is necessary to ensure that appropriate and reasonable recommendations are identified and adopted by a client. As the foundation of the financial planning process, cash flow and net worth management allows a financial planner to use the current financial situation to understand a client's past behavior more fully and to establish financial management strategies that will foster future success in reaching their goals.

Implementation of recommendations is the primary way in which a financial plan's effectiveness is measured. An implementation strategy must include enough detail to enable the client, working alone, to work through the steps necessary to implement recommendations. While it is, in practice, rare for a client to act alone, the implementation phase of the financial planning process must nonetheless be framed with appropriate detail and actionable steps. For example, it is not sufficient to say that a client should refinance their current mortgage. The implementation plan must clearly describe what type of mortgage is recommended, when the recommendation should take place, and where implementation should occur, while also providing cost data, among other factors.

The presentation of a recommendation needs to match a client's information processing style and preferences. Figure 6.13 shows how one of the recommendations developed for Chandler and Rachel can be presented within a financial plan.

Figure 6.13. Implementing a Cash Flow and Net Worth Recommendation for the Hubble Family.

Recommendation #1: Use cash from your savings account to pay off your credit card debt.	
Who:	Chandler and Rachel.
What:	Payoff the $3,500 balance on your Visa credit card and the $2,000 balance on your MasterCard credit card.
When:	On or before your next credit card payment date.
Where:	Using your online credit card account web portal, over the phone with your credit card company, or however monthly payments are currently made.
Why:	To increase discretionary cash flow by decreasing your debt payments and eliminating credit card interest paid.
How:	Log on to your credit card accounts and select the option to make a payment (if you mail in traditional monthly payments, you may use this procedure for this recommendation). Select the option to make a payment equal to the entire balance. Have funds transferred from your savings account by entering the account number and routing number linked to your savings account. If you wish to pay over the phone, call the credit card companies, notify the representative you would like to pay your balance in full, and provide the account number and routing number for your savings account.
How much:	$5,500 should be transferred from your savings account ($3,500 for the Visa balance and $2,000 for the MasterCard balance).
Effect on cash flow:	Implementing this recommendation will increase your discretionary cash flow by $5,100 annually.

Step 7: Monitor Progress and Update

The ongoing monitoring of previously implemented recommendations is a crucial step in the process of financial planning. A financial planner must be diligent about monitoring household characteristics and environmental factors in the context of cash flow and net worth planning. At the household level, regular reviews with clients should focus on determining and anticipating changes in employment status, income, and expenses. Important environmental factors to review include real and anticipated rates of inflation, interest rates, and market expectations. Interest rates, in particular, play a very important role in shaping future cash flow and net worth planning recommendations. Managing the spread between what a client pays for borrowed money versus what is earned on money the client lends to others is worth monitoring throughout the client-financial planner engagement. Financial planners who anticipate changes in the direction of inflation and interest rates can better help their clients maximize rates of return on monetary assets while minimizing borrowing expenses.

Changes to a client's circumstances should prompt a review and/or reevaluation of previously made recommendations. At a minimum, a client's cash flow and net worth situation should be monitored on an annual basis. A client's health, employment status, marital status, preferences, and attitudes can change over time. Changes almost always warrant a review of previously implemented recommendations. Figure 6.14 provides an overview of some of the factors that require ongoing monitoring for Chandler and Rachel Hubble.

Figure 6.14. Issues to Monitor in the Hubble Case.

Numerous ongoing monitoring issues are at play in the domain of cash flow and net worth planning. The following are of particular importance:

- Changes in the financial characteristics of the household, including a change in employment, change in income, or birth/adoption of a child.
- A significant change in economic perceptions, preferences, or risk tolerance for Chandler or Rachel.
- Lifestyle changes.
- Change in household or family status.
- Environmental and economic changes, such as a significant change in interest rates, market returns, inflation, or tax laws.

6.5 COMPREHENSIVE HUBBLE CASE

Cash flow and net worth analysis is a key element of nearly all financial plans. It is an important diagnostic tool that can serve as a first step in the process of determining the client's financial circumstances and identifying some of the client's largest planning needs. The following narrative is an example of how the cash flow and net worth section within a comprehensive financial plan can be written.

Cash Flow and Net Worth

Overview of Cash Flow and Net Worth:

Cash flow and net worth planning is a core element of any financial plan. In general, our firm uses a cash flow approach to financial planning, meaning that our staff analyzes your income and expenses as a starting point when developing recommendations. The goals of cash flow and net worth planning are to ensure that you have sufficient resources available to reach your financial goals and to ensure that your financial situation is stable and growing. Proper cash flow and net worth planning leads to recommendations that can help you better manage household resources in a way that brings you closer to accomplishing your financial goals.

Cash flow and net worth planning is the first section in your financial plan for a reason. The financial statements presented here summarize your current personal and financial situation. These statements also summarize how your circumstances will change once each of the recommendations presented in this plan are implemented.

Cash Flow and Net Worth Definitions:

The following definitions will be useful as you review the analysis presented in this section:

- *Dedicated expenses*: Cash flows required by contract or other similarly binding agreement or fixed expenses that generally must be paid regardless of your current or future financial position. Major categories of dedicated expenses include income tax, debt service, insurance premiums, and savings and investments.

- *Discretionary cash flow*: The amount of income remaining at the end of a period after accounting for all expenses.

- *Discretionary expenses*: Variable expenses and other outlays that you can control directly, either by the choice to spend or the amount to spend. Major categories of discretionary expenses include communication, entertainment, education, food, housing operation, household and personal care, transportation, banking and investment, and miscellaneous.

- *Financial ratios*: Financial calculations used to provide a snapshot of your current financial situation.

- *Net worth*: The result of subtracting liabilities from assets.

Planning Assumptions:

- Chandler, your salary and bonus will increase by 3 percent annually.

- Rachel, your salary will increase 3 percent annually.

- Closing costs for a new mortgage (or refinance mortgage) are equivalent to 3 percent of the remaining balance of the current mortgage.

- You are comfortable assuming a yield of 3 percent before taxes on savings and money market accounts.

- Current checking accounts do not earn interest.

Goals:

- Live a financially satisfying life.

- Increase discretionary cash flow to fund other goals.

- Establish an emergency fund of six months of total dedicated and discretionary expenses (not including taxes paid). Chandler and Rachel, you would like to achieve this goal within two years.

- Continue to increase assets and reduce debt.

Your Current Cash Flow and Net Worth Situation:

Currently, your annual household gross income is $137,310, the majority of which is earned through annual salaries and bonuses. As a household, you spend approximately $96,500 on dedicated expenses and $47,240 on discretionary expenses each year, leaving you with a negative discretionary cash flow of about $6,420.

It appears that you are using credit cards and have accumulated $5,500 of credit card debt to compensate for the $6,420 cash flow deficit. The $5,100 in credit card payments are only exacerbating your cash flow difficulties. Despite your negative cash flow position, as a household, you have made saving a priority. You are currently saving almost 22 percent of your gross income (including employer matching contributions to your 401(k) accounts). Chandler and Rachel, your diligent saving behavior has paid off. You have accumulated a net worth of $823,922 (assets of $970,150 less liabilities of $146,228).

You have sufficient monetary assets to cover nearly three months of living expenses in the event of an emergency situation; unfortunately, this is short of your goal to have six months of living expenses available.

For your reference, we have included copies of your financial statements below. The Discretionary Cash Flow Worksheet summarizes your income and expenses while the Balance Sheet Worksheet summarizes your asset and liability (net worth) situation:

DISCRETIONARY CASH FLOW WORKSHEET

Yearly Income	Current
Salary Client One	$68,466.58
Salary Client Two	$32,496.00
Qualified Cash Dividends	$1,395.50
Taxable Interest Received	$600.00
Tax-Free Interest Received	
Short-Term Capital Gains	
Long-Term Capital Gains	
Client One Business Income	
Client Two Business Income	
LLC Rental Business	
Client One Bonus Income	$34,233.30
Client Two Bonus Income	$0.00
Pension Income	
Social Security Income	
Group Benefit Income (Sec 79)	$118.00
Other Income	
Total Income	**$137,309.38**

Dedicated Yearly Expenses	Current
Mortgage Payment	$13,051.25
Automobile Payment(s)	$5,412.00
Home Equity Loan	
Student Loan(s)	
Credit Cards	$5,100.00
Loan Payment Total	**$23,563.25**
Life Insurance	$2,064.00
Disability Insurance*	$300.00
Medical Insurance*	$4,500.00
Long-Term Care Insurance	
Homeowner's Insurance	$700.00
Automobile Insurance	$2,028.00
Group Benefit Insurance	$118.00
Condo Fees	$300.00
Umbrella Liability Insurance	$175.00

Insurance Total	$10,185.00
Federal Income Taxes Paid	$19,110.00
State Income Taxes Paid	$6,266.00
FICA Paid	$10,286.00
Real Estate Taxes Paid	$1,675.00
Personal Property Taxes Paid	
Other Taxes Paid	$450.00
Tax Total	**$37,787.00**
Regular/Allocated Savings	$3,600.00
Unallocated Savings	$9,000.00
Reinvested Div/CG/Interest	$1,995.50
Retirement Plan Contributions*	$7,357.59
After-Tax Retirement Savings	$3,000.00
Savings Total	**$24,953.09**

*Pre-Tax Item

Discretionary Yearly Expenses	Current
Electricity/Utilities	$4,800.00
Other Household Utilities	
Telephone	$1,500.00
Cable/Satellite TV	$600.00
Other	$400.00
Other	
Utility Total	**$7,300.00**
Home Maintenance & Repair	
Home Improvements	$1,800.00
Other Home Expenses	$960.00
Home Expense Total	**$2,760.00**
Food at Home	$5,700.00
Clothing	$2,800.00
Laundry	
Child Care	
Personal Care	$1,200.00
Automobile Gas & Oil	$1,500.00
Automobile Repairs	

Daily Living Expense Total	$11,200.00
Non-Auto Transportation	
Bank Charges	$520.00
Entertainment & Dining	$6,000.00
Recreation & Travel	$5,700.00
Club Fees & Dues	$2,400.00
Hobbies	
Gifts & Donations	$8,300.00
Other Expense Total	$22,920.00
Unreimbursed Medical Expenses	$1,200.00
Miscellaneous Expenses	$1,860.00
Miscellaneous Expense Total	$3,060.00

Discretionary Cash Flow	
	Current
Total Income	$137,309.38
Total Dedicated Expenses	$96,488.34
Total Discretionary Expenses	$47,240.00
Discretionary Cash Flow	−$6,418.96
DCF + Unallocated Savings	$2,581.04

BALANCE SHEET WORKSHEET	
Assets	Current
Cash	
Checking Accounts	$8,500.00
Savings Accounts	$10,000.00
Certificates of Deposit	
Money Market Funds	$10,000.00
Other Monetary Assets	
Monetary Asset Total	$28,500.00
EE/I Bonds	$25,000.00
Stocks	
Bonds	
Mutual Funds	$53,000.00
Brokerage Account Investments	
Investment Real Estate	
Other Investments	
Life Insurance Cash Value	$17,100.00

Investment Asset Total	**$95,100.00**
Primary Residence	$250,000.00
Other Housing	
Housing Asset Total	**$250,000.00**
Vehicle One	$20,000.00
Vehicle Two	$15,500.00
Vehicle Three	
Other Automobiles	
Vehicle Asset Total	**$35,500.00**
Artwork	$5,000.00
Collectibles	$17,500.00
Books	
Furniture and Household Goods	$45,000.00
Sporting Equipment	
Boat	$5,800.00
Other Personal Property	$8,000.00
Personal Property Asset Total	**$81,300.00**
Client 401(k)	$203,000.00
Spouse 401(k)	$15,250.00
Client IRA	$52,000.00
Spouse IRA	$84,500.00
Other Retirement Assets	$125,000.00
Retirement Asset Total	**$479,750.00**
Loans and Money Owed	
Market Value of Business	
Business Assets	
Other Asset Total	**$0.00**
Liabilities and Debts	**Current**
Current Bills	
Other Short-Term Amounts Due	
Current Liability Total	**$0.00**
Visa Credit Card(s)	$3,500.00
MasterCard Credit Card(s)	$2,000.00
Discover Credit Card(s)	
Other Credit Card(s)	
Credit Card Liability Total	**$5,500.00**
First Mortgage	$130,332.00
Home Equity Loan	
LLC Rental Mortgages	

Housing Liability Total	**$130,332.00**
Vehicle Loan One	$10,396.00
Vehicle Loan Two	
Vehicle Loan Three	
Other Automobile Loans	
Lease Liability	
Vehicle Liability Total	**$10,396.00**
College Loans	
Life Insurance Policy Loans	
Retirement Plan Loans	
Bank Loans	
Installment Loans	
Other Loans	
Other Debt Liability Total	**$0.00**

Net Worth Calculation	
	Current
Total Assets	$970,150.00
Total Debt and Liabilities	$146,228.00
Net Worth	**$823,922.00**

You have been paying down your mortgage over the last ten years, leaving you with a current mortgage balance of $130,332. When you purchased your home, you contracted for a 7.875 percent interest rate, which, at the time, was competitive. However, interest rates have dropped over the last decade, making it worthwhile to consider refinancing alternatives. Our staff has analyzed three different refinancing options (i.e., a thirty-year, 6.5 percent mortgage; a twenty-year, 6.25 percent mortgage; and a fifteen-year, 6.0 percent mortgage). The results of the analysis are summarized below:

REFINANCE ALTERNATIVES						
Closing Cost Scenario	*Paid in Cash*	*Rolled into Loan*	*Paid in Cash*	*Rolled into Loan*	*Paid in Cash*	*Rolled into Loan*
Current Balance of Mortgage	$130,331.67	$130,331.67	$130,331.67	$130,331.67	$130,331.67	$130,331.67
Term (Years)	30	30	20	20	15	15
Rate	6.50%	6.50%	6.25%	6.25%	6.00%	6.00%
Closing Costs	$3,909.95	$3,909.95	$3,909.95	$3,909.95	$3,909.95	$3,909.95
Amount Financed	$130,331.67	$134,241.62	$130,331.67	$134,241.62	$130,331.67	$134,241.62
New Payment	$823.78	$848.50	$952.63	$981.21	$1,099.81	$1,132.81
Old Payment	$1,087.60	$1,087.60	$1,087.60	$1,087.60	$1,087.60	$1,087.60
Monthly Savings vs. Current Payment	$263.82	$239.10	$134.97	$106.39	($12.21)	($45.21)
Annual Savings	$3,165.78	$2,869.22	$1,619.63	$1,276.68	($146.55)	($542.48)
Breakeven (in Months)	15	16	29	37	Cannot Compute	Cannot Compute
Total Costs (Value of Payments + Closing Costs)	$300,472.48	$309,369.36	$232,541.37	$239,400.32	$201,876.24	$207,815.22

Cash Flow and Net Worth Recommendations:

The following tables summarize the recommendations that have been designed to help you reach your cash flow and net worth goals. As with all recommendations presented in this financial plan, our firm is available to answer any questions that might arise and to assist with specific implementation procedures.

Recommendation #1: Use cash from your savings account to pay off your credit card debt.	
Who:	Chandler and Rachel.
What:	Payoff the $3,500 balance on your Visa credit card and the $2,000 balance on your MasterCard credit card.
When:	On or before your next credit card payment date.
Where:	Using your online credit card account web portal, over the phone with your credit card company, or however monthly payments are currently made.
Why:	To increase discretionary cash flow by decreasing your debt payments and eliminating credit card interest paid.
How:	Log on to your credit card accounts and select the option to make a payment (if you mail in traditional monthly payments, you may use this procedure for this recommendation). Select the option to make a payment equal to the entire balance. Have funds transferred from your savings account by entering the account number and routing number linked to your savings account. If you wish to pay over the phone, call the credit card companies, notify the representative you would like to pay your balance in full, and provide the account number and routing number for your savings account.
How much:	$5,500 should be transferred from your savings account ($3,500 for the Visa balance and $2,000 for the MasterCard balance).
Effect on cash flow:	Implementing this recommendation will increase your discretionary cash flow by $5,100.

Recommendation #2: Refinance your mortgage to a fifteen-year, 6 percent fixed rate mortgage (pay closing costs out-of-pocket).	
Who:	Chandler and Rachel.
What:	A fifteen-year, 6 percent fixed rate mortgage. The beginning balance will be $130,332, while the new monthly payment will be $1,100.
When:	Within the next thirty to forty-five days.
Where:	At Nixa National Bank.
Why:	This recommendation is designed to decrease the amount paid in mortgage interest on an annual basis, as well as over the course of the loan period. Implementation of this recommendation will save approximately $42,000 in interest over the course of the loan, compared to your current mortgage. You will also pay off your mortgage fifty-six months earlier than under the terms of your current mortgage.

How:	Contact Mike Tyler, the senior loan officer at Nixa National Bank. Mr. Tyler has a loan application waiting for you. You will need to verify your W-2's, your last two tax returns, bank statements, and investment account statements. Nixa National Bank will have your house appraised before you sign the new loan documents. You should expect this process to take two to four weeks. Closing costs are estimated to be approximately $3,910, which should be paid using funds from the money market account.
How much:	Refinance the full $130,332 balance on the current mortgage with estimated closing costs of $3,910.
Effect on cash flow:	Implementation of this recommendation will decrease discretionary cash flow by $147 each year until the mortgage is paid off; however, the loan will be paid off sooner, freeing up cash flow later in life.

Recommendation #3: Build an emergency fund equal to six months of living expenses. To facilitate this goal, open a home equity line of credit to serve as an emergency source of income until you meet your emergency fund goal.

Who:	Chandler and Rachel.
What:	An emergency fund valued at $40,060 is needed to meet your saving goal (based on six months of dedicated and discretionary expenses [less savings and income taxes paid]). Open a $7,000 home equity line of credit.
When:	Within the next two years.
Where:	Open the home equity line of credit at Nixa National Bank.
Why:	The home equity line of credit can be considered a funding bridge to be used in the case of an emergency starting today until the emergency savings fund is completed.
How:	Assuming all financial planning recommendations presented in this plan are implemented, you will have a beginning emergency fund balance of $33,090 (monetary assets of $15,990 and life insurance cash value of $17,100). You will also have some excess cash flow each year that should be allocated towards the emergency fund. The implementation of the home equity line of credit recommendation helps put into place a safety net to supplement the emergency fund. The line of credit does not need to be used, but should a loan be taken (the line of credit is similar to a credit card), you will be responsible for paying the principal and interest, which will reduce cash flow until the loan is repaid. As such, the line of credit should only be used for emergency needs.
How much:	Six months of living expenses is equal to $40,060 ($45,592 dedicated expenses + $23,620 discretionary expenses – $16,290 total savings – $12,862 income taxes paid). You currently have $33,090 in assets saved, leaving a balance of approximately $7,000.
Effect on cash flow:	Implementation of this recommendation will decrease discretionary cash flow by $668 until the emergency fund is fully funded.

Current vs. Recommended Outcome:

Implementing the recommendation to pay off your credit card debt is a crucial first step to take early in the financial planning implementation process. Due to the high interest rates associated with credit card debt, annual payments can often be similar to the full credit card balance at the beginning of the year, yet the interest accumulates so quickly that it is difficult to pay the balance down. Paying off your credit card debt will increase your discretionary cash flow by $5,100 each year; however, your net worth will not change as both assets and liabilities decrease by $5,500. The large increase in discretionary cash flow will enable you to make significant contributions to your savings goals.

Refinancing your mortgage will increase the monthly loan payment by just a few dollars each month; however, doing so will allow for a much quicker loan repayment (almost five years earlier). Once you have paid off the mortgage, your household discretionary cash flow will increase by $13,200 annually, which can then be reallocated to other goals, dreams, and/or desires.

Currently, you have less than three months of living expenses available in the event of a loss of income or another emergency. Our firm's recommendation is to build an emergency fund equivalent to three to six months of living expenses, which matches with your stated goal of having six months of living expenses in an emergency fund. Although it is helpful to have your emergency fund available in cash, there are other strategies available to ensure emergency sources of income will be available. As noted above, our recommendation is to rely on the cash value of your life insurance and a home equity line of credit to supplement savings in the event of an emergency.

It is important to remember that financial planning recommendations are almost always interrelated. This means that implementing one recommendation will likely have a ripple effect on other areas of the financial plan. This is particularly true in relation to cash flow and net worth planning. The following provides a summary of all the recommendations made throughout this financial plan (all of which will be described in detail in later sections of the plan). This summary shows the impact of each recommendation on your cash flow situation:

- Life insurance: Purchase additional life insurance, which will increase premium expenses from $2,064 to $3,604.

- Disability insurance: Purchase additional disability insurance coverage (limits regarding coverage may exist), which will increase premium expenses from $300 to $620.

- Property and casualty insurance: Purchase additional excess liability (umbrella) insurance coverage, which will increase premium expenses from $175 to $275 (part of this increase will be offset by changes in insurance deductibles).

- Tax/Retirement: Adjust federal income tax withholdings, while also increasing retirement plan contributions, which will reduce taxes paid each year.

- Tax/Education: Begin contributing to a Section 529 plan to help fund Phoebe's college expenses, which will reduce state income taxes paid each year

- Tax: Ensure FICA withholdings are correct, which will decrease FICA taxes $10,286 to $9,975.

- Education: Begin contributing $1,800 each year to a Section 529 Plan to help fund Phoebe's college expenses, which decreased regular/allocated savings from $3,600 to $1,800.

- Retirement: Increase savings dedicated to retirement, which reduces unallocated savings from $9,000 to $0.

- Retirement: Begin saving $27,000 for retirement into tax-advantaged retirement accounts, which will increase retirement savings (this is offset partially by a decrease in after-tax retirement savings from $3,000 to $0).

The third column of the discretionary cash flow worksheet, shown below, shows the net effects of these recommendations on your household cash flow situation:

Yearly Income	Current	Recommended
Salary Client One	$68,466.58	$68,466.58
Salary Client Two	$32,496.00	$32,496.00
Nonqualified Cash Dividends	$1,395.50	$1,395.50
Taxable Interest Received	$600.00	$257.70
Tax-Free Interest Received	$0.00	$0.00
Short-Term Capital Gains	$0.00	$0.00
Long-Term Capital Gains	$0.00	$0.00
Client One Business Income	$0.00	$0.00
Client Two Business Income	$0.00	$0.00
LLC Rental Business	$0.00	$0.00
Client One Bonus Income	$34,233.30	$34,233.30
Client Two Bonus Income	$0.00	$0.00
Pension Income	$0.00	$0.00
Social Security Income	$0.00	$0.00
Group Benefit Income (Sec 79)	$118.00	$118.00
Other Income	$0.00	$0.00
Total Income	**$137,309.38**	**$136,967.08**

Dedicated Yearly Expenses	Current	Recommended
Mortgage Payment	$13,051.25	$13,197.75
Automobile Payment(s)	$5,412.00	$5,412.00
Home Equity Loan	$0.00	$0.00
Student Loan(s)	$0.00	$0.00
Credit Cards	$5,100.00	$0.00

Loan Payment Total	**$23,563.25**	**$18,609.75**
Life Insurance	$2,064.00	$3,604.00
Disability Insurance*	$300.00	$1,370.00
Medical Insurance*	$4,500.00	$4,500.00
Long-Term Care Insurance	$0.00	$0.00
Homeowner's Insurance	$700.00	$700.00
Automobile Insurance	$2,028.00	$2,028.00
Group Benefit Insurance	$118.00	$118.00
Condo Fees	$300.00	$300.00
Umbrella Liability Insurance	$175.00	$275.00
Insurance Total	**$10,185.00**	**$12,895.00**
Federal Income Taxes Paid	$19,110.00	$9,218.11
State Income Taxes Paid	$6,266.00	$5,085.24
FICA Paid	$10,286.00	$9,975.28
Real Estate Taxes Paid	$1,675.00	$1,675.00
Personal Property Taxes Paid	$0.00	$0.00
Other Taxes Paid	$450.00	$450.00
Tax Total	**$37,787.00**	**$26,403.63**
Regular/Allocated Savings (Education)	$3,600.00	$1,800.00
Unallocated Savings	$9,000.00	$0.00
Reinvested Div/CG/Interest	$1,995.50	$1,653.20
Retirement Plan Contributions*	$7,357.59	$27,000.00
After-Tax Retirement Savings	$3,000.00	$0.00
Savings Total	**$24,953.09**	**$30,453.20**
Pre-Tax Expenses		

Discretionary Yearly Expenses	Current	Recommended
Electricity/Utilities	$4,800.00	$4,800.00
Other Household Utilities	$0.00	$0.00
Telephone	$1,500.00	$1,500.00
Cable/Satellite TV	$600.00	$600.00
Other	$400.00	$400.00
Other	$0.00	$0.00
Utility Total	**$7,300.00**	**$7,300.00**
Home Maintenance & Repair	$0.00	$0.00
Home Improvements	$1,800.00	$1,800.00
Other Home Expenses	$960.00	$960.00

Home Expense Total	**$2,760.00**	**$2,760.00**
Food at Home	$5,700.00	$5,700.00
Clothing	$2,800.00	$2,800.00
Laundry	$0.00	$0.00
Child Care	$0.00	$0.00
Personal Care	$1,200.00	$1,200.00
Automobile Gas & Oil	$1,500.00	$1,500.00
Automobile Repairs	$0.00	$0.00
Daily Living Expense Total	**$11,200.00**	**$11,200.00**
Non-Auto Transportation	$0.00	$0.00
Bank Charges	$520.00	$520.00
Entertainment & Dining	$6,000.00	$6,000.00
Recreation & Travel	$5,700.00	$5,700.00
Club Fees & Dues	$2,400.00	$2,400.00
Hobbies	$0.00	$0.00
Gifts & Donations	$8,300.00	$8,300.00
Other Expense Total	**$22,920.00**	**$22,920.00**
Unreimbursed Medical Expenses	$1,200.00	$1,200.00
Miscellaneous Expenses	$1,860.00	$1,860.00
Miscellaneous Expense Total	**$3,060.00**	**$3,060.00**

Discretionary Cash Flow		
	Current	**Recommended**
Total Income	$137,309.38	$136,967.08
Total Dedicated Expenses	$96,488.34	$88,361.59
Total Discretionary Expenses	$47,240.00	$47,240.00
Discretionary Cash Flow	**-$6,418.96**	**$1,365.49**
DCF + Unallocated Savings	$2,581.04	$1,365.49

Similar to the way implementation of recommendations can alter a cash flow position, the implementation of recommendations can also change the manner in which assets and liabilities are allocated. The following summary shows how recommendations made throughout this financial plan, when implemented, will impact your net worth situation:

- Education: Fund Phoebe's Section 529 Plan with $26,100, which will require the $25,000 held in EE bonds to be reallocated. Further, the balance of the checking account will decrease from $8,500 to $7,400 due to $1,100 be used to supplement the $25,000 EE reallocation. The value of Other Investments on the balance sheet will increase from $0 to $26,100.

- Estate: Have estate planning documents drafted by an attorney (will, living trust, etc.), which will decrease savings by $2,000. (Note: the additional reduction in savings is related to paying off credit cards in full.) In total, the savings account balance will decrease from $10,000 to $2,500.

- Retirement: Surrender Rachel's annuity and invest the proceeds in a brokerage account (shown as Other Retirement Assets on the balance sheet), which will decrease the line item from $125,000 to $0. Brokerage account investment assets will increase from $0 to $123,350. (Note: the $1,650 difference between the value of the annuity and the proceeds transferred to the brokerage account is due to a tax paid upon surrendering the annuity.)

The third column of the balance sheet worksheet, shown below, shows the net effects of these recommendations on your household net worth situation:

Assets	Current	Recommended
Cash		
Checking Accounts	$8,500.00	$7,400.00
Savings Accounts	$10,000.00	$2,500.00
Certificates of Deposit		
Money Market Funds	$10,000.00	$6,090.05
Other Monetary Assets		
Monetary Asset Total	**$28,500.00**	**$15,990.05**
EE/I Bonds	$25,000.00	
Stocks		
Bonds		
Mutual Funds	$53,000.00	$53,000.00
Brokerage Account Investments		$123,350.00
Investment Real Estate		
Other Investments		$26,100.00
Life Insurance Cash Value	$17,100.00	$17,100.00
Investment Asset Total	**$95,100.00**	**$219,550.00**
Primary Residence	$250,000.00	$250,000.00
Second Home		
Third Home		
Other Housing		
Housing Asset Total	**$250,000.00**	**$250,000.00**
Vehicle One	$20,000.00	$20,000.00
Vehicle Two	$15,500.00	$15,500.00
Vehicle Three		
Other Automobiles		

Vehicle Asset Total	$35,500.00	$35,500.00
Artwork	$5,000.00	$5,000.00
Collectibles	$17,500.00	$17,500.00
Books		
Furniture and Household Goods	$45,000.00	$45,000.00
Sporting Equipment		
Boat	$5,800.00	$5,800.00
Other Personal Property	$8,000.00	$8,000.00
Personal Property Asset Total	**$81,300.00**	**$81,300.00**
Client 401(k)	$203,000.00	$203,000.00
Spouse 401(k)	$15,250.00	$15,250.00
Client IRA	$52,000.00	$52,000.00
Spouse IRA	$84,500.00	$84,500.00
Other Retirement Assets	$125,000.00	$0.00
Retirement Asset Total	**$479,750.00**	**$354,750.00**
Loans and Money Owed		
Market Value of Business		
Business Assets		
Other Asset Total	**$0.00**	**$0.00**
Liabilities and Debts	**Current**	**Recommended**
Current Bills		
Other Short-Term Amounts Due		
Current Liability Total	**$0.00**	**$0.00**
Visa Credit Card(s)	$3,500.00	
MasterCard Credit Card(s)	$2,000.00	
Discover Credit Card(s)		
Other Credit Card(s)		
Credit Card Liability Total	**$5,500.00**	**$0.00**
First Mortgage	$130,332.00	$130,332.00
Second Home		
Home Equity Loan		
Housing Liability Total	**$130,332.00**	**$130,332.00**
Vehicle Loan One	$10,396.00	$10,396.00
Vehicle Loan Two		
Vehicle Loan Three		
Other Automobile Loans		
Lease Liability		

Vehicle Liability Total	$10,396.00	$10,396.00
College Loans		
Life Insurance Policy Loans		
Retirement Plan Loans		
Bank Loans		
Installment Loans		
Other Loans		
Other Debt Liability Total	$0.00	$0.00

Net Worth Calculation		
	Current	Recommended
Total Assets	$970,150.00	$957,090.05
Total Debt and Liabilities	$146,228.00	$140,728.00
Net Worth	$823,922.00	$816,362.05

The following table summarizes how assets will be reallocated to help you reach each of your savings goals (unallocated assets represent assets that have not been directed towards one or more goals):

Asset Allocation to Goals		
	Current	Recommended
Assets Available for Goals	$586,250.00	$590,290.05
Assets Allocated to Emergency Fund	$23,500.00	$33,090.05
Assets Allocated to Retirement	$479,750.00	$478,100.00
Assets Allocated to Education	$0.00	$26,100.00
Assets Allocated to Special Goal 1	$5,000.00	$37,350.00
Assets Allocated to Special Goal 2	$0.00	$9,335.00
Assets Allocated to Special Goal 3	$0.00	$0.00
Assets Allocated to Other Needs	$0.00	$0.00
Unallocated Assets	$78,000.00	$6,315.00

Alternative Recommendations and Outcome(s):

Your current emergency fund goal is to have six months of living expenses available in the event of an emergency. Although you will have life insurance cash value and a home equity line of credit available to supplement your savings (assuming implementation of recommendations), it will be about ten years before you will have enough cash in your savings account to meet your emergency fund goal.

One way to expedite the emergency fund accumulation process involves considering ways to reduce current discretionary expenses and using the savings to fund the emergency fund. Even small expense reductions can increase cash flow. In addition, if expenses are cut, the amount needed for emergency savings will be reduced. The following table summarizes the expense items that will continue in an emergency.

Emergency Items		
	Current	Recommended
Loan Payment Total	$23,563.25	$18,609.75
Insurance Total	$10,185.00	$12,895.00
Real Estate Taxes	$1,675.00	$1,675.00
Personal Property & Other Taxes	$450.00	$450.00
Utility Total	$6,900.00	$6,900.00
Daily Living Expense Total	$11,200.00	$11,200.00
Miscellaneous Expenses	$3,060.00	$3,060.00
Emergency Items Total	$57,033.25	$54,789.75

Accounting for only crucial emergency fund expenses will decrease the annual emergency expense need from $80,120 to $54,040, making a six-month emergency fund goal $27,020. Based on this core level of expense need, your current emergency fund is sufficient.

Plan Implementation and Monitoring Procedures:

Chandler and Rachel, the recommendations presented in this section assume that you would like to maintain your current standard of living and general spending habits. Many clients are not aware of their income and expense situation, or their net worth position, until a cash flow and net worth statement has been prepared. If you would like help in developing a spending plan to identify areas where expenses can be cut, our staff would be happy to help you.

Also, we know that refinancing a mortgage can get complicated. Please notify us if you would like any assistance during the mortgage refinancing process. We are happy to provide any help possible, particularly when analyzing different refinancing options or providing financial statements. We can also provide recommendations for mortgage brokers if you would like to explore an alternative to Nixa National Bank.

Chandler and Rachel, be assured that we will conduct a review of your cash flow and net worth situation each year prior to our annual review meeting. Our staff will monitor the following factors, as these may indicate a need to update your cash flow or net worth analysis:

- Changes in the financial characteristics of the household, including a change in employment, change in income, or birth/adoption of a child.

- A significant change in economic perceptions, preferences, or risk tolerance for Chandler or Rachel.

- Lifestyle changes.

- Change in household or family status.

- Environmental and economic changes, such as a significant change in interest rates, market returns, inflation, or tax laws.

Self-Test Questions

Self-Test 1

All the following are examples of dedicated (fixed) expenses, EXCEPT:

(a) Mortgage Payment

(b) Utility Payment

(c) Student Loan Payment

(d) 401(k) Contribution

Self-Test 2

Michelle has three credit cards. Two of the cards she pays off each month, but she revolves a balance on the third card each month. She just received statements from each card company. The first card has a balance of $500. The second card has a balance of $3,500. The third card (the one she revolves month-to-month) has a balance of $900. How much should Michelle record as a liability on her net worth statements?

(a) $900

(b) $1,400

(c) $4,000

(d) $4,900

Self-Test 3

Nathan has the following assets, liabilities, and income:

- Saving Account: $5,000

- Stocks: $8,000

- Income: $39,000

- Unpaid Credit Cards: $2,000

- 3 Year Auto Loan: $9,000

What is Nathan's current ratio today?

(a) .15

(b) .40

(c) .85

(d) 2.50

Self-Test 4

All the following are examples of emergency fund expenses, EXCEPT:

(a) Home Mortgage

(b) Automobile Lease Payment

(c) Electric Bill

(d) Food Away from Home

Self-Test 5

An asset that supports a client's lifestyle is a(n):

(a) Financial asset

(b) Investment asset

(c) Use asset

(d) Dedicated asset

Self-Test Answers

Question 1: b

Question 2: a

Question 3: d

Question 4: d

Question 5: c

CHAPTER RESOURCES

Bradley, S., and Martin, M. *Sudden Money: Managing a Financial Windfall*. New York: John Wiley & Sons, 2000.

Home Affordable Refinance Program (HARP) (http://www.makinghomeaffordable.gov).

Leimberg, S. R., Jackson, M. S., and Satinsky, M. J. *Tools & Techniques of Financial Planning*, 12th Ed. Cincinnati, OH: National Underwriter Company, 2017.

CHAPTER ENDNOTE

1   For additional information see:

Griffith, R. "Personal Financial Statement Analysis: A Modest Beginning." In Proceedings of the 3rd Annual Conference of the Association for Financial Counseling and Planning Education, 3 (1985), 123–31.

Prather, C. G. "The Ratio Analysis Technique Applied to Personal Financial Statements: Development of Household Norms." *Financial Counseling and Planning,* 1 (1990): 53–69.

Lytton, R. H., E. T. Garman, and N. M. Porter. "How to Use Financial Ratios when Advising Clients." *Financial Counseling and Planning* 2 (1991): 3–23.

Chapter 7

Tax Planning

Learning Objectives

- Learning Objective 1: Calculate a client's current year tax liability.

- Learning Objective 2: Identify client characteristics that uniquely affect a client's income tax planning goals.

- Learning Objective 3: Explain the nine-step tax planning procedure and demonstrate how income taxes are determined at the federal level.

- Learning Objective 4: Explain the significance, and provide examples, of above-the-line and below-the-line deductions.

- Learning Objective 5: Identify income tax planning strategies that can be used to help clients reach their income tax planning goals.

- Learning Objective 6: Describe how a client's tax return can be used to recognize other financial planning opportunities.

7.1 THE PROCESS OF TAX PLANNING

Nearly every tax planning decision and strategy can have an impact on a client's cash flow and net worth situation. This is the primary reason tax planning occurs early in the financial planning process. Specifically, it is important to know how much discretionary cash flow exists after taxes have been calculated and before additional financial planning recommendations are made. Additionally, tax planning can serve either to increase or decrease a client's cash flow and net worth position. The following discussion describes how the financial planning process can be followed when developing and presenting a tax planning analysis.

Step 1: Understand the Client's Personal and Financial Circumstances

A review of a client's current tax situation starts by evaluating client characteristics and financial circumstances related to the tax planning process. Competent financial planners understand not only their client's tax planning goals, but each client's temperament, personality, attitudes, beliefs and values, financial knowledge and experience, and socioeconomic factors that may influence tax planning decisions. Understanding the emotional, personal, and environmental aspects of a client's situation is as important as calculating a client's yearly tax liability. For example, a client may exhibit a desire to minimize taxes paid to the government. A client may also exhibit a willingness to pay "my fair share" of the nation's tax burden, or a client may desire to avoid being audited by the IRS. Each of these personal perspectives can, and should, help shape the type of recommendations made to a client.

Figure 7.1 provides a review of the Hubbles' personal and financial circumstances related to tax planning. The information in Figure 7.1 is typical of what a financial planner should evaluate at the first step of the financial planning process.

Figure 7.1. The Hubbles' Personal and Financial Circumstances.

During your initial meeting with Chandler and Rachel, you learned the following information that can impact tax planning issues:	
Chandler Hubble	Rachel Hubble
Age: 42	Age: 42
State of residence: Missouri	State of residence: Missouri
Citizen: U.S.	Citizen: U.S.
Life status: No known life issues Income: $68,467	Life status: No known life issues Income: $32,496
Bonus: $34,233.30	Bonus: $0
Phoebe Hubble	
Age: 5	
Life status: No known life issues	

Tax Filing Status	Married Filing Jointly
Federal Marginal Tax Bracket	22%
Federal Standard Deduction Amount	$24,000
Federal Exemption Amount	$0
Total Number of Federal Exemptions	3
Number of Child Dependents Under Age 17	1
Number of Child Dependents Over Age 17	0
State Marginal Tax Bracket	5.00%
State Deduction Amount	$1,000
State Exemption Amount	$900
Tax Credit Amount	$0
Number of State Exemptions	3
Federal Income Taxes Withheld	$19,110
State Income Taxes Withheld	$6,266
Other Taxes Paid	$2,125
Mortgage Interest Paid	$10,379
Charitable Donations	$5,800
FICA Taxes Withheld	$10,286

Chandler and Rachel:
- Have a moderate to lower level of financial risk tolerance.
- Are organized.
- Use the services of tax preparer.
- Enjoy the certainty of receiving a refund every year; this is a form of forced savings.
- Have a strong charitable giving orientation.
- Are confident that Chandler's bonus will remain constant into the future.
- Expect inflation to be 3 percent each year going forward.
- Believe the basis of their investments is equal to 50 percent of fair market value.

Step 2: Identify and Select Goals

The identification of client tax planning goals tends to be relatively straightforward. Tax planning goals are often shaped by the way income is received. For example, business owners need to plan specifically for income flows, whereas non-business owners need to manage paycheck withholdings. Nearly all clients express, when asked to formalize a tax planning goal, a strong desire to minimize taxes paid. From a financial planning perspective, this goal serves to increase a client's level of discretionary cash flow. However, other client-specific factors can shape the type of tax planning goal within a comprehensive financial plan. For instance, clients may want to time the receipt of income to increase/decrease reported income in a given year. This goal is usually associated with real or anticipated changes in the tax code and/or the receipt of income that may nudge a client into a high tax bracket. Figure 7.2 provides an overview of the tax goals as they relate to the Hubble family.

Figure 7.2. The Hubbles' Tax Planning Goals.

There are several possible goals associated with the Hubble family's tax planning situation:
• Reducing tax withholdings to increase monthly discretionary cash flow. • Maximizing deductible expenses. • Maximizing the use of tax-advantaged investments. • Monitoring the impact of other financial planning recommendations on their tax situation. Another implicit outcome associated with tax planning is to ensure that the amount of FICA, federal, and state taxes withheld matches the Hubbles' liability. Any amount of over-withholding should be minimized. It is important to remember that the accomplishment of other financial goals within the comprehensive financial plan are linked to this section of the financial planning process. Specifically, investment funding, education planning, retirement, and health care expense planning are interrelated with tax planning outcomes.

Step 3: Analyze the Client's Current Course of Action and Potential Alternative Course(s) of Action

[A] Tax Planning Outcomes

Two desirable outcomes are associated with income tax planning:

- First, from a client's perspective, the assessment provides a roadmap for implementing strategies that can both reduce future tax liabilities and increase current discretionary cash flow.

- Second, from a financial planner's point of view, a tax plan can serve as a valuable client education tool. In addition to providing clients with background terms, definitions, and calculations, a tax plan can be used as a mechanism to facilitate client-financial planner discussions regarding retirement funding, insurance needs, college planning, and other client goals and expenses that can benefit from the use of tax-advantaged strategies.

Planning Reminder

Tax policy in the United States tends to be either progressive or regressive. With **progressive taxes**, the percentage of tax increases as taxable income increases. The tax rate burden in a progressive system falls disproportionately on higher-income earners. The federal income tax and the Alternative Minimum Tax (AMT) are progressive. With **regressive taxes**, the tax rate decreases proportionately as a person's taxable income decreases. The burden of tax, in a regressive system, falls on low-income earners. Self-employment and **sales taxes** are examples of regressive taxes. A 5 percent tax rate on food, for example, is proportionately more burdensome on someone earning $20,000 per year than on a person earning $100,000 annually, assuming both eat the same amount and quality of food.

When these outcomes are viewed together, it makes sense for financial planners who do not consider themselves tax experts to establish working relationships with tax professionals, such as **certified public accountants (CPAs), tax attorneys,** or **enrolled agents (EAs).** The Internal Revenue Service (IRS) recognizes these professionals as qualified to represent clients in tax disputes. A financial planner should also take the time to understand a client's knowledge of taxes and determine whether any previously undisclosed tax issues are present in the client situation. Referring a client to a CPA, attorney, or EA for complex tax help is often prudent, but such referrals do not eliminate the need to engage in tax planning within the scope of a comprehensive financial plan.

Simply relying on the help of a CPA, attorney, or EA is not enough. It is important that a financial planner has a secure understanding of current tax laws and rules. This is true because almost every aspect of financial planning is either influenced by or directly affects a client's tax situation. Consider a recommendation to increase contributions to a 401(k) retirement plan. This recommendation may appear to have only retirement planning implications but, in reality, the recommendation can also influence a client's cash flow and tax situation. Contributions to a qualified retirement plan help reduce the amount of income reportable for income tax purposes. This, in turn, helps reduce a client's annual withholding requirement, which can increase discretionary cash flow during the year.

A review of a client's current tax situation starts by evaluating client characteristics related to the tax planning process. This is just another way of saying that a financial planner needs to understand a client's tax planning goals, as well as temperament and personality, attitudes, beliefs and values, financial knowledge and experience, and related socioeconomic factors that can influence tax planning decisions.

This step in the financial planning process provides very important context for tax planning. Recent or upcoming changes in a client's household situation can affect filing status, the number of personal exemptions claimed at the state level, or the availability of adjustments, itemized deductions, or credits. Common examples of important client-specific characteristics to assess include changes in marital status, reaching significant ages for taxpayers or dependents, an inheritance, a change in employment, a salary increase or decrease, the addition of a dependent (such as the birth of a child or taking on expenses for a relative), the purchase of a second home, or the sale of a primary residence or second home. These examples of life cycle events and life transitions represent both important milestones in a client's life and potential tax planning issues.

A financial planner must also consider a client's tax situation in light of any anticipated changes in the tax code. Tax planning involves taking actions that maximize each client's situation in anticipation of household and/or tax code changes. In this regard, the process of developing tax planning strategies and recommendations begins by estimating a client's income tax liability. The steps in the estimation process are described below.

[B] The Process of Estimating a Client's Income Tax Liability

The estimation of a client's tax liability is based on identifying all sources of income. Two approaches can be used to determine a client's tax liability. The first approach uses actual IRS tax forms, such as **IRS Form 1040** and IRS Schedules A, B, C, and D. The second approach, which may be slightly less accurate but more efficient, involves using some form of tax calculator or estimator. Either approach should lead to the same conclusion: the client will receive a refund, owe nothing, or owe additional tax.

The following is the nine-step income tax calculation process that can be used when estimating a client's tax liability:

Step One: Record potential gross income.

Step Two: Exclude nontaxable income and pretax items.

Step Three: Calculate gross income.

Step Four: Subtract expenses for adjusted gross income (AGI) "above-the-line" deductions.

Step Five: Reduce taxable income using either the standard deduction or itemized deductions ("below-the-line" deductions).

Step Six: Calculate tax liability.

Step Seven: Reduce the tax liability using credits.

Step Eight: Add in other tax liabilities.

Step Nine: Determine the additional tax liability or the amount of the tax refund.

Following this nine-step tax calculation approach ensures that all income is appropriately accounted for, expenses are recorded, and appropriate tax-reduction tools and techniques are utilized. Of the nine steps, Steps Two, Four, Five, and Seven are areas where a financial planner can add the most value. At Step Two, a financial planner can help a client identify areas within the household budget that can be converted to a pre-tax expense. At Steps Four and Five, a financial planner can help a client maximize "above-the-line" and "below-the-line" deductions, or adjustments to income that occur before the determination of adjusted gross income (AGI) or itemized deductions that occur after the determination of AGI. At Step Seven, a financial planner can assist clients in maximizing available tax credits. A more detailed explanation of the steps in which a financial planner can add value to the tax planning process is presented below.

[C] Step One: Record Potential Gross Income

Step One involves identifying client income. This step in the calculation process requires a financial planner to know the delivery schedule of tax reporting forms, including Forms W2 and 1099, as well as obtaining aggregate tax reports from the client.

It is common for clients to have multiple sources of income. One common tax planning objective is to minimize a client's **average tax rate**—the average amount of each dollar earned that is paid in taxes. One way to do this involves managing a client's source and timing of income. For tax planning purposes, income can be categorized in four ways:

(1) income subject to a client's **marginal tax rate** (i.e., the tax rate at which the last dollar earned is taxed);

(2) income subject to a potentially lower tax rate;

(3) income subject to a potentially higher tax rate; and

(4) income not subject to tax.

The fourth income category is referred to as **tax-exempt income**. Examples include interest on municipal bonds, gifts, inheritances, and several forms of government provided payments, such as veterans' benefits.

To achieve the goal of reducing a client's total tax liability, a financial planner often starts with a focus on the client's **taxable income**, loosely defined as income that is usually subject to income tax. Examples of taxable income include *salaries, pensions, royalties, rent, dividends, interest, capital gains, gambling winnings, hobby income, commissions, tips, "Section 79" income,* and *business income.* Within this list, salary, pensions, non-qualified dividends, interest income, gambling winnings (net of gambling losses), hobby income, commissions, tips, and Section 79 income are subject to a client's marginal tax rate. *Royalty payments* and other business income are subject to a rate potentially higher than a client's marginal tax bracket because clients with these income sources will most likely owe self-employment tax on the earnings. Under the current tax code, investment income, such as long-term capital gains and qualified dividends, are taxed at a rate that is generally lower than a client's marginal tax bracket. The following discussion reviews the most common sources of income.

Earned income. As typically reported on a client's IRS **W-2 Form**, income earned from salaries, wages, tips, and commissions is relatively easy to document. The best and easiest way to reduce wage-based income is to increase **elective deferrals** into retirement plans, health plans, or other tax favored employer provided benefits. In addition to the tax-deferral available through participation in an employer-sponsored qualified retirement plan, an employee might also be able to purchase life, medical, dental, disability, and long-term care insurance. Contributions to a **Section 125 cafeteria plan**, if available, can also serve to reduce reported income.

Some employer-provided benefit plans also allow for payment of *unreimbursed medical expenses, childcare expenses,* or even select *transportation costs.* However, it is important to carefully monitor and account for how employer-provided fringe benefits influence a client's tax situation. Internal Revenue Code (IRC) guidelines state that any fringe benefit provided to an employee by an employer is taxable unless specifically excluded in the IRC. Figure 7.3 summarizes the tax status of many popular **fringe benefits**. More information about various employer-provided benefits is provided in applicable chapters throughout this book.

Figure 7.3. Special Rules for Determining the Tax Status of Select Fringe Benefits.

Type of Fringe Benefit	Treatment Under Employment Taxes		
	Income Tax Withholding	Social Security and Medicare (including Additional Medicare Tax when wages are paid in excess of $200,000)[1]	Federal Unemployment (FUTA)
Accident and health benefits	Exempt,[2] except for long-term care benefits provided through a flexible spending or similar arrangement.	Exempt, except for certain payments to S corporation employees who are 2% shareholders.	Exempt
Achievement awards	Exempt[2] up to $1,600 for qualified plan awards ($400 for nonqualified awards).		
Adoption assistance	Exempt[2,3]	Taxable	Taxable
Athletic facilities	Exempt if substantially all use during the calendar year is by employees, their spouses, and their dependent children, and if the facility is operated by the employer on premises owned or leased by the employer.		
De minimis (minimal) benefits	Exempt	Exempt	Exempt
Dependent care assistance	Exempt[3] up to certain limits.		
Educational assistance	Exempt up to $5,250 of benefits each year.		
Employee discounts	Exempt[3] up to certain limits.		
Employer-provided cell phones	Exempt if provided primarily for non-compensatory business purposes.		
Group-term life insurance coverage	Exempt	Exempt[2,4,6] up to cost of $50,000 of coverage. (Special rules apply to former employees.)	Exempt
Health savings accounts (HSAs)	Exempt for qualified individuals up to the HSA contribution limits.		
Lodging on your business premises	Exempt[2] if furnished on your business premises, for your convenience, and as a condition of employment.		
Meals	Exempt[2] if furnished on your business premises for your convenience; exempt if de minimis.		
No-additional-cost services	Exempt[3]	Exempt[3]	Exempt[3]

Retirement planning services	Exempt[5]	Exempt[5]	Exempt[5]
Transportation (commuting) benefits	Exempt[2] up to certain limits if for rides in a commuter highway vehicle and/or transit passes or qualified parking.		
	Exempt if de minimis.		
Tuition reduction	Exempt[3] if for undergraduate education (or graduate education if the employee performs teaching or research activities).		
Working condition benefits	Exempt	Exempt	Exempt

[1] Or other railroad retirement taxes, if applicable.
[2] Exemption doesn't apply to S corporation employees who are 2% shareholders.
[3] Exemption doesn't apply to certain highly compensated employees under a program that favors those employees.
[4] Exemption doesn't apply to certain key employees under a plan that favors those employees.
[5] Exemption doesn't apply to services for tax preparation, accounting, legal, or brokerage services.
[6] A client must include in their wages the cost of group-term life insurance beyond $50,000 worth of coverage, reduced by the amount the employee paid toward the insurance. Report it as wages in boxes 1, 3, and 5 of the employee's Form W-2. Also, show it in box 12 with code "C." The amount is subject to social security and Medicare taxes, and you may, at your option, withhold federal income tax.

Source: Internal Revenue Service: https://www.irs.gov/publications/p15b

If the benefits received from an employer exceed the limits described in the Figure 7.3, or the benefits are deemed to be nonexempt, a client's taxable income will increase. Without adjustment, a client could find that tax withholdings are insufficient to cover the tax liability. Finally, to reduce the amount of income reported, a client who is self-employed can attempt to transition personal expenses to deductible business expenses, as reported on IRS Schedule C. This can have the effect of reducing the amount of income reported, thereby reducing total income.

Identifying sources of investment income is also important. The Emergency Economic Stabilization Act of 2008 made a meaningful change to the way investors report the cost basis of mutual fund holdings. The IRS defines **cost basis** as the total cost, including transaction charges, of all shares held in an account or investment (e.g., mutual fund, exchange traded fund, individual securities). This initial cost basis is then adjusted for dividends, stock splits, distributions, depreciation, and other tax allowances. A client's basis is the amount invested, which is used to determine the amount of gain or loss (realized and/or recognized) reported by a client when an asset is sold or exchanged. In this way, under most circumstances, the higher the basis, the lower the tax liability upon the subsequent sale.

Planning Reminder

The cost basis reporting method can be changed, but only prospectively, not after a sale has occurred.

Although cost basis is typically evaluated and determined by the dollar amount paid for an asset, basis can be transferred to others when a gift or exchange is made.

- When an asset is inherited, under current tax code, the cost basis is determined either as of the decedent's date of death, or the earlier of the *alternative valuation date* or the date of transfer. In most cases, this change in basis results in a step-up.

- For gifts given prior to the donor's death, the donee will not receive the same step-up in basis. Rather, the donee will receive the original basis for gifts of appreciated assets, and a split basis for assets that have depreciated. This means that the depreciated asset has two basis valuations, the higher one used for subsequent sale gains, and the lower for subsequent sale losses.

For investment purposes, new cost basis reporting rules require investment companies to maintain cost basis information for all shares purchased on or after January 1, 2012. The IRS classifies mutual fund shares acquired before January 1, 2012, as **non-covered shares**, meaning that mutual fund companies are not required to track or report the cost basis. According to the tax code, investors may elect one of three cost basis calculation methods:

(1) specific lot identification;

(2) first in, first out (FIFO); and

(3) average cost (which is only available if the shares are identical to each other).[1]

However, on some investment company websites it is common to find a list of seven different basis options. Four of the seven are automatic instructions given by the owner of the account to the investment company based on the ability to sell specific lots. These four elections are:

(1) last in, last out (LIFO);

(2) low cost;

(3) high cost; and

(4) loss/gain utilization.

The **average cost method** is the default choice made by mutual fund companies if an investor fails to make another election. This method of reporting, as illustrated in Figure 7.4, requires an investor to track the average cost of shares acquired over a period of time.

Figure 7.4. Average Cost Method Example.

Date of Purchase	Purchase Amount	Number of Shares Purchased	Calculation	Average Price per Share
1/10/15	$2,000	50	$2,000/50	$40.00
5/15/15	$100	2	$100/2	$50.00
12/12/15	$1,500	45	$1,500/45	$33.33
Total:	*$3,600*	*97*	*$3,600/97*	*$37.11*

The FIFO (and LIFO) methods of reporting assume that shares are depleted based on the date of acquisition; with either the first (or last) shares sold first (the 1/10/15 (or 12/12/15) shares).

The **specific lot identification method** requires an investor to indicate specifically which shares were sold. This approach allows for a secondary cost basis when shares cannot be identified. For many investors, this cost basis reporting method is the most time-intensive approach to share identification. The following methods are predetermined versions of specific lot identification.

The **low-cost approach** exhausts the lowest price shares first. (In Figure 7.4, the shares purchased on 12/12/15 at $33.33 would be reported as first sold.) The **high-cost approach** assumes the highest price shares, the ones purchased on 5/15/15, are sold first. This method of reporting initially subjects an investor to smaller taxable gains (or maximum losses), while postponing larger taxable gains (or smaller losses) into the future.

The final choice is the **loss/gain utilization approach** (LGUT). This method can be somewhat complex. Basically, this approach instructs a mutual fund company to sell the shares in the following order:

(1) Shares with a short-term loss (in descending order of largest loss to smallest)

(2) Shares with a long-term loss (again, in descending order)

(3) Shares held less than one year (i.e., short-term) with no loss or gain

(4) Shares held more than one year (i.e., long-term) with no loss or gain

(5) Shares with a long-term gain (in ascending order of smallest gain to largest)

(6) Shares with a short-term gain (again, in ascending order).

Keep in mind that if the shares have an unknown cost basis–such as (potentially) those purchased prior to January 1, 2012–then those shares will be sold on a FIFO ordering with smallest share lots sold first.

Business income. Two questions arise when identifying a client's business income. First, was the client engaged in a business or simply a hobby? Second, if it is in fact a business, then was the client's engagement active or passive? The first question helps determine the output of the activity—was there the intent to make a profit? The second question looks more at input—what is the level of involvement in the activity?

A financial planner may work with a client who engages in activities where it is difficult to distinguish between a **hobby** and a business. Such situations should be monitored for tax planning opportunities. Modifying or racing cars, writing travel books, photography, and small-scale farming are examples of activities that some clients feel are more of a business than a hobby. To address this issue, the IRS has developed several rules to help determine when an activity is a hobby and when it is a business. The IRS asks whether the activity is run like a business, how much time a person spends on the activity, and whether the activity is engaged in for profit. This last hurdle is crossed if the activity results in a **profit** (income exceeds expenses resulting in a taxable gain) in three of the last five years, including the most recent year.[2]

If income is generated as the result of a hobby, the income is then reported on IRS Form 1040, and expenses associated with that hobby are deductible on IRS **Schedule A**. However, if income is generated as the result of a solely owned business, then the income and business-related expenses are reported on IRS **Schedule C**.

IRS Publication 925 provides a definitional framework for passive and at-risk "active" activities. Both terms are used to describe a client's role in the decision and management process when making an investment. The key to whether an activity is a **passive activity** is determining whether there is **material participation** in the operation. In other words, does the client work on a regular, continuous, and substantial basis in operations. This applies to the ownership and management of rental property (someone engaged in a rental real estate business should be able to document spending at least ten hours per week on the activity).

If a taxpayer fails to materially participate, losses are passive. A **passive activity loss** is limited by the amount of **passive income** reported by the taxpayer. If a loss exceeds the income generated, the amount can be carried forward only to offset future passive income.[3]

On the other hand, an **at-risk loss** is limited to the invested amount. If a loss exceeds the tax basis of the invested capital or property, the remaining loss can be carried forward into subsequent years and used against non-passive income.[4]

Unearned income or investment income. Because a financial planner has a limited number of options to help clients reduce earned income, managing unearned or investment income, such as dividends and capital gains, is an important tax planning skill. For example, following the stock market meltdown of 2008, many investors sold securities at significant losses. Some justified the sale of stocks and other investments by assuming that the losses could be used to generate tax deductions. Unfortunately, some investors found that, because they did not have offsetting capital gains, they were effectively limited to a $3,000 maximum deduction for that year. Although excess losses can be indefinitely carried forward, as this example illustrates, it is important for financial planners to help clients match losses against gains in particular years rather than having clients make investment and other financial decisions based on the client's assumptions about the tax code.

A related issue involves the timing of retirement distributions and determining how such distributions can potentially impact a client's tax situation. A client's intention to take a distribution from a **qualified retirement plan**, for example, can result in a 10 percent early withdrawal penalty tax, in addition to regular income tax, on the taxable portion of the distribution received before age 59½. Under most circumstances, clients under the age of 59½ pay a 10 percent penalty on distributions (25 percent from a SIMPLE plan during the first two years of plan participation), in addition to income taxes due. However, the 10 percent penalty may be waived under certain exceptions, including distributions:

- caused by death or disability,

- to pay for higher education expenses, and

- sometimes distributions for a first-time home purchase.

A similar 10 percent penalty also applies to distributions from annuities, IRAs, and other tax-deferred investments.

Required minimum distributions (RMDs) are another area of tax law that can influence retirement distribution decisions and the development tax planning strategies. Clients who have assets in traditional, SIMPLE, or SEP IRAs, and those with assets in a qualified defined contribution plan (excluding Roth plans), must begin taking RMDs at age 72. IRS Publication 590 provides a set of Uniform Lifetime Tables that are used to determine minimum distributions. The IRS penalty for failure to take the prescribed RMD is 50 percent of the amount that should have been withdrawn.

Although the RMD rule is straightforward, there are several interesting twists to the statute that are important to understand. Some of these include: (a) options for "stretch" IRAs that reduce the RMD and extend tax-deferred growth over a longer time period; (b) alternative calculations of RMDs for inherited spousal and non-spousal IRAs and for surviving spouses who are more than ten years younger than the decedent; and (c) the option to utilize a tax-free RMD distribution to a charity.

It is common for some clients to accumulate **employer stock** in their employer sponsored retirement plans (e.g., 401(k) plan). Although other financial planning issues are related to the decision to include company stock in a retirement plan, distributions from such plans can sometimes be eligible for special tax treatment. It is important to remember that for taxation purposes, the amount of a withdrawal from such a plan is considered in two parts: the cost basis and the accumulated value, or appreciation. The original cost basis of a withdrawal is taxed as ordinary income and therefore at the client's marginal tax rate. Any withdrawal above the cost basis amount is taxed at capital gains tax rates.

Additionally, it is important to consider that there are two options available for withdrawing accumulated company stock—each resulting in different tax outcomes, the better of which may not be intuitively obvious. Clients who anticipate being in a higher marginal tax bracket in the future should consider taking company stock distributions directly, rather than rolling assets into an IRA. The reason for this is that if the stock is rolled into a traditional IRA, the entire withdrawal amount, basis and gain, is subject to taxation at ordinary rates upon final distribution from the IRA. By taking an **in-kind, lump-sum distribution** from a qualified retirement plan and placing the assets in a **nonqualified account**, a client's stock assets become eligible for **net unrealized appreciation** (NUA) tax treatment. When this happens, the distribution is immediately taxable at ordinary income rates, but only the cost basis of the distributed amount of stock is subject to income tax, not the appreciation portion of the account. In addition, a 10 percent tax penalty may also be applicable if the client is under age 59½. This is almost the reverse of other plans, where the basis is not taxable, but the gains are. With the NUA tax treatment, a client recognizes the income rather than the gain.

Because the stock was in a qualified retirement plan, the deferred income or employee benefit dollars used to purchase the stock originally were never taxed, so income tax is owed at the time of distribution. When a client subsequently sells the stock, taxes will be due at the long-term capital gains rate on any NUA and the applicable capital gains rate (i.e., short- or long-term) on any additional appreciation. With careful planning, it may be a better option to pay income tax on the basis and capital gains tax on the appreciation later than to pay income taxes on the entire value later when using a qualified IRA account.

Planning Reminder

For tax purposes, irrevocable trusts and the estate of a decedent are considered separate tax entities. The trust may be liable for income taxes for any income that is accumulated within the trust. This is called a complex trust. **Form 1041** must be filed if a trust or estate has taxable income greater than $600, or if the estate has gross income in excess of $600, or any beneficiary of the trust or estate is a non-resident alien. Beneficiaries are taxed as if they received the income directly. For example, if an asset is sold in a trust for a long-term taxable gain, the distribution will be taxable to the beneficiary as a long-term gain.

Issues related to **income in respect of a decedent** (IRD) often come up in financial planning work. Beneficiaries of an estate may take an itemized deduction on Schedule A for the amount of estate taxes paid by the decedent's gross estate. For example, assume a client inherits an IRA worth $1 million. If the decedent pays $450,000 in estate taxes attributable to this asset, the client can deduct 45 percent of all distributions from the IRA.

When estimating and reporting potential gross income, it is important for a financial planner to account for the **Alternative Minimum Tax (AMT)**. Congress enacted the AMT to prevent wealthy taxpayers from taking advantage of preferential deductions and paying little or no tax. Clients who have high incomes and benefit from preferential provisions for regular tax purposes may have to pay the AMT. Although this tax provision was originally written with only the wealthy in mind, in recent years more individuals have found themselves liable for these alternative taxes which, in all cases, are higher than regular taxes.

To determine whether a taxpayer is subject to the AMT, a taxpayer's taxable income is altered for AMT adjustments and preferences to calculate an estimate of **alternative minimum taxable income (AMTI)**. Common adjustments and **tax preference items** that can trigger the AMT include those related to the *standard deduction, miscellaneous itemized deductions, state and local tax, accelerated depreciation of certain property, incentive* *stock options, depletion allowances, intangible drilling costs,* and certain forms of *tax-exempt interest.* Taxpayers with high enough incomes and substantial preference items in any given year might trigger the AMT. The AMT has two tax rates: 26 percent on the taxable excess of tentative minimum taxable income over an exemption amount, and 28 percent on the taxable excess above that amount. A taxpayer's regular tax liability is subtracted from the tentative minimum tax to determine the AMT.

Planning Reminder

It is important to never consider a client's current tax situation or a recommendation in isolation. A financial planning strategy that might, at first glance, appear to benefit a client's situation could have underlying tax consequences that must be fully considered for implications for other core content planning areas or for implications over a longer time horizon.

A few strategies can be used to mitigate the impact of the AMT if it appears that a client might be subject to the tax. First, preference deductions should be reviewed and reduced, if possible. For example, it may be appropriate to exercise incentive stock options over time rather than all at once. Another strategy includes exercising incentive stock options in a year when other AMT preference items are expected to be low. Clients with significant depreciation expenses should consider shifting from accelerated to straight-line depreciation. Another strategy involves accelerating current year income to help offset preference deductions. An increased bonus or salary advance could be used to increase income.

[D] Step Two: Exclude Nontaxable Income and Pretax Items

At Step Two, a financial planner can help their clients maximize income from sources that are not subject to taxation. Several analytical techniques can be used at this step in the tax-estimation process.

Careful attention should be paid to situations where a client is taking distributions from an annuity, IRA, or qualified plan. If any contribution was made using after-tax dollars, or if any of the contribution was taxed previously, a portion of the total distribution will be considered a tax-free distribution. Calculating the **exclusion ratio** can reduce the probability that a client will pay unnecessary taxes. The exclusion ratio formula is as follows:

Exclusion Ratio

$$Exclusion\ Ratio = \frac{Total\ after\mbox{-}tax\ contribution}{Total\ expected\ distributions}$$

The "total expected distributions" is calculated by multiplying the monthly distribution by the number of expected distributions (i.e., 12 per year).

Example. Assume a client expects to receive $2,000 per month over a 20-year period. If the client originally invested $300,000 on an after-tax basis, the exclusion ratio indicates that 62.5 percent of each distribution will be received tax free; that is, 37.5 percent of each distribution will be taxable.

It is possible that distributions will last longer than the expected duration used in the formula. In these situations, all the after-tax contributions are accounted for. This will result in all future distributions being fully taxable. Clients who fail to track cumulative distributions can potentially incur tax penalties at some point in the future.

Identifying opportunities to generate tax-free income is also important. **Municipal bonds** and tax-free money market accounts can be used to reduce a client's reported income. In this regard, financial planners should be adept at calculating **taxable equivalent yields** as a means of comparing taxable and tax-free fixed-income investments. An analysis may be required to determine whether, for example, municipal securities are appropriate for a client. Some bonds are exempt from federal income tax, some are exempt from state income tax, and some are fully exempt, meaning the bond holder incurs neither a federal nor state income tax liability. The following formulas should be used as a means of determining the yield needed for a taxable fixed-income investment to match that of a state and/or federally tax-free fixed income investment:

Taxable Equivalent Yield (Federal Tax-exempt)

$$TEY \ (Federal \ Tax\text{-}exempt) = \frac{Tax\text{-}exempt \ bond \ yield}{(1 - FMTB)}$$

Taxable Equivalent Yield (State Tax-exempt)

$$TEY \ (State \ Tax\text{-}exempt) = \frac{Tax\text{-}exempt \ bond \ yield}{(1 - SMTB)}$$

Taxable Equivalent Yield (Fully Tax-exempt)

$$TEY \ (Fully \ Tax\text{-}exempt) = \frac{Tax\text{-}exempt \ bond \ yield}{[1 - (FMTB + (SMTB \times (1 - FMTB)))]}$$

Where:

TEY   = Taxable Equivalent Yield

FMTB = Federal Marginal Tax Bracket

SMTB = State Marginal Tax Bracket

Another formula can be used to estimate the after-tax yield (or equivalent tax-free rate of return):

After-tax Yield

$$After\text{-}tax \ yield = Taxable \ rate \times (1 - (FMTB + (SMTB \times (1 - FMTB))))$$

Several factors should be considered when using any of the preceding formulas. For instance, it is possible and likely that over time, marginal tax rates in a particular state will change. When this happens, it is important to rerun an analysis. Also, bond rates change on a regular basis. What is an attractive tax-free rate today may be a less appealing rate tomorrow. The use of a formula is not a one-time calculation. A best practice involves conducting yield analyses on an ongoing basis. Lastly, it is important to remember that the tax-exempt status of municipal bonds does not extend to all instances, particularly within the context of the AMT.

Financial planners should also examine a client's investment holdings to identify opportunities to minimize or postpone taxation. One way to do this is to utilize **like-kind exchange** strategies. The Internal Revenue Code (IRC) addresses a dozen or more non-taxable exchanges. The two most common deal with investment property (Section 1031) and insurance policies (Section 1035).

U.S. Code Section 1031 features a provision for owners of appreciated real estate to exchange a property for a similar piece of real estate without incurring immediate taxation. For this to be an effective tax-postponing strategy, a client must exchange their property for a similar kind or class of asset. This means that 1031 exchanges can only be made using real estate. Taxes on personal property can no longer be postponed using this technique.

Planning Reminder

Keep in mind that the amount *realized* for tax purposes is often different from the amount *recognized* for tax purposes. In general, investors need only recognize for tax purposes the value of the boot received, even though they may have realized an amount greater than reported for tax purposes.

Within Section 1031, **boot** is defined as the receipt of non-like-kind property. The receipt of boot can trigger taxation. Sometimes clients attempt to exchange investment securities for personal use property. The IRS will not allow such transfers on a tax-free basis. Furthermore, real estate can be exchanged only for real estate (foreign real estate is excluded), which is defined as improved or unimproved land, buildings, warehouses, etc. For example, exchanging a mortgage for a piece of land would not be permitted under Section 1031.

U.S. Code Section 1035 provides for a tax-free insurance product exchange for owners of a life insurance policy, an endowment, or an annuity. Restrictions apply, but eligible product exchanges allow a client to avoid taxes due on the sale or redemption of an insurance product. Otherwise, the two-step process of the sale or redemption, minus the taxes owed, can result in a smaller amount for a subsequent insurance product purchase.

[E] Step Three: Calculate Gross Income

Step Three involves adding together sources of income to determine gross income that may be subject to taxation.

[F] Step Four: Subtract Expenses from AGI "Above-the-Line" Deductions

At Step Four, several different tax planning strategies are available to help clients manage tax liabilities. It is important to remember, however, that many of the benefits available in the tax code are subject to income limits. The limit most often imposed is based on **adjusted gross income (AGI)** or **modified adjusted gross income (MAGI)**. The actual definition or calculation of MAGI can vary with the tax issue in question. There are two methods used to reduce AGI. One is to minimize the amount of income reported. The other is to increase negative adjustments to income.

A financial planner should suggest ways a client can maximize their **above-the-line deductions**, which are also referred to as **adjustments to gross income**. Examples of expenses that can be used to reduce gross income include *educator expenses, student loan interest, tuition fees,* and *IRA early withdrawal penalties.* Other examples include making deductible contributions to a traditional IRA (phase-out thresholds based on income for qualified plan participation typically apply) and contributing to a *healthcare savings account* (HSA). For those who are self-employed, paying one-half of *self-employment taxes,* contributing to a self-employed retirement plan (e.g., a *Keogh* or *SIMPLE plan*), or purchasing health care insurance are additional options that can be used to reduce gross income. Adjustments to AGI provide a marginal benefit for clients. For instance, if a client is in the 24 percent marginal tax bracket, a $1,000 deduction for AGI will result in approximately $240 in tax savings.

[G] Step Five: Reduce Taxable Income using either the Standard Deduction or Itemized Deductions ("Below-the-Line" Deductions)

At Step Five, a financial planner can assist their clients to maximize below-the-line deductions. If above-the-line adjustments are either unavailable or exhausted, attention should turn to below-the-line taxable income reductions by identifying available **itemized deductions**. Three areas where many clients can increase deductions, and thereby reduce taxable income (assuming the client is not subject to the AMT), include:

(1) converting non-tax-advantaged interest paid to *deductible mortgage interest,*

(2) increasing or accelerating taxes paid in a year, and

(3) increasing gifts to charitable organizations.

The purchase, sale, or refinancing of a personal residence provides an example of how client actions can trigger tax issues that call for advanced financial planning. A married couple may exclude up to $500,000 ($250,000 for a single taxpayer) in gains on the sale of a primary residence. To receive this exclusion, the client must have owned and used the home as a personal residence for two of the past five years. This is referred to as the **holding period requirement**. Any gains exceeding the excluded amount are generally taxed at the client's capital gains tax rate.

Ownership of a home can also influence the amount of deductions available to a client. Consider the itemization of home mortgage interest. The deduction applies only to interest paid on **primary mortgage initial acquisition debt**. As of 2018, the deduction applies only to the interest paid on the first $750,000 spent to acquire, build, or improve a residence after December 15, 2017 (clients who purchased a home prior to December 2017 may deduct interest on mortgages up to $1 million). Interest paid on home equity lines of credit or loans is *not* deductible, with the follow exception: According to the

IRS, interest on a home equity loan used to build an addition to an existing home is typically deductible, while interest on the same loan used to pay personal living expenses, such as credit card debts, is not. Similar to the prior law, the loan must be secured by a client's main home or second home (known as a qualified residence), not exceed the cost of the home, and meet other requirements.

Figure 7.5 highlights common solutions used to reduce AGI either by maximizing above-the-line deductions and/or below-the-line deductions and/or tax credits. The process of selecting a strategy or finding a concentration area starts by determining whether a client is foregoing benefits because their AGI is too high.[5] For example, if AGI is too high, a client may not be able to deduct a traditional IRA contribution, make a Roth IRA contribution, deduct qualified education expenses, or claim other tax credits.

Whether a financial planner is directly involved in the preparation of a client's income tax return or indirectly involved in the analysis of a client's tax situation, as part of a comprehensive planning engagement, the financial planner may be responsible for implementing the changes necessary to increase a client's tax efficiency. The benefits for clients who use some or all of the tax liability reduction methods shown in Figure 7.5 can be mitigated or enhanced by other planning considerations.[6] Investment planning strategies that minimize tax liabilities, for example, should always be considered and accounted for when calculating a client's tax liability. Tax planning strategies should not, however, be considered in isolation. Strategies should be considered in conjunction with each client's other financial planning needs. For example, increasing a client's municipal bond allocation can be a viable strategy to reduce taxable income. However, if the tax-free rate of return offered by the bonds does not exceed the after-tax return on another fixed-income investment, the client may be better off paying taxes. To make matters even more complicated, high levels of tax-exempt interest can trigger the AMT, thus effectively reducing the availability of several deductions, including home equity interest.

Figure 7.5. Tax Planning Product and Solution Decision Tree.

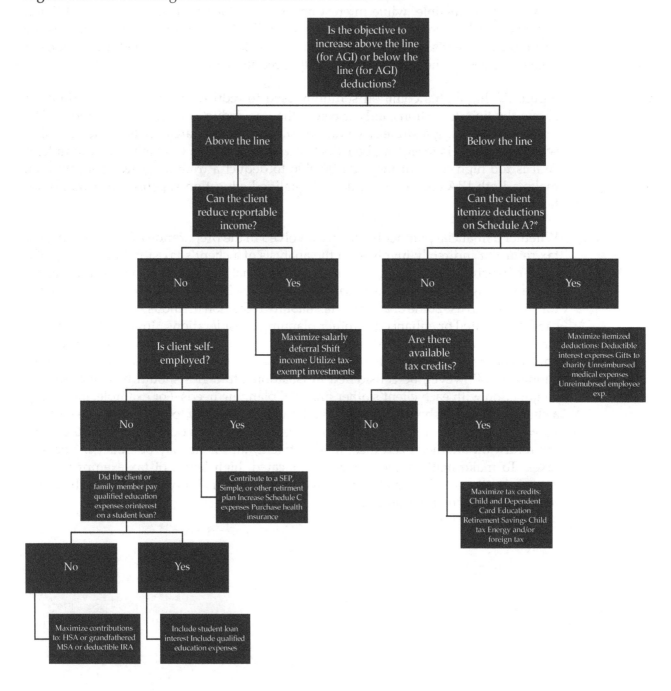

[H] Step Six: Calculate Tax Liability

Step Six involves estimating a client's tax liability. This is done using effective marginal tax rates at the time the estimate is made.

[I] Step Seven: Reduce the Tax Liability Using Credits

At Step Seven, a financial planner should take action to identify and maximize available tax credits—a dollar for dollar reduction in tax liability. A few of the most commonly used tax credits include the child and dependent care credit, the Lifetime Learning education *credit*, and the *saver's tax credit*. Maximizing available tax credits is an effective tax planning strategy because rather than reducing a client's taxable income, a tax credit reduces a client's tax liability directly. Keep in mind, however, that the availability of tax credits may depend on a client's AGI or MAGI, meeting various qualification thresholds, and potential changes in the tax code.

[J] Step Eight: Add in Other Tax Liabilities

This is an essential review step in the tax planning process. At this step, a financial planner should verify that reported withholdings are accurate, all income has been accounted for, and any other potential tax reduction strategies have been incorporated into the plan.

[K] Step Nine: Determine the Additional Tax Liability or the Amount of the Tax Refund

The last step in the tax estimation process involves determining the client's additional tax liability, or the amount of the tax refund. Details from the tax code are needed to complete this step in the tax planning process.

[L] Applying the Tax Planning Steps to the Hubbles' Situation

As a recap, the nine-step tax determination process includes: (1) recording potential gross income, (2) excluding nontaxable income and pretax items, (3) calculating gross income, (4) reducing AGI by using above-the-line deductions, (5) reducing taxable income by either the standard deduction or itemized deductions, (6) calculating the tax liability, (7) reducing tax liabilities by means of tax credits, (8) adding other tax liabilities, and (9) determining the amount owed or amount to be refunded.

The following example shows how an analysis of the Hubble family's current tax choices and needs results in a pathway to the development of tax planning recommendations. Figure 7.6, which is a screen shot of the tax planning estimation procedure using the Financial Planning Analysis Excel™ package that accompanies the book (when reviewing the spreadsheet, it is important to keep in mind that some cells are populated from other sheets in the package), provides a summary of the Hubbles' current taxation choices. This is followed by a listing of potential recommendations.

Figure 7.6. The Hubbles' Current Tax Choices and Potential Recommendations.

Federal Tax Planning Estimator	Assumption:	Married Filing Jointly
Gross Income	$137,309.38	
Long-Term Capital Gains & Qualified Dividends	$1,395.50	
Pre-Tax Retirement Contributions	$7,357.59	
Other Pre-Tax Payroll Deductions	$4,800.00	
Adjustments	$0.00	
Less Exclusions	$0.00	
Reportable Gross Income		**$126,547.29**
Less Deductions for Adjusted Gross Income		
Educator Expenses	$0.00	
One-Half Self-Employment Tax	$0.00	
Student Loan Interest	$0.00	
Archer MSA Deduction	$0.00	
Tuition Deduction	$0.00	
IRA Contribution	$0.00	
Keogh Contribution	$0.00	
Other Deductions	$0.00	
Early Withdrawal Penalty	$0.00	
Adjusted Gross Income		**$126,547.29**
Number of Children Dependents Under Age 17	1	
Number of Children Dependents Over Age 17	0	
Itemized Deductions		
Medical and Dental Expenses	$1,200.00	
AGI Medical Deduction Requirement	$9,491.05	
Amount of Deduction	$0.00	
Taxes Paid	$8,391.00	
Home Mortgage Interest	$10,379.00	
Investment Interest	$0.00	
Home Purchase Points	$0.00	
Gifts to Charity	$5,800.00	
Other Deductions	$0.00	

Total Itemized	$24,570.00	
Standard Deduction	$25,900.00	
Taxable Income		**$99,251.79**
Tax on Income		$13,069.15
Long-Term Capital Gain and Qualified Dividend Tax		$209.33
Social Security & Medicare Taxes		$9,975.28
FICA Taxes Withheld	$10,286.00	
Tax Withheld or Paid	$19,110.00	
Less Tax Credits		
Earned income tax credit (refundable)	$0.00	
Credit for child and dependent care expenses	$0.00	
Foreign tax credit	$0.00	
Adoption credit	$0.00	
Retirement savings credit	$0.00	
Education credits	$0.00	
Credit for elderly	$0.00	
Child tax credit/Credit for other dependents	$2,000.00	
Total Tax Due or (Refund)	**−$8,142.24**	

STATE INCOME TAX WORKSHEET

Assumes State Tax Linked to Federal AGI

State Marginal Tax Bracket	5.00%
State Deduction Amount	$1,000.00
State Exemption Amount	$900.00
Tax Credit Amount	$0.00
Number of Exemptions	2.00
Federal AGI	$126,547.29
State Taxable Income	$123,747.29
Before Credit Tax Liability	$6,187.36
STATE TAX LIABILITY	**$6,187.36**
State Withholdings	**$6,266.00**
(Refund) or Amount Due	−$78.64

The federal and state tax analysis shows the following:

- Chandler and Rachel are over-withholding taxes at the federal level.

  o By over-withholding taxes, Chandler and Rachel are making an interest-free loan to the government.

- For some reason, Chandler and Rachel had excess FICA taxes withheld from their pay.

- Chandler and Rachel are not taking advantage of the flexible spending account that is available.

Based on the tax analysis and observations, the following potential recommendation are worth considering:

- Chandler should adjust his W-4 so that he is withholding less on an annual basis. Chandler should also decrease his contribution to Social Security and Medicare.

- When Chandler and Rachel receive this year's tax refund, they should deposit the money in an insured bank account. The funds can then be reallocated at a later date (as described in the financial plan) to meet other financial objectives and goals.

Step 4: Develop the Financial Planning Recommendation(s)

[A] Tax Integration

Tax planning integrates with almost every other core aspect of financial planning. A financial planner should start the process of developing tax planning recommendations by reviewing a client's tax returns from at least the previous three years—this will provide insights into previously used strategies. Analysis of previous returns provides an overview of trends in income, expenses, deductions, and credits taken. Past tax returns can also indicate discrepancies in cash flow and net worth figures. Previous returns provide financial planners with needed tax loss carry-forward information. Once a thorough review of prior years' returns has been completed, the client's current-year tax situation as estimated at Step Three of the financial planning process can be used to refine recommendations. Projections for up to five years of returns may also be appropriate, depending on the nature of the client's financial planning needs and tax situation. Projections are an excellent way to inform a client about the interrelationships and tax implications of actions taken within other financial planning domains.

Planning Reminder

Unless a financial planner is also a **Certified Public Accountant** (CPA) or an **Enrolled Agent** (EA), it is prudent to include a tax planning disclaimer when presenting any tax calculations, estimates, or recommendations. A statement such as, "Before implementing the advice provided, please confirm these suggestions with your tax professional" provides some liability protection for non-tax specialist financial planners. The use of a disclaimer also helps promote collaboration with a client's other financial professionals.

As highlighted throughout this chapter, tax planning can be a complex task. Nonetheless, tax planning serves as a foundational element whenever a comprehensive financial plan is developed. Generally, only modest changes will be made to the initial recommendations developed at Step Three of the financial planning process, although it is possible that new client information or data can necessitate a reevaluation.

[B] Applying Planning Skills to the Hubble Case

As already described, there are literally hundreds of tax planning analytical techniques that can be used to identify potential tax planning strategies and products. Recommendation alternatives range from changing W-4 withholdings to reallocating investment assets to capture tax-free interest. Figure 7.7 provides a summary of the final tax planning recommendations that match the Hubble family's financial goals.

Figure 7.7. Tax Recommendations for Chandler and Rachel.

The final tax recommendations developed for the Hubble family match the preliminary recommendations identified at Step Three of the financial planning process. Specifically, Chandler and Rachel should:

- Adjust Chandler's W-4 so that he is withholding less on an annual basis. Chandler should also decrease his contribution to Social Security and Medicare to meet federal contribution guidelines.
- Deposit the money from this year's tax refund in an insured bank account. The funds will be reallocated later to meet other objectives and goals.

Step 5: Present the Financial Planning Recommendation(s)

When presenting tax planning recommendations, it is important to communicate to the client that tax calculations are estimates. As such, the client should expect to see some differences between what has been estimated and the final tax calculation made for tax filing purposes. It is also important to communicate that federal and state tax codes change on a regular basis, which necessitates the need to conduct ongoing tax planning estimates and reviews. While it is important to reduce client fears related to being audited, it is also important to remind clients that, on occasion, tax law changes may negatively impact the client's financial situation. This can be followed with an assurance that an important role of a financial planner is to help a client deal with changes and tax planning threats. Finally, as with other areas of the financial plan, it is worth noting that recommendations are made with the knowledge available at the time of the analysis and that it is likely that recommendations will be adjusted frequently or will change completely at times when new information and data is obtained.

Step 6: Implement the Financial Planning Recommendation(s)

Although some financial planners outsource the calculation and filing of client tax returns to other professionals, it is nonetheless important for financial planners to provide specific steps a client should take to maximize their financial situation. If a referral is made, the timing of the implementation should be clearly spelled out in the financial plan. This ensures that recommendations are implemented in an appropriate manner.

The presentation of a recommendation needs to match a client's information processing style and preference. Figure 7.8 shows how one of the recommendations developed for Chandler and Rachel can be presented within a financial plan.

Figure 7.8. Implementing a Tax Recommendation for the Hubble Family.

Recommendation #1: Deposit this year's income tax refund in an insured bank account.	
Who:	Chandler and Rachel.
What:	A federally insured checking or savings account.
When:	When you complete your federal and state income tax returns.
Where:	With your tax preparer or CPA.
Why:	To protect your refund and ensure that your deposit is protected by federal deposit insurance. The standard insurance amount is $250,000 per depositor, per insured bank, for each account ownership category.
How:	On your tax return (federal and state income tax returns), select the option to have your refund directly deposited into your bank account. You will need to enter the routing and account number on your tax return (our planning team can assist with this information).
How much:	Your entire tax refund. In the future, the amount deposited into the account will be much less than this year.
Effect on cash flow:	Implementation of this recommendation will not affect your cash flow; however, implementation will increase assets on your balance sheet.

Step 7: Monitor Progress and Update

The ongoing monitoring of previously made tax planning recommendations is important because any notable change in a client's financial situation, or a change in federal or state tax codes, can work to create complexity and chaos in other elements of a client's comprehensive financial plan. As such, it is important for a financial planner to monitor, at minimum, each of the following factors (if something is noted, a reevaluation of previously made recommendations should be undertaken):

- Change in a client's goals.

- Change in household status, including divorce, remarriage, birth of child, child turning age seventeen, or child attending college.

- Change in household financial status, including changes in income, loss of job, acceptance of new job, business formation, or closing of business.

- Change in employer-provided fringe benefits.

- Change in client health status.

- Elderly parent(s) moving in with client.

- The receipt and timing of income, especially in relation to ongoing investment asset allocation rebalancing.

- The potential for voluntary and required retirement plan distributions.

- The use of qualified assets for non-retirement purposes.

- Changes in marginal tax rates, deductions, and credit amounts.

Changes to a client's circumstances should prompt a review and/or reevaluation of previously made recommendations. At a minimum, a client's tax situation should be monitored on an annual basis. A client's health, employment status, marital status, preferences, and attitudes can change over time. Changes almost always warrant a review of previously implemented tax recommendations. Figure 7.9 provides an overview of some of the factors that require ongoing monitoring for Chandler and Rachel Hubble.

Figure 7.9. Issues to Monitor in the Hubble Case.

Numerous ongoing monitoring issues are at play in the domain of tax planning. At the household level, life events need to be evaluated at least on an annual basis. Some of the most important life events that may impact the Hubble family's tax situation include:

- Change in employment or promotion for Chandler or Rachel (i.e., change in income or employee benefits) or a career change.
- Purchase of a new home or second home.
- Changes related to Phoebe (i.e., her death, college scholarship, decision not to attend college, etc.).
- Pregnancy or adoption.
- Divorce.
- Chandler's parents moving in with the Hubbles or becoming tax dependents of the Hubbles.
- Opening a business.
- Selling current investment holdings.
- Receiving an inheritance.
- Receiving an unexpected financial windfall.
- Paying significant medical, property, and/or liability expenses.

7.2 COMPREHENSIVE HUBBLE CASE

Many of the recommendations made in other sections of the financial plan will have ramifications in the tax planning section of the financial plan. A tax savvy financial planner can save their clients time, money, and other resources by taking advantage of tax saving strategies. The following narrative is an example of how the tax section within a comprehensive financial plan can be written.

Taxation

Overview of Tax:

Tax planning is a topic that flows throughout all aspects of a financial plan. Nearly all financial planning recommendations are impacted by tax considerations. Financial planning strategies that provide tax savings flow directly to your cash flow statement and balance sheet. Effective tax planning can minimize the amount of taxes owed by decreasing your taxable income via deductions, credits, and pre-tax contributions, which frees up money that can be applied to your financial goals. Our team will work closely with your CPA in implementing tax planning strategies.

Tax Definitions:

The following definitions will be useful as you review the analysis presented in this section:

- *Adjusted Gross Income (AGI)*: Total income less certain deductions.

- *Flexible Spending Account (FSA)*: A tax-advantaged savings account designed to help save for certain out-of-pocket medical and dental expenses. Contributions are subtracted from gross income and a maximum contribution limit is set each year. It is important to note that contributions should be equal to or less than your expected eligible health care costs as any unspent money that remains in the FSA at the end of the plan year will be lost.

- *Marginal tax bracket*: The tax rate incurred on each additional dollar of income.

- *Tax deduction*: An expense that reduces taxable income for tax purposes.

- *Tax credit*: An expense that reduces a tax liability on a dollar-for-dollar basis.

Planning Assumptions:

- Tax filing status: Married filing jointly.

- Dividends are considered non-qualified and do not qualify for reduced tax rates.

- You are in the 5 percent Missouri tax bracket.

- You qualify for one state deduction worth $1,000 and two state exemptions valued at $900 each.

- The state calculation is based on federal adjusted gross income.

- In the event that an investment asset is sold, your basis in all after-tax investments is equal to 50 percent of the fair market value of these assets.

- All investment gains are subject to capital gains tax rates.

Goals:

- Reduce tax withholdings to increase monthly discretionary cash flow.

- Maximize deductible expenses.

- Maximize the use of tax-advantaged investments.

- Monitor the impact of other planning recommendations on the tax situation.

Your Current Tax Situation:

Based on the information provided by you, our team of financial planners has estimated your tax liability for the current tax year. Please bear in mind that our projections are estimates created for planning purposes. It is likely that the final tax estimates for tax filing purposes will be different than the values presented here.

Based on a married filing jointly tax status, you are currently in the 22 percent federal marginal income tax bracket. The state income tax rate is 5 percent.

Based on your current income, you will have a federal tax liability; however, you have a significant over-withholding of taxes from your paychecks. Your state income tax withholdings match closely with the projected tax liability.

Our tax estimates indicate that there is a small error in your FICA withholdings. You will receive the difference as an element of your federal income tax refund. The following chart shows how the tax estimates were made:

Federal Tax Planning Estimator	Assumption:	Married Filing Jointly
Gross Income	$137,309.38	
Long-Term Capital Gains & Qualified Dividends	$1,395.50	
Pre-Tax Retirement Contributions	$7,357.59	
Other Pre-Tax Payroll Deductions	$4,800.00	
Adjustments	$0.00	
Less Exclusions	$0.00	
Reportable Gross Income		$126,547.29
Less Deductions for Adjusted Gross Income		
Educator Expenses	$0.00	
One-Half Self-Employment Tax	$0.00	
Student Loan Interest	$0.00	
Archer MSA Deduction	$0.00	
Tuition Deduction	$0.00	

IRA Contribution	$0.00	
Keogh Contribution	$0.00	
Other Deductions	$0.00	
Early Withdrawal Penalty	$0.00	
Adjusted Gross Income		**$126,547.29**
Number of Children Dependents Under Age 17	1	
Number of Children Dependents Over Age 17	-	
Itemized Deductions		
Medical and Dental Expenses	$1,200.00	
AGI Medical Deduction Requirement	$9,491.05	
Amount of Deduction	$0.00	
Taxes Paid	$8,391.00	
Home Mortgage Interest	$10,379.00	
Investment Interest	$0.00	
Home Purchase Points	$0.00	
Gifts to Charity	$5,800.00	
Other Deductions	$0.00	
Total Itemized	$24,570.00	
Standard Deduction	$25,900.00	
Taxable Income		**$99,251.79**
Tax on Income		$13,069.15
Long-Term Capital Gain and Qualified Dividend Tax		$209.33
Social Security & Medicare Taxes		$9,975.28
FICA Taxes Withheld	$10,286.00	
Tax Withheld or Paid	$19,110.00	
Less Tax Credits		
Earned income tax credit (refundable)	$0.00	
Credit for child and dependent care expenses	$0.00	
Foreign tax credit	$0.00	
Adoption credit	$0.00	
Retirement savings credit	$0.00	
Education credits	$0.00	
Credit for elderly	$0.00	
Child tax credit/Credit for other dependents	$2,000.00	
Total Tax Due or (Refund)	**−$8,142.24**	

324   The Fundamentals of Writing a Financial Plan

STATE INCOME TAX WORKSHEET	
Assumes State Tax Linked to Federal AGI	
State Marginal Tax Bracket	5.00%
State Deduction Amount	$1,000.00
State Exemption Amount	$900.00
Tax Credit Amount	$0.00
Number of Exemptions	2.00
Federal AGI	$126,547.29
State Taxable Income	$123,747.29
Before Credit Tax Liability	$6,187.36
STATE TAX LIABILITY	$6,187.36
State Withholdings	$6,266.00
(Refund) or Amount Due	–$78.64

As noted in the analysis of your cash flow situation (and also in the retirement planning section of this financial plan), you are currently saving approximately $7,355 to your 401(k) accounts. Given that you are in the 22 percent marginal tax bracket, these tax-deductible contributions are saving you approximately $1,618 in taxes this year. Your contributions are still well below the maximum contribution limit permitted by the IRS, so there is potential for you to earn even larger tax benefits in future tax years.

Tax Recommendations:

The following tables summarize the recommendations that have been designed to help you reach your tax planning goals. As with all recommendations presented in this financial plan, our firm is available to answer any questions that might arise and to assist with specific implementation procedures.

Recommendation #1: Deposit this year's income tax refund in an insured bank account.	
Who:	Chandler and Rachel.
What:	A federally insured checking or savings account.
When:	When you complete your federal and state income tax returns.
Where:	With your tax preparer or CPA.

Why:	To protect your refund and ensure that your deposit is protected by federal deposit insurance. The standard insurance amount is $250,000 per depositor, per insured bank, for each account ownership category.
How:	On your tax return (federal and state income tax returns), select the option to have your refund directly deposited into your bank account. You will need to enter the routing and account number on your tax return (our planning team can assist with this information).
How much:	Your entire tax refund. In the future, the amount deposited into the account will be much less than this year.
Effect on cash flow:	Implementation of this recommendation will not affect your cash flow; however, implementation will increase assets on your balance sheet.

Recommendation #2: Decrease income tax withholdings and ensure withholdings for Social Security and Medicare are corrected.	
Who:	Chandler and Rachel.
What:	Federal and state income tax deductions from employer paychecks.
When:	Within the next thirty to forty-five days.
Where:	With your human resources office at your place of employment.
Why:	To increase monthly discretionary cash flow and maximize interest earned during the tax year. Over withholding is similar to making an interest-free loan to the federal and state government.
How:	Obtain a W-4 form from your human resources office. Ask that FICA withholdings be reviewed.
How much:	Your federal income tax withholdings should be approximately $9,000 (if you implement all recommendations presented in this plan), whereas FICA withholdings should be approximately $9,975.
Effect on cash flow:	Implementation of this recommendation will increase cash flow.

Current vs. Recommended Outcome:

You are currently in the 22 percent federal income tax bracket, and you will remain in the 22 percent tax bracket after implementing the tax planning recommendations.

Please bear in mind that tax implications from recommendations made in this section of your financial plan, as well as other sections of your financial plan, are included in the tax estimates calculated in the current vs. recommended outcome section. The recommendations from other sections of your plan that impact your tax liability are summarized below:

- Retirement: Save $16,000 ($11,000 for Chandler, $5,000 for Rachel) annually to your 401(k) accounts, and save $11,000 ($5,500 each) annually in Roth IRA accounts.

- Education: Save $1,800 annually in a Missouri 529 plan.

- Cash Flow and Net Worth: Refinance your mortgage to a fifteen-year mortgage with a 6.0 percent interest rate.

- Health Insurance: Fund a flexible spending account (FSA) with at least $600.

The figure below details the effect that our recommendations will have on your federal tax liability. Please note that the figure includes a $600 increase to your pre-tax payroll deductions to account for the recommended $600 contribution to a flexible spending account. Pre-tax retirement contributions have been adjusted to $16,000 to account for the $16,000 recommended 401(k) contributions (as described in the retirement planning section of your financial plan). You do not receive a tax deduction for Roth IRA contributions. Your home mortgage interest deduction has been adjusted to account for the recommendation to refinance to a fifteen-year mortgage at a 6 percent interest rate. More details regarding the refinance recommendation can be found in the cash flow section of your financial plan.

Federal Tax Planning Estimator	Assumption:	Married Filing Jointly
Gross Income	$137,309.38	
Long-Term Capital Gains & Qualified Dividends	$1,395.50	
Pre-Tax Retirement Contributions	$27,000.00	
Other Pre-Tax Payroll Deductions	$5,400.00	
Adjustments	$0.00	
Less Exclusions	$0.00	
Reportable Gross Income		$106,304.88
Less Deductions for Adjusted Gross Income		
Educator Expenses	$0.00	
One-Half Self-Employment Tax	$0.00	
Student Loan Interest	$0.00	
Archer MSA Deduction	$0.00	
Tuition Deduction	$0.00	
IRA Contribution	$0.00	
Keogh Contribution	$0.00	
Other Deductions	$0.00	
Early Withdrawal Penalty	$0.00	
Adjusted Gross Income		$106,304.88

Number of Children Dependents Under Age 17	1	
Number of Children Dependents Over Age 17	0	
Itemized Deductions		
Medical and Dental Expenses	$1,200.00	
AGI Medical Deduction Requirement	$7,972.87	
Amount of Deduction	$0.00	
Taxes Paid	$8,391.00	
Home Mortgage Interest	$7,669.51	
Investment Interest	$0.00	
Home Purchase Points	$0.00	
Gifts to Charity	$5,800.00	
Other Deductions	$0.00	
Total Itemized	$21,860.51	
Standard Deduction	$25,900.00	
Taxable Income		**$79,009.38**
Tax on Income		$9,070.11
Long-Term Capital Gain and Qualified Dividend Tax		$209.33
Social Security & Medicare Taxes		$9,975.28
FICA Taxes Withheld	$9,975.28	
Tax Withheld or Paid	$7,279.43	
Less Tax Credits		
Earned income tax credit (refundable)	$0.00	
Credit for child and dependent care expenses	$0.00	
Foreign tax credit	$0.00	
Adoption credit	$0.00	
Retirement savings credit	$0.00	
Education credits	$0.00	
Credit for elderly	$0.00	
Child tax credit	$2,000.00	
Total Tax Due or (Refund)	**$0.00**	

The figure below details the effect that our recommendations will have on your state tax liability. Please note that your state deduction increased from $1,000 to $2,800 to account for the $1,800 state tax deduction you will receive from the recommended $1,800 annual contribution to a Missouri 529 Plan (please see the education planning section of your plan for more details regarding this recommendation).

STATE INCOME TAX WORKSHEET	
Assumes State Tax Linked to Federal AGI	
State Marginal Tax Bracket	5.00%
State Deduction Amount	$2,800.00
State Exemption Amount	$900.00
Tax Credit Amount	$0.00
Number of Exemptions	2.00
Federal AGI	$106,304.88
State Taxable Income	$101,704.88
Before Credit Tax Liability	$5,085.24
STATE TAX LIABILITY	$5,085.24
State Withholdings	$5,085.24
(Refund) or Amount Due	$0.00

Alternative Recommendations and Outcome(s):

Please notify our team if you would like to see alternative tax recommendations or would like to see additional tax planning scenarios (including an income shifting strategy that can potentially help shelter even more income from current taxation).

Plan Implementation and Monitoring Procedures:

Our firm will contact your tax preparer to schedule a meeting about ways implement the tax planning recommendations presented in this financial plan. Our team will need you to provide authorization (in writing) for us to share information with your tax preparer and for your tax preparer to share information with our team.

Please let our team know if you have any questions as we begin implementing the tax planning recommendations. Our firm will update your tax analysis each year prior to the annual review meeting; however, please notify us if any of the following events or changes occur, as one of these factors may indicate a need to update your tax planning analysis:

- Changes in employment or a promotion (i.e., change in income or employee benefits) or a career change

- Purchase of a new home or second home

- Changes related to Phoebe (i.e., her death, college scholarship, education savings or costs, etc.)

- Pregnancy or adoption

- Divorce

- Chandler's parents moving in with you or becoming your dependents

7.3 SELF-TEST

[A] Questions

Self-Test 1

A couple, who file their taxes as married filing jointly and have taxable income of $300,000, originally purchased their home for $200,000, but because of escalating real estate prices over the past 20 years, the home is now valued at $1 million. How much should the couple project for capital gains taxes if they sell the house today?

(a) $0, they satisfy the holding period requirement

(b) 20% on $800,000

(c) 15% on $500,000

(d) 15% on $300,000

Self-Test 2

Above-the-line deductions:

(a) Are also known as adjustments to gross income.

(b) May be reduced based on AGI or MAGI.

(c) Include student loan interest and some IRA contributions.

(d) All the above statements are true about above-the-line deductions.

Self-Test 3

True or False: Tax credits, such as the Lifetime Learning credit, reduce a client's tax liability dollar for dollar, while above-the-line and below-the line adjustments result in a tax savings of approximately the amount of the deduction multiplied by the marginal tax rate.

Self-Test 4

All the following are true about business income, except:

(a) To be considered business income, the taxpayer must spend time on the endeavor and attempt to operate it as a business, not as a hobby.

(b) To be considered income, the endeavor must generate a profit (i.e., income is greater than expenses) in the most recent year and five of the last seven years.

(c) Business income and business-related expenses are reported on IRS Schedule C.

(d) Restrictions apply on carrying forward passive activity losses and at-risk losses as it applies to offsetting future passive and non-passive income.

Self-Test 5

If an investor does not elect a cost basis calculation method from the seven reporting methods, _____ becomes the default choice.

(a) Specific lot identification

(b) Average cost

(c) First in, first out (FIFO)

(d) Last in, last out (LIFO)

Self-Test 6

All the following are true, when withdrawing accumulated company stock from an employer-sponsored retirement plan, except:

(a) Assets may be rolled into a traditional IRA with the basis and appreciation taxed at ordinary income tax rates at distribution.

(b) Assets may be invested into a non-qualified account as an in-kind, lump sum distribution subject to net unrealized appreciation (NUA) tax treatment.

(c) When stock in the non-qualified account is sold, the basis is subject to ordinary income rates, the NUA is subject to long term capital gains rates, and any gain since the withdrawal will be subject to capital gains tax (i.e., short- or long-term rates).

(d) Clients who anticipate being in a higher tax bracket in the future might benefit from choosing the IRA.

[B] Answers

Question 1: d

Question 2: d

Question 3: True

Question 4: b

Question 5: b

Question 6: d

CHAPTER RESOURCES

Internal Revenue Service (www.irs.gov).

Leimberg, S. R.; J. Katz; R. Keebler; J. Scroggins; M. Jackson. *The Tools & Techniques of Income Tax Planning*, 5th Ed. Cincinnati, OH: National Underwriter Company, 2016.

Tax Facts on Insurance & Employee Benefits 2020. Erlanger, KY: National Underwriter Company.

Tax Facts on Investments 2020. Erlanger, KY: National Underwriter Company.

CHAPTER ENDNOTES

1. *IRS Publication 550, Investment Income and Expenses.* Available at: www.irs.gov/uac/about-publication-550

2. *IRS Publication 535: Business Expenses*, p. 5. Available at www.irs.gov/pub/irs-pdf/p535.pdf.

3. *IRS Publication 925, Passive Activity and At-Risk Rules.* Available at: https://www.irs.gov/publications/p925.

4. "At-risk limits," *IRS Publication 925.* Available at: www.irs.gov/publications/p925/ar02.html#en_US_2010_publink1000104672.

5. For most taxpayers, adjusted gross income (AGI) and modified adjusted gross income (MAGI) are often the same. Therefore, the terms are used interchangeably in this discussion. It is worth remembering that, for some clients, or in certain situations, there may be a difference.

6. Because of income-based phase-outs or other reasons, not all these options will be available to all clients.

Chapter 8

Life Insurance Planning

Learning Objectives

- Learning Objective 1: Describe the personal characteristics that influence the life insurance underwriting process.

- Learning Objective 2: Compare different types of life insurance policies.

- Learning Objective 3: Evaluate a client's life insurance need.

- Learning Objective 4: Explain how life insurance can be used as a business management tool.

- Learning Objective 5: Describe the role of annuities in a client's financial plan.

8.1 THE PROCESS OF LIFE INSURANCE PLANNING

The origins of personal financial planning can be traced back to insurance professionals' attempts to streamline the process of integrating insurance into a client's overall financial situation. This began in the late 1960s. Before this time, financial planning as a profession, or even a codified process, existed only on a firm-by-firm basis. It is not surprising that the insurance industry had such a strong impact on the financial planning profession from the beginning. Life insurance is, after all, a major component of every comprehensive financial plan. Protecting a client's current assets and lifestyle should be a primary goal of every financial planner. Without first protecting a client's current financial situation, all other suggestions, goals, strategies, and recommendations can be undone by a serendipitous twist of fate. The following discussion describes how the financial planning process can be followed when developing and presenting a life insurance analysis.

8.2 STEP 1: UNDERSTAND THE CLIENT'S PERSONAL AND FINANCIAL CIRCUMSTANCES

A client's life insurance need is typically assessed early in the financial planning process. The logic for the placement of a life insurance analysis within the financial planning process is simple: clients must be adequately insured to cover the fiscal and psychological costs of premature death. This is especially true if a client is married and/or has dependents, a significant life partner, a business, or other financial obligations that carry forward after the client's death, such as a substantial ownership interest in a private firm.

Central to the analysis of a client's current life insurance situation—and all aspects of the financial planning process—is a thorough knowledge of the client's personal and financial circumstances. To complete a comprehensive assessment, this knowledge must encompass an understanding of:

1. the financial goals and objectives to be met by the insurance coverage in the event of premature death;

2. a broad range of personal characteristics that could affect the need for insurance;

3. appropriate product recommendations; and

4. documentation and review of any coverage currently available to the client.

Life insurance strategies and recommendations must be evaluated against certain client **risk classification factors** that determine the availability and cost of insurance. Although financial planners might not be expected to be familiar with specific company underwriting methods, a general knowledge of the factors considered is critical to effective planning. When reviewing a client's risk characteristics, financial planners should consider the following factors:

- Lifestyle:

  o Using tobacco, alcohol, or drugs.

  o Convictions for reckless driving, driving under the influence of alcohol or drugs, or receiving multiple speeding tickets.

  o Participating in sensation-seeking activities, including skydiving, scuba diving, or mountain climbing.

  o Personal character or household financial situation.

- Occupation:

  o Working in a hazardous profession or occupation.

  o Piloting commercial, private, or military aircraft.

- Medical condition or history:

  o Gender, age, height, and weight.

  o Family medical history.

Individuals who, because of any of these factors, have a higher than standard **risk of mortality** will typically be considered **substandard risks**. Depending on the company and the underwriting and reinsurance standards, client insurability factors could result in:

- a denial of the policy application;

- increased policy costs because of the risk factors; or

- the inclusion of riders that exclude certain causes of death or reduce the benefits to the premiums paid, policy reserve accumulations, or the greater of the two.

To summarize, life insurance planning, in particular, exemplifies the need for a broad exploration of a client's lifestyle, personal, and demographic profile. A financial planner must collect the quantitative and qualitative data necessary to conduct a realistic needs assessment that will provide the coverage necessary to fulfill the client's goals. Throughout the life insurance planning process, the financial planner or planning team must demonstrate genuine client empathy, balanced with rigorous analytical skills.

Figure 8.1 provides a review of the Hubbles' personal and financial circumstances related to life insurance planning. The information in Figure 8.1 is typical of what a financial planner should evaluate at the first step of the financial planning process.

Figure 8.1. The Hubbles' Personal and Financial Circumstances.

Chandler Hubble	Rachel Hubble
Age: 42	Age: 42
State of residence: Missouri	State of residence: Missouri
Citizen: U.S.	Citizen: U.S.
Life status: No known life issues	Life status: No known life issues
Phoebe Hubble	
Age: 5	
Life status: No known life issues	

- Chandler and Rachel currently pay $172 per month in life insurance premiums.
- The Hubbles' temperament, personality, and risk tolerance make life insurance an appropriate product for their financial plan.
  - The Hubbles' beliefs and values about the importance of protecting family and providing for Phoebe's education may influence their life insurance purchase decisions. The fact Rachel's family did not provide an inheritance for Rachel might influence Rachel's attitudes about life insurance needs.
  - Because Chandler and Rachel have been responsible in recognizing the need and purchasing policies both at work and privately, the Hubbles' financial situation suggests a higher than average financial knowledge and experience. This is also supported by their clearly articulated views about the many premature death issues.
- The history of cancer in Rachel's family and the death of her parents at relatively young ages may influence her attitude about the need for life insurance.
- Chandler, Rachel, and Phoebe are healthy.
- No one in the family uses tobacco, alcohol, or drugs.
- There have been no convictions for reckless driving, driving under the influence of alcohol or drugs, or receiving multiple speeding tickets.
- Chandler and Rachel do not participate in sensation-seeking activities.
- Chandler and Rachel do not work in hazardous professions or occupations.
- Chandler and Rachel are not commercial, private, or military pilots.
- There is the possibility that Rachel may exhibit substandard insurability risks in the future.
- Chandler and Rachel have a strong desire to take care of the surviving spouse financially in the event of death.
- In the case of joint deaths, Chandler and Rachel would like Phoebe's future education and lifestyle costs accounted for through the purchase of insurance.

8.3 STEP 2: IDENTIFY AND SELECT GOALS

Life insurance planning plays a vital role in the development of a comprehensive financial plan. A client's life insurance need is normally evaluated early in the financial planning process to determine the fiscal and emotional costs associated with a client's premature death. Without proper levels of insurance in place—and funded—a client's entire financial plan could potentially collapse in the event of premature death. If this were to happen, the results could be dramatic. At a minimum, lack of insurance or inadequate insurance can result in liquidity constraints and unfunded tax liabilities.

As such, it is important to identify and select life insurance goals that are appropriate for a particular client. Generally, clients do not have the knowledge or skills to fully articulate their life insurance goals. It is up to a client's financial planner to help guide the establishment of realistic life insurance goals. Figure 8.2 provides an overview of life insurance goals as they relate to the Hubble family.

Figure 8.2. The Hubbles' Life Insurance Goals.

> **Although neither Chandler nor Rachel specifically articulated a life insurance goal, life insurance planning was an important reason prompting them to engage in financial planning. When thinking about their life insurance situation, Chandler and Rachel have the following goals:**

- Determine whether a need exists for additional life insurance.

- Evaluate current policies to ensure that each policy is appropriately priced.

- Confirm that survivors will be protected financially in the event either Chandler or Rachel were to prematurely pass.

Other goals include:

- Pay off all liabilities at the death of the first spouse.

- Maintain a standard of living equivalent to the present time for the surviving spouse.

- Account for the possibility that Rachel's health may deteriorate in the future, making her a substandard risk.

- Maintain adequate life insurance protection to ensure that retirement and education funding goals are achieved in the case of the death of either Chandler or Rachel.

8.4 STEP 3: ANALYZE THE CLIENT'S CURRENT COURSE OF ACTION AND POTENTIAL ALTERNATIVE COURSE(S) OF ACTION

[A] Determining the Need for Life Insurance

The loss of a family member or a person who provides financial support to others can result in financial and emotional trauma. Life insurance can certainly help mitigate the financial loss. Life insurance, within a financial plan, is typically used to help a client's survivors (1) pay for the final expenses of the client (decedent) and/or (2) maintain the same standard of living enjoyed prior to the death of the insured. The need for life insurance is predicated on three basic notions:

1. People earn money during their working lives.

2. The money a client earns supports a desired standard of living.

3. A client's desired standard of living should not need to change because of the death of a household earner.

The first step in the process of analyzing a client's current situation involves determining whether a client needs life insurance, and if so, the amount of coverage needed. Figure 8.3 shows the types of questions that can be used to determine financial responsibility, net worth, charitable giving, and insurability factors to consider when deciding whether a client has a current need for life insurance.

Figure 8.3. Decision Tree for Determining a Client's Need for Life Insurance.

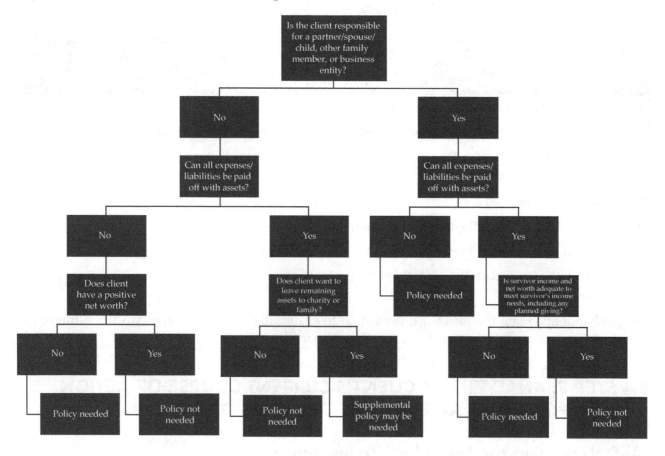

A primary concern should be whether a client is responsible for the financial welfare of another person (e.g., a spouse, partner, child, or parent) or business entity. If the answer is no, the financial planner should determine whether the client's net worth is large enough to meet all final expenses (e.g., medical, burial, tax, and other needs). If net worth is sufficient, and the client has no other legacy goals, then coverage may not be needed unless there are reasons to justify putting a policy in place to ensure future access to coverage.

If a client is projected to have a net worth in excess of final expenses, the issue of charitable donations (or other legacy gifts) should be considered. Similarly, if the client would like to be a benefactor to another person or organization, then life insurance coverage could be warranted. However, if the answer to all these questions is negative, the recommendation to purchase life insurance purchase can be postponed. If this is the case, the financial planner should continue to regularly monitor future circumstances to determine whether and when the need for coverage might arise.

The same issues must be considered if a client has financial dependents. If this is the situation, net worth must be sufficient to meet final expenses, the survivor's future income needs, and if relevant, any planned legacy transfer or charitable gift(s). Otherwise, life insurance protection may be needed. Finally, in the event assets are sufficient to satisfy all anticipated expenses, the need for life insurance as an estate tax planning tool must be considered.

Assuming a client needs life insurance, the analysis process proceeds to answering the following question: "How much life insurance does the client need?" It is likely that the typical financial planning client already has one or more forms of life insurance. Nearly all clients come to the financial planning engagement with some type of **employer-provided group coverage**, unless the client is self-employed. When analyzing the current situation, the financial planner's role involves determining whether the amount of current coverage is sufficient to meet the client's current and future financial goals and objectives.

Numerous approaches can be used to evaluate a client's insurance need. However, five methods are commonly used to estimate a client's gross life insurance need. These methods include the:

- needs-based analysis approach;

- simple income multiplier approach;

- human life value approach;

- capital retention approach; and

- income retention approach.

Planning Reminder

Anyone who is fully insured under Social Security is eligible to have their surviving spouse, and sometimes children, receive a lump sum death benefit of $255. Obviously, this lump sum payment is insufficient to pay for most final expenses; however, this is the maximum benefit through Social Security.

The most challenging, and arguably the most accurate of the methods for determining a client's insurance need, is the needs-based analysis approach. The easiest method, but also the most arbitrary, is the income multiplier approach. The human life value approach, the capital retention approach, and the income retention approach all rely on time value of money estimations.

One reason multiple methods are used to estimate life insurance needs is that each client's circumstances can make one assessment approach superior to another at any given time. As such, calculations made on behalf of a client should be periodically updated. Furthermore, understanding the flaws and adjustments for each method is crucial for preparing a thorough and defensible life insurance needs assessment. Each method for estimating life insurance needs is described below.

[B] Needs-Based Analysis Approach

Of the five methods commonly used to estimate a client's life insurance need, the **needs-based analysis approach** is the most complicated but arguably the most accurate. Nearly all financial planners use some form of a needs-based analysis to estimate their clients' life insurance needs.

Planning Reminder

Given the inherent complexity associated with the needs-based analysis procedure, none of the certification examinations in the domain of financial planning test the use of the technique.

It is important to note that there is no standard formula or set of formulas commonly used when conducting a needs-based analysis. Every financial planner either uses a firm approved methodology or an approach that has been personally developed with experience. A needs-based analysis should be designed to provide an estimate of the level of insurance needed based on the following:

- final expenses (e.g., medical bills and funeral expenses);

- estate settlement expenses, including federal and state estate taxes and other settlement expenses (e.g., publication and mailing, administration, income taxes);

- debt reduction (e.g., mortgage, credit card, auto, or other consumer debt);

- transitional expenses (e.g., education or retraining for the survivor, childcare or homemaker services, or other transitional needs);

- special needs funding (e.g., education of the children, gifts or donations);

- household expenses to maintain or readjust standard of living goals for the survivor, while the children are at home, if applicable;

- household expenses to maintain or readjust standard of living goals for the survivor after the children leave home, if applicable;

- funding to supplement the survivor's needs from age sixty to full retirement age, if needed; and

- funding to supplement or provide for the survivor's retirement.

Use of a life insurance needs-based analysis is predicated on a thorough investigation of a client's preferences and expectations and an earnest attempt to quantify client goals and desires over the life cycle. Furthermore, a reasonable attempt should be made to project the exact cost of all future goals and the probable rate of return and effects of inflation.

Given the number of time value of money calculations involved in the analysis, care should be taken when projecting the future cost of a client's goals. Additionally, caution should be used when determining which goals to fund (e.g., college costs, donations, etc.). It may be unwise to suggest funding certain goals through insurance proceeds (e.g., total mortgage payoff or excessive college expense funding) that in all likelihood would not have been available absent the death of the spouse, partner, or child. Furthermore, a financial planner should consider how a client's feelings of grief, guilt, or other emotional distress might affect how life insurance proceeds will be used.

Figure 8.4 shows the inputs and calculations needed to complete a basic needs-based analysis. In this example, the data inputs come from the initial client data intake form. The calculations (shown in bold/italic) are either summations or present value of annuity due calculations.

Figure 8.4. Input and Calculation Requirements for a Basic Need-Based Life Insurance Analysis.

Client's Income	Dollar Amount
Client's Age	Years
Survivor's Income	Dollar Amount
Survivor's Age	Years
Final Expenses	Dollar Amount
Estate Administration	Dollar Amount
Federal Estate Taxes	Dollar Amount
State Estate Taxes	Dollar Amount
Other Final Needs	Dollar Amount
Credit Card Debt	Dollar Amount
Dollar Amount	Dollar Amount
Automobile Debt	Dollar Amount
Mortgage Debt	Dollar Amount
Other Debt	Dollar Amount
Transitional Child Care Expenses	Dollar Amount
Other Transitional Needs	Dollar Amount
Household Expenses Need in the Event of Death	Dollar Amount

Capital Retention Replacement Ratio	Percent
Investment Rate of Return	Percent
Marginal Tax Bracket (State & Fed.)	Percent
Inflation Rate	Percent
Tax-Adjusted Rate of Return	Percent
Real Rate of Return	Percent
While Children Are at Home	
Number of Survivors	Number
Expense Reduction Ratio	Percent
Household Expense Need	Dollar Amount
Social Security Survivor Benefits	Dollar Amount
Other Income	Dollar Amount
Income Need	Dollar Amount
Years Until Youngest Child Turns 18	Number
Value of Need	*Present Value of Annuity Due*
Educational Needs	
Educational Expenses for Children/Grandchildren	Dollar Amount
From Time Children Leave to Age 60 for Survivor	
Number of Survivors	Number
Expense Reduction Ratio	Percent
Household Expense Need	Dollar Amount
Social Security Survivor Benefits	Dollar Amount
Other Income	Dollar Amount
Income Need	Dollar Amount
Years From Last Child 18 to Age 60	Number
Value of Need	*Present Value of Annuity Due*
Investment Rate of Return in Retirement	Percent
Marginal Tax Bracket (State & Fed.)	Percent
Inflation Rate	Percent
Real Retirement Rate of Return	Percent
From Age 60 to Full Retirement	
Survivor's Full Retirement Age	Years
Age at Death	Years

Income Need While Retired (a)	Dollar Amount
Age 60 Social Security Benefit (b)	Dollar Amount
Other Income (c)	Dollar Amount
Survivor's Earnings (d)	Dollar Amount
Income Need	$a - b - c - d$
Value of Need	*Present Value of Annuity Due*
From Full Retirement to Death	
Income Need While Retired (a)	Dollar Amount
Social Security Benefit (b)	Dollar Amount
Other Income (c)	Dollar Amount
Survivor's Earnings (d)	Dollar Amount
Income Need	$a - b - c - d$
Value of Need	*Present Value of Annuity Due*
Needs Summary	
Immediate Needs	Dollar Amount from Above
While Children Are at Home	Dollar Amount from Above
Educational Needs	Dollar Amount from Above
From Time Children Leave to Retirement for Survivor	Dollar Amount from Above
From Age 60 to Full Retirement	Dollar Amount from Above
From Full Retirement to Death	Dollar Amount from Above
TOTAL GROSS NEED (x)	*Sum of Needs*
Assets and Insurance Available for Need	
Insurance Values (a)	Dollar Amount
Retirement Savings (b)	Dollar Amount
Other Savings (c)	Dollar Amount
Other Assets (d)	Dollar Amount
Total (e)	$a + b + c + d$
NET NEED	$x - e$

[C] Income Multiplier Approach

The **income multiplier approach** is a widely used life insurance needs analysis method. Financial planners like this method because of its ease in assessing the life insurance need. Financial planners who use this technique multiply the insured's current income by a multiplication factor to arrive at an insurance need. Virtually any number from five to twenty-five can be used. For most situations, multiples between five and fifteen are typical, but a financial planner might be able to justify using twenty-five as this multiplier will result in policy proceeds that provides gross salary replacement income for life (assuming a 4 percent payout). The multiplier is usually determined by evaluating a number of issues, including age (or years until retirement) of the insured, number and ages of financial dependents, amount and types of debt, percentage of household income lost, and availability and continuity of a survivor's income. The more factors that increase the need, the higher the multiplier used.

For example, a multiplier of twelve might be appropriate for a client with several dependent children or other ongoing financial demands. A multiplier of seven might be appropriate for an individual with no financial dependents and a low level of debt and final expenses. However, a multiple of fifteen may be inadequate for clients who are living well beyond their financial means or have a desire to leave a large legacy to children or charity. The choice of multiplier is very subjective and almost always based on a financial planner's past experience in similar situations. The formula for this method is:

Current Need = Insured's Current Gross Income × Chosen Multiplier

Planning Reminder

Life insurance benefits are typically received by the beneficiary income tax free. So, while either gross income or net income can be used for a life insurance needs analysis, using gross income can overstate the amount of income actually received.

Although gross income typically is used with this approach, net income can also be easily substituted. In either case, care must be taken when applying this formula as the only means of determining life insurance coverage needs. Because of the extremely general nature of this approach, even after years of experience, financial planners rarely use this as the sole measure of a client's insurance need. However, as noted earlier, this type of assessment approach can provide a quick, ballpark estimate before completing a more in-depth analysis.

[D] Human Life Value Approach

The **human life value (HLV) approach** is used to determine the amount of income expected to be provided by the insured that would need to be replaced upon the death of the insured. This approach is estimated using two inputs: (1) the current income of the insured, and (2) the years remaining until the projected retirement of the insured. This estimated income level can then be fine-tuned for self-maintenance costs, taxes, associated life insurance costs, other assets, or any other reasonable adjustment. The calculation involves solving for the present value of the lost income stream using a present value of annuity calculation, where:

Present Value of an Annuity (PVA)

$$PVA = \frac{PMT}{i} \left[1 - \frac{1}{(1 + i)^n} \right]$$

PVA = present value of an annuity

PMT = insured's current income

i = projected after-tax rate of return on investment assets

n = insured's remaining work-life = (projected retirement age – current age)

If used, the estimate should be recalculated annually or whenever a major career or lifestyle event occurs (e.g., career change, promotion, raise, loss of job, etc.) that results in a change in income. Recalculation is needed because the basic form of the HLV approach suffers from a major shortcoming; namely, the insured's income is assumed to remain static for the life of the survivor. However, it is possible to automatically adjust for this weakness by using a growing annuity formula and an estimation of the insured's expected annual salary growth rate (g), as shown below:

Present Value of a Growing Annuity Due

$$PVGA = \frac{PMT_1}{(i-g)} \left[1 - \frac{(1+g)^n}{(1+i)^n} \right]$$

Keep in mind that there are two other flaws associated with the HLV approach. First, it does not consider other sources of income. Second, it does not consider to what extent an insured's income supports the family. Although normally associated with the income-retention approach, using a **replacement ratio** (also known as a **family member support ratio**) to determine the annual income need for the survivor(s) is one method that can be used to adjust for any possible overstatement in required income. Although little data exists on best practices, financial planners often use replacement ratios ranging from a high of 100 percent to a low of 70 percent. Commonly used standards of practice suggest that within a two-person household, the death of one adult reduces expenses by approximately 30 percent. As household size increases, the percentage reduction in total living expenses declines. For example, for a surviving family of two, three, or four members, the expected reduction in expenses is 26 percent, 22 percent, and 20 percent, respectively. Expenses are generally reduced by only 2 percent with each additional surviving family member.

In addition to household size, other important factors shape the choice of a replacement ratio. These factors include the survivor's earnings potential, the projected rate of return that can be earned on insurance proceeds, and other family issues, such as the need to eliminate debt or save for future goals. The more favorable the future looks for the survivor, the lower the replacement ratio that can be selected.

Planning Reminder

If the goal is merely to replace income until retirement (with the assumption being that at that time the survivor will begin income distributions from retirement assets), recalculation or the purchase of a **declining balance term insurance** policy can be appropriate because, as time goes by, there will be fewer years until retirement. As the name implies, a declining balance term insurance policy is one where the annual premium remains constant, but the face value of the policy declines yearly. These policies are typically associated with mortgage products.

[E] Capital Retention Approach

Similar to the HLV method, the **capital retention approach** bases the needs calculation on the current income of the insured. Unlike the HLV approach, the capital retention approach uses a **perpetuity** (i.e., an annuity payable forever) to determine the need. This estimation method assumes the survivor does not want to liquidate investment assets for current income. In other words, the capital is "retained." This income or payment level can be adjusted for self-maintenance costs, taxes, associated life insurance costs, or any other reasonable adjustment. Once the desired payment is determined, the resulting net income need is then divided by the projected rate of return that can be generated from an investment portfolio, as shown in the following formula:

Present Value of Perpetuity (PVP)

$$PVP = \frac{PMT}{i} + \text{first year's payment to make equation an annuity due}$$

PMT = insured's current gross income

i = projected rate of return on investment assets

The weakness associated with the capital retention approach is that it considers the income stream to continue in perpetuity. This is obviously not the case because people do not live forever. As a result, this approach can overestimate the required amount of insurance coverage needed. This flaw is compounded if an unreasonable discount rate is used. If the **discount rate** (i.e., what the client is projected to earn on any investments) is overestimated, the formula will understate the coverage need.

Because the capital retention approach assumes that a client's income needs to continue indefinitely, this calculation method normally results in the highest estimate of a life insurance need. However, this approach also virtually guarantees that the survivor will not outlive available capital. As a conservative estimate, the capital retention method is the best for ensuring that future generations will receive an inheritance. Therefore, if providing for multiple generations is the goal, this life insurance estimation approach is worthy of consideration.

[F] Income Retention Approach

Unlike the previous two approaches, the **income retention approach** bases the needs estimate on the expected income needs of the survivor. As such, this estimation procedure accounts for income earned or received by the survivor between the death of the insured and the retirement of the survivor. Beginning with the gross income of the insured, reductions can be made for:

1. any continuous income earned by the survivor;

2. the income taxes associated with the insured's income;

3. any preretirement benefits received from Social Security or pensions; and

4. other reasonable adjustments (e.g., annuity payments, interest, or dividend income).

The amount of insurance purchased is assumed to cover only the net amount of income lost. As such, this life insurance estimation approach often yields the lowest approximation of the required insurance coverage. The following formula can be used to estimate the income retention need:

Present Value of an Annuity

$$PVA = \frac{PMT}{i} \left[1 - \frac{1}{(1 + i)^n} \right]$$

PVA = present value of an annuity

PMT = survivor's net income need after considering all sources of continuing income)

i = projected after-tax rate of return on investment assets

n = survivor's remaining work-life = (projected retirement age – current age)

Although the formula for this approach is the same as the HLV method, a financial planner who uses this methodology must first complete an assessment of the client's family annual income need (i.e., total annual expenses and savings). Once the amount for a single year has been determined, the financial planner can use the present value of an annuity formula to calculate the required amount of current coverage that will provide adequate supplementary income over the survivor's future working lifetime. If there is a high probability that the survivor will remarry, and thus will not be overly dependent on insurance proceeds to maintain a standard of living, the income retention approach might be the most appropriate method to consider, despite the estimation of the lowest insurance coverage need.

[G] Common Adjustments to the Annuity Calculations

Although each of the life insurance calculation approaches discussed thus far is based on one or more present value equations, there are subtle differences among the methodologies, primarily in how the payment is determined. With the human life value and capital retention approaches, the payment (PMT) in the time value of money formula is based on the insured's gross or net income. With the income retention approach, the PMT is based on current required replacement income (i.e., gross income reduced by any sources of continuing cash flow available to the survivor). Another difference between the income retention approach and the human life value approach is that the number of years for the projection period (n) is based on the *survivor's* remaining working life, rather than the insured's remaining working life. The distinguishing characteristic of the methods discussed thus far is that each can be altered to consider additional client specific information.

A common adjustment involves changing each formula to account for **beginning-of-period payments** rather than the typical end-of-year convention. Adding a $(1+i)$ to the basic form of the appropriate formula adjusts for this change. Making this adjustment increases the present value outcome by exactly one year of interest to account for the funds being withdrawn before expenses, instead of at the end of the year *after* the expenses. When using the beginning-of-period convention, it is customary to refer to the equation as an **annuity due** rather than as an ordinary annuity.

Another common adjustment involves applying a growth rate to the formula, thus creating a **growing annuity**. All the other variables remain the same, as in the previous equations, apart from an additional variable (i.e., that the insured's income would have continued to increase). This affects the present value need by assuming that the decedent's income would have increased at a fixed rate over the projected time period. The growth variable (g) should be a reasonable estimate of the average annual increase. This adjustment will always result in a higher present value need and, therefore, is a more conservative approach to life insurance needs analysis planning. The following growth-adjusted formula can be used to estimate this conservative approach:

Present Value of a Growing Annuity Due

$$PVGAD = \frac{PMT_1}{(i-g)}\left[1 - \frac{(1+g)^n}{(1+i)^n}\right](1+i)$$

This growth-adjusted formula can provide a more realistic measure of a client's life insurance need by assuming that the client's income will increase over time. By assuming a salary growth rate equivalent to the inflation rate, the insured's life insurance need will increase. As such, it is more likely that the assets provided from the life insurance settlement will be sufficient to provide the surviving household or partner an increasing stream of income over the survivor's life.

Planning Reminder

In some cases, financial planners substitute a household's current living expenses less the survivor's earnings for current income. The decision to make this input choice will depend on a client's unique situation. The use of current living expenses will likely increase the amount of insurance needed. An alternative consideration involves whether current living expenses are defined to include or exclude savings. Including current savings for the cost of education, for example, will increase, and potentially over-estimate, the insurance need.

For example, assume a client:

- earns a current annual income of $75,000;
- expects a 7 percent average after-tax return;
- anticipates a salary growth rate of 4 percent; and
- desires to work another twenty years.

With these assumptions, the amount of suggested life insurance coverage increases from about $850,000 to about $1,160,000 using the human life value approach. The increase is based on including a salary growth rate. Adding a growth rate is prudent if a client's salary is assumed to increase over the life cycle. However, because of this assumption, the total amount of insurance needed will initially be greater, which may lessen the need to purchase additional life insurance in the future.

Another issue worthy of consideration is where the proceeds of a policy are invested. Generally, if the proceeds are taken as a lump sum and invested in taxable accounts, the growth and/or income attributable to the account could be eligible for lower capital gains and qualified dividend tax rates. However, if the proceeds are left on deposit with the insurance company and paid as an installment or life annuity, then any interest received will be taxed at the beneficiary's marginal tax bracket.

Why does this matter when calculating a life insurance need? The reason comes down to the following insight: the survivor can spend only after-tax income. Therefore, some discussion on how insurance proceeds will be received and taxed should be incorporated into meetings with clients. IRS Publication 525, *Taxable and Nontaxable Income*, should be consulted for additional information on the extent to which life insurance proceeds are taxed.

[H] Determining the Additional Amount of Insurance a Client Should Purchase

Each of the estimation methods described above can be used to determine a client's gross life insurance need. To answer the question of how much life insurance a client needs to purchase (i.e., **net life insurance need**), currently available life insurance coverage(s) and selected assets should be subtracted from the gross need amount. First, the additional insurance need is calculated by subtracting the current face value of all in-force life insurance policies from the gross need, as shown below:

Additional insurance need = Gross estimated insurance need – Face value of in-force policies

Second, in nearly all cases, a client's retirement assets, other investments, or additional resources can be used to reduce the gross amount of insurance required. For example, a client may wish, after consulting with their financial planner, to use the equity in a principal residence to reduce the gross life insurance need. Another client, on the other hand, could determine, after consulting with their financial planner, that a conservative estimate of gross need less current insurance is most appropriate. Whatever the case or client, it is the financial planner's responsibility to help clients consider the complexities involved in determining which assets to use in case of death. Furthermore, the true emotional and financial impact of tapping the equity established in a principal residence must be carefully considered. In a worse-case scenario, this could mean selling the family home, which is a very significant lifestyle change following the loss of a loved one.

Ideally, a client's financial situation will be modeled using each of the preceding life insurance estimation approaches to determine the amount of insurance needed.

In practice, however, few financial planners use more than one or two of these methods. A reasonable approach involves triangulating results from at least three of the calculation methods. Figure 8.5 shows a hypothetical range of results from the different calculation methods that can be averaged into a dollar amount.

Triangulation would take, for instance, the human life value ($520,116), the capital retention ($1,242,164), and the needs-based analysis approach results ($2,415,936), add them, and divide the sum by three. The average result, in this case $1,392,739, would flatten out the significant variances resulting from each method. Triangulation can provide a more realistic indication of an insurance need. Note that the triangulation result based on the three approaches is somewhere in the middle. In this regard, it is similar to the average need of $924,008 shown in Figure 8.5, which is the average of all five methods. However, taking an average has its own drawbacks because each method is based on unique assumptions.

Figure 8.5. Client's Triangulated Net Life Insurance Need Based on Different Analysis Methods.

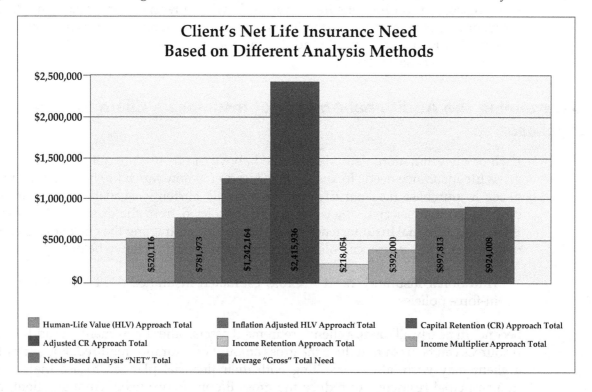

Planning Reminder

Life insurance is sold in units. Each unit is equal to $1,000. Someone, for example, who purchases 100 units of insurance is purchasing $100,000 in face value coverage.

Once a client's insurance need has been determined, that number must be converted into the most cost-effective purchase amount. **Face value break points** (e.g., more or less than $100,000 or more or less than $1 million), can significantly affect the cost of coverage. Insurance companies refer to these price differentials as **insurance bands**, where more insurance could actually cost less than a lower amount in the previous band, or below the break point.

Example. Assume an insurance company's pricing bands are $500,000 to $999,999, followed by $1 million to $1,999,999, etc. Based on a projected need of $895,000, buying $1 million of coverage could actually be less expensive than purchasing $900,000 in coverage because the cost of $1,000 in coverage decreases with progressively higher bands. Asking about break points or bands, or experimenting with different amounts, may provide significant cost savings and potentially more protection.

The following example shows how an analysis of the Hubble family's current life insurance choices and needs results in a pathway to the development of life insurance recommendations. Figure 8.6 provides a summary of the Hubbles' current life insurance choices. Figure 8.6 also shows a screen shot of the life insurance estimation procedure using the Financial Planning Analysis Excel™ package that accompanies the book. Potential recommendations are also provided.

Figure 8.6. The Hubbles' Current Life Insurance Choices and Potential Recommendations.

Type of policy	Policy 1 Whole-life*	Policy 2 Whole-life*	Policy 3 Group term	Policy 4 Group term
Insurance company	Manhattan Insurance Company	Manhattan Insurance Company	Great Plains Assurance and Protection Corporation	Virginia Highland Life Insurance Company
Rating	A.M. Best: A	A.M. Best: A	A.M. Best: A	A.M. Best: A
Equivalent after-tax rate of return	5.50%	5.50%	0%	0%
Death benefit	$100,000	$100,000	1 x salary (not including bonus)	4 x salary (not including bonus)
Person insured	Chandler	Rachel	Chandler	Rachel
Owner	Chandler	Rachel	Chandler	Rachel
Beneficiary	Rachel	Chandler	Rachel	Chandler
Cash value	$8,750	$8,350	$0	$0
Premium amount	$92	$80	Company paid	Company paid
Payment frequency	Monthly	Monthly	NA	NA

*At the beginning of last year, the cash value of the Hubbles' whole-life policies equaled $7,850 for Chandler and $7,500 for Rachel. Chandler and Rachel both received a dividend in the policy equal to $250.

LIFE INSURANCE NEEDS ANALYSIS ESTIMATOR Assumptions		
Insured's Name	Chandler	Rachel
Insured's Earned Income	$102,699.88	$32,496.00
Insured's Age	42	42
Survivor's Earned Income	$32,496.00	$102,699.88
Survivor's Age	42	42
Final Expenses	$10,500.00	$10,500.00
Estate Administration	$13,500.00	$13,500.00
Federal Estate Taxes	$0.00	$0.00
State Estate Taxes	$0.00	$0.00
Other Final Needs	$10,000.00	$10,000.00
Credit Card Debt	$5,500.00	$5,500.00
Installment Debt	$0.00	$0.00
Automobile Debt	$10,396.00	$10,396.00
Mortgage Debt	$130,332.00	$130,332.00
Other Debt	$0.00	$0.00
Transitional Child Care Expenses	$0.00	$0.00
Other Transitional Needs	$25,000.00	$25,000.00
Household Expenses Needed in the Event of Death	$115,000.00	$115,000.00
Capital Retention Replacement Ratio	100%	100%
Investment Rate of Return	7.75%	7.75%
Marginal Tax Bracket (State & Fed.) Before Retirement	30.00%	30.00%
Marginal Tax Bracket (State & Fed.) After Retirement	25.00%	25.00%
Inflation Rate	3.00%	3.00%
Tax-Adjusted Rate of Return Before Retirement	5.43%	5.43%
Real Rate of Return Before Retirement	2.35%	2.35%
Real Rate of Return During Retirement	2.73%	2.73%
While Children Are at Home		
Number of Survivors	2.00	2.00
Expense Reduction Ratio	100.00%	100.00%
Household Expense Need	$115,000.00	$115,000.00
Social Security Survivor Benefits	$35,160.00	$19,104.00
Other Income	$0.00	$0.00
Income Need	$47,344.00	$0.00

Years Until Youngest Child Turns 18	13	13
Value of Need	$537,297.74	$0.00
Educational Needs		
Educational Expenses for Children/Grandchildren	$40,806.38	$40,806.38
From Time Children Leave to Age 60 for Survivor		
Number of Survivors	1.00	1.00
Expense Reduction Ratio	100.00%	100.00%
Household Expense Need	$115,000.00	$115,000.00
Social Security Survivor Benefits	$0.00	$0.00
Other Income	$0.00	$0.00
Income Need	$82,504.00	$12,300.12
Years From Last Child 18 to Age 60	5	5
Value of Need	$393,973.85	$58,735.64
From Age 60 to Full Retirement		
Survivor's Full Retirement Age	67	67
Survivor's Age at Death	95	95
Income Need While Retired	$115,000.00	$115,000.00
Survivor's Age 60 Social Security Benefit	$16,765.00	$0.00
Other Income	$0.00	$0.00
Survivor's Earnings	$0.00	$0.00
Income Need	$98,235.00	$115,000.00
Value of Need	$635,177.67	$743,578.48
From Full Retirement to Death		
Income Need While Retired	$115,000.00	$115,000.00
Survivor's Social Security Benefit	$23,448.00	$26,400.00
Other Income	$0.00	$0.00
Survivor's Earnings	$0.00	$0.00
Income Need	$91,552.00	$88,600.00
Value of Need	$1,824,373.85	$1,765,548.80
Needs Summary		
Immediate Needs	$205,228.00	$205,228.00
While Children Are at Home	$537,297.74	$0.00
Educational Needs	$40,806.38	$40,806.38
From Time Children Leave to Retirement for Survivor	$198,244.19	$29,555.26
From Age 60 to Full Retirement	$229,736.32	$268,943.63
From Full Retirement to Death	$444,313.44	$429,987.01
TOTAL GROSS NEED	$1,655,626.08	$974,520.29
Assets and Insurance Available for Need		
Insurance Values	$168,466.58	$229,984.00
Retirement Savings	$255,000.00	$224,750.00

Other Savings	$0.00	$0.00
Other Assets	$100,000.00	$100,000.00
Total	$523,466.58	$554,734.00
NET NEED	**$1,132,159.50**	**$419,786.29**
ALTERNATIVE LIFE INSURANCE NEEDS APPROACHES		
HUMAN LIFE VALUE APPROACH		
Gross Need	$1,463,035.10	$462,929.35
Net Need (Subtracting Current Insurance & Assets)	*$939,568.52*	*$0.00*
INFLATION-ADJUSTED HUMAN LIFE VALUE APPROACH		
Gross Need	$1,969,386.34	$623,147.55
Net Need (Subtracting Current Insurance & Assets)	*$1,445,919.76*	*$68,413.55*
CAPITAL RETENTION APPROACH		
Gross Need	$1,995,785.23	$631,500.61
Net Need (Subtracting Current Insurance & Assets)	*$1,472,318.65*	*$76,766.61*
CAPITAL RETENTION APPROACH ALTERNATIVE		
Gross Need	$2,659,781.83	$2,729,985.71
Net Need (Subtracting Current Insurance & Assets)	*$2,136,315.25*	*$2,175,251.71*
INCOME RETENTION APPROACH		
Ratio Reduced Current Living Expenses Until Retirement	$115,000.00	$115,000.00
Investment Income Until Retirement	$19,258.75	$17,617.69
Spouse Income Until Retirement	$32,496.00	$102,699.88
Pre-Retirement Social Security and Other Survivor Benefits	$0.00	$0.00
Yearly Income Need	$63,245.25	$0.00
Gross Need	$1,212,799.19	$0.00
Net Need (Subtracting Current Insurance & Assets)	*$982,815.19*	*$0.00*
10x GROSS INCOME APPROACH		
Net Need	$1,026,998.80	$324,960.00
Net Need (Subtracting Current Insurance & Assets)	*$503,532.22*	*$0.00*
Weighted Average Need	**$1,230,375.58**	**$391,459.74**
Needs Approach, HLV, CR, & IR Average	**$1,131,715.46**	**$124,138.22**

The analysis of the Hubbles' current life insurance situation suggests that:

- Chandler is underinsured.

- Rachel is underinsured.

- Based on an analysis of the yearly price per thousand coverage estimate (described later in the chapter), the Hubbles' current permanent life insurance policies are fairly priced.

Based on the life insurance situational analysis and observations, the following potential recommendation are worth considering:

- Chandler should purchase $1,250,000 in additional life insurance coverage.

- Rachel should purchase at least $400,000 in additional life insurance coverage.

- Chandler and Rachel should retain and maintain all current life insurance policies.

8.5 STEP 4: DEVELOP THE FINANCIAL PLANNING RECOMMENDATION(S)

There are a multitude of life insurance planning recommendations, both product and strategic, that can be used to help a client reach their financial goals. An important aspect of the financial planning process involves identifying and recommending prospective life insurance planning strategies that can be used to meet a client's unique financial situation and life goals. Recommending life insurance strategies focused on helping a client reach their financial goals provides an excellent pathway for developing and strengthening the financial planner-client relationship.

A financial planner should exhibit the skills to transform the analysis of a client's situation into actionable recommendations. In order to effectively formulate recommendations, a financial planner must have an understanding of the terms and concepts associated with life insurance and the products and services offered in the life insurance marketplace. The following discussion highlights the basic information needed to develop insurance planning recommendations.

[A] Life Insurance Terms and Definitions

Once all currently in-force policies have been identified, it is important to document the ownership, or titling, of each. Whenever a life insurance contract is underwritten, three parties must be identified within the contract. The **policy owner** is the person or entity who has the right to name one or more beneficiaries. The owner is also entitled to all participating dividends and has the responsibility for paying the insurance premium. Policy owners can, at their discretion, surrender, transfer, or cancel the policy. A policy owner is any person or entity with an insurable interest in the insured. This means the owner can be the insured, a family member, an employer, or a trust. The policy owner must provide evidence of an **insurable interest**, which is defined as possibly incurring a financial loss resulting from the death of the insured. The **insured** named in a policy is the person whose death prompts payment of the insurance policy's face value.

A policy **beneficiary** is the person or entity (e.g., trust, business, or nonprofit organization) that receives the proceeds from a policy at the death of the insured. Two types of beneficiaries exist. The first is a **primary beneficiary**. This is the person or entity that receives the proceeds of a life insurance policy when the insured dies. A beneficiary can be designated revocable (can be changed) or irrevocable. When a beneficiary is named irrevocable, the owner cannot change the beneficiary on the policy without the prior consent of the irrevocable beneficiary. Naming an irrevocable beneficiary also changes the policy owner's rights. The owner cannot receive dividends, take a loan against the policy, pledge the policy as collateral for a debt, or surrender the policy without the written permission of the irrevocable beneficiary. These examples of the right to change, use, modify, or benefit from a policy are typically referred to as **incidents of ownership**.

The second type of beneficiary is a **contingent beneficiary**. A contingent beneficiary is entitled to receive the proceeds of an insurance policy in the event the primary beneficiary predeceases the insured. Married clients with children often list their minor children as contingent beneficiaries to life insurance policies. Unfortunately, this can be a costly mistake, both financially and in relation to the speed at which policy proceeds can be distributed. Most states prohibit a child under the age of eighteen directly controlling monetary assets. Therefore, most insurance companies will not pay benefits directly to a minor. Because children cannot legally receive a death benefit, if a guardian or a trust (with the minor as the beneficiary) has not been named in a will, then the court will appoint a guardian or require that a trust be established to manage the proceeds from the life insurance payout. The insurance company can hold the assets for the child until a court-approved or court-appointed guardian is named to oversee the distribution and investment of insurance proceeds for the minor child. Without proper planning for the distribution of the proceeds to a minor child, the court can require that funds be held in an FDIC-insured account. This safe alternative could, however, preclude sufficient earnings to meet the child's future needs.

Planning Reminder

Dividends earned on life insurance and endowment policies are typically not taxable. The IRS considers dividends a return of premium to the client. However, dividends are taxable *if* total dividends received exceed total premiums paid. This is rarely the case. And, if dividends remain with the insurance company, and the dividends earn interest, the interest is fully taxable.

An individual can be the owner, insured, and beneficiary of the same policy; however, this is not generally recommended. The most common form of ownership is for the insured to own the policy. However, estate tax consequences should be considered. The **face amount of the policy** (i.e., the dollar value of the policy when issued to be received by the beneficiary) will be included in the gross estate of an insured owner who possesses any incidents of ownership. The policy proceeds will also be included in the gross estate if the insured or "my estate" or "for the benefit of my estate" is named as the beneficiary. This might not be an estate tax problem immediately due to the unlimited marital deduction. However, the additional value could increase the estate value for the surviving spouse, thus making the distribution subject to estate taxes (often referred to as a **second to die** issue). On the other hand, if the proceeds are payable to children of the insured with the insured as owner, the proceeds may be subject to estate tax if the value of the estate exceeds the estate tax exclusion.

Even when each party of an insurance contract is a separate person or entity, another problem, known as a **Goodman Triangle** or an **unholy trinity**, can occur. Consider a situation where a wife owns a policy in which the husband is the insured and non-minor children are the beneficiaries. When the husband dies, the children will receive the insurance proceeds on a tax-free basis; however, the surviving spouse, as the owner, could owe a federal gift tax on the policy proceeds if the amount exceeds the annual gift exclusion and the total amount of the wife's gifts exceeds the lifetime gift tax exemption amount. The situation can become more troublesome if the wife, while the husband is still alive, transfers ownership of the policy or changes the beneficiaries, both of which are legal actions available to owners.

Planning Reminder

An adjustment that can be made to all of the life insurance estimation approaches presented in this chapter is to base the calculations on after-tax income. This makes sense, because, in most cases, life insurance proceeds are received by the beneficiary income tax free. This methodology yields a more direct comparison to the income the survivor will actually be able to spend. To do this, simply substitute the after-tax income for the payment (PMT) previously shown. Although this adjustment has merit, care must be taken not to overestimate the tax advantages of life insurance proceeds. Generally, if the proceeds are received from a life insurance contract because of the death of the insured, the benefits are not considered taxable income and do not have to be reported. However, any earnings received on the death benefit would be considered taxable income. In other words, the periodic income derived from the invested settlement proceeds is taxable to the extent that it exceeds the original basis of the investment.

[B] Transferring Policy Ownership

Two methods are available to change the ownership of a policy. Ownership can be transferred to another individual/entity or to a trust. Transfer to another individual or entity with an insurable interest as a gift is irrevocable, and the value of the policy proceeds will be brought back into the estate if the transfer occurs within three years of the owner's death. If the current cash value plus any unearned premiums paid at the time of the gift exceed the annual gift tax exclusion, gift taxes may be assessed and will be due upon the death of the original owner. Gift splitting with a spouse is allowed.

The second alternative is to establish an **irrevocable life insurance trust**, or **ILIT**, and transfer the policy ownership. To remove the policy from the estate, an owner must give up all incidents of ownership. There are costs related to establishing and managing an ILIT. With an ILIT, an owner can ensure that premiums are paid, and with careful planning for the trust, the insured can gift money to the trust up to the annual exclusion amount to pay the premiums. The new owner should immediately update the contract beneficiary form. Owning life insurance in an ILIT is a very effective way to mitigate tax and privacy issues for domestic partners. Keep in mind that the use of an ILIT is most appropriate for cash value policies. Term policies are rarely transferred to an ILIT.

[C] Common Types of Insurance Products

An important step in the life insurance planning process, and certainly a step that must be completed before a financial planner can recommend additional or alternative life insurance, involves having a clear understanding of the different life insurance products available in the marketplace. Although there are numerous types and classifications of life insurance policies offered in the market, most fall within one of the following six categories:

1. **Term life insurance**: The most basic and least expensive life insurance policy, term life insurance provides coverage for a specific number of years, usually at a fixed annual premium rate. Although term policies can be renewable (this is an optional rider), new policies usually cost more because the premium on term policies is tied to the age of the client. Older clients, holding all other factors constant, pay higher premiums. To overcome the problem of clients having to renew at higher premium costs and for longer terms than desired, some insurance companies offer term policies that continue until age sixty-five, a client's expected retirement age, or longer.

2. **Return-of-premium term insurance**: As the name implies, a return-of-premium term insurance policy refunds up to 100 percent of total premiums paid if the policy is held to the end of the term and the insured has not passed. In situations where a policy is terminated prematurely, only a portion of the premiums paid will be returned.

3. **Whole life insurance**: As the most basic form of **cash value insurance** (sometimes referred to as **permanent insurance**), a whole life policy combines lifetime insurance protection with a continual buildup of cash value. Effectively, a portion of each premium payment is used to fund premiums associated with the purchase of life insurance, the costs associated with management of the policy, and cash value accumulation. A unique feature associated with whole life insurance is the level lifetime premium. Loans can be taken against the accrued cash value.

4. **Universal life insurance**: As an alternative cash value policy, universal life insurance allows a policy owner to increase, defer, or decrease the annual premium, and to withdraw the accrued cash value (although this will reduce the policy's **death benefit**, which is defined as the policy's face value minus outstanding loans and other expenses credited against the policy). Universal life insurance also allows a policy owner to change the face value periodically without **proof of insurability**. Like its cousin, whole life insurance, universal life policies build cash value on a guaranteed return basis (approximately 3 to 4 percent annually) beyond a nominal level.

5. **Variable life insurance**: Variable life insurance offers policy owners a fixed annual premium; however, unlike whole- or universal life policies, a variable contract provides an opportunity to earn higher returns on the cash value of the policy. Accrued cash can be invested in stock, bond, and money market investments through subaccount funds. As such, the cash value and death benefit associated with a variable life insurance policy can and will fluctuate over time. It is important to note that insurance companies rarely guarantee cash values within variable products.

6. **Variable universal life insurance (VUL)**: As the name implies, variable universal life insurance is a blended product that borrows features from universal and variable contracts. A VUL, as the product is sometimes known, offers policy owners flexible premiums and a wide variety of investment options within the cash account. As with all cash value policies, outstanding loans accrue interest and reduce the death benefit when paid.

[D] Choosing Between Cash Value and Term Policies

Before recommending specific life insurance strategies and products, a financial planner should consider whether a client's current and projected needs are best met through a term or cash value policy. Figure 8.7 compares important attributes associated with term and cash value polices.

The decision between a term policy and a cash value policy should include several important considerations. Figure 8.8 illustrates the general decision process used to select a life insurance product. The first issue is the goal of the policy. Will the policy be purchased to cover a temporary or permanent need? If the need is permanent or very long term, perhaps greater than 20 years, a client might want to consider a low-cost, cash value policy. Furthermore, if a financial planner determines that a client's current health status is poor, or has the potential to deteriorate significantly, a cash value policy could be an appropriate recommendation. Cash value policies generally last for the life of a client (or at least to age 100). Therefore, no additional medical tests will be required to maintain the policy, even if the client's subsequent risk class would make insurance prohibitively expensive. Keep in mind that some term policies are **guaranteed renewable** and do not require new medical tests, making this product an alternative recommendation.

The review cannot stop at the client's current health condition. Determining a client's family health history, lifestyle, and occupational risk factors can offer insights into the choice of a permanent or temporary type of coverage. For a client who reports numerous issues that could affect the underwriting decision, a permanent type of insurance might be more appropriate than a term policy. On the other hand, if a client needs the maximum level of coverage at the lowest premium rate, a term policy will likely be a more appropriate recommendation.

Figure 8.7. Comparison of Term and Cash Value Insurance Policy Characteristics.

Characteristic	Term Renewable	Cash Value			
		Whole life	Variable	Universal	VUL
Length of policy	1–30 years	Life of insured*	Life of insured*	Life of insured*	Life of insured*
Premium from year to year	Fixed or increasing	Fixed	Fixed	Flexible	Flexible
Cash value	No	Yes	Yes	Yes	Yes
Guaranteed cash value	NA	Yes	No	No	No
Interest earned on cash value	NA	Fixed	Based on investments chosen	Based on annually adjusted fixed rate	Based on investments chosen
Death benefits	Guaranteed	Guaranteed	Guaranteed minimum (may be less than face value)	Option A: guaranteed; Option B: guaranteed minimum (may be less than face value)	No guarantee (may be greater than or less than face value)
Ability to skip premiums	No	No	No	Yes	Yes

*Some policies terminate at a specified, but very advanced, age–typically no earlier than 95 years old.

NA = not applicable

Figure 8.8. Decision Tree for Choosing between a Cash Value Policy (CVP) and a Term Policy.

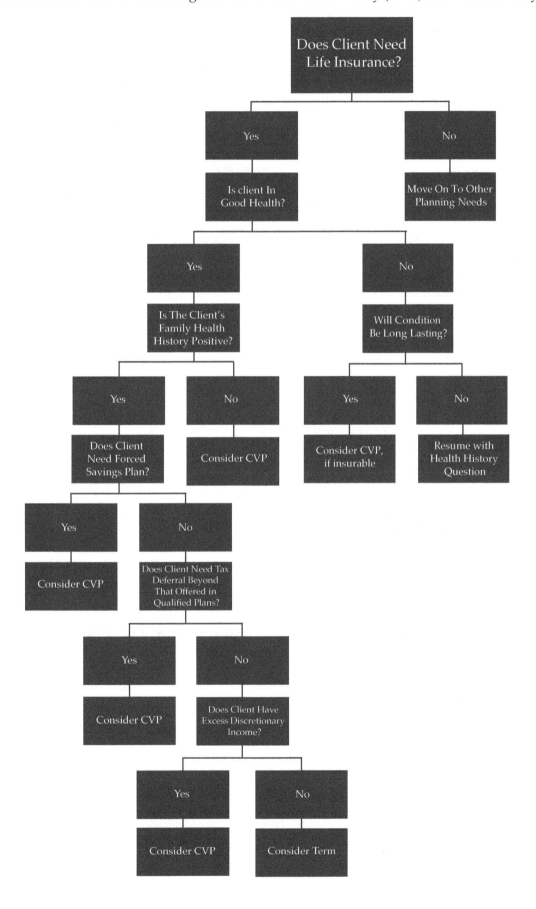

Medical history and coverage period are just two factors to consider when determining the type of policy to recommend. Cash value policies offer a savings component that is not generally available in a term policy. Under certain circumstances, a client might need the forced savings or investment availability of a cash value policy. Access to and the amount of tax-advantaged investments a client has available should also be considered. Clients who earn significant yearly income may find that they are unable to take full advantage of 401(k), 403(b), 457(b), and other qualified defined contribution plans, leaving high levels of income subject to taxation. This is especially true for business owners. High income earning clients may need a way to invest a significant amount of money each year into other tax-deferred investments. Life insurance can serve this purpose. However, it is important to note that putting too much money into a life insurance contract can violate the seven-pay test and result in the contract being classified as a **modified endowment contract** (with less favorable tax treatment).

Finally, it is worth noting that term life policies can be used to provide coverage at a fraction of the cost of a cash value policy if the client's lifestyle, occupation, and health status suggest no underwriting concerns. A term policy recommendation is appropriate when a client:

- qualifies for but does not maximize contributions to defined contributions plans, individual retirement accounts, and other forms of tax-advantaged investments;

- is not a business owner; and

- needs only temporary insurance coverage.

When a cash value policy is considered, a few more considerations must be addressed. The following questions can be used to guide the decision-making process:

- Will the policy be funded in full at the time of purchase or over the life of the contract?

- Will the cash value policy offer an array of investment choices through subaccounts or simply be a "savings account" with the rate of return controlled by the insurance company?

- If a cash value insurance policy is selected, will it be whole life, universal life, variable life, or variable universal life (VUL)?

The decision tree shown in Figure 8.9 can be used to gauge which cash value policy might be the most appropriate for a client.

Figure 8.9. Decision Tree to Guide the Choice of Cash Value Policy.

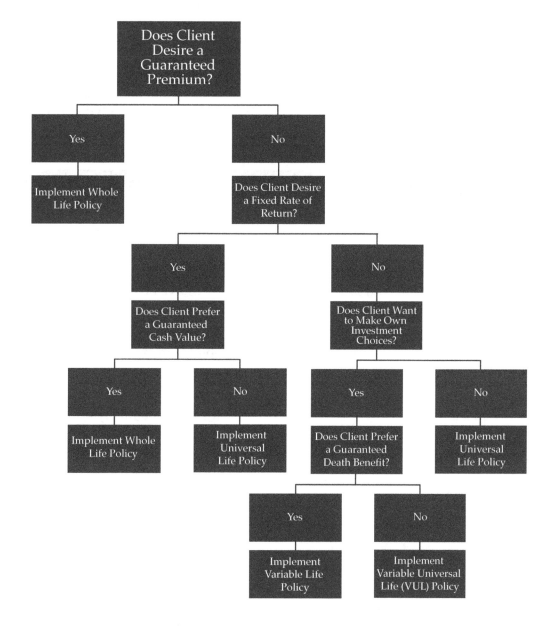

[E] Evaluating an Existing Policy

Once all currently in-force coverage has been identified, an analysis will likely show that some policies should be retained while others should be replaced, canceled, or otherwise altered. Financial planners who make policy replacement recommendations without conducting a **policy replacement analysis** are overlooking an important element of professional responsibility. It is very important to review whether the forms and types of insurance held by a client are appropriate to meet a client's current and longer-term needs. If changes can be made to existing policies to better meet a client's needs, then every attempt should be made to do so.

There may be times when existing policies must be replaced. Changes in tax laws, insurance company strength, and client financial capacity all may warrant a policy change. It is important that financial planners assess the financial strength and default risk of insurance companies before making a recommendation to clients. Five third-party rating agencies and each agency's ratings are shown in Figure 8.10. It is a best practice for financial planners to encourage the use of products from companies rated "A" or higher by any of the rating agencies. A financial planner may need to recommend replacing insurance products issued by companies with lower ratings.

Figure 8.10. Third-Party Insurance Company Rating Agencies.

Rating Agency	Safety Ratings	Criteria
A.M. Best	A++ to F	Insurance company's ability to meet policyholder and contractual obligations based on four size categories.
Demotech's	A" (Unsurpassed) to S (Substantial) to M (Moderate) to L (Licensed)	Measures of solvency
Fitch Ratings	AAA to D	Insurance company's claims-paying ability, financial fundamentals, capitalization, debt rating leverage, and asset quality.
Moody's	Aaa to C	Insurance company's ability to meet policyholder obligations by focusing on investment portfolio and asset/liability structure.
Standard & Poor's	AAA to C	Insurance company's claims-paying ability.
Weiss Ratings	A to F	Adherence to general accounting principles.

Next, attention can turn to policy cost considerations. Term policies can be compared on the basis of premium dollars per $1,000 of coverage, as long as comparisons are for similar periods and face amounts. The complexity of cash value policies demands more rigorous review. Financial planners use a number of methodologies to evaluate the cost-effectiveness of cash value life policies. Commonly used methods include the **traditional net cost method,**[1] the **interest-adjusted net cost method,**[2] the **internal rate of return yield method,**[3] and the **yearly price per thousand method** (also known as the **yearly rate of return method**).[4] One approach that provides a quick insight into the "maintain or replace" question for a cash value policy is based on the yearly-price-per-thousand formula.

The yearly-price-per-thousand formula is effective in determining the cost per thousand a client pays for a policy. Using established benchmark costs, it is possible to compare cash value policies based on the age of the insured. This method is particularly well suited for analyzing whole life and universal life insurance policies.

The information needed to calculate the yearly-price-per-thousand formula is generally available from the insurance company underwriting the policy. The **yearly-price-per-thousand method formula** is:

$$YPT = \left[\frac{\left[(PMT + CV_0) * (1 + i) \right] - (CV_1 + Div)}{(DB - CV_1) * (0.001)} \right]$$

YPT = yearly cost per thousand in coverage

PMT = annual premium payment

CV_0 = cash value at the beginning of the year

CV_1 = cash value at the end of the year

i = projected after-tax rate of return

Div = current policy dividend

DB = death benefit (most often face value)

The interest rate used in the formula should be the rate of interest that a financial planner and client estimate could be earned in another investment with similar safety and liquidity characteristics as those offered in a life insurance policy. The rate of return should be equivalent to a net after-tax yield. Once the cost per thousand of coverage is calculated, this amount is compared to benchmark price recommendations shown in Figure 8.11.

Figure 8.11. Benchmark Premium Prices Based on the Yearly-Price-per-Thousand Formula.

Age of Client	Yearly Price per $1,000 (Benchmark)
Less than 30	$1.50
30–34	$2.00
35–39	$3.00
40–44	$4.00
45–49	$6.50
50–54	$10.00
55–59	$19.00
60–64	$29.00
65–69	$39.00
70–74	$50.00
75–79	$80.00
80–84	$129.00

Source: Adapted from Belth, J. M. *Life Insurance: A Consumer's Handbook*, 2nd Ed. (Bloomington, IN: Indiana University Press, 1985).

There are three rules associated with the yearly-price-per-thousand formula:

1. If the cost is less than the benchmark price, the client should maintain the policy.

2. If the cost is greater than the benchmark price but less than two times the benchmark price, the client should still retain the policy.

3. Only when the cost per thousand is greater than two times the benchmark price should a client consider replacing or exchanging a policy; the new policy should be priced favorably according to the yearly-price-per-thousand formula guidelines.

Planning Reminder

Underwriting issues are an important consideration in the decision to replace an insurance policy. The cost of insurance, based on the YPT formula, may be high suggesting that the policy should be replaced. However, a review of a client's insurability factors might suggest that it would be a mistake to cancel the policy because the client might either be unable to purchase or afford a new policy because of the higher risk classification. A core financial planning rule is this: policies should only be canceled or terminated after a new policy is in place.

Example. In the following example, the yearly-price-per-thousand formula was calculated for a whole life policy owned by Adam. Adam is 36 years old. He pays $6,120 in annual premiums. The cash value at the beginning of the year was $475, whereas the cash value at the end of the year was $500. The policy does not pay a dividend. Adam is willing to assume a 6.90 percent after-tax rate of return.

$$\text{YPT} = \left[\frac{\left[(6{,}120 + 475) * (1.069) \right] - (500 + 0)}{(500{,}000 - 500) * (0.001)} \right] = \$13.11$$

As shown above, Adam is currently paying $13.11 per $1,000 of life insurance coverage, whereas the recommended benchmark for a male his age is $3.00 per $1,000 of life insurance coverage. Given that the premium cost per $1,000 of coverage is more than four times greater than the recommended yearly-price-per-thousand benchmark, a recommendation to replace the policy (assuming the coverage is needed) should be made. However, additional analyses might also be warranted to gain a better understanding about why Adam's premium is so high. It could be that Adam is a very poor underwriting risk, in which case his financial planner may not be able to obtain a policy quote with a lower premium.

This type of analysis offers the client several benefits. First, Adam might be able to stop paying for an overpriced policy. If true, the premium savings can then be used to purchase additional life insurance, if needed, or redirected to fund other financial goals. Second, if Adam is a poor underwriting risk, this could uncover additional planning needs. There may be a need for a larger emergency fund, to increase life coverage on other financial dependents, or to alter lifestyle or other habits to mitigate the detrimental underwriting factors. Alternative sources of insurance through Adam's employer or other groups could offer additional coverage.

Keep in mind that replacing or consolidating policies, for any reason, must be done with care. A financial planner must ensure that this recommendation is handled in the most advantageous manner possible, so that the client does not lose protection or incur undue additional expense. Furthermore, it is important that any existing policy not be terminated until a new policy is permanently in place.

[F] Policy Nonforfeiture Options

Both state and federal laws offer options for terminating life insurance policies. State laws specify standard nonforfeiture options that insurance companies must offer policyholders. Further, the Internal Revenue Code offers certain tax advantages for policy ownership. These consumer protections are briefly considered below.

A **nonforfeiture provision** is available to owners of cash value life insurance policies. This provision provides a policy owner the ability to use the cash value of a policy to maintain some life insurance coverage without paying additional premiums or subjecting the cash value to current income taxation. Owners of cash value policies have three broad alternatives if premium payments are discontinued (i.e., canceled policy), as shown in the Figure 8.12.

The hypothetical policy in the sample nonforfeiture table is for a thirty-five-year-old male smoker with a policy face value amount of $10,000. The client's nonforfeiture options include the following:

1. The client can request that the insurance company return the **cash surrender value** of the policy, as shown in the second column of Figure 8.12. After ten years this would be $1,719. The value of the cash received in excess of the net paid premiums is subject to federal and state income taxation.

2. The cash value of the policy can be used to purchase a fully **paid-up cash value policy**. This will result in a significantly reduced face value policy, as shown in the third column. If this choice is made after ten years, the new policy face value will be $3,690. The benefit, however, is that no additional premiums will have to be paid.

3. The cash value can be used to purchase a **fully paid term policy**. The face value of the original cash value policy is retained in this case. The length of the term policy is then determined by the amount of the cash value available in the policy. If this election is made after ten years, a $10,000 face value policy will be in effect for nineteen years and seventy-eight days.

A nonforfeiture recommendation should not be implemented until a thorough analysis has been conducted and any new policy is in force. The analysis may need to include consultations with both insurance and tax professionals. Second, life insurance obtained by using a nonforfeiture option may likely be costly compared to policies available in the marketplace. Nevertheless, the continued insurance protection might be a better alternative than the cash value, depending on the need for cash or the amount of taxes due.

Figure 8.12. Sample Whole Life Insurance Nonforfeiture Table.

End of Policy Year	Cash/Loan Value	Paid-up Insurance	Extended-term Insurance Years	Days
1	$14	$30	0	152
2	$174	$450	4	182
3	$338	$860	8	65
4	$506	$1,250	10	344
5	$676	$1,640	12	360
6	$879	$2,070	14	335
7	$1,084	$2,500	16	147
8	$1,293	$2,910	17	207
9	$1,504	$3,300	18	177
10	$1,719	$3,690	19	78
11	$1,908	$4,000	19	209
12	$2,099	$4,300	19	306
13	$2,294	$4,590	20	8
14	$2,490	$4,870	20	47
15	$2,690	$5,140	20	65
16	$2,891	$5,410	20	66
17	$3,095	$5,660	20	52
18	$3,301	$5,910	20	27
19	$3,508	$6,150	19	358
20	$3,718	$6,390	19	317
Age 60	$4,620	$7,200	18	111
Age 65	$5,504	$7,860	16	147

Source: Sample Life Insurance Policy. Education and Community Services, American Council of Life Insurance, Washington, DC.

Although the insurance company will issue a 1099-R, showing the gross payout from surrendering the policy, financial planners should calculate the tax consequences when advising a client on their options. To determine if taxes are due, calculate whether the gross proceeds from the policy exceed the cost basis. Any taxable gain is subject to ordinary income tax and should be reported on the applicable income tax form as other income. The following example illustrates the tax estimation process for a $250,000 policy for a thirty-five-year-old non-smoker, who paid $4,430 in annual premiums for ten years.

Total premiums paid:	$44,300
Total dividends received:	–$12,404
Cost basis:	$31,896
Cash surrender value:	$55,487
Cost basis:	–$31,896
Taxable gain:	$23,591

Individual client situations, such as premiums paid for additional benefit riders or any outstanding loan amounts, can change the calculation. For example, dividends are not taxed upon surrender as dividends are normally considered to be a rebate or return of premium. This is true regardless of whether the dividends are taken as cash, used to pay premiums, or used to purchase additional paid-up coverage. If the cash surrender value does not exceed the cost basis, then the proceeds are received tax free and any "loss" does not offset gains from other investments. In the example above, the insured would owe $5,898 in taxes, assuming a 25 percent marginal tax bracket.

[G] Section 1035 Exchanges

A **Section 1035 exchange** is an alternative to using a nonforfeiture option. An exchange is especially useful if a policy has taxable appreciation. A Section 1035 exchange offers more options for policy replacement. Internal Revenue Code Section 1035 allows for a policy owner to exchange a life insurance policy (contract) for another life insurance contract on a tax-free basis. In general, a Section 1035 exchange allows a policy owner to transfer the cash value from one policy to another without paying taxes on the distribution. This is substantially similar to a tax-free "rollover" of a policy's cash value.

The following specific types of Section 1035 exchanges are allowed:

1. a currently owned life policy for a newly issued policy;

2. an endowment contract policy for another endowment contract, with certain restrictions, or for an annuity contract;

3. a currently owned life policy for an annuity contract;

4. an annuity contract for another annuity contract; or

5. an annuity or life insurance contract for a long-term care contract.

Using a 1035 exchange strategy, it is possible to replace a currently owned policy for another newly issued policy by the same or another insurance company. The process of transferring policies on a tax-free basis is analogous to conducting a custodian-to-custodian rollover of qualified retirement plan assets. Although Code Section 1035 can be used to exchange life insurance policies, the majority of Section 1035 exchanges involve annuity contracts. Nevertheless, a Section 1035 tax-free exchange strategy should be considered whenever a currently owned cash value policy is disadvantaged in terms of performance or premium cost. It is important to keep careful records of the exchange for tax purposes and to be certain the new policy is in force before cancelling the original policy.

[H] Accelerated Death Benefits and Viatical Settlements

Chronically or terminally ill clients have several options available to access policy funds prior to death. Policy provisions, known as a **living benefit rider** or **accelerated death benefit**, may be available, depending on the policy. Another option, known as a **viatical settlement**, involves the sale of a life insurance policy to a third party. In either case, the funds can be used to pay for medical or pharmaceutical expenses, caregiving, or living expenses. These options benefit individuals who have exhausted other funds or need the insurance proceeds to make end of life accommodations more comfortable. For federal income tax purposes, the amount received by an insured client from an accelerated death benefit or a viatical settlement is treated as an amount paid under the life insurance contract by reason of the insured's death and thus is generally tax-free. For more information see IRS Publication 525, *Taxable and Nontaxable Income*.

Although exact definitions may change from company to company, an insurance company may pay **accelerated death benefits** to the insured when the insured is critically, chronically, or terminally ill. This is done with a policy feature or a rider(s) that is added to the policy either at the time of purchase or, in some cases, to a preexisting policy. If added, the cost of the rider must be considered relative to the client's perceived need or medical history, and cost comparisons among companies should be considered.

In the case of a policy feature or rider, a portion of the face value of the policy (e.g., typically a stated amount or percentage, such as 25 to 95 percent) is paid to the client once certain medical circumstances have been documented. The balance of the policy is paid at the death of the insured. Some states set specific limits on the percentage amount that can be paid out, while some restrictions are set by insurance companies. Service or interest charges may apply, and there may be requirements that the policy be in effect for a stated period before accelerated benefits are available. Accelerated death benefits paid to the chronically ill on a per diem or other periodic basis are excludable up to a limit that change annually.

For definition purposes, a person with a **chronic illness** is one who has been medically certified, within the previous twelve months, to require:

1. substantial assistance because of the inability to perform at least two activities of daily living (i.e. eating, toileting, transferring, bathing, dressing, and continence); or

2. substantial supervision because of cognitive impairment.

Critical illness benefits are triggered by a diagnosis of specifically listed conditions. A diagnosis of expected death within two years typically triggers terminal illness benefits. **Viatical settlements** occur when a terminally ill insured client sells a life insurance policy to a third party. Settlement values vary greatly, but a payout of 40 to 85 percent of the death benefit is typical, depending on the insured's life expectancy. A viatical settlement provides the dying person with immediate funds that can be used to pay medical expenses. The face value of the policy is paid to the viatical holder at the death of the insured. Individual state law is used to define what is meant by the term terminal illness. Generally, someone has a **terminal illness** if life expectancy is twenty-four months or less from the date that a physician certifies that death is reasonably expected as a result of the insured's illness or physical condition. When considering a viatical settlement, it is important to consider immediate benefits to the insured, the household, and caregivers compared to the longer-term effect of limited or no insurance proceeds for the beneficiary. If selected, the cost of the viatical settlement should be compared across different companies to get the maximum benefit for the client.

[I] Life Settlements

For elderly clients who no longer need life insurance or estate tax protection, or can no longer afford the premium costs, **life settlements** or selling a policy to a life settlement company may be a viable financial planning alternative. To be worthwhile, the settlement must be for more than the cash surrender value. If a life settlement is taken, the client benefits from the immediate availability of the funds that can be used to supplement income or meet expenses and bills. Additionally, the client avoids the premiums required to maintain the policy, which is a form of future savings or an addition to the client's cash flow. At the death of the insured, the face value of the policy is paid to the settlement company.

When considering a life settlement, it is important to recognize that life settlement companies prefer that the insured be at least sixty-five to seventy years old with a policy providing a minimum face value of $250,000. Some settlement companies will consider $100,000 policies, depending on the age and health of the insured. Other guidelines apply that could affect the availability of a settlement offer. Policy owners with a life expectancy of less than twelve years are preferred, but those in declining health could receive a higher offer. The policy should have been in force for two years, and the client should be expected to live for at least two more years. Contingent on the cost basis of the policy, the cash surrender value, and the settlement offer, the life settlement payment could be taxable. If a life insurance policy is surrendered or sold for a lump sum amount prior to the death of the insured, any amount received in excess of the net premiums paid will be considered taxable as income. Losses are not recognized for tax purposes. Fees or commissions also apply, so it is important to consider offers from multiple settlement firms to get the maximum benefit for the client.

[J] Annuities

Annuities, once considered the product choice of retirees and highly risk-averse investors, have increasingly gained popularity as a way to lock in higher rates of return while reducing portfolio volatility risk. For many investors, annuity products have replaced fixed-income holdings in asset allocation models. Given the importance and use of annuities, it is important for financial planners to understand the definitions and general operating characteristics of these products in the context of investing and insurance planning.

Annuities are products marketed and sold by insurance companies. Annuities come in two general forms: deferred and immediate income, although it is also possible to purchase hybrid annuity products. A **deferred annuity** is a tax-deferred investment that can be funded with a lump sum contribution, a series of payments, or a combination of these two approaches. When a deferred annuity is purchased, the owner must choose either a fixed or variable annuity option. Investors who are interested primarily in security and complete minimization of variability in the investment account typically purchase a **fixed annuity**. Fixed deferred annuities are similar to certificates of deposit in that the insurance company provides a guaranteed interest rate on the account balance for a fixed number of years. However, unlike certificates of deposit, FDIC insurance does not apply. At the end of the period, the interest rate credited to the account can be changed.

Variable deferred annuities tend to be popular with younger and more aggressive investors. The term **variable annuity** refers to the type of investments held within the annuity account. Whereas a fixed deferred annuity provides a guaranteed interest rate on assets held in the annuity, the rate of return on a variable product is based on the investments held in the account. Usually, variable products offer mutual funds and guaranteed investment contracts as investment options. It is very important to note that, unlike typical mutual funds that can often be purchased without a commission, fund and investment choices within annuity products tend to be more expensive. Insurance companies typically charge fees and expenses above and beyond what the funds levy. Furthermore, almost all deferred annuity products contain **early distribution penalties** that can last up to fifteen years, meaning any distribution will be reduced by the **surrender charge**. Together, fees, expenses, and surrender charges make annuity products an expensive investment alternative.

Financial planners often recommend either a fixed or variable deferred annuity product to clients who have maximized the use of qualified retirement plans and other tax-deferred investment alternatives. Because a 10 percent penalty could be imposed on distributions before age fifty-nine-and-half, these products are inappropriate for clients seeking short-term or emergency fund investment choices. It is also important to remember that annuities avoid probate by means of a beneficiary designation. Account values can be paid as a lump sum (over a period not to exceed five years) or as a lifetime stream of income at the death of the annuitant. A beneficiary spouse can elect to assume ownership of the annuity, thus maximizing the tax deferral of the product.

Immediate income annuities represent a large segment of the annuity marketplace. Income annuities are usually purchased by retirees or others who need a guaranteed (although not federally insured) source of income for life or a fixed period. The primary difference between a deferred annuity and an income annuity is that immediate income annuity holders receive income from the annuity on a regular basis rather than deferring income to a later period. (A deferred annuity can be converted to an income annuity at a future point in time.) When a fixed-income annuity is purchased, the insurance company guarantees an income stream for a predetermined period. Some annuity products can even include a **cost-of-living rider**, which is a form of inflation protection. It is important to note, however, that this guarantee is based on the insurer's claims-paying ability and financial strength. As is the case when purchasing any insurance product, financial planners should always assess the strength of an insurance company before basing a purchase recommendation on either the rate of return offered or the commission paid to the financial planner.

Although not as popular as fixed-income annuities, **immediate variable annuity** products are also available. To maintain certain tax advantages, insurance companies are required to guarantee income for life from a variable annuity; however, insurance companies are not required to guarantee the amount of each payment. In effect, the level of payout from a variable annuity will depend on the investment choices made in the account. This product is most appropriate for younger clients who have a relatively high tolerance for financial risk.

Distributions and rules associated with immediate annuities can get quite complex. Income payments from annuity products vary by company, but generally a client's gender, age, and purchase value are used to estimate either guaranteed or projected income from an annuity product. Those who choose a variable annuity may receive more or less than the projected annual income amount based on the underlying performance of the investments in the account. When a client is married, a **joint and survivor's annuity distribution** choice can be selected. A 100 percent and 50 percent survivor benefit is traditional.

> *Example.* To illustrate the distribution of annuity income, consider a sixty-one-year old male client who purchases a $500,000 immediate fixed-income annuity.[5]

- A typical non-survivor annuity product will guarantee him a monthly payment of $2,248. At death, his spouse, also age sixty-one, will receive no benefit.

- A 100 percent guaranteed lifetime survivor benefit option will reduce the monthly income stream to $1,984, with all payments continuing for the life of the spouse.

- A 50 percent survivor option will generate a dollar amount between these two extremes, say, $2,100 per month in current income, which will leave $1,050 per month to the surviving spouse, with all payments ending at her death.

Many financial planners and clients worry about the irrevocable nature of immediate income annuity products. Although it is true that if a traditional product is purchased (thus maximizing current monthly income) all asset values held in the annuity will revert to the insurance company at the death of the owner or last beneficiary, certain income distribution alternatives reduce the possibility of purchasing an annuity, receiving a few payments, passing away, and forfeiting the present value of the asset. Today, most insurance companies provide a ten- or twenty-year **guaranteed payout schedule.** Using the preceding example, if the client purchased a 100 percent survivor product with a twenty-year payout guarantee, the initial monthly payment would be $2,181 per month. If both the husband and wife were to pass away in less than twenty years, the insurance company would guarantee distributions to additional beneficiaries until the twenty-year period was fulfilled.

As this discussion highlights, the use of annuity products in a client's financial plan has grown beyond the retiree market. Today, financial planners commonly incorporate fixed-income annuity products into portfolios as a substitute for traditional fixed-income holdings. The risk-return tradeoff (the risk being the financial stability of the insurance company) must always be considered, but in cases where a guaranteed long-term fixed rate is needed, an annuity could be an important tool in the insurance and financial planning process. For clients who have maximized other forms of deferred savings, variable annuity products that allow financial planners to actively manage portfolio assets can also be powerful investment tools.

[K] Life Insurance Strategies for Small Business Owners

Life insurance plays an extremely important role for the owner of a small or closely held business, especially when the business is the primary source of income and perhaps the bulk of a client's net worth. When an owner dies, revenue can decline or cease and there may not be an easy way to extract value from the business to support the deceased's survivors. Many typical estate planning needs are amplified in the case of business ownership. Without an effective estate plan, including a **business succession plan**, the business may have to close or be liquidated to pay estate taxes. With the proper use of life insurance, a business owner can plan to provide the liquidity needed to pay any estate tax liability.

Beyond immediate liquidity needs, there are two additional reasons that life insurance is so critically important to small business owners: (1) key person insurance to protect the company and (2) buy-sell funding agreements to protect partners and co-owners.

Key person insurance is life insurance on the vital person or persons who are crucial to the financial success of a business. The purpose of key person insurance is to help a company survive the financial loss associated with the death of the person who makes the business operate efficiently and profitably. The business might not be viable without the services of the owner or another key person. Therefore, to ensure the continuation of the business, it is common for the company to purchase a life insurance policy on the **key employee**(s), pay the premium(s), and be the beneficiary of the policy(ies). If the insured dies, the company receives the face value of the insurance. The company can then use insurance proceeds for expenses until a replacement manager can be found, or if necessary, pay off debts, distribute money to investors, pay severance to employees, or buy out the ownership interests of other owners. Proceeds can also be used to close the business in an orderly fashion. In a tragic situation, key person insurance provides companies with options other than immediate bankruptcy.

A **buy/sell agreement** reduces the number of difficulties a business faces when an owner dies by allowing the business to continue. The agreement is typically between the owners, an owner and a family member, the owners and the business entity, or an owner and employees.

Buy-sell agreements are typically defined as either a cross-purchase plan or an entity purchase plan. In either case, in a partnership the agreement facilitates the surviving partners' purchase of the deceased partner's business interest from the heirs or the estate at an agreed-upon price. Buy-sell agreements work similarly for limited liability companies (LLC) and LLC members, and for corporations and corporate shareholders.

With a **cross-purchase plan,** each partner, not the partnership, buys a life insurance policy on each of the other partners. Each partner owns, pays the premiums, and is the beneficiary of the insurance policies on the other partners in an amount equal to each partner's investment or business equity as set forth in the buy/sell agreement. At a partner's death, the other partners purchase the deceased partner's interest in the partnership using the insurance proceeds.

In an **entity purchase plan** the individual partners enter into an agreement with the **partnership** (the legal entity representing the business), which owns, pays the premiums, and is the beneficiary of the policies. At a partner's death, the partnership purchases the deceased partner's interest in the partnership. This plan only works when more than two partners are involved.

It is important that whatever plan is chosen, it include a funding method. There are several options for the future business owner to fund a buy-sell agreement, including borrowing funds, establishing a savings account within the company, or establishing an employee stock ownership plan. However, the death of an owner typically creates a significant financial burden on the business and its remaining partners. To mitigate this risk, many buy-sell agreements are established to be funded with the proceeds of life insurance, although life insurance used in this manner can be very expensive because the size of the policy tends to be quite large.

A buy/sell agreement is typically executed as follows:

- An agreement is prepared that sets forth the entity or the prospective business owner's obligation to buy, the price of the business, and the method of payment. (The price should be periodically reviewed based on a current valuation of the business.)

- The entity or the prospective business owner purchases, funds, and is named the beneficiary of a life insurance policy on the current owner, as the insured.

- Upon the death of the owner, the death benefit of the insurance policy is used to buy the business, shares, or interest from the decedent's estate.

Because two-party partnerships are automatically dissolved with the death of one partner, a buy-sell agreement is especially important. This business continuation method can be used with partnerships, limited liability companies, or closely held private corporations.

[L] Applying Planning Skills to the Hubble Case

Generally, only modest changes will be made to the initial recommendations developed at Step Three of the financial planning process, although it is possible that new client information or data can necessitate the need for a reevaluation. Figure 8.13 provides a summary of the final life insurance recommendations that match the Hubble family's financial goals.

Figure 8.13. Life Insurance Recommendations for Chandler and Rachel.

Note: The final life insurance recommendations developed for the Hubble family match the preliminary recommendations identified at Step Three of the financial planning process. Specifically, Chandler and Rachel should:

- Maintain Currently Held Policies

    o Based on this recommendation, Rachel and Chandler should keep currently owned life insurance policies. Each has group term life insurance provided by an employer; each has a whole life policy with a face value of $100,000.

    o The permanent insurance provides long-term coverage to meet expenses, including final medical expenses, burial expenses, adjustment period expenses, and miscellaneous taxes due.

    o This approach also works to cover Rachel in case her health deteriorates. This strategy also provides some protection in case she leaves her current employer and loses her group term insurance.

    o Chandler and Rachel should consider making cross gifts of their privately purchased policies in order to reduce future estate tax liabilities. An explanation of the three-year gifting rule should be provided.

    o A contingent beneficiary for each policy should be named, such as Phoebe, but with provisions in each person's will describing how to manage funds should Chandler or Rachel die before Phoebe reaches the age of majority.

- Purchase a $1,250,000 Twenty-Year Level Term Insurance for Chandler

    o Chandler has an additional life insurance need of approximately $1,250,000.

        ♦ This need is temporary.

        ♦ In the event that Chandler lives until retirement, his financial plan will provide for future expenses.

        ♦ A twenty-year term policy matches the duration of the family's two largest cash flow expenses: the mortgage and college savings.

        ♦ In twenty years, the mortgage will be paid off, assuming a fifteen-year refinance recommendation is implemented. Further, Phoebe will have completed college. At that time, the family's need for a large amount of insurance will have diminished.

        ♦ The policy should be purchased with a disability premium waiver rider.

        ♦ It may be possible to purchase a policy for $960 per year in premium (more or less depending on provider).

        ♦ Rachel should own the policy.

            ▪ This ownership titling procedure will keep the face value of the policy out of Chandler's estate should he predecease Rachel.

            ▪ Rachel should be named as the beneficiary with a minor's trust for Phoebe as the contingent beneficiary.

- Purchase a $400,000 Twenty-Year Level Term Insurance for Rachel

  - Rachel has an additional life insurance need of approximately $400,000.

    - This need is temporary.

    - In the event that Rachel lives until retirement, her financial plan will provide for future expenses.

    - A twenty-year term policy matches the duration of the family's two largest cash flow expenses: the mortgage and college savings.

    - In twenty years, the mortgage will be paid off, assuming a twenty-year refinance recommendation is implemented. Further, Phoebe will have completed college. At that time, the family's need for a large amount of insurance will have diminished.

    - The policy should be purchased with a disability premium waiver rider.

    - It may be possible to purchase a policy for $580 per year in premium (more or less depending on provider).

    - Chandler should own the policy.

      - This ownership titling procedure will keep the face value of the policy out of Rachel's estate should she predecease Chandler.

      - Chandler should be named as the beneficiary with a minor's trust for Phoebe as the contingent beneficiary.

8.6 STEP 5: PRESENT THE FINANCIAL PLANNING RECOMMENDATION(S)

The presentation of life insurance recommendations should begin by reviewing the risk classification factors used in the life insurance underwriting process. Client lifestyle characteristics, such as using tobacco, alcohol, or drugs; a history of reckless driving; and participating in sensation-seeking activities are indicators of potential underwriting problems. These same factors, as well as a client's tolerance for risk and financial product preferences, help shape the development of recommendations. These factors should be presented to and reviewed with the client.

The life insurance analysis procedures used to estimate an insurance need should also be reviewed. Although clients may not ask, it is important for a financial planner to be able to articulate the assumptions underlying the use of a needs-based, human life value, capital retention, income retention, and simple income multiplier approach. As noted earlier in the chapter, rather than relying on one or two of these assessment techniques, the final recommendation should be one based on a triangulation of results.

Additionally, the presentation of recommendations should include information about the financial strength of the insurance companies underwriting the recommended products. A competent financial planner should be able to identify the advantages and disadvantages associated with different policy types and companies.

Figure 8.14 highlights some of the important factors to consider when presenting life insurance recommendations to Chandler and Rachel Hubble.

Figure 8.14. Factors to Consider When Presenting Life Insurance Recommendations.

An important consideration when presenting life insurance recommendations to Chandler and Rachel involves confirming that the twenty-year term on Chandler's policy matches the Hubbles' expectations and preferences. Additionally, it is important to document that Chandler and Rachel can afford the additional premiums associated with the purchase recommendation.

Steps should also be taken to explain the importance of beneficiary designations. Specifically, Chandler and Rachel should be counseled to understand that it is counterproductive to have insurance proceeds payable to their estates. Given Phoebe's age, Chandler and Rachel should also consider adding a contingent beneficiary to each policy. Alternatives can also be suggested, such as naming a trust or Phoebe's guardian as the beneficiary for the benefit of Phoebe. Care must be exercised in naming the guardian. These decisions should meet the wishes of the family and be coordinated with the estate plan for Chandler and Rachel.

8.7 STEP 6: IMPLEMENT THE FINANCIAL PLANNING RECOMMENDATION(S)

When implementing life insurance recommendations, it is very important to be clear about who is responsible for actual implementation. The action could be the responsibility of the financial planner and the financial planner's staff, or it could be the responsibility of the client, working with an insurance agent or broker. Prior to implementation, a financial planner should double check policy and contract features, as well as consider income and estate tax implications. Such considerations are important when implementing recommendations for new insurance products, as well as when conducting periodic reviews of previously implemented recommendations. An important role played by a financial planner includes working with the client and insurance, tax, and estate planning professionals, as applicable, to formulate or mitigate insurance planning issues.

During the implementation process, it is important to remember that the decision to purchase either a term or cash value policy is more complicated than just implementing a "buy term and invest the difference" strategy. Information in this chapter shows that every insurance recommendation should be based on a client's need for a policy. Permanent cash value policies might be more appropriate when a client has a long-term enduring financial need. In situations where the financial need is shorter and temporary, term insurance may be more appropriate. Other factors to review prior to implementation of recommendations include understanding the medical history of the client and their family. Additionally, the aspect of forced savings can be important for some clients, resulting in an implementation strategy that requires very explicit instructions related to premium payments.

The presentation of a recommendation needs to match a client's information processing style and preferences. Figure 8.15 shows how one of the recommendations developed for Chandler and Rachel can be presented within a financial plan.

Figure 8.15. Implementing a Life Insurance Recommendation for the Hubble Family.

Recommendation #1: Purchase a twenty-year $1,250,000 term life insurance policy with Chandler as the insured.	
Who:	Chandler.
What:	Twenty-year annually renewable convertible term life insurance policy with Rachel named as the owner and primary beneficiary. The policy should include a disability waiver.
When:	Within the next thirty to forty-five days.
Where:	Our firm will provide you with specific quotes that satisfy your requirements.
Why:	To ensure financial and medical security for your family.
How:	Our firm will assist by discussing the underwriting issues, required application, and medical information.
How much:	$1,250,000.
Effect on cash flow:	The purchase will reduce cash flow by the estimated annual premium of $960.

8.8 STEP 7: MONITOR PROGRESS AND UPDATE

It is important for life insurance recommendations to be reviewed and monitored on an ongoing basis. A key element associated with the monitoring process involves conducting a policy replacement analysis, especially when a client owns a cash value life insurance policy. The yearly price per thousand method formula can be used to estimate the appropriate cost of a cash value life insurance policy. Benchmarks developed by Joseph Belth can be used to determine if a policy should be replaced.

In situations where a policy does need replacement, or when a client may no longer need coverage, nonforfeiture techniques can be used manage insurance holdings. The use of Section 1035 exchange techniques is also an important aspect of life insurance monitoring.

It goes without saying that a client's unique characteristics and preferences should be evaluated on an ongoing basis. Changes to a client's circumstances should prompt a review and/or reevaluation of previously made recommendations. At a minimum, a client's need for life insurance should be monitored annually. A client's health, employment status, marital status, preferences, and attitudes can change over time. Changes almost always warrant a review of previously implemented recommendations. Figure 8.16 provides an overview of some of the factors that require ongoing monitoring for Chandler and Rachel Hubble.

Figure 8.16. Issues to Monitor in the Hubble Case.

Numerous ongoing monitoring issues are at play in the domain of life insurance planning. It is important to evaluate the financial strength of each insurance company in which the Hubble family has a policy. At the household level, life events also need to be evaluated at least on an annual basis. Some of the most important life events that may impact the Hubble family's life insurance needs include:

- Change in employment or promotion for Chandler or Rachel (i.e., change in income or employee benefits) or a career change.

- Purchase of a new home or second home.

- Changes related to Phoebe (i.e., her death, college scholarship, decision not to attend college, etc.).

- Inheritance from Chandler's parents.

- Pregnancy or adoption.

- Divorce.

- New, more dangerous hobbies or jobs.

- Disability of a family member.

8.9 COMPREHENSIVE HUBBLE CASE

Recommendations related to life insurance coverage is a key element within most comprehensive financial plans. Life insurance planning is one area of the general insurance planning process that can be analyzed and managed by a financial planner, even if the financial planner is not an insurance agent or broker. Ensuring that a client has necessary insurance in place is a key element to strengthening a client's financial capacity. The following narrative is an example of how the life insurance section within a comprehensive financial plan can be written.

Life Insurance

Overview of Life Insurance:

Life insurance planning is an essential part of nearly all comprehensive financial plans, especially when a family is responsible for the financial welfare of dependents. The premature death of a spouse or loved one can be devastating. A loss will only be compounded if survivors are left with insufficient funds to maintain their standard of living and meet other end-of-life expenses. Life insurance can be used to:

- Maintain or increase a survivor's standard of living.

- Provide adequate funds to pay for final expenses such as funeral costs.

- Provide liquidity while the decedent's estate is being settled.

- Pay off a survivor's debt.

- Fund client-specific goals.

Life Insurance Definitions:

The following definitions will be useful as you review the analysis presented in this section:

- *1035 exchange*: Allows a policy owner to transfer the cash value from one policy to another without paying taxes on the distribution.

- *Needs-based analysis approach*: An in-depth method of analysis used to determine how much life insurance coverage a person needs. This is the preferred method used to project the financial needs and costs of a client in the event of a premature death. These needs are discounted for inflation, taxes, and potential investment returns in order to provide the most precise and accurate estimate possible.

- *Non-forfeiture provision*: Gives a policy owner the ability to use the cash value of a policy to maintain some life insurance coverage without paying additional premiums or subjecting the cash value to current income taxation.

- *Replacement ratio*: An assumption used to reduce the amount of annual income needed by survivors.

- *Term life insurance*: Provides coverage for a specific number of years, usually at a fixed annual premium rate.

- *Whole life insurance*: Combines lifetime insurance protection with a continual buildup of cash value. A portion of each premium payment is used to fund premiums associated with the purchase of life insurance, the cost associated with management of the policy, and cash value accumulation.

- *Yearly-price-per-thousand method*: This formula is used to evaluate the cost-effectiveness of cash value life policies.

  - An estimate using the method is based on a benchmark for your age group, which suggests that annual premiums for cash value life insurance should cost between $4 and $8 for every $1,000 of coverage you purchase.

Planning Assumptions:

- Assets available at Chandler's death include his IRA and 401(k) plan.

- Assets available at Rachel's death include her IRA, her 401(k) plan, the annuity, and her IRA rollover account.

- You will need $115,000 in before-tax yearly income to fund total household expenses at the death of either Chandler or Rachel.

- You are willing to allocate $100,000 of your non-retirement investment assets towards survivor needs.

- In the case of death, the surviving spouse will invest any cash settlements in a moderately conservative after-tax portfolio. *In the event of death, you want this assumption to supersede all other rate-of-return assumptions used in other calculations.*

- You would like to assume a 30 percent combined state and federal tax bracket until the surviving spouse retires.

- You would like to assume a 25 percent marginal tax bracket while in retirement.

- You would like to pre-fund retirement and education objectives, even in the event of a spouse death.

- For insurance planning purposes, the surviving spouse will need approximately $115,000 per year (in today's dollars) when Chandler and Rachel retire.

- You feel that allocating $20,000 for final debts (e.g., credit card, auto loans, etc., but not the mortgage), $1,500 for final illness costs, $9,000 for funerals, $13,500 for estate administration costs, $10,000 for other short-term needs, and $25,000 for a spousal adjustment period will meet final expense needs.

- You would like to pay off mortgage debt in the event of a spouse death.

- Social Security benefits, in the event of either Chandler's or Rachel's death, are as follows:

  - $17,580 yearly to Phoebe until age eighteen if Chandler dies.

  - $17,580 additional yearly to Rachel until Phoebe turns age eighteen if Chandler dies.

  - $23,448 yearly to Rachel from age sixty to age sixty-seven if Chandler dies.

- ○ $23,448 yearly to Rachel from age sixty-seven to age ninety-five if Chandler dies.

- ○ $9,552 yearly to Phoebe until age eighteen if Rachel dies.

- ○ $9,552 additional yearly to Chandler until Phoebe turns age eighteen if Rachel dies.

- ○ $0 to Chandler from age sixty to sixty-seven if Rachel dies.

- ○ $26,400 yearly to Chandler from age sixty-seven to ninety-five if Rachel dies.

- Life expectancy for both is age ninety-five.

You currently have life insurance through your employers and through private policies. Information about each policy is shown below:

Type	Policy 1 Whole Life*	Policy 2 Whole Life*	Policy 3 Group Term	Policy 4 Group Term
Insurance Co	Manhattan Insurance Company	Manhattan Insurance Company	Great Plains Assurance and Protection Corporation	Virginia Highland Life Insurance Company
Rating	A.M. Best: A	A.M. Best: A	A.M. Best: A	A.M. Best: A
Equivalent After-Tax Rate of Return	5.50%	5.50%	0%	0%
Death Benefit	$100,000	$100,000	1 x salary (Not Including Bonus)	4 x salary (Not Including Bonus)
Person Insured	Chandler	Rachel	Chandler	Rachel
Owner	Chandler	Rachel	Chandler	Rachel
Beneficiary	Rachel	Chandler	Rachel	Chandler
Cash Value	$8,750	$8,350	$0	$0
Premium Amount	$92	$80	Company paid	Company paid
Payment frequency	Monthly	Monthly	N/A	N/A

Goals:

- Determine whether a need exists for additional life insurance.

- Evaluate current policies to ensure that each policy is appropriately priced.

- • Confirm that survivors will be protected financially in the event either Chandler or Rachel prematurely pass.

Your Current Life Insurance Situation:

Chandler and Rachel, you each currently have one whole life insurance policy purchased privately through the Manhattan Insurance Company and one term policy you obtained through the Great Plains Assurance and Protection Corporation, which is provided by your employer.

- • Chandler, you have $100,000 worth of whole life insurance coverage and $68,467 of group term life insurance.

- • Rachel, you have $100,000 of whole life insurance coverage and $129,984 of group term life insurance.

Based on an analysis of different life insurance needs estimates, it was determined that Chandler needs additional life insurance coverage in the range of $1,000,000 to $1,400,000, whereas Rachel needs additional coverage ranging from $100,000 to $500,000. The following tables highlight the inputs and calculations used to arrive at these conclusions:

LIFE INSURANCE NEEDS ANALYSIS		
Assumptions		
Insured's Name	Chandler	Rachel
Insured's Earned Income	$102,699.88	$32,496.00
Insured's Age	42	42
Survivor's Earned Income	$32,496.00	$102,699.88
Survivor's Age	42	42
Final Expenses	$10,500.00	$10,500.00
Estate Administration	$13,500.00	$13,500.00
Federal Estate Taxes	$0.00	$0.00
State Estate Taxes	$0.00	$0.00
Other Final Needs	$10,000.00	$10,000.00
Credit Card Debt	$5,500.00	$5,500.00
Installment Debt	$0.00	$0.00
Automobile Debt	$10,396.00	$10,396.00
Mortgage Debt	$130,332.00	$130,332.00
Other Debt	$0.00	$0.00
Transitional Child Care Expenses	$0.00	$0.00

Other Transitional Needs	$25,000.00	$25,000.00
Household Expenses Needed in the Event of Death	$115,000.00	$115,000.00
Capital Retention Replacement Ratio	100%	100%
Investment Rate of Return	7.75%	7.75%
Marginal Tax Bracket (State & Fed.) Before Retirement	30.00%	30.00%
Marginal Tax Bracket (State & Fed.) After Retirement	25.00%	25.00%
Inflation Rate	3.00%	3.00%
Tax-Adjusted Rate of Return Before Retirement	5.43%	5.43%
Real Rate of Return Before Retirement	2.35%	2.35%
Real Rate of Return During Retirement	2.73%	2.73%
While Children Are at Home		
Number of Survivors	2.00	2.00
Expense Reduction Ratio	100.00%	100.00%
Household Expense Need	$115,000.00	$115,000.00
Social Security Survivor Benefits	$35,160.00	$19,104.00
Other Income	$0.00	$0.00
Income Need	$47,344.00	$0.00
Years Until Youngest Child Turns 18	13	13
Value of Need	$537,297.74	$0.00
Educational Needs		
Educational Expenses for Children/Grandchildren	$40,806.38	$40,806.38
From Time Children Leave to Age 60 for Survivor		
Number of Survivors	1.00	1.00
Expense Reduction Ratio	100.00%	100.00%
Household Expense Need	$115,000.00	$115,000.00
Social Security Survivor Benefits	$0.00	$0.00
Other Income	$0.00	$0.00
Income Need	$82,504.00	$12,300.12
Years From Last Child 18 to Age 60	5	5
Value of Need	$393,973.85	$58,735.64
From Age 60 to Full Retirement		
Survivor's Full Retirement Age	67	67
Survivor's Age at Death	95	95
Income Need While Retired	$115,000.00	$115,000.00

Survivor's Age 60 Social Security Benefit	$16,765.00	$0.00
Other Income	$0.00	$0.00
Survivor's Earnings	$0.00	$0.00
Income Need	$98,235.00	$115,000.00
Value of Need	**$635,177.67**	**$743,578.48**
From Full Retirement to Death		
Income Need While Retired	$115,000.00	$115,000.00
Survivor's Social Security Benefit	$23,448.00	$26,400.00
Other Income	$0.00	$0.00
Survivor's Earnings	$0.00	$0.00
Income Need	$91,552.00	$88,600.00
Value of Need	**$1,824,373.85**	**$1,765,548.80**
Needs Summary		
Immediate Needs	$205,228.00	$205,228.00
While Children Are at Home	$537,297.74	$0.00
Educational Needs	$40,806.38	$40,806.38
From Time Children Leave to Retirement for Survivor	$198,244.19	$29,555.26
From Age 60 to Full Retirement	$229,736.32	$268,943.63
From Full Retirement to Death	$444,313.44	$429,987.01
TOTAL GROSS NEED	**$1,655,626.08**	**$974,520.29**
Assets and Insurance Available for Need		
Insurance Values	$168,466.58	$229,984.00
Retirement Savings	$255,000.00	$224,750.00
Other Savings	$0.00	$0.00
Other Assets	$100,000.00	$100,000.00
Total	**$523,466.58**	**$554,734.00**
NET NEED	**$1,132,159.50**	**$419,786.29**
ALTERNATIVE LIFE INSURANCE NEEDS APPROACHES		
HUMAN LIFE VALUE APPROACH		
Gross Need	$1,463,035.10	$462,929.35
Net Need (Subtracting Current Insurance & Assets)	*$939,568.52*	*$0.00*
INFLATION ADJUSTED HUMAN LIFE VALUE APPROACH		
Gross Need	$1,969,386.34	$623,147.55
Net Need (Subtracting Current Insurance & Assets)	*$1,445,919.76*	*$68,413.55*

CAPITAL RETENTION APPROACH		
Gross Need	$1,995,785.23	$631,500.61
Net Need (Subtracting Current Insurance & Assets)	*$1,472,318.65*	*$76,766.61*
CAPITAL RETENTION APPROACH ALTERNATIVE		
Gross Need	$2,659,781.83	$2,729,985.71
Net Need (Subtracting Current Insurance & Assets)	*$2,136,315.25*	*$2,175,251.71*
INCOME RETENTION APPROACH		
Ratio Reduced Current Living Expenses Until Retirement	$115,000.00	$115,000.00
Investment Income Until Retirement	$19,258.75	$17,617.69
Spouse Income Until Retirement	$32,496.00	$102,699.88
Pre-Retirement Social Security and Other Survivor Benefits	$0.00	$0.00
Yearly Income Need	$63,245.25	$0.00
Gross Need	$1,212,799.19	$0.00
Net Need (Subtracting Current Insurance & Assets)	*$982,815.19*	*$0.00*
10x GROSS INCOME APPROACH		
Net Need	$1,026,998.80	$324,960.00
Net Need (Subtracting Current Insurance & Assets)	*$503,532.22*	*$0.00*
Weighted Average Need	$1,230,375.58	$391,459.74
Needs Approach, HLV, CR, & IR Average	$1,131,715.46	$124,138.22

The following table summarizes the analysis conducted on the cost of your whole life insurance policies. The cost of your whole life insurance coverage falls within accepted benchmarks for your age group.

Cost Per $1,000 Formula: Insurance Replacement Analysis		
	Chandler	Rachel
Annual Premium	$1,104.00	$960.00
Cash Value at Beginning of Year	$7,850.00	$7,500.00
Cash Value at End of Year	$8,750.00	$8,350.00
After Tax Rate of Return	5.50%	5.50%
Policy Dividend	$250.00	$250.00
Death Benefit	$100,000.00	$100,000.00
Cost Per Thousand	$4.89	$3.55
Recommended Price	$4.00	$4.00
Is Price of Current Policy Reasonable?	*Yes*	*Yes*

Life Insurance Recommendations:

The following tables summarize the recommendations that have been designed to help you reach your life insurance goals. As with all recommendations presented in this financial plan, our firm is available to answer any questions that might arise and to assist with specific implementation procedures.

Recommendation #1: Purchase a twenty-year $1,250,000 term life insurance policy with Chandler as the insured.	
Who:	Chandler.
What:	Twenty-year annually renewable convertible term life insurance policy with Rachel named as the owner and primary beneficiary. The policy should include a disability waiver.
When:	Within the next thirty to forty-five days.
Where:	With your insurance professional or with an online provider that our firm can recommend (our staff will provide you with specific information and guidance throughout the process).
Why:	To ensure financial and medical security for your family.
How:	Consult your insurance professional or our firm can assist you with identifying an online provider. Our firm will assist by discussing the underwriting issues, required application, and medical information.
How much:	$1,250,000.
Effect on cash flow:	The purchase will reduce cash flow by the estimated annual premium of $960.

Recommendation #2: Purchase a twenty-year $400,000 term life insurance policy with Rachel as the insured.	
Who:	Rachel.
What:	Twenty-year annually renewable convertible term life insurance policy with Chandler named as the owner and primary beneficiary. The policy should include a disability waiver.
When:	Within the next 30 to 45 days.
Where:	With your insurance professional or with an online provider that our firm can recommend (our staff will provide you with specific information and guidance throughout the process).
Why:	To ensure financial and medical security for your family.
How:	Consult your insurance professional or our firm can assist you with identifying an online provider. Our firm will assist by discussing the underwriting issues, required application, and medical information.
How much:	$400,000.00.
Effect on cash flow:	The purchase will reduce cash flow by the estimated annual premium of $580.

Current vs. Recommended Outcome:

Currently, you do not have sufficient life insurance coverage to meet the needs of the surviving spouse if one of you were to pass away. Implementation of the recommendations will fill your current life insurance gap. Note that if you surrender your whole life insurance policies and purchase term life insurance policies, the annual total cost of life insurance premiums will decrease. the following is an *alternative* that we can discuss; however, given potential health issues in the future, the current recommendation calls for you to hold your cash value policies.

Alternative Recommendations and Outcome(s):

An alternative life insurance recommendation has been developed:

Alternative #1: Surrender your current whole life insurance policies and replace with twenty-year term annually renewable convertible life insurance policies.	
Who:	Chandler and Rachel.
What:	Two $100,000 Manhattan Insurance Company Whole life insurance policies.
When:	After you purchase new term life insurance policies.
Where:	Directly with the Manhattan Insurance Company (our staff will provide you with specific information and guidance throughout the process).
Why:	To increase cash flow available for saving.
How:	If this recommendation is implemented, additional term life coverage will be needed. The cost of the additional insurance will be totally offset by the reduction in premiums on the current policies.
How much:	$200,000 of whole life insurance coverage.
Effect on cash flow:	Annual cash flow will increase by approximately $1,900 (Cost of premiums for whole life [$2,064] minus the estimated cost of replacement term life policies [$164]).

As noted above, given Rachel's potential health status, this strategy is not recommended because Rachel will potentially have difficulty obtaining additional coverage in the future. Maintaining these permanent forms of insurance will ensure that your family has minimal coverage into the future. Additionally, the policies are appropriately priced.

Plan Implementation and Monitoring Procedures:

It is important that the recommendations presented in this section be implemented within the next thirty to forty-five days. Once you obtain your new life insurance policies, please send our firm copies of the policies so that we may maintain these for our records. Our firm will update your life insurance needs analysis each year prior to the annual review meeting; however, please notify us if any of the following events or changes occur, as one of these issues may indicate a need to reevaluate your life insurance situation:

- Change in employment or promotion for Chandler or Rachel (i.e., change in income or employee benefits) or a career change.

- Purchase of a new home or second home.

- Changes related to Phoebe (i.e., her death, college scholarship, decision not to attend college, etc.).

- Inheritance from Chandler's parents.

- Pregnancy or adoption.

- Divorce.

- New, more dangerous hobbies or jobs.

- Disability of a family member.

8.10 SELF-TEST

[A] Questions

Self-Test 1

Akmed is fifty-three years old and married to Janine who is age thirty-nine. They have four children, ages three, seven, nine, and eleven. Akmed earns $135,000 per year. Given these facts, which of the following would be an appropriate income multiplier when estimating his insurance need?

(a) Five

(b) Seven

(c) Twelve

(d) Twenty

Self-Test 2

Pam, age fifty, earns $165,000 per year. She plans to retire at age sixty-seven. If she can earn an annual rate of return equal to 8% how much life insurance does she need today using the HLV approach (rounded)?

(a) $750,000

(b) $1,000,000

(c) $1,500,000

(d) $2,500,000

Self-Test 3

Abed is forty years old and is married to Sonya, also age forty. Abed earns $290,000 per year, whereas Sonya earns $100,000 annually. If they plan to retire at age sixty-seven and can earn 7% on their investment assets, how much is Abed's life insurance need using the income retention approach (rounded)?

(a) $1,200,000

(b) $2,300,000

(c) $3,000,000

(d) $3,500,000

Self-Test 4

Which of the following require a life insurance policy owner to make a fixed premium payment?

(a) A whole life policy.

(b) A variable life policy.

(c) A universal life policy.

(d) All of these policies require a fixed premium payment.

Self-Test 5

Which of the following is an example of an incidents of ownership?

(a) The right to change the beneficiary.

(b) The ability to modify the contract.

(c) The right to use the policy as collateral.

(d) All the above.

Self-Test 6

When a policy is sold to a third party using a viatical settlement procedure, the policy owner

(a) will receive less than the face value of the policy.

(b) will receive the face value ofIe policy.

(c) will receive more than the face value of the policy.

(d) will receive the future value of foregone premiums.

Self-Test 7

Swarn would like to purchase a product that will provide him with lifetime income starting immediately. For planning purposes, he would like a guaranteed income stream for the remainder of his life. Swarn should purchase a(n):

(a) Deferred Annuity.

(b) Variable Annuity.

(c) Immediate Fixed Income Annuity.

(d) Immediate Variable Income Annuity.

Self-Test 8

What type of buy/sell agreement exists when each partner buys a life insurance policy on each of the other partners?

(a) Entity purchase plan.

(b) Cross-purchase plan.

(c) Key person plan.

(d) Cross purpose plan.

[B] Answers

Question 1: c

Question 2: c

Question 3: b

Question 4: c

Question 5: d

Question 6: a

Question 7: c

Question 8: b

8.11 CHAPTER RESOURCES

Baldwin, B. *The New Life Insurance Investment Advisor.* New York: McGraw Hill, 2002.

Belth, J. M. *Life Insurance: A Consumer's Handbook*, 2nd Edition. Bloomington, IN: Indiana University Press, 1985.

General life insurance and tax source: 2022 *Tax Facts on Life Insurance & Employee Benefits.* Cincinnati, OH: National Underwriter Company, published annually.

Leimberg, S. R., Buck, K., and Doyle, R. J. *The Tools & Techniques of Life Insurance Planning*, 7th Edition. Cincinnati, OH: National Underwriter Company, 2017.

New York Department of Financial Services (https://www.dfs.ny.gov/consumers/life_insurance/glossary_terms).

CHAPTER ENDNOTES

1. The traditional net cost method subtracts total premiums paid from a policy's projected dividends plus the cash surrender value. What remains is divided by the projected holding period. This equates to an annual cost of ownership. One criticism of this methodology is that the calculation does not account for the time value of money associated with premium payments. This evaluation procedure is not widely used because the calculation often results in a negative cost of ownership.

2. This method of evaluation adjusts the traditional net cost estimate for the time value of money associated with premium payments.

3. Sometimes called the **net payment cost index**, this approach assumes that premiums and policy dividends are accrued over a set period of time, typically 20 years, with a fixed rate of return (e.g., 4%) paid on the policy cash value. Total dividends are then subtracted from the total of all premium payments. This figure is then averaged, using a time value of money adjustment, to estimate an average annual net premium cost.

4. Joseph Belth originally developed the yearly price per thousand method. A complete description of the method can be found in: Belth, J. M. *Life Insurance: A Consumer's Handbook*, 2nd Edition. Bloomington, IN: Indiana University Press, 1985.

5. Calculations based on estimates from Fidelity Investments Guaranteed Income Estimator. https://digital.fidelity.com/prgw/digital/gie/.

Chapter 9

Health Insurance Planning

Learning Objectives

- Learning Objective 1: Evaluate a client's health insurance situation and circumstances.

- Learning Objective 2: Integrate health insurance into a client's risk management strategy.

- Learning Objective 3: Conduct a health insurance needs analysis.

9.1 THE PROCESS OF HEALTH INSURANCE PLANNING

Helping clients make choices that maximize benefits, reduce costs, increase tax-advantaged purchases, and facilitate peace of mind are excellent reasons to incorporate health insurance planning into a comprehensive review of a client's financial situation. Information needed to conduct a health insurance analysis typically is obtained during the initial client data gathering phase of the financial planning process. The following discussion highlights how the financial planning process can be used when conducting a health insurance analysis.

9.2 STEP 1: UNDERSTAND THE CLIENT'S PERSONAL AND FINANCIAL CIRCUMSTANCES

The first step in the health insurance planning process involves reviewing, with the client, relevant personal and financial information. It is important to discuss a client's family health situation prior to making health insurance recommendations. This type of discussion can strengthen the client-financial planner relationship and lead to the development and presentation of integrative recommendations.

Each client's financial, physical, and emotional situation is unique. Client situational factors need to be evaluated carefully when assessing and selecting appropriate health care plans, products, and services. Although the number of situational factors is almost limitless, this chapter highlights the need for financial planners to consider, at a minimum, the following client characteristics: (a) family health status and related health history; (b) family demographics, which can trigger insurance needs; (c) assets available for use in case of a catastrophic health claim; (d) lifestyle choices that can affect the availability of insurance benefits; (e) working in a hazardous profession or occupation; and (f) concerns over future unemployment, career changes, or retirement.

Figure 9.1 provides a review of the Hubbles' personal and financial circumstances related to health insurance planning. The information in Figure 9.1 is typical of what a financial planner should evaluate at the first step of the financial planning process.

Figure 9.1. The Hubbles' Personal and Financial Circumstances.

Chandler Hubble	Rachel Hubble
Age: 42	Age: 42
State of residence: Missouri	State of residence: Missouri
Citizen: U.S.	Citizen: U.S.
Health status: No known health issues	Health status: No known health issues
Phoebe Hubble	
Age: 5	
Health status: No known health issues	

- Health insurance is provided for the entire family through a group health insurance policy offered through Chandler's work. The health provider, Peacock & Peacock, is a health maintenance organization. Chandler pays $375 a month in premiums for this coverage through his company's Section 125 plan. The plan allows for pretax premium payments.

- The policy has an annual deductible of $450 and a stop-loss limit of $3,000. Under the policy, doctors' visits cost $20 per appointment to the primary care physician and $40 per visit to specialists, and for emergency treatment a $100 copayment is required. Monthly prescriptions are $10 for generic brands and $25 for other brands. There is no copayment for hospitalization in semiprivate accommodations, and private rooms are provided when medically necessary. The original lifetime ceiling for services, per family member, was $2 million; however, with the passage of the Patient Protection and Affordable Care Act limits have been removed.

- Over the past several years the Hubbles have averaged about $50 per month in dental and eye care expenses, which Chandler and Rachel pay out of discretionary cash flow. A flexible spending account for health costs is available through Chandler's employer. Chandler and Rachel have not funded this account in the past because of uncertainty related to "use it or lose it" rules.

9.3 STEP 2: IDENTIFY AND SELECT GOALS

Identifying and refining health insurance goals does not lend itself to an easy financial calculation. In some respects, this aspect of financial planning can best be described as a combination of art and science. Generally, a client's health insurance goals include having access to insurance coverage, obtaining coverage that is affordable, funding anticipated and unexpected expenses, and obtaining any tax advantages available. The goal development process will likely be driven by a combination of a client's psychological needs (e.g., decreasing the financial fears associated with disease and discomfort) and purely quantifiable medical costs. Goals should be developed that help the client deal with not only the financial realities associated with health care but also the worries associated with the unknown.

Although the Hubble family already has health insurance coverage, it is worthwhile to identify and review their health insurance goals. Figure 9.2 provides a summary of these goals.

Figure 9.2. The Hubbles' Health Insurance Goals.

When thinking about their health insurance situation, Chandler and Rachel arrived at the following goals:
• Maintain appropriate health insurance coverage through Chandler's employer.
• Take advantage of any tax-advantaged plans that may be available through Chandler's or Rachel's employer, or through a private provider.
• Continue to ensure that any health coverage is appropriate in terms of cost and coverage.

9.4 STEP 3: ANALYZE THE CLIENT'S CURRENT COURSE OF ACTION AND POTENTIAL ALTERNATIVE COURSE(S) OF ACTION

Health insurance is a topic that goes beyond traditional analytic procedures. When working with clients, financial planners should anticipate the fear of economic loss associated with the cost of health care and related **out-of-pocket expenses**, which are defined as the amount of unreimbursed expenses one must pay before insurance reimbursement and the **deductible** a client must pay before insurance benefits begin. Health insurance is a complex form of insurance, primarily because policies are offered via employers, private health insurance contracts, and governmental exchanges. Although financial planners may or may not sell the actual insurance they recommend, it is nevertheless important that financial planners understand the basic issues involved in medical insurance planning and policy selection.

Analyzing a client's current health insurance need is relatively straightforward, but each client's unique situation must be considered. Issues to reflect upon during this step of the financial planning process include:

- family health status and related health history;

- family demographics that could trigger insurance needs;

- assets available for use in case of a catastrophic health claim;

- lifestyle choices that could influence the availability of insurance benefits;

- working in a hazardous profession or occupation; and

- concerns about future unemployment, career changes, or retirement.

Planning Reminder

Clients that have children who (1) are approaching age twenty-six and (2) do not have access to an employer-provided plan should encourage their clients' children to purchase a short-term individual health insurance policy or use a Health Insurance Exchange to obtain a policy.

An additional action to take, when analyzing a client's current health coverage situation, focuses on reviewing the client's current coverage and/or availability and use of tax-advantaged accounts. Gathering a variety of information about a client's health insurance situation is an important task associated with ensuring that a thorough analysis is conducted.

Before considering specific health insurance planning strategies, a financial planner should determine whether a client's current and short-term needs are best met through a traditional indemnity health insurance plan, a managed care plan option, or a high deductible health plan (HDHP), which can be structured after either model. **Managed care** plan options attempt to control access to and coordination of services while promoting efficient, high-quality care, all with the objective of controlling health care costs. The standard in- or out-of-network methods common to nearly all managed care plans differ from traditional indemnity plans where the insured can obtain services from any provider, but typically at a higher premium and/or service fee. Figure 9.3 provides a comparison of the five primary health insurance plans available in the marketplace.

As shown in Figure 9.3, **preferred provider organization** (PPO) plans, **point-of-service (POS) plans,** and **health maintenance organization** (HMO) plans are three common managed care designs. A PPO offers the most flexibility for those seeking health care, whereas an HMO is typically the most restrictive. The hybrid POS plan shares features of a PPO and HMO, whereas an **exclusive provider organization** (EPO) plan is similar to but more restrictive in its provider network than an HMO.

Figure 9.3. Comparison of Health Insurance Plans.

Plan Type	Traditional Indemnity Plan	Preferred Provider Organization (PPO)	Point-of-service (POS) Plan	Health Maintenance Organization (HMO)	High-Deductible Health Plan (HDHP)
Cost	Highest	Middle-high	Middle-low	Lowest of managed cost plans	Lowest of all plans available
Physician Choice	Least restrictive, but restrictions are increasing to control costs	Restricted to network; may go outside network with higher deductible and copayment	Restricted, but insured may see out-of-network provider for additional cost	Restricted	Depends on whether the HDHP is an indemnity, PPO, POS, or HMO plan, but certain requirements must be met to qualify as a HDHP. Offers copays for office visits only after the deductible has been met.
Hospital Choice	Least restrictive, but restrictions are increasing to control costs	Restricted to network; may go outside network with higher deductible and copayment	Restricted to network	Restricted	Similar to a physician choice plan, the choice depends on whether the HDHP is an indemnity, PPO, POS, or HMO plan, but certain requirements must be met to qualify as a HDHP. Offers copays for office visits only after deductible has been met.

Appropriate for Whom?	Households that demand maximum choice	Households that would like some choice but with lower expenses than a traditional plan	Households that use medical services frequently, but occasionally visit out-of-network providers	Households that use medical services frequently	Households that are: • Generally healthy and medical expenses are limited to preventive care OR not healthy and typically hit the lower limits on catastrophic coverage in other plans and incur out-of-pocket expenses for exclusions (e.g., drug or other costs); • Financially disciplined savers who can fund the annual maximum of the HSA to cover expenses; and • Comfortable with in-network providers to maximize savings.
Among Firms Offering Health Benefits, Availability of this Plan[1]	3 percent	50 percent	24 percent	16 percent	23 percent
Estimated Annual Group Plan Cost for a Family	$20,000+	$19,500	$18,297	$17,978	$16,737

[1] Source: Kaiser Family Foundation. 2016 Employer Health Benefits Survey. Available at: https://www.kff.org/health-costs/report/2016-employer-health-benefits-survey/: Because some firms offer more than one type of plan, columns do not sum to 100 percent

Sources:

- Lyke, B., & Peterson, C. L. (2009). Tax-Advantaged Accounts for Health Care Expenses: Side-by-Side Comparison. Washington, DC: Congressional Research Service.

- IRS Publication 969, Health Savings Accounts and Other Tax-Favored Health Plans.

- U.S. Department of the Treasury. Resource Center-Health Savings Accounts (HSAs). Available at: https://www.treasury.gov/resource-center/faqs/Taxes/Pages/Health-Savings-Accounts.aspx

Keep in mind that health insurance choices typically are limited to plans offered by a client's employer and that plan changes are severely restricted. While it may be possible to obtain coverage outside of an employer's plan, the cost to do so may be too high for most clients. Even so, it is important to explore client preferences that reflect both quantitative aspects of the analysis as well as qualitative or more intangible preferences. The latter may supersede cash flow issues, when something as personal as family health care is at stake.

Figure 9.4 identifies decision criteria to help address which type of health plan—traditional indemnity, PPO, POS, or HMO—may be the most appropriate for a client. It is important to note that the same options can also be offered as a HDHP, so the decision criteria and research on the plan should be similar once the HDHP alternative has been chosen. Helping a client choose the type of health insurance that best matches the client's lifestyle, health situation, medical usage, and anticipated wellness is an important consideration when making health insurance recommendations.

Figure 9.4. Health Insurance Plan Decision Tree.

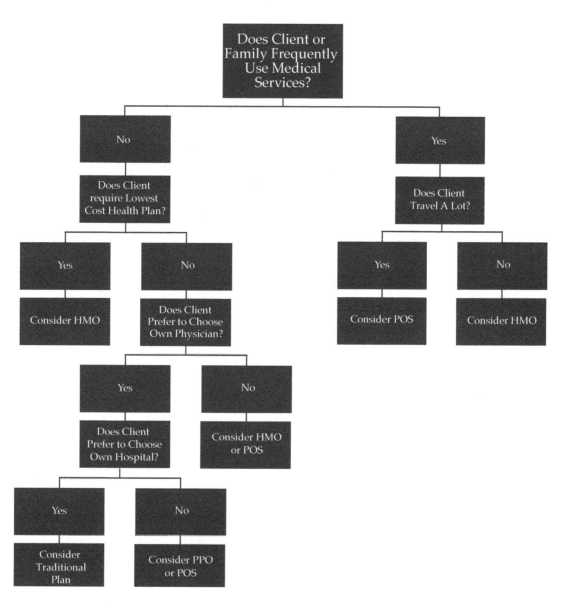

Based on the preceding analyses, the following observations and potential recommendations are worth considering:

- Currently, the Hubbles purchase their family health insurance through Chandler's employer. The HMO policy is relatively inexpensive. Chandler and Rachel are able to pay the premiums easily from discretionary cash flow. Because the policy is funded on a pre-tax basis, the after-tax cost is even lower. The Hubble family should:

  o Continue to utilize the HMO through Chandler's employer.

  o Establish an FSA at the next enrollment period.

    ♦ Fund the FSA up to at least $600 for the year ($50 per month). Given that Chandler and Rachel have not used the FSA in the past, they may need some additional education about the benefits of this strategy. For example, Chandler and Rachel may feel more comfortable making a small contribution that is sure to be spent rather than risk funds that may not be used. Over time, as they gain confidence and experience, they should consider increasing the annual FSA contribution.

    ♦ Implementation will result in a tax benefit equal to approximately $226 ($600 pretax contribution × [30 percent state and federal tax rate + 7.65 percent FICA tax rate]).

9.5 STEP 4: DEVELOP THE FINANCIAL PLANNING RECOMMENDATION(S)

The development of health insurance recommendations, within a comprehensive financial plan, can encompass a multitude of products and services. A competent financial planner should be able to transform the analysis of a client's situation into actionable recommendations. The following discussion highlights some of the important concepts, tools, and techniques that can be incorporated into the recommendation development process.

[A] Terminology of Health Insurance

It is important to have a clear understanding of the different terms and phrases associated with health insurance. The following include some of the most widely used health insurance terms and definitions:

- current **deductible**—amount the insured pays before the insurance company contributes to a claim;

- current **copayment**—fixed fee the insured pays for services in addition to what the insurance company will pay;

- current **coinsurance**—percentage of service expense paid by the insured above the deductible amount (e.g., if a plan has a 20 percent coinsurance clause, the insured is responsible for paying the deductible and 20 percent of each bill up to the maximum annual stop-loss limit);

- current **stop-loss limit**—the maximum amount of out-of-pocket expenses paid by an insured, which includes deductibles, copayments, and coinsurance (i.e., **cost sharing**);

- excluded coverage—what a plan will not pay for (e.g., elective cosmetic surgery); and

- current annual premium—the cost of insurance.

[B] The Patient Protection and Affordable Care Act

The Patient Protection and Affordable Care Act of 2010 changed the health care planning environment dramatically. The law established **Health Insurance Exchanges**, expanded Medicaid coverage, and provided incentives for employers to offer health insurance. Additionally, the law strengthened consumer protections, limited premium increases, encouraged preventive care, and initially required all Americans to purchase health insurance. Even though the Act had a minimal impact on most financial planning clientele—few clients lost their insurance coverage or encountered reduced coverage—the law did introduce several new points to consider when incorporating health insurance analyses into a client's financial plan. The following discussion highlights these factors. More information about these and other features of the Act can be found at www.healthcare.gov.

- The Act effectively eliminated insurance restrictions based on pre-existing conditions; waiting periods are now prohibited.

- Programs are now in place to help those who are age fifty-five or older obtain insurance prior to enrolling in Medicare at age sixty-five.

- Tax credits up to 50 percent of employer contributions to health insurance plan premiums help small businesses offer plans.

- Children up to age twenty-six may stay on their parents' insurance regardless of financial dependence, student status, marital status, employment, or residency (some states, like New York, have even more generous laws).

- Lifetime limits on coverage are now prohibited.

- The Act banned rescissions in which insurance companies could drop someone from coverage due to a paperwork mistake after the insured person got sick.

- Health insurance plans must now provide preventative services without copayments, coinsurance, or deductibles.

- The Act formalized an appeals process for individuals and groups who feel that their insurance company has denied a claim in error.

- The choice of a primary care provider is now guaranteed, assuming the provider is available to accept new patients.

- Direct access to OB/GYN services is guaranteed; further, insurance companies can no longer force an insured to use a network OB/GYN service provider.

- The Act prohibits employer sponsored plans from excluding employee participation based on salary or income.

- Lower income households may receive subsidies to make health insurance premiums more affordable.

- The Act guarantees everyone access to health insurance without regard to age, sex, occupation, or health status.

[C] Health Savings and Flexible Spending Accounts and Other Plans

Another choice that aligns with the selection of a health insurance policy is the use of a tax-advantaged account to fund out-of-pocket medical expenses. Because these decisions must be coordinated, it is important that financial planners be aware of the features of each to help clients effectively manage costs. Four primary tax-advantaged accounts exist: (a) **health care flexible spending arrangement** (FSA), (b) **health reimbursement account** (HRA), (c) **health savings account** (HSA), and (d) **Archer medical savings account** (MSA).

A health care FSA may be funded through a voluntary salary reduction agreement. Employment tax and federal income tax withholding are not deducted from an employee's contribution. The employer may also contribute. An FSA may be used to reimburse the participant for qualified medical expenses.

Planning Reminder

If a client is funding both an FSA and an HSA, funds from the FSA should be exhausted first so that funds can remain in the HSA for the future. Similarly, to the extent that qualified expenses could be reimbursed from an FSA or an HRA, expenses from the FSA should be used first, typically to maintain the HRA balance.

An HSA is a tax-exempt trust or custodial account set up in conjunction with a HDHP that allows the participant to be reimbursed for qualified medical expenses. As a reminder, a HDHP has a higher annual deductible compared to other health plans, which means participants must pay more of their health care costs. HSAs can be used to meet these expenses.

Planning Reminder

A **cafeteria plan** (also known as a **Section 125 plan**) provides company or organizational participants an opportunity to receive certain employee benefits on a pretax basis. Participants in a cafeteria plan must be permitted to choose among at least one taxable benefit (such as cash) and one qualified benefit. According to the IRA, a qualified benefit is a benefit that does not defer compensation and is excludable from an employee's gross income under a specific provision of the tax code (without being subject to the principles of constructive receipt). Qualified benefits include the following:

- Accident and health benefits.

- Adoption assistance.

- Dependent care assistance.

- Group-term life insurance coverage.

- Health savings accounts (including distributions to pay long-term care services).

A section 125 plan is the only means by which an employer can offer employees a choice between taxable and nontaxable benefits without the choice causing the benefits to become taxable.

An HRA receives contributions from the employer only (employees may not contribute); however, contributions are not included in a participant's income. Reimbursements from an HRA that are used to pay qualified medical expenses are not taxed.

Finally, MSA eligibility is restricted to employees of small employers and the self-employed, which rules out participation for many taxpayers. MSAs have been phased out and replaced with HSAs, except for those who were eligible prior to December 31, 2007. MSA funding can continue, assuming the owner is still eligible, or the Archer MSA can be rolled over into an HSA. Figure 9.6 compares aspects of these accounts.

Figure 9.6. Comparison of Tax-Advantaged Accounts.

	HSA	MSA	HRA	FSA
PRE-TAX EMPLOYEE CONTRIBUTION?	Yes	Yes, but only if employer does not contribute	No contribution from employee allowed	Yes
MAY ASSETS IN ACCOUNT BE INVESTED?	Yes, using IRA instruments	Yes, using IRA instruments	No	No
EMPLOYER CONTRIBUTIONS ALLOWED?	Yes	Yes	Yes	Yes
ROLLOVER ALLOWED?	Yes	Yes	No	No
MUST ACCOUNT BE LINKED TO HDHP?	Yes	Yes	No	No
MAY ACCOUNT ASSETS BE ROLLED OVER?	Yes	Yes	Yes	A limited dollar amount may be rolled over to the new year*
MAY ACCOUNT ASSETS BE USED FOR OVER-THE-COUNTER MEDICINES AND MENSTRUAL CARE?	Beginning in 2020, account assets may be used to purchase over-the-counter medications and receive reimbursement without the necessity of a prescription–assuming their employer's plan documents allow for these expenses. In addition, expenses for menstrual care products may be paid for from assets. Vitamins, dietary supplements, and cosmetic procedures are not reimbursable, but expenses for herbal remedies or a weight loss program, if prescribed by a physician as medically necessary, can be covered.			

* An employer may offer those with remaining FSA assets a 2½-month grace period for the use of assets or a $500 maximum allowable carryover option, but not both.

Source: U.S. Bureau of Labor Statistics: www.bls.gov/opub/mlr/cwc/consumer-driven-health-care-what-is-it-and-what-does-it-mean-for-employees-and-employers.pdf

[D] Medicare Planning and Eligibility

Medicare is available for people age sixty-five years of age or older, younger people with disabilities, and those with end-stage renal disease (i.e., permanent kidney failure requiring dialysis or a transplant). Medicare has three primary parts. Part A is a hospital insurance plan. Part B is a voluntary medical insurance plan with a monthly premium. Part D is a prescription drug benefit. Those who have not paid Medicare taxes for at least ten years or were never married may not be eligible for Part A, but they may be able to purchase coverage if they are age sixty-five or older and a citizen or permanent resident of the United States. A brief description of Parts A, B, and D follows. To learn more about these coverage and changes to Medicare plans and benefits, see www.medicare.gov.

Medicare Part A, hospital insurance, helps cover costs for inpatient care in hospitals, critical access hospitals, and skilled nursing facilities. Benefits for nursing facilities are available only following a related three-day hospital stay. Part A also covers hospice care for the terminally ill and some home health services prescribed by a doctor, including durable medical equipment and supplies. In addition to services and supplies covered as part of hospital or skilled nursing home care, Part A includes coverage for pints of blood received at a hospital or skilled nursing facility. Although the costs of some benefits are fully covered, coinsurance and deductibles also may apply.

Medicare Part B, medical insurance, provides benefits for doctors' services, outpatient hospital care, some home health services, and some other medical services excluded from Part A, such as the services of physical and occupational therapists or speech pathologists. Part B helps pay for these covered services and diagnostic testing and supplies when these services are judged to be medically necessary. The listing of covered services is extensive, ranging from ambulance services when medically necessary to transplants, yet restrictions and limitations on services apply.

The base monthly Part B premium varies by income. The monthly premium is generally deducted from a retiree's Social Security, Railroad Retirement, or Civil Service retirement check. In addition to the monthly premium for Part B, annual deductible and coinsurance provisions (20 percent) also apply. Effective in 2007, premium charges for Medicare Parts B and D, Medicare prescription drug coverage, are **means tested**. Some programs are available to reduce Part B premiums for those with limited income.

A **Medicare doughnut hole**, or coverage gap, may exist for those with **Medicare Part D** coverage and high prescription drug costs. The gap is based on the dollar amount that a client must pay out of pocket for medication costs (typically referred to as the **initial coverage period**). Beginning in 2020, the coverage gap is capped at 25 percent of the cost of prescription drugs until the annual out-of-pocket spending limit is met. Different gap costs are associated with covered generic drugs and covered brand-name drugs purchased in the doughnut hole. Keep in mind that individuals in the doughnut hole enter catastrophic coverage after their out-of-pocket expenses for drugs on the plan's formulary, or list of covered drugs, reaches the stated annual limit, and Part D payment for prescriptions resumes until the end of the year. The money spent on drugs that are not covered on the plan's formulary does not count toward the catastrophic coverage threshold. Medicare Part D coverage resets each year on January 1st.

The **Medicare + Choice program**, which is sometimes referred to as **Medicare Part C**, is an alternative to traditional Medicare programs. Part C coverage was ushered in as part of the Medicare Prescription Drug, Improvement, and Modernization Act of 2003. Medicare Part A and Part B coverage is required to be eligible. Medicare + Choice plans allow consumers to seek benefits through a private health maintenance organization (HMO), a special needs plan for targeted audiences, a private fee-for-service plan (PFFS) through a private insurance company, or a preferred provider organization (PPO). Part C plans may include extra benefits such as prescription drugs, dental care, and routine physical and vision services.

Originally enacted in 1997, this program has been renamed the **Medicare Advantage Program** and was expanded in 2006 to offer more choices for both urban and rural consumers. For example, Congress created **special needs plans** to allow insurance companies to target enrollment to special needs individuals, including those who are (a) institutionalized, (b) dually eligible, and/or (c) suffering from severe or disabling chronic conditions. To identify Medicare Advantage Programs available in a geographic area and any extra benefits offered by these plans, visit the Medicare Personal Plan Finder at www.medicare.gov.

The **Medicare Advantage MSA** is an Archer MSA for those who are enrolled in Medicare Part A and Part B and have a HDHP that meets Medicare guidelines. This tax-exempt trust or custodial account is funded by the Medicare program—no personal contributions are allowed—to pay for qualified medical expenses of the account holder. Funds in the account can earn interest or dividends, grow tax-deferred, and are not taxed if used for qualified medical expenses. Medicare Advantage MSAs are administered through the Medicare program (See www.medicare.gov or IRS Publication 969).

A variety of expenses are excluded under Medicare Part A and Part B. Some exclusions affect only select groups of Medicare beneficiaries (e.g., exclusions for acupuncture, cosmetic surgery, or health care received outside the United States). Other exclusions for routine physicals, eye care, foot care, dental care, hearing aids, or custodial care at home or in a nursing home affect far more consumers. Starting in 2011, cost sharing (e.g., copayments, coinsurance, and deductibles) for select Medicare covered preventive services are prohibited.

It is important that financial planners and their clients be fully informed of both exclusions and covered services to more accurately project medical costs. A client who assumes that they are covered may find themselves exposed to unreimbursed costs if services are needed. Such knowledge can help financial planners develop strategies to cover these expenses with private sources of insurance, such as **Medigap coverage**, or through self-insurance techniques. Clients who overestimate the cost of care may unnecessarily limit their lifestyle, gifting, or spending for other goals to save more for future medical costs.

[E] Applying Planning Skills to the Hubble Case

Similar to other insurance topics, only modest changes will generally be made to the initial recommendations developed at Step Three of the financial planning process, although it is possible that new client information or data can necessitate the need for a reevaluation. Figure 9.7 provides a summary of the final health insurance recommendations that match the Hubble family's financial goals.

Figure 9.7. Health Insurance Recommendation for Chandler and Rachel.

The final health insurance recommendations developed for the Hubble family match the preliminary recommendations identified at Step Three of the financial planning process. Specifically, Chandler and Rachel should:
• Continue to utilize the HMO through Chandler's employer.
• Establish an FSA at the next enrollment period.
◦ Fund the account up to $600 for the year ($50 per month). Implementation will result in a tax benefit equal to approximately $225.90 ($600 × [30 percent state and federal tax rate + 7.65 percent FICA tax rate]).

9.6 STEP 5: PRESENT THE FINANCIAL PLANNING RECOMMENDATION(S)

Although the number of planning alternatives available to financial planners when dealing with client health care issues is somewhat limited, there are ample opportunities to recommend strategies that increase client cash flow and maximize client well-being. Exploring concepts related to the use of *health savings accounts*, *flexible spending arrangements*, *high-deductible insurance plans*, *Medigap* policies, and, of course, understanding provisions related to PPACA, provides a useful way to identify and recommend appropriate and reasonable health insurance strategies matched to a client's situation.

Planning Reminder

Supplemental Medicare insurance is known as **Medigap**. Medigap policies are managed by private firms. A Medigap policy can help pay what Medicare Part A does not cover, such as copayments, coinsurance, and deductibles (policies purchased by those new to Medicare can no longer be used to pay Part B deductibles). Some Medigap policies cover services not available with Medicare. Before recommending a Medigap policy, a financial planner should consider the following issues:

• The client must be enrolled in Medicare Part A and Part B.

• Premiums for a policy are made to an insurance company, not the government.

• All standardized policies are guaranteed renewable, which means the insurance company cannot cancel a policy as long as premiums are paid.

• Policies sold after January 1, 2006 do not pay for prescription drugs; instead, clients should purchase Part D coverage through Medicare.

• It is illegal to sell a Medigap policy to someone who is enrolled in a Medicare Advantage Plan.

If a particular insurance plan is the only one available to a client, then actions taken to recommend a health insurance plan stop, aside from perhaps establishing a flexible spending account. The second, and maybe more important, way a financial planner can offer advice is in cases where more than one health plan is available, either by one employer, or for couples or partners, across both employers. If multiple plans are available, then a similar cost-benefit analysis should be conducted. For instance, some organizations provide employees with the choice of a traditional indemnity plan, a managed care plan (e.g., HMO, PPO, POS, or EPO), and/or a high-deductible health plan. To maximize benefits and control costs, a thorough analysis is needed, perhaps with the assistance of personnel from human resources or employee benefits or an independent health care insurance specialist.

Based on this information, a financial planner and client can begin to take action to adequately protect the health of the client's household while minimizing or eliminating duplicative coverage. It is also important to recognize that the choice of plan may change over the life cycle. Decisions about the *coordination of benefits* between two plans must also be considered, as well as the option for each spouse/partner to carry an individual plan, if no coverage is required for children. However, care must be taken when a high-deductible health plan is used because coverage through any other health plan is not permitted. Exceptions to this rule include accident, disability, dental, vision, long-term care, or specified disease insurance (e.g., cancer coverage).

Figure 9.8 highlights some of the important factors to consider when presenting health insurance recommendations to Chandler and Rachel Hubble.

Figure 9.8. Factors to Consider When Presenting Health Insurance Recommendations.

As noted previously, it is important for financial planners to possess a working knowledge of terms such as traditional indemnity, managed care (e.g., HMO, PPO, POS, and EPO plans), and high-deductible health plans. Although each of these terms represents a type of health insurance coverage, each plan is distinct, offering advantages and disadvantages for clients. Other important concepts include: (a) deductibles, (b) copayment levels, (c) coinsurance requirements, (d) policy stop-loss limits, (e) excluded coverages, (f) out-of-network restrictions, (g) premiums, and (h) access to COBRA and HIPAA benefits. Competent financial planners should not only know and use basic health insurance terms correctly, as well as understand provisions associated with health insurance products, financial planners must also be able to summarize plan strengths and weaknesses using client learning and processing preferences.

9.7 STEP 6: IMPLEMENT THE FINANCIAL PLANNING RECOMMENDATION(S)

Financial planners who are engaged in writing a comprehensive financial plan should follow an implementation checklist. The presentation of a recommendation should match a client's information processing style and preferences. Figure 9.9 shows how one of the recommendations developed for Chandler and Rachel can be presented within a financial plan. Keep in mind that in the Hubbles' situation, much of the implementation must be undertaken by either Chandler or Rachel, although the financial planner should be available to assist and answer questions.

Figure 9.9. Implementing an FSA Recommendation for the Hubble Family.

Recommendation #1: Maintain your HMO health insurance policy but begin funding a Flexible Spending Account (FSA) for health care with an amount equal to your average annual medical expenses.	
Who:	Chandler and Rachel.
What:	A Flexible Spending Account (FSA) for health care, which is funded with pretax salary withdrawals.
When:	Prior to your employer's account form due date (this date is generally two weeks prior to the start of your open enrollment period).
Where:	At your human resources representative's office or online through your employer's open enrollment website.
Why:	To ensure financial and medical security for your family.
How:	Consult your human resources representative who will assist you with filling out the required forms to begin payroll deductions to fund the FSA.
How much:	You should contribute $50 monthly ($600 annually) to the FSA for the year. Once you are comfortable with using an FSA, consider increasing your contributions to $1,650 annually ($600 vision and dental + $450 deductible + $240 copay + $360 prescriptions).
Effect on cash flow:	This contribution will save you approximately $226 in taxes per year ($600 pretax contribution x [30 percent state and federal tax rate + 7.65 percent FICA tax rate]). If you increase your contribution to $1,650, you will save approximately $621 in taxes ($1,650 pretax contribution x [30 percent state and federal tax rate + 7.65 percent FICA tax rate]).

9.8 STEP 7: MONITOR PROGRESS AND UPDATE

Monitoring health insurance recommendations is an ongoing task, with a special point of emphasis during the months of October and November of each year, or when plan renewals take place. Health insurance reviews become important, as well, whenever a client or client's family experiences a change in life or employment circumstances. Events such as loss of job, a new job, divorce, remarriage, death of a spouse or family member, transition of a child off a health plan, birth of a child, retirement, or any other significant life change will necessitate a review of health insurance coverages.

Monitoring of implemented recommendations becomes even more important as clients transition from working life toward retirement. Clients nearing retirement face many new challenges and opportunities. One common source of anxiety among those considering retirement deals with health care costs and health insurance alternatives. Even clients who continue to work past age sixty-five must grapple with health insurance issues. Financial planners need a firm understanding of the key rules, guidelines, products, and services targeted toward seniors. Specifically, understanding how Medicare and Medigap policy coverage affects health insurance planning is essential. The monetary and psychic costs associated with hastily made Medicare and Medigap choices can easily come back to haunt clients and their financial advisors.

Although there is minimal ongoing monitoring needed in the Hubble case, this step in the process still needs to be addressed. Figure 9.10 provides a summary of ongoing monitoring issues facing the Hubble family.

Figure 9.10. Issues to Monitor in the Hubble Case.

Out-of-pocket expenses for medical care and expenses should be monitored on an annual basis. Adjustments to the FSA should be made using forecasts of the following year's expenses. Additionally, the health status of Chandler, Rachel, and Phoebe should be updated each year to ensure that the appropriate type and level of coverage is being used to meet their needs. Given the highly volatile nature of the health insurance marketplace, it is also important to monitor changes in state and federal laws and changes in premium rates.

9.9 COMPREHENSIVE HUBBLE CASE

Health insurance coverage is often overlooked in the financial planning process because policies are generally employer provided. Typically, a financial planner has little control over the selection of the product or coverage. Health insurance planning, however, should not be overlooked when developing a comprehensive financial plan. Adequate policy provisions, as well as other aspects of coverage and the potential for future changes, should be evaluated and monitored.

This is particularly true in relation to the Hubble case. Strategies using Section 125 plans and FSA alternatives should be developed based on the Hubbles' annual health care spending patterns, deductibles, and copayments. Although it is unlikely that a financial planner would recommend that either Rachel or Chandler purchase a private insurance policy, a cost analysis of other available policies offered during the open enrollment periods might be appropriate. The family's goal of living a financially satisfying life must be weighed against the relative costs of health care options.

To summarize, health insurance coverage is an important topic to address in a financial plan. Ensuring that a client has necessary insurance in place is a key element to strengthening a client's financial capacity. The following narrative is an example of how the health insurance section within a comprehensive financial plan can be written.

Health Insurance

Overview of Health Insurance:

Health insurance is extremely important as a way to manage risk within a financial plan. Medical debt is one of the top three reasons that people file for bankruptcy in the United States. There are distinct types of health insurance coverage options, so it is important to consider your choices to ensure you have cost effective and adequate health insurance coverage in place. Your choice of health care alternatives affects your access to and payment for care. There are several tax-advantaged savings accounts specifically designed for medical expenses. Utilizing these accounts can provide significant tax savings.

Health Insurance Definitions:

The following definitions will be useful as you review the analysis presented in this section:

- *Out-of-pocket expenses*: The maximum amount of unreimbursed expenses you must pay on an annual basis.

- *Deductible*: Amount you must pay before insurance benefits begin.

- *Copayment*: Fixed fee you pay for services in addition to what the insurance company will pay.

- *Coinsurance*: Percentage of service expenses paid by you above the deductible amount.

- *Stop-loss limit*: The maximum amount of out-of-pocket expenses you will pay, which includes deductibles, copayments, and coinsurance, or what PPACA refers to as cost sharing.

Planning Assumptions:

- Current employment and health insurance coverage continues until retirement.

- Health insurance costs and out-of-pocket expenses will increase at the rate of inflation (3 percent per year) until the end of the plan.

- Family members are in good health with no diagnosed chronic health conditions.

- All family members visit health care providers annually for preventative care and each family member adheres to a healthy lifestyle.

- Chandler and Rachel do not have access to any other types of health insurance plans through their employers other than their current HMO plan.

Goals:

- Maintain appropriate health insurance coverage through Chandler's employer.

- Take advantage of any tax-advantaged plans that may be available through Chandler's or Rachel's employer, or through a private provider.

- Continue to ensure that any health coverage is appropriate in terms of cost and coverage.

Your Current Health Insurance Situation:

Health insurance coverage for your family of three is currently purchased through Chandler's employer. You have a health maintenance organization (HMO) plan that allows you to pay your monthly premiums of $375 on a pretax basis. Dental and vision insurance coverage is not included.

Based on the data you provided, your household is paying:

- $600, average expenses, for dental and eye care;

- $4,500 in health insurance premiums;

- $450 annually for medical deductibles;

- $240 annually in medical copayments; and

- $360 annually for prescriptions.

Health Insurance Recommendation:

The following table summarizes the primary recommendation that aligns with your health insurance planning goals. As with all recommendations presented in this financial plan, our firm is available to answer any questions that might arise and to assist with specific implementation procedures.

Recommendation #1: Maintain your HMO health insurance policy but begin funding a Flexible Spending Account (FSA) for health care with an amount equal to your average annual medical expenses.	
Who:	Chandler and Rachel.
What:	A Flexible Spending Account (FSA) for health care, which is funded with pretax salary withdrawals.
When:	Prior to your employer's account form due date (this date is generally two weeks prior to the start of your open enrollment period).
Where:	At your human resources representative's office or online through your employer's open enrollment website.

Why:	To ensure financial and medical security for your family.
How:	Consult your human resources representative who will assist you with filling out the required forms to begin payroll deductions to fund the FSA.
How much:	You should contribute $50 monthly ($600 annually) to the FSA for the year. Once you are comfortable with using an FSA, consider increasing your contributions to $1,650 annually ($600 vision and dental + $450 deductible + $240 copay + $360 prescriptions).
Effect on cash flow:	This contribution will save you approximately $226 in taxes per year ($600 pretax contribution x [30 percent state and federal tax rate + 7.65 percent FICA tax rate]). If you increase your contribution to $1,650, you will save approximately $621 in taxes ($1,650 pretax contribution x [30 percent state and federal tax rate + 7.65 percent FICA tax rate]).

Current vs. Recommended Outcome:

Your current health insurance coverage remains the same if you implement the health insurance recommendation. However, implementation will result in meaningful tax savings ($226 annually), which can be used to help fund other financial goals. It is important to note that contributions to flexible spending accounts do not rollover every year (this is often referred to as the "use it or lose it" rule). However, even if you do not spend all the money you contributed to an FSA in a given year, your tax savings will offset any potential loss as long as your expenses are more than $954 each year.

Alternative Recommendations and Outcome(s):

This analysis and resulting recommendation assumes that your employer(s) do not provide any other health insurance plan(s) other than Chandler's HMO plan. If this assumption is not correct, we recommend that you provide us with information on the other health care plan options available to you. Our firm will conduct a thorough analysis in conjunction with your human resources representative to compare the costs of coinsurance, copayments, deductibles, and the network of providers available. If you have access to a high-deductible health plan (HDHP), the use of this coverage should be evaluated. A HDHP provides the lowest premium option coupled with an opportunity to contribute to a Health Savings Account (HSA). Contributions to HSAs are tax-deferred and are tax-free if used for qualified medical expenses. You will not lose the funds that you contribute each year, even if you do not use the contributions on an annual basis. Any funds that remain in the HSA after the age of sixty-five can be used for any purpose without penalty.

Plan Implementation and Monitoring Procedures:

Prior to your open enrollment period, please review all health plan information in conjunction you're your employer's human resources personnel and/or our firm's staff. Monitor the dates for open enrollment so that you can implement any changes in plan selection and/or enroll in the FSA. Our firm will conduct a health insurance review during the fourth quarter of each year to coincide with your open enrollment period.

9.10 SELF-TEST

[A] Questions

Self-Test 1

Which of the following health insurance plans offers the greatest flexibility in terms of health care provider choice and facility use?

(a) PPO.

(b) Traditional Indemnity.

(c) HMO.

(d) HDHP.

Self-Test 2

It is January 2, 20XX and Sherman was just injured in a ski accident. He has $3,500 in hospital bills. His insurance policy has a $500 deductible, 20 percent coinsurance clause, and $1,500 stop-loss provision. How much will Sherman's insurance company pay for this claim?

(a) $800.

(b) $1,200.

(c) $2,400.

(d) $3,500.

Self-Test 3

Which of the following Medicare coverages is typically a free benefit starting at age sixty-five?

(a) Part A.

(b) Part B.

(c) Part D.

(d) All the above.

Self-Test 4

Kristy recently started working for a new employer. When she was hired she signed up for a high deducible health insurance plan. In order to obtain the greatest flexibility and maximize pre-tax dollars when paying for medical expenses, Kristy should also contribute to:

(a) An HSA.

(b) An FSA.

(c) A PPACA.

(d) A Medicare Supplemental Plan.

Self-Test 5

Which of the following is not a provision of the Patient Protection and Affordable Care Act?

(a) Lifetime limits on health insurance payments are prohibited.

(b) The choice of a primary care provider is guaranteed.

(c) Direct access to OB/GYN services is guaranteed.

(d) The use of an FSA to pay for non-prescription drugs is prohibited.

[B] Answers

Question 1: b

Question 2: c

Question 3: a

Question 4: a

Question 5: d

9.11 RESOURCES

Health insurance cost information (www.nchc.org).

Health savings account information (www.treasury.gov/resource-center/faqs/Taxes/Pages/Health-Savings-Accounts.aspx).

IRS Publication 969, Health Savings Accounts and Other Tax-Favored Health Plans.

Medicare information (www.medicare.gov).

Patient Protection and Affordable Care Act (PPACA) of 2010 (www.dol.gov/ebsa/healthreform).

Chapter 10

Disability Insurance Planning

Learning Objectives

- Learning Objective 1: Explain the role of disability insurance in a client's comprehensive financial plan.

- Learning Objective 2: Calculate a client's short- and long-term disability insurance need.

- Learning Objective 3: Understand the tax implications associated with different disability policies.

- Learning Objective 4: Identify appropriate disability planning recommendations based on a client's goals, resources, and household characteristics.

10.1 THE PROCESS OF DISABILITY INSURANCE PLANNING

The Americans with Disabilities Act defines a **disability** as broadly meaning a physical or mental impairment that substantially limits a person's major life activities.[1] Among those of working age, more are likely to become disabled than to die in any given year. As illustrated in Figure 10.1, the probability of becoming disabled for ninety days or longer is significantly greater than the probability of death, until a client reaches age sixty or older, although on a continually decreasing basis. This information is important for a financial planner to understand because it illustrates the need for disability insurance across time.

Figure 10.1. Probability of Death and Disability by Age.

Current Client Age	Probability of Death prior to Age 67[1]	Probability of Disability (Lasting 90 Days or Longer) prior to Age 65[2]
25	24%	54%
30	23%	52%
35	22%	50%
40	21%	48%
45	20%	45%
50	18%	39%
55	15%	32%
60	9%	9%

1. Calculation is a summation of the probability of death at every age from the current age to age at death. Social Security Administration, *Actuarial Publications, Period Life Figure*. Available at http://www.ssa.gov/oact/STATS/table4c6.html.
2. National Association of Insurance Commissioners, *1985 Individual Disability Figure A and B* as reported by Kenneth Black, Jr., and Harold D. Skipper, Jr., in *Life & Health Insurance*, 13th Edition. Upper Saddle River, NJ: Prentice Hall, 2000, 1411. Often referenced as 85CIDA or 85CIDB.

Reported **incidence of disability** can vary greatly from the unadjusted data presented in Figure 10.1.[2] Data in Figure 10.1 include disability from all sources. Figure 10.2 shows probabilities of disability, by age, based on accident or illness. The probabilities are lower, yet large enough to warrant concern when viewed holistically within a client's financial plan.

Figure 10.2. Probability of Disability from Accident or Illness by Age.

Current Client Age	Probability of Disability (Lasting 90 Days or Longer) prior to Age 65
25	40.3%
30	38.5%
35	36.5%
40	34.0%
45	30.5%
50	26.2%
55	20.5%

Source: New York Life, *Disability Income Worksheet.* Based on data from the 1985 National Association of Insurance Commissioners' Individual Disability Figure A. Available at: https://www.actuary.org/files/IDTWG_Table_Report_Dec_2013.pdf

Various occupations exhibit different incidences of disability. As such, when determining whether to issue a policy and the applicable premium, underwriters consider the **likelihood of disability** based on the insurance applicant's profession. As shown below, there are four basic classifications for disability insurance underwriting. Figure 10.3 shows the associated probabilities of disability by classification for male and females.

- Class 1—Professional;

- Class 2—Skilled;

- Class 3—Nonhazardous or light manual labor; and

- Class 4—Hazardous or heavy manual labor.

Figure 10.3. Probability of Disability by Occupational Class and Gender.

Occupational Class	Probability of Disability (Lasting 90 Days or Longer) prior to Age 65, Male	Probability of Disability (Lasting 90 Days or Longer) prior to Age 65, Female
1	18.0%	26.2%
2	33.3%	38.2%
3	46.1%	48.9%
4	411.2%	52.3%

Source: Centers for Disease Control and Prevention. Report available at: https://www.cdc.gov/ncbddd/disabilityandhealth/features/key-findings-community-prevalence.html

As illustrated in these figures, the incidence of disability varies based on many factors, including but not limited to gender, age, lifestyle, and occupation.[3] The purpose of this chapter is to review a method for determining a client's disability insurance need and to consider the way in which a needs analysis can be transformed into one or more recommendations within a comprehensive financial plan. Additionally, the discussion that follows describes how the financial planning process can be followed when developing and presenting a disability insurance analysis.

10.2 STEP 1: UNDERSTAND THE CLIENT'S PERSONAL AND FINANCIAL CIRCUMSTANCES

The first step in the disability insurance planning process involves reviewing, with the client, relevant personal and financial information. It is important to discuss a client's family health situation prior to making disability insurance recommendations. This type of discussion can be used to reinforce the client-financial planner relationship, leading to the development and presentation of integrative recommendations.

Any number of client-specific characteristics and factors can affect a client's need for disability income replacement coverage, including (1) the number of wage earners in the household; (2) whether the client is providing support for minor children or disabled adults; (3) the availability of assets or credit; (4) whether the client qualifies for Social Security Disability Insurance; (5) the hazard level of the client's job and whether they are self-employed; (6) the client's lifestyle choices; and (7) the client's risk tolerance.

By exploring the possible future need for disability income protection and currently available coverage, a financial planner can help inform their client about issues that can influence the recommendation and implementation of disability income protection strategies. Gathering a variety of information about a client's personal and household characteristics, as well as any in-force disability policies, is a critically important task associated with a thorough analysis of a client's situation. This information also serves as the foundation for identifying appropriate strategies and recommendations.

Figure 10.4 provides a review of the Hubbles' personal and financial circumstances related to disability insurance planning. The information in Figure 10.4 is typical of what a financial planner should evaluate at the first step of the financial planning process.

Figure 10.4. The Hubbles' Personal and Financial Circumstances.

Chandler Hubble	Rachel Hubble
Age: 42	Age: 42
State of residence: Missouri	State of residence: Missouri
Citizen: U.S.	Citizen: U.S.
Disability status: No known disability issues	Disability status: No known disability issues
Phoebe Hubble	
Age: 5	
Disability status: No known disability issues	

- Chandler and Rachel pay $25 per month in disability insurance premiums.
- Chandler and Rachel will receive no Social Security disability benefits in the event of disability.
- Chandler and Rachel plan to continue to save for other financial planning goals in the event of a disability.
- Any cash settlements received will be invested using a moderately conservative asset allocation approach.
- Chandler and Rachel will use a 70 percent income replacement ratio in case of disability.
- The applicable before-tax investment return is 7.75 percent.
- Chandler and Rachel are automatically covered for disability through employer provided plans. Rachel also pays for additional long-term disability coverage through her employer.
- Information about each policy is shown below:

Type of Policy	Policy 1 Group	Policy 2 Group	Policy 3 Group	Policy 4 Group
Insurance company	Mid-America Disability Assurance Corporation	All-World Life and Disability Company	Mid-America Disability Assurance Corporation	All-World Life and Disability Company
Rating	A.M. Best: A	A.M. Best: A	A.M. Best: A	A.M. Best: A-
Person insured	Chandler	Rachel	Chandler	Rachel
Wait periods (days)	0 days	0 days	90 days	90 days
Benefit period	90 days	90 days	To age 65	To age 65
Disability benefit	100 percent of salary and bonus	100 percent of salary and bonus	60 percent of salary and bonus	70 percent of salary and bonus
Definition	Own occupation	Own occupation	Own occupation	Modified own occupation
Benefit frequency	Biweekly	Monthly	Biweekly	Monthly
Premium amount	Company paid	Company paid	Company paid	$25 monthly (purchased through employer with pretax dollars)
Premium payment frequency	NA	NA	NA	Monthly

10.3 STEP 2: IDENTIFY AND SELECT GOALS

Few clients enter a financial planning engagement thinking about the need for disability insurance or contemplating strategies to replace income in the event of a disability. This does not mean, however, that disability planning should receive less attention in the financial plan development process. It is important for a financial planner to provide guidance to help their clients avoid risks posed by a potential disability. Disability insurance is a tool that increases as client's financial risk capacity. When viewed broadly, financial **risk capacity** refers to a client's ability to withstand unexpected financial shocks. The possibility of needing to replace household income in the event one or more primary wage earners in a family were to become disabled is one such financial shock. Having adequate disability coverage in place can help a household deal with the various financial obligations associated with disability. Figure 10.5 provides an overview of disability income replacement goals as they relate to the Hubble family.

Figure 10.5. The Hubbles' Disability Insurance Goals.

Possible disability income replacement goals for the Hubble family include:
• Replacing enough income to meet daily household expenses while continuing to save for other goals in the event of the disability of Chandler, Rachel, or both.
• Maintaining adequate funds (emergency or non-qualified) sufficient to cover any short-fall of income during a period of short-term or long-term disability for Chandler, Rachel, or both.
• Protecting the Hubble household from a significant reduction in their standard of living should one or both earners become disabled.

10.4 STEP 3: ANALYZE THE CLIENT'S CURRENT COURSE OF ACTION AND POTENTIAL ALTERNATIVE COURSE(S) OF ACTION

Calculating the appropriate amount of disability insurance to recommend requires consideration of income and expenses, assets available to support a client's lifestyle (e.g., bank accounts, undrawn lines of credit, cash value life insurance, etc.), and employee benefits (e.g., vacation and sick leave, Family Medical Leave Act (FMLA) availability, group disability policies, etc.). For example, a client might not have access to a short-term disability policy, but one may not be needed because of a generous leave policy provided by an employer or the availability of liquid assets in the form of an emergency fund.

Several factors determine the amount of *long-term* disability coverage needed. A client may wish to opt for a larger monthly replacement percentage and a longer elimination period or a lower replacement ratio and a shorter elimination period for roughly the same cost. In either case, it is often assumed the client has assets that can be used to cover a gap or shortfall in benefits. Additionally, if there is another earner in the household, and the household can meet monthly expenses on the income of the remaining earner, there might be less need for coverage, resulting in less coverage being purchased.

Five questions should be answered when evaluating an existing or new disability policy:

(1) How restrictive is the definition of disability?

(2) How long must the insured wait before benefits are paid?

(3) How much of a client's expenses (measured as a percentage of gross or net income) will be replaced during the benefit period?

(4) Will the benefits remain fixed or is it possible for benefits to increase with the rate of inflation?

(5) How long will the benefits continue?

There are many valid approaches financial planners can use to estimate the disability insurance need of a client. A simple approach, with an accompanying example, is shown in Figure 10.6. In this example, the proposed policy for a hypothetical client (not the Hubble family) is assumed to provide long-term coverage with a ninety-day elimination period (the **elimination period** is the time between the diagnosis of the disability and the contractual point when benefits are paid). As illustrated, the estimate can be calculated using annual or monthly figures (note that in this example the monthly estimates are rounded); however, since disability insurance is typically issued on a monthly dollar replacement basis, the monthly estimates may be more appropriate for most client situations.

Figure 10.6. Basic Approach to Estimate Disability Insurance Need.

Inputs	Yearly Example	Monthly Example	Monthly Calculation
Determine Household Income or Expense Need in the Event of a Disability	$90,000	$7,500	
Determine an Appropriate Income Replacement Ratio	80%	80%	
Estimate Net Household Income Needed	$72,000	$6,000	$7,500 × 80%
Determine Income While Insured is Disabled	$50,000	$4,167	
Calculate Disability Need	$22,000	$1,833	$6,000 – $4,167
Long-Term Disability Benefits	$0	$0	
Social Security Disability Benefits	$0	$0	
Estimate Earnings from Assets while Insured is Disabled	$12,000	$1,000	
Sum of Disability Benefits + Earnings	$12,000	$1,000	$0 + $0 + $1,000
Calculate Long-Term Disability Insurance Need	$10,000	$833	$1,833 – $1,000
Estimate Short-Term (90 Day) Elimination Period Need	$5,500	$5,500	$1,833 × 3
Current Emergency Fund Value	$10,000		
Short-Term Disability Insurance Need	$0		$5,500 – $10,000

As illustrated in this example, this hypothetical client has a long-term disability need in the amount of $833 in monthly benefits. This estimate assumes that the policy will begin paying benefits ninety days after the diagnosis of a covered disability. The emergency fund needed to cover the first ninety days of disability comes to $5,500; because the client has $10,000 currently saved, no short-term disability coverage is needed at this time.

A key figure for determining a disability insurance need is the **income replacement ratio**. The ratio is typically 60 percent to 70 percent of earned income. For example, assume that a client currently earns $90,000 per year before taxes. Using a 70 percent income replacement ratio, the client's total annual disability need will be $63,000 of available, or after-tax, income. This amount is equivalent to the client's after-tax income before the disability, assuming a 30 percent combined federal and state marginal tax bracket. However, this seemingly straightforward estimation procedure is complicated by three additional factors:

1. Disability insurance pays a fixed amount of monthly indemnity, but the amount that can be purchased is limited to prevent over-insurance, or the disincentive to return to work. In other words, disability insurance will pay a percentage of a client's pre-disability income each month, but the percentage of income replacement that the client can purchase is limited to avoid a situation where income remains at pre-disability levels but expenses decrease, effectively increasing income due to the disability.

2. Disability policies often have a **disability integration clause**, which is used to protect against the moral hazard of over-insurance by instituting an offset for other benefits. This prevents people from receiving more income due to a disability than they would have received without a disability.

3. Disability benefits can be subject to income tax depending on how the recipient paid the premiums and whether the premiums were paid with pretax or post-tax dollars. If the benefits are taxable, the client will need a higher income replacement ratio because some of the monthly benefit will be decreased by taxes.

In general, long-term policies are more important than short-term policies within a client's financial plan. A basic outcome of the financial planning process is the development and funding of an emergency savings fund or the identification of emergency sources of income. Self-insurance is often the best option for managing a short-term disability. By planning to use emergency funds, including cash assets, short-term liquid securities, or available lines of credit, clients can avoid the additional cost of short-term coverage. This strategy can provide an additional incentive to build and maintain an emergency fund and lines of credit.

The greatest financial risk for most clients is an extended period of disability. As such, a general best practice is to recommend the purchase of a long-term disability policy that provides benefits until age 65 or 67, when Social Security and other retirement benefits can be used to fund income needs. Short-term coverage, although important and perhaps the less expensive of the two options, should be a secondary consideration.

The following example shows how an analysis of the Hubble family's current disability insurance choices and needs can result in a pathway to the development of recommendations. Figure 10.7 provides a summary of the Hubbles' current disability insurance choices. Potential recommendations are also provided.

Figure 10.7. The Hubbles' Current Disability Insurance Choices and Potential Recommendations.

DISABILITY NEEDS ANALYSIS		
ASSUMPTIONS		
Client's Name	Chandler	Rachel
Client's Income	$102,699.88	$32,496.00
Length of Short-Term Disability (Months)	3.00	3.00
Length of Long-Term Disability (Months)	276.00	276.00
Does Client Have Short-Term Disability Policy? 1 = yes; 0 = no	1	1
Does Client Have Long-Term Disability Policy? 1 = yes; 0 = no	1	1
Short-Term Elimination Period (Months)	0	0
Long-Term Elimination Period (Months)	3.00	3.00
Short-Term Benefit Period (Months)	3.00	3.00
Long-Term Benefit Period (Months)	273.00	273.00
Value of Assets to be Used for an Elimination Period	28,500.00	28,500.00
Value of Other Assets to be Used for Disability Needs	$0.00	$0.00
Household Income Replacement Ratio	70.00%	70.00%
Yearly Expense Needs In Disability	$94,637.12	$94,637.12
Continuing Earned Household Income While In Disability	$32,496.00	$102,699.88
Before-Tax Investment Return	7.75%	7.75%
Federal Marginal Income Tax Bracket	25.00%	25.00%
State Marginal Income Tax Bracket	5.00%	5.00%
Monthly After-Tax Investment Income	$0.00	$0.00
After-Tax Continuing Income While In Disability	$22,747.20	$71,889.92
Yearly Shortfall While In Disability	$71,889.92	$22,747.20
Monthly Income Shortfall	*$5,990.83*	*$1,895.60*
SHORT-TERM DISABILITY		
Monthly Tax-Free Short-Term Disability Benefits	$0.00	$0.00
Monthly Tax-Free Short-Term Social Security Disability Benefits	$0.00	$0.00
Monthly Taxable Short-Term Disability Benefits	$8,558.33	$2,708.00
Monthly Other Taxable Benefits or Income for Short-Term Disability Use	$0.00	$0.00
Monthly Investment Earnings	$0.00	$0.00
Total Monthly Short-Term Income Available While In Disability	*$5,990.83*	*$1,895.60*
Monthly Short-Term Disability Need	$0.00	$0.00
Assets Needed to Fund Short-Term Disability Need	$0.00	$1,895.60
Does Client Have Sufficient Elimination Period Assets to Meet Short-Term Disability?	Yes	Yes

LONG-TERM DISABILITY		
Monthly Tax-Free Long-Term Disability Benefits	$0.00	$0.00
Monthly Tax-Free Long-Term Social Security Disability Benefits	$0.00	$0.00
Monthly Taxable Long-Term Disability Benefits	$5,135.00	$1,895.60
Monthly Other Taxable Benefits or Income for Long-Term Disability Use	$0.00	$0.00
Monthly Investment Earnings	$0.00	$0.00
Total Monthly Long-Term Income Available While In Disability	$3,594.50	$1,326.92
Monthly Long-Term Disability Need	2,396.33	568.68
Assets Needed to Fund Long-Term Disability Need	$643,669.57	$134,332.04
Does Client Have Sufficient Monetary and Investment Assets to Meet Long-Term Disability Needs?	No	No
SUMMARY		
Monthly Short-Term Disability: How Much is Needed?	$0.00	$0.00
Monthly Long-Term Disability: How Much is Needed?	$2,396.33	$568.68

The analysis of the Hubbles' current disability insurance situation shows a short-term disability need exists for Chandler and Rachel; however, this need can be offset by assets held in the Hubbles' growing emergency fund. On the other hand, the analysis shows that Chandler and Rachel have a long-term disability insurance need as well. Chandler's long-term need is approximately $2,400 per month, whereas Rachel's need is approximately $570 per month. These figures are based on the general recommendation that clients do not rely on Social Security disability benefits. Rather, Social Security disability benefits should supplement an existing long-term policy.

Based on this analysis, the following potential recommendations are worth considering:
- Chandler should obtain additional disability coverage (as much as possible up to $2,400 monthly) in the event of a long-term disability.
  - Chandler should explore whether he can purchase a private long-term disability policy or whether he can purchase life insurance with a disability income rider.
- Rachel should obtain additional disability coverage (as much as possible up to $570 monthly) in the event of a long-term disability.
  - Rachel should explore whether she can purchase a private long-term disability policy or whether she can purchase a life insurance policy with a disability income rider.

Planning Reminder

When an initial disability analysis indicates that a client needs coverage in excess of 70 percent of income, it may be necessary to reevaluate the client's situation because it is generally not possible to purchase policies that provide more than 70 percent income replacement. Possible adjustments to an analysis include reducing expenses and adjusting goal funding needs. Rather than purchase additional insurance coverage, a client may need to increase savings.

10.5 STEP 4: DEVELOP THE FINANCIAL PLANNING RECOMMENDATION(S)

[A] Types of Disability Insurance Policies

Disability insurance planning may be the most important, yet most frequently overlooked, topic in a client's comprehensive financial planning. This often happens because disability insurance tends to be provided to clients as a component of an employee benefits package. Because the incidence of personal bankruptcy has been closely linked to both medical expenses and job loss, it is important for financial planners to exhibit appropriate disability planning skills. Disability insurance can provide the necessary funding to help a client avoid, or at least mitigate, a potentially devastating monetary loss that could result in bankruptcy.

For the purposes of disability insurance planning, a disability policy can be classified broadly as either own-occupation or any-occupation coverage. With an **own-occupation policy**, a claimant is considered disabled and therefore eligible for benefits if they are unable to perform the duties required by the person's original or "own" job. Under an **any-occupation policy**, claimants are considered eligible to collect benefits only if the disability is severe enough to keep them from performing the duties required for any meaningful work. Any-occupation is the stricter classification in that it will be much more difficult for a claimant to be eligible to receive benefits under the policy.

Although own-occupation policies are appropriate for nearly all clients, finding such a policy is becoming increasingly difficult. Several insurance companies have either stopped offering own-occupation policies or significantly reduced the number of policies issued on a yearly basis. When and if an own-occupation policy can be obtained, the annual premium can be quite expensive. To meet the needs of the market while protecting the underwriting profitability of insurance companies, some firms now offer only modified own-occupation or split-definition disability policies. A **modified own-occupation** policy is one that pays only if an insured is unable to engage in their chosen occupation and is also unable to work in a reasonable alternative occupation— or one for which the client is qualified by education, training, or experience. A **split-definition policy** incorporates the preceding modified own-occupation definition with a short- and long-term disability definition. Specifically, to obtain benefits, the insured must be unable to engage in their own occupation for a certain period of time, usually two years. After the specified period, benefits are continued if the insured is unable to engage in a suitable and reasonable occupation.

In addition to these classifications of disability, a policy provision called a **residual benefits rider** is typically available for purchase. This rider offers added protection for partial disability or for claimants who can return to work on a part-time basis. Nearly all policies also provide a **cost-of-living adjustment rider** that continues to increase benefits as inflation increases. The addition of these two riders will increase the premium paid.

Clients may have access to resources in addition to traditional disability income replacement policies. An employee that becomes disabled might have unused sick or personal leave that can be used for a short-term disability. In addition, a client might have access to or be eligible for **Social Security Disability Income** (SSDI) and/or **workers' compensation insurance**. To be eligible for SSDI, a worker must be totally disabled and expect the disability to last for at least twelve continuous months. To be eligible for workers' compensation, the event that precipitated the disability must have occurred at work or when functioning in a working capacity.

[B] Other Disability Insurance Coverage Definitions

Before formulating a disability insurance recommendation, it is important to recognize definitions and standard long-term disability policy options. Some of these key terms are summarized in Figure 10.8.

Figure 10.8. Long-Term Disability Policy Definitions and Options Available.

Term	Description	Options Available	Typical Selection
Elimination period	Period of time the insured must be totally disabled before benefits can begin.	30, 60, 90, 180, or 365 days	Minimum: 180 days Preferred: Matched to short-term policy benefit period, paid leave available, or savings.
Benefit period	Period of time the insurance company is obligated to pay the monthly disability benefits.	3, 5, 10, or 20 years, until age 65, or lifetime	Minimum: 5 years Preferred: Age of eligibility for Social Security/Medicare
Qualification period	Period of time the insured must be totally disabled before residual benefits can begin.	Same as elimination period	Minimum: 180 days Preferred: 30 days
Definition of occupation	Determines the conditions under which disability income benefits are paid.	Own occupation or any occupation	Own occupation is preferred but should be coordinated with residual benefit rider.
Residual benefit rider	Pays a partial benefit when the insured is not totally disabled.		Recommended, but coordinated with definition of occupation.
Cost-of-living adjustment (COLA) or inflation rider	Total disability and residual benefits each year are increased by a specified percentage.		Recommended for maximum coverage, but expensive.

[C] Disability Policy Riders

Financial planners who provide disability recommendations should be familiar with the most common policy provisions that help ensure continuity or continuation of coverage. Some of the most widely used riders include the following:

- A **group disability replacement rider** guarantees a client the ability to convert a certain percentage of their group disability benefit into an individual plan, thus making the group long-term disability policy portable.

Planning Reminder

Clients should focus on purchasing a policy with an annual inflation adjustment to the benefit. Regardless of the percentage of income initially replaced, long-term benefits can quickly become eroded by inflation.

- A **waiver-of-premium clause** pays all future premiums in the event of disability.

- A **guaranteed-renewable disability provision** protects the insured from policy cancellation by allowing the insured to renew a policy without proof of insurability.

- If available, a **noncancelable disability provision** allows for the guaranteed renewal of a policy at a predetermined premium—an essential provision for controlling costs.

- A **recurrent disability provision** states that if the insured were to become disabled again within six months or up to one year, the disability will be considered a continuation of the previous claim. Without a recurrent disability provision, an insurance company can impose another elimination period before beginning benefits a second time.

- A **residual disability provision** continues benefits for those who are either still or once again actively engaged in their occupation, but because of a sickness or injury, continue to suffer from either a loss of time and/or productivity or a loss of income.

[D] Tax Implications Associated with the Receipt of Disability Benefits

The choice of a private or employer-provided policy can have a significant impact on the taxation of benefits. The **taxability of disability benefits** is primarily based on who pays the annual premium during the plan year in which the disability occurs. There are six basic premium payment scenarios that are used to determine the extent of taxability. These are shown in Figure 10.9.

Figure 10.9. Taxability of Disability Insurance Benefits Matrix.

Scenario	Type of Policy	Premiums Paid by	Premiums Included in Income	Taxability of Benefits
1	Group	Employer	No	Yes
2	Group	Both	No	Yes
3	Group	Employer	Yes	No*
4	Group	Both	Yes	No*
5	Group	Employee	Yes	No*
6	Individual	Owner	N/A	No

* Taxes will be due on the portion of benefits attributable to any employer-paid premiums over the preceding three policy years.

If a client is insured through a group plan paid for completely by their employer, and the client elects to exclude employer contributions from taxable income, any future benefits received will be fully taxable to the employee. For employees who irrevocably elect to include employer contributions as income (making the benefits taxable in the current year), any benefits resulting from a disability occurring during the plan year will avoid taxation, prorated to the portion of employer-provided premium contributions made over the preceding three policy years. If the premium cost is shared between the employer and the employee (i.e., a **contributory disability plan**), taxes will be due on the portion of benefits attributable to the employer-paid premiums over the preceding three policy years. If the premium is paid completely by the insured with after-tax dollars, all benefits will be received tax free.

When developing a disability insurance recommendation, it is very important that financial planners consider whether a client is better served paying taxes on the premiums received today or the benefits received in the future. Helping clients financially prepare for financial uncertainties is a basic tenet of financial planning, and in this case, client characteristics, such as marital/partner situation, type of employment, self-employment, or recreational pursuits must be considered.

[E] Insurance Company Selection Criteria

Given the long-term nature of most disabilities, it is important to match a product recommendation for a client with an insurer that is financially strong and stable. While it is possible to conduct an independent evaluation of an insurer, nearly all practicing financial planners rely on a **rating service** to help guide the selection of an insurance provider. Five third-party rating agencies and each firm's range of ratings are shown in Figure 10.10. As is the case with life insurance recommendations, a best practice involves the use of products from companies rated "A" or higher by any of the rating agencies.

Figure 10.10. Third-Party Insurance Company Rating Agencies.

Rating Agency	Safety Ratings	Criteria
A.M. Best	A++ to F	Insurance company's ability to meeting policyholder and contractual obligations based on four size categories.
Demotech's	A'' (Unsurpassed) to S (Substantial) to M (Moderate) to L (Licensed)	Measures of solvency
Fitch Ratings	AAA to D	Insurance company's claims-paying ability, financial fundamentals, capitalization, debt rating leverage, and asset quality.
Moody's	AAA to C	Insurance company's ability to meet policyholder obligations by focusing on investment portfolio and asset/liability structure.
Standard & Poor's	AAA to C	Insurance company's claims-paying ability.
Weiss Ratings	A to F	Adherence to general accounting principles.

[F] Estimating Individual Disability Policy Premiums

It is often difficult to obtain a disability insurance quote without undergoing the full underwriting process. However, it is possible to estimate premium costs for an average high-quality policy when writing a comprehensive financial plan in which disability insurance is not the primary client objective.

The cost generally comes close to between 1 percent and 3 percent of a client's annual gross earned income.[4] Premiums are tied the applicant's occupational riskiness and the number of supplemental riders added to the policy.

The definition of disability or type of policy selected is the other primary determinant of cost. It is a financial planner's responsibility to adjust the premium estimate to match the needs of each client based on the elimination period, benefit period, and monthly benefit chosen. Extending the elimination period will lower the premium.

Planning Reminder

Given the relatively high probability that a client may experience a disability, it is important to use a **liability release form** if a client declines a recommendation to purchase disability insurance. A liability release should be signed by the client. This provides some protection against potential litigation. Should the client, the client's spouse, or other family members question the lack of contingency planning to protect the household from a temporary or long-term loss of income, the financial planner will be able to document the client's choice. The client's signature on the liability release acknowledges that the financial planner made a recommendation that was declined.

[G] Disability Insurance for High-Income Earners and Business Owners

High-income earners may become accustomed to a certain lifestyle. A disability can create serious financial repercussions. Multiple mortgages, private school tuition for children, and domestic help can all be considered fixed expenses not easily continued in the event of a disability. Many disability insurance policies limit the maximum monthly benefit regardless of the stated percent of coverage. This is especially prevalent in group policies. For example, a group disability policy might impose an absolute limit of $6,000 for monthly benefits or limit the amount of earned income includable in the benefits calculation to $120,000 of annual income. In either case, a high-income earner could face a situation where the group disability policy covers far less than the stated 60 percent of income.

Although many high-income earners might also have a sizable net worth that can provide adequate unearned or investment income to fill an earnings gap, others may not have nearly enough to support their current lifestyle, which could create undue hardship on the earner's family. A high-income earner should consider purchasing a **supplemental disability income policy**. These policies, although expensive, offer a much higher income limit—in some cases, $1 million or more—and are normally underwritten by specialty insurers, such as Lloyd's of London.

In addition to filling an income gap, a supplemental policy can provide an extra layer of financial protection that replaces a larger percentage of total compensation (e.g., incentive pay, bonuses, or commissions). Although moral hazard prohibitions limit any policy from providing benefits greater than earned income, a supplemental policy can offer additional guarantees and enhanced portability.

The issue of disability insurance covering only earned income creates an additional issue for self-employed business owners—not all of whom are high-income earners. Business owners often overlook the fact that their business generates income attributable to the owners' efforts that are not covered under disability income insurance definitions of personal, earned income. An example of this is a business that generates $250,000 of revenue per year based on the activities of the owner, with the owner drawing a salary of only one-half this amount, choosing to reinvest the remainder in the company. The reinvestment will decrease or possibly stop because of a lost-time injury or illness. Unfortunately, the income will not be replaced under a standard disability insurance policy. Strategies to prepare for this uncertainty are available, but the critical point is not to overlook these issues when advising self-employed business owners and other high-income earners.

[H] Applying Planning Skills to the Hubble Case

As noted throughout each insurance discussion presented in this book, only modest changes generally need to be made to the initial recommendations developed at Step Three of the financial planning process, although it is possible that new client information or data can necessitate the need for a reevaluation. Figure 10.11 provides a summary of the final disability insurance recommendations that match the Hubble family's financial goals.

Figure 10.11. Disability Insurance Recommendations for Chandler and Rachel.

> **The final disability insurance recommendations developed for the Hubble family match the preliminary recommendations identified at Step Three of the financial planning process.**
>
> - Chandler has sufficient short-term disability coverage but has insufficient long-term disability coverage.
>   - Recommend that Chandler obtain disability coverage equal to approximately $2,400 monthly in the event of a long-term disability. Chandler should explore whether he can purchase a private long-term disability policy or whether he can purchase life insurance with a disability income rider.
> - Rachel has sufficient short-term disability coverage but has insufficient long-term disability coverage.
>   - Recommend that Rachel obtain coverage equal to approximately $570 monthly in the event of a long-term disability. Rachel should explore whether she can purchase a private long-term disability policy or whether she can purchase a life insurance policy with a disability income rider.
> - Keep in mind that a general recommendation is that clients should not rely on Social Security disability benefits, but rather to consider Social Security benefits only as a supplement to an existing long-term policy. Similarly, clients should not rely on worker's compensation benefits. In order to qualify for worker's compensation, the disability must occur on the job.

10.6 STEP 5: PRESENT THE FINANCIAL PLANNING RECOMMENDATION(S)

Numerous possible strategies can be recommended based on a client's circumstances and the quality of any in-place disability policies. Recommendations should generally center on a client's willingness and capacity to sustain the loss of income. Clients need be made aware that most disabilities not only reduce income but also increase expenses; therefore, recommendations should consider the likelihood and severity of any possible disability. Finally, strategies should also consider appropriate policy provisions (e.g., inflation riders, classifications of disability, residual benefit clauses) that make the most sense for a client, because a client living in a dual-earner household or one with adequate access to assets might not need the same amount of coverage or a policy with many added provisions.

Figure 10.12 highlights some of the principal factors to consider when presenting disability insurance recommendations to Chandler and Rachel Hubble.

Figure 10.12. Factors to Consider When Presenting Disability Insurance Recommendations.

> **Some desired outcomes associated with the presentation of disability insurance recommendations include (1) educating Chandler and Rachel about potential future issues associated with an income shortfall due to a short- or long-term disability and (2) helping Chandler and Rachel prepare for this uncertainty using a combination of cost-effective and tax-effective insurance and self-insurance strategies.**

There are several client-specific characteristics and factors that will influence the way in which recommendations are presented to Chandler and Rachel. Some of these factors include:

- Temperament and personality, interpreted as a positive or negative view of life in determining the extent to which random events might influence the Hubbles' decisions about buying disability insurance. For example, some clients think the risk of disability is too small to worry about. A financial planner should attempt to determine what fears Chandler and Rachel have about becoming disabled.
- The Hubbles' risk tolerance or other attitudes, as an aversion to risk may encourage some clients to perhaps buy more disability insurance than is needed, whereas a client who is more risk tolerant may prefer to gamble that such insurance is unnecessary. Experiences with Rachel's parents might influence these issues.
- The history of cancer in Rachel's family and the death of her parents at relatively young ages might influence her attitude about disability insurance.

The following assumptions should also be reviewed prior to and during the presentation of recommendations:

- The Hubbles are automatically covered for short-term disability through employer-provided plans. Chandler has an employer-provided long-term disability insurance plan.
- Rachel also pays for long-term disability coverage through her employer.
- Chandler and Rachel will receive no Social Security disability benefits in case of a disability.
- Chandler and Rachel plan to continue to save for other financial planning goals in the event of a disability.
- Any cash settlements received will be invested using a moderately conservative asset allocation approach.

10.7 STEP 6: IMPLEMENT THE FINANCIAL PLANNING RECOMMENDATION(S)

Implementing disability income replacement recommendations should be a primary focus when insurance issues are being dealt with in the financial plan development process. When choosing the platform in which to implement recommendations, a financial planner should consider each of the following:

- Definitions of disability and occupation.

- The elimination period requirements.

- Any pre-existing condition exclusions.

- Recurrent disability provisions.

- Residual disability provisions.

- COLA provisions.

- Partial or residual benefit provisions.

- Disability replacement riders.

- Waiver of premium clauses.

- Guaranteed renewable provisions.

- Noncancelable provisions.

- Social Security riders.

- Benefits integration.

- Split-definition policies.

As noted in earlier chapters, the implementation of recommendations is the primary way in which a financial plan's effectiveness is measured. An implementation strategy must include enough detail to enable the client to work through the steps necessary to implement recommendations.

When working with Chandler and Rachel, there are a quite a few recommendations that can be proposed, with different costs and possible outcomes associated with each. The presentation of recommendations needs to match the information processing styles and preferences of Chandler and Rachel. Figure 10.13 shows how one of the recommendations developed for Chandler and Rachel can be presented within a financial plan.

Figure 10.13. Implementing a Disability Insurance Recommendation for the Hubble Family.

Recommendation #1: Obtain quotes and purchase a private supplemental long-term disability policy for the maximum permissible income replacement percentage.	
Who:	Chandler.
What:	(A) An annually renewable convertible disability insurance policy. The policy should include a disability waiver and a disability income rider. (B) Private supplemental long-term disability insurance policies are not always available. Determine whether a private insurance company is willing to write a policy that provides benefits in addition to the long-term disability policy provided by your employer.
When:	Within the next thirty to forty-five days.
Where:	With your insurance professional or with an online provider that our firm can recommend (our staff will help you when working with outside professionals).
Why:	To ensure financial security for your family in the event of a disability. For a specified period of time, the disability income rider will pay out a monthly income of 1 percent of the coverage amount of the insurance policy in the event of a permanent disability.
How:	Consult your insurance professional or our firm can assist you when working with an online provider. Our firm will assist by discussing the underwriting issues, required application, and medical information.
How much:	(A) $2,400 monthly. (B) Maximum available benefit amount.
Effect on cash flow:	Estimated annual cost: $900. • Although an extreme consideration, Chandler should also explore using disability insurance premium dollars to purchase other employer-provided benefits with pre-tax dollars, which will then free up cash flow to purchase additional disability coverage in the private market. Chandler should also ask if group disability premiums can be paid with after-tax dollars, so that any future benefits received will not be taxable (a further tax analysis will be needed if this is an option).

10.8 STEP 7: MONITOR PROGRESS AND UPDATE

Numerous ongoing monitoring issues are at play in the domain of disability insurance planning. It is important to evaluate the financial strength of each insurance company in which a client has a policy, as well as the financial stability of insurance companies in which a new policy can be purchased. If disability insurance is provided through an employer, any change in employment could influence how much coverage the client is able to obtain. At the household level, disability triggers need to be evaluated at least on an annual basis. Figure 10.14 provides a summary of ongoing monitoring issues facing the Hubble family.

Figure 10.14. Issues to Monitor in the Hubble Case.

Some of the most important disability events that may impact the Hubble family's disability insurance needs include:
• Health status and health choices. • Family health history, including coronary artery disease, cancer, and early-onset Alzheimer's. • Employment status or change in type of employment. • New, more dangerous hobbies or jobs. • Divorce. • Change in health status for Chandler or Rachel. • Death of Chandler or Rachel. • Changes in cash flow. • Changes in net worth. • Changes in emergency fund or other non-qualified assets.

10.9 COMPREHENSIVE HUBBLE CASE

Disability insurance coverage is an important topic that should be addressed in a comprehensive financial plan. In addition to life insurance, this is one insurance topic that can be analyzed and managed by a financial planner, even if the financial planner is not an insurance agent or broker. Ensuring that a client has the necessary disability insurance in place is a key element to strengthening a client's financial capacity. The following narrative is an example of how the disability insurance section within a comprehensive financial plan can be written.

Disability Insurance

Overview of Disability Insurance:

Planning for a disability is an important part of your financial plan. People in your age group have a 30 to 34 percent probability of being disabled for more than ninety days prior to reaching age sixty-five. Short-term disability policies cover short periods of lost income. The policies typically offer from six months up to a maximum of two years of benefits. Long-term disability policies provide benefit coverage for as little as three years or as much as a lifetime, although policies typically offer coverage until a specific age, such as sixty-five or sixty-seven. By design, disability insurance products that offer long-term disability benefits will never provide 100 percent income replacement. The reason is that a replacement ratio this high increases fraudulent claims by incentivizing some insured individuals to take more risk in order to become disabled (generally, disability coverage is limited to 70 percent of income). This section of your financial plan discusses options to compensate for a potential decline in income in the event of a disability.

Disability Insurance Definitions:

The following definitions will be useful as you review the analysis presented in this section:

- *Elimination period*: Period of time the insured must be totally disabled before benefits can begin.

- *Benefit period:* Period of time the insurance company is obligated to pay monthly disability benefits.

- *Qualification period*: Period of time the insured must be totally disabled before residual benefits can begin.

- *Definition of occupation*: Determines the conditions under which disability income benefits are paid.

- *Residual benefit rider*: Pays a partial benefit when the insured is not totally disabled.

- *Cost of living (COLA) rider*: Ensures that total disability and residual benefits each year are increased by a specific percentage.

Planning Assumptions:

- As a family, you will receive no Social Security disability benefits.

- Chandler and Rachel, you plan to continue to save for other financial planning goals in the event of a disability.

- Any cash settlements received will be invested using a moderately conservative asset allocation approach (approximately 7.75 percent).

- In the event that either Chandler or Rachel is disabled, household expenses are expected to be $115,000 per year (in today's dollars).

- As a family, you want to replace 70 percent of the disabled person's income in the event of a disability.

Goals:

- Determine whether your disability insurance policies are best suited to your needs and whether additional coverage is necessary.

Your Current Disability Insurance Situation:

Currently, you both own a short-term and a long-term disability policy. Your short-term disability policies will provide 100 percent salary and bonus income replacement for the first ninety days of a disability. If you are still unable to return to work after ninety days, your long-term disability policies will provide benefits equal to 60 percent of Chandler's salary and bonus if he is disabled and 70 percent of Rachel's salary if she is disabled. Both of Chandler's disability policies provide protection in the case that he is unable to return to work in his own occupation. Even if he is able to work in a different occupation, he will still receive his disability benefits.

Rachel's short-term disability policy also provides protection in the case that she is unable to work in her own occupation; however, her long-term disability policy is a modified own occupation policy. This means that the policy will only pay benefits if Rachel is unable to engage in her own chosen occupation and is also unable to work in a reasonable alternative occupation or an occupation that she is qualified for in terms of education, training, or experience.

Modified-own occupation policies are significantly less expensive than own-occupation policies. Additionally, modified-own occupation policies are much easier to obtain in the marketplace. Please bear in mind that since your insurance premiums are paid by your employer or purchased with pretax dollars, any disability benefits you receive will be taxable; therefore, your disability coverage will need to be sufficient to cover your living expenses and the income tax liability resulting from the receipt of the disability benefits.

We have analyzed your current disability policies to determine whether the coverage you have is sufficient to meet your needs in the event that either or both of you become disabled and are unable to return to your current occupations, either for a short period of time or permanently. The table below shows details of the analysis.

The analysis shows that Rachel's current disability coverage is insufficient to meet your family's income needs in the event that Rachel becomes disabled. Your family will have a monthly income shortfall of $570 ($6,840 annually). If Chandler were to become disabled, your family will need an additional $2,400 per month ($28,800 annually) in order to meet your family's needs.

DISABILITY NEEDS ANALYSIS		
ASSUMPTIONS		
Client's Name	Chandler	Rachel
Client's Income	$102,699.88	$32,496.00
Length of Short-Term Disability (Months)	3.00	3.00
Length of Long-Term Disability (Months)	276.00	276.00
Does Client Have Short-Term Disability Policy? 1 = yes; 0 = no	1	1
Does Client Have Long-Term Disability Policy? 1 = yes; 0 = no	1	1
Short-Term Elimination Period (Months)	0	0
Long-Term Elimination Period (Months)	3.00	3.00
Short-Term Benefit Period (Months)	3.00	3.00
Long-Term Benefit Period (Months)	273.00	273.00
Value of Assets to be Used for an Elimination Period	28,500.00	28,500.00
Value of Other Assets to be Used for Disability Needs	$0.00	$0.00
Household Income Replacement Ratio	70.00%	70.00%
Yearly Expense Needs In Disability	$94,637.12	$94,637.12
Continuing Earned Household Income While In Disability	$32,496.00	$102,699.88
Before-Tax Investment Return	7.75%	7.75%
Federal Marginal Income Tax Bracket	25.00%	25.00%
State Marginal Income Tax Bracket	5.00%	5.00%
Monthly After-Tax Investment Income	$0.00	$0.00
After-Tax Continuing Income While In Disability	$22,747.20	$71,889.92
Yearly Shortfall While In Disability	$71,889.92	$22,747.20
Monthly Income Shortfall	**$5,990.83**	**$1,895.60**
SHORT-TERM DISABILITY		
Monthly Tax-Free Short-Term Disability Benefits	$0.00	$0.00
Monthly Tax-Free Short-Term Social Security Disability Benefits	$0.00	$0.00
Monthly Taxable Short-Term Disability Benefits	$8,558.33	$2,708.00
Monthly Other Taxable Benefits or Income for Short-Term Disability Use	$0.00	$0.00
Monthly Investment Earnings	$0.00	$0.00
Total Monthly Short-Term Income Available While In Disability	*$5,990.83*	*$1,895.60*
Monthly Short-Term Disability Need	$0.00	$0.00
Assets Needed to Fund Short-Term Disability Need	$0.00	$1,895.60
Does Client Have Sufficient Elimination Period Assets to Meet Short-Term Disability?	Yes	Yes
LONG-TERM DISABILITY		
Monthly Tax-Free Long-Term Disability Benefits	$0.00	$0.00
Monthly Tax-Free Long-Term Social Security Disability Benefits	$0.00	$0.00
Monthly Taxable Long-Term Disability Benefits	$5,135.00	$1,895.60

Monthly Other Taxable Benefits or Income for Long-Term Disability Use	$0.00	$0.00
Monthly Investment Earnings	$0.00	$0.00
Total Monthly Long-Term Income Available While In Disability	*$3,594.50*	*$1,326.92*
Monthly Long-Term Disability Need	$2,396.33	$568.68
Assets Needed to Fund Long-Term Disability Need	$643,669.57	$134,332.04
Does Client Have Sufficient Monetary and Investment Assets to Meet Long-Term Disability Needs?	No	No
SUMMARY		
Monthly Short-Term Disability: How Much is Needed?	**$0.00**	**$0.00**
Monthly Long-Term Disability: How Much is Needed?	**$2,396.33**	**$568.68**

Disability Insurance Recommendations:

The following tables summarize the recommendations that have been designed to help you reach your disability insurance goals. As with all recommendations presented in this financial plan, our firm is available to answer any questions that might arise and to assist with specific implementation procedures.

Recommendation #1: Obtain quotes and purchase a private supplemental long-term disability policy for the maximum permissible income replacement percentage.	
Who:	Chandler.
What:	(A) An annually renewable convertible disability insurance policy. The policy should include a disability waiver and a disability income rider. (B) Private supplemental long-term disability insurance policies are not always available. Determine whether a private insurance company is willing to write a policy that provides benefits in addition to the long-term disability policy provided by your employer.
When:	Within the next thirty to forty-five days.
Where:	With your insurance professional or with an online provider that our firm can recommend (our staff will provide you with specific information and guidance throughout the process).
Why:	To ensure financial security for your family in the event of a disability. For a specified period of time, the disability income rider will pay out a monthly income of 1 percent of the coverage amount of the insurance policy in the event of a permanent disability.
How:	Consult your insurance professional or our firm can assist you when working with an online provider. Our firm will assist by discussing the underwriting issues, required application, and medical information.
How much:	(A) $2,400 monthly or (B) Maximum available benefit amount.
Effect on Cash flow:	Estimated annual cost: $900.

Recommendation #2: Obtain quotes and purchase a private supplemental long-term disability policy for the maximum permissible income replacement percentage.	
Who:	Rachel.
What:	(A) An annually renewable convertible disability insurance policy. The policy should include a disability waiver and a disability income rider. (B) Private supplemental long-term disability insurance policies are not always available. Determine whether a private insurance company is willing to write a policy that provides benefits in addition to the long-term disability policy provided by your employer.
When:	Within the next thirty to forty-five days.
Where:	With your insurance professional or with an online provider that our firm can recommend (our staff will provide you with specific information and guidance throughout the process).
Why:	To ensure financial security for your family in the event of a disability. For a specified period of time, the disability income rider will pay out a monthly income of 1 percent of the coverage amount of the insurance policy in the event of a permanent disability.
How:	Consult your insurance professional or our firm can assist you when working with an online provider. Our firm will assist by discussing the underwriting issues, required application, and medical information.
How much:	A) $570 monthly or B) Maximum available benefit amount.
Effect on Cash flow:	Estimated annual cost: $170.

Current vs. Recommended Outcome:

Implementation of these recommendations will cause a decrease in discretionary cash flow; however, implementation ensures that in the event of a disability, your family's standard of living will remain similar to what it is today. You will not need to reallocate assets from other goals to meet your retirement needs. Additionally, implementing the disability insurance recommendations will minimize your financial stress during a difficult time period and ensure that your family is protected financially.

Alternative Recommendations and Outcome(s):

An alternative to purchasing a supplemental long-term disability policy involves adding a disability income rider to any life insurance policy purchases (see the life insurance section of this plan). A disability income rider will generally pay a benefit equivalent to 1 percent of the face value of the policy as a monthly benefit. A disability income rider will reduce the value of the insurance received by a beneficiary should disability payments need to be made. This means that the face value amount of insurance needs to increase. Specifically, if this alternative is accepted, Chandler should purchase a term life insurance policy with an additional face value of $240,000, whereas Rachel should purchase a term life insurance policy with an additional face value of $57,000. Implementing this alternative recommendation will increase the cost of each insurance policy.

Another alternative involves exploring whether your employers can increase benefits provided in existing long-term disability policies. It may be possible to increase disability coverage with an additional pretax cost. If this is an option, please provide our firm with the contact information of your human resources representative. We will contact the person to determine the options available to modify your current disability policies in order to meet your needs.

Plan Implementation and Monitoring Procedures:

Please notify us if you would like assistance in locating and obtaining quotes for the products recommended above (our firm is not licensed to sell insurance products, but we do have referral agreements with highly regarded insurance brokers in the area). The savings from implementing other recommendations in this plan should be used to pay for the additional long-term disability coverage your family needs. Under this financial plan, you can reallocate some of your cash flow to pay for the cost of additional long-term disability coverage.

As your income changes and the cost of living increases, it will be important to reevaluate your disability coverage annually to ensure that coverage is still sufficient and to determine whether additional coverage needs to be purchased. Our firm will request updated documents prior to the next annual review meeting to update the analysis.

10.10 SELF-TEST

[A] Questions

Self-Test 1

Juwan is thinking about the appropriate income replacement ratio for his client who is married. The client works in an office, is healthy, and provides approximately 25 percent of household income. Given these details, which of the following would be an appropriate income replacement ratio assumption?

(a) 25 percent.

(b) 30 percent.

(c) 70 percent.

(d) 100 percent.

Self-Test 2

Haley would like to recommend a disability policy that uses the broadest definition of disability. Which policy definition fits this criterion?

(a) Any-occupation.

(b) Own-occupation.

(c) Modified own-occupation.

(d) Split-definition.

Self-Test 3

A policy provision that waives the elimination period within a policy contract if an insured is subsequently disabled within six months of an original disability is called a:

(a) Residual disability provision.

(b) Renewability provision.

(c) Recurrent disability provision.

(d) Disability replacement provision.

Self-Test 4

Lamar is estimating the potential cost of a disability policy that is designed to replace 70 percent of a client's $150,000 annual income. What is the minimum dollar premium Lamar should forecast when formalizing his disability insurance recommendation?

(a) $1,050 yearly.

(b) $1,500 yearly.

(c) $2,100 yearly.

(d) $4,500 yearly.

Self-Test 5

Emily owns her own business. The business generates a net income of $400,000 each year; however, Emily takes only $75,000 each year as income. The remainder of the business income is reinvested. If Emily purchases a traditional disability policy, using a 60 percent income replacement ratio, what is the maximum yearly benefit Emily can expect to receive if she were deemed disabled?

(a) $240,000

(b) $195,000

(c) $75,000

(d) $45,000

[B] Answers

Question 1: c

Question 2: b

Question 3: c

Question 4: b

Question 5: d

10.11 CHAPTER RESOURCES

Council for Disability Awareness. http://www.disabilitycanhappen.org.

Disability Insurance Glossary. https://doi.nv.gov/Consumers/Disability-Insurance/.

General disability insurance information. https://www.healthcare.gov/glossary.

Information about Medicare (www.medicare.gov).

Social Security Benefit Calculator (disability, retirement, survivor): http://www.socialsecurity.gov/planners/benefitcalculators.htm.

Blair, J., Kiner, M., and Thomas, M. 2022 *Social Security & Medicare Facts*. Erlanger, KY: National Underwriter Company, 2022.

CHAPTER ENDNOTES

1.   U.S. Equal Employment Opportunity Commission, *Facts About the Americans With Disabilities Act*. http://www.eeoc.gov/eeoc/publications/fs-ada.cfm.

2.   "Report of the Committee to Recommend New Disability Figures for Valuation," *Transactions of the Society of Actuaries*, 37 (1985): 449–601. http://www.soa.org/library/research/transactions-of-society-of-actuaries/1985/january/tsa85v3713.pdf.

3.   Maleh, J., and Bosley, T. *Disability and Death Probability Figures for Insured Workers Born in 1997*. https://www.ssa.gov/OACT/NOTES/ran6/an2017-6.pdf.

4.   Estimate adapted from data published publicly by AffordableInsuranceProtection.com, *How Much Does Disability Insurance Cost?* http://www.affordableinsuranceprotection.com/disability_premiums.

Chapter 11

Long-Term Care Insurance Planning

Learning Objectives

- Learning Objective 1: Evaluate a client's long-term care insurance need.

- Learning Objective 2: Describe activities of daily living that are commonly used to document the need for long-term care.

- Learning Objective 3: Perform a long-term care insurance needs analysis.

- Learning Objective 4: Develop a long-term care plan that incorporates insurance, savings, and the use of household assets.

11.1 THE PROCESS OF LONG-TERM CARE INSURANCE PLANNING

Once known as *nursing home insurance*, **long-term care insurance** continues to be redefined. Policies can cover a range of services from home health care, an adult care center, in-home care, assisted living care, skilled nursing care, hospice care, or some combination of these needs. Information needed to conduct a long-term care insurance analysis typically is obtained during the initial client data gathering phase of the financial planning process.

Long-term care facilities provide for the progression of **chronic care** or care that may be continuous or long-term. Long-term care facilities run the gamut from basic assisted living homes that provide only domestic help to facilities with twenty-four-hour medical staff capable of dispensing medication and handling minor medical emergencies. Facilities also offer a variety of living conditions, including group arrangements, semiprivate living quarters, and private rooms or even suites. (With increased amenities and privacy come higher costs.) Because long-term care (LTC) is not purely "medical care" and is not provided in a hospital, health insurance typically offers no coverage (hospitals provide **acute care**, or care that is immediate or short-term). It is also important to remember that Medicare offers only limited coverage under certain conditions.

LTC costs can be staggering for some households. LTC costs vary widely by geographic area. States such as Alaska, Massachusetts, and New York have, on average, higher costs of living, which means facilities in these states are correspondingly more expensive. An outcome associated with LTC planning is helping clients anticipate and deal with the costs of future care, as well as assisting client conceptualize how future medical expenses can impact the stability of a financial plan. The following discussion highlights how the financial planning process can be followed when conducting a LTC needs analysis.

11.2 STEP 1: UNDERSTAND THE CLIENT'S PERSONAL AND FINANCIAL CIRCUMSTANCES

The first step in the long-term care insurance planning process involves reviewing, with the client, relevant personal and financial information. It is important to discuss a client's family health situation prior to making LTC insurance recommendations. This type of discussion can enhance the client-financial planner relationship, which can, in turn, promote the development and presentation of integrative recommendations.

It is important for financial planners to understand their clients' individuals needs and circumstances prior to estimating a LTC insurance need. The process of LTC insurance planning starts with a review of the following client factors:

- family health status and related health history;

- family demographics and preferences that can affect the need for care;

- assets available for care expenses, as well as the goals competing for those assets; and

- lifestyle and profession or occupational choices that could affect the future need for long-term care.

For example, the likelihood of developing Alzheimer's disease, the most common type of dementia, is greater for someone with a first-degree relative (i.e., a parent or sibling) who has the disease. For an individual with more than one first-degree relative diagnosed, the risks of the disease are even greater. Further complicating the evaluation is consideration of the continuum of care that may begin at home, transition to an assisted living facility, and finally progress to a skilled nursing facility or what is typically called a *nursing home*.

Figure 11.1 provides a review of the Hubbles' personal and financial circumstances related to LTC insurance planning. The information in Figure 11.1 is typical of what a financial planner should evaluate at the first step of the financial planning process.

Figure 11.1. The Hubbles' Personal and Financial Circumstances.

Chandler Hubble	Rachel Hubble
Age: 42	Age: 42
State of residence: Missouri	State of residence: Missouri
Citizen: U.S.	Citizen: U.S.
Long-Term Health status: No known health issues Occupation: Low risk	Long-Term Health status: No known health issues Occupation: Low risk
Phoebe Hubble	
Age: 5	
Long-Term Health status: No known health issues	

- Rachel is the youngest child of a very large family. She has four brothers and three sisters. Her mother Jenny passed away when Rachel was age thirty. Her father Terrance passed away three years later. Both died of cancer.
- Chandler is the only child in his family. His parents, both aged sixty-five, are healthy and living in Springfield.
- Household net worth: $823,922.
- Household income: $139,435 (rounded).
- Chandler and Rachel are willing to set aside $200,000 in net worth (today's dollars) to meet any potential LTC needs.

11.3 STEP 2: IDENTIFY AND SELECT GOALS

As described above, a thorough understanding of client situational characteristics is necessary to appropriately analyze a client's need to purchase LTC insurance or self-insure. Although planning for the uncertainty of LTC needs is not an exact science, financial planners typically focus on two issues: the client and the client's resources. Specifically, a client's age, health, family health history, lifestyle choices, and occupational choices (i.e., risk triggers) can directly influence the likelihood of needing LTC services. A client's financial and personal resources (network of family or friends) directly affect decisions regarding how to provide or pay for any necessary LTC services.

A client's preferences are an important factor shaping LTC planning goals. Although Chandler and Rachel did not explicitly mention long-term planning concerns during the initial data-gathering phase of the financial planning engagement, Chandler and Rachel did provide some guidelines to be used when making estimates. LTC insurance planning assumptions and LTC planning goals are highlighted in Figure 11.2.

Figure 11.2. The Hubbles' Long-Term Care Insurance Goals.

> **When thinking about their long-term care insurance situation, Chandler and Rachel have a simple goal: to ensure that they can meet future LTC needs through a combination of insurance and savings, assuming the following:**
>
> - Annual nursing home expenses in the area are currently $65,000.
> - The average age for those entering an assisted living facility is age seventy-five, with an assumed average length of stay of approximately three years.
> - The average age for those entering a nursing home is eight-three, with an assumed average stay of approximately two years.
> - Chandler and Rachel would like to cover six years of total expenses in the event either were to enter a facility.
> - Long-term care expenses have been increasing at 5 percent per year.
> - In the event either Rachel or Chandler enters a nursing home, they are willing to allocate $200,000 from their net worth (today's dollars) to help pay for LTC expenses.
> - Assets for use in funding LTC expenses will grow at a modest 5.5 percent after-tax rate of return.

11.4 STEP 3: ANALYZE THE CLIENT'S CURRENT COURSE OF ACTION AND POTENTIAL ALTERNATIVE COURSE(S) OF ACTION

The need for LTC insurance is based on (a) client preferences; (b) net worth; and the projected need for care based on age, personal health, family health history, lifestyle choices, and occupational choice. The first two factors may be easily identified, while the last factor can be more time consuming to identify. All significantly influence the projected cost of care and the amount of insurance to be purchased. Five policy considerations should be evaluated when quantifying the amount of insurance coverage to purchase:

1. range of services covered and benefit amount;

2. coverage period;

3. method in which benefits are paid (i.e., pool-of-money or indemnity);

4. elimination period; and

5. inflation rider to increase coverage limits.

Financial planners who are asked to evaluate an existing (or new) LTC policy should first determine whether the client really needs coverage or if self-insurance is a better option. Then, factors that determine the amount of insurance needed, as well as other riders that affect coverage, should be reviewed. If the decision to discontinue a policy is made, a client usually has the option to (1) let the policy lapse; (2) exercise the nonforfeiture clause, if available; (3) exercise a contingent benefits nonforfeiture provision, if available; or (4) exercise a Section 1035 exchange for another, more suitable LTC insurance contract. With the last option, care must be taken because the new policy premium will reflect the client's current age.

The actual steps required to determine a LTC insurance need are relatively straightforward. The calculation process for a hypothetical client (not the Hubble family) is show in Figure 11.3. The following inputs are needed: current age of client, assumed age at need, annual cost of care today, the LTC inflation rate, the value of any funds set aside for LTC expenses, the before tax-rate of return, the client's marginal tax bracket, and the expected increase in future savings for long-term expenses.

Figure 11.3. Estimating a Client's Long-Term Care Insurance Need.

Client Data Input	Data Input Example	Calculation
Current Age	60	
Age LTC Benefits Begin	65	
Annual LTC Inflation Rate	3%	
Number of Years Benefits are Needed	3	
Before-Tax Rate of Return	8%	
Marginal Tax Bracket	24%	
Annual Increase in Savings	0%	
Current Dollars Set Aside for LTC Needs	$50,000	
Estimate Annual Cost of LTC	$50,000	Calculate FV of Cost: N = 5 I/Y = 3 PV = $50,000 CPT FV = $57,964

Estimate Total LTC Need (based on three years stay in nursing home)		Calculate Need on First Day of Care: 1) Determine After-Tax Return: $8\% \times (1 - .25) = 6.08\%$ 2) Calculate Serial Rate: $(1.0608 / 1.03) - 1 = 2.99\%$ 3) Calculate PV (Annuity Due): N = 3 I/Y = 2.99 PMT = $57,964 PV = $168,892
Calculate Current Value of Assets Set Aside for LTC Needs	$50,000	Calculate FV of Assets: N = 5 I/Y = 8 PV = $50,000 FV = $73,466
NET LTC NEED		Determine Difference Between Need and Resources: $168,892 - $73,466 = $95,426
Note: This calculation approach assumes the client uses assets from an emergency savings fund to pay for services during a policy's elimination period.		

Keep in mind that nearly every input used in a LTC calculation is an assumption. As such, the derived estimates should be used only as a starting point in further discussions with clients. As illustrated in this example, this hypothetical client needs to identify sources of funding that will pay total benefits equal to $95,426. This is the total amount they will pay for three years of LTC needs. If the client's net worth is high enough, it may be possible to self-insure the need. For risk-averse clients, and those with limited assets, purchasing a LTC insurance policy may be appropriate.

The following example shows how an analysis of the Hubble family's current LTC insurance choices and needs results in a pathway to the development of recommendations. Figure 11.4 provides a summary of the Hubbles' current LTC insurance choices. Potential recommendations are also provided.

Figure 11.4. An Analysis of the Hubbles' Current Long-Term Care Insurance Need and Potential Recommendations.

LONG-TERM CARE ANALYSIS	
ASSUMPTIONS	
Cost of Care Today	$65,000.00
Age Today	42
Age of LTC Need	75
Years Until Need	33
Years of Stay	6
LTC Inflation Rate	5.00%

Before-Tax Rate of Return	5.50%
Marginal Tax Bracket	30.00%
After-Tax Rate of Return	3.85%
Salary Inflation Rate	3.00%
Value of Assets Set Aside	$200,000.00
CALCULATIONS	
Cost of LTC at Age of Need	$325,207.26
Cost of Total Stay for One Person	$2,006,066.30
Cost for Couple (Joint Stay)	$4,012,132.60
FV of Assets	$695,736.08
Net LTC Need Per Person	**$1,310,330.22**
Net LTC for Couple	**$3,316,396.52**

Based on the LTC planning assumptions and the estimation procedure shown above, the Hubbles face a projected LTC deficit at age seventy-five of $1,310,330 (rounded) per person. After evaluating the preceding analysis, the following potential recommendations are worth considering:

- Chandler and Rachel should postpone purchasing LTC coverage until age fifty at the earliest.
- Given Rachel's family history, she has the greatest need for coverage, although both Chandler and Rachel should consider purchasing LTC insurance at a later point.

Chandler and Rachel have two options when it comes to meeting any LTC funding shortfall:

- purchase a LTC insurance policy; given their age, the annual premium for a highly-rated policy should be quite low (under $200 per month per person); or
- postpone the LTC insurance purchase and increase the value of assets set aside today to pay for LTC needs (i.e., self-insure some of the need).

11.5 STEP 4: DEVELOP THE FINANCIAL PLANNING RECOMMENDATION(S)

The development of LTC insurance recommendations, within a comprehensive financial plan, can encompass a multitude of products and services. A competent financial planner should continually develop and refine skills needed to transform the analysis of a client's situation into actionable recommendations. The following discussion highlights some of the important concepts, tools, and techniques that can be incorporated into the recommendation development process.

[A] Activities of Daily Living

Eligibility for LTC insurance benefits is based on functional ability, cognitive ability, or medical necessity. Functional ability is determined by the insured's capability when performing certain **activities of daily living (ADLs)**, which measure the ability to perform routine personal care functions. Benefits begin when the insured is unable to perform *two* of the six activities (some policies may combine toileting and continence and require three of five ADLs) listed below:

1. Eating.

2. Toileting (e.g., getting to, from, on, and off the toilet).

3. Transferring from a bed to a chair.

4. Bathing.

5. Dressing.

6. Maintaining continence (e.g., ability to control bladder and bowel movements).

A **cognitive disability**, such as Alzheimer's disease or other dementias or organic cognitive disorders, is another eligibility trigger and one of the primary reasons for admission to a care facility today. The Alzheimer's Association reports, based on numerous studies, that at least half of elderly adult day care clients, almost half of nursing home residents, and as many as two-thirds of residents in assisted living facilities have Alzheimer's disease or another form of dementia.[1] Such mental incapacities are isolated triggers and should not be linked to any ADLs.

Medical necessity is the final qualification for LTC insurance eligibility. A client is eligible for LTC benefits if, as the result of an illness, injury, or chronic condition, the insured requires medically necessary care and assistance. Some policies require that a company representative perform the screening, but others allow the client's physician to conduct the assessment, which is typically considered the better option.

[B] Tax-Qualified Policies

Beyond the issue of eligibility for policy benefits is the related issue of policy eligibility for favorable tax treatment. The **Health Insurance Portability and Accountability Act (HIPAA)** of 1996, along with Internal Revenue Code (IRC) Section 7702B, set forth the requirements for LTC policies to be considered "qualified" and therefore eligible for the premiums to be tax deductible and the benefits in excess of premiums paid to be excluded from income. To be considered a qualified policy, the benefit payment must be contingent on:

1. a chronic illness that lasts for at least ninety days;

2. the loss of at least two ADLs; and

3. severe cognitive impairment or impairment that requires supervision.

Tax qualification under HIPAA also precludes medical necessity as a stand-alone trigger for benefit payment. In addition to these benefit-related requirements, to claim the cost of premiums as a tax deduction, the insured must also itemize tax deductions and claim medical expenses that exceed the adjusted gross income (AGI) limitation.

The primary benefit associated with purchasing a tax-qualified policy is that the premiums may be tax-deductible, whereas no portion of the premium cost is a tax-deductible expense if the policy is not tax qualified. The advantages of purchasing a non-tax-qualified policy include unlimited benefits, less restrictive qualification for benefits, and a shorter qualification period. Given the AGI limitation and the age-based maximum deductibility of premium limits, this cost-reduction strategy only works for clients who have substantial additional out-of-pocket medical expenses.

> *Example.* A fifty-year-old single client with an AGI of $100,000 per year would need to have more than $7,500 of other IRS Schedule A unreimbursed medical expenses to receive any tax benefit associated with paying a LTC premium.

Regardless of the situation, the cost associated with the more restrictive benefit qualification should be addressed when making a recommendation. It would be a disservice to the client, given the negligible tax savings, if the client was not eligible for benefits under a qualified plan but would have been eligible for benefits under a nonqualified plan. This assessment is perhaps one of the most complex and subjective of any of the core financial planning content areas, and perhaps one of the most difficult to discuss.

[C] Triggers Associated with Long-Term Care Needs

Certain personal, family, and lifestyle **risk triggers** should be closely reviewed when evaluating the potential need for LTC coverage. In some cases, for example, family health history may be the most important evaluative factor for a financial planner to understand when helping a client evaluate a potential need. Anticipating the probability of incurring assisted living or skilled nursing facility expenses, based in part on family history, can help guide the development of recommendations. Furthermore, awareness of a genetic health issue can also help a financial planner determine when a policy should be purchased.

Specifically, the following risk triggers should be considered:

- personal health status (e.g., diabetes, alcoholism, high blood pressure);

- related family health history (e.g., coronary artery disease, cancer, Alzheimer's disease, or Parkinson's disease);

- lifestyle choices (e.g., high-risk activities, tobacco or other drug usage); and

- working in a hazardous profession or occupation (e.g., steel worker, firefighter).

These triggers could compromise a client's future health status and increase the likelihood of needing chronic care or custodial care. Considered in conjunction with the client's care preferences and biases, both client and financial planner will have a better idea of what challenges or financial demands the future may hold.

In addition to risk triggers, a client's age is another important factor when considering the need for and future cost of LTC insurance. According to the American Association for Long-Term Care Insurance (AALTCI), only 3 percent of insurance claimants are under age sixty, compared to more than 50 percent of claimants who are eighty years of age or older. Almost a third of claimants are between the ages of seventy and seventy-nine.[2] As these data indicate, as a client ages, the likelihood of needing services becomes more relevant. This phenomenon, known as **adverse selection**, increases the tendency for persons with a greater chance of loss to seek coverage.

Adverse selection is controlled by insurance companies through the underwriting process, which results in higher premiums for those with greater need or an increased likelihood of making a policy claim. As a result, the older the client, the higher the periodic premiums, but the fewer premiums paid. The younger the purchaser, the lower the periodic premium, but the greater the number of premiums paid—unless a fixed-pay policy is chosen.

Clients under the age of forty typically are advised to *postpone* the purchase of a LTC policy because the cost/benefit tradeoff makes LTC coverage unfavorable for young clients. A young person who owns a policy is unlikely to make use of services in the near future. As such, the opportunity cost associated with premium payments usually outweighs the benefits of being insured. Beyond the financial savings of delaying the purchase, clients under the age of forty are also more likely to have living parents or other family members who could help provide care in the event of a disability or illness that would otherwise have required a stay in a care facility.

Conversely, clients over the age of fifty-five typically should consider purchasing some sort of LTC coverage or set aside assets to self-insure a potential need. The reduced availability of an extended family network or of family members to care for an older adult, the increased immediacy of need, and the cost of a long-term stay in a care facility make LTC insurance at this stage of life very important for some clients. These same factors can be relevant regardless of a client's age. For example, a younger client with no extended family network, spouse, or partner to provide care may need and want a policy simply for peace of mind, so that if care is needed, coverage would be available.

By age sixty-five, a client should have a reasonable idea about their individual likelihood of need, as well as their ability to self-insure the need. After age seventy, policy cost and physical condition may eliminate the insurance option. As reported by *Consumer Reports*, a plan that costs a fifty-year-old $1,625 annually could cost a sixty-year-old $3,100 and a seventy-year-old $7,575. This, of course, assumes the older client will qualify for coverage. One out of four sixty-five-year-olds fails the physical needed for coverage, which results in rejection for long-term-care insurance. At age seventy-five, one in three is rejected.[3]

[D] Long-Term Care Insurance Purchase Strategies

Once the need for LTC insurance has been established, attention must turn to the quantification of that need. Just as the determination of a need is not always straightforward, neither is the decision regarding the amount of coverage to purchase. The continuum of services covered; differences in the respective costs of those services; and uncertainty regarding when, where, and how long services may be needed confound discussions on the amount of coverage. Additional factors, such as the age of the client, spouse or partner, and the corresponding cost of coverage purchased now or later should be considered. Several policy provisions are available to tailor a policy to a client's needs, but these will generally add to premium costs. Conversely, it is important to remember that restricting coverage too much in an effort to reduce premiums may render the policy virtually ineffective.

When purchasing a LTC policy, the client and financial planner should consider several factors. The first issue is the range of services covered and the corresponding actual benefit amount. Nearly all comprehensive LTC insurance policies, or **integrated policies**, cover a range of services, although the amount of coverage will vary by policy. The client may use **home care**, **adult day care**, **assisted living care**, **nursing home care**, or **hospice care** until the maximum benefit or the stated period expires.

The choice of maximum benefit is typically based on nursing home costs. Coverage amounts for other services vary and may be the same as the nursing home amount, a percentage of that amount contingent on the type of care used, or a smaller stated per-day coverage amount contingent on the service. Some policies cover only the insured, but others offer coverage for couples—a difference that can significantly affect the amount of coverage needed when matched to the needs of the client(s). Finally, it is important to note that policy benefits can be limited to a specific coverage, such as facility-only or home-care only.

Planning Reminder

It is important to note that it is not necessary for a client to purchase 100 percent of the daily need. Often the best strategy is one that blends the use of insurance with a spending contribution from client assets. A client, for example, with a $200 daily need may be best served by purchasing a policy with a $100 daily inflation-adjusted benefit combined while spending down assets in the amount of $100 per day.

Nearly all LTC policies provide a specified **per-day benefit**. This amount can range from less than $100 to more than $300 per day. The appropriate amount should be based on a thorough review of facility costs in the area where the care is most likely to be received.

The second factor when quantifying coverage need is the length of the coverage period. Policies generally offer coverage periods between two (or, in some states, a minimum of three) and five to seven years, although some may offer coverage for a lifetime (these policies can be prohibitively expensive). The length of coverage must be matched to the individual client's projected need for coverage, available resources, and ability to pay for the premiums.

The third factor to consider when quantifying coverage need is how a policy pays the benefit. Some policies pay a full daily limit regardless of actual charges for LTC services after the *elimination period* (the period of time from the point of a LTC diagnosis to the point at which benefits begin) has been met . In other words, the full cost of a day of service is "exhausted" regardless of actual cost, and with some older policies any excess benefit is generally lost. Most policies pay the actual amount of charges incurred up to the daily limit chosen. Still other policies provide a set dollar benefit that is not measured by calendar usage, but rather by a lifetime maximum dollar amount.

For example, a four-year, $100-per-day policy would list a total benefit of $146,000 (4 × 100 × 365). But the insured's actual benefit received could vary depending on the type and length of care.

If a policy is a **pool-of-money policy**, also known as an **expense-reimbursement contract**, then regardless of the benefit per day received, the policy will, using the example from above, pay $146,000 prior to expiration. If the policy is a **stated period policy**, or **indemnity policy**, however, then the contract will pay only for the specified period of years, whether or not the client receives the maximum $100-per-day benefit. In other words, the only way to receive the full $146,000 is to be eligible for the maximum per-day benefit for the full four years. A pool-of-money policy refers to the maximum lifetime benefit amount. A stated-period policy refers to benefits indemnified or paid over a period of time.

Benefits from an individually owned LTC policy are typically received tax free, except for benefits from an indemnity policy. Benefits are subject to federal tax only if the amount paid exceeds the higher of the cost of qualified long-term care or an IRS determined rate that varies by year.[4]

Clearly, a pool-of-money, or expense-reimbursed, contract is superior to an indemnity contract. A pool-of-money policy might allow a client to extend a four-year benefit to longer-term coverage if the reimbursement does not require the maximum daily amount. In addition to direct reimbursement for services, other plans feature a per-diem cash payment based on the daily benefit amount and the number of eligible days in a payment cycle, regardless of the type of services used once eligibility is established. The cash payment option offers more flexibility because the recipient of the benefits determines how the money is spent.

Planning Reminder

Long-term care costs continue to outpace inflation. It is reasonable to assume an annual cost of care increase between 4 percent and 5 percent annually when estimating a client's LTC need.

The fourth factor to consider when quantifying the need for LTC insurance is the **elimination period** of the policy. This factor affects the amount of proposed coverage, the cost of coverage (the longer the waiting period, the lower the premium), and the client resources available to pay for care during the waiting period. Almost all policies have waiting periods before benefits are payable ranging from zero days (known as **first-dollar coverage**) to, more commonly, fifteen to ninety days, although the elimination period can be as long as one year.

Insurance companies define the days that count toward the elimination period or deductible differently, with the primary consideration being *days of service*, meaning how long the insured receives paid care, or simply calendar days. Some policies count actual qualifying service days or weeks (based on a defined number of qualifying days within a week), and may count only consecutive days or random qualifying days over a period of time. Other policies calculate the elimination period based on other factors, including previous stays in a care facility within the last twelve months, a hospital stay immediately preceding a move to a care facility, or a change in the insured's health.

The fifth factor to consider when quantifying coverage need is an inflationary increase in the cost of LTC services. Although this can be important for any client, it is especially important for younger clients because the difference between increasing service costs and policy benefits must be drawn from personal assets. An **inflation rider** provides an annual automatic increase in coverage limits in one of two primary ways. Some policies refer to an inflation rider as a **cost-of-living adjustment**, or **COLA**. The annual inflation factor can be a simple fixed percentage, a compound fixed percentage, or it can be based on the Consumer Price Index or other measure of inflation. Policies typically offer a 2 percent to 5 percent inflationary increase, but other options may be available. Both the amount and kind of increase and the kind of factor influence the cost of the rider, with choices that yield a greater increase in benefits, level of protection, or greater cost.

Two more options for increasing coverage are available. Each can affect the amount of coverage purchased initially. A different inflation protection approach is a **guaranteed purchase option** that allows the insured to increase daily coverage automatically at periodic intervals (e.g., every three to five years) with no evidence of insurability. This provision offers additional flexibility, but it does increase the premium based on the insured's age at the time of exercise. If the option is not exercised, it is typically lost. Another option is to choose a significantly higher daily benefit than currently needed, with the idea that the cost of care will increase to or exceed the benefit amount. This can be more cost effective than adding an inflation rider. But higher-than-expected out-of-pocket costs may be necessary if the cost of care increases more than anticipated and no other inflation protection has been included.

Planning Reminder

When selecting an inflation rider, a compound fixed percentage increase is recommended, unless the client is sixty years of age or older, when a simple fixed percentage option may offer sufficient protection. Keep in mind that clients should be cautioned that waiting until this age to purchase a policy will increase the cost and, depending on health status, could render them uninsurable. A second caution is also warranted. The inflationary increase should be automatic, not contingent on the insurability of the client, as some policies require.

Incidental to the consideration of inflationary increases in the cost of care is the issue of future premium costs relative to retirement income available. For those on a fixed income, premiums that were once affordable can, over time, become prohibitively expensive. Without a well-diversified retirement plan and ample savings, purchasing LTC insurance that will subsequently lapse may not be the most productive use of premium dollars.

As a general rule, purchasing LTC insurance typically does not make financial sense for those under age forty. Many financial planners with clients in the forty to fifty-five age range take a "wait-and-see" approach before recommending coverage. With college or wedding costs for those who have children, as well as the need to accelerate retirement savings, discretionary cash flow may be insufficient to meet all financial goals.

Even so, while there may be many reasons to delay the purchase of LTC insurance, an early purchase could be in a client's best interest. By purchasing a policy while younger and still working, a client can effectively lock in a lower lifetime premium, which will allow the client to allocate more income to meet other financial obligations. For example, if a forty-five-year-old client purchased a twenty-pay policy, then the client's LTC needs would be funded before or near the time of retirement. This would free up cash flow during retirement and protect the client from future premium increases.

Whereas a client's risk profile and age can offer insights into the need for LTC insurance, a more definitive answer may come from the client's available monetary resources for use when funding care services. Assuming a client is at least age forty, and that there is evidence to suggest that long term-care may be needed in the future, a client's situation analysis hinges on the choice between retaining the risk and insuring the risk. The following rules can be used to help a financial planner, in consultation with a client, determine If LTC insurance should be purchased:

> **Rule 1:** If a client has a net worth between $500,000 and $2 million, exclusive of the value of their home, a LTC policy may be worth considering. A client fitting this profile may not have sufficient resources to fully self-insure the need. If an extended stay in a care facility is needed, the cost will significantly reduce the client's net worth. Lifetime premiums, as a percentage of net worth, often indicate the need for LTC coverage.

> **Rule 2:** Clients with a net worth in excess of $2 million, exclusive of their home value, should consider self-insuring. Clients with this level of net worth can often afford to self-insure the risk of entering a care facility or fund needed services while remaining at home. Assuming an average stay in a care facility, usually quoted as thirty months, it is unlikely that this cost would deplete assets below $1 million for most clients, thus preserving wealth for other goals.

> **Rule 3:** Clients with a net worth less than $500,000, exclusive of home value, should consider self-insuring or purchasing a **partnership plan** (these plans shelter some assets from Medicaid asset restrictions). Although this rule seems harsh, a client at this level of net worth would be expected to spend down assets and use Medicaid benefits to pay for an extended period of care, if necessary. The cost of premiums, in comparison to such a modest level of net worth, makes purchasing a policy inefficient. However, clients living in a **partnership plan** state could purchase a lower-cost, state-certified policy and protect a predetermined level of assets while remaining Medicaid eligible. In addition to Medicaid qualification restrictions, clients could lose control over care decisions, and in-home care typically is not an option.

As with all rules, exceptions apply. For example, consider a client with a net worth of $2 million who wants to preserve the money for a charitable or family legacy. To protect this wish, the client could purchase a LTC policy, even though the cost of care is otherwise affordable. Another exception would be a married couple with $750,000 in assets who decides that the much younger spouse would care for the older spouse should chronic care be required. As long as the couple jointly reaches an informed decision, the choice to self-insure should be honored. Figure 11.5 summarizes how a client's age, family health history, or current financial situation can generally be incorporated into determining the need for LTC insurance.

Figure 11.5. Long-Term Care Insurance Planning Decision Tree.

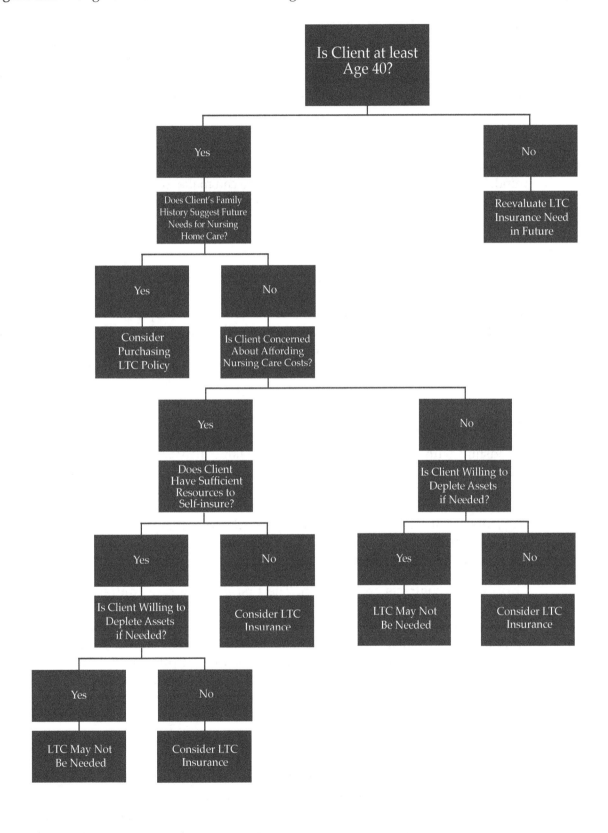

[E] Hybrid Policies

This chapter has focused almost entirely on the use of stand-alone LTC insurance policies. It is possible, however, to recommend the purchase of **linked-benefit** (or hybrid) life and annuity products. These products offer clients the certainty of a base policy—death or annuity benefits, respectively—coupled with the availability of LTC coverage, if needed. These products are very popular because this type of coverage helps clients manage the risk of paying for but not requiring LTC protection, at the same time offering the certainty of estate protection or a policy benefit for heirs. Health underwriting may be less stringent or unnecessary—a benefit for some clients, but if a single-sum payment approach is used, the premium may be a deterrent. Keep in mind, however, that individual policy features can make hybrid policies less favorable than purchasing two separate policies if both are needed.

[F] Continuing Care Retirement Communities

According to AARP, a **continuing care retirement community (CCRC)** combines independent living, assisted living, memory or special care, and skilled nursing home care in a tiered approach for those who want to prepare for health care need transitions. Rather than moving from one facility to another as health care needs change, a retiree enters a CCRC as an independent person living in a single-family home or apartment. When the need arises, the person may transfer to assisted living or nursing care facilities within the community. For couples who need different types of care, the community can accommodate both needs while promoting independence and togetherness. Many CCRC residents prefer the notion of living in one location with an available continuum of care. Family members also like the idea of consistent friendships within the community as well as familiarity with the caregiving services. This flexibility comes at a cost. CCRCs can be expensive. Clients who wish to consider this type of living arrangement in retirement should contemplate the costs and plan accordingly. According to AARP, some CCRCs require nonrefundable entrance fees (e.g., $100,000 to $1 million) and monthly maintenance charges (e.g., $2,000 to $5,000).[5] It is also common for the monthly fee to increase over time and as the health care needs of the resident change.

Three CCRC contracts are common. The first is a **life care contract,** also called an **extensive contract**. This provides unlimited assisted living, medical treatment, and skilled nursing care over a resident's lifetime with no additional charges. A **modified contract** offers residents a choice of services for a predetermined period of time. At the end of that time period, additional services may be purchased. Finally, a **fee-for-service contract** provides access to a CCRC, but once assisted living and/or skilled nursing care is needed, the resident will be required to pay market rates for additional services and care.

When working with clients to select the appropriate CCRC facility, it is important to consider factors associated with the financial viability of the CCRC, as well as other licensing and inspection reports. Qualitative issues to consider include facilities and grounds, staff, food, transportation, and interests shared with other residents. Third-party accreditation and review standards are available, such as from the Commission on Accreditation of Rehabilitation Facilities/Continuing Care Accreditation Commission (CARF/CCAC), or LeadingAge.

[G] A Liability Release Form

Similar to the situation with disability insurance planning, it is important to use a **liability release form** (client disclaimer) if a recommendation to postpone coverage is made or in situation when a client declines a recommendation to purchase LTC insurance. A liability release should be signed by the client. This provides some protection against potential litigation. Should the client, the client's spouse, or other family members question the lack of contingency planning to protect the household from a loss in assets, the financial planner will be able to document the client's choice. The client's signature on the liability release acknowledges that the financial planner made a recommendation that was declined. An example of the language to include in a form is as follows:

Long-Term Care Insurance is a generally recommended product the can help protect your assets, savings, retirement, and estate plan.

On this date, my financial planner and I discussed long-term care insurance and how it can provide protection in the event of a long term sickness or accident that would require an extended stay in a nursing home or extended home health care.

CLIENT NAME: _____

REPRESENTATIVE NAME: _____

DATE: _____

At this time, I have made the decision not to purchase long-term care coverage, and I am aware that my assets are fully exposed and subject to liquidation if a long-term care need arises. I also understand that long-term care insurance is an underwritten product and that a change in my future health status could impact my eligibility for coverage at a later date.

_____
Client Signature Date

_____
Representative Signature Date

This form is evidence that [name of financial planner] presented Long-Term Care Insurance as a financial planning alternative to the client and for file documentation.

[H] Applying Planning Skills to the Hubble Case

In general, only modest changes will need to be made to the initial recommendations developed at Step Three of the financial planning process, although it is possible that new client information or data can necessitate a reevaluation. Figure 11.6 provides a summary of the final life insurance recommendations that match the Hubble family's financial goals.

Figure 11.6. Long-Term Care Insurance Recommendations for Chandler and Rachel.

> **The final LTC insurance recommendations developed for the Hubble family match the preliminary recommendations identified at Step Three of the financial planning process. Specifically, the Hubbles should:**
>
> - Postpone the purchase of LTC insurance until Chandler and Rachel are each at least age fifty or older.
> - If, at that time, the decision is made to purchase LTC insurance, Chandler and Rachel should consider using a combination of insurance benefits and spending down assets.
> - If the decision to purchase is made in the future, Chandler and Rachel should each purchase a separate policy. It is important to point out to them that the cost of coverage at that time cannot be known with certainty.
>   - The daily future need is anticipated to be approximately $129 per day ($773,047/6 years = $128,841 yearly or $128,841/365 = $353 daily).
>   - When Chandler and Rachel are over the age of fifty, each should purchase a policy with a $300 daily benefit and a six-year payment option, with an inflation rider.
>   - The cost at that time for Chandler is estimated to be approximately $400 per month.
>   - The cost of Rachel at that time is estimated to be approximately $490 per month.
>   - If a need arises, Chandler and Rachel should spend down available investment assets to make up any difference between actual daily costs and the insurance benefit.

11.6 STEP 5: PRESENT THE FINANCIAL PLANNING RECOMMENDATION(S)

As illustrated in this chapter, financial planners have multiple options when working with clients to customize LTC planning recommendations to individual client needs. Strategies reflect differences in products available, product coverage and features, and the tax or other advantages associated with different products. Other strategies focus on client education to help clients choose between LTC product options and self-insurance options. For many clients, a combination of strategies may be needed.

Although the calculation of a client's LTC need is relatively straightforward, presenting data and accompanying recommendations can be more challenging. Clients rarely look forward to talking about and planning for disability, hospitalization, institutionalization, or death. These discussions are, nonetheless, important for financial planners who provide comprehensive financial planning services. Without adequate steps taken when a client is healthy, a LTC need in the future can wipe away years of saving and planning.

As was the case with life insurance, the presentation of LTC recommendations should include information about the financial strength of the insurance companies underwriting the recommended products. A competent financial planner should also be able to identify the advantages and disadvantages associated with different policy types and companies.

Figure 11.7 highlights some of the other key factors to consider when presenting LTC insurance recommendations.

Figure 11.7. Factors to Consider When Presenting Long-Term Care Insurance Recommendations.

As noted throughout each of the insurance chapters, it is important for financial planners to possess a working knowledge of insurance and LTC insurance terms and concepts. When presenting recommendations, however, financial planners should take steps to avoid the use of jargon and overly specialized insurance and medical terms in the context of LTC needs. Few clients look forward to planning for the potential need for LTC services. If LTC is needed, clients like Chandler and Rachel intuitively know that their physical and mental health will have declined significantly. As such, this topic is one that needs to be addressed with empathy and care. It may take several meetings (or years) to help these clients deal with the potentiality of one day needing LTC help. Given the importance of the funding needed to pay for expenses, ongoing discussions with Chandler and Rachel are recommended. Summarizing each recommendation's strengths and weaknesses is one way to help Chandler and Rachel (as well as other clients) understand the vital role LTC planning can play in shaping the achievement of lifetime financial goals.

11.7 STEP 6: IMPLEMENT THE FINANCIAL PLANNING RECOMMENDATION(S)

Financial planners should base LTC recommendations on a thorough review of a client's situation and projected needs. Although most insurance companies will sell policies to clients between the ages of eighteen and eighty-four who are in reasonably good health and able to care for themselves, the implementation of a purchase recommendation usually occurs when a client is age fifty or older. Unlike life insurance or health insurance that everyone eventually uses, LTC insurance is truly a gamble. The analysis of a client's current situation begins by answering two important questions:

1. Does the client's current health, family medical history, or personal situation suggest that LTC may be needed in the future?

2. Does the client have sufficient monetary resources or a family support network to "self-insure" in the event that LTC may be needed in the future?

Notice that the first question does not address a client's financial situation. This ordering is purposeful and based on the subjective factors that help characterize a client's situation and affect the pending decision. The emotion surrounding a client's decision to purchase LTC insurance is second only to the decision to purchase life insurance. There is little reason to consider an objective assessment of the financial ramifications of LTC without first addressing a client's fears, preferences, and even cultural biases about care.

Some of the concerns clients might face center not only on who will care for them, but also who will care for those for whom they have traditionally provided care and support. Guilt about the possibility of being unable to care for family can be a very powerful emotion. Other concerns surrounding a diagnosis or the need for custodial care might be more egocentric, such as feelings of shame, inadequacy, or failure. Women, who tend to live longer than men, may be in greater need of paid care services. Similarly, single individuals, because of the lack of a family network, might require paid care services. The loss of privacy and the potential reversal of family roles are additional concerns, especially between parents and children. Besides these intrinsic barriers, home design, space limitations, or the geographic location of family members can pose even greater barriers for LTC alternatives.

Although such fears may seem rational to clients or their children (if involved in the decision-making process), these fears can create barriers to open communication during the financial planning process. For example, a recent survey of adults aged eighteen to ninety revealed that more than 90 percent of respondents had not talked to their spouses, adult children, or parents about any of the following: preferred LTC options, the role of family members in managing care, and how to pay for LTC.[6] Eighty-six percent of respondents in the same survey felt it was important for their financial professional to discuss LTC with them, but only 9 percent of respondents had actually done so.[7]

A financial planning professional must be able to adequately empathize with these issues while encouraging clients to fully explore the biases that may shape decisions about LTC needs as a pathway to recommendation implementation. This could start by helping clients confront their understanding, or lack of knowledge, of the protection and limitations of Medicare, Medicaid, private insurance, and personal assets. Clients might also be ignorant of the range of care available or the associated costs. Allowing time for the discussion to evolve and approaching the conversation with sensitivity to the emotional and cognitive needs of the client are good strategies to encourage client action.

Beyond these considerations, the presentation of a LTC insurance recommendation should match a client's learning style and reference. Figure 11.8 shows how the LTC recommendations developed for Chandler and Rachel can be presented within a financial plan.

Figure 11.8. Implementing a Long-Term Care Recommendation for the Hubble Family.

Recommendation #1: When you reach age fifty-five, consider the purchase of a long-term care policy with a ninety-day elimination period and a six-year benefit period.	
Who:	Chandler and Rachel.
What:	Two long-term care policies with a ninety-day elimination period and a six-year benefit period provided by the same insurance provider.
When:	Once Phoebe begins college.
Where:	With your insurance professional or with an online provider that our firm can recommend.
Why:	To ensure financial security for your family and minimize the risk that long-term care costs will deplete your assets and prevent you from reaching your goals.

How:	Consult your insurance professional (our staff can assist you with this task). Our firm will assist by discussing underwriting issues, required application, and medical information.
How much:	Purchase a policy with a $300 daily benefit and a six-year payment option, with an inflation rider. It is expected that at the time of implementation: • The cost for Chandler will be approximately $400 per month. • The cost of Rachel will be approximately $490 per month. • You will receive a 10 to 30 percent discount by insuring jointly with the same insurance provider. • You will need to maintain an emergency fund equal to the length of the elimination period.
Effect on cash flow:	The purchase will decrease annual cash flow by approximately $10,680 at the time of purchase.

11.8 STEP 7: MONITOR PROGRESS AND UPDATE

The aging of the baby boom generation, coupled with a steady increase in life expectancy, is fueling a rapid increase in the cost of and need for care for the elderly. This continuum of care includes home health care services, care at an adult day care center, in-home care, assisted living care, skilled nursing care, hospice care, and in some instances, a combination of these needs. As the annual cost of LTC in the United States approaches $200 billion, providing care becomes either a direct client expense that financial planners must help their clients fund or an indirect expense paid for by the tax-funded Medicare and Medicaid programs. Thus, it is important for financial planners to help clients prepare to fund future LTC expenses, for themselves or extended family members, as part of the comprehensive financial planning process. Central to LTC planning is client education on the possible contribution of Medicare, Medicaid, insurance products, and self-insurance to meet future needs. This is an element of ongoing plan monitoring.

As a reminder, LTC insurance contracts typically are established as reimbursement plans that provide for a specific amount of coverage, or as indemnity plans that pay for a specific period of time. Given the way in which policies have been priced, the number of insurance carriers offering long-term coverage has fluctuated over the years, as have the terms and benefits offered in policies. While it is unlikely that a client's policy will be cancelled, there is the potential for increased premiums if the insurance company finds that, across insureds, a rate increase is needed. This situation should be monitored by a financial planner whose clients own a LTC policy. Related to this, then, is the need for a financial planner to continually shop the marketplace for new policies that offer better benefits at a lower premium cost. It is equally important to monitor the appropriateness of previously selected elimination periods, the inflation rider, the nonforfeiture clause, and premium provisions. Figure 11.9 provides a summary of ongoing monitoring issues facing the Hubble family.

Figure 11.9. Issues to Monitor in the Hubble Case.

> **Several client-specific factors and household characteristics should be monitored on at least an annual basis while Chandler and Rachel wait to reevaluate their need for LTC insurance, including:**
>
> - The health of Rachel and Chandler; any unexpected negative change in health status should prompt an immediate reevaluation of the LTC insurance need.
> - A meaningful change in net worth.
> - A negative change in the health status of related family members (where the change in health may be hereditary).
> - Significant changes in the long-term insurance marketplace, including potential limitations on the issuance of policies or stricter underwriting guidelines, which should prompt a reevaluation of the Hubbles' LTC insurance need.
> - Changes in the attitudes, preferences, or concerns of Chandler or Rachel.

11.9 COMPREHENSIVE HUBBLE CASE

Unlike other forms of insurance where there is little flexibility in policy selection, a financial planner can play an important role in helping clients prepare for and select appropriate forms of LTC insurance. The presentation of a LTC analysis is, therefore, an important element in a well-written comprehensive financial plan. The following narrative is an example of how the life insurance section within a comprehensive financial plan can be written. Notice that this section of the financial plan has a space for the clients to sign an acknowledgement that the benefits and risks associated with postponement of the purchase of LTC insurance has been explained.

Long-Term Care Insurance

Overview of Long-Term Care Insurance:

Long-term care insurance provides coverage in the event that an insured needs care for an extended period of time due to a chronic condition. The cost of long-term care in a nursing home facility can be quite high, with costs increasing at a faster pace than inflation. See the assumptions listed below for more information and statistics about long-term care insurance in the local area.

It is worth noting that long-term care insurance is becoming increasingly expensive and more difficult to obtain. As a result, long-term care insurance is not suitable for everyone. Long-term care insurance is generally recommended for clients with a net worth between $500,000 and $2,000,000, exclusive of the value of the home, as there may not be sufficient resources to self-insure and the cost of an extended stay in a long-term care facility could significantly reduce net worth. The time to start considering the purchase of long-term care insurance is generally between the age of forty and fifty-five. Prior to age forty, the probability that the lifetime costs of long-term care insurance will exceed the benefits of purchasing the insurance is very high; however, starting after age fifty-five, the cost of premiums can become prohibitively expensive.

Long-Term Care Insurance Definitions:

The following definitions will be useful as you review the analysis presented in this section:

- *Activities of daily living (ADLs):* An ADL measures someone's ability to perform routine personal care functions. There are six ADLs: eating, toileting, transferring from a bed to a chair, bathing, dressing, and maintaining continence.

- *Benefit period*: Period of time the insurance company is obligated to pay a monthly disability benefits.

- *Elimination period:* Period of time from the point of a LTC diagnosis to the point at which benefits begin.

- *Risk triggers*: Events, characteristics, or factors that can compromise a person's future health status and increase the likelihood of needing chronic care or custodial care. Examples include personal health status, related family health history, lifestyle choices, and working in a hazardous profession or occupation.

Planning Assumptions:

- Annual nursing home expenses are currently $65,000.

- The average age for those entering as assisted living facility is seventy-five, with an assumed average length of stay of approximately three years.

- The average age for those entering a nursing home is eighty-three, with an assumed average stay of approximately two years.

- As a family, you would like to cover six years of total expenses in the event either Chandler or Rachel enter a facility.

- Long-term care expenses have been increasing at 5 percent per year.

- In the event either Rachel or Chandler enters a nursing home, you are willing to allocate $200,000 from your net worth (today's dollars) to help pay for LTC expenses.

- Assets for use in funding long-term care expenses will grow at a modest 5.5 percent after-tax rate of return.

Goal:

- Ensure that you can meet future long-term care needs through a combination of insurance and savings.

Your Current Long-Term Care Insurance Situation:

Currently, you do not own long-term care insurance, but you are at an age where many people begin to consider whether long-term care insurance is an appropriate choice. Rachel, your family history suggests that you need to be proactive in screening for potential health issues. Chandler, your family health history is positive. Even so, there are many considerations, in addition to family history, that play a role in determining the appropriateness of long-term care insurance, including your work environment and lifestyle choices.

At this point, given your age and health status, you are in a position to postpone the purchase of long-term care insurance for approximately a decade. Should a long-term care need arise, you will need to reallocate assets to help offset expenses. Our team will monitor changes in the long-term care insurance policy market and your long-term care needs on an ongoing basis.

Long-Term Care Insurance Recommendation:

The following table summarizes the LTC recommendation that was developed to help you reach your long-term care insurance goal. As with all recommendations presented in this financial plan, our firm is available to answer any questions that might arise and to assist with specific implementation procedures.

Recommendation #1: When you reach age fifty-five, consider the purchase of a long-term care policy with a ninety-day elimination period and a six-year benefit period.	
Who:	Chandler and Rachel.
What:	Two long-term care policies with a ninety-day elimination period and a six-year benefit period provided by the same insurance provider.
When:	Once Phoebe begins college.

Where:	With your insurance professional or with an online provider that our firm can recommend (our staff will provide you with specific information and guidance throughout the process).
Why:	To ensure financial security for your family and minimize the risk that long-term care costs will deplete your assets and prevent you from reaching your goals.
How:	Consult your insurance professional (our staff can assist you with this task). Our firm will assist by discussing underwriting issues, required application, and medical information.
How much:	Purchase a policy with a $300 daily benefit and a six-year payment option, with an inflation rider. It is expected that at the time of implementation: • The cost for Chandler will be approximately $400 per month. • The cost of Rachel will be approximately $490 per month. • You will receive a 10 to 30 percent discount by insuring jointly with the same insurance provider. • You will need to maintain an emergency fund equal to the length of the elimination period.
Effect on cash flow:	The purchase will decrease annual cash flow by approximately $10,680 at the time of purchase.

Current vs. Recommended Outcome:

Currently, you are self-insuring a potential long-term care need. Since you are young and in excellent health, the likelihood of needing care in the near future is very low. By postponing the purchase of long-term care insurance until you both reach the age of fifty-five, you will be in a position to allocate available cash flow to other needs, including retirement and education expenses.

Alternative Recommendations and Outcome(s):

Once you reach age fifty-five and Phoebe begins college, it is likely that your net worth will be large enough to make self-insurance a viable alternative to purchasing long-term care insurance. It is likely that your long-term care need will look very different in the future given changes to your net worth and changes to the long-term care insurance market. If your net worth is in excess of $2 million at that time (adjusted for inflation), you should consider allocating additional assets and savings towards a self-insurance pool that can be used to offset any potential long-term care expenses. This strategy will help ensure that you will be more likely to have additional assets in the event that one or both of you needs long-term care. At the end of your LTC need, any amount remaining in the self-insurance pool can be used for estate and legacy planning goals.

Plan Implementation and Monitoring Procedures:

A long-term care analysis should be conducted annually as your income, net worth, health status, and other factors change. Our firm will continue to monitor changes in the long-term care insurance market, including average lengths of stay, premium prices, and long-term care inflation rates. This analysis will be conducted prior to each annual review meeting.

Long-Term Care Insurance Recommendation Documentation:

Please sign and date the following form. The form confirms that you agree with the recommendation to postpone the purchase of long-term care insurance, and that the recommendation has been explained to you, with the benefits and risks associated with postponement fully described, and that you have read and understand this section of your financial plan.

Long-Term Care Insurance is a generally recommended product the can help protect your assets, savings, retirement, and estate plan.

On this date, my financial planner and I discussed long-term care insurance and how it can provide protection in the event of a long term sickness or accident that would require an extended stay in a nursing home or extended home health care.

CLIENT NAME: _____

REPRESENTATIVE NAME: _____

DATE: _____

At this time, I have made the decision **not** to purchase long-term care coverage, and I am aware that my assets are fully exposed and subject to liquidation if a long-term care need arises. I also understand that long-term care insurance is an underwritten product and that a change in my future health status could impact my eligibility for coverage at a later date.

_____
Client Signature Date

_____
Representative Signature Date

This form is evidence that [name of financial planner] presented Long-Term Care Insurance as a financial planning alternative to the client and for file documentation.

11.10 SELF-TEST

[A] Questions

Self-Test 1

Graham is age 49 and single. He has a net worth of $2.1 million. Assuming that he has no confirmed legacy or gifting plans, which of the following statements is true in relation to his long-term care insurance need?

(a) To be extra safe, Graham should purchase a LTC insurance policy today.

(b) Graham has the net worth to self-insurance a current or future LTC need.

(c) When Graham enters retirement he should immediately purchase a $100 per day LTC policy.

(d) Graham should begin spending down assets and/or create a gifting plan to ensure that he can used Medicaid benefits in the event of a LTC need.

Self-Test 2

Which of the following forms of care is not covered in a traditional long-term care policy?

(a) nursing home care.

(b) dementia care.

(c) hospice care.

(d) surgical care.

Self-Test 3

Pat has arthritis. She has trouble getting out of bed each morning, but she manages to make it through the day with the help of pain medications and a walker. Does Pat qualify for long-term care?

(a) Yes, because she cannot perform an ADL.

(b) No, because she still has functional abilities.

(c) Yes, because arthritis is an overarching trigger of benefits.

(d) No, because she does not yet exhibit dementia.

Self-Test 4

The optimal age to consider purchasing LTC insurance is:

(a) Age forty.

(b) Age fifty-five.

(c) Age sixty-five.

(d) Age seventy.

Self-Test 5

A LTC policy that that will make payments for a specified period of years, whether or not the insured receives the maximum daily benefit, is called

(a) an indemnity policy.

(b) a pool-of-money policy.

(c) an expense-reimbursement contract.

(d) an any-care policy.

[B] Answers

Question 1: b

Question 2: d

Question 3: b

Question 4: b

Question 5: a

11.11 CHAPTER RESOURCES

AARP (www.aarp.org).

Administration on Aging (www.aoa.gov).

American Association for Long-Term Care Insurance (www.aaltci.org).

Commission on Accreditation of Rehabilitation Facilities/Continuing Care Accreditation Commission (CARF/CCAC) (www.carf.org/Providers.aspx?content=content/Accreditation/Opportunities/AS/CCAC.htm).

Comparison of Nursing Homes (www.medicare.gov/NHcompare).

Comprehensive long-term care insurance information (www.longtermcarelink.net).

LeadingAge (www.leadingage.org).

Long-term Care Partnership Plans (ltcpartnershiponly.com/index.html).

Medicare (www.medicare.gov).

National Clearinghouse for Long-term Care Information (www.longtermcare.gov).

Weiss Ratings (www.weissratings.com).

Patient Protection and Affordable Care Act (PPACA) of 2010 (www.dol.gov/ebsa/healthreform).

CHAPTER ENDNOTES

1. Alzheimer's Association, "2020 Alzheimer's Disease Facts and Figures." https://www.alz.org/alzheimers-dementia/facts-figures.

2. American Association for Long-Term Care Insurance, *2018 LTCi Sourcebook*. www.aaltci.org/long-term-care-insurance/learning-center/fast-facts.php.

3. "Do You Need Long-term-care Insurance? (CR Investigates)," *Consumer Reports* (2004). www.accessmylibrary.com/coms2/summary_0286-19498415_ITM.

4. American Association for Long-Term Care Insurance, *Long-term Care Insurance Tax-deductibility Rules*. www.aaltci.org/long-term-care-insurance/learning-center/tax-for-business.php.

5. AARP, *Continuing Care Retirement Communities: What They Are and How They Work*. www.aarp.org/relationships/caregiving-resource-center/info-09-2010/ho_continuing_care_retirement_communities.html.

6. AgeWave/Harris Interactive, *America Talks: Protecting Our Families' Financial Futures*. https://agewave.com/what-we-do/landmark-research-and-consulting/research-studies/america-talks-protecting-our-families-financial-futures/

7. *Ibid*.

Chapter 12

Property and Casualty Insurance Planning

Learning Objectives

- Learning Objective 1: Evaluate a client's property and casualty insurance need.

- Learning Objective 2: Identify liability exposures associated with the ownership of property.

- Learning Objective 3: Assess a client's need for property replacement and liability insurance coverage.

- Learning Objective 4: Compare different homeowner's and personal automobile insurance policies.

- Learning Objective 5: Recommend appropriate property and casualty insurance policies.

12.1 THE PROCESS OF PROPERTY AND LIABILITY INSURANCE PLANNING

Ensuring that a client has adequate levels of property, casualty, and liability insurance is an important step in the development of a client's financial plan. The role of property and casualty insurance planning within the comprehensive financial planning process sometimes gets relegated to a quick review, especially when compared to life, disability, and long-term care planning issues. This is unfortunate. Although often overshadowed, issues related to property loss and liability exposure can influence almost every other aspect of a client's financial situation. The following discussion highlights how the financial planning process can be followed when conducting a property and casualty insurance needs analysis.

12.2 STEP 1: UNDERSTAND THE CLIENT'S PERSONAL AND FINANCIAL CIRCUMSTANCES

Managing risks involves identifying, analyzing, and ranking a client's personal, household, and family lifestyle for potential threats that could lead to a monetary loss and identifying methods to reduce or eliminate the impact of that loss. In its simplest form, this is the premise underlying **risk management** methodologies. The success of any risk management method is contingent on timing. Recognizing a client's **risk exposure** after a loss has occurred is pointless. Thus, it is essential to take the time before a loss occurs to carefully evaluate risk exposures. As shown in Figure 12.1, there are five risk management and reduction techniques that can be used to control client property and casualty risks: (1) **risk retention**, (2) **risk avoidance**, (3) **risk reduction**, (4) **risk sharing**, and (5) **risk transference**. Insurance contracts represent an example of transferring and/or sharing risk with a third party.

Figure 12.1. Risk Management and Reduction Techniques.

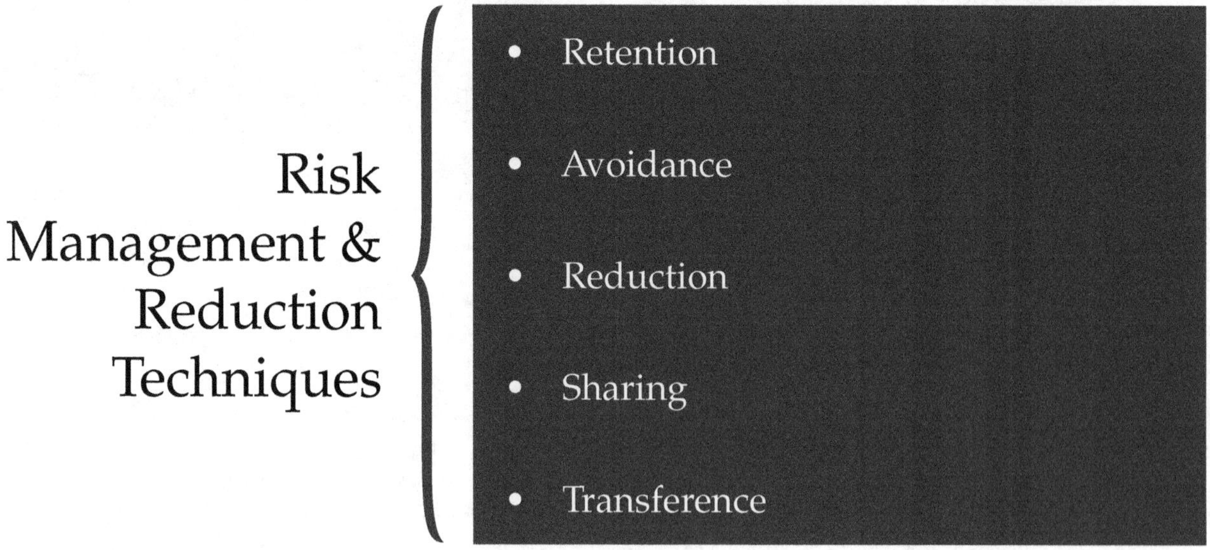

Planning Reminder

Deductible and premium amounts move inversely. Increasing the deductible reduces the annual premium. Increased discretionary cash flow resulting from a reduction in premiums can be used to build an emergency fund to offset future insurance costs and losses. A homeowner's policy deductible of the *lesser* of $1,000 or 1% of the value of the dwelling is not uncommon.

It is important to keep in mind that although recommendations will differ based on each client's unique situation, the fundamentals of property and casualty insurance planning apply to all clients. Thus, identifying and recommending appropriate and reasonable insurance strategies becomes an important way to help clients protect property, assets, and future income. It is imperative that financial planners adequately review and evaluate a client's personal, household, and family lifestyle issues as a way to identify threats that could lead to economic loss.

Figure 12.2 provides a review of the Hubbles' personal and financial circumstances related to property and casualty insurance planning. The information in Figure 12.2 is typical of what a financial planner should evaluate at the first step of the financial planning process.

Figure 12.2. The Hubbles' Personal and Financial Circumstances.

- Over the past several years, Chandler and Rachel have taken steps to purchase insurance to meet different life, health, and property contingencies. They are still uncertain whether these policies are best suited to their needs.
- Chandler and Rachel have split-limit PAP coverage of 100/300/50 on both cars, in addition to $100,000 of uninsured/underinsured motorist coverage.
  - Automobile insurance is provided by Missouri Valley Insurance Corporation (A.M. Best Rating: A).
  - Deductibles are $500 for comprehensive coverage and $500 for collision coverage. This insurance includes medical payments, car rental coverage, and towing.
- The Hubbles currently have an HO-3 policy with a $100,000 liability limit that provides replacement value on contents through an endorsement underwritten by Missouri National Insurance (A.M. Best rating: A).
  - The Hubbles' home is currently insured for $225,000.
  - The replacement value of the home is equal to the fair market value.
  - Chandler and Rachel do not know if the HO policy has an inflation endorsement.
  - The HO policy deductible is $500.
  - The HO policy premium is $700 per year.
- Three years ago, their insurance agent recommended that Chandler and Rachel purchase a $500,000 umbrella insurance policy. The premium for the policy is $175 per year.
- Chandler and Rachel own other property (e.g., boat, jewelry, collectibles, etc.) that may require additional insurance coverage.

12.3 STEP 2: IDENTIFY AND SELECT GOALS

Information and client-specific factors used to assess the need for property and casualty insurance tend to focus on the assets and lifestyle of a client's household. Rarely do clients have specific property and casualty insurance goals. Instead, clients most often have questions regarding the appropriate coverage for property replacement and liability protection.

An important task associated with identifying and selecting goals involves recognizing property that needs to be protected and the possible risk exposures associated with a client's activities and those of other family members. The risk management and control process is an ongoing activity. Financial planners can strengthen the client-financial planner relationship by periodically updating client information to maintain and improve a client's property and casualty insurance protection. Minimally, financial planners should at regular intervals review client data related to (a) the names and addresses of all household members; (b) dwelling construction type; (c) dwelling or outbuilding improvements or additions; (d) changes in car ownership; (e) liability policy limits; (f) policy deductibles; and (g) homeowners and personal automobile policy schedules and endorsements. This information will help clarify a client's property and casualty insurance needs and goals.

Although Chandler and Rachel voiced just a few insurance goals during the initial data intake meeting, Chandler and Rachel do have several insurance objectives that can be used to guide the property and casualty insurance planning process. Figure 12.3 summarizes the Hubbles' current property and casualty insurance goals.

Figure 12.3. The Hubbles' Property and Liability Insurance Goals.

Neither Chandler nor Rachel have given much thought to property and casualty insurance planning. In the past, Chandler and Rachel have relied on their insurance agent to guide them when making insurance choices. Based on a review of their situation, the following goals emerged as important:

- Minimize personal liability exposures.
- Minimize liability exposures resulting from the use of their property.
- Maintain appropriate property and casualty insurance coverage on a year-to-year basis.
- Obtain replacement cost coverage for property that may be currently underinsured.
- Purchase additional coverage to ensure that Chandler and Rachel are adequately covered in the case of property loss or liability claim.
- Continue to ensure that any property, casualty, and liability coverage is appropriate in terms of costs.

12.4 STEP 3: ANALYZE THE CLIENT'S CURRENT COURSE OF ACTION AND POTENTIAL ALTERNATIVE COURSE(S) OF ACTION

[A] Assessing a Client's Current Situation and Risk

Typically, a client's property and casualty insurance plan will have been designed by another professional, most often an insurance agent or broker. Financial planners can play a valuable role by providing an independent evaluation of current coverages.

It is important to keep in mind that, for many clients, a substantial portion of net worth is associated with home equity and non-investment asset ownership. Uninsured damage or liability claims against a client's property ownership status can adversely impact the client's lifestyle and financial goal achievement. Without adequate liability coverage, for instance, a single accident or event could place a family's financial future in jeopardy and negatively impact their capacity to fund other financial goals. In today's increasingly litigious society, it is imperative that clients be protected from financial losses associated with personal property and casualty claims.

Planning Reminder

Dangerous attractive nuisances, like a swimming pool or a yard trampoline that attract children or others to a client's home, represent a perilous opportunity for loss that requires additional insurance, especially liability coverage.

A major step in the insurance planning process involves assessing and discussing a client's unique property and casualty insurance exposures and/or the risks clients face. Despite the fact that a client may have consulted with other insurance professionals, it is common to find insurance oversights that if left unresolved could leave a client financially vulnerable.

As shown previously in Figure 12.1, five primary risk reduction techniques should be considered when analyzing a client's property and casualty insurance situation. Two of these techniques deal with reducing the likelihood of loss, whereas two deal with reducing the cost of loss. There is one additional possibility: risk retention. **Risk retention** involves having a client accept the loss or gain resulting from a risk. Risk retention is an appropriate risk management strategy when the costs associated with insurance are significantly greater than the potential losses involved. By definition, any risk that is not prevented, avoided, or transferred is retained by the client. Sometimes retention is the only way to handle risk. There may be no economically viable option to prevent a risk or to indemnify a client for it (e.g., acts of war). Retention may also be the best way to deal with risks that are predictable and not costly.

Clients who do not want or cannot afford to retain the risk of loss should consider reducing or eliminating the risk. The two primary methods of reducing, or controlling, the likelihood of a loss include **risk avoidance** and **risk reduction**. However, both avoiding and reducing risk require a client to alter behavior, possessions, or their personal, household, or working environment. For instance, to avoid an auto theft loss, the client could choose not to own a car. This approach to risk management may not be practical or even possible. Instead, the client may seek to reduce the likelihood of loss by safeguarding the car with a vehicle alarm or tracking system. This is an example of risk reduction.

If controlling the likelihood of loss is impractical, a client can **indemnify** the loss by sharing the cost associated with the risk with another person or organization, typically an insurance company. The two primary indemnification methods include **risk transferring** and **risk sharing**. Both methods establish an agreement or contract (e.g., an *indemnity* or *hold-harmless agreement* or *insurance contract*) prior to a loss. The agreement outlines the moral and financial responsibilities of both parties. When contractually transferring risk, clients (ideally with the help of their financial planner) must identify potential risks, determine the likelihood of loss, and calculate the estimated financial exposure associated with that risk. The insurance company determines the uncertainties, probabilities, and costs associated with insuring the risks. **Insurance** is most often the preferred risk management mechanism when risks pose the possibility of moderate or high financial loss but the anticipated frequency of loss is low or unpredictable.

Even in the presence of insurance, a financial planner should nudge their clients towards risk control strategies. **Risk control** is an ongoing process that involves identifying and analyzing the severity and likelihood of potential loss exposures. A key element associated with risk control is understanding the following concepts: maximum possible loss, maximum probable loss, and typical losses, as well as the likelihood of each. The **maximum possible loss** is the largest loss that can occur. Theoretically, for liability purposes, there is no limit on the maximum possible loss because there generally is no way to be certain what a jury might award. The **maximum probable loss** is the greatest loss that has the highest probability of occurring. The **typical loss** is the one that occurs most frequently.

Planning Reminder

Personal property valued at more than $2,500 should be covered by a policy endorsement. Items to be scheduled include jewelry, guns, collectibles, coins, stamps, gold, silver, and other valuable items.

Safeguarding against a maximum possible loss requires insurance to cover **catastrophic losses**, regardless of how likely or unlikely it is that a catastrophic event might occur. When analyzing a client's **homeowner's (HO)** and **personal automobile policy (PAP)** coverage, a financial planner should make certain that the limits of liability and property coverage shield the client from a potentially bankrupting financial responsibility. Additionally, clients may need coverage for property that requires additional coverage. An **endorsement** changes a policy by modifying the scope of coverage, specifying some unique loss exposure, or adding insureds or locations for coverage. Typical endorsements, depending on the insurer, include guaranteed replacement cost coverage, inflation protection, identity theft, or modified coverage of assets that are included or *scheduled* for coverage, such as musical instruments or jewelry.

A thorough knowledge of a client's personal and financial situation is central to all aspects of financial planning, but nowhere is this more evident than when planning for property and casualty insurance. Seemingly mundane—and in some cases intrusive—questions about a client's home, personal property, pets, hobbies, vehicles, and driving habits must be considered. To complete a comprehensive assessment, a financial planner and client must explore issues related to the client's lifestyle, the client's **aversion to risk**—the client's willingness to take financial risk when the outcome of the risk is both unknown and potentially negative—property owned, and the ways in which property is used by members of the insured's household, including residence employees. This information provides the basis for determining property and casualty insurance needs, as well as appropriate product recommendations.

A key step in the assessment of a client's current situation focuses on gathering, summarizing, and analyzing all currently in-force property and casualty policies. This entails conducting a comprehensive review of a client's HO, PAP, excess liability, and other miscellaneous policies. A basic checklist that can be used for this task is shown in Figure 12.4.

Figure 12.4. Questions to Use When Assessing Property and Liability Insurance Coverage.

Assessing Homeowners Insurance Coverage	Yes	No
Is client's home insured for 100% replacement value rather than market value?		
Is coverage on the home at least 80% of the estimated replacement value?		
Has the home recently been appraised for its estimated replacement value?		
Does the policy have an inflation endorsement?		
Does the policy have a building code, sewer back-up, identity theft, or other endorsement?		
Has client made a household possessions inventory?		
Does client have a video or pictures to supplement the inventory?		
Is the household possessions inventory/documentation held in a safe place outside of the home?		
Does client's homeowner's policy have adequate contents insurance protection?		
Does client need special coverage for collectibles and other hard-to-replace items?		
Does client have written appraisal for expensive items (silver, jewelry, furs, etc.)?		
Does client have endorsements or individual policies for these items?		
Does client carry comprehensive (open perils) coverage on household contents?		
Does client carry replacement cost coverage on household contents?		
Does client need/have coverage for any watercraft?		
Does client need extended theft coverage?		
Is coverage for medical payments to others sufficient?		
Is liability coverage sufficient? Is it coordinated with an umbrella policy?		
Does the deductible match client's ability to pay out of pocket for losses?		

	Yes	No
Have all available discounts been taken?		
Does client own any seasonal residences that might need special insurance treatment?		
Does client own an historic home that might need special insurance treatment?		
Assessing Automobile Insurance Coverage	**Yes**	**No**
Are liability limits sufficient? Are they coordinated with an umbrella policy?		
Is coverage for medical payments to others sufficient?		
Is uninsured and under-insured motorist's coverage sufficient to protect the client, if needed?		
Does client still need comprehensive or collision coverage, given the age of the vehicle(s)?		
Does client have coverage for any off-road or recreational vehicles?		
Do deductibles match client's ability to pay for losses from cash flow or assets?		
Have all available discounts been taken?		
Assessing Liability Insurance Coverage	**Yes**	**No**
Does client have an umbrella liability policy?		
Does client have potential liability exposure from serving as an officer or director of a for-profit or not-for-profit organization?		
Does client have potential liability exposure resulting from volunteer activities?		
Does client have a nanny, housekeeper, or lawn/garden help?		
Are liability homeowners and auto policies coordinated with client's umbrella policy?		
Assessing Need for Flood and Earthquake Insurance	**Yes**	**No**
Does client need, or qualify for, flood insurance?		
If maximum losses were incurred, could client afford to pay damages from cash flow and/or assets?		
Does client need/have earthquake insurance?		
Can client afford the premium for flood or earthquake insurance?		

Two issues should guide the review. First, is the current level of coverage sufficient to insure property losses fully? Second, is the client adequately protected against liability claims? A negative or unsure answer requires the issue to be considered in greater depth.

[B] The HO Policy and the 80 Percent Rule

Two out of every three homes in the United States are underinsured. The average amount of under-insurance is approximately 22 percent, with some homes underinsured by 60 percent or more.[1] As these statistics suggest, it is imperative that financial planners assess each client's home insurance coverage to ensure adequate reimbursement for potential losses.

Planning Reminder

Although 80 percent coverage is the minimally acceptable level of coverage on a structure, 100 percent coverage with an inflation endorsement is a standard planning recommendation.

Some homeowner's policies include an **80 percent rule** (or *coinsurance rule*) to determine the level of reimbursement when a loss is incurred. *Every financial plan should include an 80 percent rule analysis.* The 80 percent rule provides a way to verify whether an HO policy limit is sufficient to provide full replacement for a major loss. Based on the replacement value of the residence at the time of loss, if the amount of coverage is equal to 80 percent of the replacement cost, then full replacement of the damaged portion will be paid, up to the limits of the policy less the deductible, with no reduction for depreciation. As noted above, if the insured does not carry insurance equal to at least 80 percent of the replacement cost, the insured is penalized through a coinsurance clause when the loss is paid.

Planning Reminder

Financial planners should remind clients that insurance is based on **replacement cost**, which is defined as the actual amount needed to rebuild or repair property, rather than the **fair market value** of the property. Market value may be higher or lower than the replacement cost, depending on the geographic area in which the home is located. Although it is always a good idea to recommend a 100 percent replacement cost policy with inflation protection, it is essential that the 80 percent rule be met. Otherwise, a client may not be completely reimbursed for future losses or damage. Recommending an additional **inflation endorsement** ensures that property coverage automatically adjusts annually in response to rising prices. Some policies may include inflation protection without an additional endorsement.

If the amount of insurance on a structure, divided by 80 percent of the applicable replacement cost, is equal to or greater than 1.0, then the homeowner will be reimbursed for the lesser of the replacement cost or the amount of the policy. However, if the amount of insurance on the structure, divided by 80 percent of the applicable replacement cost, is less than 1.0, then the insured will not qualify for full repair or replacement. If an insured is penalized, the insured will be paid the actual cash value of the part of the structure damaged or destroyed less the deductible *or* the reimbursement amount calculated using the following formula:

$$\frac{\text{Amount of HO Insurance Coverage}}{80\% \times \text{Replacement Cost}} \times \text{Value of Loss} = \text{Value of the Claim} - \text{Deductible}$$

Example. Assume, for example, that a client owns a home with a replacement value of $190,000. Unfortunately, over the years the policy has not kept pace with the rising values of construction, with the home being currently insured for only $130,000 with a $500 deductible. If the insured incurs a loss of $20,000, the insurance company will value the claim at only $16,605, as shown below:

$$\left(\frac{\$130,000}{80\% \times \$190,000} \times \$20,000 \right) - \$500 = \$17,105 - \$500 = \$16,605$$

Planning Reminder

The deductible amount will be subtracted from all settlements, regardless of whether the insured has met the 80 percent rule. **Actual cash value settlements** typically depreciate a property to account for its age. **Replacement cost settlements** typically do not include depreciation.

The $2,895 not reimbursed on the $20,000 claim is considered to be the client's **coinsurance penalty**. However, this is the reimbursement before applying the $500 deductible. Therefore, the actual amount received by the client will be $16,605. To maintain full reimbursement to the limit of the policy, the home should have been insured for a minimum of $152,000 ($190,000 multiplied by 80 percent).

In general, it is important to remember three rules when evaluating the current coverage limits on a client's home: (1) the 80 percent rule applies primarily to partial losses; (2) if the actual cash value exceeds the 80 percent rule limit, the insured receives the larger amount; and (3) the total reimbursement will never exceed the face amount of the policy less the deductible.

Figure 12.5 provides guidance on how the 80 percent rule can impact client outcomes in the event of a loss. Most other coverage levels are determined as a percentage of the coverage on the structure. It is important to note that the ripple effect of under-insurance can have a significant impact on large losses.

Figure 12.5. Coverage and Coinsurance Illustration.

Possible Coverage and Coinsurance Outcomes					
Amount of Insurance Coverage	Coverage Ratio to Property Value	Reimbursement Amount for Total Loss	Insured Coinsurance Percentage	Reimbursement Amount for Partial* Loss	Insured Coinsurance Penalty
$250,000	100%	$247,500	0%	$47,500	0%
$200,000	80%	$197,500	20%	$47,500	0%
$150,000	60%	$147,500	$(1-(60/80))$ or 25%	$35,000	25%
$100,000	40%	$97,500	$(1-(40/80))$ or 50%	$22,500	50%
Based on a home value of $250,000 and an HO policy with a $2,500 deductible. * $50,000 loss					

The following summary is based on an analysis of the Hubble family's current property and casualty insurance choices and needs. This analysis summary can be used to facilitate the development of recommendations. Potential recommendations based on the analysis are also provided.

- Currently, the Hubble family purchases property and casualty insurance through Missouri Valley Insurance Corporation. Chandler and Rachel are pleased with the products and services provided by the insurance company and agent; however, Chandler and Rachel are open to additional insurance recommendations.

- At this time, Chandler and Rachel meet the 80 percent rule (they are currently insured for 90 percent of replacement value). The Hubbles also have $100,000 in liability protection, combined with a $500,000 excess liability policy. This coverage may be too low.

- Chandler and Rachel may be required by the insurer to increase their HO policy liability coverage to $300,000 in order to raise the umbrella policy limit. With a split limit coverage of 100/300/50, Chandler and Rachel have minimally acceptable coverage for their vehicles. Financial planners typically recommend that a family increase the liability portion to at least $100,000 ($300,000 may be needed to obtain a high limit umbrella policy).

Based on the insurance assumptions presented in the case and the summary from above, the following potential recommendations are worth considering:

- Increase insurance on the home to 100 percent of replacement value, including an inflation rider.

- Purchase endorsements on some personal property, as needed.

- Increase umbrella policy limit to $1 million.

- Purchase insurance on the boat, motor and trailer, including liability insurance.

- Consider increasing, at a minimum, the property damage liability on the auto policy, and possibly all liability limits if the cost is not prohibitive.

- An increase in deductibles across policies is also recommended. Increasing deductibles will decrease premium costs. If a need should arise, assets held within the Hubbles' emergency fund can be used to meet deductible expenses.

12.5 STEP 4: DEVELOP THE FINANCIAL PLANNING RECOMMENDATION(S)

The development of property and casualty insurance recommendations, within a comprehensive financial plan, can encompass a multitude of products and services. A competent financial planner should continually develop and refine skills needed to transform the analysis of a client's situation into actionable recommendations. The following discussion highlights some of the important concepts, tools, and techniques that can be incorporated into the recommendation development process.

[A] Premium Considerations

Answering the question of how much a client needs in property and casualty insurance coverage is not a straightforward process. Most insurance experts agree on the need to transfer risk through insurance, but how much of that risk to transfer or the amount of protection to purchase is often a matter of interpretation.

For instance, a client with a high net worth and an elevated willingness to take financial risk may be able to self-insure a risk, whereas purchasing insurance may be the more appropriate solution for a client with less risk capacity. Other factors unique to the individual client household should also be considered, including: type of construction and local construction costs, access to and quality of community fire protection, occupancy and use of the home, and home safety features, driving history and preferences, and general liability exposure. Clients who enhance existing safety features throughout their life may qualify for additional discounts. Policy type and the limits of coverage affect the cost of all policies. As such, issues surrounding the cost to replace a home and its contents, as well as other property, including vehicles, boats, planes, motorcycles, etc., should be carefully reviewed when formulating insurance recommendations.

Beyond a lender's requirement for HO insurance or the state-mandated requirement of PAP insurance to license a vehicle, nearly all clients think of property insurance in the context of replacing damaged, lost, or stolen property. Although the monetary impact of property loss may be significant, by far the greater risk comes from liability claims resulting from the actions of the insured or members of the insured's household.

Factors that can affect the need for property and casualty insurance parallel the issues that influence underwriting and rating procedures used to determine insurance costs. Although the factors that insurance companies use vary for HO and PAP insurance, two consistent and very important issues must be considered when determining the level of insurance coverage to recommend.

First is the territory or location of the property. Aside from moving, this factor is beyond the insured's control when purchasing HO or PAP insurance. Location, for example, influences the need for flood insurance or earthquake coverage. Retrofitting or modernizing a home to improve its disaster resistance may reduce policy costs and the potential for loss.

Second is the client's **insurance score**, which is calculated from data collected by the major national credit bureaus. The Federal Trade Commission defines an insurance score as a numerical summary of a person's past credit delinquencies, bankruptcies, debt ratio, credit-seeking behavior, credit history, and use of credit.[2] These factors are shown in Figure 12.6.

Figure 12.6. Factors Associated with a Client's Insurance Score.

Insurance companies typically use insurance scores to estimate whether a person is (1) likely to make premium payments and (2) how many claims someone is, in all likelihood, going to file over any period of time. A client's insurance score tends to be inversely correlated with claim costs. In other words, the lower the client's insurance score, the higher the likely cost of future claims and thus a higher insurance premium. For clients with credit problems, efforts to reduce the reliance on credit and making timely payments can, over time, improve their credit and insurance scores, both of which can impact other aspects of the client's financial life, primarily by reducing the cost insurance premiums.

[B] HO Policy Considerations

HO policies are generally packaged as **standard policy forms**. Figure 12.7 compares seven of the most widely available HO policy forms. An important feature that differentiates HO policies is protection from **perils**. A **named perils policy** protects against economic loss resulting from perils that are specifically named within a policy. **Open peril** is a term used to describe an **all-risk policy** that covers losses from all causes unless specifically excluded in the insurance contract. These exclusions typically include flood, earthquake, war, nuclear accident, and mold. Corresponding to these types of policies is the related issue of **burden of proof**. With a named perils policy, the homeowner (or renter) must provide evidence that the loss was caused by a named peril listed in the policy. In contrast, with the open peril policy, a loss is covered unless the insurance company can provide evidence that the loss was excluded from the policy.

Once the type of policy is selected, both homeowner and renter have choices on the level of protection offered, or the policy's loss settlement clause. Some policies use **actual cash value** (ACV) as the basis for replacing property. Although typically applied to replacement of possessions, ACV may also apply to claims on a structure. Actual cash value provides reimbursement based on the replacement value of the property less depreciation. Older property, whose age exceeds the specified useful life of "x" years, has little or no reimbursement value. Consequently, reimbursement could be pennies on the dollar relative to the value of the loss or the amount needed for even minimal replacement. Keep in mind that the term market value refers to reimbursement based on the value of similar items in the secondary market, whereas replacement cost coverage pays for a similar new product.

A **replacement cost coverage endorsement** provides for lost, stolen, or destroyed property to be replaced with equivalent property with no reductions for depreciation. Although slightly more expensive, replacement cost coverage is recommended in most situations.

Although not available in every state or from every insurance company, homeowners also may have the choice of **guaranteed replacement cost** or **extended replacement cost** for claims on the structure. With both, the amount paid on a claim to replace or repair the structure may exceed the amount of coverage on which the premium is based. Guaranteed replacement coverage pays the full amount, while extended replacement coverage pays a specified amount, typically 20 to 25 percent above the policy coverage limit. These endorsements protect the insured in the case of a total loss or when a natural disaster may cause widespread market increases in construction costs. It is important to note that costs of upgrading a home to comply with current building codes are not typically included.

For clients who rent or own a condominium or cooperative, the 80 percent rule is not an effective measure of coverage. Other factors must be considered. Foremost is the named perils coverage on contents, which some clients may wish to extend to protect against all risks except specific exclusions. Clients protected by an HO-4 or HO-6 policy should include replacement cost and inflation guard endorsements for maximum protection.

Condominium or cooperative owners must consider the level of coverage on unit property for which they are responsible, such as built-in cabinetry, appliances, or other surface treatments (e.g., carpet, tile, wallpaper, etc.) relative to their actual cash value or replacement cost decision. Upgrading to replacement cost and inflation guard protection offers broader protection, but it will increase premium costs as well.

Figure 12.7. Typical HO Policy Forms and Coverage.

Seven Forms of Homeowners Policies*						
Form	Part A Dwelling	Part B Other Structures	Part C Personal Property	Part D Loss of Use	Part E Typical Personal Liability Limit	Part F Typical Medical Payments to Others Limit
Broad Form (HO-2) Named 16 perils policy***	Replacement value	10% of dwelling coverage	50% of dwelling coverage; actual cash value	30% of dwelling coverage	$100,000	$1,000 per person per incident
Special Form (HO-3) Named 16 perils policy for personal property	Replacement value	10% of dwelling coverage	50% of dwelling coverage; actual cash value	30% of dwelling coverage	$100,000	$1,000 per person per incident
Contents Form (HO-4) Named 16 perils policy for personal property***	Does not apply	Does not apply	Usually stated in dollar amount; actual cash value	30% of personal property coverage	$100,000	$1,000 per person per incident
Comprehensive Form (HO-5) All perils, except specific exclusions	Replacement value	10% of dwelling coverage	50% of dwelling coverage; actual cash value	30% of dwelling coverage	$100,000	$1,000 per person per incident
Unit Owner's Form (HO-6) Named 16 perils policy***	$1,000 – $5,000 minimum limited to semi-permanent features in the unit	Does not apply or included in Part A	Usually stated in dollar amount; actual cash value	50% of personal property coverage	$100,000	$1,000 per person per incident
Modified Coverage Form (HO-8) Named 11 perils policy**	Market value of structure or cost to repair replace with functional equivalent	10% of dwelling coverage	50% of dwelling coverage; actual cash value	10% of dwelling coverage	$100,000	$1,000 per person per incident

Table Notes:
* This summary is based on the standard Insurance Service Office (ISO) policy forms used throughout the United States. Policy variations may apply as some insurers use American Association of Insurance Services (AAIS) forms, while some insurers design their own forms, and in some instances, state mandated modifications may apply. For more information see www.iso.com. HO-1 policies are generally no longer available.
** The named 11 perils typically include: (1) Fire or lightning; (2) windstorm or hail; (3) explosion; (4) riot or civil commotion; (5) damage caused by aircraft; (6) damage caused by vehicles; (7) smoke; (8) vandalism or malicious mischief; (9) theft; (10) volcanic eruption; and (11) falling objects.
*** The additional five perils (leading to a total of 16) include: (12) weight of ice, snow or sleet; (13) accidental discharge or overflow of water or steam from within plumbing, heating, air conditioning, automatic fire-protective sprinkler system, or from a household appliance; (14) sudden and accidental tearing apart, cracking, burning, or bulging of a steam or hot water heating system, an air conditioning or automatic fire-protective system; (15) freezing of a plumbing, heating, air conditioning, automatic, fire-protective sprinkler system, or of a household appliance; and (16) sudden and accidental damage from artificially generated electrical current (does not include loss to a tube, transistor or similar electronic component). See the Insurance Information Institute at http://www.iii.org/policymakers/home/ for more information.

[C] Coverage for Overlooked Personal Property

Beyond the basic limits of Part C coverage for personal property, as shown in Figure 12.7, additional coverage is available for select items that are either inadequately covered or excluded from coverage under an HO policy. Personal assets valued at $2,500 or more, such as jewelry, furs, firearms, collectibles/collections, musical instruments, art, precious and semiprecious metals, securities held in physical form, and business assets, may require additional coverage. Although a basic HO policy provides some coverage, the value of such items can quickly exceed the limits of coverage depending on the asset and the insurance company.

The provisions to extend personal property coverage come through a **personal property endorsement**, or rider on an existing polity, or the addition of a **floater policy** (the term rider refers to the document that changes the amount of coverage from the underlying contract). Originally called an **inland marine policy**, a floater is a separate mini-policy that "floats" coverage for an asset that frequently changes location—most often jewelry, firearms, art, or musical instruments. A **personal article, personal effects policy**, or **personal property policy** (different companies use different terms) works in much the same way as a personal property endorsement. Whereas an endorsement is an extension of an HO policy, a floater is a separate policy that may or may not be written by the same company and often has different features, including all risks coverage. This type of separate policy may benefit a client because the coverage allows for more flexibility in coverage limits and deductibles. The endorsement may be written to increase coverage on a specific asset basis, a class of asset basis, or a blanket basis for all classes of personal property otherwise limited in the policy.

In order to obtain coverage and receive full reimbursement, a recent receipt for the purchase or a professional appraisal may be necessary. These costs, as well as the time and effort to complete a well-documented possessions inventory, may discourage some clients. But a quick tally of the potential financial losses, without the additional coverage, may persuade clients to add endorsements or floaters. Annual client reviews should include questions about any new property to ensure that adequate ongoing coverage is in place.

[D] Insurance Exclusions

When developing recommendations, it is important to consider **property exclusions** that may be relevant. For example, theft of property typically is excluded from coverage for college-age students who vacate their dorm rooms or apartments for more than forty-five days during the summer or for alternative educational opportunities. Although an obscure circumstance, this question, as well as others, relating to coverage for property moved by a college student away from the insured residence should be considered because policies vary. Clients who operate a home business will find that insurance restrictions may require the addition of a **home business insurance endorsement**. HO policies typically include up to $2,500 of coverage for business property kept at home, but standard coverage characteristically excludes many business exposures from liability claims and losses of high-value business property.

Planning Reminder

A standard HO policy may or may not provide coverage for "off-premises" property, such as a storage facility. And, if covered, the perils may be limited. Some storage facilities provide coverage, but clients should be warned: "Before you store, be sure you know." For example, banks do *not* insure safe deposit box contents, so a jewelry floater is needed.

Clients often worry about issues related to medical claims resulting from property ownership. The **medical payments coverage** (Part F) and **liability coverage** (Part E) of an HO policy extend beyond situations on the insured's property to liability losses caused by the activities of the insured, the activities of a residence employee in the course of employment, and the activities of an animal owned or cared for by the insured. It may be wise to increase the medical payments or liability coverage based on the athletic participation or hobbies of household members, as well as pet ownership. For example, some states have passed legislation making the owner of a dog that bites someone *strictly liable* for the injuries. Information about dog ownership often is considered when underwriters are rating and offering insurance coverage. Homeowners with swimming pools also may pay higher insurance premiums. Pools are generally considered to be an **attractive nuisance**. A knowledgeable insurance professional should be consulted to explore these issues and to ensure sufficient protection, either through the HO policy or in conjunction with an excess liability policy, which is described in more detail later in the chapter.

[E] Other Coverage Options

Standard HO policies typically provide reimbursement for losses associated with fire (including wildfires), windstorms, hail, and freezing pipes. Standard policies, however, exclude damage caused by disasters, such as flooding and earthquakes, and for those who live in hurricane coastal areas, windstorms. Clients who live in areas prone to flooding must consider **flood coverage**. A lender may, in fact, require **flood insurance** before a mortgage can be acquired. Floods are the most common and widespread of all natural disasters, except for fire. The federal flood insurance requirement applies to any structures located in an eligible community or one that is designated a Special Flood Hazard Area in the emergency program.

The national flood insurance program is administered by the Federal Insurance and Mitigation Administration, which is part of **FEMA (Federal Emergency Management Agency)**. An insurance agent or broker may issue a policy directly from the **National Flood Insurance Program (NFIP)**, or a client may secure coverage from a **write your own (WYO) company**. WYO companies are private insurance companies that provide flood insurance under a special arrangement with the NFIP. WYO companies provide and service policies, while the NFIP retains the risk, thus expanding the availability of flood protection to more homeowners and communities. Policies are also available for renters and condominium unit owners.

Flood insurance provides reimbursement for the overflow of inland or tidal waters and surface waters. Mudslides caused by a flood are also covered. Flood insurance will not cover damage from rain, snow, hail, sewer back-ups, or water damage that results from something a homeowner can control. As with all types of property insurance, premiums reflect the risk of loss, and a deductible does apply. According to the National Flood Insurance Program, the average annual cost of a flood insurance policy is $700.[3] The maximum deductible may be set by the mortgage lender, but as with other insurance, increases to the deductible will result in a reduced annual premium.

Even though all states have experienced earthquakes of varying magnitudes, neither the government nor mortgage lenders mandate coverage. **Earthquake insurance** provides catastrophic coverage for those who live in areas prone to earthquakes. These policies also provide coverage for landslides, mudslides, mudflows, mine subsidence, or other earth movement. Earthquake policies typically have deductibles equal to 10 to 25 percent of the policy limit. Some policies apply the deductible separately to the contents, the structure, and any unattached buildings, so care must be taken to carefully evaluate these policies.

As with all types of property insurance, premiums reflect the risk of loss, including location and the probability of an earthquake, as well as building materials and other structural considerations. Premiums for a $500,000 home in a high-risk earthquake community can run as high as $2,000 a year, with a deductible equal to 10 percent of the limit of coverage. In other parts of the country, an earthquake endorsement can be purchased for much less.

Some financial planners advise clients to self-insure against earthquake losses. Other financial planners argue that the cost of insurance, plus the deductible, is reasonable considering the unpredictability and potential magnitude of earthquake damage. The value of the home and potential replacement costs relative to the client's total net worth should be a major consideration.

[F] PAP Considerations

Driver characteristics, such as age, gender, marital status, and driving record, use of an automobile, and number and types of vehicles covered are considerations in

PAP insurance price and coverage recommendations. How vehicles are used (e.g., for pleasure, commuting to work, or business or farm activities) significantly influences PAP prices and the liability limits needed. Driver education and **good student discounts** may be used to reduce premiums for households with young drivers, as may the discount for a college student away from home without a car.

As shown in Figure 12.8, New Hampshire is the only state that does not have compulsory liability insurance minimums. Aside from the fact that **state minimum liability requirements** are generally inadequate, attention to the liability limits in a PAP is important for another reason. Typically, the **split-limit liability coverage** selected is the same amount of **uninsured** or **underinsured motorists insurance** offered by the policy.

As a reminder, the split limit dollar amounts indicate the maximum coverage provided by the insurance company. For example, a 25/50/25 policy will pay $25,000 in medical bills per person to others involved in an accident (assuming the insured is at fault), with a maximum of $50,000 paid for all medical expenses. Additionally, the insurance company will pay a maximum of $25,000 in property damages to others involved in an accident. **Bodily injury coverage** and **property damage coverage** protect the insured from losses sustained as a result of an accident with an uninsured or underinsured driver.

Studies by the Insurance Research Council, as reported by the Insurance Information Institute, suggest that approximately 13 percent of U.S. drivers may be uninsured. In Oklahoma, Florida, Mississippi, New Mexico, Michigan, and Tennessee, reportedly 20 percent or more of drivers are uninsured.[4] Clients who reside in areas where there is a concentration of uninsured drivers may want to consider higher limits for uninsured or underinsured motorists insurance. While a few states require uninsured motorist coverage, only Connecticut, Illinois, Maryland, Minnesota, Nebraska, New Jersey, North Carolina, North Dakota, Oregon, South Dakota, and Virginia require drivers to carry underinsured motorist coverage.

Figure 12.8. State Minimum PAP Split-Limit Liability Requirements.

State/District	Split-limit Liability Minimums	State/District	Split-limit Liability Minimums
Alabama	25/50/25	Montana	25/50/20
Alaska	50/100/25	Nebraska	25/50/25
Arizona	25/50/15	Nevada	25/50/20
Arkansas	25/50/25	New Hampshire	25/50/25*
California	15/30/5	New Jersey	15/30/5
Colorado	25/50/15	New Mexico	25/50/10
Connecticut	25/50/25	New York	25/50/10
Delaware	25/50/10	North Carolina	30/60/25
Florida	10/20/10	North Dakota	25/50/25
Georgia	25/50/25	Ohio	25/50/25
Hawaii	20/40/10	Oklahoma	25/50/25

Idaho	25/50/15	Oregon	25/50/20
Illinois	25/50/20	Pennsylvania	15/30/5
Indiana	25/50/25	Rhode Island	25/50/25
Iowa	20/40/15	South Carolina	25/50/25
Kansas	25/50/25**	South Dakota	25/50/25
Kentucky	25/50/25	Tennessee	25/50/15
Louisiana	15/30/25	Texas	30/60/25
Maine	50/100/25 + minimum of $1,000 for medical payments	Utah	25/65/15
Maryland	30/60/15	Vermont	25/50/10
Massachusetts	20/40/5	Virginia	25/50/20
Michigan	20/40/10	Washington	25/50/10
Minnesota	30/60/10	Wash D.C.	25/50/10
Mississippi	25/50/25	West Virginia	25/50/25
Missouri	25/50/25	Wisconsin	25/50/10
		Wyoming	25/50/20

Note: Some states allow the minimum requirement to be met with a combined single-limit policy. Coverage amounts vary by state. Some states require medical payments coverage; amounts vary by state.

*New Hampshire does not require the purchase of auto insurance, but drivers must be able to prove they can meet the New Hampshire Motor Vehicle Financial Responsibility Requirements in the event of an "at-fault" accident.

Data source: The Insurance Information Institute. Available at http://www.iii.org/issues_updates/compulsory-auto-uninsured-motorists.html

[G] Other PAP Considerations

In addition to understanding the basic components of a traditional PAP, financial planners are sometimes required to help clients deal with insurance issues related to leased cars and those where the insured is considered to be *upside-down*, meaning that they owe more on the car than the car is worth in the marketplace. An auto loan/lease coverage endorsement provides coverage for the potential gap between the actual cash value of an auto and the amount the insured owes on the auto loan or lease. If a vehicle is deemed a total loss after an accident, the owner may owe more on the vehicle than the insurance will pay as its actual cash value. **Guaranteed auto protection (GAP)** pays the difference between the actual cash value settlement and the remaining balance on the loan or lease.

Planning Reminder

Although not common, some states allow owners to self-insure for auto losses. High net worth clients who drive exotic cars sometimes forego replacement due to damage and instead focus on paying liability claims only. To do so, the client will need to post a liability bond for an amount determined by the state where the vehicle is housed.

Renting a car while on business or for personal reasons causes many clients anxiety. Whether to purchase the insurance offered by rental car companies can be a confusing issue. Normally, clients who carry collision coverage—a policy provision which covers damage to a policy holder's auto resulting from physical contact with another object—on their personal car will find that the coverage extends to rental cars as well. Usually comprehensive coverage also carries over to a rental car. This coverage provides reimbursement for non-collision damage or theft of the automobile; however, it is important to advise clients that they are responsible for paying the policy deductible and that the insurance company will consider the policy to be excess coverage, meaning the insurance company will look first to see whether the insured purchased coverage from the rental car company before paying a claim.

Drivers who have many claims on file with their insurance company, and those who are highly risk averse, should consider purchasing insurance as part of the rental agreement. Rental car insurance is known as a **loss damage waiver (LDW)** or a **collision damage waiver (CDW)**. Purchasing an LDW/CDW allows the insured to walk away from an accident, or if the car is stolen or vandalized, without having to pay a deductible, unless the rental company can show that the driver was reckless or driving while under the influence of drugs or alcohol. Costs for LDW/CDWs average between $10 and $40 per day. Sometimes clients will ask financial planners whether **accidental death and/or personal property insurance coverage** should be purchased when renting a car. Normally, the answer is no. The cost of accidental death insurance can be very high, and most often, reimbursement for lost personal property falls under a client's HO policy.

[H] Excess Liability (Umbrella) Coverage

Although clients often think of insurance as a tool to reimburse property losses, financial planners should be quick to point out that liability coverage may be a more important need for clients. Typical HO and PAP coverage provides basic levels of liability protection. Often, however, these limits are too low. In some states, for example, someone may drive legally with as little as $5,000 in liability coverage. Although it is possible and prudent for clients to purchase additional liability coverage of $300,000 to $500,000 on individual HO, PAP, or watercraft policies, additional—and perhaps more cost-effective—coverage should be purchased through an **excess liability** or **umbrella liability policy**. These policies provide coverage for losses above HO and PAP liability limits. Higher HO and PAP liability coverage is typically required before an excess liability policy can be purchased. Umbrella contracts are not standardized, so coverage can vary. These insurance contracts also typically provide **personal injury coverage** (e.g., claims alleging **libel**, **slander**, or **invasion of privacy**) that may not be included in other policies.

Although $1 million is a typical minimum policy available in the marketplace, financial planners often recommend $2 million to $5 million in coverage. It is appropriate to roughly match the umbrella protection, at a minimum, to the client's net worth. But other factors, such as earnings potential, risk tolerance, personal risk and lifestyle profile, and the availability of assets to be attached to pay for a claim beyond the coverage of the policy, also must be considered.

[I] Homestead Exemptions

Many states provide homeowners with the opportunity to protect a portion of home equity in a personal residence from creditors, which can include liability claims. This protection is provided through a **homestead exemption** or **declaration**. Protection may or may not be automatic, depending on the state. To qualify, a client must live in the residence, and it may be necessary to file a form with the local municipality. Equity protection amounts and guidelines vary by state.

[J] Recommendation Guidelines

When developing a financial plan it is important to provide clients with estimates of premiums associated with current and recommended strategies. The following represent broad generalizations that can be used to estimate how much a client can expect to pay when raising policy limits and how much can be saved by increasing deductibles.

Unlike health and disability insurance, it is difficult to generalize rules regarding HO policy premiums in relation to liability limits and deductibles. Although there are no standardized rules, the following guidelines can be used to estimate HO premium costs:

- $300,000 dwelling / $300,000 liability: $321 increase from a $100,000 liability limit policy.

- $400,000 dwelling / $300,000 liability: $376 increase from a $100,000 liability limit policy.

- $500,000 dwelling / $300,000 liability: $419 increase from a $100,000 liability limit policy.

These policy cost increases can be offset somewhat by changing the policy deductible. A client can save approximately 5 percent for every $500 increase in their HO deductible (it is important to account for future claims by adjusting the client's emergency fund). Financial planners must also consider other coverage costs, including flood and earthquake coverage, and they must be aware that some insurance companies apply a separate deductible for wind damage (e.g., 1 percent of the replacement value of the home).

Figure 12.9 shows estimates of premium reductions associated with increasing an HO policy deductible by state. The dollar amounts in the body of the figure represent the average premium cost by deductible.

Figure 12.9. Premium Costs Associated with Deductible by State.

State	$500 Deductible	$1,000 Deductible	% Reduction from $500	$1,500 Deductible	% Reduction from $500	$2,000 deductible	% Reduction from $500	$2,500 deductible	% Reduction from $500	$ Savings from $500 to $2,500	Average $ saved for every $500	Average % saved for every $500
Alabama	$2,521	$2,314	–8.21%	$2,232	–11.46%	$2,208	–12.42%	$2,213	-12.22%	$308	$79.50	3.04%
Alaska	$974	$908	–6.78%	$837	–14.07%	$828	–14.99%	$815	-16.32%	$159	$39.75	4.08%
Arizona	$884	$813	–8.03%	$738	–16.52%	$691	–21.83%	$660	-25.34%	$224	$56.00	6.33%
Arkansas	$2,226	$2,063	–7.32%	$1,905	–14.42%	$1,906	–14.38%	$1,775	-20.26%	$451	$112.75	5.07%
California	$896	$793	–11.50%	$763	–14.84%	$681	–24.00%	$675	-24.67%	$221	$55.25	6.17%
Colorado	$1,552	$1,417	–8.70%	$1,260	–18.81%	$1,073	–30.86%	$1,137	-26.74%	$415	$103.75	6.68%
Connecticut	$996	$902	–9.44%	$840	–15.66%	$795	–20.18%	$788	-20.88%	$208	$52.00	5.22%
DC	$765	$706	–7.71%	$663	–13.33%	$621	–18.82%	$611	-20.13%	$154	$38.50	5.03%
Delaware	$777	$748	–3.73%	$704	–9.40%	$684	–11.97%	$670	-13.77%	$107	$26.75	3.47%
Florida	$3,838	$3,575	–6.85%	$3,515	–8.42%	$3,246	–15.42%	$3,164	-17.56%	$674	$168.50	4.40%
Georgia	$1,225	$1,103	–9.96%	$1,040	–15.10%	$966	–21.14%	$1,105	-9.80%	$120	$30.00	2.45%
Hawaii	$399	$337	–15.54%	$321	–19.55%	$279	–30.08%	$288	-27.82%	$111	$27.75	6.95%
Idaho	$661	$622	–5.90%	$601	–9.08%	$578	–12.56%	$565	-14.52%	$96	$24.00	3.63%
Illinois	$1,204	$1,053	–12.54%	$1,000	–16.94%	$912	–24.25%	$906	-24.75%	$298	$74.50	6.19%
Indiana	$1,314	$1,198	–8.83%	$1,118	–14.92%	$967	–26.41%	$1,003	-23.67%	$311	$77.75	5.94%
Iowa	$1,325	$1,205	–9.06%	$1,101	–16.91%	$1,056	–20.30%	$1,025	-22.64%	$300	$75.00	5.66%
Kansas	$2,142	$1,939	–9.48%	$1,802	–15.87%	$1,653	–22.83%	$1,557	-27.31%	$585	$146.25	6.83%
Kentucky	$1,416	$1,355	–4.31%	$1,265	–10.66%	$1,195	–15.61%	$1,144	-19.21%	$272	$68.00	4.80%
Louisiana	$3,158	$2,979	–5.67%	$2,911	–7.82%	$2,732	–13.49%	$2,643	-16.31%	$515	$128.75	4.08%
Maine	$777	$721	–7.21%	$701	–9.78%	$665	–14.41%	$658	-15.32%	$119	$29.75	3.80%
Maryland	$939	$866	–7.77%	$831	–11.50%	$741	–21.09%	$731	-22.15%	$208	$52.00	5.54%
Massachusetts	$1,330	$1,190	–10.53%	$1,161	–12.71%	$1,083	–18.57%	$1,062	-20.15%	$268	$67.00	5.04%
Michigan	$1,156	$1,073	–7.18%	$1,005	–13.06%	$952	–17.65%	$919	-20.50%	$237	$59.25	5.13%
Minnesota	$1,451	$1,333	–8.13%	$1,205	–16.95%	$1,156	–20.33%	$1,108	-23.64%	$343	$85.75	5.93%
Mississippi	$2,390	$2,290	–4.18%	$2,239	–6.32%	$2,112	–11.63%	$2,117	-11.42%	$273	$68.25	2.86%
Missouri	$1,852	$1,722	–7.02%	$1,730	–6.59%	$1,598	–13.71%	$1,538	-16.95%	$314	$78.50	4.23%
Montana	$1,244	$1,175	–5.55%	$1,107	–11.01%	$1,039	–16.48%	$1,012	-18.65%	$232	$58.00	4.64%
Nebraska	$1,727	$1,583	–8.34%	$1,610	–6.77%	$1,513	–12.39%	$1,441	-16.56%	$286	$71.50	4.13%
Nevada	$774	$703	–9.17%	$639	–17.44%	$615	–20.54%	$586	-24.29%	$188	$47.00	6.04%
New Hampshire	$790	$680	–13.92%	$647	–18.10%	$589	–25.44%	$593	-24.94%	$197	$49.25	6.23%
New Jersey	$779	$711	–8.73%	$681	–12.58%	$656	–15.79%	$642	-17.59%	$137	$34.25	4.40%
New Mexico	$1,282	$1,197	–6.63%	$1,072	–16.38%	$1,063	–17.08%	$988	-22.93%	$294	$73.50	5.71%
New York	$1,068	$935	–12.45%	$899	–15.82%	$845	–20.88%	$830	-22.28%	$238	$59.50	5.57%

North Carolina	$904	$773	–14.49%	$712	–21.24%	$555	–38.61%	$555	-38.61%	$349	$87.25	9.65%
North Dakota	$1,399	$1,354	–3.22%	$1,350	–3.50%	$1,284	–8.22%	$1,266	-9.51%	$133	$33.25	2.38%
Ohio	$962	$864	–10.19%	$807	–16.11%	$779	–19.02%	$737	-23.39%	$225	$56.25	5.87%
Oklahoma	$2,851	$2,651	–7.02%	$2,583	–9.40%	$2,479	–13.05%	$2,331	-18.24%	$520	$130.0	4.55%
Oregon	$700	$643	–8.14%	$605	–13.57%	$583	–16.71%	$573	-18.14%	$127	$31.75	4.54%
Pennsylvania	$891	$801	–10.10%	$743	–16.61%	$697	–21.77%	$671	-24.69%	$220	$55.00	6.17%
Rhode Island	$1,397	$1,205	–13.74%	$1,172	–16.11%	$1,047	–25.05%	$1,007	-27.92%	$390	$97.50	6.98%
South Carolina	$1,517	$1,402	–7.58%	$1,314	–13.38%	$1,255	–17.27%	$1,227	-19.12%	$2u90	$72.50	4.78%
South Dakota	$1,579	$1,379	–12.67%	$1,282	–18.81%	$1,204	–23.75%	$1,168	-26.03%	$411	$102.75	6.51%
Tennessee	$1,620	$1,521	–6.11%	$1,446	–10.74%	$1,328	–18.02%	$1,323	-18.33%	$297	$74.25	4.58%
Texas	$2,037	$1,945	–4.52%	$1,894	–7.02%	$1,828	–10.26%	$1,734	-14.87%	$303	$75.75	3.72%
Utah	$699	$642	–8.15%	$605	–13.45%	$581	–16.88%	$562	-19.60%	$137	$34.25	4.90%
Vermont	$638	$589	–7.68%	$556	–12.85%	$511	–19.91%	$496	-22.26%	$142	$35.50	5.56%
Virginia	$1,043	$959	–8.05%	$934	–10.45%	$876	–16.01%	$851	-18.41%	$192	$48.00	4.60%
Washington	$701	$653	–6.85%	$612	–12.70%	$572	–18.40%	$554	-20.97%	$147	$36.75	5.24%
West Virginia	$1,377	$1,288	–6.46%	$1,206	–12.42%	$1,138	–17.36%	$1,116	-18.95%	$261	$65.25	4.76%
Wisconsin	$829	$788	–4.95%	$759	–8.44%	$707	–14.72%	$698	-15.80%	$131	$32.75	3.98%
Wyoming	$991	$976	–1.51%	$943	–4.84%	$868	–12.41%	$850	-14.23%	$141	$35.25	3.53%

Note: Data adapted from insurance.com; data accurate as of 2021/2022.

Similar estimates should be made when making PAP recommendations. The discussion that follows is based on the assumption that a client currently has a policy with split-limit coverage of 50/100/50. As a reminder, the first two numbers refer to bodily injury liability, which pays the hospital bills of anyone an insured injures. The first number is the per-person limit. The second is the per-accident limit. The third number is the property damage liability limit, which can be used to repair or replace the property of others involved in an accident.

When deciding how much liability insurance to recommend, a financial planner typically starts with three options:

- The client's state required minimum to drive legally.

- 50/100/50.

- 100/300/100.

A financial planner can then focus on balancing coverage with premiums. In relation to this task, one can assume that the nationwide average cost for *state minimum liability coverage* is $574. Increasing the minimum coverage to $50,000/$100,000/$50,000 raises the average to $644 (an additional $70 per year [$6 monthly]).

If a $100,000/$300,000/$100,000 split-limit policy, with comprehensive and collision coverage and a $500 deductible, is recommended, the average premium cost is $1,758, which is $1,184 more per year or about $99 per month compared to a state minimum liability policy. Figure 12.10 shows the estimated costs for a 50/200/50 policy by state:

Figure 12.10. PAP Premium Costs by State.

State	Cost for State Minimum	COST FOR 50/200/50 COVERAGE
Alabama	$498	$545
Alaska	$412	$420
Arizona	$578	$707
Arkansas	$449	$479
California	$606	$752
Colorado	$553	$604
Connecticut	$891	$972
DC	$839	$949
Delaware	$843	$943
Florida	$828	$1,100
Georgia	$684	$754
Hawaii	$485	$558
Idaho	$377	$415
Illinois	$493	$545
Indiana	$430	$466
Iowa	$326	$354
Kansas	$464	$496
Kentucky	$669	$756
Louisiana	$771	$955
Maine	$355	$359
Maryland	$853	$901
Massachusetts	$520	$651
Michigan	$1,855	$1,919
Minnesota	$614	$663
Mississippi	$413	$477
Missouri	$546	$601
Montana	$447	$487
Nebraska	$393	$426
Nevada	$717	$945
New Hampshire	$424	$447
New Jersey	$846	$1,025
New Mexico	$479	$536
New York	$867	$960
North Carolina	$438	$481
North Dakota	$423	$453
Ohio	$406	$427
Oklahoma	$418	$455

Oregon	$674	$724
Pennsylvania	$502	$584
Rhode Island	$738	$921
South Carolina	$617	$673
South Dakota	$323	$362
Tennessee	$462	$514
Texas	$538	$565
Utah	$565	$596
Vermont	$398	$434
Virginia	$380	$424
Washington	$537	$587
West Virginia	$541	$608
Wisconsin	$401	$450
Wyoming	$328	$354

In general, a client can save approximately 9 percent annually in premium costs by raising their deductible from $500 to $1,000 or 16 percent from $500 to $2,000.

[K] Applying Planning Skills to the Hubble Case

Generally, only modest recommendation changes from those made at Step Three of the financial planning process will be needed at this point, although it is possible that new client information or data might necessitate a reevaluation. Figure 12.11 provides a summary of the final property and casualty insurance recommendations that match the Hubble family's financial goals.

Figure 12.11. Property and Liability Insurance Recommendations for Chandler and Rachel.

The final property and casualty insurance recommendations developed for the Hubble family match the preliminary recommendations identified at Step Three of the financial planning process. Specifically, the Hubbles should:

- Increase policy limits and coverage on their home. The replacement cost of the home is within the 80 percent coinsurance limit, but the policy limits on some items may be lower than the value of the family's possessions. A new policy with appropriate coverage limits should be obtained. Rather than rely on meeting the 80 percent rule, Chandler and Rachel should ensure their home for 100 percent of replacement value. An inflation endorsement should also be included in the policy. Further, the liability coverage should be increased from $100,000 to $300,000 and coordinated with the umbrella policy.

  o This strategy also includes a recommendation to increase the annual deductible from $500 to $1,000, although 1 percent of the coverage is sometimes recommended. Increasing the deductible will help offset the increase in annual premium associated with upgrading the policy and adding endorsements.

  o An A. M. Best (or other third-party source) insurance company rating should be confirmed and explained to the client.

- Increase excess liability coverage held by Chandler and Rachel. The umbrella policy should be increased from $500,000 to $1,000,000. Implementation of this recommendation will provide increased protection from losses caused by personal liability from injury or damages to others (including property damage). Required minimum liability coverage on the PAP, HO, and boat policies must be increased in order to purchase the higher limit umbrella policy.

- Increase PAP liability coverage. A review of the Hubbles' auto coverage shows that Chandler and Rachel are adequately insured for loss and damage to their vehicles. However, the current policy does not provide sufficient personal liability protection without the addition of the umbrella coverage. The PAP liability coverage should be increased to 100/300/300, at a minimum, or if Chandler and Rachel are particularly risk averse, they should consider an increase to 300/500/300 (the $300,000 liability limit corresponds to the increase in the umbrella policy). It is also important to confirm that the current new policy has uninsured and underinsured motorist coverage. Implementing this recommendation will provide additional protection from losses arising from uninsured or underinsured motorists. Chandler and Rachel should consider increasing the PAP deductible to $1,000 to help offset other premium increases.

12.6 STEP 5: PRESENT THE FINANCIAL PLANNING RECOMMENDATION(S)

Although financial planners often collaborate with licensed insurance agents to manage their client's risk exposures, financial planners can still play a significant direct role in the insurance planning process. It is important for financial planners to exhibit knowledge of typical liability exposures resulting from property ownership and the activities of a client's household. Financial planners also need to exhibit competence when comparing different HO and PAP insurance products and provisions designed to reduce client risk exposures. Through the data collection and discovery process, financial planners can develop a profile of a client's situation that enables the financial planner to advise clients on: (a) forms of coverage, (b) policy provisions, (c) excess liability planning, (d) flood/earthquake coverage, and (e) factors associated with premium rate determinations.

Figure 12.12 highlights some of the important factors to consider when presenting property and casualty insurance recommendations to Chandler and Rachel Hubble.

Figure 12.12. Factors to Consider When Presenting Property and Casualty Insurance Recommendations.

> Consider the way in which a recommendation to increase excess liability, or umbrella, policy coverage can be presented. This product is an essential tool that can be used to help a client manage their exposure to insurance risks. Typically, financial planners recommend clients purchase at least $1 million in excess liability protection, although higher limits are sometimes more appropriate. To qualify for an umbrella policy, a client will be required to increase liability limits in their HO and PAP policies. The presentation of this recommendation can sometimes be confusing to a client. First, some clients have a difficult time envisioning the need for such coverage. Second, some clients balk at the potential increase in premiums associated with the recommendation. Additionally, implementation requires additional meetings outside of the financial planning environment, which can be perceived as time consuming. As such, when presenting this recommendation, a financial planner should stress ways the increased premium can be mitigated by adjusting deductibles. Additionally, the presentation should be focused on helping a client understand the benefits associated with enhanced liability protection. Steps should also be taken to help the client deal with underwriting issues. This can include working as an intermediary between the client and their insurance company/agent.

12.7 STEP 6: IMPLEMENT THE FINANCIAL PLANNING RECOMMENDATION(S)

Each recommendation within the property and casualty section of a financial plan should be presented in a way that facilitates implementation. Figure 12.13 shows how a recommendation to purchase $1,000,000 of excess liability coverage can be presented.

Figure 12.13. Implementing an Excess Liability Recommendation for the Hubble Family.

Recommendation #2: Increase your umbrella liability insurance coverage to $1 million.	
Who:	Chandler and Rachel.
What:	Excess liability/umbrella insurance policy with a $500 deductible.
When:	Within the next thirty to forty-five days.
Where:	With your insurance professional or with an online provider that our firm can recommend.
Why:	To ensure financial security and liability protection for your family.
How:	Consult your insurance professional (or our firm can assist you in selecting an online provider).
How much:	Increase coverage from $500,000 to $1,000,000.
Effect on cash flow:	Your excess liability/umbrella insurance premium will increase by approximately $100 annually.

12.8 STEP 7: MONITOR PROGRESS AND UPDATE

A client's property and casualty insurance situation should be monitored at least annually or whenever a major purchase (e.g., new car, home, or expensive personal property) is made. At a minimum, the following should be included in the monitoring process:

- Recalculation of the 80 percent rule.

- Evaluation of appropriateness of personal property endorsements.

- Evaluation of coverage of other property owned by client, including boats and recreational vehicles.

- Evaluation of a client's personal automobile policies.

- Recalculation of the appropriate level of excess liability coverage needed.

- Evaluation of ways insurance premiums can be reduced, including a review of policy discounts and the use of policy deductibles.

- Recalculation of the client's emergency fund to ensure that deductibles can be met if needed.

Each year, at a minimum, the Hubble family's HO, PAP, other property, and liability situation should be reviewed. Figure 12.14 provides a summary of ongoing monitoring issues facing the Hubble family.

Figure 12.14. Issues to Monitor in the Hubble Case.

Any of the following events should trigger a reevaluation of the Hubbles' property and casualty insurance coverage situation:
• The purchase of a new car or other vehicle.
• The purchase of expensive jewelry or other personal items.
• Major home improvements.
• Phoebe obtaining a driver's permit or license.
• Replacing the boat with a new or larger used boat.
• A change in policy limits, coverages, or exclusions.

12.9 COMPREHENSIVE HUBBLE CASE

Property and liability insurance coverage sometimes fails to receive enough attention in written comprehensive financial plans. The reason is that unless a financial planner is also an insurance agent or broker, many of the recommendations made to improve a client's situation fall outside the practice domain of the financial planner. Property and liability insurance planning, however, should not be overlooked within the financial planning process. Adequate policy provisions, as well as other aspects of coverage and the potential for future changes, should be evaluated and monitored across time. The following narrative is an example of how the property and casualty insurance section within a comprehensive financial plan can be written.

Property and Casualty Insurance

Overview of Property and Casualty Insurance:

Property and casualty coverages include several types of insurance policies, including homeowner's, auto, and umbrella (also known as excess liability insurance). Having sufficient liability coverage is becoming more important in our increasingly litigious culture. Accidents are frequent occurrences and being held liable for an accident can seriously damage a family's financial security and ability to meet life's goals. Premium costs for property and casualty coverage are based on a family's insurance score. Insurance scores take into account factors such as past credit delinquencies, bankruptcies, debt ratios, credit-seeking behavior, credit history, and the use of credit. Managing your credit well can result in significant insurance premium savings.

Property and Casualty Insurance Definitions:

The following definitions will be useful as you review the analysis presented in this section:

- *Endorsement*: An extension of a policy that covers the value of goods above standard policy limits. Specifically, an endorsement refers to the actual change in coverage.

- *Floater*: A separate mini-policy that "floats" coverage of an asset that frequently changes location.

- *Replacement cost*: The actual amount needed to rebuild or repair property (not the market value of the property).

- *Rider*: This policy extension is sometimes used synonymously with the term endorsement, but technically, a rider refers to the document that changes the amount of coverage from the underlying contract.

Planning Assumptions:

- You do not live in a flood zone or an area that has a significant risk of flooding.

- You live in an area that is at risk for tornadoes.

- You do not live in an area that is subject to moderate or major earthquakes.

Goals:

- Minimize personal liability exposures.

- Minimize liability exposures resulting from the use of personal property.

- Maintain appropriate property and casualty insurance coverage on a year-to-year basis.

- Obtain replacement cost coverage for property that may be currently underinsured.

- Purchase additional coverage to ensure that family asset and liability exposures are adequately covered in the case of property loss or liability claim.

- Continue to ensure that any property, casualty, and liability coverage is appropriate in terms of costs.

Your Current Property and Casualty Insurance Situation:

The following table summarizes your current property and casualty insurance policy situation:

Summary of Chandler and Rachel's Current Property and Liability Insurance Coverage				
Type	HO-3	Auto	Auto	Excess Liability
Insurance Company	Missouri National Insurance	Missouri Valley Insurance Corporation	Insurance Corporation	Missouri National Insurance
Premium Amount	$700	$500	$500	$175
Premium Frequency	Annually	Semi-annually	Semi-annually	Annually
Liability Coverage	$100,000	100/300/50	100/300/50	$500,000

- Currently, your home is insured with an HO-3 Special Form homeowner's policy. This policy covers losses to the dwelling and other structures for open perils protection (all perils, except flood, earthquake, war, and nuclear attack are included in the policy).

- Personal property is limited to named perils protection, which means losses occurring as a result of a specific named perils (e.g., fire, lightning, theft) are covered.

- You have an endorsement that provides replacement coverage on your home's contents, but it is unclear whether or not the policy has an inflation endorsement.

- The deductible on the homeowner's policy is $500. You do not have additional endorsements or personal articles policies to cover your valuable items beyond the applicable policy limits.

- Both auto policies provide full protection (liability, medical expense, uninsured/ underinsured motorists, and damage to your auto). Each has a $500 deductible for comprehensive coverage and a $500 deductible for collision coverage.

As a reminder, at your earliest convenience, please provide us with your insurance policy documents and declaration pages. We have provided general recommendations in this section of the plan, but more details about these policies are required in order to conduct a more in-depth analysis.

Property and Casualty Insurance Recommendations:

The following tables summarize the recommendations that have been designed to help you reach your homeowner's, personal automobile, and casualty/liability insurance goals. As with all recommendations presented in this financial plan, our firm is available to answer any questions that might arise and to assist with specific implementation procedures.

Recommendation #1: Bundle your homeowner's and auto policies with the same insurance provider to receive a discount and reduce the cost of premiums. Determine whether your insurance provider offers any other discounts for which you may be eligible.

Who:	Chandler and Rachel.
What:	Homeowner's and auto insurance policies.
When:	Within the next thirty to forty-five days.
Where:	With your insurance professional or with an online provider that our firm can recommend.
Why:	To ensure financial security for your family.
How:	Consult your insurance professional (or our firm can assist you in selecting an online provider).
How much:	Bundling can decrease your homeowner's and auto insurance premiums by approximately 15 percent.
Effect on cash flow:	Bundling will save you approximately $105 on car insurance and $285 on homeowner's insurance annually.

Recommendation #2: Increase your umbrella liability insurance coverage to $1 million.

Who:	Chandler and Rachel.
What:	Excess liability/umbrella insurance policy with a $500 deductible.
When:	Within the next thirty to forty-five days.
Where:	With your insurance professional or with an online provider that our firm can recommend.
Why:	To ensure financial security and liability protection for your family.
How:	Consult your insurance professional (or our firm can assist you in selecting an online provider).
How much:	Increase coverage from $500,000 to $1,000,000.
Effect on cash flow:	Your excess liability/umbrella insurance premium will increase by approximately $100 annually.

Recommendation #3: Increase the deductible and the liability coverage on your homeowner's insurance policy to $300,000 and add an inflation endorsement.

Who:	Chandler and Rachel.
What:	HO-3 policy insurance policy with coverage equal to 100% of the replacement cost of your home, with a $1,500 deductible, $300,000 liability coverage, and an inflation endorsement.
When:	Within the next thirty to forty-five days.

Where:	With your insurance professional or with an online provider that our firm can recommend.
Why:	To ensure financial security and liability protection for your family.
How:	Consult your insurance professional (or our firm can assist you in selecting an online provider).
How much:	Increase liability coverage from $100,000 to $300,000 and increase your deductible from $500 to $1,500.
Effect on cash flow:	Increasing the deductible will offset the cost of increasing the recommended liability coverage, resulting in no change to cash flow.

Recommendation #4: Create a household possessions inventory list and supplement the list with pictures and videos.

Who:	Chandler and Rachel.
What:	Detailed household inventory list that documents information, such as make, model, and serial number of the items in your home.
When:	Within the next six months.
Where:	Create the inventory list based on property held in your home. After the list has been created, ensure the form is kept in a safe place outside your home, such as a safety deposit box.
Why:	To facilitate insurance claims processing and to maximize the payout of your homeowner's insurance policy in the event your home is damaged or destroyed or property is lost or stolen.
How:	Make a detailed list and take pictures of the items or make a video.
How much:	This list should include as many items as possible. If possible, make two copies of the list and keep the copies in different locations; also, include serial numbers of property when appropriate.
Effect on cash flow:	This recommendation will not impact your cash flow.

Current vs. Recommended Outcome:

The table below summarizes the recommended changes to your current property and casualty insurance situation:

Comparison of Property and Liability Insurance Coverage Options						
Type of Coverage	Homeowner's Policy		Automobile Policy		Umbrella Policy	
	Existing	Suggested	Existing	Suggested	Existing	Suggested
Total Liability Coverage Limit	$100,000	$300,000	100/300/50	100/300/100	$500,000	$1,000,000
Property Damage Coverage	Replacement Cost	Replacement Cost	Actual Cash Value	Actual Cash Value	N/A	N/A

Property Damage Deductible(s)	$500	$1,500	$500 (Comprehensive) & $500 (Collision)	$1,000 (Comprehensive) & $500 (Collision)	Unknown	$500
Medical Payments	$1,000	$1,000	Unknown	$3,000	N/A	N/A
Annual Premium	$700	$700	$2,000	$1,900	$175	$275
Premium Cost with Bundling Discount (15%)	N/A	$595	N/A	$1,615	N/A	N/A

- Your homeowner's insurance premium will remain approximately the same. This result is based on increasing the deductible to offset the cost of the additional liability insurance.

- Your auto insurance premium is estimated to decrease slightly if you increase your comprehensive coverage deductible as recommended above.

  o The savings from increasing your auto insurance deductible will offset the additional cost of the umbrella insurance premium.

- Your umbrella insurance premium will increase because you are doubling the liability coverage; however, the increased premium will be partially offset by increasing the liability limits on your homeowner's insurance policy.

- If you implement the recommendation to bundle your homeowner's policy and auto insurance policy, you will generate an additional $390 of cash flow annually, which can be used to build your emergency fund and save towards other goals.

- Overall, these adjustments to your property and casualty insurance policies will increase your insurance protection. However, since your deductibles will also increase, you will need to have a sufficient emergency fund on hand to pay potential deductibles; this has been factored into the emergency fund analysis presented earlier in this financial plan.

Alternative Recommendations and Outcome(s):

Once you provide our team with more detailed information on your current insurance policies, the recommendations above may be altered. For example, it may be necessary to purchase additional endorsements to cover your valuables, collectibles, and other property that exceed policy limits. For example, any personal property valued at $2,500 or more should be insured separately. For planning purposes, adding additional property will cost approximately $300 annually.

Currently, you own a boat that is not adequately insured. Your umbrella policy will provide you with liability protection in the event of an accident. However, you will not receive any payouts for medical payments to others or property damage. Given that the boat is fifteen years old, it may not be worthwhile to insure the boat for physical damage protection since the cost to repair the boat may exceed the value of the boat. Further discussion is warranted to determine how important the boat is to you, how you are currently using the boat, and whether or not you would want to have the boat repaired if it was damaged.

This analysis assumes that you do not live in a flood zone; however, if this assumption is not true, we recommend that you purchase flood insurance. Flood insurance provides a reimbursement for the overflow of inland or tidal waters and surface waters. Flood insurance is administered by the Federal Insurance and Mitigation Administration. Flood insurance can be purchased directly from the National Flood Insurance Program (NFIP) or from a private insurance company which has a special arrangement with the NFIP.

Plan Implementation and Monitoring Procedures:

Savings resulting from reducing your auto and homeowner's insurance premiums should be used to pay for the increased cost of your umbrella insurance policy (and any supplemental endorsements and/or floaters). It is important to comparison shop and evaluate quoted rates when purchasing insurance. Our team can assist with this activity. All other recommendations can be implemented with the assistance of your insurance agent.

12.10 SELF-TEST

[A] Questions

Self-Test 1

Toni has an HO policy with open perils coverage. Which of the following causes of a loss would not be covered?

(a) Fire

(b) Earthquake

(c) Theft

(d) Both b and c

Self-Test 2

Sienna owns a condominium in a college town. What type of HO policy does she need?

(a) HO 1

(b) HO 3

(c) HO 6

(d) HO 8

Self-Test 3

Which of the following assets would likely need a separate floater policy to fully insure for the value?

(a) Shotgun valued at $3,500.

(b) Golf clubs valued at $1,000.

(c) Guitar valued at $200.

(d) All the above.

Self-Test 4

When Wookjae went to his basement the other day he noticed that he had several inches of water near the main drain. Which of the following potential causes would not be covered under his HO policy?

(a) An overflowing toilet on the first floor.

(b) Sewer back-up, and he did not have the water back up and sump overflow endorsement.

(c) A leak in his roof as a result of damage sustained during a major rainstorm.

(d) All of the above.

Self-Test 5

Jim's wife recently hit a light pole in a parking lot. The accident was clearly his wife's fault. Jim can make a claim on his PAP using what coverage provision?

(a) Collision for the car; property damage liability for the light pole.

(b) Property damage liability for the car and light pole.

(c) Comprehensive for the car; out of pocket payment for the light pole.

(d) None of the above; the damage to both the car and the pole will be covered by the parking lot's commercial policy.

[B] Answers

Question 1: b

Question 2: c

Question 3: a

Question 4: b

Question 5: a

12.11 CHAPTER RESOURCES

Insurance Institute for Business and Home Safety (www.disastersafety.org).

Insurance Information Institute (www.iii.org).

National Flood Insurance Program (floodsmart.com or www.fema.gov/nfip/ or 1-800-638-6620).

Policy Forms Used by the Top 10 Homeowners' Insurance Groups in Nevada (doi.nv.gov/scs/Homeowners.aspx). Nevada is one of only a few states offering this service to consumers, but other states are expected to follow this initiative.

Property Casualty Insurers Association of America (www.pciaa.net/web/sitehome.nsf/main).

United Policyholders™ Empowering the Insured (www.uphelp.org).

CHAPTER ENDNOTES

1.   Nationwide Insurance Company. *Underinsurance: A Common Problem.* http://www.nationwide.com/underinsurance.jsp.

2.   Federal Trade Commission, *Credit-based Insurance Scores: Impacts on Consumers of Automobile Insurance.* www.ftc.gov/os/2007/07/P044804FACTA_Report_Credit-Based_Insurance_Scores.pdf, p. 1.

3.   National Flood Insurance Program, Policy Rates. https://www.floodsmart.gov/floodsmart/pages/residential_coverage/policy_rates.jsp.

4.   Insurance Information Institute. *Uninsured Motorists.* www.iii.org/fact-statistic/uninsured-motorists.

Chapter 13

Investment Planning

Learning Objectives

- Learning Objective 1: Describe how the concepts of risk and return serve as the foundation of investment planning.

- Learning Objective 2: Identify investment asset classes that are most often used within diversified household portfolios.

- Learning Objective 3: Describe the different types of investment/financial risks and how to measure each risk.

- Learning Objective 4: Calculate measures of modern portfolio theory.

- Learning Objective 5: Explain how portfolio performance can be measured and assessed.

- Learning Objective 6: Develop an investment policy statement that incorporates strategic and tactical investment strategies.

13.1 THE PROCESS OF INVESTMENT PLANNING

While nearly every financial planning topic requires a thorough understanding of a client's unique personal and financial circumstances, this is perhaps most important in the domain of investment planning. A financial planner should possess the skills to be able to assess and evaluate five client-centered factors that help shape the way investment planning is conceptualized

Step 1: Understand the Client's Personal and Financial Circumstances

The first step in the investment planning process involves reviewing, with the client, relevant personal and financial information. As with other financial planning topics, this type of discussion can strengthen the client-financial planner relationship and lead to the development and presentation of integrative recommendations.

Any number of client-specific characteristics and factors can affect a client's need for investment products and services. The following personal and financial issues are of particular importance:

(1) a client's financial risk tolerance,

(2) a client's expectations about future market conditions,

(3) a client's financial knowledge and experience in the markets,

(4) a client's goal time horizon, and

(5) a client's financial capacity to deal with uncertain outcomes.

The first three factors represent subjective client characteristics. The last two are quantitative in nature. Once these foundational elements have been identified and assessed, the investment planning process typically moves on to determining an appropriate required rate of return needed to help a client meet their financial goals. Ideally, a client's subjective and objective characteristics—what can be termed as a client's **risk profile**—will match the return requirement. For example, assume a client needs to generate a 9 percent annualized rate of return to reach their financial objective. Obtaining this level of return matches well with a client who has a high tolerance for risk, reasonable expectations about possible gains and losses, an expansive knowledge and experience of the markets, a long time horizon, and the financial ability to withstand short-term financial losses. It is possible, however, for a client's risk profile to conflict with a required rate of return need. When this occurs, it is up to the financial planner to engage their client in discussions related to the five client-centered factors listed above, as well as possibly altering the client's goal(s) to come into alignment with their risk profile. Once the client's risk profile matches the required rate of return need, asset classes can be selected, and the financial planner can finalize combinations of these asset classes into a cohesive portfolio or, in some cases, multiple portfolios. As illustrated in this example, and given the importance of these factors, the measurement and use of each factor will be explored in more detail below.

The first three factors can be measured using a scale or subjective attitude measurement. In most situations, risk attitude, expectations, financial knowledge, and experience are assessed during the initial data gathering phase of the financial planning process. A more complete understanding of these and other client-centered factors should emerge from the evolving client-financial planner relationship. The last two factors, time horizon and financial capacity to withstand risk (or loss), typically come into perspective during the cash flow and net worth planning phase of the financial planning process, and during discussions with clients. As noted earlier in this book, goals should be defined specifically. Risk capacity, when used as a guide in investment planning, tends to be quantitative and most often based on measured financial ratios and assessments of client-specific factors, such as income stability, strength of insurance coverages, and the presence of an emergency fund or sources of income.

It is essential to consider both qualitative and quantitative client-specific characteristics before and during the development of investment strategies. An increased focus on the codification of investment policy statements is an example of focusing on the holistic needs of a client. For example, an investment plan, client communication, and client education might, of necessity, be quite different for a highly emotional and reactive client who is unduly influenced by short-term market trends than for a client who has a more tolerant, long-term outlook.

Arguably, the most important client-specific characteristics within the investment planning process is a client's **risk tolerance**, which can be defined as the maximum level of uncertainty a client is willing to accept when making an investment decision that entails the possibility of a loss. Developing an understanding of, and an appreciation for, both the time and psychological dimensions of risk is essential before a financial planner can confidently say they have mastered the intricacies of investment planning.

Keep in mind that it is possible for a client to have both a long time horizon and a low tolerance for risk. A quandary arises when this phenomenon is observed. Some financial planners tend to discount a client's risk attitude and focus instead on the client's time horizon. This approach (referred to as a goal-based model) often results in portfolio recommendations that provide a high expected rate of return with associated risks that exceed a client's comfort level. An alternative approach is one focused on aligning a client's need to take risk with their tolerance to do so. To help mitigate the influence of **risk-averse behavior**, a financial planner must be willing to explain to clients that goal achievement may be impossible with a given time horizon if the client is unwilling to accept higher uncertainty in relation to returns. A financial planner may find, even after such a discussion, that the client is unwilling to accept more risk. This will result in a reformulation of the client's investment goal, which is, in the long run, better that forcing a high risk/return portfolio on a risk averse client who will be likely to abandon the portfolio when faced with prolonged losses.

Another important client-specific characteristic that influences investment planning decisions are a client's **expectations**. Expectations include perceptions of a financial planner's abilities and skill set, the general economy, and most notably, achievable rates of return. A best practice involves not competing in the marketplace based on generating the highest possible rates of return. Instead, the best financial planners work daily to manage client expectations regarding performance and risk in relation to reasonable benchmarks.

Consider a financial planner who suggests an allocation designed to achieve a 10 percent annualized rate of return but only manages to generate an 8 percent annualized return. The 8 percent return might be considered poor, average, or excellent in relation to the market environment. In fact, this level of return may be superior to almost all other strategies available; however, clients working with this financial planner might very well be disappointed. Some clients terminate financial planning relationships because expectations fail to meet reality. Appropriate coaching to manage expectations on the part of a financial planner is a key element associated with investment planning success.

Planning Reminder

Expectations and attitude assessments can provide only a starting point in client-financial planner discussions. It is important to remember that questionnaires and scale items are not necessarily prescriptive in and of themselves; it takes a financial planner's insights and experience to decipher the impact that temperament, personality, attitudes, and beliefs have and will have on the investment planning process.

Think about another financial planner who consistently informs clients that a 6 percent annualized rate of return is the target. With this set as the expectation, the financial planner manages over the course of three to five years to generate an 8 percent annualized return for clients. Clients working with this financial planner are likely to feel that they have received a bonus. This demonstrates the importance of managing client expectations when it comes to investment planning. While all financial planners should attempt to maximize returns while minimizing risks, in some cases it is wiser to under-promise and over-deliver.

To summarize, an investment plan should be tempered by a client's expectations and satisfaction with their current financial situation. Managing expectations requires a financial planner not only to measure, but also to understand a client's view of market trends, both past and future. It is therefore necessary to account for investment and economic expectations when developing investment plans. A client's outlook, be it negative or positive, should be used as a moderating factor when developing an investment plan.

Figure 13.1 provides an example of the type of questions that can be used to measure a client's expectations about the future economy, the client's level of financial satisfaction, their level of financial knowledge, and financial confidence. Answers to the first question are particularly important when developing investment planning strategies. If a client truly believes that the economy will perform worse in the future, and if the financial planner concurs, the level of risk taken to meet a financial goal should be reduced accordingly. Similar adjustments, either positive or negative, can be made based on responses to the other questions. For instance, if a client is dissatisfied with their career, this could be an indicator that a career change is possible or that the potential for significant promotions or salary increases may be limited. It would be imprudent, in this situation, to invest a client's assets too aggressively—thereby reducing **marketability** (i.e., the size and activity of a market that allows for an asset to be sold quickly) and **liquidity** (i.e., how quickly assets can be converted to cash)—if there is a possibility that those assets might be needed to fund job search expenses and other costs. Furthermore, the **financial capacity** to withstand **financial risk** (i.e., uncertainty and/or variability of returns) and the availability of assets to invest should be realistically assessed.

Figure 13.1. Examples of Expectation and Satisfaction Questions.

1. Over the next five years, do you expect the U.S. economy, as a whole, to perform better, worse, or about the same as it has over the past five years?
    a. Perform better
    b. Perform worse
    c. Perform about the same

2. How satisfied are you with your current level of income?
    1 2 3 4 5 6 7 8 9 10
    Lowest level   Highest level

3. How confident are you that your current level of income is sufficient to cover your overall financial needs?
    1 2 3 4 5 6 7 8 9 10
    Lowest level   Highest level

4. How satisfied are you with your present overall financial situation?
    1 2 3 4 5 6 7 8 9 10
    Lowest level   Highest level

5. Overall, how satisfied are you with your current job or position within your chosen career?
    1 2 3 4 5 6 7 8 9 10
    Lowest level   Highest level
6. How likely are you to change jobs or careers within the next 3 to 5 years?
    1 2 3 4 5 6 7 8 9 10
    Very Unlikely   Very Likely

7. Rate yourself on your level of knowledge about personal finance issues and investing.
    1 2 3 4 5 6 7 8 9 10
    Lowest level   Highest level

8. How comfortable are you investing in the stock market?
    1 2 3 4 5 6 7 8 9 10
    Not At All Comfortable   Very Comfortable

Additionally, a financial planner is expected to know the investment marketplace and a client's level of **investment knowledge and experience**. Beyond the regulatory requirements of understanding a client's knowledge level, a financial planner will have fewer objections to overcome if they can present investment alternatives that the client already understands or has experience with. The last question from Figure 13.1 can be helpful to determine how much to reduce the variance of returns or overall volatility of a portfolio based on knowledge and experience.

Although the qualitative factors of investment planning are critical to the long-term viability of a plan, two quantitative factors—time horizon and risk—may be more important in the short term. Suggesting that a client invest heavily and aggressively in a retirement account is certainly sound advice if a client is fifty years old, risk tolerant, and retirement funding is the client's primary goal. But making the same suggestion to an equally risk tolerant twenty-five-year-old who does not have an emergency fund might ignore the time available to realize the goal or the financial capacity to take on the risk associated with this plan.

Planning Reminder

Occasionally, a client's risk tolerance is so low that a financial planner has almost no choice but to recommend very liquid insured assets (e.g., savings account, CDs, and money market deposit accounts). In some cases, a client might require the sole use of FDIC insured bank accounts. It is then up to the financial planner to optimize the client's earning power while maintaining complete FDIC coverage of the client's accounts. For very risk-averse clients, an annuity may also be an appropriate asset suggestion. Annuities can be used as a tool to convince a client to invest in the market with a small safety net.

Of the five client-centered factors, **time horizon** tends to be the easiest to document. Time horizon can be defined as the time period between goal formation and goal achievement. For instance, someone who starts planning for retirement at age twenty-five will find that time allows for great investment flexibility. Someone else who waits until age fifty to plan for retirement will most likely discover that their investment alternatives are limited. The longer the time period between goal establishment and achievement, the less aggressively a client will need to invest to maintain the same likelihood of goal success. Another way of viewing a longer time horizon is that a client can invest less money on a periodic basis, at a higher expected rate of return, because there is less need to worry about short-term uncertainty (i.e., volatility).

For example, assume that two clients have the same goal of saving one million dollars by age sixty-five. Both have $250 per month available to save. One client is twenty-five years old. The other is thirty-five years old. In this example, the older client will need to earn an average annualized rate of return of close to 13 percent to reach their goal. This is possible, but at what level of risk? Comparatively, the younger client needs only to average about 9 percent annualized to achieve the same goal. This is also possible, even probable—and at a much lower level of risk. As this example illustrates, the longer the time horizon, and the more a client can devote to saving and investing for the goal, the higher the likelihood that the client will accomplish the goal. Because **risk and return** in the securities markets are highly positively correlated (i.e., risk and return generally move in the same direction), those with longer time horizons are often in a better position to take on risk in pursuit of goal achievement.

Finally, a client's financial capacity to deal with the negative outcomes associated with risk taking is a principal factor to consider when formulating investment plans. **Risk capacity** measures the amount of financial cushion or the safety net available to a client both before and after an investment decision has been implemented. Some clients are inadequately prepared to take risks with their investments because of lack of discretionary cash flow, a marginal emergency fund, lack of insurance, or a combination of factors. Documenting and assessing a client's risk capacity is especially important when tempering initial portfolio risk profiles based on time horizon and risk attitude. Factors that increase risk capacity include having:

(a) adequate insurance in place and funded,

(b) a well-funded emergency fund,

(c) a stable source of household income,

(d) low debt, and

(e) high savings.

Figure 13.2 provides a review of the Hubbles' personal and financial circumstances related to investment planning. The information in Figure 13.2 is typical of what a financial planner should evaluate at the first step of the financial planning process.

Figure 13.2. The Hubbles' Personal and Financial Circumstances.

Chandler Hubble	Rachel Hubble
Age: 42	Age: 42
State of residence: Missouri	State of residence: Missouri
Citizen: U.S.	Citizen: U.S.
Life status: No known life issues	Life status: No known life issues

- Before meeting with you, Chandler and Rachel completed a confidential risk tolerance questionnaire downloaded from http://pfp.missouri.edu/research_IRTA.html. The results from the risk quiz suggest that both Chandler and Rachel have a moderate to low level of financial risk tolerance.
- Chandler and Rachel are interested in ideas that can improve their current portfolio returns without taking excessive risk.
- Chandler has made it very clear that he is extremely apprehensive about investing and feels that he tends to be risk averse.
- Rachel, on the other hand, feels comfortable taking additional risks if she is confident that she can earn higher returns.
- The Hubbles' risk tolerance and other attitudes must be reflected in any recommendations made to Chandler and Rachel. Other values, preferences, and attitudes, such as "not deserving to be rich," or fear of not being adequately prepared for old age could significantly impact the types of investment recommendations implemented by Chandler and Rachel.
- Going forward, it would be helpful to gain an understanding of how current investment holdings were chosen.
- Chandler's and Rachel's conscientiousness in past savings/investments suggests the discipline needed to accomplish investment objectives.

Step 2: Identify and Select Goals

The development of an investment plan is typically based on four elements:

(1) an analysis of client circumstances,

(2) a review and projection of external economic factors,

(3) the investment goal(s) of the client, and

(4) the time frame for goal achievement.

Of these four elements, a client's goal(s) and goal time horizon are of primary importance. The type of investment plan developed and presented to a client is primarily shaped by the goal(s) and time frame(s) identified by the client, taking into account the client's risk tolerance, expectations, attitudes, and risk capacity. Because client goals change, so must investment recommendations. An investment plan can best be described as a "living record" in that the assets comprising the plan can and will change, as will the proportion of total portfolio assets allocated to each asset. An investment plan can and should change in response to client-driven events and economic changes. Ultimately, the soundness of investment choices is one of the primary determinants of success or failure in realizing financial planning goals.

Figure 13.3 provides an overview of investment goals as they relate to the Hubble family.

Figure 13.3. The Hubbles' Investment Goals.

Although there are several implied investment planning goals within the case narrative, the following stand out as being of primary concern for Chandler and Rachel:

- Develop an investment plan for Phoebe's college education fund.
- Increase tax-advantaged investing.
- Develop and manage household portfolios to match the Hubble family's time horizon, risk capacity, and risk tolerance for each of the major goals in their plan, including: (1) retirement planning, (2) special situation planning, and (3) an emergency fund.

Step 3: Analyze the Client's Current Course of Action and Potential Alternative Course(s) of Action

Analyzing a client's current investment management situation and developing investment recommendations involves a combination of qualitative and quantitative assessments. To this end, investment planning is as much an art as it is a logical system based on fixed rules. A financial planner must understand a client's perspectives on wants (ideals) and needs (reality), as well as a broad range of personal and household circumstances that can influence investment decisions.

The first step in the analysis of a client's current investment planning situation focuses on determining and quantifying the client's financial goal(s) and planning needs.

Temperament, personality, attitudes, and beliefs are particularly salient factors in the development of efficient, effective, client specific recommendations. Too often, investment planning decisions are based initially on assets available and a client's rate of return need, with insufficient consideration of other client factors that are instrumental to informing the products and strategies chosen.

Regardless of what financial planning model is used for investment planning, specific investment goals should be reviewed. If goals have not been determined, it is essential to do so before proceeding with any investment planning. Without a clear understanding of the goal(s) (e.g., new home, retirement, college funding, emergency fund, etc.), when funding is needed (e.g., next year, ten years, at age sixty-five, etc.), and the amount of funding needed, it is unrealistic to assume that an investment plan can be drafted that will remain valid over time.

Planning Reminder

Financial planning studies conducted over the past decade have generally concluded that, holding other factors constant, clients with low levels of financial knowledge tend to view risk differently than clients with a high degree of financial knowledge. This view of risk is commonly referred to as **risk perception**, which is different from risk tolerance. It has been shown that risk tolerance does not dramatically move up or down in the same way that risk perceptions change.

Once a client's personal and household characteristics have been identified and assessed and goals identified, the next step in the investment analysis phase of the financial planning process entails documenting and evaluating all investment plans currently in place. This should occur regardless of whether assets are allocated or unallocated for a specific goal. An initial assessment should focus on the client's stage in the **financial life cycle** (e.g., whether a client is closer to the beginning or end of their working life) and whether current investment plans match life-cycle objectives and other client characteristics. It must be noted that changing **family dynamics** (e.g., delayed marriage, remarried, or re-partnered families) can limit the usefulness of the life-cycle approach, but even broad generalizations can be very important when discussing investment plans with clients. The financial life cycle is typically conceptualized in three stages:

(1) protection,

(2) accumulation, and

(3) distribution.

These categorizations provide direction and meaning by helping clients understand and anticipate how each financial decision can influence subsequent decisions. The following discussion highlights how a client's investment focus, or overall objective, can change as a client progresses through life-cycle stages.

Planning Reminder

One way to assess a client's risk capacity involves conducting a financial ratio analysis. Determining how many ratios meet prescribed benchmarks and the availability of an emergency fund can provide insight into a client's risk capacity. Excess capacity gives a client additional flexibility when combining assets into a long-term investment plan.

During the **protection stage** of the life cycle, a client's focus should be on developing a budget and emergency fund to meet unexpected expenses. Financial planners add value to the client-financial planner relationship by helping clients build risk capacity at this stage of the life cycle.

At the **accumulation stage** of the life cycle, a client's focus changes to building wealth. This stage can last decades. A client's goal(s) typically shape actions taken during the accumulation stage. A financial planner's responsibility is to recommend actions that will enable the client to meet savings objectives as efficiently as possible. By closely monitoring the client's investment profile for changes, and reallocating the portfolio as necessary, a financial planner can safely and effectively guide the client through this challenging stage of the client's financial life.

The **distribution stage** of the life cycle represents a notable change in short- and long-term planning. This is the point at which a client transitions from accumulating assets to reach a goal to using assets to fund a goal. At this point in the life cycle, a financial planner's role changes as well. Investment recommendations tend to focus on capital preservation, titling and gifting strategies, and estate issues related to investment assets.

[A] Determining a Client's Investment Profile

Once a client's stage in the life cycle has been identified, and the client's risk tolerance, expectations about future market conditions, knowledge and experience, time horizon, and risk capacity have been assessed, a financial planner can begin to combine this information into an **investment profile**. Initially, this can be estimated by evaluating a client's time frame and risk tolerance for goal achievement. Figure 13.4 illustrates how the combination of time frame and risk tolerance can be used to categorize a client into a risk and return profile.

Figure 13.4. Portfolio Risk Guidelines Based on Client Time Horizon and Risk Tolerance.

Time Frame	High Risk Tolerance	Moderate Risk Tolerance	Low Risk Tolerance
10+ years	Aggressive	Moderately Aggressive	Moderate
7 to 10 years	Moderately Aggressive	Moderate	Moderate
3 to 7 years	Moderate	Moderate	Moderately Conservative
1 to 3 years	Moderately Conservative	Moderately Conservative	Conservative
Less than 1 year	Conservative	Conservative	Conservative

It is important to remember that clients typically have more than one goal, each with a different time horizon. This implies that multiple investment strategies may need to be designed. It is also useful to remember that the guidelines shown in Figure 13.4 must be tempered by the financial planner's assessment of a client's attitudes, expectations, and risk capacity. For example, the categorization of a client who has a high capacity to take on risk will be different than the categorization of a client who has limited risk capacity. Given this caveat, however, the guidelines provide some broad direction to guide the development of investment recommendations.

Example. A client is saving for retirement in twenty years. After taking a risk-tolerance assessment quiz, it becomes apparent that the client is neither a real risk taker nor a risk avoider. Given the length of time as the primary factor, an aggressive portfolio could still be prescribed as a starting point in client discussions.

Knowing only a client's time frame and risk tolerance is not enough to formulate an investment profile or an investment plan. These factors alone tell less than half the story. To get a full picture of a client's investment profile, it is also important to assess a client's investment attitudes and investment expectations. For instance, some clients might be open to holding any type of investment within their portfolio, while others may prefer to employ screens to eliminate certain types of investments or asset classes. Screens related to socially responsible investing, religious beliefs, or political affiliations are examples of how attitudes and values can affect the structure of an investment plan. Other considerations need to be evaluated as well. It is often helpful, for example, to know whether a client is content with regard to the current level of investment income generated by investments, taxes paid on investment earnings, and the level of volatility associated with holdings. Figure 13.5 presents a sample of attitudinal questions a financial planner can ask to obtain a better understanding of what might be driving a client to seek help with investments.

Figure 13.5. Client Investments Attitude Questionnaire.

Name _____ Investment Attitudes Questionnaire					
Place an X in the box to the right that reflects your first reaction to the statement.	Strongly Disagree	Disagree	Neutral	Agree	Strongly Agree
1. Keeping pace with inflation is important to me.					
2. I am comfortable borrowing money to make a non-home purchase investment.					
3. Diversification is important to investment success.					
4. The current return I am making on my investments is acceptable.					
5. I need to earn more spendable income from my investments.					
6. I am comfortable with the volatility I experience with my current portfolio.					
7. Reducing the amount of taxes paid on my investments is a top priority.					
8. I am willing to risk being audited by the IRS in exchange for higher returns.					
9. I am willing to risk being audited by the IRS in exchange for paying less tax.					
10. My friends would tell you that I am a real risk taker.					

Planning Reminder

Today's litigious environment suggests that financial planners—even those whose investment advice is secondary to their planning activities—should use an IPS to disclose and document the professional expectations for the management and investment of client assets. Practicing full disclosure with a client signed IPS is a prudent procedure because it establishes a mutually agreed-upon standard of conduct while reducing the possibility of a future lawsuit brought by a client who claims misrepresentation or inferior performance.

The process of documenting a client's investment preferences and evaluating alternatives is the basis of constructing an investment policy statement. An **investment policy statement (IPS)** is a document used to acknowledge agreement with and willingness to follow the parameters guiding the investment or management of a client's assets. An IPS, normally written by a financial planner and signed by both the financial planner and client, integrates a client's risk tolerance, risk capacity, and investment philosophy with the financial planner's proposed investment methods to establish parameters for investment strategies. A sample IPS is provided in Appendix 13A.

Some financial planners develop multiple IPS forms individually matched to the investment management plan aligned with different client goals. For example, two investment policy statements might be necessary for managing retirement assets if risk tolerance factors and acceptable investment management strategies are very different between a client and their spouse. Regardless of the number of IPS documents, or where the IPS is situated in a comprehensive financial plan, its inclusion is not only a necessity to lessen financial planner liability through appropriate planning disclosure, but an IPS also serves as a link to the financial planning process and as a reminder to the client and financial planner of the importance of adhering to established investment guidelines.

[B] Matching a Client's Investment Profile to Portfolio Alternatives

Taken together, a client's investment profile, consisting of time frame, risk tolerance, knowledge, expectations, and risk capacity, can be used as the basis for better understanding a client's current situation. Once this phase of the current situation analysis is concluded, it is appropriate to next evaluate portfolio characteristics in more detail. Specifically, it is important to document whether a client's current portfolio matches the client's investment profile and goals.

Example. Assume a client has a long-term time horizon, a moderate level of risk tolerance and financial knowledge, generally positive attitudes and expectations regarding investing, and an intermediate level of risk capacity, but a portfolio that is invested fairly conservatively. A financial planner may rightly conclude that additional portfolio risk could—and probably should—be taken by the client, thus increasing the expected return of the portfolio.

An important question that should be asked before conducting a current situation investment planning analysis is whether a client needs to make a portfolio change to better meet their financial goals. There is no definite, quantitative way to answer this question, but there are approaches that can be employed to make the process easier.

One approach that is often used to quantify how a portfolio corresponds to a client's investment profile is to document relevant portfolio characteristics using a standardized form, and then compare these characteristics to market benchmarks. Figure 13.6 is an example of a form that can be used in this process.

Figure 13.6. Investment Profile and Portfolio Summary Form.

Investment Profile and Portfolio Summary Form			
Client Investment Profile			
Qualitative	Circle the appropriate response.		
Risk tolerance	High	Moderate	Low
Knowledge/experience	High	Moderate	Low
Market expectations	Positive	Neutral	Negative
Quantitative			
Time horizon	Long	Intermediate	Short
Risk capacity	High	Moderate	Low
Client risk profile*		Client allocation profile**	
Portfolio Measures	**Current Statistics**	**Benchmark Statistics**	**Comparison to Benchmark**
Targeted portfolio allocation profile**			
Observed portfolio allocation profile**			
Portfolio statistics			
Beta			
Alpha			
R^2			
Sharpe ratio			
Treynor ratio			
Fixed income measures			
Bond duration			
Average bond quality			
Asset allocation (%)			
Cash			
U.S. stock			
Foreign stock			
Bond			
Other			

Sensitivity analysis					
3-year average return					
Worst 1-year loss					
Best 1-year gain					
Does portfolio match investment profile?	Yes	No	Yes	No	
* Scale: 5: High; 4: Above average; 3: Moderate; 2: Below average; 1: Low					
** Scale: 6: Aggressive growth; 5: Growth; 4: Moderate growth; 3: Balanced growth; 2: Conservative growth; 1: Income					

This form begins by documenting the factors that influence a client's investment profile. An investor's profile, based on these factors, is then determined. This form uses a five-point investment risk-profile scale: High = 5; Above average = 4; Moderate = 3; Below average = 2; Low = 1. A financial planner then matches these classifications with recommended portfolio allocations.

The client portfolio allocation profile becomes the basis for choosing a benchmark portfolio. Benchmark statistics should then be entered into the table. For example, if a financial planner determines that a client's investment profile falls in the moderate range, then statistics for a balanced growth portfolio should be entered in the benchmark column. Next, relevant portfolio statistics should be summarized, and actual portfolio statistics should then be compared to the benchmark.

[C] Using Financial Market Benchmarks to Document a Client's Investment Situation

A **market index** can be used by financial planners to track the performance of a select group of equities, bonds, or other investment assets. Economists use the performance of market indexes as a **leading economic indicator**. Financial planners, on the other hand, find indexes to be useful as benchmarks or standards of measurement for client portfolio performance. For a meaningful comparison, it is important to select a **benchmark** that most closely matches both the type of security or asset and the corresponding level of risk associated with a portfolio.

The simplest method for determining the best benchmark is to first find one or more benchmarks that seem to have a general fit; for example, the S&P 500 index can be used as a benchmark for a large market capitalization portfolio. Next, it is best to perform a linear regression of historical returns of the asset versus the historical returns of the benchmark. A financial planner can then review the **coefficient of determination (R^2)**—a statistic that indicates the amount of explained variance in portfolio performance that is accounted for by the index—for each regression and select the benchmark that results in the largest R^2. When evaluating R^2, it is important to remember that values can run a continuum from zero to one. The closer R^2 is to 1.0 indicates that more variability in returns of the asset is explained by variability in returns of the benchmark.

It is common to benchmark portfolio performance. To gauge overall portfolio performance, the returns for several indexes, reported over the same period, can be matched proportionately to the assets in the portfolio. In other words, weighted average returns can be used to compare the portfolio and matching benchmarks for corresponding market sectors. Information to track the performance of most securities over time should be readily available, either free from online sources or from a financial planner's custodian, broker dealer, or other third-party source. Although numerous indexes track different market segments (nationally, regionally, and internationally), some of the most commonly used indexes are listed in Figures 13.7 and 13.8. It is worth noting that a decision to purchase or sell a security should not be based solely on performance relative to a benchmark. Security selection and portfolio development issues should consider other aspects of a client's situation as well.

Figure 13.7. Select Widely Used Equity Market Indexes.

Corresponding Index by Provider				
Market Sector All U.S. stocks	S&P/Barra S&P Total Mkt	Russell 3000	Morgan Stanley Market 2500	1Wilshire/DJ Wilshire 5000
U.S. Equity (Size segmented)				
Mega-cap	—	—	—	DJIA 30
Large-cap	S&P 500	1000	Large-cap 300	Wilshire 750
Mid-cap	S&P 400	Mid-cap	Mid-cap 450	Wilshire 500
Small-cap	S&P 600	2000	Small-cap 1750	Wilshire 1750
U.S. Equity (Style segmented)				
Large growth	Barra Growth	1000 Growth	—	Target large Growth
Mid-growth	—	Mid-cap Growth	—	Target large value
Large value	Barra Value	1000 Value	—	Target mid-growth
Mid-value	—	Mid-cap Value	—	Target mid-value
U.S. Equity (Sector segmented)				
Consumer	S&P Consumer	—	—	—
Health care	S&P Health Care	—	—	DJ Health Care
Utilities	S&P Utilities	—	—	—
Financials	S&P Financials	—	—	DJ Insurance
Technology	S&P Technology	—	—	DJ Telecom
International Equity (Region segmented)				
Global	S&P Global 1200	—	AC World Index	—
International (non-emerging)	S&P 700	—	AC World Index (Ex. U.S.)	DJ Developed Mkts
Emerging market	IFCI	—	Emerging Markets	DJ Emerging Mkts & DJ Latin America

In some situations, a benchmark analysis can lead to quick and apparent conclusions. For example, a portfolio that carries a higher risk profile, as measured by **beta**, a lower annualized rate of return, and hence a negative **alpha** compared to the benchmark should lead to the conclusion that the client is taking too much risk for the return received. When faced with this situation, a financial planner should implement steps to reallocate the client's portfolio.

However, not all analyses are that simple. During the early 2000s, for instance, portfolios that were over-weighted in bonds and cash tended to outperform portfolios that were balanced more heavily in equities. These fixed-income heavy portfolios almost always showed betas that were lower, alphas that were higher, and returns that were superior to balanced portfolio indexes. On paper, these portfolios looked better than what was actually the case going forward. Over the long run, it is worth remembering that risk and return are positively related. In the short term, this relationship might not hold true. To believe that risk and return will continue to be uncorrelated—as many investors did during the global recession that lasted from 2008 through 2012—can lead to a serious underachievement of client goals if and when the risk/return relationship reverts to normal.

Figure 13.8. Select Widely Used Fixed-Income Market Indexes.

Corresponding Index by Provider			
Market Sector	**S&P**	**2Wilshire/DJ**	**Barclay's**
All U.S. bonds	—	—	*U.S. Universal*
U.S. Treasury (Term segmented)			
Long-term	BG Cantor U.S. T-bond	—	
Intermediate	—		U.S. Treasury
Short-term	BG Cantor U.S. T-bill		—
TIPS	BG Cantor U.S. TIPS		U.S. Treasury TIPS
Corporate Debt (Quality segmented)			
U.S. Investment Grade	—	—	U.S. Long Credit
U.S. High-Yield	—	—	U.S. Corp High-Yield
International (Region segmented)			
Global	—	—	Multiverse
International	Int'l Corp Bond	—	Global Aggregate
Emerging market	—	—	Global Emerging Markets
Specialty			
Real Estate (REITS)	U.S. REIT	3Wilshire RESI*	—
Global Real Estate	—	Global RESI*	—
U.S. municipal	Municipal Bond	—	U.S. Municipal
U.S. mortgage-backed	—	—	U.S. MBS
*Real Estate Securities Index			

[D] Determining a Client's Required Rate of Return

There are times when investment decisions must be based on projected investment outcomes rather than current attitudes and financial circumstances. In such cases, rather than making allocations that happen to result in a certain rate of return, a financial planner and client can allocate a portfolio to achieve the necessary rate of return. This type of **reverse engineering** has advantages if all goes as planned; however, if the results are not achieved, then maintaining client satisfaction can become more difficult because the client might be less comfortable with the level of risk exposure or the amount of volatility associated with recommended investments.

An example of reverse engineering can be seen with a thirty-five-year-old client who wants to retire at age sixty-five with $1 million. If she has $250 to invest monthly, the portfolio must be allocated to achieve an annual rate of return of nearly 13 percent (ignoring the impact of income taxes). This rate of return is the **required rate of return** that achieves the objective. The return estimate does not consider the client's risk tolerance or risk capacity. Calculating this required rate of return requires the following inputs:

- Future Value: $1 million

- Present Value: $0

- Periodic payment: $250

- Number of periods: 360 [(65-35) × 12]

In practice, using a required rate of return to dictate an investment or asset allocation recommendation, rather than basing a recommendation on a client's risk profile, can cause problems. Specifically, if the risk associated with the investment choice exceeds a client's willingness to take financial risk and/or the client's financial capacity to withstand a financial loss, the client may sell the investment when faced with a significant loss. If this occurs, the client will move further away from goal achievement. As such, using required rates of return as an investment planning model should be used only for a knowledgeable client with the capacity to accept the risk.

[E] Comparative Risk Statistics[1]

A financial planner plays an important role at the third step of the financial planning process as it relates to investment planning. Specifically, a financial planner should perform a performance and risk analysis on currently held positions. An evaluation of this analysis will provide insight into how closely portfolio holdings align with a client's risk need and ultimate goal achievement.

Performance measures of excess performance can be separated into two categories: absolute measures and ratio measures. As summarized in Figure 13.9, various measures categorize risk differently and provide a more specific description of what risk is: **total risk** versus **downside risk** or **systematic risk** versus **unsystematic risk**:

- Total risk is a measure that quantifies the general likelihood of an unexpected outcome.

- Downside risk limits the quantification of risk to both unexpected and negative outcomes.

- Systematic risk measures quantify the risk inherent in the entire market.

- Unsystematic risk quantifies the risk associated with a single asset or asset class within a market.

Precision of measurement is important for a financial planner when developing investment recommendations and when attempting to make assessments about the effectiveness of portfolio management or asset selection choices. The more active the financial planner is in attempting to mitigate a specific type of risk, or maximize a return based on a particular investment philosophy, the more precise the financial planner must be in isolating those variables to make accurate comparisons.

Figure 13.9. Summary of Commonly Used Portfolio Risk Measures.

Name (Symbol)	Definition/Formula
Variance (σ^2) and Std. deviation (σ)	These are absolute measures of the average variability or spread of periodic returns. This measures the *total risk* of unanticipated outcomes. $$\sigma^2_i = \frac{1}{T-1} \sum_{t=1}^{T} (r_{i,t} - \bar{r}_1)^2 \qquad \sigma = \sqrt{\sigma^2}$$
Semi-variance (σ^2) and Semi-deviation (σ)	These are absolute measures of the average variability or spread of periodic returns that do not meet the targeted return: *downside risk*. $$\sigma^2_i = \frac{0.5}{T-1} \sum_{t=1}^{T} (r_{i,t} - \bar{r}_1)^2 \qquad \sigma = \sqrt{\sigma^2}$$ Formulas assume "normal" distribution.
Coefficient of variation (CV)	This is a measure of dispersion of a probability distribution. It is defined as the ratio of the standard deviation (σ) to the mean (μ). $$CV = \frac{\sigma}{\mu}$$
Coefficient of determination (R^2)	This is a measure of systematic, or market-related, variability. R^2 ranges from 0 to 100 and reflects the percentage of an asset's movements that are explained by movements in the benchmark. The remainders (residuals) are a rough measure of the *unsystematic* component of risk. *Linear regression-based*
Beta (σ)	The beta coefficient is a measure of a security's volatility relative to the market. This is a "relative" measure of volatility. Because beta reflects only the market-related or *systematic* portion of a security's risk, it is a narrower measure than standard deviation. $$\beta = \frac{\sigma_{i,M}}{\sigma^2_M}$$

[F] Comparative Portfolio Statistics

There are five performance statistics commonly used when making risk-adjusted, return-based portfolio evaluations. Each statistical tool is described in greater detail below.

[1] Sharpe Ratio

The **Sharpe ratio** standardizes portfolio performance in excess of the risk-free rate by the standard deviation of the portfolio. Higher Sharpe ratio scores are indicative of better risk-adjusted performance. However, the ratio is not useful unless an investor has a comparable portfolio to judge the score against. Additionally, because the Sharpe ratio uses a measure of **total risk** (i.e., standard deviation), a financial planner should use this method primarily for comparing **undiversified portfolios** or concentrated positions. The Sharpe ratio can be calculated using the following formula:

$$S_i = \frac{R_i - R_f}{\sigma_i}$$

Where:

S_i = Sharpe ratio

R_i = Actual return of the asset (or portfolio)

R_f = Risk-free rate

σ_i = Standard deviation of asset (or portfolio)

Example: First, assume that Laini's portfolio achieved an average annual return of 12 percent with an annualized standard deviation of 16 percent, and the market portfolio achieved an annual return of 13 percent with a standard deviation of 18 percent. Second, assume that a risk-free opportunity returned 5 percent per year. Applying the formula, Laini's Sharpe ratio would be 0.437.[2] But what does this mean? Without a point of comparison, it is hard to tell. A comparison portfolio is needed. If, for example, the Sharpe ratio of the market was 0.444, one can say that Laini's portfolio provided an inferior return compared to the market portfolio.

[2] Modigliani Measure

The **Modigliani measure** (M^2), which calculates the absolute amount of risk-adjusted return within a portfolio, is based on the Sharpe ratio. The Modigliani measure helps put a portfolio's results into perspective by providing an intuitive estimate of what the return should have been given the amount of total risk taken. The calculation starts with the Sharpe ratio and then applies a risk adjustment to convert the Sharpe back into percentage return form, adding the risk-free rate, then subtracting the return of the market.

$$M^2_i = \left[R_f + \sigma_m \left(\frac{(R_i - R_f)}{\sigma_i} \right) \right] - R_m$$

Where:

M² = Modigliani measure

R_f = Risk-free rate

R_i = Return of the asset or portfolio

σ_m = Standard deviation of the market or benchmark

σ_i = Standard deviation of the asset or portfolio

R_m = Return on the market

Example. Returning to the previous example and based on the formula, Laini's M² measure is –0.125 percent. Although her portfolio's returns were 1 percent less than the market with a standard deviation less than the market, her risk-adjusted return remained negative. In other words, the M² measure provides an estimate of her risk-adjusted return. This coincides with the fact that the Sharpe ratio was lower than the market. This measure nicely quantifies the exact amount of risk-adjusted performance achieved by an investor.

[3] Treynor Index

The **Treynor index** is also a measure of standardized risk-adjusted performance. Instead of using standard deviation as a measure of absolute volatility, the formula uses *beta* as a measure of **systematic risk**—risk that cannot be reduced through diversification. Just like the Sharpe ratio, the Treynor index outcome is useful only in terms of comparing one portfolio to another. Because the Treynor uses a systemic measure of risk, this index should be used only with well-diversified portfolios. A Treynor index score can be calculated using the following formula:

$$T_i = \frac{R_i - R_f}{\beta_i}$$

Where:

T_i = Treynor index

R_p = Actual return of the portfolio (the return of an investment $_{(Ri)}$ can also be used in this formula)

R_f = Risk-free rate

β_i = Beta

Example. Assume Jack's portfolio return was 12 percent, the risk-free rate was 3 percent, and the beta of Jack's portfolio was 0.85. The Treynor index for the portfolio would be 0.106.[3]

[4] Jensen's Alpha

Another useful statistic is **Jensen's alpha** or the **Jensen Performance Index**. **Alpha** measures the relative under- or over-performance of a portfolio compared to a benchmark—typically a representative, diversified market portfolio. Alpha measures the difference between the actual returns of a portfolio and the portfolio's expected risk-adjusted performance. The following formula is used to determine the Jensen's alpha of a portfolio:

$$\alpha = R_p - [R_f + \beta (R_m - R_f)]$$

Where:

α = Alpha (derived from the assumption of investment risk)

R_p = Actual return of the portfolio (the return of an investment $_{(Ri)}$ can also be used in this formula)

R_f = Risk-free rate

β = Beta

R_m = Return on the market

Notice that the calculation is based on the CAPM ($R_f + \beta(R_m - R_f)$). A positive alpha indicates that a portfolio exceeded expectations on a risk-adjusted basis. A negative alpha suggests that a portfolio underperformed the market on a risk-adjusted basis. A reallocation of assets might be warranted if a portfolio shows a long history of significant underperformance.

Example. Returning to Jack's portfolio from the previous example, if Jack actually earned a rate of return of 12 percent over the three-year period, he could conclude that on a risk-adjusted basis he did better than expected. His portfolio would have generated a positive alpha of 1.35 percent.[4] If the portfolio were managed by a financial planner, Jack could conclude that his financial planner added value above what would have been expected given the risk taken.

[5] Information Ratio

The **information ratio** can be used to estimate the excess return of a portfolio (alpha) generated by active management compared to the standard deviation (tracking error of alpha) generated by active management. This is most useful when a financial planner is attempting to outperform a benchmark through superior asset selection or market timing. The information ratio differs from other ratios in that the benchmark is no longer the risk-free asset, as assumed in the Sharpe ratio and Treynor index. The information ratio can be calculated using the following formula.[5]

$$IR = \frac{(r_p - r_B)}{\sqrt{Var\ (r_p - r_B)}} = \frac{\alpha}{\varepsilon_T}$$

Where:

IR = Information ratio

α = Alpha (derived from active management, not solely investment risk) where alpha is the difference between the portfolio return and the benchmark return

ε_T = Tracking error of alpha where the error is the standard deviation of the alpha return

Each of these measures is based on concepts imbedded in **modern portfolio theory**. This theory introduced the process of mean-variance optimization, its related statistics, and various other investment rules which can be used to determine whether a client's portfolio is efficient. While data can and should be used to guide portfolio choices, professional judgment must also play a role in the decision-making process. Experience, knowledge, and skill help a financial planner determine whether a portfolio is appropriate for a client's needs within the context of the current economic situation, client attitudes and expectations, and an analysis of risk tolerance and risk capacity. The integrated nature of these, and other factors, makes investment planning challenging. Figure 13.10 provides a summary of the relative portfolio performance measures as illustrated in this chapter. Appendix 13B provides details on other performance measures and statistics.

Figure 13.10. Summary of Relative Portfolio Performance Measures.

Name (Symbol)	Definition/Formula
Sharpe ratio	A measure of risk-adjusted performance calculated by dividing the excess return of a portfolio by a measure of *total risk*. Higher values are desirable. This measure is most appropriate when analyzing portfolios where unsystematic risk is still prevalent. $$S_i = \frac{R_i + R_f}{\sigma_i}$$
Modigliani measure (M^2)	A measure of risk-adjusted performance that results in a percentage measure for under- (negative values) or over- (positive values) performance, based on *total risk* within the asset or portfolio. $$M^2_i = \left[R_f + \sigma_m \left(\frac{(R_i - R_f)}{\sigma_i} \right) \right] - R_m$$
Treynor index	A measure of risk-adjusted performance calculated by dividing the excess return of a portfolio, return beyond the risk-free rate, by its beta. Higher values are desirable and indicate greater return per unit of *systematic* risk. This measure is most appropriate when analyzing portfolios where only systematic risk remains. $$T_i = \frac{R_i - R_f}{\beta_i}$$

Jensen's alpha (α)	Return in excess of capital asset pricing model (CAPM) return. Alpha is the difference between the security's actual performance and the performance anticipated in light of the security's *systematic risk* (beta) and the market's behavior.[6] $$\alpha = R_p - [R_f + \beta\,[(R_m - R_f)]]$$
Information ratio	A measure of risk-adjusted performance calculated by dividing the excess risk-adjusted return (alpha) of a portfolio by the tracking error (standard deviation of alpha). Higher values are desirable. This measure is most appropriate when analyzing actively managed portfolios where either market timing or asset selection is being used in an attempt to exceed a benchmark. $$IR = \frac{(r_p - r_B)}{\sqrt{Var\,(r_p - r_B)}} = \frac{\alpha}{\varepsilon_T} \text{ or } IR = \frac{\alpha}{\varepsilon_T}$$

The following example shows how an analysis of the Hubble family's current investment choices and needs can be used as a pathway to the development of investment planning recommendations. Figure 13.11 provides a summary of the Hubbles' investment management choices. Potential recommendations are also provided.

Figure 13.11. The Hubbles' Current Investment Choices and Potential Recommendations.

The case narrative provides detailed information about the Hubble family's current investment alternatives and choices. Some of the relevant data that can be used to build an investment profile for Chandler and Rachel includes the following:
- Both Chandler and Rachel have a generally moderate to conservative financial risk tolerance.
- Chandler and Rachel are holding cash reserves in bank, checking, and money market accounts to meet emergency needs. There may be opportunities to reallocate assets going forward.
- Chandler and Rachel are investing in a moderately aggressive portfolio for Phoebe's college costs.
- Chandler and Rachel are investing conservatively for special needs (the home addition and gallery start-up costs). Assets are being held in a bank account.
- Chandler and Rachel are comfortable assuming a moderately conservative rate of return prior to retirement and a conservative rate of return after retirement.
- Chandler and Rachel are interested in ideas that can improve the family's current return situation without taking excessive risk. However, Chandler has made it very clear that he is extremely apprehensive about investing and feels that he tends to be risk averse. Rachel feels comfortable taking additional risks if she is confident that she can earn higher returns.
- The following represent expected rates of return for planning purposes:

Expected Rates of Return*			
	Expected After-tax Total Rate of Return*	Maximum Portfolio Risk	
		Beta (indexed to S&P 500)	Standard Deviation
Conservative	5.25%	< 0.40	< 7.0
Moderately conservative	7.75%	< 0.80	< 9.0
Moderately aggressive	10.00%	0.80 < 1.00	< 13.0
Aggressive	12.14%	> 1.00	> 13.0

*Note that these returns include capital appreciation, dividends, and interest received.
** Assumes a combined federal and state tax rate of 30 percent.

- Mutual fund (investment) choices are limited to the following:

Equity Funds					
Fund	Investment Objective	Historical Before-Tax Rate of Return	Standard Deviation	Correlation (r) with Equity Market	Yield
Value Fund	Large Cap	9.00%	12.00%	0.95	3.00%
Growth Fund	Large Cap	10.20%	15.00%	0.90	2.00%
Eastside Fund	Mid Cap	8.40%	10.00%	0.92	2.00%
Konza Fund	Mid Cap	9.20%	13.00%	0.91	1.75%
Sagebrush Fund	Small Cap	11.20%	21.00%	0.80	0.50%
Rocket Fund	Small Cap	14.00%	22.00%	0.75	0.00%
Consumer Fund	Small Cap	8.75%	11.00%	0.99	2.50%
Acquisitions Fund	Mid Cap	7.50%	5.20%	0.20	4.00%
International Fund	International (EAFA Index)	10.00%	11.20%	0.50	2.00%
Haley G&I Fund	Large Cap	8.00%	10.00%	0.90	3.20%
Graham Fund	Real Estate & Precious Metals	4.10%	12.00%	0.10	2.00%

Bond Funds					
Fund	Investment Objective	Historical Before-Tax Rate of Return	Standard Deviation	Correlation (r) with Bond Market	Yield
Ruth Fund	Government Bond	4.80%	4.90%	0.85	4.00%
Cardinal Fund	Corporate Bond	5.20%	5.10%	0.90	4.80%
Clock Fund	Corporate Bond	6.00%	6.20%	0.98	5.40%
Ely Fund	Government Bond	6.10%	6.05%	0.92	6.00%
Companion Fund	High Yield	7.00%	13.00%	0.80	6.10%
States Fund	Government Bond	5.70%	6.00%	0.75	4.00%
Barrister Fund	Money Market	3.00%	0.00%	0.00	3.00%

- The following cash and cash equivalent assets are also available:

Cash and Cash Equivalent Asset	Yield
Savings Accounts	2.00%
Money Market Accounts	3.00%
Money Market Mutual Funds	3.00%
State of Missouri Municipal Money Market Accounts and Funds	2.30%
One-Year Certificates of Deposit	3.50%

- Market index data for each asset class is shown below:

Market Indexes			
Index	Before-Tax Rate of Return	Standard Deviation	Yield
T-Bills	4.00%	2.00%	4.00%
Equity Market	8.80%	11.00%	2.50%
Bond Market	6.10%	6.50%	6.10%
Other Indexes			
Treasury coupon bonds	5.00%	6.00%	5.50%
Treasury zero-coupon bond "strips"	6.00%	6.50%	0.00%
Investment-grade corporate coupon bonds	7.00%	7.00%	7.00%
Investment-grade corp. zero-coupon bonds	7.50%	8.00%	0.00%
High-yield corporate bonds	9.00%	12.00%	9.00%
International bonds	10.00%	15.00%	10.00%
U.S. large-cap equity	10.00%	18.00%	2.25%
U.S. small-cap equity	12.00%	+20.00%	<1.00%
Developed international equity	15.00%	+25.00%	≈0.00%
* RoR and Yields may not reflect current market conditions.			

- Other investments available for use when advising Chandler and Rachel include:

  o   The Potsdam Fixed Annuity, which has a current guaranteed yield of 5 percent; the guaranteed yield period will end in two years.
  o   The Bostonian Variable Annuity, which allows investments in all equity and bond funds shown above as well as the cash and cash equivalents. This annuity has a guaranteed investment contract that currently yields 5 percent.

- Chandler and Rachel would like to assume a 30.0 percent combined state and federal tax bracket until retirement and a 25.0 percent combined state and federal marginal tax bracket during retirement.
- If an investment asset is sold, Chandler and Rachel would prefer to assume (for tax purposes) that the basis in all after-tax investments is equal to 50 percent of the fair market value of these assets, and that all investment gains are subject to capital gains tax rates.
- Chandler and Rachel would also like to assume that any interest earned from savings is reinvested, rather than being spent on household expenses; additionally, Chandler and Rachel prefer to assume that all dividends and capital gains from other investment assets are also reinvested.

Specific data linked to each goal is as follows:

- Emergency Fund:

  o   Ultra-short-term time horizon.
  o   Low risk tolerance.
  o   Chandler and Rachel expect to place assets in safe and secure investments.
  o   Chandler and Rachel expect investments to perform well regardless of economic situation.
  o   Chandler and Rachel currently have the risk capacity to meet this goal.

• Retirement Planning:
o Long-term time horizon. o As a couple, Chandler and Rachel have a moderately-conservative risk tolerance. o Chandler and Rachel are willing to invest in any security as long as total portfolio risk remains in the moderately-conservative range. o Chandler and Rachel expect their personal as well as regional and national economies to remain healthy into the forecasted future. o Chandler and Rachel have a healthy and growing risk capacity for this goal.
• Education Planning:
o Long-term time horizon. o As a couple, Chandler and Rachel have a moderately-conservative risk tolerance. o Chandler and Rachel are willing to invest in any security as long as total portfolio risk remains in the moderately-aggressive range. o Chandler and Rachel expect their personal as well as regional and national economies to remain healthy into the forecasted future. o Chandler and Rachel have a healthy and growing risk capacity for this goal.
• Home improvement and art gallery planning:
o Long-term time horizon. o As a couple, Chandler and Rachel have a moderately-conservative risk tolerance. o Chandler and Rachel are willing to invest in any security as long as total portfolio risk remains in the moderately-aggressive range. o Chandler and Rachel expect their personal as well as regional and national economies to remain healthy into the forecasted future. o Chandler and Rachel have a healthy and growing risk capacity for this goal.

An analysis of the available investments is shown below. In the analysis, T-bills are assumed to be the risk-free rate of return.

Fund	Objective	RoR	SD	Corr (r)	Yield	r*r	Beta	CAPM	Sharpe	Treynor	Alpha	Beta to Equities
Indexes												
T-Bills	n.a.	4.00%	2.00%	1.00	4.00%	n.a.	n.a.	n.a.	n.a.	n.a.	n.a.	
Equity Market	n.a.	8.80%	11.00%	1.00	2.50%	n.a.	n.a.	n.a.	n.a.	n.a.	n.a.	
Bond Market	n.a.	6.10%	6.50%	1.00	5.30%	n.a.	n.a.	n.a.	n.a.	n.a.	n.a.	
Equity Funds												
Value Fund	Large Value	9.00%	12.00%	0.95	3.00%	0.90	1.04	8.97%	0.4167	0.0482	0.03	
Growth Fund	Large Growth	10.20%	15.00%	0.90	2.00%	0.81	1.23	9.89%	0.4133	0.0505	0.31	
Eastside Fund	Medium Value	8.40%	10.00%	0.92	2.00%	0.85	0.84	8.01%	0.4400	0.0526	0.39	
Konza Fund	Medium Growth	9.20%	13.00%	0.91	1.75%	0.83	1.08	9.16%	0.4000	0.0484	0.04	
Sagebrush Fund	Small Value	11.20%	21.00%	0.80	0.50%	0.64	1.53	11.33%	0.3429	0.0471	(0.13)	
Rocket Fund	Small Growth	14.00%	22.00%	0.75	0.00%	0.56	1.50	11.20%	0.4545	0.0667	2.80	
Consumer Fund	Index Fund	8.75%	11.00%	0.99	2.50%	0.98	0.99	8.75%	0.4318	0.0480	(0.00)	
Acquisitions Fund	Specialized	7.50%	5.20%	0.20	4.00%	0.04	0.09	4.45%	0.6731	0.3702	3.05	
International Fund	International	10.00%	11.20%	0.50	2.00%	0.25	0.51	6.44%	0.5357	0.1179	3.56	
Haley G&I Fund	Growth & Income	8.00%	10.00%	0.90	3.20%	0.81	0.82	7.93%	0.4000	0.0489	0.07	
Graham Fund	Commodities	4.10%	12.00%	0.10	2.00%	0.01	0.11	4.52%	0.0083	0.0092	(0.42)	
AVERAGES		9.12%	12.95%	0.72	2.09%	0.61	0.88	8.24%	0.4106	0.0825	0.88	
Bond Funds												
Ruth Fund	Short-Term Bonds	4.80%	4.90%	0.85	4.00%	0.72	0.64	5.35%	0.1633	0.0125	(0.55)	0.38
Cardinal Fund	Intermediate-Term Bonds	5.20%	5.10%	0.90	4.80%	0.81	0.71	5.48%	0.2353	0.0170	(0.28)	0.42
Clock Fund	Long-Term Bonds	6.00%	6.20%	0.98	5.40%	0.96	0.93	5.96%	0.3226	0.0214	0.04	0.55
Ely Fund	Ginnie-Mae Bonds	6.10%	6.05%	0.92	6.00%	0.85	0.86	5.80%	0.3471	0.0245	0.30	0.51
Companion Fund	International Bonds	7.00%	13.00%	0.80	6.10%	0.64	1.60	7.36%	0.2308	0.0188	(0.36)	0.95
States Fund	Municipal Bonds	5.70%	6.00%	0.75	4.00%	0.56	0.69	5.45%	0.2833	0.0246	0.25	0.41
AVERAGES		5.80%	6.88%	0.87	5.05%	0.76	0.91	5.90%	0.2637	0.0198	(0.10)	0.53

The following potential recommendations, based on an evaluation of the preceding analysis, emerge and are worth considering:
- Given their current marginal tax bracket, Chandler and Rachel should consider investing in tax-free municipal securities for the fixed-income portion of their taxable portfolio.
- Chandler and Rachel currently are not meeting their required rate of return objective for retirement. As such, they should consider reallocating their portfolio more aggressively.
- Chandler and Rachel are not saving enough or earning enough to meet their education funding objective. They should consider reallocating their educational portfolio more aggressively.
- Chandler and Rachel are not saving enough or earning enough to meet their special needs objectives. They should consider reallocating their portfolio more aggressively.

Step 4: Develop the Financial Planning Recommendation(s)

The next step in the investment planning process involves developing financial planning recommendations. Recommendations should flow directly from the analysis of the client's current investment positions and situation. It is important that a client understands why certain investments and asset allocation approaches are recommended. Investments are bought and sold not only because of changing investor goals, risk attitudes, and time horizons, but also because of changing environmental factors. **Environmental asset allocation factors**, such as the current and prospective economic environment, represent investment constraints not usually controllable by a client or financial planner. The process of economically based asset allocation can be outlined by asking the following questions:

- What have been the recent and long-term returns of various asset classes?

- Are domestic interest rates (currently and projected) rising or falling?

- What is the difference in stock yields and bond yields?

- Is projected monetary policy and fiscal policy conducive to strong long-term growth?

- Will the dollar rise or fall in value relative to foreign currencies?

- What are projected domestic and international growth rates?

- Will inflation or rising commodity prices stunt growth domestically or internationally?

- Will foreign investments offer superior risk-adjusted returns?

A financial planner must be careful not to overwhelm a client with too much financial or economic information, although avoiding any discussion about the market and/or economic environment can be equally problematic. The inclusion of environmental factors into the investment selection process begins by segregating assets into a two-by-two investment selection matrix as shown in Figure 13.12.

Figure 13.12. Investment Selection Matrix.

		Goal	
		Appreciation	**Income**
Inflation	High	Commodities	Real estate
	Low	Stocks	Bonds

The matrix consists of stocks, bonds, commodities, and real estate (hard assets, such as collectibles, are typically not considered to be traditional investment assets because their value is determined primarily by supply and demand). Each of the categories offers advantages and disadvantages. By considering the impact of economic conditions—particularly inflation—a financial planner can optimize portfolio allocation choices by changing the weight of a particular class of assets.

There tends to be a dynamic interaction between a client's need for current income and the need to generate capital appreciation. Typically, financial planners recommend real estate and bond holdings to maximize the income potential of a portfolio. Stock and commodity holdings are used to maximize the appreciation potential. An example of an allocation that might perform equally well in times of high or low inflation is a portfolio split 25 percent among each asset class. However, this might not be efficient if a client needs to maximize current income. If this were the case, a financial planner would need to change the portfolio based on both the state of the economy and the client's goal.

Environmental factors can play a role in shaping recommendations to invest domestically or internationally. The primary outcome associated with including foreign investments in a portfolio is risk reduction (i.e., a decrease in the **systematic risk** associated with investing in only one country or region). However, superior returns can also be achieved through international investments by capitalizing on changes in **currency exchange rates** or higher international growth rates associated with emerging or recovering markets. In either case, adding international diversification to **an asset allocation framework** can increase the overall risk-adjusted return of a client's portfolio.

Another environmental issue pertains to the current and projected interest rate environment. The rule for fixed-income securities is that as rates rise, bond values fall. Therefore, a financial planner should take steps to allocate a portfolio that is not overly sensitive to rising or falling interest rates. Analytical tools such as duration and sensitivity analyses can be used for these purposes.

The following discussion highlights the importance of other concepts, tools, and techniques that can be incorporated into the recommendation development process.

[A] Asset Classifications

Asset allocation represents the way a client's investment dollars are spread among different financial asset classes. **Financial assets** can be broken into many categories for asset allocation purposes, based on either a client's preferences or current and projected market conditions. Figure 13.13 provides a summary of some of the most popular asset classes and a suggested use for each.

Figure 13.13. Summary of Investments by Asset Classification.

Equities (stocks). The primary purpose of equity investing is to generate capital appreciation. Stocks have historically had the highest asset returns after adjusting for inflation. A secondary purpose is the generation of current income through dividend payments.

Sub-classifications:

- Large-cap—stocks with a market capitalization over $10 billion. These stocks are typically mature, dividend-paying companies.

- Mid-cap—stocks with a market capitalization between $2 billion and $10 billion. These stocks may not pay dividends, but mid-cap stocks have higher growth rate prospects than large-cap companies.

- Small-cap—stocks with a market capitalization under $2 billion. These stocks typically do not pay dividends; they tend to be fast-growing companies that retain earnings to fuel growth.

Debt (bonds). The primary purpose of debt investing is the generation of current income. Bonds typically pay interest on a regular and recurring basis without the possibility of interest reinvestment. A secondary purpose is the possibility of capital appreciation in a declining interest rate environment.

Sub-classifications:

- Treasury/government agency—bonds issued by the Treasury Department or a federal government agency.

- Municipal—bonds issued by state and local governments, which can be further classified as general obligation bonds or revenue bonds.

- Corporate—bonds issued by public corporations, which can be further classified as investment-grade or high-yield issues.

- Zero coupon—bonds sold at a discount to par value that do not pay a periodic payment. Typically, these bonds are issued by the federal government in the form of Treasury Strips; however, other zero-coupon issues are available.

International assets. The primary purpose associated with the use of international assets is capital appreciation, especially during times of superior international growth. Sub-classifications include the equity and debt of both developed markets and emerging markets.

Commodities. The primary purpose of investing in commodity assets, for the average investor, is capital appreciation, especially in times of rapid hard asset price growth. Commodities can serve as an inflation hedge. Sub-classifications include precious metals, natural resources, energy products, livestock, and agricultural products.

Real estate. The primary purpose of real estate investing is the generation of current income. Real estate investment trusts (REITs) typically pay dividends on a regular and recurring basis. Capital appreciation, as a secondary focus, is possible with some forms of direct real estate investment. Sub-classifications include raw land, agricultural, commercial, residential, and mortgage-backed obligations.

[B] Riskiness and Potential Returns of Different Financial Assets

When allocating a client's financial assets, financial planners must consider not only the asset classes available, but also client characteristics and external asset allocation factors. Client characteristics help financial planners answer two questions:

(1) What is the client's goal—current income, capital appreciation, or capital preservation?

(2) How aggressively allocated does the portfolio need to be to achieve the goal?

Aggressiveness can be loosely defined as the amount of additional risk a portfolio must take on in order to achieve a corresponding incremental increase in potential returns. In other words, the more aggressive the portfolio, the greater the expected return of the portfolio, but the higher the anticipated volatility or risk.

Figure 13.14 summarizes the risk and return characteristics of commonly used investments. The level of aggressiveness required within an asset allocation structure depends heavily on the difference between the current value of invested assets and the desired level of invested assets. From a time value of money perspective, there are two factors that control the difference between the amount of money initially (or periodically) invested and the desired future value of the portfolio: rate of return and time horizon. Unless a client can delay the realization of a goal, or is willing and able to invest more money, a financial planner's only choice is to increase the aggressiveness of the portfolio in an attempt to achieve a greater rate of return.

Figure 13.14. Summary of Investment Characteristics by Investment Type.

Asset	Risk (Aggressiveness)			Potential Return	
	Liquidity	Marketability	Risk	Current Income	Capital Appreciation
Direct Investment					
Cash	High	High	Low	Low	None
Savings accounts	High	High	Low	Low	None
Certificates of deposit	Moderate	High	Low	None	Low to average
Treasury bills	High	High	Low	None	Low to average
Treasury bonds	High	High	Low	Low to average	Low to average

EE and I savings bonds	High	High	Low	None	Low to average
HH savings bonds	High	High	Low	Low to average	None
Federal agency bonds	High	High	Low	Average	Average
Municipal bonds	Moderate	Moderate	Moderate	Average	Average
Investment-grade corporate bonds	Moderate	High	Moderate	Average	Low
Speculative-grade corporate bonds	Moderate	Moderate	Moderate	High	Low to high
Zero-coupon bonds	Moderate	Moderate	Moderate	None	Average to high
Preferred stock	Moderate	Moderate to high	Moderate	Average to high	None to low
Common stock	Moderate to high	High	Moderate to high	Low to average	Low to high
Collectibles (coins, stamps, art, etc.)	Low	Low to moderate	High	None	Dependent on supply and demand
Precious metals	Low to moderate	Moderate	Moderate to high	None	Dependent on supply and demand
Real estate	Low	Low	High	Low to high	Dependent on supply and demand

Indirect Investment

Money market funds	High	High	Low	Low to average	None
Bond funds/ ETFs	High	High	Low	Average to high	Low to average
Stock funds/ ETFs	High	High	Moderate	Low to average	Average to high

Commodity funds	Moderate to high	Moderate to high	High	Low to average	Low to high
Real estate investment trusts (REITs)	Moderate to high	Moderate to high	High	Average to high	Low to average
Derivative Investment					
Options and warrants	Low	Low to moderate	High	None to average	Dependent on underlying security
Futures	Low	High	High	None	Dependent on underlying contracts

[C] Structuring a Portfolio

Once classes of appropriate assets have been selected, a financial planner must determine how to combine them into a cohesive portfolio. **Portfolio construction** begins with the client and is based on a client's goal(s) and risk profile. The development of portfolio recommendations should focus on maximizing returns while minimizing risks. This can be done by targeting a specific risk level. It is then up to the financial planner to optimize the return. Risk can be quantified either by **standard deviation** or beta.

Financial planners should use caution when attempting to risk-weight a portfolio. **Beta**, which is a risk measure relative to a benchmark, is accurate only if the asset allocation model matches well with the benchmark from which it was calculated. As such, risk-weighting only works if the R^2 of a portfolio, relative to the benchmark, is very high (i.e., .80 or greater).

A second issue arises from the fact that the **capital asset pricing model (CAPM)** derives beta using a linear regression model. Because all asset class betas are linear, the beta of a targeted portfolio becomes the weighted average beta of the underlying asset classes. The following example illustrates this issue.

Example. Assume a client has an asset allocation of 50 percent domestic equities, 25 percent international equities, 10 percent commodities, and 5 percent each to real estate, bonds, and cash. Based on the data shown in Figure 13.15, this portfolio has a beta of 0.88 as indexed to the S&P 500. This portfolio has a standard deviation of almost 24 percent. The standard deviation of the S&P 500, during the same period, is just slightly more than 21 percent. Although the portfolio exhibits less systematic risk than the market, it produces more total variability in returns. It turns out that it is possible to construct a portfolio with a higher beta but a lower standard deviation.

Figure 13.15. Sample Risk and Return Statistics.

Asset	10-year Arithmetic Average Return	5-year Standard Deviation	Asset Beta vs. Best Index
Equity 1	7.00	20.21	0.757
Equity 2	8.41	19.08	0.887
International equity	9.29	28.51	1.046
Real estate	17.10	35.19	1.131
Commodity	14.59	39.42	0.682
Real estate bond	5.93	3.18	1.058
Treasury bond	6.32	3.77	1.066
Corporate bond 1	14.33	13.09	1.372
Corporate bond 2	3.57	11.33	0.850
Money market	3.50	1.78	0.211

[D] Strategic and Tactical Asset Allocation Models

Strategic asset allocation is the process of setting target (percentage) allocations for each asset class based on the long-term objective of the portfolio. The portfolio is then periodically rebalanced back to the original asset allocation percentages. Periodic adjustments are necessary because different asset classes appreciate and depreciate at varying rates and times in the market cycle. This is the basis of a **buy-and-hold investing strategy**, where strategic asset allocations change only as the client's goals and needs change.

Historically, a standard **three-asset-class model** has predominated, where a portfolio is divided among domestic equities, debt, and cash. However, based on continued research and considering recent economic events, a more diversified approach is becoming more prevalent. A **five-asset-class model** is often used to derive normative portfolio recommendations. In addition to the original three asset classes, real estate and commodities are often included when developing a strategic asset allocation. Greater emphasis is also being placed on international equities and debt holdings.

Example. If a client wants a portfolio designed for maximum capital appreciation with tax minimization, with a secondary goal of maintaining purchasing power over an extended period of time, a financial planner might recommend a portfolio that is comprised of 50 percent domestic equities, 25 percent international equities, 10 percent commodities, and 5 percent each to real estate, zero-coupon bonds, and cash. This allocation can be rebalanced annually to maintain these targets until a change in the client's situation dictates a reallocation. For instance, if a client were to lose their job, it might be prudent to alter the composition of the portfolio to reduce volatility. In the long run, strategic allocations are the most important determinant of total return for a broadly diversified portfolio.

Some financial planners prefer using a **tactical asset allocation** approach. Tactical allocation allows for a more active management style by setting a range of percentages in each asset class (e.g., a domestic equity range of 45 percent to 60 percent rather than a fixed target of, say, 50 percent). The use of a range gives a financial planner the ability to be more opportunistic about changing allocations to match current market conditions.

Based on economic forecasts, tactical allocations attempt to add value by overweighting asset classes that are expected to outperform on a relative basis and underweighting those expected to underperform. The value added can be measured with alpha. **Alpha** is calculated by subtracting expected returns (usually estimated using the capital asset pricing model) from actual portfolio returns. This should not be confused with attempting to **time the market** (i.e., predicting short-term swings in the market); rather, tactical asset allocation allows for changes to an allocation when longer-term economic conditions might favor one asset class over another. For instance, having 5 percent of a portfolio invested in real estate might make very good sense over the long-term, but not having as much or any exposure to real estate in 2008 would have turned out to be a very wise tactical move at that time.

To some extent, tactical asset allocation is a **dynamic allocation strategy** that actively adjusts the apportionment of a portfolio based on short- and long-term market forecasts, with the objective of increasing appreciation potential. **Sector rotation** is a basic form of tactical asset allocation in which an investor attempts to outperform a market index, such as the S&P 500, by tracking the economic cycle. Sector rotation, as in investment approach, was first introduced as a way to incorporate National Bureau of Economic Research (NBER) data on the business cycle into investment decisions. Proponents of the strategy use their analyses of the current phase of the business cycle, and relative currency valuations, to anticipate industrial and household demand for goods and services. For example, during an economic contraction, demand for commodities typically decreases, which then relaxes the general price pressure on downstream goods.

Another form of tactical allocation is the construction of **core-and-satellite portfolios**. The core-and-satellite investing style, as shown in Figure 13.16, is designed to maximize returns while minimizing **trading expenses** and **tax liabilities**. The approach comprises two types of investments: **core holdings** and **satellite investments** (i.e., speculative or rotational). Financial planners who use this strategy first decide how much to allocate to core portfolio investments, which are those that an investor intends to hold through a number of business and market cycles. This is essentially the investor's strategic allocation. Often, core investments are held as index positions. Core investments are rarely managed tactically, resulting in high tax efficiency. The remainder of the assets can then be dedicated to the satellite portion of the portfolio. Satellite holdings are actively managed. These investments tend to be short-term holdings that allow a financial planner to position assets tactically for maximum capital gain potential.

Figure 13.16. A Core-and-Satellite Portfolio.

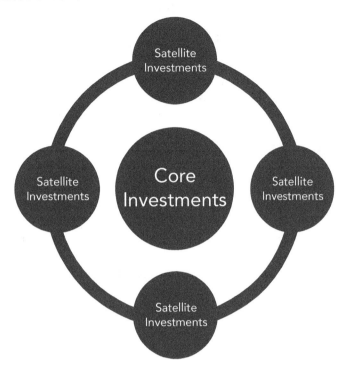

This portfolio management approach is used to add "excess returns" (i.e., alpha) by enhancing the return of an asset class upswing by adding exposure to that class of assets. When a financial planner increases a position in or exposure to a market rotation, they are adding leverage. For example, if a portfolio has a "normal" strategic allocation that results in a portfolio beta of 0.8, and the market increases 12 percent when the risk-free rate is 2 percent, then, according to the **capital asset pricing model (CAPM)**, the portfolio should rise only 10 percent.[7] However, if the portfolio has a beta of 1.1, then the CAPM would suggest that the portfolio should rise by 13 percent.[8] If the financial planner mistimes the market and increases the beta just before a market downturn of 12 percent, then the portfolio will be expected to lose slightly more than 13 percent.[9]

[E] Alternative Investments

Alternative investments are designed to provide investors with portfolio diversification. **Hedge funds** represent the best known type of alternative investment. Hedge funds are pooled investments that attempt to add diversification to an investor's portfolio or to meet a specific investment objective (e.g., purchasing distressed securities, engaging in arbitrage, or implementing equity long-short positions). Given their regulatory status, hedge funds are private and open only to **accredited investors**. According to the Securities and Exchange Commission (SEC), "An *accredited investor*, in the context of a natural person, includes anyone who (a) earned income that exceeded $200,000 (or $300,000 together with a spouse) in each of the prior two years, and reasonably expects the same for the current year, *or* (b) has a net worth over $1 million, either alone or together with a spouse (excluding the value of the person's primary residence)".[10] Hedge funds also tend to have high expense ratios and restricted levels of marketability and liquidity.

Private equity funds raise money and invest in privately held companies. Once the private company issues an initial public offering or is acquired by another firm, the fund is liquidated. Private equity can also include **venture capital funds** that invest in start-up companies. Similar to private equity funds, **private placement debt funds** exist to allow investors an opportunity to diversify into non-rated debt securities issued by private companies. **Hard asset funds** invest in physical assets, such as real estate and commodities. Some hard asset funds invest in assets with limited markets, including wine, art, coins, and stamps. A **funds of funds** is another alternative investment that is sometimes used by investors to create diversification. As the name implies, these funds buy shares in other mutual funds.

Each of the alternatives described here tend to be available to institutional and sophisticated investors. **Liquid alternative funds** can be used by other investors to obtain similar market diversification and performance. Liquid alternative funds use non-traditional investment strategies, hedging techniques, and leverage to enhance performance. Downsides associated with all the investments discussed here include high fees, general lack of transparency in day-to-day holdings, and restrictions on the type of client that may invest. Before recommending an alternative investment or service, a financial planner must perform a **due diligence** investigation focusing on expenses, fees, distribution restrictions, tax liabilities, and the long-term performance of the fund's manager.

[F] Applying Planning Skills to the Hubble Case

As with other topics within a comprehensive financial plan, only modest changes will be made to the initial investment management recommendations developed at Step Three of the financial planning process, although it is possible that new client information or data can necessitate the need for a reevaluation and more significant changes. Figure 3.17 provides a summary of the final investment management recommendations that match the Hubble family's financial goals.

Figure 13.17. Investment Recommendations for Chandler and Rachel.

While there are many different possible recommendations that can help Chandler and Rachel Hubble reach their financial goals, the following strategies represent one potential approach. Each recommendation is linked to the Hubble family's investment goals. In general, the recommendations correspond to those developed at Step Three of the financial planning process.					

Emergency fund recommendations:

- Emergency fund assets should be held in cash and cash equivalent investments, such as savings and checking accounts, money market mutual funds, money market accounts, and other short-term investments. Some emergency funds may be placed in savings bonds.
- It is also possible to designate the cash value from the family's life insurance policies as an emergency fund source, assuming there is not a recommendation to cancel these policies.
- The saving goal is to obtain six months of fixed and variable expenses, excluding taxes, in one or more accounts.

Retirement investment recommendations:

- The following portfolio reallocation recommendation, built using a strategic management approach, can be used to manage retirement assets:

	Weight	Asset Return	Weighted Return	Asset Beta	Weighted Beta
Haley G&I Fund	55.00%	8.00%	4.400%	0.82	0.451
Ely Fund	25.00%	6.10%	1.525%	0.51	0.128
International Fund	13.00%	10.00%	1.300%	0.51	0.066
Value Fund	7.00%	9.00%	0.630%	1.23	0.086
Portfolio	**100.00%**		**7.855%**		**0.731**

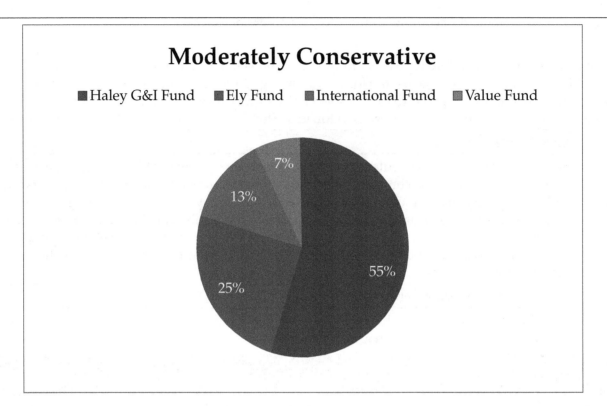

Moderately Conservative

■ Haley G&I Fund   ■ Ely Fund   ■ International Fund   ■ Value Fund

7%

13%

25%

55%

Note that there are no tax implications associated with the reallocation of 401(k) and IRA assets if this portfolio is used.

Education investment recommendations:

- The following portfolio reallocation recommendation, built using a strategic management approach, can be used to manage educational assets:

	Weight	Asset Return	Weighted Return	Asset Beta	Weighted Beta
Value Fund	20.00%	9.00%	1.800%	1.04	0.208
Growth Fund	20.00%	10.20%	2.040%	1.23	0.246
Konza Fund	20.00%	9.20%	1.840%	1.08	0.216
Rocket Fund	15.00%	14.00%	2.100%	1.5	0.225
International Fund	15.00%	10.00%	1.500%	0.51	0.077
Acquisitions Fund	10.00%	7.50%	0.750%	0.09	0.009
Portfolio	**100.00%**		**10.030%**		**0.981**

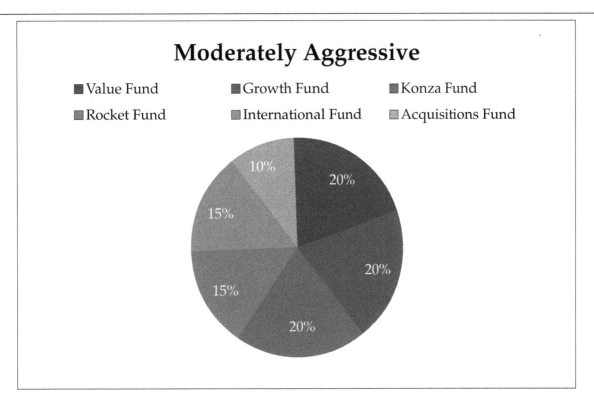

The non-qualified assets used in this portfolio may be subject to capital gains taxes. The annual earnings on assets held in non-qualified account will also be taxable, which will reduce subsequent year income projections.

Home improvement and art gallery investment recommendations:

- The following portfolio reallocation recommendation, built using a strategic management approach, can be used to manage home improvement goal assets:

	Weight	Asset Return	Weighted Return	Asset Beta	Weighted Beta
Value Fund	20.00%	9.00%	1.800%	1.04	0.208
Growth Fund	20.00%	10.20%	2.040%	1.23	0.246
Konza Fund	20.00%	9.20%	1.840%	1.08	0.216
Rocket Fund	15.00%	14.00%	2.100%	1.50	0.225
International Fund	15.00%	10.00%	1.500%	0.51	0.077
Acquisitions Fund	10.00%	7.50%	0.750%	0.09	0.009
Portfolio	**100.00%**		**10.030%**		**0.981**

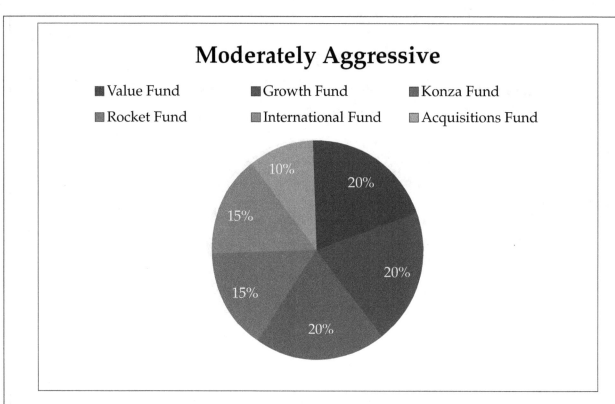

Note: The non-qualified assets used in this portfolio may be subject to capital gains taxes. The annual earnings on assets held in non-qualified account will also be taxable, which will reduce subsequent year income projections.

Step 5: Present the Financial Planning Recommendation(s)

Clients tend to seek the help of a financial planner for investment planning guidance to increase the capital appreciation potential of their investments, to increase the amount of current income earned from their investments, and/or to reduce the amount of taxes paid on their investments. However, clients are often unaware of what might be necessary to increase their real, risk-adjusted, or after-tax returns. As noted in this chapter, nothing is more important than a financial planner's skill in matching one or more investment alternatives to a client's objective. Although the tendency when dealing with investments is to focus on specific products, this chapter illustrates the importance of following a procedure of portfolio management. Financial planners and clients often find that the simplest strategy makes for the best recommendation.

Figure 13.18 highlights some of the important factors to consider when presenting investment recommendations to Chandler and Rachel Hubble.

Figure 13.18. Factors to Consider When Presenting Investment Recommendations.

When presenting investment recommendations to a client, it is worth remembering that the client may be apprehensive about investing given that returns are unknown and volatile. In other areas of financial planning, the outcome of recommendations is easily anticipated. For example, recommending the purchase of an insurance policy will provide known protections for a client according to the terms of the policy purchased. With investing, a recommended portfolio will be designed to achieve an expected risk and return profile. That being said, the possibility of variance from the expected return is significant, even for portfolios that are carefully constructed according to the principles described in this chapter. It is important to manage a client's expectations and to communicate that the portfolio will not achieve the expected return each and every year. It may be helpful to provide ongoing educational interventions with clients, either individually or through group meetings, about investing principles. Familiarity influences risk perception, so helping a client feel more familiar with investing principals may help the client learn to be more comfortable taking risk.

As noted in the communication and counseling chapter, it is always a good idea to consider the learning and information processing preferences of clients. A best practice calls for including visual aids, such as pie charts, dynamic graphs, and other visual materials, in the investment section of a financial plan, as well as when the plan is being presented in person. Many clients, particularly visual learners, appreciate the inclusion of figures and graphs when receiving investment recommendations. Visual and written materials can be used to provide a client with a broader understanding of investment and portfolio recommendations, which may help to prevent the client from becoming overwhelmed with the intricacies of implementing investment recommendations.

Step 6: Implement the Financial Planning Recommendation(s)

In many ways, the development and presentation of investment planning recommendations is the most important part of the systematic financial planning process. This is particularly true in the context of investment planning. Although there may be a temptation to develop complex and intricate recommendations, this is not always appropriate or even necessary. Lack of implementation by a client is the leading cause of plan failure. Making plans relatively easy to implement is important. Some of the best planning strategies accomplish more than one objective, such as hedging inflation while providing current income or maximizing long-term appreciation while minimizing tax consequence. As such, it is imperative that recommendations be easily understood, conceptually valid, and cost effective. As discussed in this chapter, it is of paramount importance when developing or choosing strategies to remember that a client's goals should dominate the decision-making process. Financial planners should always solicit a client's collaboration in decision making and implementation. For the majority of investment planning recommendations, a client should be able to quickly understand the reasoning behind each suggestion and the potential outcomes associated with implementation. This means that answers to the core implementation questions of who, what, when, where, why, how, and how much should be clear, concise, and understandable.

The presentation of a recommendation needs to match a client's information processing style and preferences. Figure 13.19 shows how one of the recommendations developed for Chandler and Rachel can be presented within a financial plan.

Figure 13.19. Implementing an Investment Recommendation for the Hubble Family.

Recommendation #1: Place emergency fund assets in cash and cash equivalent investments.	
Who:	Chandler and Rachel.
What:	Cash and cash equivalents include savings and checking accounts, money market mutual funds, money market accounts, savings bonds, and other short-term investments. Our recommendation also involves designating the cash value from your life insurance policies as an emergency fund source.
When:	Within the next thirty to forty-five days.
Where:	Nixa National Bank.
Why:	Cash and cash equivalents are appropriate this goal because these assets match your ultra-short time horizon, your risk tolerance, and the need for liquidity.
How:	Continue to hold cash assets at Nixa National Bank. Use excess cash flow to fund the emergency fund.
How much:	Six months of total dedicated and discretionary expenses, excluding taxes.
Effect on cash flow:	This recommendation has no immediate impact on cash flow; savings is already accounted for as an ongoing household expense.

Step 7: Monitor Progress and Update

As discussed in this chapter, when allocating a client's assets, financial planners must consider not only the asset classes available, but also client characteristics and environmental asset allocation factors. In terms of ongoing monitoring of investment recommendations, client characteristics, which involve the goal of the client's portfolio and how aggressively the assets in the portfolio can be allocated within the risk comfort level of the client, are of primary importance. Changes to a client's financial, employment, household, or family situation all warrant a reevaluation of previously made investment recommendations.

Additionally, environmental factors pertaining to the current and prospective economic landscape must be monitored on an ongoing basis. Interpreting the influence of economic and market changes is an important financial planning function. At a minimum, a financial planner should regularly monitor environmental factors including asset class returns, domestic interest rates, stock and bond yields, monetary and fiscal policies, and inflation. Actual or anticipated changes in one or more of these factors can be enough to warrant a reevaluation of previously made recommendations.

Changes in or to a client's circumstances should prompt a review and/or reevaluation of previously made recommendations. At a minimum, a client's investment and portfolio situation (particularly the risk and return profile of investment holdings) should be monitored on an annual basis. It is important to monitor investment performance to ensure that goal achievement is still achievable across time. A client's health, employment status, marital status, preferences, and attitudes can change over time. Changes almost always warrant a review of previously implemented recommendations. Figure 13.20 provides an overview of some of the factors that require ongoing monitoring for Chandler and Rachel Hubble.

Figure 13.20. Issues to Monitor in the Hubble Case.

> **Given the number of assumptions, inputs, and market factors that can potentially impact one or more investment recommendations, a financial planner working with Chandler and Rachel Hubble must be diligent in monitoring implemented recommendations. The following represent the types of household level data that should be reviewed periodically:**
>
> - Any changes to the Hubble family's financial situation or status.
> - Any event that might change Chandler's and Rachel's risk capacity, including job status changes, loss or increase in bonus, or a change in insurance coverage.
> - The possibility of obtaining scholarship funding to help offset college expenses or other changes related to Phoebe as she ages.
> - The possibility of receiving an inheritance or other windfall.
> - A meaningful change in risk perceptions or risk tolerance for either Chandler or Rachel.
> - A change in the time horizon associated with any goal.
> - Any macro-economic event that might impact the family (e.g., a change in federal or state tax policy).
> - Pregnancy or adoption.
> - Divorce.
>
> Almost daily monitoring of the investment markets (including interest rates and inflation) is an important financial planning task associated with this step in the financial planning process. Significant changes (actual or anticipated) related to inflation, interest rates, tax laws, and/or estate laws should prompt a reevaluation of previously made recommendations. Issues related to elections, local, state, and federal policies, international trade, terror threats, and war need to also be monitored and evaluated in the context of the Hubbles' goal achievement.

13.2 COMPREHENSIVE HUBBLE CASE

Investment planning is a fundamental element within nearly all comprehensive financial plans. It is quite common for financial planners to spend the majority of their day-to-day practice dealing with investment planning topics, including developing strategies, monitoring the markets, and working with clients who have questions and concerns about market events. For some financial planners, a portion of annual pay is tied to investment performance through the sale of investment products and/or through the management of investment returns. As such, it is common for the investment planning section of a financial plan to be long and detailed. The following narrative is an example of how the investment section within a comprehensive financial plan can be written.

Investments

Overview of Investments:

At XYZ Financial Planning, investment planning and management occurs on a daily basis as our team of financial planning professionals monitors the markets and client portfolios. Important activities associated with investment management practices involves monitoring your portfolio's cash needs, rebalancing portfolio assets, monitoring market performance, and proactively allocating assets in anticipation of market events. Our firm's portfolio recommendations are shaped by the following five client-centered factors: (1) your financial risk tolerance, (2) your expectations about future market conditions, (3) your financial knowledge and experience in the markets, (4) your goal time horizon, and (5) your financial capacity to deal with uncertain outcomes.

Investment Definitions:

The following definitions will be useful as you review the analysis presented in this section:

- *Beta*: A measure of uncertainty, or risk, associated with an investment. Beta is useful when comparing the riskiness of an investment relative to a benchmark.

- *Equities (stocks)*: The primary purpose of equity investing is to generate capital appreciation. Stocks have historically had the highest asset returns after adjusting for inflation. A secondary purpose is the generation of current income through dividend payments.

- *Bonds*: Fixed-income securities that provide income and possibly capital gains. Generally, bonds are considered to be less risky than equities.

- *Certificate of Deposit (CD)*: A bank issued time deposit that pays a fixed rate of interest for a predetermined time period. CDs are federally insured up to $250,000 per account holder per institution.

- *Risk capacity*: Represents the amount of financial cushion or the safety net available to a client both before and after an investment decision has been implemented.

- *Risk tolerance*: The maximum level of uncertainty a client is willing to accept when making an investment decision that entails the possibility of a loss.

- *Time horizon*: The desired amount of time until the client would like to achieve the goal.

Planning Assumptions:

- Rachel's annuity is invested 100 percent in the Potsdam Fixed Annuity earning 5 percent (no other investment alternatives are available within the annuity). Rachel, you originally purchased the annuity when you were thirty-four years of age. The annuity has a seven-year declining withdrawal penalty.

- Chandler and Rachel, your traditional IRAs are invested in one-year certificates of deposit (CD) maturing in a few months. The CDs yield 3.5 percent annually. The renewable rate is also 3.5 percent.

- In the event that an investment asset is sold, your preference is to assume that the basis in all after-tax investments is equal to 50 percent of the fair market value of these assets, and that all investment gains are subject to capital gains tax rates.

Goals:

- Develop an investment plan for Phoebe's education fund.

- Evaluate tax-advantaged investing alternatives.

- Develop and manage household portfolios to match the time horizon, risk capacity, and risk tolerance of Chandler and Rachel for (1) retirement, (2) special situation needs, and (3) an emergency fund.

Your Current Investment Situation:

The table below summarizes the holdings, the market value, and the current yield of your current cash and investment assets:

Hubble Current Portfolio Summary			
Account	Investment Holding	Market Value	Current Yield
Savings Account	Cash	$10,000	3.00%
Checking Account	Cash	$3,500	0.00%
Money Market Account	Cash	$10,000	3.00%
Checking Account (for art gallery savings)	Cash	$5,000	0.00%
Investment Account	EE Bonds	$25,000	3.5% Deferred
Investment Account	Haley G&I Fund	$19,000	3.20%
Investment Account	Konza Fund	$13,000	1.75%
Investment Account	Ruth Fund	$13,000	4.00%
Investment Account	Sagebrush Fund	$8,000	0.50%
Chandler's 401(k)	Consumer Fund	$69,000	8.75%
Chandler's 401(k)	Graham Fund	$134,000	4.10%
Rachel's 401(k)	Rocket Fund	$15,250	14.00%
Rachel's Rollover IRA	Ruth Fund	$32,500	4.80%
Rachel's Traditional IRA	Certificate of Deposit	$52,000	3.50%
Conservative Annuity	Potsdam Fixed Annuity	$125,000	5.00%

Chandler, you are apprehensive about investing. Rachel, you feel comfortable taking additional risk if you are confident you can earn higher returns. Based on the results of the risk tolerance questionnaire you completed, our team has determined that, as a household, you have a combined moderate to low level of financial risk tolerance.

The following recommendations are based on your goals, time horizon, risk tolerance, general risk capacity, and available investment alternatives:

Investment Recommendations:

The following tables summarize the recommendations that have been designed to help you reach your investment planning goals. As with all recommendations presented in this financial plan, our firm is available to answer any questions that might arise and to assist with specific implementation procedures.

Recommendation #1: Place emergency fund assets in cash and cash equivalent investments.	
Who:	Chandler and Rachel.
What:	Cash and cash equivalents include savings and checking accounts, money market mutual funds, money market accounts, savings bonds, and other short-term investments. Our recommendation also involves designating the cash value from your life insurance policies as an emergency fund source.
When:	Within the next thirty to forty-five days.
Where:	Nixa National Bank.
Why:	Cash and cash equivalents are appropriate this goal because these assets match your ultra-short time horizon, your risk tolerance, and the need for liquidity.
How:	Continue to hold cash assets at Nixa National Bank. Use excess cash flow to fund the emergency fund.
How much:	Six months of total dedicated and discretionary expenses, excluding taxes.
Effect on cash flow:	This recommendation has no immediate impact on cash flow; savings is already accounted for as an ongoing household expense.

Recommendation #2: Reallocate retirement funding assets.	
Who:	XYZ Financial Planning.
What:	The following investment portfolio, designed using a strategic management approach, is recommended for your retirement assets. The portfolio should be allocated to the Haley G&I Fund (55 percent), the Ely Fund (25 percent), the International Fund (13 percent), and the Value Fund (7 percent).
When:	Within the next thirty to forty-five days, after the Investment Policy Statement (IPS) has been signed (an example of an IPS is illustrated in Appendix 13A).
Where:	Investment recommendation implementation will occur at the office of XYZ Financial Planning.
Why:	The portfolio shown below has historically generated a rate of return that matches the retirement funding need.
How:	After reviewing the investment recommendations, sign the Investment Policy Statement. Upon your signature, XYZ Financial Planning staff members will begin the allocation process.
How much:	All assets currently allocated to retirement savings, plus all additional contributions.
Effect on cash flow:	Implementation of this recommendation has no impact on cash flow.

Note: There will be no tax implications associated with the reallocation of 401(k) and IRA assets if this portfolio is used.

Retirement Portfolio

	Weight	Asset Return	Weighted Return	Asset Beta	Weighted Beta
Haley G&I Fund	55.00%	8.00%	4.400%	0.82	0.451
Ely Fund	25.00%	6.10%	1.525%	0.51	0.128
International Fund	13.00%	10.00%	1.300%	0.51	0.066
Value Fund	7.00%	9.00%	0.630%	1.23	0.086
Portfolio	100.00%		7.855%		0.731

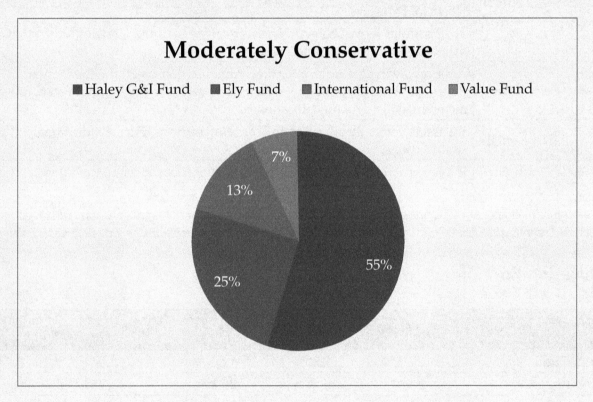

Moderately Conservative

Haley G&I Fund   Ely Fund   International Fund   Value Fund

Recommendation #3: Reallocate education funding assets.	
Who:	XYZ Financial Planning.
What:	The following investment portfolio, designed using a strategic management approach, is recommended for your education planning assets. The portfolio should be allocated to the Value Fund (20 percent), the Growth Fund (20 percent), the Konza Fund (20 percent), the Rocket Fund (15 percent), the International Fund (15 percent), and the Acquisitions Fund (10 percent).
When:	Within the next thirty to forty-five days, after the Investment Policy Statement (IPS) has been signed (an example of an IPS is illustrated in Appendix 13A).
Where:	Investment recommendation implementation will occur at the office of XYZ Financial Planning.
Why:	The portfolio shown below has historically generated a rate of return that matches the education fund need.
How:	After reviewing the investment recommendations, sign the Investment Policy Statement. Upon your signature, XYZ Financial Planning staff members will begin the allocation process.
How much:	All assets currently allocated to education savings, plus all additional contributions.
Effect on cash flow:	Implementation of this recommendation has no impact on cash flow.

The non-qualified assets used in this portfolio may be subject to capital gains taxes. The annual earnings on assets held in non-qualified account will also be taxable, which will reduce subsequent year income projections.

Education Portfolio

	Weight	Asset Return	Weighted Return	Asset Beta	Weighted Beta
Value Fund	20.00%	9.00%	1.800%	1.04	0.208
Growth Fund	20.00%	10.20%	2.040%	1.23	0.246
Konza Fund	20.00%	9.20%	1.840%	1.08	0.216
Rocket Fund	15.00%	14.00%	2.100%	1.5	0.225
International Fund	15.00%	10.00%	1.500%	0.51	0.077
Acquisitions Fund	10.00%	7.50%	0.750%	0.09	0.009
Portfolio	100.00%		10.030%		0.981

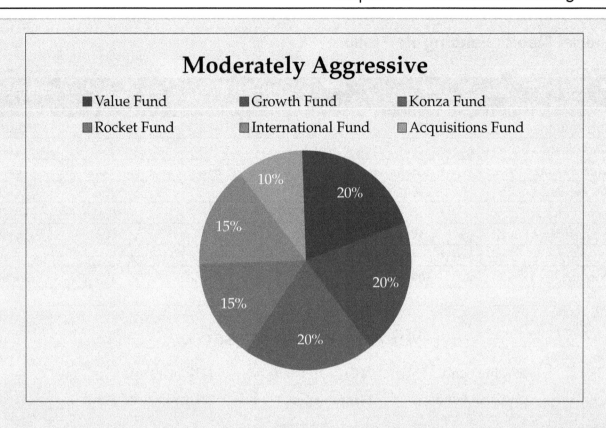

Recommendation #4: Reallocate special needs funding assets (investments for home improvement and art gallery).	
Who:	XYZ Financial Planning.
What:	The following investment portfolio, designed using a strategic management approach, is recommended for your special needs funding assets. The portfolio should be allocated to the Value Fund (20 percent), the Growth Fund (20 percent), the Konza Fund (20 percent), the Rocket Fund (15 percent), the International Fund (15 percent), and the Acquisitions Fund (10 percent).
When:	Within the next thirty to forty-five days, after the Investment Policy Statement (IPS) has been signed (an example of an IPS is illustrated in Appendix 13A).
Where:	Investment recommendation implementation will occur at the office of XYZ Financial Planning.
Why:	The portfolio shown below has historically generated a rate of return that matches the special needs funding requirement.
How:	After reviewing the investment recommendations, sign the Investment Policy Statement. Upon your signature, XYZ Financial Planning staff members will begin the allocation process.
How much:	All assets currently allocated to special needs funding savings, plus all additional contributions.
Effect on cash flow:	Implementation of this recommendation has no impact on cash flow.

Note: The non-qualified assets used in this portfolio may be subject to capital gains taxes. The annual earnings on assets held in non-qualified account will also be taxable, which will reduce subsequent year income projections.

Special Needs Funding Portfolio

	Weight	Asset Return	Weighted Return	Asset Beta	Weighted Beta
Value Fund	20.00%	9.00%	1.800%	1.04	0.208
Growth Fund	20.00%	10.20%	2.040%	1.23	0.246
Konza Fund	20.00%	9.20%	1.840%	1.08	0.216
Rocket Fund	15.00%	14.00%	2.100%	1.50	0.225
International Fund	15.00%	10.00%	1.500%	0.51	0.077
Acquisitions Fund	10.00%	7.50%	0.750%	0.09	0.009
Portfolio	100.00%		10.030%		0.981

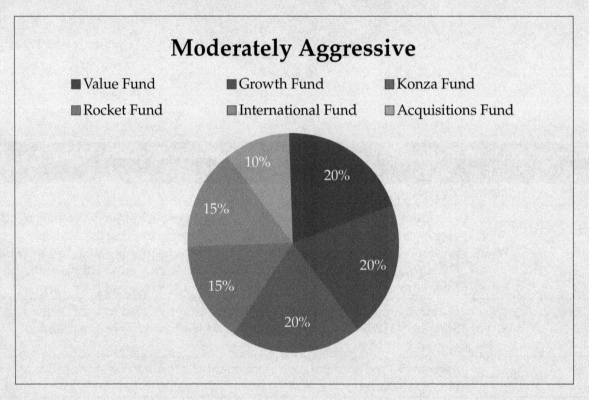

Current vs. Recommended Outcome:

Chandler and Rachel, the rate of return you are earning on investments across each of your portfolios is generally too low to meet stated financial objectives and goals. The new portfolio allocations recommended above have been designed to achieve a rate of return that matches your household risk tolerance and goal time horizons.

Alternative Recommendations and Outcome(s):

The portfolio recommended for Phoebe's education savings is approximate at this point. The actual investment options available in the MOST 529 plan may not match exactly with the mutual funds used in the portfolio recommendation. Our team will work to match available 529 plan funds to those in the portfolio recommendation. Once you have opened the 529 plan for Phoebe, please provide our team with a list of the available investments.

Plan Implementation and Monitoring Procedures:

As an element of the financial planning agreement, you will receive investment portfolio reports every quarter by mail or secure email (depending on your stated communication preferences). Additionally, you will be able to see your investment account performance at any time by logging into your secured custodian account. Our firm's client portal also provides a live summary of investment returns across all your investment accounts. It is important to note that the investment returns reported across portfolios is net of financial planning and asset management fees.

As noted throughout this financial plan, there is volatility risk inherent in investing. You can expect to see investment and portfolio returns and performance fluctuate daily; for this reason, our team suggests that you monitor your investment performance monthly, rather than daily. In any event, our team is available at any time to answer questions about your investment holdings.

Moving forward, please notify our team if any of the following events or changes occur, as changes may indicate a need to reevaluate your investment portfolio allocations:

- Any changes to your family's financial situation or status.

- Any event that might change your risk capacity, including job status changes, loss or increase in bonus, or a change in insurance coverage.

- The possibility of obtaining scholarship funding to help offset college expenses or other changes related to Phoebe as she ages.

- The possibility of receiving an inheritance or other windfall.

- A meaningful change in your risk perceptions or risk tolerance.

- A change in the time horizon associated with any goal.

- Pregnancy or adoption.

- Divorce.

13.3 SELF-TEST

[A] Questions

Self-Test 1

An investor's willingness to engage in a risky financial behavior in which she can lose money is called:

(a) risk perception.

(b) risk preference

(c) risk tolerance.

(d) risk capacity.

Self-Test 2

Ted is hoping to identify an index to benchmark his portfolio performance. He has determined the following R^2 values for four indexes. Which is the best index to use as his benchmark?

(a) S&P 500: $R^2 = .78$

(b) NASDAQ: $R^2 = .85$

(c) Wilshire 5000: $R^2 = .82$

(d) IFCI: $R^2 = .77$

Self-Test 3

Avery would like to retire in twenty years. If she needs $6.4 million on her first day of retirement, what is her required rate of return assuming she can save $5,000 per month?

(a) 3.14%

(b) 4.84%

(c) 7.90%

(d) 9.78%

Self-Test 4

CJ would like to purchase an asset that provides relatively high liquidity with high marketability. All the following assets are appropriate, EXCEPT:

(a) U.S. equities.

(b) Treasury securities.

(c) Corporate bonds.

(d) Real estate.

Self-Test 5

A financial planner is attempting to determine the required rate of return for a portfolio. What is the expected return, based on the CAPM, using the following assumptions?

- Return of the Market = 12 percent

- Portfolio Return = 11 percent

- Risk Free Rate = 3 percent

- Portfolio Beta = .80

(a) 9.40 percent

(b) 14.20 percent

(c) 11.00 percent

(d) 12.60 percent

[B] Answers

Question 1: c

Question 2: b

Question 3: a

Question 4: d

Question 5: b

CHAPTER RESOURCES

Benninga, S. *Financial Modeling*, 3rd Ed. Boston: MIT Press, 2008.

Boone, N., and L. Lubitz. *Creating an Investment Policy Statement.* Denver, CO: FPA Press, 2004.

California Debt and Investment Advisory Commission. *Issue Brief, Duration*, CDIAC# 06-10, 2007.

Ellis, C. D. *Investment Policy: How to Win the Loser's Game.* New York: McGraw-Hill, 1993.

FinaMetrica Risk Profiling System (www.riskprofiling.com/home).

FINRA Mutual Fund Expense Analyzer (apps.finra.org/fundanalyzer/1/fa.aspx).

Guy, J. W. *How to Invest Someone Else's Money*. Chicago: Irwin, 1994.

Investment Risk Tolerance Quiz (http://pfp.missouri.edu/research_IRTA.html).

Leimberg, S., et al. *The Tools and Techniques of Investment Planning,* 4th Ed. Cincinnati, OH: National Underwriter Company, 2017.

Murray, N. *Behavioral Investment Counseling*. Mattituck, NY: The Nick Murray Company, Inc., 2008.

Shefrin, H., and Mario B. "Behavioral Finance: Biases, Mean-Variance Returns, and Risk Premiums." *CFA Institute Conference Proceedings Quarterly*. June (2007): 4–11. Available at: www.ifa.com/pdf/behavioralfinancecp.v24.n2.pdf.

Siegel, L. B. *Benchmarks and Investment Management*. Charlottesville, VA: CFA Institute, 2003.

Susan Bradley's Sudden Money Institute (www.suddenmoney.com).

Trone, D. B., Allbright, W. R., and Taylor, P. R. *The Management of Investment Decisions*. Chicago: Irwin, 1996.

CHAPTER ENDNOTES

1. Additional modern portfolio statistics are described in greater detail in Appendix 13B.

2. Sharpe Ratio: $(12 - 5)/16$

3. Treynor Index: $[(0.12 - 0.03)/0.85]$

4. Jensen's Alpha: $(12\% - 14.65\%)$

5. If a financial planner achieved an annual alpha of 2.5 percent with an annualized tracking error of 6.25 percent, then the information ratio would be 0.4. What does 0.4 mean? Generally, a positive estimate is good sign.

6. The formula is shown with return of the portfolio (R_p) as an input; however, the return of an investment (R_i) can also be used in this formula.

7. CAPM: $[2\% + (0.8 \times (12\% - 2\%))]$

8. CAPM: $[2\% + (1.1 \times (12\% - 2\%))]$

9. CAPM: $[2\% + (1.1 \times (-12\% - 2\%))]$

10. Source: https://www.investor.gov/introduction-investing/general-resources/news-alerts/alerts-bulletins/investor-bulletins/updated-3.

Chapter 14

Education Planning

Learning Objectives

- Learning Objective 1: Estimate a client's education funding need.

- Learning Objective 2: Describe the features of different education saving plans.

- Learning Objective 3: Explain the tax benefits associated with providing and obtaining financial assistance for higher education costs.

- Learning Objective 4: Develop strategies a client can use to meet an education funding goal.

14.1 THE PROCESS OF EDUCATION PLANNING

As the cost of a college education and college loan debt reach unprecedented heights, planning one's own, a child's, or a grandchild's higher education funding need has grown in importance within the context of comprehensive financial planning. Financial planners have responded by assuming a more proactive role that goes beyond the projection of costs and needed investments to helping clients plan to maximize need- and merit-based aid, to choose tax-advantaged accounts, and to creatively combine strategies that help clients balance the cost of education against the need to fund other financial objectives and goals. The purpose of this chapter is to highlight how the financial planning process can be followed when conducting an education funding analysis.

14.2 STEP 1: UNDERSTAND THE CLIENT'S PERSONAL AND FINANCIAL CIRCUMSTANCES

A wide range of client characteristics, circumstances, and factors, both qualitative and quantitative, affect planning for education funding and the type of recommendations ultimately made. Unknown household and environmental information, and a generally brief time between determining a need and using funding, complicate the planning process. Layered onto what is already a complicated topic, educational goals tend to be highly emotional topics for parents, close family members, and children. Given the emotional latency that educational objectives prompt among some clients, it is important for a financial planner to help their clients balance the allocation of household resources in a way that ensures education and other goals receive similar treatment in a financial plan. As with all topic areas in financial planning, client attitudes, values, and expectations can influence planning assumptions, but in some ways, this is especially true in relation to education planning. Clients can sometimes, for example, be swayed by their desire to help a child at the expense of the client's own long-term well-being. Thus, it is important that financial planners take the time to fully explore client characteristics and circumstance factors as a foundation for the planning of education funding needs. In the context of this observation, Figure 14.1 provides a review of the Hubbles' personal and financial circumstances related to education planning. The information in Figure 14.1 is typical of what a financial planner should evaluate at the first step of the financial planning process.

Figure 14.1. The Hubbles' Personal and Financial Circumstances.

- Phoebe Hubble is five years old and in good health.
- Chandler and Rachel Hubble are committed to providing some financial assistance to help offset future college costs for Phoebe.
- Education planning may take priority over any other short-term goals or wants.
- The risk tolerance for Chandler and Rachel will influence the chosen strategy to meet the education planning goal, as well as the investment preferences within any education plan or product used to fund college costs.
- Chandler and Rachel believe "working in college builds character and workplace skills," and "paying for college increases appreciation for and dedication to an education." The clear implication is that while Chandler and Rachel have a strong desire to help pay Phoebe's college expenses, they may be open to limiting help to paying tuition, fees, room, and board. "Other" expenses may be Phoebe's responsibility.

> - Some of Chandler and Rachel's assumptions about education may reflect a lack of accurate knowledge about private college costs (depending on the size and reputation of the college), or the actual monthly or annual saving requirements to achieve their stated goal of funding all costs before Phoebe begins college. It is, thus, important to provide information at this stage of the planning process that can be used to help Chandler and Rachel refine their education funding goal(s).

14.3 STEP 2: IDENTIFY AND SELECT GOALS

The complexity of planning for college education funding and the variety of alternative approaches that can be presented often make it difficult for clients to choose and implement the most effective strategies. Financial planners are in an ideal position to help their clients explore the emotional issues underlying education goals and understand the advantages and disadvantages associated with different schooling alternatives. Access to and control of funds, the timeline for accumulating and disbursing funds, the effect on financial aid, and tax implications should be primary considerations when helping a client formalize an educational funding goal. Tax consequences include (1) tax-deferred versus taxable growth; (2) tax-free versus taxable withdrawals; (3) annual income tax reductions from state taxes, a possible federal adjustment for interest paid on student loans, and the credit for costs incurred; and (4) shifting of assets to potentially reduce or avoid estate taxes. Figure 14.2 provides an overview of education funding goals as they relate to the Hubble family.

Figure 14.2. The Hubbles' Education Goals.

> Chandler and Rachel were able to provide direct insights into their hopes and dreams for Phoebe's future education. When thinking about Phoebe's education situation, Chandler and Rachel stated the following goal:
>
> - Provide 100 percent of Phoebe's college education costs. Information that can be used to help further define the goal includes:
>   - Chandler and Rachel have a strong commitment to education. Although not their primary goal, providing funding for Phoebe is important and all attempts at meeting the goal should be considered.
>   - Phoebe is a bright and enthusiastic child and she shows an aptitude for learning. Her parents want to support this aptitude.
>   - She is actively involved in sports and plays the piano; there may be opportunities in the future to obtain scholarships based on her interests.
>   - Chandler and Rachel are proactive and are willing to sacrifice today in order to reach future goals.
>   - Identifying education planning strategies that can be recommended and implemented is important.
>   - Periodically monitoring the progress Chandler and Rachel are making towards the funding goal is important.

14.4 STEP 3: ANALYZE THE CLIENT'S CURRENT COURSE OF ACTION AND POTENTIAL ALTERNATIVE COURSE(S) OF ACTION

Many interrelated steps are involved in the analysis of a client's education planning situation. To complete not only an education funding assessment but also a comprehensive financial plan, it is essential that a client's goals and objectives guide the process. It is possible—and likely—that a wide range of personal client beliefs and expectations will affect the education funding analysis and the type of recommendations ultimately made. Client attitudes and beliefs, especially as these factors are converted into financial planning assumptions, may be more important and potentially more problematic in relation to education planning compared to other core content planning areas.

Planning Reminder

If a client's education funding assets are held in a **Coverdell Education Savings Account** (**CESA**), and the assets are not used for educational purposes, any distributions become fully taxable and subject to a 10 percent penalty. This hints at the importance of fully considering the choices associated with asset placement when considering college funding.

Understanding a client's characteristics and household preferences should precede any quantitative analyses or the identification and review of strategies. Just as strategies in any financial planning area must be matched to a client's needs, this customization must also be considered in education planning. The timing of planning efforts, the assumptions needed (which can vary dramatically depending on the timing), and client characteristics can disqualify the use of some otherwise beneficial strategies.

As such, it is worth noting again that education funding and planning strategies and recommendations must be matched well with a client's personal beliefs and values. Compared to their financial planner, parents, guardians, or other family members may hold different attitudes about how to pay for education expenses, either for themselves or their children. Planning the educational needs of a client's child generally must be balanced with planning for other household goals—most often, retirement. A thorough assessment to determine and quantify education planning needs can help clients make decisions that are in closest alignment with a wide range of goals.

Two fundamental questions require answers when conducting an education funding analysis:

(1) How much will the education cost?

(2) How will these costs be paid?

Many underlying factors need to be considered when addressing these questions. Foremost among these is framing the goal of 'college' broadly to include education, higher education, or post-secondary education. These terms allow clients to acknowledge that their children might or might not be interested in college, but that other options such as trade, technical, or arts programs may be a more appropriate choice. For some clients, the topic of paying for education can focus on the cost of private elementary or secondary school rather than public education. The following questions offer one way to explore some of the client-specific factors that underlie education planning:

- Do you plan to save enough to pay for higher education before the child enters the educational program?

- Do you plan to pay for the educational program after or while the child is enrolled in the educational program?

- Do you expect others to pay for some or all the child's education?

- Do you plan to use a combination of sources (e.g., personal, family, loans) to pay for the child's education?

Once a client has defined the direction of the education planning effort, focused planning with the client can begin. Thoroughly and openly discussing these questions can help a financial planner and client explore the range of client characteristics that impact education planning decisions. For example, some clients may firmly refuse to fully pay for college costs, although they may be financially capable of doing so. Based on their values and attitudes, some clients may want the child to contribute through earnings or loans. Other clients might insist on funding college costs to the exclusion of other planning needs. In these situation, clients may believe that it is important to leave college with little or no debt. Although these scenarios are extreme, each illustrates how personality, values, attitudes, experience, and socioeconomic descriptors converge to influence education planning efforts.

> *Example.* Clients who plan to accumulate funding before a child enters college will likely initiate disciplined savings early and focus on the desired amount. Those who plan to pay during or after the student attends college may be doing so by necessity or choice—because of a failure to start early, competing financial goals, life events that prevented or interrupted savings, or any number of other reasons. These clients may have few reservations about incurring debt through public or private sources, or postponing other goals to contribute to educational expenses. They, as well as clients who plan on someone else paying, may expect the child to contribute through borrowing or working while in school. Other clients may view student loan debt or employment during the academic year as an unnecessary burden on their child.

Planning Reminder

The guidance given to a client who believes strongly that a child will receive financial assistance or not attend college will differ significantly from that given to a client committed to saving. Clients who trust that their child will receive financial aid for merit or need should consider funding retirement as an alternative goal or as a contingent source of education funding.

In addition to the child, others may be asked to help fund educational costs, including providers of **scholarships** and **grants** based on need, aptitude (e.g., scholastic, athletic, artistic), or interest (e.g., leadership, community service). Other family members might also be expected to contribute to a child's educational funding need before, during, or after college through direct or indirect gifts, trusts, or estate distributions. A combination of funding sources may sometimes result in an optimal funding solution.

The choice of which or how much of each goal to fund is complicated by the uncertainty of the assumptions used when determining education funding needs. Prior to quantifying this need, financial planners should first understand what priority a client places on education planning and which assumptions to include in the planning process. For some clients, education funding will be the highest priority. For others, education funding will rank below other financial planning goals. Many of these issues can be revealed during the data-gathering discovery and the goal identification phase of the financial planning process, but if not, then a discussion focused on education planning should occur. Specific issues to address with a client include:

- determining how much value a client or household places on attending institutions of higher education;

- prioritizing education planning within the comprehensive planning framework;

- establishing the primary reason education funding is desired, including feelings of obligation or benevolence, as well as tax considerations (e.g., preferences for tax-advantaged savings opportunities to defer or avoid income taxes, availability of income tax adjustments, or credits reductions in estate taxes);

- establishing guidelines regarding what the client or household believes is a reasonable amount to pay for a college education for one or more dependents;

- identifying the level of control a client wants to retain in the management of assets devoted to education funding needs;

- assessing a child's probability of receiving a scholarship or grant based on unique skills, abilities, or interests; and

- determining a child's expectation of receiving financial aid.

Of these factors, some are wholly determined by the client, and as such, a financial planner should respect a client's answers without judgment. Other fact-based considerations, such as preferences regarding taxes and control over accounts, can be used by financial planners to directly influence strategic recommendations. Once a financial planner has a relatively complete understanding of a client's perceived roles, attitudes, and preferences underlying education planning, the next step in the analysis process is to determine the cost of the goal.

Once a client's specific education funding goal(s) has been established, the gross education funding need should be determined. A determination of whether or not the client is on track to meet the goal(s) should follow next. The analysis can be guided by the following questions:

(1) When will the child(ren) begin college?

(2) What type of college might the child(ren) want or be encouraged to attend?

(3) How much are college costs increasing annually for this type of college?

(4) What are the projected costs for the targeted college when the child(ren) begins college?

(5) How much of the projected college cost does the client intend to provide?

(6) How much of the projected cost does the client expect to be funded by scholarships, grants, and loans?

(7) Does the client currently have assets earmarked for this goal?

(8) How much is the client, or other family members, currently saving for this goal?

(9) Does education planning include funding for graduate education? (If yes, the preceding questions must be reconsidered for this scenario.)

Assessing a client's educational funding needs is a relatively straightforward procedure. Figure 14.3 illustrates the information needed to complete a basic education funding needs analysis, the likely source of data, and the calculations required.

Planning Reminder

A key analytical task when conducting a college funding needs analysis involves accurately assessing the current cost of college attendance. The U.S. government provides estimates of college costs at collegecost.ed.gov. This site can also be used to estimate tuition inflation rates.

In order to complete the analysis, a financial planner must determine the rate of return most likely to be generated on assets and savings dedicated to the goal. This return assumption should match the client's financial risk tolerance and funding need. The choice of a single rate-of-return figure may be overly simplistic because it is possible for clients to use a combination of before- and after-tax investments earmarked for education, and/or use an age-based portfolio where the rate of return will decrease over time as risk is removed from the portfolio and goal realization nears. It is also likely that some investments (e.g., U.S. Savings Bonds and Section 529 plans) will generate tax-free returns. Once individual account returns have been determined, a financial planner can then calculate the weighted-average return on which to base future value calculations.

Figure 14.3. Summary of Data and Calculations Required for a College Savings Needs Analysis.

Data Needed for Analysis	Source of Data
Rate of return	Client/financial planner assumption
Years to complete college	Client/financial planner assumption
Initial additional periodic savings amount	Client/financial planner assumption
Initial periodic increase in savings amount	Client/financial planner assumption
Annual cost of college today	Financial planner research
College expense inflation rate	Financial planner research
Current age of child	Client data
College age of child	Client data
Present value of assets currently saved	Client data

Calculations Required for Analysis	Completed by
College real interest rate	Financial planner
Future value cost of college	Financial planner
Future value of assets currently saved	Financial planner
Future value of additional periodic savings	Financial planner

Other information needed to complete an analysis includes the assumed rate of inflation for tuition and other college expenses, the child's current age, expected age when entering college, and the number of years of college to be funded. The current cost of the college of choice is needed. Finally, the amount of assets already saved, and a projected annual savings amount, must be determined. The following is a step-by-step process[1] that can be used to conduct an education funding analysis:

Step One

Determine the future value (FV) cost of education for a single year at the time the child begins college, using the future value equation below, where the present value (PV) is the current annual cost of college, the interest rate (i) is the projected annual increase (inflation rate) in college cost, and n is the number of years until college begins.

Future value of a lump sum

$$FV = PV (1 + i)^n$$

Step Two

Find the total cost of education (all years) at the time the child begins college using the present value of a growing annuity equation, where the payment (PMT) is the first-year cost of college as calculated in Step One. Because college tuition is normally paid as an annuity, the annual increase in college cost is the growth rate (g), the estimated rate of return becomes the interest rate (i), and n is the number of years in college. This estimate is an annuity due because college tuition is typically paid at the beginning of each semester.

Present value of a growing annuity

$$PV = \frac{PMT}{i - g}\left(1 - \frac{(1 + g)^n}{(1 + i)^n}\right)(1 + i)$$

Step Three

To determine the cost of college today (as if the client were going to set aside the requisite amount immediately), calculate the present value (PV) of the total cost of education discounted from the first year of college back to today, using the present value of a lump sum equation, where the future value (FV) is the total cost in Step Two. The interest rate (i) is the estimated rate of return, and n is the number of years until college begins.

Present value of a lump sum

$$PV = \frac{FV}{(1 + i)^n}$$

Step Four

If funding has already been dedicated to the goal, this amount should be subtracted from the total present cost of education in Step Three. The result is the **funding shortfall**, which is the lump sum amount needed immediately to meet the education goal.

Funding Shortfall = Total Need – Amount Already Dedicated

Step Five

If the client plans to fund the shortfall on a periodic basis, the financial planner needs to determine the monthly savings required until college begins. This amount can be estimated using a present value of an annuity payment formula, where the present value (PV) is the lump sum amount in Step Four. The inputs for the formula include the expected rate of return (i) and the anticipated growth rate of the periodic payment (g), if applicable. Again, n is the number of years until college begins.

Present value of an annuity payment

$$PV = \frac{PMT}{i - g}\left(1 - \frac{(1 + g)^n}{(1 + i)^n}\right)$$

Rearranging the formula to isolate PMT yields the payment required to achieve the savings goal:

$$PMT = \frac{PV(i - g)}{\left(1 - \frac{(1 + g)^n}{(1 + i)^n}\right)}$$

The resulting payment is the required periodic payment, assuming that the client wants to save enough to achieve the goal without regard to other funding sources.

Example. To illustrate this process, assume the current annual cost of college is $12,000, and to ensure adequate funding, assume an annual cost increase of 5 percent per year both before and during college. Assume the child will begin college in exactly four years, will attend for four years, and has no money set aside for the goal. Finally, assume an effective annual rate of return of 8.30 percent.[2] What is the required savings amount if the client is going to set aside the entire amount today? What is the required monthly savings amount?

Step One. Determine the future value cost of education for the first year of school:

$$FV = PV (1 + i)^n$$

or

$$FV = \$12,000(1.05)^4 = \$14,586.08$$

Input	Keystroke	Result
0	[PMT]	PMT = 0.00
12000 [+/−]	[PV]	PV = −12,000.00
5	[I/Y]	I/Y = 5.00
4	[N]	N = 4.00
[CPT]	[FV]	FV = 14,586.08

Note: The PV is input as a negative figure because an investment is an assumed outflow. For this step, the inflation rate is treated as an interest rate to determine the "inflated" cost of the goal.

Step Two. Find the total cost of education (for all years) needed at the time the child begins college:

$$PV = \frac{PMT}{i - g}\left(1 - \frac{(1 + g)^n}{(1 + i)^n}\right)$$

or

$$PV = \frac{\$14,586.08}{0.083 - 0.05}\left(1 - \frac{(1.05)^4}{(1.083)^4}\right)(1.083) = \$55,731.37$$

Input	Keystroke	Result
14586.08	[PMT]	PMT = 14,586.08
0	[FV]	FV = 0.00
3.1429*	[I/Y]	I/Y = 3.1429
4	[N]	N = 4.00
[CPT]	[PV]	PV = –55,731.37**

*The calculator needs a serial rate to handle growing annuities.

**Disregard the negative sign in the solution.

Step Three. Determine the present value of the savings required as a lump sum:

$$PV = \frac{FV}{(1+i)^n}$$

or

$$PV@T_0 = \frac{\$55,731.37}{(1.083)^4} = \$40,512.20$$

Input	Keystroke	Result
0	[PMT]	PMT = 0.00
55731.37	[FV]	FV = 55,731.37
8.30	[I/Y]	I/Y = 8.30
4	[N]	N = 4.00
[CPT]	[PV]	PV = –40,512.20*

*Disregard the negative sign in the solution.

Step Four. Estimate the savings shortfall:

Since nothing has been saved to date, the lump sum amount needed immediately to meet the education goal equals $40,512.20 ($40,512.20 – $0).

Step Five. Determine the monthly savings needed to meet the education goal:

To solve for a monthly payment, the equivalent monthly rate for both the rate of return and the rate of payment growth, if applicable, must be used.

$$PMT = \frac{PV(i-g)}{\left(1 - \frac{(1+g)^n}{(1+i)^n}\right)}$$

or

$$PMT = \frac{\$40{,}512.20(0.00667)}{\left(1 - \dfrac{1}{1.00667^{48}}\right)} = \$989.02$$

Input	Keystroke	Result
40512.20	[PV]	PV = 40,512.20
0.667*	[I/Y]	I/Y = 0.667**
48	[N]	N = 48.00
0	[FV]	FV = 0
[CPT]	[PMT]	PMT = –989.02***

*0.667 represents an effective annual rate (EAR) of 8.30 or 8.0/12.

**To calculate the monthly payment, either the interest rate must be in input as a monthly EPR or the number of payments per year must be reset to 12.

***Disregard the negative sign in the solution.

The last step in the analysis involves subtracting out any current monthly savings from the estimate. Because the client in this example was not saving towards the goal, the monthly savings needed to meet the education goal equals $989.02.

The following example shows how an analysis of the Hubble family's education funding goal results in a pathway to the development of recommendations. Figure 14.4 provides a summary of the Hubbles' current education choice and potential recommendations. Figure 14.4 also shows a screen shot of the education savings estimation procedure using the Financial Planning Analysis Excel™ package that accompanies the book. Potential recommendations are also provided.

Figure 14.4. The Hubbles' Current Education Choices and Potential Recommendations.

- In-state tuition at a desirable private university for four years will cost $10,000 per semester, including room and board (in today's dollars).
- Tuition costs are increasing at 5 percent per year.
- Chandler and Rachel are willing to invest in a moderately aggressive portfolio for this goal before Phoebe begins college and during her college years.
- Chandler and Rachel want all college savings to be accumulated before Phoebe begins college.
- The Hubble family will stop saving for college expenses once Phoebe begins college.
- No assets are currently targeted for college savings needs.
- Chandler and Rachel would prefer to invest in tax-advantaged investments to pay for college, if possible.

Based on these inputs, the total amount needed to fund Phoebe's college is $140,874.70 (the amount needed on her first day of college), as shown below:

COLLEGE SAVINGS ANALYSIS

ASSUMPTIONS	
Child/Scenario Name	**Phoebe**
Combined Federal and State Marginal Tax Bracket	30.00%
Assumed After-Tax Rate of Return Before College	7.00%
Assumed Before-Tax Return of Tax-Advantaged Plans	10.00%
Assumed Rate of Return After College Begins	10.00%
Assumed College Expense Inflation Rate	5.00%
Age	5
College Age	18
Years In College	4
Yearly Cost of College TODAY	$20,000.00
Value of After-Tax Assets Saved Today	
Value of Tax-Advantaged Assets Saved	
Annual After-Tax Savings	
Annual Tax-Advantaged Savings	
Annual Savings Growth Rate	3.00%
CALCULATIONS	
College Serial After-Tax Interest Rate Before College Starts	1.9048%
College Serial Before-Tax Rate Before College Starts	4.7619%
College Serial Interest Rate After College Starts	4.7619%
FV of College	$37,712.98
FV of Assets	$0.00
FV of Savings	$0.00
Gross Assets Needed (1st Day of College) without Savings	$162,547.67
Assets Needed (1st Day of College)	$140,874.71
BEFORE-TAX ASSET CALCULATION	
Present Value of Assets Needed	$40,806.38
BEFORE-TAX SAVINGS REQUIREMENTS	
Annual Level Savings Needed	$5,744.66
Serial Adjusted Savings Needed*	$4,282.03
AFTER-TAX ASSET CALCULATION	
Present Value of Assets Needed	$58,458.00
AFTER-TAX SAVINGS REQUIREMENTS	
Annual Level Savings Needed	$6,994.55
Serial Adjusted Savings Needed*	$5,118.94

*Serial adjusted savings require that the amount saved for college increases each year by the savings growth rate.

Based on the preceding analysis, the following potential recommendations are worth considering as a way to help the Hubble family meet their education funding goal:

- If Chandler and Rachel do not allocate current assets towards this goal, they need to save approximately $5,745 at the end of each year until Phoebe begins college in thirteen years.

- The Hubble family should consider establishing a 529 plan in the state of Missouri. Establishing the plan will:
  - Allow for a state income tax deduction for the amount contributed.
  - Generate tax-deferral of earnings.
  - Allow for tax-free distribution of earnings if funds are used to pay for qualified educational expenses.

- Transfer the savings bonds held by Chandler and Rachel into the 529 plan for Phoebe.

14.5 STEP 4: DEVELOP THE FINANCIAL PLANNING RECOMMENDATION(S)

[A] Discussing Alternatives for College Funding

Financial planners and their clients have numerous alternatives available for use in the college funding and general education planning process. In addition to commonly used education planning accounts, less common and less advantageous funding alternatives include the cash value available in an insurance policy, a home equity loan or line of credit, and the use of investment accounts. Unlike Section 529 plans and other qualified educational savings accounts, these alternatives lack significant educational funding income tax benefits.

It behooves a financial planner to encourage clients to also pursue a variety of grants, loans, scholarships, and other financial aid sources to help fund higher education expenses. It is possible to seek funding through private education loans or even family or personal loans. Although some clients may hold a strong preference for or against, a recommendation to encourage a student to fund part of the cost of college through summer jobs or on- or off-campus employment during the school term should also be considered. Finally, some students pursue careers associated with loan forgiveness programs as a means to defray after-college loan repayment. Being familiar with federal loan repayment alternatives is an important financial planning attribute.

As noted above, few other core financial planning content areas offer so many unique strategies that can be used to align with a client's goals and preferences. The following discussion highlights some of the important concepts, tools, and techniques that can be incorporated into the recommendation development process.

[B] College Funding Considerations

[1] Multi-goal Funding Alternatives

Clients who wish to fund a child's or another family member's educational costs often face conflicting choice outcomes. Clients in this situation must sometimes decide whether to save for potential college costs or fund retirement plans. The time horizons for saving for these goals are generally different, with overlaps being common. Furthermore, a child may decide not to go to college or to go to a more or less expensive college, or the child may end up qualifying for a scholarship or other form of financial aid.

One method that can be used to hedge the possibility that college expenses will be lower than expected, funded through other means, or simply unneeded, is to fund both goals in one account. This means that future college costs, coupled with retirement funding needs, can be combined into one or more tax-deferred contribution plans. An employer-sponsored retirement plan, a Roth IRA, or a traditional IRA can be used to fund a portion of or all projected college costs.

For example, all client contributions to a **Roth IRA** can be withdrawn at any time without incurring taxation. Keep in mind, however, that if a client dips into *account earnings* to pay qualified higher education expenses before retirement, the distributed earnings will generally be taxable, and if the account has not been open for at least five years, the distribution may also be subject to a penalty.

The situation is different for a traditional IRA. Any withdrawals from a traditional IRA will be taxable (except to the extent the distribution is attributable to nondeductible contributions, determined on a pro rata basis). To the extent the withdrawal is used to pay qualified higher education expenses, the penalty tax on early distributions will not apply. In general, for purposes of the education exception to the penalty tax on early distributions, distributions are covered only to the extent that distributions do not exceed qualified higher education expenses for the taxpayer, the taxpayer's spouse, or the child or grandchild of either. Eligible expenses include tuition, fees, books, supplies, and room and board for a student attending undergraduate or graduate school at least half-time.

Planning Reminder

There is no hard-and-fast rule regarding the best time to convert a traditional IRA to a Roth IRA (**Roth conversion**); however, there is a worst possible time—while a client's children are in college. Qualified retirement accounts are excluded from assets when calculating the **expected family income** (EFC) for financial aid; however, income derived from those sources is not. So, although a distribution from IRAs to pay qualified educational expenses is allowable and will not trigger a tax penalty, it will count as income and could affect the income component of the EFC the following year.

A lesser-known consideration is the tax impact of conversion. Converting a traditional IRA to a Roth IRA is a taxable event. In other words, the amount of the conversion is typically taxable as ordinary income in the year of conversion, although there have been numerous temporary changes to this rule. So, a financial planner must consider long-term tax implications of IRA distributions and conversions to the account owner, as well as the near-term financial aid implications to the dependent student of the account owner.

[2] Section 529 Plans

According to the Securities and Exchange Commission's Office of Investor Education and Advocacy, a **Section 529 plan** is a tax-advantaged savings plan designed to encourage education savings. Section 529 plans are sponsored by individual states and by educational institutions. There are two types of plans: (1) *prepaid tuition plans* and (2) *education savings plans*. Educational savings plans are the most popular. Savings can be used to pay for qualified higher education expenses, including tuition, mandatory fees, and room and board. Assets from education savings plans can also be used to pay up to $10,000 per year per beneficiary for tuition at any public, private, or religious elementary or secondary school. Typical investment alternatives include mutual funds and exchange traded funds. Like most other tax-favored savings alternatives, contributions are capped per beneficiary on an annual basis.

While contributing to a 529 plan can be a good way to save for a child's or grandchild's college educational expenses, there are times when money saved in a 529 plan is not used. When this occurs, clients have several options.

- One alternative is to withdraw the account balance as cash; however, doing so will cause the client to owe tax on the earnings, plus a penalty equal to 10 percent on account earnings.

- Another option is keep the money in the 529 plan; doing so will allow a beneficiary to use the funds for graduate school expenses.

- An alternative is to change the recipient beneficiary; the only requirement is that the new beneficiary be a family member.

- A fourth option involves the use of up to $10,000 to pay down existing student loan debt.

In situations where 529 plan assets remain unspent because a beneficiary received a scholarship, it is possible for the client to withdraw money up to the value of the scholarship. Of course, some or all of the withdrawal will be taxable, but the distribution will not be penalized. The same holds true if the beneficiary becomes disabled or dies. Finally, clients should not feel rushed to make any changes to a 529 plan as long as the named beneficiary is still alive. The assets will continue to grow on a tax-free basis until used or withdrawn. In rare cases when no future beneficiary is anticipated, the client may decide to donate the account to a charity and receive a tax deduction (assuming the client itemizes deductions).

[3] Coverdell Education Savings Accounts

A **Coverdell Education Savings Account** (CESA) can be used to help parents and grandparents save for a qualified beneficiary's education expenses. A CESA is a trust or custodial account set up for the purpose of paying qualified education expenses for a designated beneficiary. Principal and earnings from the account can be used to pay qualified higher education expenses, including tuition, fees, books, supplies, and equipment required for enrollment or attendance. Other expenses include amounts contributed to a qualified tuition program and room and board expenses. Distributions can be used to pay expenses at public, private, and religious elementary and secondary schools, as well as for postsecondary education expenses. This means that, unlike other tax-advantaged programs, a CESA can be used to pay for private day school expenses.

The designated beneficiary of a CESA must be under the age of eighteen when the account is established, unless the beneficiary has special needs. Any balance in a CESA must be distributed within thirty days after the date the beneficiary reaches age thirty, unless the beneficiary has special needs. There is no limit to the number of CESAs that can be established for one beneficiary. However, contributions can be made only in cash, and the total contributions made to all CESAs for any beneficiary in one tax year cannot be greater than $2,000. This means, for example, that a client cannot contribute $2,000 to an account while a grandparent contributes another $2,000. Also, contributions to CESAs are restricted by income phase-out rules.

The primary education planning advantage associated with a CESA is that a distribution is tax free to the extent the distribution does not exceed the beneficiary's qualified education expenses. If a distribution does exceed the beneficiary's qualified education expenses, a portion of the distribution will be taxable. A CESA can be rolled over into a Section 529 plan. Also, the **American Opportunity tax credit** or the **Lifetime Learning tax credit** can be claimed for certain qualified higher education expenses in the same year in which the student receives a tax-free withdrawal from a CESA. However, the distribution cannot be used for the same educational expenses for which the credit was taken.

Two limitations are associated with this educational savings approach. First, many financial planning clients could find that their income exceeds threshold limits, making contributions out of the question. Second, and more importantly, the annual $2,000 contribution limit severely restricts the usefulness of this tool in accumulating assets for education.

To maximize this type of account, a client must start saving early in a child's life and save the maximum allowable each year. If, for instance, a client saved $2,000 each year for fifteen years earning a 9 percent average annual return, the account would be worth $58,722 at the end of the period, which may not cover all educational costs. Also, if assets are not used by the child's thirtieth birthday, and are not assigned to a close family member, the client will incur an income tax and a 10 percent penalty on earnings that accumulated on a tax-free basis within the account.

[4] Series EE and Series I Savings Bonds

A client (or grandparent) who owns **EE savings bonds** or **I savings bonds** can use the bonds, on a tax-free basis, to help pay for a child's (or grandchild's) college tuition. The amount that can be contributed—used to purchase bonds—on a yearly basis is higher ($30,000 for married clients) than the amount that can be contributed to a CESA or traditional or Roth IRAs.

Individuals must meet certain requirements for distributions from EE and I savings bonds to be tax free. First, a client must be at least twenty-four years old on the first day of the month in which the bond was purchased. Second, when using bonds for a child's education, the bonds must be *registered in the client's and/or spouse's name*. A child can be listed as a beneficiary on the bond, but not as a co-owner. Third, if a client uses bonds for the client's own education, the bonds must be registered in the client's name. Finally, if a client is married and uses the bonds for educational purposes, the client must file a joint return to qualify for the exclusion.

Unlike distributions from CESAs, only payments made to postsecondary institutions, including colleges, universities, and vocational schools that meet the standards for federal assistance (such as guaranteed student loan programs) qualify for the program. **Qualified educational expenses** include tuition and fees such as lab fees and other required course expenses. Expenses paid for any course or other educational activity involving sports, games, or hobbies qualify only if required as part of a degree- or certificate-granting program. The costs of books, room, and board are not considered qualified expenses. Savings bonds can be used to fund qualified state tuition plans, such as a Section 529 plan. When determining the amount of qualified expenses, a client must reduce the amount of total expenses by the amount of scholarships, fellowships, employer-provided educational assistance, and other forms of tuition reduction received. Finally, expenses must be incurred during the same tax year in which the bonds are redeemed.

To exclude the interest from gross income, a client must use both the principal and interest from bonds sold to pay qualified expenses. If the amount of eligible bonds cashed in during the year exceeds the amount of qualified educational expenses paid during the year, the amount of excludable interest will be reduced using a pro rata formula. For example, assume that bond proceeds equal $20,000 ($16,000 principal and $4,000 interest) and qualified educational expenses are $16,000. The amount of interest that can be excluded is $3,200 ([$16,000 purchases ÷ $20,000 proceeds] × $4,000 interest).

Like most tax benefits, certain household income limitations apply. The full interest exclusion is available only to clients with modified adjusted gross income (which includes the interest earned) under certain limits. Also, savings bonds are included as a parent asset, which can increase the expected family contribution used in financial aid formulas. Furthermore, the rate of return for EE and I bonds has been historically low, which limits a client's ability to fund expenses from interest earned. The early withdrawal penalty during the first five years of ownership and the relatively low rate of return require that this strategy be implemented well in advance of when the funds are needed.

[5] Student Financial Aid Alternatives

Financial aid comes in three basic forms: (1) **scholarships**, (2) **loans**, and (3) **grants**. Nearly all scholarships offered in the United States are university or program specific. However, a number of national scholarships are available. Scholarships can be either need or merit based. Students interested in scholarships should generally apply through their university, college, and academic unit.

Federal student loans are available as **Stafford loans** (Perkins loans were discontinued in 2015). Stafford loans are federally sponsored loans that can be used to pay educational expenses. Prior to July 2010, Stafford loans were offered under the Federal Family Education Loan Program, and funds were provided by private banks and credit unions. But after passage of the Health Care and Education Reconciliation Act of 2010, the Federal Direct Loan Program handles all Stafford loan processing, while the federal government provides funding directly through participating schools.

There are two types of Stafford loans: **subsidized** and **unsubsidized**. A subsidized Stafford loan is a **need-based loan** where the federal government pays the interest for the student on the loan as long as the student is enrolled at least half-time. Unsubsidized Stafford loans are available to all students (who are eligible for federal aid) regardless of need. An unsubsidized Stafford loan accrues interest from the date of disbursement. Both loans offer payment deferral, meaning the student is not required to make interest payments while attending college at least half-time, and both offer a six-month grace period after the deferment period ends before repayment is required.

Annual loan limits for undergraduate students are determined by their grade level and dependency status. Interest rates on Stafford Loans are quite reasonable—the rates are set periodically by Congressional Act.[3] Some currently enrolled students may hold a **Perkins loan**, which is a need-based loan that charges a flat 5 percent interest rate, allows repayment to be deferred until nine months following graduation, and features a ten-year repayment period.[4] These loans were discontinued after 2015.

Parents, rather than students, are eligible to use a **Parent Loan for Undergraduate Students (PLUS)**. A PLUS loan can be taken out for an amount equal to the difference between the college-defined cost of attendance and all other financial aid received. For loans disbursed prior to July 2006, the interest was variable based on market conditions and capped at 9 percent; however, loans disbursed since that time have rates ranging from less than 7 percent to more than 9 percent annually.[5] A primary difference between Stafford and PLUS loans is that PLUS loans require repayment beginning approximately sixty days after the loan is fully disbursed rather than being deferred until graduation.

All Direct Loan Program loans offer a variety of **repayment plans**, as listed below:

- *Standard repayment*: up to ten years, with a minimum monthly payment of $50.[6]

- *Extended repayment*: up to twenty-five years, with the option of fixed or graduated payments (increasing every two years); must have more than $30,000 in qualifying debt to be eligible).[7]

- *Graduated repayment*: up to ten years (or twenty years if also qualified under the extended plan) with payment increasing every two years. Later payments are prohibited from being more than three times any other payment on the loan.[8]

- *Income contingent repayment*: an applicant income-based formula capped at 20 percent of discretionary income with a repayment period of twenty-five years, after which any outstanding balance is forgiven but taxed as current income.[9] The annual payment calculation is based on adjusted gross income (AGI), plus spouse's income (if applicable), family size, and the total amount of Federal Direct Loans.

- *Income based repayment*: maximum repayment period can exceed ten years, but it is only available to those experiencing partial financial hardship. Under certain circumstances, loan cancellation may be available.[10] Payments may adjust annually matched to income. Partial financial hardship is determined using a calculation where, under a standard ten-year repayment plan for all eligible loans, the total annual payment due exceeds 15 percent of discretionary income.[11] The Health Care and Education Reconciliation Act, passed in 2010, reduced the maximum payment percentage from 15 to 10 percent and also reduced the forgiveness of any remaining loan balance from twenty-five years to twenty. These changes were effective for new borrowers of new loans made on or after July 1, 2014.[12]

Planning Reminder

Pay-As-You-Earn repayment plans generally limit debt repayments to 10 percent of the borrower's discretionary income, but never more than the standard ten-year repayment plan amount. Visit the Federal Student Aid website to learn more about repayment options: https://studentaid.ed.gov/sa/repay-loans/understand/plans/income-driven.

Beginning in 2015, any U.S. citizen who has ever borrowed money using a federal government loan, either for college or graduate school, can enroll in the **pay-as-you-earn** debt repayment program. This program sets the maximum monthly debt repayment equal to 10 percent of a borrower's **discretionary income**, which is defined as adjusted gross income (AGI) less one-hundred and 50 percent of the poverty level. Under the rules, payments can be made for twenty years. For those with graduate student debt, the repayment period can be extended to twenty-five years. At the end of the period (i.e., either twenty or twenty-five years), any remaining balance is forgiven; however, all amounts forgiven are subject to regular income taxes. Two things are worth remembering. First, parents who took out loans to pay for a child's college costs are not eligible for pay-as-you-earn. Second, while this repayment plan appeals to many people, it is important that clients be reminded that more interest will be paid over the life of the loan.

[6] The FASFA Form

For most forms of financial aid, some component of need or expected contribution is used to determine eligibility or availability. Financial planners can serve as a valuable resource to families applying for student aid by understanding the inputs needed to complete the **Free Application for Federal Student Aid (FASFA)** form. A financial planner and their client must determine not only the amount of money that will be available for college expenses, but who will control the money. Ownership is important because the percentage of assets required to fund college costs depends on whether the assets are held in a child's, parent's, or guardian's name. Dependent students are expected to contribute 20 percent of assets and 50 percent of income to education expenses, whereas parents are expected to contribute 22 percent to almost one half of assets and nearly 3 percent to more than 5 percent of income.[13] These amounts differ for independent students.

Armed with some knowledge of the financial aid system, a financial planner can advise parents regarding how to work more proactively with high school staff and targeted college financial aid programs to determine more accurately the likelihood of merit- or need-based financial assistance. The same strategy can be applied to identifying institutions, both public and private, that could offer the most assistance given the student's profile. Finally, this information, plus projected payment scenarios, can help clients feel more comfortable about taking on education loan debt for themselves or their children.

[7] Asset Ownership Considerations

Tax and education planning may be the most difficult financial objectives to jointly optimize because many of the most attractive options from an ongoing income tax liability perspective (e.g., Section 529 plans, CESAs) can interfere with the ability to also claim an education tax credit. Figure 14.5 summarizes how the form of asset ownership can impact financial aid and the use of tax credits.

Figure 14.5. Potential Impact of Asset Ownership on Financial Aid and Tax Credits.

Education Savings Plan	Assets Owned by the Dependent Student	
	Change in Expected Family Contribution	American Opportunity and Lifetime Learning Tax Credit Impact
UGMA/UTMA	Increased (20% of balance)*	No impact
§ 529 savings plan (UGMA/UTMA)	Increased (2.6% – 5.6% of balance) *	Expenses paid with distribution cannot be claimed for tax credit**
Coverdell Education Savings Account (CESA)	Increased (2.6 %– 5.6% of balance) *	Expenses paid with distribution cannot be claimed for tax credit**
Crummey trust****	Increased (20% of balance)*	No impact
Assets Owned by the Parent		
§ 529 savings plan	Increased (2.6% – 5.6% of balance)*	Expenses paid with distribution cannot be claimed for tax credit**
Series EE savings bonds (tax-free education withdrawals)	Increased (2.6% – 5.6% of balance)*	Expenses paid with distribution cannot be claimed for tax credit**
Retirement plans	None	No impact
Variable universal life insurance	None	No impact
Assets Owned by Others (e.g., Grandparent) but with Student as Beneficiary		
§ 529 savings plan	None***	Expenses paid with distributions cannot be claimed for tax credit**

*   Hurley, J. F. (2011). *Family guide to college savings 2011–2012*, JFH Innovative, LLC, Pittsford, NY.

**   Clients may take distributions from these plans. However, distributions must be spent on expenses not already claimed with the American Opportunity or Lifetime Learning Credits.

*** Distributions from plans owned by a third party will be added back as income on the FAFSA.

**** A Crummey trust allows the beneficiary a window of opportunity to access the gift made, thereby completing the gift and removing the donated amount from the estate of the donor, although the intent is for the money to remain in the trust for a specified purpose or time period.

[8] Summary

Figure 14.6 illustrates some of the decisions that can influence the choice of college funding alternatives. When reviewing the decision alternatives, it is important to remember that one or more strategies will likely be needed to achieve a client's education funding goal(s). Different strategies should be fully evaluated relative to a client's situation before combining them into a recommendation.

Figure 14.6. Decision Tree for Select Education Funding Strategies.

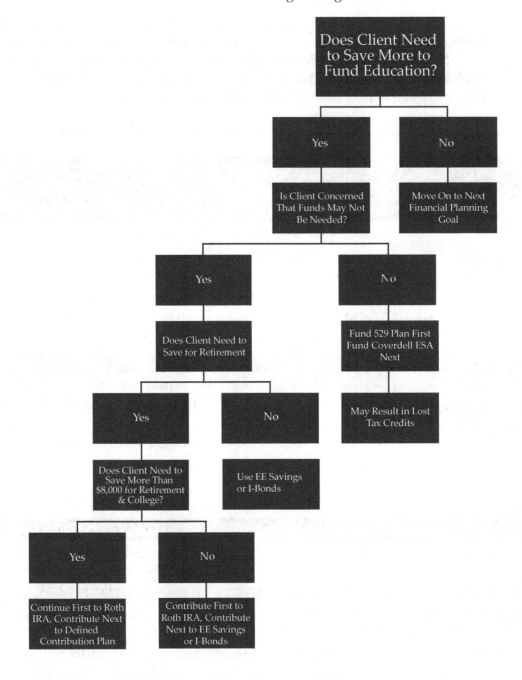

[C] Applying Planning Skills to the Hubble Case

Generally, only modest changes will need to be made to the initial recommendations developed at Step Three of the financial planning process, although it is possible that new client information or data can necessitate a reevaluation. Figure 14.7 provides a summary of the education planning recommendations that match the Hubble family's financial goals.

Figure 14.7. Education Recommendations for Chandler and Rachel.

> **The final education recommendations developed for the Hubble family match the preliminary recommendations identified at Step Three of the financial planning process. Specifically, Chandler and Rachel should:**

- Open a Missouri 529 Plan and invest in the Vanguard Growth Portfolio, which, at the time of publication, matches the Hubbles' return need for a moderately aggressive portfolio returning 10 percent annually.
- Assuming all other requirements for the ownership of the bonds are met, Chandler and Rachel should cash in the $25,000 EE Bonds and transfer these funds to the 529 account using a Transfer/Rollover Form. Because the Hubbles' income may be too high for the interest to be tax exempt, IRS Form 8815 must be completed to calculate the excludable savings bond interest and to ensure that the redemption of the savings bonds is appropriately tracked as being rolled over to a 529 plan, resulting in a tax-free distribution of interest. If Chandler and Rachel fail to use a rollover, some tax may be due on the distribution, based on a face value of $25,000, a purchase price of $15,000, and $10,000 in interest.
- Based on the original analysis, the Hubbles need to save $140,874.70 by the time Phoebe starts college. Given the original savings need, additional estimates were undertaken. A solution emerged. It was determined that goal funding is possible if Chandler and Rachel allocate $25,000 from the EE savings bonds, $1,100 from savings, and $1,800 annually towards the goal in a 529 plan.

Other education funding options include:
- Sell non-qualified assets, and paying the capital gains taxes, as a way to initially fund a 529 plan, followed by monthly or annual contributions.
- Sell non-qualified assets to yield the required $40,806 after capital gains taxes to fully fund a 529 plan; however, because Missouri does not offer the carry forward tax advantage, the tax benefit would be limited to the current year deduction.
- Maximize funding to Roth IRAs for Chandler and Rachel, with the idea that, if needed, funds could be withdrawn to fund or supplement funding for education.
- Fund a Coverdell Education Savings Account as a supplement because of the broader definition of allowable expenses, including K-12 costs, and the flexibility in investment options.
- Discuss with Chandler and Rachel the importance of continuing to fund retirement, despite the importance placed on the education funding goal. A 401(k) loan could be an option to pay for Phoebe's college.
- Discuss with Chandler and Rachel the tradeoffs associated with paying for a private college education compared to funding a state school's tuition.
- Contribute to a Uniform Gift to Minors Act Account (UGMA) which offers the advantage that the money does not have to be used for college expenses in the event that Phoebe decides not to attend college; issues to consider include the kiddie-tax and the loss of control of account assets when Phoebe turns age eighteen. Additionally, holding assets in an UGMA account can have a negative effect on financial aid.

14.6 STEP 5: PRESENT THE FINANCIAL PLANNING RECOMMENDATION(S)

Education funding is a primary concern for many financial planning clients. Often the need to identify strategies to fund a child's or another family member's educational costs is this issue that prompts a client to seek professional financial planning services. Although parents tend to be the most interested in education planning, this is not the only group that can be involved. Frequently, grandparents and relatives have a stake in helping a family plan for a child's education. A grandparent's objective may be strictly to help fund their grandchildren's education. On the other hand, the objective might include reducing their taxable estate. So, depending on the client and situation, education planning can be important to clients with young children, clients with children who are about to enter college, and clients with grandchildren. It is important, therefore, to identify the presenting and associated reasons a client is seeking education funding advice. In this regard, it is important for financial planners to exhibit a working knowledge of the variety of tax-advantaged and non-tax-advantaged options available for individuals and families as clients plan for future educational expenses. Taxes, timing, assets, income, competing financial goals, and a host of other considerations serve to further complicate a seemingly simple question, "How do we pay for college expenses?" Anticipating this and other questions is a proven approach to help facilitate the delivery of education funding recommendations.

Figure 14.8 highlights some of the important factors to consider when presenting education recommendations to the Hubble family.

Figure 14.8. Factors to Consider When Presenting Education Recommendations.

An important consideration when presenting education recommendations to Chandler and Rachel involves confirming all the assumptions made in the education planning analysis. It is also important to keep in mind that the calculations and resulting recommendations were made based on Chandler and Rachel's stated objectives and agreed upon assumptions. It is very likely that changes to the education planning analysis will need to be made as assumptions and objectives change across time. When presenting the financial planning recommendations, it is important to communicate that the recommendations are adaptable, and as Phoebe ages, she may have personal goals that influence the funding outcome. Additionally, it is worth bearing in mind that education planning can be confusing to clients given the vast number of educational savings vehicles available and the tax ramifications involved with different strategies. A best practice involves presenting two or three education planning recommendations that, in the view of the financial planner, best meet a client's needs, rather than overwhelming the client with too many alternatives. If a client wishes to discuss additional recommendations, their financial planner can always present new options at a later date.

14.7 STEP 6: IMPLEMENT THE FINANCIAL PLANNING RECOMMENDATION(S)

Financial planners can add value to the client-financial planner relationship by helping clients understand the importance of acting quickly to implement education funding recommendations. Essentially, every moment counts. The longer a client waits to implement recommendations, the more complex and expensive future recommendations become. Given the complex nature of the products typically used in an education funding plan, and the associated tax implications, it is important to present recommendations clearly and concisely. Particular care needs to be given to documenting who is responsible for implementation. Timeframes for implementation should also be featured.

The presentation of all education funding recommendations should match a client's learning style and preferences. Figure 14.9 shows how the 529 Plan recommendation developed for the Hubble family can be presented within a comprehensive financial plan.

Figure 14.9. Implementing an Education Recommendation for the Hubble Family.

Recommendation #1: Contribute $26,100 of your current savings to a section 529 plan for education funding and contribute $1,800 to the account each year until Phoebe begins college (at age eighteen).	
Who:	Chandler or Rachel (account owner) and Phoebe (beneficiary).
What:	A Section 529 plan for educational savings. All contributions should be invested in the Vanguard Growth Portfolio.
When:	Contribute $26,100 prior to the end of the current tax year and contribute $1,800 annually (or $150 monthly) until Phoebe begins college. The EE savings bonds should be redeemed ($25,000), with the proceeds deposited into the 529 college savings plan within sixty days of receiving the distribution. Doing so will make the distribution a tax-free event.
Where:	Missouri's MOST 529 plan, your state's provider of Section 529 plans. The MOST website can be found at https://www.missourimost.org.
Why:	If you use all assets held in the 529 plan before turning age seventy-two to fund qualified educational expenses, distributions can be received tax free (in addition, you will receive a state tax deduction for each contribution). Qualified expenses for a 529 plan include tuition, fees, computer technology, books, and room and board. 529 plan contributions are considered gifts to the beneficiary, but contributions under the federal gift tax contribution limit qualify for a gift tax exclusion (you will not incur gift taxes if this recommendation is implemented).
How:	The process for establishing a 529 plan is as follows: (1) establish a MOST 529 account; (2) cash in the Series EE savings bonds and transfer the funds to the 529 account using a Transfer/Rollover Form. You can open a section 529 plan account online by visiting the Missouri's MOST website (https://www.missourimost.org/). You will need to provide your Social Security number, your birth date, your beneficiary's (Phoebe) Social Security number, and your beneficiary's (Phoebe) birth date; (3) choose the Vanguard Growth Portfolio option. Note that in the future, you may change the beneficiary of the account if needed.

How much:	Contribute $25,000 using the EE savings bonds and $1,100 from your checking account prior to the end of the current tax year. Thereafter, contribute $1,800 annually (or $150 monthly). Your ongoing, annual savings will come from cash flow, which is accounted for in your spending plan.
Effect on cash flow:	This investment will decrease available cash flow by $1,710 each year (the $1,800 contribution is offset by state tax savings of $90).

14.8 STEP 7: MONITOR PROGRESS AND UPDATE

Changes to a client's circumstances should prompt a review and/or reevaluation of previously made recommendations. This is true across financial planning topics, but this rule is particularly relevant in relation to education funding outcomes. At a minimum, a client's education funding plan should be monitored on an annual basis. Changes in a client's attitudes, expectations, objectives, and/or changes in the investment markets, warrant a review of previously implemented recommendations. Figure 14.10 provides an overview of some of the factors that require ongoing monitoring for Chandler and Rachel Hubble.

Figure 14.10. Issues to Monitor in the Hubble Case.

Numerous ongoing monitoring issues are at play in the domain of education planning. It is important to evaluate these (and other) factors on an ongoing basis:

- The type of college Phoebe would like to attend (i.e., in-state, out-of-state, public, private).
- The inflation rate associated with education costs.
- Changes in tax legislation regarding education savings vehicles.
- Change in marital status.
- The receipt of gifts or inheritances.
- A change in the savings objectives of Chandler and/or Rachel.
- The birth or adoption of another child.

14.9 COMPREHENSIVE HUBBLE CASE

Education planning is an important topic within a financial plan that typically involves a client's goal of funding a child's or grandchild's educational costs. Estimating the future cost of education, and presenting strategies that will assist a client reach their education funding goal(s), indicates financial planning competency. The following narrative is an example of how the education section within a comprehensive financial plan can be written.

Education

Overview of Education:

Although education planning is not a component of every financial plan, for those who would like to help fund the educational expenses of a child, grandchild, or other family member, it is important to begin planning for these financial outlays as soon as possible. On average, tuition costs have been increasing 5 percent to 6 percent each year. There are myriad ways to save for college expenses using tax-advantaged savings vehicles, non-tax-advantaged savings investments, and/or a combination of techniques depending on your personal and financial circumstances and your college savings goals.

Education Definitions:

The following definitions will be useful as you review the analysis presented in this section:

- *Financial aid:* Money provided for education expenses from sources other than the student or the student's family. Financial aid comes in three basic forms: scholarships, loans, and grants.

- *Section 529 plan:* A tax-advantaged savings plan designed to encourage saving for college education. These plans are sponsored by states, state agencies, or educational institutions. Savings can be used for tuition, books, and other education-related expenses. Each state has its own rules regarding tax benefits.

Planning Assumptions:

- In-state college tuition for four years will cost $10,000 per semester, including room and board.

- Tuition costs are increasing 5 percent per year.

- As a family, you are willing to invest in a moderately aggressive portfolio (a portfolio that generates a return of approximately 10 percent on an annualized basis) for this goal, before Phoebe begins college and during her college years.

- As a family, you want all college savings to be accumulated before Phoebe begins college, and therefore, you plan to stop saving for college expenses once Phoebe begins college.

- No assets are currently targeted for college savings needs.

- You prefer to invest in a tax-advantaged investment to pay for college, if possible.

Goals:

- Provide 100 percent of Phoebe's college education costs.

- Choose appropriate education saving vehicles to meet educational funding need (you prefer to invest in tax-advantaged investments to pay for college, if possible).

Your Current Education Situation:

You recently started thinking about saving for Phoebe's higher education needs. As such, no money has been saved for this goal thus far. Without any additional adjustments, our estimates indicate that you need to accumulate approximately $141,000 by the time Phoebe enters college to fully fund educational expenses. As shown in the table below, this will require annual savings of approximately $5,700.

COLLEGE SAVINGS ANALYSIS	
ASSUMPTIONS	
Child/Scenario Name	Phoebe
Combined Federal and State Marginal Tax Bracket	30.00%
Assumed After-Tax Rate of Return Before College	7.00%
Assumed Before-Tax Return of Tax-Advantaged Plans	10.00%
Assumed Rate of Return After College Begins	10.00%
Assumed College Expense Inflation Rate	5.00%
Age	5
College Age	18
Years In College	4
Yearly Cost of College TODAY	$20,000.00
Value of After-Tax Assets Saved Today	
Value of Tax-Advantaged Assets Saved	
Annual After-Tax Savings	
Annual Tax-Advantaged Savings	
Annual Savings Growth Rate	3.00%
CALCULATIONS	
College Serial After-Tax Interest Rate Before College Starts	1.9048%
College Serial Before-Tax Rate Before College Starts	4.7619%
College Serial Interest Rate After College Starts	4.7619%
FV of College	$37,712.98
FV of Assets	$0.00
FV of Savings	$0.00
Gross Assets Needed (1st Day of College) without Savings	$162,547.67
Assets Needed (1st Day of College)	$140,874.71
BEFORE-TAX ASSET CALCULATION	
Present Value of Assets Needed	$40,806.38
BEFORE-TAX SAVINGS REQUIREMENTS	
Annual Level Savings Needed	$5,744.66
Serial Adjusted Savings Needed*	$4,282.03
AFTER-TAX ASSET CALCULATION	
Present Value of Assets Needed	$58,458.00

AFTER-TAX SAVINGS REQUIREMENTS	
Annual Level Savings Needed	$6,994.55
Serial Adjusted Savings Needed*	$5,118.94

Serial adjusted savings require that the amount saved for college increases each year by the savings growth rate.

Education Recommendations:

It is possible to fully fund your education goal without significantly adjusting your current financial situation. The following table summarizes the recommendation that was designed to help you reach your education funding goal. As with all recommendations presented in this financial plan, our firm is available to answer any questions that might arise and to assist with specific implementation procedures.

Recommendation #1: Contribute $26,100 of your current savings to a section 529 plan for education funding and contribute $1,800 to the account each year until Phoebe begins college (at age eighteen).	
Who:	Chandler or Rachel (account owner) and Phoebe (beneficiary).
What:	A Section 529 plan for educational savings. All contributions should be invested in the Vanguard Growth Portfolio.
When:	Contribute $26,100 prior to the end of the current tax year and contribute $1,800 annually (or $150 monthly) until Phoebe begins college. The EE savings bonds should be redeemed ($25,000), with the proceeds deposited into the 529 college savings plan within sixty days of receiving the distribution. Doing so will make the distribution a tax-free event.
Where:	Missouri's MOST 529 plan, your state's provider of Section 529 plans. The MOST website can be found at https://www.missourimost.org/.
Why:	If you use all assets held in the 529 plan before turning seventy-two to fund qualified educational expenses, distributions can be received tax free (in addition, you will receive a state tax deduction for each contribution). Qualified expenses for a 529 plan include tuition, fees, computer technology, books, and room and board. 529 plan contributions are considered gifts to the beneficiary, but contributions under the federal gift tax contribution limit qualify for a gift tax exclusion (you will not incur gift taxes if this recommendation is implemented).
How:	The process for establishing a 529 plan is as follows: (1) establish a MOST 529 account; (2) cash in the Series EE savings bonds and transfer the funds to the 529 account using a Transfer/Rollover Form. You can open a section 529 plan account online by visiting the Missouri's MOST website (https://www.missourimost.org/). You will need to provide your Social Security number, your birth date, your beneficiary's (Phoebe) Social Security number, and your beneficiary's (Phoebe) birth date; (3) choose the Vanguard Growth Portfolio option. Note that in the future, you may change the beneficiary of the account if needed.

| How much: | Contribute $25,000 using the EE savings bonds and $1,100 from your checking account prior to the end of the current tax year. Thereafter, contribute $1,800 annually (or $150 monthly). Your ongoing, annual savings will come from cash flow, which is accounted for in your spending plan. |
| Effect on cash flow: | This investment will decrease available cash flow by $1,710 each year (the $1,800 contribution is offset by state tax savings of $90). |

Current vs. Recommended Outcome:

Currently, you are not allocating savings towards education expenses for Phoebe. Without appropriate savings, Phoebe may need to rely on financial aid and student loans to cover college expenses, if she chooses to attend college. In order to meet your goal of covering all of Phoebe's college expenses, you will need to follow the savings schedule outlined in the recommendation above. The following table shows how implementation of the recommendation will lead to goal achievement

COLLEGE SAVINGS RECOMMENDATIONS	
ASSUMPTIONS	
Child/ Scenario Name	Phoebe
Combined Federal and State Marginal Tax Bracket	30.00%
Assumed After-Tax Rate of Return Before College	7.00%
Assumed Before-Tax Return of Tax-Advantaged Plans	10.00%
Assumed Rate of Return After College Begins	10.00%
Assumed College Expense Inflation Rate	5.00%
Age	5
College Age	18
Years In College	4
Yearly Cost of College TODAY	$20,000.00
Value of After-Tax Assets Saved Today	
Value of Tax-Advantaged Assets Saved	$26,100.00
Annual After-Tax Savings	
Annual Tax-Advantaged Savings	$1,800.00
Annual Savings Growth Rate	3.00%
CALCULATIONS	
College Serial After-Tax Interest Rate Before College Starts	1.9048%
College Serial Before-Tax Rate Before College Starts	4.7619%
College Serial Interest Rate After College Starts	4.7619%
FV of College	$37,712.98
FV of Assets	$90,104.28
FV of Savings	$51,010.39
Gross Assets Needed (1st Day of College) without Savings	$162,547.67
Assets Needed (1st Day of College)	($239.96)

BEFORE-TAX ASSET CALCULATION	
Present Value of Assets Needed	($69.51)
BEFORE-TAX SAVINGS REQUIREMENTS	
Annual Level Savings Needed	($9.79)
Serial Adjusted Savings Needed*	($7.29)
AFTER-TAX ASSET CALCULATION	
Present Value of Assets Needed	($99.58)
AFTER-TAX SAVINGS REQUIREMENTS	
Annual Level Savings Needed	($11.91)
Serial Adjusted Savings Needed*	($8.72)

* Serial adjusted savings require that the amount saved for college increases each year by the savings growth rate.

Saving $1,800 each year will provide funds to cover four years of college education expenses assuming tuition remains approximately $10,000 (today's dollars) per semester and that a 10 percent annualized rate of return can be earned on 529 plan assets.

Using a 529 college savings plan as a savings vehicle provides several advantages. You can control how the funds are spent and retain ownership of the money in the account. You can change the beneficiary at any time. You will not pay any immediate state or federal income tax on the earnings in the account. If the withdrawals you make are for qualified education expenses, you can avoid paying federal and Missouri state tax on the withdrawals. In Missouri, you can deduct up to $8,000 ($16,000 if filing taxes jointly) of MOST 529 Plan contributions on your state income tax return. These tax savings will allow you to increase your savings for other goals or free up cash flow that can be spent elsewhere.

Alternative Recommendations and Outcome(s):

It is possible to meet your education savings goal by splitting contributions into the 529 plan. For example, you could allocate $16,000 into the account this year, $12,000 into the account next year, and $1,800 into the account each year until Phoebe begins college. This strategy provides a state tax deduction equivalent to the contribution for each year the contribution is made. The benefit associated with this strategy is that you can maximize the state tax deduction over several years. The disadvantage associated with this strategy is that you will need to pay federal and state taxes on the growth of education savings assets held outside the 529 plan.

If Phoebe decides to postpone or not attend college, you may change the beneficiary to a grandchild or other family member, if desired. You may also withdraw the funds, but distributions will be subject to a 10 percent tax penalty and you will owe state and federal income taxes on the earnings withdrawn. For the same reason, if it becomes very likely that Phoebe will receive financial aid or a scholarship for college, it may be necessary to invest ongoing contributions outside the section 529 plan or suspend savings altogether.

Plan Implementation and Monitoring Procedures:

It is very likely that this education savings plan will need to be updated to account for changes in assumptions and to account for Phoebe's own college goals as her educational objectives begin to take shape. Our firm will provide you with the necessary paperwork to cash in the Series EE bonds and roll the funds into a 529 plan account. Once the initial lump sum has been transferred, you will need to set up the ongoing monthly or annual contributions to the account. Our firm will provide ongoing guidance about the investments in your 529 plan and incorporate these investment assets into your overall investment plan (as described in the separate investment management agreement). We will include performance data from your 529 plan account in quarterly reports and may recommend changes to your investment allocation if necessary.

14.10 SELF-TEST

[A] Questions

Self-Test 1

Which of the following inputs into a college savings needs analysis is an assumption best estimated by a financial planner, rather than a client?

(a) When the client's child will begin college.

(b) The average annual rate of tuition inflation.

(c) The number of years the client's child will stay in college.

(d) Each of these inputs should be a financial derived input.

Self-Test 2

When calculating the total cost of education, a financial planner should

(a) assume a beginning payment for tuition.

(b) assume an ending payment for tuition.

(c) use a constant $100,000 future value.

(d) make the estimate using quarterly compounding of returns.

Self-Test 3

Liana has been saving for retirement using a traditional IRA. She likes the IRA because she has been able to deduct all contributions on her Form 1040. She would like to know what will happen if she takes a $20,000 distribution to help pay for her son's college tuition.

(a) The full amount of the distribution will be taxable.

(b) The full amount of the distribution will be subject to the 10 percent early withdrawal penalty.

(c) If she rolls the distribution into a Roth IRA prior to paying for her son's tuition, both the tax and penalty will be waived.

(d) Both (a) and (b).

Self-Test 4

Dora has agreed to help her daughter pay for tuition at a state college. Which of the following loan choices may Dora use to obtain money for her daughter's tuition expense?

(a) A Stafford Unsubsidized Loan.

(b) A Perkins Loan.

(c) A PLUS Loan.

(d) Either (a) or (c).

Self-Test 5

Which of the following will have the greatest negative impact on a family's ability to obtain financial aid?

(a) A grandparent's 529 plan held for one of the family's children.

(b) A $10,000 529 plan account balance held by a parent for a child.

(c) $20,000 held in an UGMA account.

(d) $250,000 held in a 401(k) plan by a parent.

[B] Answers

Question 1: b

Question 2: a

Question 3: a

Question 4: c

Question 5: c

14.11 CHAPTER RESOURCES

Department of Education, Overview of the Student Loan Program. https://studentaid.gov/.

Department of Education. https://studentaid.ed.gov/sa/repay-loans/understand/plans.

Information about education tax credits: www.irs.gov/publications/p970/ch02.html#d0e1386.

Information about student financial aid: www.fafsa.ed.gov.

Information about interest rates and fees on PLUS loans: www.edvisors.com/college-loans/federal/parent-plus/interest-rates/

Hurley, J. F. *Family Guide to College Savings 2018–2019*. Miami, FL (savingforcollege.com).

Equal Justice Works. *Partial Financial Hardship*. Available at: www.equaljusticeworks.org/resources/student-debt-relief/income-based-repayment/partial-financial-hardship.Student loan repayment plans: https://studentaid.gov/manage-loans/repayment/plans

Information about student loans: www.finaid.org/loans/studentloan.phtml.

CHAPTER ENDNOTES

1. This process assumes that periodic savings payments occur at the end of each period; that periodic savings payments for college will cease when the child begins college; and the annual college expense payment occurs at the beginning of each school year. Each of these assumptions can be changed to fit a client's individual situation, but corresponding changes in the calculations will be necessary.

2. An effective annual rate (EAR) of 8.30 percent is equivalent to an 8 percent rate compounded monthly.

3. Department of Education, Student Loans Overview, *Fiscal Year 2012 Budget Request*. Available at: www2.ed.gov/about/overview/budget/budget12/justifications/s-loansoverview.pdf, p. S-12.

4. FinAid, The Smart Student™ Guide to Financial Aid. *Student Loans*. Available at: www.finaid.org/loans/studentloan.phtml.

5. See "Interest Rates and Fees on PLUS Loans": www.edvisors.com/college-loans/federal/parent-plus/interest-rates/

6. Department of Education. Federal Student Aid. Direct Loans. *Repayment Plans*. Available at: www.direct.ed.gov/RepayCalc/dlindex2.html.

7. Department of Education, Repayment Plans.

8. *Ibid*.

9. *Ibid*.

10. *Ibid*.

11. Equal Justice Works. *Partial Financial Hardship*. Available at: www.equaljusticeworks.org/resources/student-debt-relief/income-based-repayment/partial-financial-hardship.

12. FinAid, The Smart Student™ Guide to Financial Aid. *Health Care and Education Reconciliation Act of 2010*. Available at: www.finaid.org/educators/20100330hcera.phtml.

13. Hurley, J. F. *Family Guide to College Savings 2011–2012* (Pittsford, NY: JFH Innovative, 2011).

Chapter 15

Retirement Planning

Learning Objectives

- Learning Objective 1: Describe the importance of retirement planning within a comprehensive financial plan.

- Learning Objective 2: Identify factors that influence the establishment of retirement goals.

- Learning Objective 3: Describe the process involved when conducting a retirement capital needs analysis.

- Learning Objective 4: Understand the tax implications associated with different retirement saving plans.

- Learning Objective 5: Identify appropriate retirement planning recommendations that can be used to help a client reach their retirement objectives, accounting for client goals, resources, and household characteristics.

15.1 THE PROCESS OF RETIREMENT PLANNING

When viewed historically, **retirement planning**—the process of helping a client to define and prepare for retirement by developing strategies for asset accumulation, asset distribution, and monitoring of plan progress—can be seen as a relatively new phenomenon. Prior to the industrial revolution, people rarely planned to retire in the way retirement is defined today, nor did they live as long or spend as many years as possible in retirement. Nearly everyone worked until they could work no longer. Those who did outlive their working careers relied on the charity of family, friends, religious groups, or community sources for assistance with elder needs. Today, beyond leaving one's primary source of employment, retirement can mean pursuing part-time or full-time employment in the same or a different occupation. Retirement can also mean pursuing leisure or volunteer activities. Although retirement activities can vary widely, for many people, retirement represents a different phase of one's evolving life. From a financial planning perspective, this creates both opportunities and challenges.

For nearly all clients, planning and saving for retirement requires a significant commitment, especially in relation to allocating household resources towards this goal. In addition to issues related to the use of cash flow to build a retirement nest egg, clients, working with their financial planner, must also grapple with questions related to housing preferences, health issues, recreational choices, and overall lifestyle factors as they plan for retirement. Clients who postpone tasks associated with retirement planning will find that the strategies, tools, and techniques available to reach retirement goals diminish as the day of retirement nears. Financial planners can serve their clientele well by promoting early and ongoing retirement planning activities. The purpose of this chapter is to describe how the financial planning process can be applied when conducting a retirement planning analysis.

15.2 STEP 1: DOCUMENT THE CLIENT'S PERSONAL AND FINANCIAL CIRCUMSTANCES

Prior to beginning a quantitative retirement analysis, either pre- or post-retirement, it is important to review lifestyle and client characteristics that may impact retirement planning assumptions. Client characteristics to consider—from the perspective of the client and spouse, partner, or significant other—include the following:

- attitude about retiring, or specifically about retiring early;

- motivation for retiring or retiring early;

- willingness to continue working for another firm or in a different profession;

- willingness to establish a consulting practice or other business venture;

- types of personal, leisure, or volunteer activities that the individual(s) will engage in while retired;

- health status;

- willingness to relocate, either to a specific designation or to a lower-cost area; and

- willingness or need to provide support for other family members (e.g., children, grandchildren, parents, in-laws).

Although financial planners who work with pre-retirees should analyze the following quantitative financial factors to assess a client's retirement readiness, those considering early retirement must carefully consider these issues:

- ability of the accumulated asset base, plus other forms of income, to provide adequate retirement income;

- impact of early retirement on Social Security benefits;

- impact of early retirement on defined benefit plan distributions;

- effect of retirement on health benefits;

- impact of early retirement on the working status of a spouse or partner;

- tax implications of lump-sum benefits (e.g., unused sick and vacation days) received from an employer; and

- relocation and retirement transition expenses.

Figure 15.1 provides a review of the Hubbles' personal and financial circumstances related to retirement planning. The information in Figure 15.1 is typical of what a financial planner should evaluate at the first step of the financial planning process.

Figure 15.1. The Hubbles' Personal and Financial Circumstances.

Chandler Hubble	Rachel Hubble
Age: 42	Age: 42
Retirement Age: 62	Retirement Age: 62
State of residence: Missouri	State of residence: Missouri
Citizen: U.S.	Citizen: U.S.
Life status: No known life issues	Life status: No known life issues

- Chandler and Rachel appear to be conscientious, as reflected in being organized, thorough, disciplined, and achievement-oriented. These attributes will help them be proactive in relation to implementing retirement planning recommendations.

- The risk tolerance and investment preferences of Chandler and Rachel will influence the choice of retirement planning strategies recommended in the financial plan.

- Other attitudes and beliefs about retirement may influence the Hubbles' approach to funding retirement. Attitudes, personality, and interests are evident in their stated life goal: being active contributors to the community (especially youth efforts).

- Chandler and Rachel feel that they have other talents and dreams that should be pursued during retirement. Chandler loves golfing, gardening, and traveling. His dream is to teach aspiring young golfers on a volunteer basis during retirement.

- If she is successful as an art gallery owner, Rachel plans to donate any net revenue from the art gallery to local youth groups to enhance creative learning.

- Rachel loves to paint and attend art shows. In addition, Rachel would like to improve her golf game so that Chandler would enjoy playing more golf with her.

- Neither Chandler nor Rachel has a strong desire to travel in retirement. Chandler travels enough now, and he would prefer to enjoy life in Southwest Missouri during retirement.

- Chandler and Rachel do, however, plan on taking an occasional trip, especially to go and see their daughter if she is not living in Springfield.

- Chandler's and Rachel's experiences with other retirees, such as their parents or others, may influence their plans.

- The Hubbles' assumptions about retirement reflect Chandler's and Rachel's financial knowledge and experience, which may limit a comprehensive understanding of the actual amount of saving/investing needed to accumulate enough assets to sustain retirement until age ninety-five.

- The Hubbles' preference to receive Social Security benefits as early as possible may be based on assumptions that do not fully take into account the permanent reduction in benefits. Increasing the Hubbles' knowledge may change this preference, or at least help them to make the most informed decision relative to their situation.

15.3 STEP 2: IDENTIFY AND SELECT GOALS

Although retirement planning entails a high degree of quantitative analyses, it is essential that financial planners account for client-specific circumstances and environmental factors that could uniquely influence the establishment of retirement planning goals. The following lifestyle issues commonly impact the process associated with developing retirement planning goals: client retirement attitudes, early retirement aspirations, postretirement work attitudes, leisure activity hopes and dreams, health status, and relocation preferences. Environmental factors include job security, investment market conditions, the stability of the housing market, and possible employer restructuring, among other factors.

Although Chandler and Rachel have many years until they will be in a position to retire from paid working life, now is a good time to begin preparing for retirement. Figure 15.2 provides an overview of retirement goals as they relate to the Hubble family.

Figure 15.2. The Hubbles' Retirement Goals.

> **Chandler and Rachel came to the financial planning process with relatively well-defined retirement planning goals. When discussing their retirement situation, Chandler and Rachel indicated the following goals:**
>
> - Chandler and Rachel have expressed a strong desire to retire at age sixty-two, but it is more important that they do not deplete assets over their lifetime.
> - Chandler and Rachel plan to build a small addition to their home and fill it with art; if built today, the addition would cost $20,000. Rachel would like to then open a small art gallery in downtown Springfield. She estimates the cost of the gallery would be $80,000 if opened today.
> - Keep in mind that Chandler and Rachel need to balance their desire to retire early with the fact that they have limited savings and assets available to meet this and all other financial goals and identified planning needs.
> - Chandler and Rachel are willing to postpone retirement to age sixty-five if this action will allow them to fully fund the cost of Phoebe's education, save for the house addition and art gallery, and enjoy their lifestyle while maintaining sufficient financial flexibility that they are not anxious about money today or depleting their assets in the future.

15.4 STEP 3: ANALYZE THE CLIENT'S CURRENT COURSE OF ACTION AND POTENTIAL ALTERNATIVE COURSE(S) OF ACTION

[A] Documenting the Client's Current Retirement Planning Situation

Analyzing a client's current retirement planning situation involves documenting and evaluating all relevant current retirement planning strategies. This type of analysis should consider four questions:

(1) Is the amount of money the client is saving enough to meet the goal?

(2) Is the client optimizing the asset class mix to ensure the best risk-adjusted return?

(3) Is the client utilizing the optimal types of accounts (i.e., qualified or pretax versus non-qualified or post-tax) to ensure the best tax-adjusted return?

(4) Is the client maintaining adequate financial flexibility to meet changing goals or emergencies?

Although the first question may be the most important to review early in the accumulation phase of retirement planning, the fourth question becomes more important as a client nears or enters retirement. The second and third questions represent important planning issues across the life cycle, as well as issues that might need to be reconsidered because of changes in the economy or market or tax policy changes.

[B] The Capital Needs Analysis

Conducting a retirement capital needs analysis is a key aspect embedded in the retirement planning process. The steps involved in conducting a needs analysis (be it a capital depletion, capital preservation, or inflation-adjusted model) requires the application of time value of money concepts. It is each financial planner's responsibility to develop assumptions related to rates of return, inflation, life expectancy, and timing of payments, and once established, to balance these assumptions against each client's retirement aspirations and financial goals. Keep in mind that depending on an individual financial planner's business model and scope of services provided, retirement planning services can focus on one or two perspectives: the employer's or the employee's. In some situations, a client can be both. Additionally, financial planners often advise clients who are employed by a firm where plan benefits are limited. In these cases, financial planners must seek better alternatives because of plan limitations.

There are numerous approaches that can be used to estimate the amount needed for retirement. The following discussion highlights one approach that can used to determine whether a client is on track to meet their retirement goal.

[C] Calculating a Retirement Need

Once a client and their financial planner have finalized one or more retirement goal(s), incorporating lifestyle and income desires, and considering both the active and inactive years associated with aging, attention must turn to quantifying the cost of the projected retirement need. Fundamentally, retirement planning involves:

1. documenting a client's specific retirement income funding goal;

2. determining the gross amount needed to pay for expenses over a client's life expectancy; and

3. determining whether the client is on track to meet their asset accumulation objective given all other assumptions about the funding situation.

Although the analytical approach may appear straightforward, these three elements of the projection must be accurately matched to each client's unique situation.

The retirement needs analysis process begins by calculating an income or living expense **replacement ratio**. This is a measure used to estimate a client's **retirement income funding goal**. An accepted generalization is that a client will need 70 percent to 80 percent of currently available income in retirement to maintain their lifestyle. That is, the target should be to replace at least 70 percent of current income on the client's first day of retirement. In general, low- and high-income earning households need the highest replacement ratios.

> *Example.* Assume a client currently earns $169,000 annually. If it is determined that the client needs to replace 80 percent of this amount in retirement, the income funding goal becomes $135,200. This amount should be reduced by guaranteed sources of retirement income, such as expected defined benefit payments, Social

Security benefits, and annuity payments. The result is the dollar amount needed in a capital needs analysis. Because the figure is in today's dollars, a future value estimate must occur using (1) an inflation rate assumption and (2) the number of periods between the retirement date and the current period as the period input.

Determining the gross pool of assets needed over a client's life expectancy involves conducting a traditional **retirement capital needs analysis**. This projection determines the capital needed from all sources to support a client's estimated retirement income requirement, while accounting for the effects of inflation over a client's life expectancy. Three types of **capital needs analyses** are typically used by financial planners:

(1) Capital depletion.

(2) Capital preservation.

(3) Inflation-adjusted capital preservation.

Each approach is based on relatively simple time value of money equations. However, a financial planner must first make several assumptions, in consultation with the client, before estimating a client's retirement planning need. These include the following:

- The first assumption involves determining whether contributions toward the retirement goal will grow or remain fixed. That is to say, will each subsequent payment increase by a predetermined amount, such as the inflation rate? In effect, this assumption comes down to using a fixed annuity or a geometric varying annuity assumption.

- A second assumption involves the length of the retirement period or the number of years that the client will engage in saving for the goal.

- The third assumption involves determining the rate of return expected during retirement.

Once these calculation inputs have been determined, the financial planner—again working closely with their client—must calculate the amount of the first retirement payment. The amount of this payment should be based on the client's current (or projected) income. The projection can simply be an estimated target value, such as a dollar figure (e.g., $100,000), or a percentage of current living expenses using a replacement ratio. Once all variable inputs are known, the financial planner can calculate the amount required to fully fund the level of savings needed on an annual basis to meet the accumulated asset objective as of the retirement date.

To facilitate the presentation of these calculations, two loosely defined terms can be used. The first is a **retirement annuity**, which is the amount of money required to fund a client's retirement over a given period. The second is a **legacy pool**. This is the amount of money that a client wants or hopes to leave unspent at the end of the retirement period. Typically, this is the amount the client wants to bequeath to other people and/or organizations.

The most basic needs analysis approach is called the **capital depletion approach**. This approach assumes that at the end of the retirement planning period no additional client assets will remain available to the client or heirs. In other words, the legacy pool will be zero.

> *Example:* Assume a client desires to fund a retirement account with enough money to last thirty years. The financial planner knows that the client wants the first payment to be $100,000, to be received at the beginning of the first year of retirement. [The $100,000 figure can either be an assumption or it can be based on taking a client's current household income multiplied by the income replacement ratio, less any guaranteed forms of retirement income, such as Social Security, and inflated to the date of retirement (i.e., a future value calculation)]. A further assumption is the financial planner knows that subsequent payments are to increase 4 percent annually to keep pace with anticipated inflation. Assuming an effective annual rate of return of 10 percent, how much, in total assets, will the client need at retirement? Using the present value of a growing annuity formula, it can be determined that the client requires $1,492,564, as shown below:

Present value of a growing annuity

$$PVGA_n = \frac{PMT_1}{(i-g)}\left[1 - \frac{(1+g)^n}{(1+i)^n}\right](1+i)$$

Where

$i = 10$ percent

$g = 4$ percent

$PMT_1 = \$100,000$

$n = 30$

$$PVGA_n = \frac{\$100,000}{(0.10-0.04)}\left[1 - \frac{(1.04)^{30}}{(1.10)^{30}}\right](1.10) = \$1,492,564$$

The capital depletion approach results in the smallest retirement annuity need because it is assumed the client will deplete the account over the course of retirement. Many clients are uncomfortable with the fundamental assumption of depleting all assets over their life expectancy. First, there is the possibility of outliving the available assets. Second, the capital depletion approach leaves nothing as a legacy to heirs or charities. In cases where the minimum capital depletion scenario can be satisfied with asset projections, a financial planner should also calculate the retirement need using the **capital preservation approach**.

To determine the legacy pool needed to preserve a client's capital so that the client's asset base does not decline during retirement, a financial planner must conduct one additional time value of money calculation. As with the previous method, the retirement annuity figure must be estimated. The legacy pool should then be added to the present value of the retirement annuity to determine a new amount needed on the first day of retirement. In effect, the present value of the legacy pool grows while the present value of the retirement annuity is depleted. At the end of the planning period, the client should have exactly the same nominal amount available that they had on the first day of retirement. The following example illustrates the steps necessary to estimate a capital preservation retirement annuity.

> *Example*. Return to the previous example where a client requires a growing annuity with a beginning payment of $100,000. However, in addition, the client desires to leave a legacy equal to the beginning value of the retirement annuity. Given these assumptions, the client needs to accumulate an additional $85,537 by the first day of retirement.[1] This is the amount that will result in a future value equal to $1,492,564 at the client's death. Using this approach, the client needs a total of $1,578,101 saved at retirement ($1,492,564 + $85,537). The present value of a lump sum is used to solve for the additional amount needed.

Present Value

$$PV_n = \frac{FV}{(1 + i)^n}$$

Where

$i = 10$ percent

FV = $1,492,564 (the amount needed to fund the retirement annuity)

$n = 30$

$$PV_n = \frac{\$1,492,564}{(1.1)^{30}} = \$85,537$$

In cases where capital preservation can be achieved, a third retirement needs estimation can be used: the **inflation-adjusted capital preservation approach**. It may be possible not only to preserve a client's assets, but also to account for inflation such that at life expectancy the real value of the retirement assets is equal to the nominal value at retirement. The following illustration example extends the case from above.

> *Example*. Again, the client requires a growing annuity with a beginning payment of $100,000. However, in addition, the client wishes to leave a legacy with an ending purchasing power equal to the beginning purchasing power of the retirement annuity. To maintain equivalent purchasing power, the client needs to a have an additional $277,429 saved at the time of retirement. The estimate replaces the nominal i with the serial rate (see below). Using this approach, the client needs a total of $1,769,993 saved on the first day of retirement ($1,492,564 + $277,429).

Serial Rate

$$\text{Serial Rate} = \frac{(1 + i)}{(1 + g)} - 1$$

$$\text{Serial Rate} = \frac{(1.10)}{(1.04)} - 1 = 5.77\%$$

Using the serial rate, the following present value equation is used to calculate the required additional amount needed to preserve the purchasing power of the client's legacy:

$$PV_n = \frac{FV}{(1 + i)^n}$$

Where

$i = 5.77$ percent

FV = \$1,492,564 (the inflation-adjusted amount desired at the end of retirement)

$n = 30$

$$PV_n = \frac{\$1,492,564}{(1.0577)^{30}} = \$277,429$$

Planning Reminder

The Social Security Administration provides information on estimating a client's life expectancy. The following website can be used to obtain an estimate of a client's life expectancy: socialsecurity.gov/planners/lifeexpectancy.html

Once the retirement annuity figure has been determined, a financial planner must then estimate the future value of retirement assets and savings. These assets will be used, in most client situations, to generate income as an element of the retirement annuity. Making appropriate rate of return, inflation, and tax rate assumptions is important at this stage of the analysis.

Assume, for example, that a client currently has twenty-four years remaining until retirement, can earn an annualized rate of return equal to 7 percent, has 401(k) assets of \$86,000, and is saving \$9,000 per year (including employer matching contributions). Using these figures, a financial planner can estimate the future values as follows:

- 401(k) = \$436,224

- savings = \$523,590

These amounts should then be subtracted from the capital needs analysis estimate to determine a surplus or shortfall need. If a shortfall exists, a time value of money calculation can be used to pinpoint the amount of additional annual savings needed.

[D] Retirement Distribution Calculations

Almost all retirement planning calculations are based on the assumption that a client is in the process of saving for retirement. It is, however, equally important to understand how to estimate appropriate retirement distribution amounts for those who are already retired. There are multiple ways to calculate the optimal withdrawal strategy for a client. Some financial planners use a simple heuristic, such as the **4 percent rule**, which states that a retiree can safely withdraw 4 percent of the value of savings each year during retirement. The academic literature offers a multitude of similar strategies, ranging from withdrawals based on increasing equity holdings over retirement to reducing the safe distribution to 4 percent or less, and in some cases, including reverse mortgages and home equity in distribution estimates.

Two other approaches are widely used to determine the appropriate distribution from accumulated assets. The first is based on a **deterministic model**. Deterministic models use a static, or constant, mean return throughout the modeling period. The output is a very elementary projection on which to base a safe withdrawal strategy. The second is called a **stochastic model**. Stochastic models add variability to distribution calculations. The following discussion highlights the steps necessary to estimate withdrawals using a *deterministic model*.

1. *Determine the value of the pool of available assets at the beginning of retirement.* Although not all client assets will be used to fund retirement (home equity is often excluded), assets that can be used should be valued at the market value as of the projected date of retirement.

2. *Choose a reasonable after-tax rate of return for retirement.* A financial planner should always take into account a client's risk tolerance, expectations, time horizon, and preferences, including asset class limitations, when establishing a rate of return projection. The return should not subject a client's assets to risks beyond those necessary to achieve a desired standard of living.

3. *Choose a realistic average rate of inflation during retirement (or determine the client's desired rate of increase for the retirement annuity).* Although not always the case, using a conservative estimate is a best practice (i.e., slightly overstate projected inflation). Just as investment losses are more detrimental early in the withdrawal period, high inflation early during a withdrawal period can create a quicker depletion of assets, making it problematic that a client can maintain their standard of living.

4. *Calculate the inflation-adjusted rate of return applicable to the client using the serial interest rate formula:*

$$\text{Serial Rate} = \frac{(1 + i)}{(1 + g)} - 1$$

5. *Determine the client's life expectancy.* A client's individual life expectancy can be estimated using a Period Life Expectancy Table. If a client is married, the client's and spouse's joint and survivor life expectancy (i.e., how long at least

one of the two will live, or until both will be deceased) can be determined using a joint and survivor life expectancy table. These tables should be used as a starting point in an analysis. Other important information, including a client's ancestral life expectancy patterns, current health status, occupation, and hobbies, can be used to increase or decrease assumptions regarding a client's life expectancy. For financial planners who want a conservative estimate, using a table factor life expectancy and adding at least five years can be a practical approach.

6. *Calculate the withdrawal amount.* There are two basic methods that can be used at this step of the estimation process. Both methods can be adjusted to account for inflation to preserve purchasing power. If inflation is accounted for, withdrawals will increase each year to reflect inflation. The first method assumes a depletion of all assets at the end of the client's life expectancy (i.e., at the end of retirement), which is referred to as the **capital depletion withdrawal method.** This approach is based on a growth-adjusted present value of an annuity due calculation.

Example: Assume a client has retirement assets equal to $500,000 at the time of retirement, that yearly distributions will increase by 4 percent, assets will earn 8 percent annually, and retirement is planned to last for twenty years, at which time assets will be depleted. As shown below, and using the serial rate, the amount that can be withdrawn at the beginning of the first year equals $34,947. This amount must then be increased by 4 percent in each succeeding year.

$$\text{Serial Rate} = \frac{(1+i)}{(1+g)} - 1 = \frac{1.08}{1.04} - 1 = 3.846\%$$

$$\$500,000 = \frac{\text{PMT}}{0.03846}\left(1 - \frac{1}{1.03846^{20}}\right)(1.03846)$$

$$\text{PMT} = \frac{\$500,000 \times 0.03846}{(1 - 1.03846^{-20}) \times 1.03846} = \$34,947$$

Where

$i = 3.846$ percent

FV = 0

PV = $500,000

n = 20

Solving for PMT also returns approximately $34,947, which is an annuity due estimate.

The second distribution approach is called the **capital preservation method.** This approach assumes that a client's assets at retirement will be preserved throughout the client's lifetime. The capital preservation method can also increase the yearly payment to reflect inflation. Payments can be determined using a present value of a growing perpetuity due calculation.

> *Example.* Assume a client has retirement assets equal to $500,000 at the time of retirement, that yearly distributions will increase by 4 percent, assets will earn 8 percent annually, and retirement is planned to last for twenty years, at which time assets will still be equal to the inflation-adjusted future value of $500,000. As shown below, the amount that can be withdrawn at the beginning of the first year equals $18,519. This amount, which is significantly less than the capital depletion withdrawal method, will then increase by 4 percent in each succeeding year. Using the same serial rate as before:

$$\$500,000 = \frac{PMT}{0.03846}\left(1 - \frac{1}{1.03846^{20}}\right)(1.03846) + \frac{\$500,000(1.04^{20})}{1.08^{20}}$$

$$\$500,000 = \frac{PMT}{0.03846}\left(1 - \frac{1}{1.03846^{20}}\right)(1.03846) + \$235,050.77$$

$$\$500,000 - \$235,050.77 = \frac{PMT}{0.03846}\left(1 - \frac{1}{1.03846^{20}}\right)(1.03846)$$

What is actually available to support retirement is the difference in the $500,000 saved and the $235,051 needed to ensure the inflation-adjusted future value of the account.

$$PMT = \frac{\$264,949.23 \times 0.03846}{(1 - 1.03846^{-20}) \times 1.03846} = \$18,519$$

Where

$i = 3.846$ percent

$FV = 0$

$PV = \$264,949.23$

$n = 20$

Solving for PMT also returns approximately $18,519.

In other words, the present value of the account continues to increase in perpetuity by the rate of inflation. As a result, if the account is increasing in value at a rate equal to increases in the annual withdrawal, then it turns out to be a simple present value of a growing perpetuity.

$$\$500{,}000 = \frac{PMT}{0.08 - 0.04} \ (1.08)$$

$$PMT = \frac{\$500{,}000 \times (0.08 - 0.04)}{1.08} = \$18{,}519$$

Planning Reminder

Keep in mind that a calculator cannot easily handle a growing annuity problem using time value of money (TVM) keys because there is a future value involved and serial rates typically cannot be used to directly solve for future values. Therefore, the present value of the remaining balance must be subtracted before beginning an analysis. As a reminder, a TVM calculator should be set to beginning-of-period payments.

A **non-random deterministic withdrawal model** can also be developed to help a client gain an idea of how long their retirement account balance(s) will exist into the future. Figure 15.3 illustrates how Excel™ can be used to project estimated withdrawal amounts for a client who enters retirement at age sixty-five with $100,000 in assets. The data in Figure 15.3 are based on the following assumptions:

- 5 percent annualized before-tax rate of return.

- 3 percent annualized inflation rate.

- 4 percent annual distribution rate.

- a distribution rate that increases by the rate of inflation.

- a required minimum distribution (RMD) based on the Uniform Lifetime Table.[2]

Figure 15.3. Deterministic Withdrawal Illustration.

Age of Client	Beginning Balance	Yearly Distribution	Distribution Rate (percent)
65	$500,000	$20,000	4.00
66	504,000	20,600	4.09
67	507,570	21,218	4.18
68	510,670	21,855	4.28
69	513,256	22,510	4.39
70	515,283	23,185	4.50
71	516,702	23,881	4.62
72	517,462	24,597	4.75
73	517,508	25,335	4.90
74	516,781	26,095	5.05

75	515,220	26,878	5.22
76	512,759	27,685	5.40
77	509,328	28,515	5.60
78	504,853	29,371	5.82
79	499,257	30,252	6.06
80	492,455	31,159	6.33
81	484,361	32,094	6.63
82	474,880	33,057	6.96
83	463,914	34,049	7.34
84	451,359	35,070	7.77
85	437,103	36,122	8.26
86	421,030	37,206	8.84
87	403,015	38,322	9.51
88	382,928	39,472	10.31
89	360,629	40,656	11.27
90	335,972	41,876	16.46
91	308,801	43,132	13.97
92	278,952	44,426	15.93
93	246,253	45,759	18.58
94	210,519	47,131	22.39
95	171,557	48,545	28.30
96	129,163	50,002	38.71
97	83,119	51,502	61.96
98	33,198	33,198	100.00
99	0	0	0.00

The first column in Figure 15.3 shows the client's age from sixty-five to an assumed death at age ninety-nine. The second column shows the client's account balance adjusted for each annual withdrawal and account earnings. The third column shows the annual 4 percent distribution, adjusted for inflation. The effective distribution rate shown in the last column can be estimated by dividing the yearly distribution amount by the beginning balance. Over time, the effective distribution rate will rise in response to inflation.

The use of a stochastic retirement withdrawal model is another way financial planners make retirement withdrawal estimates. Stochastic modeling, or what is known as **Monte Carlo modeling**, has gained favor as a projection tool for withdrawal analyses. A stochastic approach randomizes rate-of-return, inflation, and life expectancy assumptions using thousands of data point observations to estimate features of plan success or failure. The primary drawback to stochastic models is the need to use software or advanced data worksheet applications. While certainly not impossible, it would be very time intensive to use a calculator as a stochastic modeling tool.

The following illustration shows how an analysis of the Hubble family's current retirement choices and needs can lead to the development of actionable recommendations. Note that this is a traditional capital needs analysis. Figure 15.4 provides a summary of the Hubbles' current retirement choices and planning assumptions. A screen shot of the retirement needs analysis estimation procedure using the Financial Planning Analysis Excel™ package that accompanies the book is also shown. Potential recommendations are also provided.

Figure 15.4. The Hubbles' Current Retirement Choices and Potential Recommendations.

Globally-accepted planning assumptions include the following:
- The global inflation rate before and after retirement is 3 percent annually.
- Life expectancy is age ninety-five (although some planners/clients assume age one hundred).
- Chandler and Rachel are unwilling to reduce their projected life expectancy unless absolutely required to achieve their age at retirement objective.

Client-specific or financial planner-generated planning assumptions include the following:
- Chandler and Rachel believe they will receive Social Security benefits, and they want to access their benefits at the earliest opportunity.
- Chandler and Rachel have a strong desire to leave as large an estate as possible for the benefit of Phoebe at their death, and as such, they would very much like to minimize the depletion of their retirement assets.
- Chandler and Rachel plan to increase contributions to their retirement accounts by 3 percent each year. Rachel would like to add a small addition to their home for art. If built today the addition would cost $20,000.
- Rachel would also like to open a small art gallery. She estimates the cost of the gallery would be $80,000 if opened today.
  - They are saving $1,800 per year towards the art gallery goal and have $5,000 saved.
  - The Hubbles are willing to invest in a moderately aggressive portfolio (expected before tax rate of return of 10 percent) to fund the art gallery and house addition.
- Chandler and Rachel will need approximately 85 percent of their current earned before-tax income (in today's dollars) when they retire.
- Chandler and Rachel are willing to reallocate retirement assets and savings to earn a 7.75 percent rate of return prior to retirement.
- Once retired the Hubbles would like to assume an average rate of return of 5.25 percent.
- Regardless of nominal tax rates, Chandler and Rachel would like to assume a 25 percent marginal tax bracket while in retirement.
- Chandler and Rachel are willing to assume that the taxes they will need to pay in retirement are accounted for in the rates of return provided in the case.
- The Hubbles want to retire at age sixty-two, but it is more important that they do not deplete their assets over their lifetime.
- Full Social Security benefits at age sixty-seven are projected to be $42,000.
- Chandler and Rachel are willing to reallocate assets and savings to meet their retirement objective.
- The Potsdam Fixed Annuity has a current guaranteed yield of 5 percent, but the guaranteed yield period will expire in two years.
- The Bostonian Variable Annuity allows investments in all funds and cash and cash equivalents listed in the case narrative. The annuity has a guaranteed investment contract that currently yields 5 percent.

The following spreadsheet shows how the assumptions and data inputs can be used to conduct a current situation capital needs analysis for the Hubble family (excluding the home addition and art gallery). As shown in the analysis, Chandler and Rachel will need approximately $4,950,370 on their first day of retirement to meet their income need, assuming a capital depletion methodology. At the family's current level of savings, Chandler and Rachel will be short by more than $967,000. Without making any adjustments, Chandler and Rachel will need to begin saving an additional $21,750 per year to meet their retirement goal. For capital preservation, Chandler and Rachel need approximately $5,865,100 on the first day of retirement to meet their income and legacy need. Chandler and Rachel will fall $1,882,600 short of meeting this goal. In order to achieve a capital preservation goal, Chandler and Rachel need to save an additional $42,292 each year until retirement.

CAPITAL NEEDS ANALYSIS	
Assumes that income and savings grow at a constant rate prior to retirement	
Assumes Social Security benefits do not begin before retirement	
ASSUMPTIONS	
Current Household Earned Income	$135,195.88
Other Retirement Income Excluding Social Security (today's dollars)	
Non-Tax Deferred Retirement Assets (Stocks & Bonds)	
Tax Deferred Retirement Assets (e.g., 401k)	$479,750.00
Tax-Free Retirement Assets (e.g., Roth)	
Tax Deferred Annual Savings (e.g., 401k) Including Employer Matching Contributions	$10,386.47
After Tax Annual Savings Specifically Allocated to Retirement Needs	$3,000.00
Tax-Free Savings Contributions (e.g., Roth)	
Other Annual Savings Specifically Allocated to Retirement Needs	
Retirement Income Replacement Ratio	85%
Age	42
Retirement Age	62
Age to Begin Social Security Benefits	62
Life Expectancy	95
Years Until Retirement	20
Years in Retirement	33
Inflation Prior to Retirement	3.00%
Inflation After Retirement	3.00%
Growth Rate of Savings	3.00%
Growth Rate of Salary	3.00%
Assumed Return While Retired	5.25%
Assumed Rate of Return Before Retirement	7.75%
Inflation Adjusted Retirement Return	2.18%
Inflation Adjusted Pre-Retirement Return	4.61%

CALCULATIONS	
Ratio Reduced Income Need (Today's Dollars)	$114,916.50
FV of Ratio Reduced Income Need @ Retirement Age	$207,551.98
FV of Non-Deferred Retirement Assets	$0.00
FV of Tax-Deferred Retirement Assets	$2,134,816.55
FV of Tax-Free Retirement Assets	$0.00
FV of Tax-Deferred Savings	$578,087.18
FV of After-Tax Savings	$166,973.11
FV of Tax-Free Savings	$0.00
FV of Other Savings	$0.00
FV of Social Security Benefits	$1,102,656.70
Total Retirement Assets/Savings Available on First Day of Retirement	$3,982,533.53
CAPITAL DEPLETION METHOD	
Amount Needed on FIRST DAY of RETIREMENT for CAPITAL DEPLETION	$4,950,371.19
Additional Net Assets Needed @ Retirement	$967,837.66
Additional Level Annual Savings Needed	**$21,742.21**
CAPITAL PRESERVATION METHOD	
Assets Needed on FIRST DAY of RETIREMENT for CAPITAL PRESERVATION	$5,865,133.61
Additional Net Assets Needed @ Retirement	$1,882,600.08
Additional Level Savings Needed (Capital Preservation)	**$42,292.10**

Based on an evaluation of the preceding analyses, there are a number of possible recommendations that can be presented to Chandler and Rachel to help close the gap between what is needed and what they have accumulate in terms of retirement assets. The following recommendations are worthy of consideration:

- Redeem Rachel's annuity and invest the proceeds in mutual funds, ETFs, or a brokerage account to increase portfolio returns.

   o Although the stated return is a fixed rate of 5.0 percent annually, an analysis of the annuity suggests that the annual return, net of fees, is 1.28% (PV = –$90,000, FV = $125,000, N = 96, PMT = –$250). Given that the annuity has $11,000 of earnings ($125,000 current value – $90,000 initial purchase – $24,000 contributions), capital gains taxes are estimated to be $1,650 ($11,000 capital gains x 15 percent capital gains tax rate). Managing these assets outside of an annuity will likely generate a higher after-tax return.

- Use a Section 1035 exchange strategy to move Rachel's annuity from a fixed account product to a variable annuity product to increase the return and continue to defer capital gains taxes.

- Reallocate retirement assets and savings to increase returns from 5.24 percent currently to 7.75 percent before retirement and 5.25 percent after retirement.

- Reallocate assets to earn a higher rate of return to achieve the retirement goal or the home addition/art gallery goal.

- Contribute to Roth IRAs to increase the Hubbles' tax diversity during retirement.

- Increase Chandler and Rachel's contributions to employer-provided plans or other accounts.

- Increase savings to other tax-qualified accounts, such as Chandler and Rachel's employer-provided accounts, to fund the home addition and art gallery. Reaching the maximum annual contribution limit is not a concern at this time.

- Earmark some available non-qualified assets as retirement savings.

- Earmark some of the available non-qualified assets for the home addition and art gallery goals, perhaps even completely funding these goals depending on the amount allocated and the assumed rate of return.

- Fund a variable universal life insurance policy to supplement other retirement savings strategies. This product can be used as a source of funding for education, retirement, or other goals, depending on the product costs and the funding allowed relative to the death benefit.

- Defer taking Social Security benefits until Full Retirement Age or until age seventy to maximize retirement income. It is important to communicate to Chandler and Rachel that Social Security benefits can begin months or years before or after retirement; the starting date for Social Security benefits does not need to coincide with the starting date of retirement. The following analysis provides further details regarding this potential recommendation:

  o It will take approximately one hundred and twenty-five months beyond age seventy to recover the $147,840 of benefits Chandler would have received and the $87,360 of benefits Rachel would have received between age sixty-two and age seventy. Since Chandler and Rachel expect to live beyond age eighty, which is assumed in the case narrative, they should defer benefits until age seventy, as documented below:

Social Security Break Even Analysis		
	Chandler	Rachel
Monthly Benefit at Age 62	$1,540.00	$910.00
Total Benefits Between Age 62 and 70	$147,840.00	$87,360.00
Difference in Monthly Benefits from Age 62 to 70	$1,188.00	$702.00
Months to Break Even	124.4	124.4
Years to Break Even	10.4	10.4

15.5 STEP 4: DEVELOP THE FINANCIAL PLANNING RECOMMENDATION(S)

[A] Determining Retirement Goals

Developing retirement planning strategies and recommendations involves integrating qualitative and quantitative client characteristics and factors into actionable plans. It is important to determine at the outset a client's goals, dreams, and aspirations for retirement. Where clients want to live, what they want to do, and how they will spend or donate money are all critically important factors to know before making recommendations. Examples of quantitative factors include asset values and savings amounts, and assumptions related to rates of return, inflation, and life expectancies. Once these factors have been reviewed, it is time to consider outputs from needs analysis estimates to quantify the client's retirement planning situation.

At the end of the retirement needs analysis, a financial planner will know whether a client is on track to meet retirement goals, based on all planning assumptions. If a client is projected to meet their household's need, few changes in the plan may be needed. If, on the other hand, a client's current retirement assets and savings approach are insufficient to meet stated goals, it will be necessary to help the client implement changes to meet the retirement objectives.

Keep in mind that planning for retirement can encompass decades of planning to identify and implement the most effective accumulation and distribution strategies responsive to changing financial, economic, and tax environments. The following discussion highlights some of the important concepts, tools, and techniques that can be incorporated into their recommendation development process.

[B] Tax-Deferred Plans and IRAs

The use of tax-deferred plans and IRAs is premised on the notion that saving money on a tax-deferred basis is one of the best ways to accumulate wealth for retirement. The choice of which type of plan to use—an employer-sponsored plan or an IRA—is complicated. Figure 15.5 illustrates a decision tree to help determine funding priorities based on plan type.

Figure 15.5. Choosing between a Defined Contribution Plan and IRA Contributions.

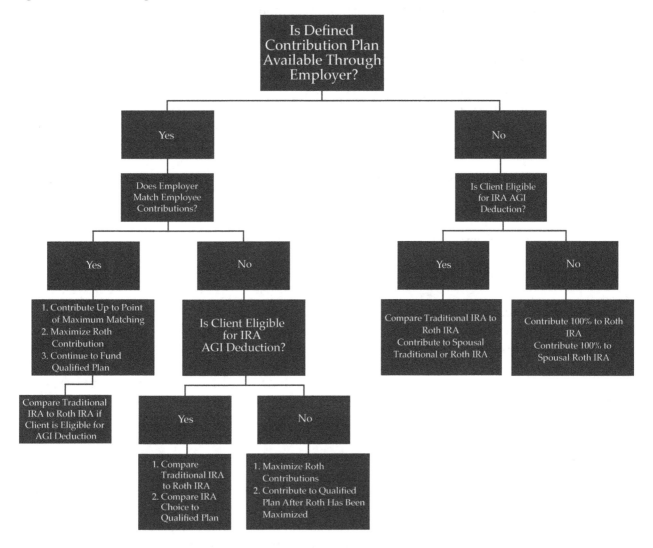

As shown in the decision tree, clients should be encouraged to contribute to a defined contribution plan when employer matching is available. Maximizing the match is important. If, for example, an employer matches dollar-for-dollar on the first 4 percent of contributions, it would be ill-advised to pass up this offer. In effect, the employer is guaranteeing the client an immediate 100 percent return on contributions up to 4 percent, and that is before any earnings are generated from the contribution.

Next, benefits associated with employer-sponsored plans should be compared to advantages offered by an **Individual Retirement Arrangement** (or account) (**IRA**). In many situations, contributing either to a tax-deductible or Roth IRA may be more beneficial than contributing to a defined contribution plan. If eligible, the tax-deductible plan offers immediate income tax savings and tax-deferred growth (similar to a 401(k)/403(b)/457 plan), whereas the Roth IRA offers the advantages of tax-deferred growth and tax-exempt earnings if qualified distribution rules are followed.

Once deductible or Roth IRA contributions have been maximized, clients who can afford additional contributions up to the maximum allowable limits should contribute to qualified and other employer retirement plans (e.g., 403(b) and 457 plans). These plans provide immediate income tax reduction and tax deferral on account growth.

A limitation associated with this strategy is that not all clients will be able to fully implement each stage of the recommendation. This is especially true for a **highly compensated employee (HCE)**, which is defined as anyone who was a 5 percent owner of a firm at any time during the year or anyone who receives Internal Revenue Service (IRS) defined high compensation (the figure changes yearly but is more than $120,000) and, if elected by the employer, is in the top 20 percent of employees based upon compensation. A **key employee** is:

(a) an officer with relatively high income (e.g., more than $175,000);

(b) a 5 percent owner; or

(c) a 1 percent owner with high compensation.

Planning Reminder

In 2016, the Department of Labor (DOL) introduced new rules that influence the way financial planners provide advice regarding retirement plans. According to the DOL, a financial planner who provides recommendations to clients regarding ERISA regulated retirement plans or IRAs must provide advice using **fiduciary investment standards**. Recommendations made either directly or indirectly fall under the fiduciary rule. Financial planners who receive some compensation in the form of commission need to pay particular attention to this rule. Best interest standards still apply for advice and recommendations made in traditional asset management and brokerage situations.

Highly compensated employee contributions to a 401(k) plan can be limited by the contributions made by non-highly-compensated employees. Also, high-income clients typically cannot deduct traditional IRA contributions, and they may be unable to contribute to a Roth IRA. Other considerations include potential penalties associated with early withdrawals and the possibility of paying higher taxes if the client's marginal rate is higher once distributions begin. Other clients may not have available discretionary cash flow to benefit from multiple accounts.

[C] Insurance Company Products in Retirement Planning

Nearly every client has a fear of outliving their household's asset base in retirement. In the academic community this is known as **shortfall risk**, or the percentage of time a portfolio will run short of the money needed to pay distributions. Several tradeoffs exist when making distribution choices in retirement to deal with shortfall risks. Some financial planning experts recommend the prudent use of annuities.[3] The use of **annuities** can reduce shortfall risk significantly. The difference in risk falls from close to zero with 100 percent annuitization to 6 percent without the use of annuities. Second, the use of annuities reduces a client's gross estate significantly. Whereas without annuitization someone can expect their final estate to be larger than the starting portfolio value, the use of annuities reduces this amount dramatically. In other words, when thinking about shortfall risks, retirees must choose between legacy and security. Retirees who are more interested in retirement income security, versus leaving heirs or charitable institutions a legacy, should consider the use of annuitization as a retirement planning distribution tool.

Annuitized distributions provide a way to manage retirement income. **Annuitization** is basically an underwriting process where the issuer of an annuity—in the United States this must be an insurance company—determines the likely remaining life span of the annuitant, thereby calculating the cost of guaranteeing the stream of periodic payments to the annuitant. The annuity product is an insurance wrapper of sorts that guarantees the payment stream, but the client's assets are used to make the payments.

Annuitization provides greater certainty of income for longer periods of time while also reducing the asset base subject to required minimum distributions (RMDs) because the IRS requires that annuity contracts comply with IRS requirements regarding RMDs. This effectively increases the after-tax rate of return for assets held in annuity accounts.

Annuitization is essentially an irrevocable choice of planned distribution. Annuities are typically sold in one of three basic forms: fixed period, single lifetime, or joint lifetime. Annuitization shifts the shortfall risk to the underwriter because it is possible for the annuitant to outlive the principal, even though the annuitant cannot outlive the payment stream (assuming a life annuity). Because of underwriting requirements and the guarantees provided, canceling or surrendering an annuity contract can be quite expensive, so the choice of an annuitized distribution should be made carefully.

Annuity payments are based on two factors:

(1) The assets underlying the contract.

(2) The desired length of time the contractually obligated payments last.

Two basic categories of annuities are available: fixed and variable. In return for a lump sum payment or series of payments, a **fixed annuity** provides an income stream based on a fixed, guaranteed interest rate, similar to a fixed income security or bank account. This option carries very little to no market risk. **Variable annuity** products, on the other hand, can offer clients more inflation protection in exchange for an element of risk. Instead of providing a client with a fixed rate of return, variable annuities make payments based on the returns generated from the value of the securities in the portfolio. This option can offer a higher payout if market conditions are favorable, but in exchange the annuitant must accept a certain degree of market risk and payout variability.

A case can be made against retirees' use of annuities. The case is strongest against life annuities. A **life annuity** pays out either a fixed or inflation-adjusted stream of income for as long as the annuitant lives. If all goes as planned, in other words, if a client dies when expected based on the mortality tables, then the annuity purchase provides an actuarially appropriate return. However, if the client outlives the forecast, then the insurance company must continue to pay, in which case the client reaps a windfall. If the client dies prematurely, any remaining principal balance in the annuity is forfeited at death (note that it is possible to purchase a term certain rider that ensures a minimum number of payments; however, this option will decrease the payment). As a result, life annuities generally appeal only to individuals who have an above-average life expectancy and those who exhibit high risk aversion.

A compelling case can be made for the use of a **guaranteed annuity**. A **fixed payment** (or **period-certain**) **annuity** provides either a fixed or inflation-adjusted payout for a specific number of years, usually five, ten, twenty, or thirty years, regardless of how long the annuitant lives. In this case, the annuitant could outlive the payment stream, but if the annuitant were to die prematurely a secondary beneficiary would continue to receive payment until the end of the guaranteed period. The use of guaranteed annuities is warranted as a retiree's income increases, risk aversion increases, and overall equity and bond market volatility intensify.[4]

Planning Reminder

Some annuities combine certain aspects of both life and guaranteed annuities. **Guaranteed lifetime annuities**, as the name implies, provide lifetime income to a client. Most lifetime annuities cease payments upon the client's death (as the name implies). However, it is possible to obtain annuities with a guaranteed minimum number of distribution years. These products are sometimes referred to as **life with period certain annuities**. If an annuitant were to die during the "period certain," then payments would continue to a secondary beneficiary until the end of that period.

[D] Normal, Early, and Delayed Social Security Claiming Strategies

While the normal Social Security retirement age is sixty-seven, for those born in or after 1960, many clients hold a goal of retiring earlier. It is possible to receive Social Security benefits prior to one's full retirement age. Age sixty-two is the earliest age at which Social Security retirement benefits can be received.

A retiree's monthly benefit is reduced by 5/9 of one percent for every month of early retirement for the first thirty-six months, and by 5/12 of one percent for every month in excess of thirty-six. Someone whose full retirement age is sixty-six and claims benefits at age sixty-four, for example, will receive a reduction in benefits of approximately thirteen percent ($5/9 \times 0.01 \times 24$). Someone whose full retirement age is sixty-seven and who claims benefits at age sixty-two will receive a 30 percent reduction in benefits, as shown below:

$$[(5/9 \times 0.01 \times 36) + (5/12 \times 0.01 \times 24)]$$

Clients also may also delay the receipt of Social Security benefits. Doing so results in a permanent increase in benefits. The actual increase depends on the age of the client, but generally a worker can expect between a 6.5 percent and 8 percent increase in benefits for every year of deferment between the worker's full retirement age and age seventy.

[E] Qualified Employee Plans

Employer-provided retirement plans can be broadly categorized as either qualified or non-qualified. **Qualified retirement plans** are recognized and described in the Internal Revenue Code (IRC). Qualified plans provide employees and employers certain tax advantages because they meet qualifications established in tax law and reported in the IRC. Contributions to an employee's qualified retirement plan are generally excluded from current taxable income. Further, employers enjoy an immediate tax deduction for contributions made to a qualified retirement plan for the firm's employees. Although certain rules place limits on contributions, it is possible for some employers to offer more than one kind of plan.

Qualified retirement plans can be further differentiated into two categories: defined benefit plans and defined contribution plans. A **defined benefit plan**, or **pension plan,** provides a specific guaranteed benefit at retirement that is usually calculated using a **unit-benefit formula**, which is typically based on a percentage of salary and years of service. For example, a benefit of 2 percent of final pay (or a combination of final years' pay) for each year of service up to twenty-five years is common. Using this formula, someone who has worked at a firm for twenty years would be eligible to receive 40 percent of final pay as a yearly benefit in retirement for the remainder of the retiree's life. Keep in mind that joint and survivor benefits are not provided automatically under ERISA-covered defined benefit or cash-balance plans.

A **defined contribution** plan provides an individual account for each participant and offers benefits to employees based on the value of the account upon retirement. The most usual form of employer-provided retirement plan in the United States is the defined contribution plan.

A widely used qualified plan is a 401(k) plan. A **401(k) plan** offers employees the opportunity to contribute pretax dollars to their accounts. Many plans provide some form of matching contribution by the employer. A 401(k) plan can also include a **Roth 401(k)** feature, which allows the contribution of after-tax dollars. Two specialized types of 401(k) plan designs are available: the **SIMPLE 401(k) plan** and a **safe harbor 401(k) plan**.

Defined contribution plans include all profit-sharing plans, as well as stock bonus plans and employee stock ownership plans (ESOP). Money purchase plans and target benefit plans are also included. Certain types of retirement plans are not technically qualified plans, yet each operates in a comparable manner and provides tax-deferred earnings growth. Examples include simplified employee pension accounts (SEP accounts) and Keogh plan accounts for small businesses, 403(b) tax-sheltered annuities for nonprofit employers, and 457 plans for state, local, and municipal government employers. Figure 15.6 provides summary data for each of these defined contribution plans.

Figure 15.6. A Comparison of the Funding Characteristics of Defined Contribution Plans for 2022.

Plan Type	Maximum Contribution per Participant (Elective Deferral)	Maximum Annual Addition[1] per Participant (based on Max. Compensation of $305,000)[2]	Mandatory Yearly Employer Contributions?	CODA/401(k) Permitted?	Forfeitures Generally Required to Be Distributed?	In-Service Withdrawals Allowed?	Immediate, Mandatory Vesting for Employer Contributions?
	Large-employer-sponsored plans
Money purchase	After-tax allowed	The lesser of 100% of income or $61,000	Yes	No	Yes	No, but loans are allowed	No
Target benefit	Not allowed	The lesser of 100% of income or $61,000	Yes	No	Yes	No	No
Profit-sharing	Not allowed	The lesser of 100% of income or $61,000	No[3]	Yes	Yes	Yes	No
Stock bonus	$61,000	The lesser of 100% of income or $61,000	No[3]	Yes	Yes	Yes	No
ESOP	$61,000	The lesser of 100% of income or $61,000	No[3]	Yes	Yes	Yes	No
401(k)[4]	$20,500 + $6,500 age 50+ catch-up	The lesser of 100% of income or $61,000	No	NA	No	Yes	No
Roth 401(k)	$20,500 + $6,500 age 50+ catch-up (after-tax)	The lesser of 100% of income or $61,000	No	NA	No	Yes; after five years of participation, or age 59½	No
Thrift and savings	Varies	The lesser of 100% of income or $61,000	Generally, yes	No	Yes	Yes	No
403(b)[4]	$20,500 + $6,500 age 50+ catch-up	The lesser of 100% of income or $61,000	No	No	No	Yes	Yes
457[4]	$20,500 + $6,500 age 50+ catch-up or 100% of compensation	$20,500 or 100% of compensation	Not allowed	No	NA	Yes; unforeseen emergency only	NA
	Small-business-sponsored Plans
SEP[5]	Not allowed	The lesser of 25% of net earnings or $61,000	No	No	NA	Yes; same as IRA	Yes
SARSEP/ 408(k)[6]	The lesser of 25% of compensation or $20,500	The lesser of 25% of net earnings or $61,000	No	No	NA	Yes; same as IRA	Yes
Keogh[5] money purchase	Employees may not contribute	Up to 25% of earned income	Yes	No	Yes	No	No

Keogh[5] profit-sharing	Employees may not contribute	Up to 25% of earned income	No[3]	No	Yes	Yes; after 5 years of participation, or age 59½	No
SIMPLE IRA	$14,000 + $3,000 age 50+ catch-up	See[7] below	Yes	No	NA	Yes; same as IRA	Yes
SIMPLE 401(k)[4, 8]	$14,000 + $3,000 age 50+ catch-up	$21,400 or $24,400 age 50+	Yes	Yes	NA	Yes; same as IRA	Yes

1. Annual additions are equal to the sum of employer contributions, employee contributions, both deductible and nondeductible, and unvested forfeitures. The maximum combined contribution to a defined contribution plan for a participant aged 50 or higher in 2022 is $67,500, consisting of the sum of $61,000 plus a $6,500 "catch-up" contribution.
2. There is an additional limitation on the maximum amount of employer contribution that is tax-deductible to the employer.
3. No mandatory annual employer contributions required, but employers must make substantial and regular contributions.
4. A targeted, non-refundable tax credit for low- to moderate-income savers is available for 401(k), 403(b), 457(b), and IRA contributions.
5. SEP and KEOGH: the effective maximum contribution percentage considers net earnings instead of total compensation.
6. Salary Reduction (SAR) SEPs have not been eligible for new establishment since 1997.
7. For a SIMPLE IRA, employers must make either a dollar-for-dollar matching contribution up to 3 percent of an employee's compensation (can elect to lower the percentage to no less than 1 percent for no more than 2 out of 5 years ending in the current year), or 2 percent of compensation for all eligible employees earning at least $5,000 regardless of elected salary reductions.
8. The maximum total contribution to a SIMPLE 401(k) plan is equal to the salary deferral + 3 percent contribution based on maximum IRS salary limit + catch-up contributions). The maximum permitted contribution for a SIMPLE 401(k) plan is the maximum elective deferral plus the 3 percent matching contribution.

[F] Applying Planning Skills to the Hubble Case

A primary financial planning focus for Chandler and Rachel Hubble involves issues related to retirement planning. In other financial planning domains, only modest changes are typically needed to recommendations developed at Step Three of the financial planning process. In terms of retirement planning, it is possible for financial recommendations to take on new dimensions at this stage of the financial planning process. Figure 15.7 provides a summary of the final retirement planning recommendations made in the sample financial plan. It is worth noting that other solutions can be used to help Chandler and Rachel achieve their retirement goals. Also, it is important to recognize new client information or data received during the financial planning process may necessitate the need for a reevaluation of the Hubbles' retirement need.

Figure 15.7. Retirement Recommendations for Chandler and Rachel.

The final retirement recommendations developed for the Hubble family match several of the preliminary recommendations identified at Step Three of the financial planning process. Specifically, Chandler and Rachel should:

- Plan to retire at age sixty-two, assuming the following recommendations are implemented:
- Open Roth IRA accounts and begin contributing each year.

- Increase savings to their 401(k) accounts. Based on the retirement planning analysis, Chandler and Rachel need to save a minimum of $21,742 to meet a capital depletion model of retirement or $42,292 to meet a capital preservation model of retirement. Given the Hubble's cash flow situation, it is recommended that Chandler and Rachel save $27,000 (an amount between the capital depletion and capital preservation need) to fund retirement needs at age sixty-two, assuming that retirement savings will increase by 3 percent each year and assuming that other retirement recommendations are implemented. The recommendation calls for the Hubbles to increase 401(k) contributions to $16,000, in addition to each making a contribution of $5,500 to a Roth IRA account. Note that if the Hubbles choose to not implement one or more of the retirement recommendations described here (i.e., defer Social Security benefits until age seventy, surrender Rachel's annuity, etc.), the retirement savings need should be re-estimated to account for changes to the assumptions).
- Allocate $37,350 in currently held mutual fund assets to the Art Gallery goal. Similarly, Chandler and Rachel should allocate $9,335 of mutual fund assets to the Home Addition goal.
- Surrender the annuity owned by Rachel, pay the tax, and invest the proceeds into a mutual fund portfolio earmarked for retirement. A review of the annuity distributions (Step Three of the financial planning process) revealed that the net return generated by the annuity is less than 1.3 percent annually, indicating that much of the 5 percent fixed annual return is being absorbed by fees. Chandler and Rachel would be better off financially foregoing the tax-deferred returns in favor of achieving higher returns in a taxable account.
- Defer Social Security benefits until age seventy. Although Rachel and Chandler stated a desire to begin Social Security benefits at age sixty-two, a further analysis (Step Three of the financial planning process) revealed that delaying Social Security benefits is a financially optimal strategy. In general, the longer a client's life expectancy, the more beneficial it is to delay taking Social Security benefits, although it may be advantageous to take Social Security benefits at or before Full Retirement Age if a client has a short life expectancy.

15.6 STEP 5: PRESENT THE FINANCIAL PLANNING RECOMMENDATION(S)

Clients, such as the Hubble family, are increasingly turning to financial planners to help answer questions about funding future retirement costs. Issues related to the timing of savings, the taxation of benefits, and issues related to capital depletion and longevity risk drive many people to seek the services of a competent financial planner. As such, it is important for financial planners to exhibit a working knowledge of the variety of tax-advantaged and non-tax-advantaged options available for individuals and families as clients plan for retirement. Taxes, timing, assets, income, competing financial goals, and a host of other considerations serve to further complicate a seemingly simple question, "Are we on track to reach retirement?" Anticipating this and similar questions is a proven approach to help facilitate the delivery of retirement planning recommendations.

Figure 15.8 highlights some of the important factors to consider when presenting retirement recommendations to Chandler and Rachel Hubble.

Figure 15.8. Factors to Consider When Presenting Retirement Recommendations.

Often, the retirement planning narrative within a financial plan is one of the longest and most complex sections. There are a wide range of potential reactions that a client may have when presented with retirement planning recommendations. If a client finds saving easy or is already in a good position for retirement, recommendations will likely be met with a positive reaction, especially if strategies are presented in a way that matches the client's learning and processing preferences.

Many times, however, recommendations may be met with resistance or anger. An unfavorable reaction may be the result of any number of factors. For example, a client may be skeptical about a savings need estimate. This number, accounting for taxes and inflation and encompassing expenses for several decades, may be a larger lump sum than the client expected to need. Initially, a client may feel overwhelmed, believing that their retirement goals are out of reach. It is important to address the client's reaction and respond to their concerns.

If a client feels like retirement is unattainable, they are unlikely to follow through on implementing recommendations even if retirement goals are actually realistic. Retirement can also be a difficult subject for some clients because of the need to make present sacrifices (in the form of savings) for future benefits. Many people struggle to conceptualize what the future will look like.

When presenting recommendations, it can be useful to help a client identify what the costs of not preparing adequately for retirement could be. This takes the focus away from discussions of sacrifice to a talk about solutions that can be implemented today to make the future easier. Another strategy involves highlighting the tax savings associated with using tax-advantaged retirement accounts to save for retirement. Few clients enjoy paying taxes. Tax savings can be framed as a current benefit, making saving an easier task.

In certain cases, a financial planner's judgment may lead them to make recommendations that are not in line with a client's stated wishes. This can happen for several reasons but most likely it will occur when a client's goal is unrealistic or an alternative assumption will lead to a financially superior outcome. In these cases, it is important to show a client multiple scenarios based on new assumptions and inputs. This may require additional dialogue and discussions focused on providing additional information to a client.

15.7 STEP 6: IMPLEMENT THE FINANCIAL PLANNING RECOMMENDATION(S)

The presentation of a retirement planning recommendation needs to match a client's information processing style and preferences. Relatedly, the presentation should help the client clearly identify the way in which one or more retirement goals will be achieved upon product or service implementation. While it is true that the majority of recommendations related to retirement planning tend to be complex, and often integrative from a multiple-step perspective, every effort should be taken to make each recommendation as easy to implement as possible. This means explicitly addressing the who, what, when, where, why, how, and how much questions related to implementation.

Figure 15.9 shows how one of the recommendations developed for Chandler and Rachel can be presented within a financial plan.

Figure 15.9. Implementing a Retirement Recommendation for the Hubble Family.

Recommendation #1: Make a contribution to Roth IRA accounts each year.	
Who:	Chandler and Rachel.
What:	Two new Roth IRA accounts with a low fee custodian. Our firm utilizes Roth arrangements with Vanguard and Charles Schwab Institutional; however, other custodians may be used.
When:	Before the end of the current tax year, you should begin making contributions, followed by similar contributions each year when Chandler receives his bonus.
Where:	Through our financial planning office. Our team will provide paperwork for your signature to open the appropriate accounts.
Why:	Your new IRA accounts will have an extensive array of investments from which to choose. Our team will provide direct advice on the appropriate investments to use within the accounts. Roth IRAs provide tax diversification benefits as withdrawals are tax-free in retirement (although contributions are not tax-deductible).
How:	Our firm will provide paperwork for your signature to open these accounts. Once opened, we encourage you to set up automatic contributions from your checking account for the recommended annual contribution.
How much:	Although the annual contribution limit is higher, contribute $5,500 annually beginning in 20XX. This amount should be contributed to Chandler's Roth IRA and Rachel's Roth IRA, for a total annual contribution of $11,000.
Effect on cash flow:	Implementation of this recommendation will reduce discretionary cash flow by $11,000 annually.

15.8 STEP 7: MONITOR PROGRESS AND UPDATE

Although the tendency among some financial planners—and their clients—is to focus on conducting a needs analysis and then deriving appropriate recommendations based on the analysis, it is important to keep in mind that once one or more recommendations have been implemented, monitoring aspects of a client's retirement plan should be an ongoing task. Numerous personal, household, and environmental factors can interact to prompt changes in a client's retirement planning situation. This is true for clients in the accumulation phase of retirement, as well as those clients who are using withdrawal strategies. Any significant changes in model inputs, such as inflation, interest rates, rates of return, or tax laws, should trigger an immediate review of a client's retirement plan. Equally important are factors related to a client's health, employment, marital, or family status. The key takeaway is that the initial needs analysis is just a starting point when helping a client reach their retirement goals. It is likely that adjustments in accumulation or withdrawal strategies will be needed over time.

Financial planners also need to monitor state and federal tax laws and retirement plan rules. Rules related to qualified plan and IRA distributions are complex. Factors related to early retirement, job transfers, and the use of plan assets for non-retirement purposes can each have an impact on a client's retirement plan, as well as tax and cash flow implications. Understanding what might trigger a taxable distribution and federal tax penalty is considered a minimal standard of competency for financial planners. In addition, the ability to identify and calculate required minimum distributions, exceptions to distribution rules, and QDRO exemptions is an essential skill for financial planners. Finally, understanding issues related to IRA rollovers and annuity distribution alternatives represent a characteristic of competency among financial planners.

As with other financial planning topics, changes to a client's circumstances should prompt a review and/or reevaluation of previously made retirement recommendations. At a minimum, a client's progress towards retirement goal achievement should be monitored on an annual basis. A client's health, employment status, marital status, preferences, and attitudes can change over time. When these and other changes occur, the retirement plan should be reviewed. Changes almost always warrant a review of previously implemented recommendations. Figure 15.10 provides an overview of some of the factors that require ongoing retirement plan monitoring for Chandler and Rachel Hubble.

Figure 15.10. Issues to Monitor in the Hubble Case.

Numerous ongoing monitoring issues are at play in the domain of retirement planning. At the household level, life events need to be evaluated at least annually. Some of the most important life events that may impact the Hubble family's retirement needs include:

- Change in employment (i.e., change in demands, stress, etc.) or promotion for Chandler or Rachel (i.e., change in income or employee benefits) or a career change.
- Purchase of a new home or second home.
- Changes related to Phoebe (i.e., her death, college scholarship, decision not to attend college, etc.).
- Inheritance or receipt of sizable gift from Chandler's parents or other relatives.
- Pregnancy or adoption.
- Divorce.
- Death or disability of a family member.
- Change in health status.
- Winning the lottery.
- Change in life dreams or goals.
- A significant change in investment market returns and/or risks.
- Changes in tax policy (at the state and federal level).

15.9 COMPREHENSIVE HUBBLE CASE

Retirement planning is, for nearly all clients, a primary reason to seek the help of a financial planner. This is certainly the case for Chandler and Rachel Hubble. The following narrative is an example of how the retirement section within a comprehensive financial plan can be written.

Retirement

Overview of Retirement:

Retirement planning often emerges as one of the most important goals clients have when seeking the help of a financial planner. Planning for retirement is growing in importance as access to pension plans continues to shrink, life expectancies grow longer, and the number of years in retirement continues to rise. Conceptualizing and planning for retirement can be overwhelming; however, using tools, techniques, and assumptions grounded in decades of data and research, it is possible to create a roadmap leading to a fulfilling retirement. Our job is to help you make your retirement dreams a reality.

Retirement Definitions:

The following definitions will be useful as you review the analysis presented in this section:

- *Brokerage account*: A type of taxable account that is housed at a brokerage firm. You can hold a variety of investment products within a brokerage account. Gains and losses are subject to capital gain tax rates, whereas other income is subject to regular taxation.

- *Traditional Individual Retirement Arrangement (IRA)*: A tax advantaged retirement account; contributions are tax deductible, and earnings within the account grow tax-deferred until withdrawals are made during retirement.

- *Roth individual retirement arrangement (Roth IRA)*: A tax advantaged retirement account; contributions are not tax deductible but earnings (and contributions) can be withdrawn tax-free during retirement in certain rules are met. .

- *401(k)*: A 401(k) plan offers employees the opportunity to contribute pretax dollars to an employer-sponsored account. Many 401(k) plans provide some form of matching contribution from the sponsoring employer.

Planning Assumptions:

- Rachel would like to build a small addition to your home and fill it with art. If built today, the addition will cost $20,000.

- Rachel would also like to open a small art gallery. You estimate the cost of the gallery will be $80,000 if opened today.

- You are willing to invest in a moderately aggressive portfolio to fund the art gallery and house addition.

- You will need approximately 85 percent of your current earned, before-tax, income (in today's dollars) when you retire.

- You prefer to assume a moderately conservative rate of return prior to retirement, which is 7.75 percent.

- You also prefer to assume a conservative rate of return once retired, which is 5.25 percent.

- You are willing to assume that the taxes you will need to pay in retirement are accounted for in the rates of return provided in the case.

- Your Social Security retirement age is age sixty-seven (both Chandler and Rachel).

- You do not want to deplete all of your assets over your lifetime.

- Your life expectancy is age ninety-five. You are unwilling to reduce your projected life expectancy.

- You are willing to reallocate assets and savings to meet your retirement objective.

- You believe that your incomes will increase at the rate of inflation into the future.

- You plan to increase contributions to your retirement accounts by 3.0 percent each year.

- The primary insurance amount for Chandler at age sixty-seven is $2,200 in today's dollars.

- The primary insurance amount for Rachel at age sixty-seven is $1,300 in today's dollars.

- Annual benefits will increase by 8 percent for each year that Social Security benefits are deferred between age sixty-seven and age seventy.

Goals:

- As a family, you would like to retire at age sixty-two.

- You want to be self-sufficient in retirement (you will need 85 percent of your current earned before-tax income in today's dollars when you retire; you do not wish to deplete your assets over your lifetime).

- Rachel would like to turn her love of collecting art into a small business.

- Rachel would also like to build a small addition to your home and fill it with art.

- You want to plan on taking occasional trips during retirement.

- You would like to begin receiving Social Security benefits as soon as possible.

Your Current Retirement Situation:

At the moment, you have $479,750 saved for retirement in tax-deferred retirement assets. This means that you received an income tax deduction for your contributions to these retirement accounts and the account earnings are growing on a tax-deferred basis until you begin making withdrawals (in retirement). The distributions from these accounts will be taxed at income tax rates in effect at retirement. A summary of your current retirement account balances is shown below:

Chandler's 401(k)	$203,000.00
Rachel's 401(k)	$15,250.00
Chandler's IRA	$52,000.00
Rachel's IRAs	$84,500.00
Rachel's Annuity	$125,000.00
Retirement Asset Total	**$479,750.00**

Chandler and Rachel, your employers provide a matching contribution for contributions to 401(k) accounts in which you are making contributions.

- Chandler, your employer matches 100 percent of your contribution up to 3 percent of base salary but only for contributions made to the Graham Fund. Currently, Chandler is contributing 6 percent of base pay ($4,108 annually) to the 401(k) account, 3 percent to the Graham Fund and 3 percent to the Consumer Fund.

- Rachel, your employer provides a 50 percent match up to 6 percent of base salary. Rachel is currently contributing 10 percent of base pay ($3,250 annually) to the 401(k) account.

- Based on these contributions, Chandler you are receiving an annual $2,054 matching contribution, whereas Rachel you are receiving an annual $975 matching contribution.

As a family, you are also saving $250 each month ($3,000 annually) to Rachel's conservative annuity. The annuity was purchased seven years ago for $90,000. You have contributed $24,000 since purchasing the annuity. The annuity is worth $125,000 today. Although this product guarantees a 5 percent fixed rate of return, the net return has been less than 1.3 percent annually, indicating that a large portion of the gains are going towards paying fees related to the annuity.

Your retirement contributions to all retirement accounts (including employer matching contributions) total $13,387. This amount is equivalent to approximately 10 percent of your gross earned income.

Your stated goal is to begin receiving Social Security benefits at age sixty-two, the earliest you can begin receiving benefits. If you begin taking Social Security benefits at age sixty-two, Chandler's monthly social security benefit is estimated to be $1,540 in today's dollars, whereas Rachel's monthly Social Security benefit is estimated to be $910 in today's dollars. Waiting until age sixty-seven will increase benefits to $2,200 and $1,300, respectively. Postponing Social Security benefits until age seventy will increase benefits to $2,728 and $1,612, respectively.

As a family, you have two special goals that you would like to achieve during retirement: (1) opening an $80,000 (in today's dollars) art gallery for Rachel and (2) building a $20,000 (in today's dollars) addition to your home. Chandler and Rachel, you have saved $5,000 thus far and are saving $1,800 each year for the art gallery. You have not started saving for the addition to your home.

The table below shows the retirement analysis of your current situation:

CAPITAL NEEDS ANALYSIS	
Assumes that income and savings grow at a constant rate prior to retirement	
Assumes Social Security benefits do not begin before retirement	
ASSUMPTIONS	
Current Household Earned Income	$135,195.88
Other Retirement Income Excluding Social Security (today's dollars)	
Non-Tax Deferred Retirement Assets (Stocks & Bonds)	
Tax Deferred Retirement Assets (e.g., 401k)	$479,750.00
Tax-Free Retirement Assets (e.g., Roth)	
Tax Deferred Annual Savings (e.g., 401k) Including Employer Matching Contributions	$10,386.47
After Tax Annual Savings Specifically Allocated to Retirement Needs	$3,000.00
Tax-Free Savings Contributions (e.g., Roth)	
Other Annual Savings Specifically Allocated to Retirement Needs	
Retirement Income Replacement Ratio	85%
Age	42
Retirement Age	62
Age to Begin Social Security Benefits	62
Life Expectancy	95
Years Until Retirement	20
Years in Retirement	33
Inflation Prior to Retirement	3.00%
Inflation After Retirement	3.00%
Growth Rate of Savings	3.00%
Growth Rate of Salary	3.00%
Assumed Return While Retired	5.25%
Assumed Rate of Return Before Retirement	7.75%
Inflation Adjusted Retirement Return	2.18%
Inflation Adjusted Pre-Retirement Return	4.61%
CALCULATIONS	
Ratio Reduced Income Need (Today's Dollars)	$114,916.50
FV of Ratio Reduced Income Need @ Retirement Age	$207,551.98
FV of Non-Deferred Retirement Assets	$0.00
FV of Tax-Deferred Retirement Assets	$2,134,816.55
FV of Tax-Free Retirement Assets	$0.00
FV of Tax-Deferred Savings	$578,087.18
FV of After-Tax Savings	$166,973.11
FV of Tax-Free Savings	$0.00
FV of Other Savings	$0.00
FV of Social Security Benefits	$1,102,656.70
Total Retirement Assets/Savings Available on First Day of Retirement	$3,982,533.53

CAPITAL DEPLETION METHOD	
Amount Needed on FIRST DAY of RETIREMENT for CAPITAL DEPLETION	$4,950,371.19
Additional Net Assets Needed @ Retirement	$967,837.66
Additional Level Annual Savings Needed	**$21,742.21**
CAPITAL PRESERVATION METHOD	
Assets Needed on FIRST DAY of RETIREMENT for CAPITAL PRESERVATION	$5,865,133.61
Additional Net Assets Needed @ Retirement	$1,882,600.08
Additional Level Savings Needed (Capital Preservation)	**$42,292.10**

Retirement Recommendations:

The following tables summarize the recommendations that have been developed to help you reach your retirement funding goals. As with all recommendations presented in this financial plan, our firm is available to answer any questions that might arise and to assist with specific implementation procedures.

Recommendation #1: Make a contribution to Roth IRA accounts each year.	
Who:	Chandler and Rachel.
What:	Two new Roth IRA accounts with a low fee custodian. Our firm utilizes Roth arrangements with Vanguard and Charles Schwab Institutional; however, other custodians may be used.
When:	Before the end of the current tax year, you should begin making contributions, followed by similar contributions each year when Chandler receives his bonus.
Where:	Through our financial planning office. Our team will provide paperwork for your signature to open the appropriate accounts.
Why:	Your new IRA accounts will have an extensive array of investments from which to use. Our team will provide direct advice on the appropriate investments to choose within the accounts. Roth IRAs provide tax diversification benefits as withdrawals are tax-free in retirement (although contributions are not tax-deductible).
How:	Our firm will provide paperwork for your signature to open these accounts. Once opened, we encourage you to set up automatic contributions from your checking account for the recommended annual contribution.
How much:	Although the annual contribution limit is higher, contribute $5,500 annually beginning in 20XX. This amount should be contributed to Chandler's Roth IRA and Rachel's Roth IRA, for a total annual contribution of $11,000.
Effect on cash flow:	Implementation of this recommendation will reduce discretionary cash flow by $11,000 annually.

Recommendation #2: Contribute $16,000 annually from cash flow to your 401(k) retirement accounts, with retirement savings increasing by 3 percent each year.	
Who:	Chandler and Rachel.
What:	Your retirement contributions should be made to Chandler's 401k account and Rachel's 401(k) account.
When:	Adjust contributions before the end of the current tax year.
Where:	Through the online 401(k) portal with each employer (our firm can assist with website navigation).
Why:	Based on our estimates, as a family, you need to save at least $21,742 to meet a capital depletion model of retirement (this assumes no assets remain at the end of retirement). Based on your goals and cash flow situation, it is possible to save more. Our analysis indicates that you should save a total of $27,000 each year, which will allow retirement at age sixty-two, leaving a small legacy at the end of retirement. In combination with maximized contributions to Roth IRA accounts, you should contribute $16,000 to your 401(k) accounts. In addition, this level of contribution will help reduce future tax liabilities. Withdrawals will be taxed at ordinary income rates in effect at the time of distribution. This level of contribution will enable you both to continue receiving maximum employer matching contributions.
How:	Contact your human resources office or call the administrator of your 401(k) plan. Implementation will require you to complete a 401(k) Contribution Enrollment/Deferral Change Form (our firm can assist with this paperwork).
How much:	Although the annual contribution limit is higher, Chandler, you should contribute $11,000 to your 401(k) annually, whereas Rachel, you should contribute $5,000 to your 401(k) annually.
Effect on cash flow:	Implementation of this recommendation will reduce discretionary cash flow by $16,000 annually (before any tax adjustment is made).

Recommendation #3: Allocate $37,350 held in mutual funds to the Art Gallery goal and allocate $9,335 held in mutual funds to the Home Addition goal.	
Who:	Chandler and Rachel.
What:	Reallocate general mutual fund holdings towards special retirement goals. For management purposes, our firm will segregate the reporting of return and risk data related to the holdings used for these goals.
When:	Within the next thirty days.
Where:	Through our financial planning office. We recommend maintaining current holdings. Our team will make a special note of the way each fund is earmarked and report separate return and risk data to you quarterly.
Why:	The current goals are underfunded. Earmarking mutual fund assets towards these goals ensures that money will be available to open the art gallery and add to the house at retirement.

How:	Because our firm currently manages your investment portfolio, the earmarking of funds can be completed by our staff.
How much:	In total, $46,685 should be allocated toward these goals ($37,350 for the art gallery and $9,335 for the home addition).
Effect on cash flow:	Implementation of this recommendation will not affect cash flow.

Recommendation #4: Surrender Rachel's annuity, use the proceeds to pay associated capital gains taxes, and invest the remainder in a brokerage account allocated for retirement goals.

Who:	Rachel.
What:	Rachel's individual, conservative fixed-annuity contract invested in the Potsdam Fixed Annuity. The new brokerage account should be owned by Rachel as the annuity was in Rachel's name.
When:	Within thirty to forty-five days.
Where:	Begin with the custodian of your annuity. Our team will assist you in completing the paperwork to surrender the funds from the annuity.
Why:	Although the annuity does grow on a tax-deferred basis, the annual return (net of fees) is less than 1.3 percent. In order to meet your retirement goals, you need to earn a higher rate of return. Although you will be giving up the tax-deferral, the value of the tax benefits will be outweighed by earning a higher rate of return. Withdrawal penalties expired one year ago, so it is possible to now withdraw the funds without penalty.
How:	Contact the custodian of the annuity. Our team will assist you in completing the paperwork to surrender the annuity. Once the distribution has been received, we will assist in allocating the proceeds into suitable mutual funds.
How much:	The annuity is currently worth $125,000. Given that the annuity has $11,000 of earnings ($125,000 current value – $90,000 initial purchase – $24,000 contributions), capital gains taxes are estimated to be $1,650 ($11,000 capital gains x 15 percent capital gains tax rate). The remaining value, $123,350, should be invested according to the provisions of your family investment policy proposal (IPS).
Effect on cash flow:	Implementation of this recommendation will not affect cash flow as taxes will be paid from the asset sale rather than cash flow.

Recommendation #5: Retire at age sixty-two but defer Social Security benefits until age seventy.

Who:	Chandler and Rachel.
What:	Postpone Social Security benefits until age seventy rather than age sixty-two or age sixty-seven.

When:	Once you reach age seventy, you should apply for benefits no more than four months before the date you want your benefits to start. Bear in mind that benefits are paid the month after benefits are due. (If your benefits start in April, you will receive your first benefit payment in May.)
Where:	Your local Social Security Administration office.
Why:	To maximize your Social Security benefit, which will be your only guaranteed source of income available until your death. This strategy maximizes Social Security benefits while maintaining future cost-of-living adjustments (COLAs).
How:	You can apply for benefits online, by phone, or in person at your local Social Security office. Our staff will help with the process.
How much:	Your Social Security benefit will increase by 8 percent each year that you defer benefits between age sixty-seven and age seventy. If you defer your benefits until age seventy, we estimate Chandler will receive $2,728 (in today's dollars) each month, whereas Rachel will receive $1,612 (in today's dollars) each month.
Effect on cash flow:	Implementation will have no immediate effects on current cash flow; however, future cash flow at age seventy will be $22,680 (in today's dollars) greater than if benefits start at age sixty-two.

Current vs. Recommended Outcome:

If you do not increase your savings for retirement, we estimate that you will have an asset shortfall of approximately $968,000 on the first day of retirement. If you wish to leave a legacy equivalent to your initial retirement savings amount, the shortfall is $1,883,000.

By implementing the retirement recommendations described above, you will have approximately $5,436,000 available on the first day of retirement to meet your retirement goals. Although our recommendations will likely not preserve your assets completely, we estimate you will have approximately $2,632,000 of assets remaining at age ninety-five. The table below illustrates your retirement situation assuming each recommendation is implemented:

RETIREMENT PLANNING RECOMMENDATIONS	
Assumes that income and savings grow at a constant rate prior to retirement	
Assumes Social Security benefits do not begin before retirement	
ASSUMPTIONS	
Current Household Earned Income	$135,195.88
Other Retirement Income Excluding Social Security (today's dollars)	
Non-Tax Deferred Retirement Assets (Stocks & Bonds)	$123,350.00
Tax Deferred Retirement Assets (e.g., 401k)	$354,750.00
Tax-Free Retirement Assets (e.g., Roth)	
Tax Deferred Annual Savings (e.g., 401k) Including Employer Matching Contributions	$19,028.88
After Tax Annual Savings Specifically Allocated to Retirement Needs	

Tax-Free Savings Contributions (e.g., Roth)	$11,000.00
Other Annual Savings Specifically Allocated to Retirement Needs	
Retirement Income Replacement Ratio	85%
Age	42
Retirement Age	62
Age to Begin Social Security Benefits	70
Life Expectancy	95
Years Until Retirement	20
Years in Retirement	33
Inflation Prior to Retirement	3.00%
Inflation After Retirement	3.00%
Growth Rate of Savings	3.00%
Growth Rate of Salary	3.00%
Assumed Return While Retired	5.25%
Assumed Rate of Return Before Retirement	7.75%
Inflation Adjusted Retirement Return	2.18%
Inflation Adjusted Pre-Retirement Return	4.61%
CALCULATIONS	
Ratio Reduced Income Need (Today's Dollars)	$114,916.50
FV of Ratio Reduced Income Need @ Retirement Age	$207,551.98
FV of Non-Deferred Retirement Assets	$548,889.26
FV of Tax-Deferred Retirement Assets	$1,578,585.03
FV of Tax-Free Retirement Assets	$0.00
FV of Tax-Deferred Savings	$1,059,103.60
FV of After-Tax Savings	$0.00
FV of Tax-Free Savings	$612,234.73
FV of Other Savings	$0.00
FV of Social Security Benefits	$1,637,920.25
Total Retirement Assets/Savings Available on First Day of Retirement	$5,436,732.87
CAPITAL DEPLETION METHOD	
Amount Needed on FIRST DAY of RETIREMENT for CAPITAL DEPLETION	$4,950,371.19
Additional Net Assets Needed @ Retirement	($486,361.68)
Additional Level Annual Savings Needed	**($10,925.98)**
CAPITAL PRESERVATION METHOD	
Assets Needed on FIRST DAY of RETIREMENT for CAPITAL PRESERVATION	$5,865,133.61
Additional Net Assets Needed @ Retirement	$428,400.75
Additional Level Savings Needed (Capital Preservation)	**$9,623.91**

Please bear in mind that your Social Security benefits will be reduced by 30 percent if you start receiving benefits at age sixty-two. You will also be losing the 8 percent increase in benefits between age sixty-seven and age seventy. If you begin taking Social Security benefits at age sixty-two, Chandler's monthly Social Security benefit is estimated to be $1,540 in today's dollars, whereas Rachel's monthly

Social Security benefit is estimated to be $910 in today's dollars. If you defer benefits until age seventy, we estimate Chandler will receive $2,728 (in today's dollars) each month, whereas Rachel will receive $1,612 (in today's dollars) each month. As noted above, it is financially optimal for you to defer Social Security benefits until age seventy. If you prefer to begin Social Security benefits at age sixty-two, the long-term viability of your retirement plan will be jeopardized. You would need to save an additional $1,100 each year in order to have sufficient retirement savings by age sixty-two (and your retirement assets would be depleted at the end of your plan). The following graphs illustrate how the two Social Security strategies will affect the depletion of asset over the retirement period.

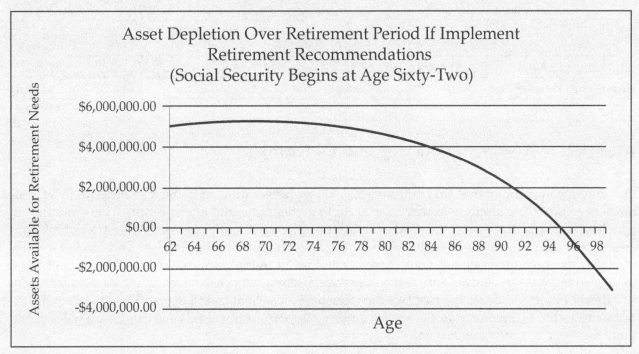

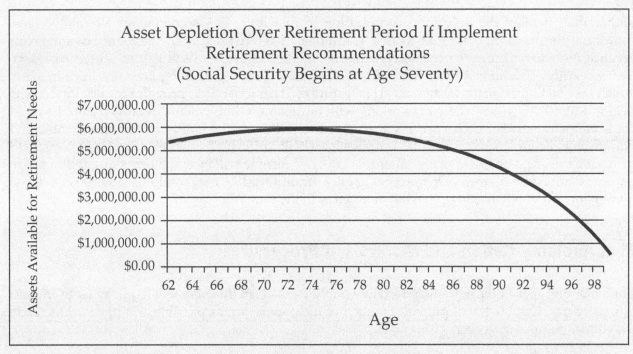

In addition, we conducted a break-even analysis for your Social Security benefits. Based on the analysis, it will take approximately one hundred and twenty five months beyond age seventy to recover the $147,840 of benefits Chandler would have received and the $87,360 of benefits Rachel would have received between age sixty-two and age seventy; therefore, if you expect to live beyond age eighty, you should defer benefits until age seventy. The following table contains the details of the Social Security break-even analysis:

Social Security Break Even Analysis		
	Chandler	Rachel
Monthly Benefit at Age 62	$1,540.00	$910.00
Total Benefits Between Age 62 and 70	$147,840.00	$87,360.00
Difference in Monthly Benefits from Age 62 to 70	$1,188.00	$702.00
Months to Break Even	124.4	124.4
Years to Break Even	10.4	10.4

Alternative Recommendations and Outcome(s):

Our core recommendation is that you save $27,000 each year until retirement in order to meet your retirement goals (assuming you defer Social Security benefits until age seventy). This amount will enable you to maintain your standard of living in retirement and preserve a large portion of your assets for a legacy transfer to Phoebe while minimizing your current tax liability. This level of savings will also allow you to maintain your current standard of living until retirement. Alternatively, you may wish to save a smaller amount to increase your discretionary cash flow and increase your current standard of living. If this is the case, we recommend you save at least $18,360 ($7,360 to your 401(k) accounts and $11,000 to your Roth IRA accounts) each year. At this level of savings, you will deplete your assets by the end of retirement.

Rather than making the maximum contribution to two Roth IRA accounts, an alternative is to contribute the maximum amount to two Traditional IRAs instead. Roth IRAs are advantageous because these arrangements provide certainty as to the tax rate you will pay in retirement—zero percent. With a Traditional IRA, you will pay tax based on the prevailing tax rates in retirement, which may be higher than current rates. This feature of Traditional IRAs provides uncertainty. Assets held in Roth IRAs will permit you (working with our team) to implement a relatively sophisticated tax saving strategy. For each year in retirement, you will have the ability to combine taxable and non-taxable income to keep marginal tax rates low. If all or most of your retirement assets are held in Traditional IRAs or 401(k) plans, all or most of your income will be taxable, making it difficult to reduce taxation in retirement. On the other hand, a Traditional IRA may minimize your taxes prior to retirement, but you may end up paying more taxes in the long run.

Plan Implementation and Monitoring Procedures:

Implementing each of the retirement recommendations made in this plan will require a large amount of paperwork. Our team will prepare as much of the paperwork as possible and have forms ready for your signatures as needed.

Alternatively, we are happy to mail forms to you (with return postage included) if you wish to begin implementation prior to the next meeting. If you prefer to receive the forms electronically, we can send forms to you using a secure link.

Throughout implementation, we will ensure that we are mindful of tax implications, and we will communicate with you about the tax consequences associated with implementing any current or future recommendations.

Please let us know if you have any questions as we begin implementing the retirement planning recommendations. In the meantime, you can expect to receive reminder emails when retirement contributions are due. Going forward, our team will monitor changes to tax legislation. We will let you know how these changes impact you or if changes to your retirement plan may be required. As with other aspects of this financial plan, we will update your retirement plan and assumptions each year prior to your annual review meeting; however, please notify us if any of the following events or changes occur, as one of these issues may indicate a need to reevaluate your retirement situation:

- Change in employment (i.e., change in demands, stress, etc.) or promotion for Chandler or Rachel (i.e., change in income or employee benefits) or a career change.

- Purchase of a new home or second home.

- Changes related to Phoebe (i.e., her death, college scholarship, decision not to attend college, etc.).

- Inheritance or receipt of sizable gift from Chandler's parents or other relatives.

- Pregnancy or adoption.

- Divorce.

- Death or disability of a family member.

- Change in health status.

- Winning the lottery.

- Change in life dreams or goals.

- A significant change in investment market returns and/or risks.

- Changes in tax policy (at the state and federal level).

15.10 SELF-TEST

[A] Self-Test Questions

Self-Test 1

An annuity that provides a beneficiary with a stream of income that has little market risk is known as a:

(a) Variable annuity.

(b) Period-certain annuity.

(c) Life annuity.

(d) Fixed annuity.

Self-Test 2

Thalia's full retirement age is sixty-seven. She plans to retire at age sixty-three. Based on this, how much will her Social Security benefit be reduced?

(a) 5 percent.

(b) 20 percent.

(c) 25 percent.

(d) 30 percent.

Self-Test 3

Sarita participates in a defined benefit pension plan. Her firm uses the following unit-benefit formula: 2 percent of final pay for each year of service. If Sarita works for 20 years and has a final year income of $160,000 how much will she receive from the pension?

(a) $58,000.

(b) $64,000.

(c) $4,800,000.

(d) $6,400,000.

Self-Test 4

The capital needs analysis approach that accounts for the real preservation of capital held in retirement accounts is called the:

(a) Capital Depletion Approach.

(b) Captial Preservation Approach.

(c) Inflation-Adjusted Captial Preservation Approach.

(d) Geometrical Varying Annuity Distribution Approach.

Self-Test 5

Which of the following is a commonly used replacement ratio when conducing a retirement needs analysis?

(a) 70 percent.

(b) 85 percent.

(c) 95 percent.

(d) 100 percent.

[B] Self-test Answers

Question 1: d

Question 2: c

Question 3: b

Question 4: c

Question 5: a

15.11 CHAPTER RESOURCES

Baldwin, B., *The New Retirement Investment Advisor* (New York: McGraw Hill, 2002).

Belth, J. M. *Retirement: A Consumer's Handbook,* 2nd Edition. Bloomington, IN: Indiana University Press, 1985.

General retirement and tax source: *Tax Facts on Retirement & Employee Benefits* (Cincinnati, OH: National Underwriter Company, published annually).

Leimberg, S. R., Buck, K., and Doyle, R. J. *The Tools & Techniques of Employee Benefit and Retirement Planning*, 17th Edition. Cincinnati, OH: National Underwriter Company, 2021.

CHAPTER ENDNOTES

1.   In practice, this extra amount is segregated from a client's other retirement assets and left to grow at the post-retirement rate of return. At the end of the client's retirement period, the original dollar amount should be worth approximately $1,492,564. Any yearly tax liability is assumed to be paid from regular cash flows.

2.   IRS Publication 590, Appendix B, Table III, Uniform Lifetime Table.

3.   J. J. Spitzer, "Managing a Retirement Portfolio: Do Annuities Provide More Safety?" *Journal of Financial Counseling and Planning,* 20(1) (2009): 58–69.

4.   M. A. Milevsky and V. R. Young, "Annuitization and Asset Allocation," *Journal of Economic Dynamics & Control,* 31 (2007): 3138–3177.

Chapter 16

Estate Planning

Learning Objectives

- Learning Objective 1: Describe the importance of estate planning within a comprehensive financial planning plan.

- Learning Objective 2: Identify influential client characteristics and questions that help determine a client's estate planning goal(s).

- Learning Objective 3: Estimate a client's potential gift and estate tax liability.

- Learning Objective 4: Identify estate planning strategies that can be used to help a client reach their estate planning goal(s).

16.1 THE PROCESS OF ESTATE PLANNING

In some respects, estate planning is the most integrative of the core financial planning topics. Almost every aspect of a client's financial life either impacts or is impacted by the estate planning decisions made by a client. Additionally, each client's unique characteristics help shape the type of recommendations that a financial planner makes in relation to estate planning questions. Some clients have a stated goal to minimize gift and estate taxes. Other clients desire privacy above other issues. Still other clients wish to share their wealth with family and community organizations. These examples suggest that no single strategy or tool is always appropriate when framing an estate plan. It is very important that a financial planner, working with their clients and collaborative professionals, develop recommendations that can be implemented in a way that maximizes each client's unique personal and financial circumstances. The following discussion describes how the financial planning process can be used when conducting an estate planning analysis.

Step 1: Understand the client's Personal and Financial Circumstances

The first step in the estate planning process involves reviewing relevant personal and financial information with the client. As is the case with all other financial planning topics, this type of discussion can strengthen the client-financial planner relationship and lead to the development and presentation of integrative recommendations.

A wide range of client-specific characteristics and factors can affect a client's estate planning situation, including the client's age, family situation, health status, charitable intentions, and overall quality of life expectations. Other issues to consider include:

- Change in employment or income status

- Pregnancy or adoption

- Separation

- Divorce

- Receipt of an inheritance

- Receipt of a large gift

- Receipt of life insurance proceeds

- New information related to a client's health situation or insurance coverage

- Disability

- Retirement

- Change in a child's status (e.g., attending school/college, no longer a financial dependent, etc.)

- Purchase of expensive assets

- Payment of large debts

These and other factors combine to shape a client's estate planning needs, desires, and financial planning focus. Figure 16.1 provides a review of the Hubbles' personal and financial circumstances related to estate planning. The information in Figure 16.1 is typical of what a financial planner should evaluate at the first step of the financial planning process.

Figure 16.1. The Hubbles' Personal and Financial Circumstances.

Chandler Hubble	Rachel Hubble
Age: 42	Age: 42
State of residence: Missouri	State of residence: Missouri
Citizen: U.S.	Citizen: U.S.
Life status: No known life issues	Life status: No known life issues
One child: Phoebe, age 5	One child: Phoebe, age 5

- Although neither Chandler nor Rachel have stated worries related to estate planning, it is important to frame discussions and recommendations in a way that reduces emotions surrounding incapacity or mortality.

- Chandler's and Rachel's general low level of financial risk tolerance may influence their preference for estate planning strategies at the time of recommendation implementation.

- Other attitudes, beliefs, and experiences with family or friends may influence the urgency for estate planning.

- Their stated view that paying an attorney is costlier than the benefit gained needs to be addressed early in the general financial/estate planning process.

- Chandler's and Rachel's assumptions about Rachel's sister as an appropriate guardian may influence how quickly they act to implement estate planning recommendations.

Step 2: Identify and Select Goals

Estate planning deals with the ownership and distribution of client assets. From a financial planning perspective, **estate planning** involves helping clients make decisions about the accumulation, preservation, and ultimate distribution of assets. Estate planning also involves providing advice about other end-of-life decisions, including custodial and guardianship situations for incapacitation or minor children.

Estate planning is an essential part of any well-conceived financial plan. An estate planning analysis can identify potential weaknesses in a client's financial situation that can reduce assets available for beneficiaries, charities, or other legacy goals. Steps taken to determine a client's estate planning goals, analyze a client's situation, and to develop estate planning recommendations can serve multiple outcomes. First, working through the estate planning process can create insights into ways of maximizing client assets while minimizing taxes and estate settlement costs. Second, a well-crafted estate plan can protect a client's privacy. Third, estate planning can help ensure that legacy goals are achieved. Fourth, estate planning can provide clients with peace of mind by confirming that their final financial and life wishes will be enacted. An estate plan should accomplish three objectives:

(1) provide a strategy for the cost-effective transfer of assets in a way that is consistent with a client's wishes through the preservation of the estate;

(2) provide for survivors or other financial or charitable needs; and

(3) allow for a client's final wishes regarding incapacitation and other end-of-life decisions to be fulfilled.

As described at Step One of the financial planning process, in order to meet these objectives—and before embarking upon a quantitative review of a client's estate planning situation—it is important for a financial planner to identify client characteristics, preferences, and wishes that can be used to guide the formalization of estate planning goals. Obtaining a clear idea of a client's values, social position, and cultural perceptions related to incapacity and death can help shape an estate plan. In addition, asking questions related to privacy desires, feelings about taxation and charitable giving, and special needs are important in shaping estate planning recommendations.

Reviewing life and death preferences is a foundational step when identifying estate planning goals. A number of questions can be used to determine a client's estate planning preferences and better assess client estate planning and estate liquidity needs. Answers to these questions directly impact the size or distribution of an estate. In situations where an estate is not large enough to trigger estate tax issues, other financial possibilities must be considered, especially if these issues can threaten to reduce a client's estate, or if not planned for properly, can create other problems for heirs.

Before considering these questions, it is important to clarify whether the client—and, if applicable, the spouse or partner—is a U.S. citizen. Specifically, planning needs differ for noncitizens or resident aliens. Citizenship can affect asset titling, gifts, estate transfers, and estate taxes. Property owned in the United States must be probated in a U.S. court, so similar considerations apply. It is generally important for noncitizens to have U.S. estate planning documents, even if documents were prepared in another country. Another critical consideration is a client's marital status, primarily because estate planning for domestic partners can get complicated.

Additional questions to determine a client's estate planning goal(s) include:

- Does the client wish to avoid probate (i.e., the legal and public procedure that validates a will and the distribution of assets as described in a will) or reduce probate assets?

- Is reduction of state death taxes a primary client need?

- Is protection of assets from creditors a concern?

- Is reduction of income taxes a primary client need?

- Does the client wish to leave some or most of the estate to a spouse or partner?

- Are there special needs (e.g., mental or emotional health issues, mental capacity or disability, physical disabilities) or other financial management issues that must be considered?

- Does the client have a desire to leave some or most of their estate to children? If yes, are the beneficiaries minor children or children with special needs, regardless of age?

- If an estate is to be left to children, will each child share equally, and if a child should predecease the parent, how will that child's share be distributed?

- Does the client wish to leave some or most of the estate to other dependents besides a spouse, a partner, or children? If yes, are there special needs (e.g., mental or emotional health issues, mental or physical disabilities) or other financial management issues that must be considered?

- Does the client wish to leave a charitable bequest? If charitable giving is a priority, which organizations are most important?

- Does the client have financial or managerial ties to a small business or a closely or privately held business that must be planned for within or outside of the estate plan?

- Which assets will be used to pay for final expenses and debt reduction?

- Is preplanning for a medical situation or emergency or long-term care an important client objective?

- Does the client have any special wishes that should be accounted for in the estate plan?

Each of these questions can lead to an in-depth discussion between a financial planner and client—and in some cases spouses, partners, or other family members—about life goals, legacies, estate planning objectives, and end-of-life issues. Answers to these, and similar questions, can then be used as background for establishing estate planning goals and initiating an assessment of a client's estate plan.

Figure 16.2 provides an overview of some of the most important estate planning goals as identified by Chandler and Rachel.

Figure 16.2. The Hubbles' Estate Planning Goals.

> Estate planning is an important reason Chandler and Rachel sought the help of a financial planner. Issues related to premature death and/or incapacity, as well as ensuring that Phoebe (age five) will have appropriate guardianship in the event of Chandler's and Rachel's death, prompted the Hubbles' engagement in the financial planning process. When thinking about their estate planning situation, Chandler and Rachel have the following goals:
>
> - To prepare for future events, such as incapacity or death, that can impact the family's financial situation.
>
> - Adequately provide for Phoebe in the event of Chandler's and Rachel's death.
>
> - To minimize estate settlement costs, such as probate, inheritance, and estate taxes.
>
> - To avoid probate and maintain privacy of their financial affairs.
>
> - To ensure that Chandler's and Rachel's end-of-life wishes, both to protect the family and the family's financial situation, are known and planned for to the fullest extent possible.

Step 3: Analyze the Client's Current Course of Action and Potential Alternative Course(s) of Action

Four steps are associated with describing and estimating a client's gift and estate tax situation.

- First, the value of the client's gross estate must be estimated.

- Second, the taxable estate must be calculated by subtracting from the gross estate funeral and administrative expenses, debts, taxes, charitable donations, and any marital transfers.

- Third, the value of taxable lifetime gifts must be added back into the taxable estate figure—unless the gift taxes were paid at the time the gift was made. This results is what is known as the *adjusted taxable estate*.

- The fourth step involves determining the tax payable. To arrive at this figure, the estate's remaining exclusion amount is subtracted from the adjusted taxable estate. What remains is subject to taxation. Alternatively, the tax can be calculated first with the applicable credit amount, then subtracted to determine the remaining liability.

[A] The Estate Tax Calculation

It is worth remembering that although a client's values, social position, or culture are influential factors in determining and quantifying a client's situation across all primary financial planning content areas, these types of personal characteristics are particularly relevant in estate planning. Sensitivity to a client's family, cultural, and religious/spiritual beliefs and attitudes is an important financial planner skill. Estate planning needs can run the gamut from providing care to a family member or pet to determining the optimal donation to a charity. The primary estate planning calculation centers on estimating a client's potential federal estate tax liability. The calculation hinges on the value of a client's **taxable estate** (i.e., the taxable value of assets owned by a decedent at their death) relative to the federal estate tax threshold).

The **estate tax** is a levy on a client's right to transfer property at death. The tax is based on the value of a client's taxable estate at the time of death. A client's taxable estate is the gross estate less allowable deductions.

The gross estate includes the fair market value of all property that a client owned or had an incidence of ownership in at the time of death, or in some cases, within three years of death. IRS Form 706 is used to account for these assets. The **fair market value of assets** at a client's death (or as of an alternative valuation date) is used to determine the gross estate. Assets included in the gross estate consist of cash and securities, real estate, revocable trusts, business interests, and other assets, as listed below:

- life insurance proceeds payable to the estate or, if the client held incidents of ownership in the policy, to the client's heirs;

- the value of certain annuities payable to the estate or heirs;

- the value of certain property transferred within three years before death; and

- trusts or other interests established by the client or others in which the client had certain interests or powers.

A client's **taxable estate** is determined by subtracting certain deductions from the gross estate. Allowable deductions include outstanding mortgages and other debts, as well as the following deductions:

- expenses associated with estate administration, including funeral expenses paid out of the estate, debts owed at the time of death, taxes, and certain estate losses;

- marital deductions, including all property passing to a surviving spouse;

- charitable deductions; and

- a state death tax deduction.

It is important to deduct only the portion of a liability attributable to the deceased client. Only the part of a deceased client's debt attributable to a listed asset is deductible. For example, married couples holding a principal residence as **joint tenants with right** of survivorship (JTWROS) can list only half of the fair market value of the property as an asset. As such, the deceased client can deduct only one-half of the outstanding mortgage balance.

Planning Reminder

Keep up to date on estate tax rates, the marital deduction, the unified credit, and other important data by visiting the IRS website yearly: www.irs.gov/Businesses/Small-Businesses-&-Self-Employed/Estate-Tax

A **marital deduction** is available for the value of all property that passes from one spouse to another. Under current law, the marital deduction is unlimited, meaning that one spouse is entitled to leave all their assets to a spouse free of estate and gift taxes. A **charitable deduction** is available for the value of property that passes to a charity or qualified non-profit organization.

After the net amount is computed, **adjusted taxable gifts** or the value of lifetime taxable gifts made after 1976 are added to this figure, resulting in the taxable estate. The tax is then computed on the new balance or taxable estate (tax is also calculated on the adjusted taxable gifts and subtracted from the tax on the taxable estate). The tax is then reduced by the available **unified credit** and other available credits, such as the credit for prior taxes paid or a foreign death tax credit. A **credit**, in this case, is similar to an income tax credit. It is this dollar amount that reduces or eliminates a tax.

An additional tax may be necessary for **income in respect of a decedent (IRD)**. This tax is based on any income that the deceased client was entitled to receive prior to death, but was not actually received until after death. Examples of IRD include salary earned but not paid until after a client's death, retirement account distributions, royalties, rents, dividends, interest, and other similar forms of income. IRD items must be included in the decedent's gross estate. The beneficiary of the income is then taxed at the beneficiary's marginal tax rate. However, the beneficiary might be able to deduct their portion of any estate taxes generated by the inclusion of the IRD.

Figure 16.3 summarizes the steps involved when calculating a client's potential estate tax liability.

Figure 16.3. Estate Planning Calculation Process.

STEP	CALCULATION	NOTES				
1.	Calculate Gross Estate	Calculation is based on the fair market value at date of death or alternate date value of the decedent's ownership interest.				
2.	Calculate the Taxable Estate	Subtract Funeral/Burial Expenses, Estate Administration and Legal Expenses, Outstanding Liabilities, Income Taxes, Executor Fees, Charitable Contributions, and other reductions, including the Qualified Marital Transfer, directly attributable to the decedent.				
3.	Add back Adjusted Taxable Gifts					
4.	Estimate Tax liability based on Estate and Gift Tax Rates	For Taxable Estates Between ...	And ...	You will Pay This Amount of Tax ...	Plus, You will Pay This Percentage on the Amount in Excess of the Lower Limit	
		$0	$9,999	$0	18%	
		$10,000	$19,999	$1,800	20%	
		$20,000	$39,999	$3,800	22%	
		$40,000	$59,999	$8,200	24%	
		$60,000	$79,999	$13,000	26%	
		$80,000	$99,999	$18,200	28%	
		$100,000	$149,999	$23,800	30%	
		$150,000	$249,999	$38,800	32%	
		$250,000	$499,999	$70,800	34%	
		$510,3010	$749,999	$155,800	37%	
		$750,000	$999,999	$248,300	39%	
		$1,000,000	-----------	$345,800	40%	
5.	Subtract Tax on Adjusted Taxable Gifts					
6.	Equals Tentative Estate Tax					
7.	Subtract Credits					
8.	Equals Estate Tax Liability					

The following example shows how an analysis of the Hubble family's current estate planning choices and needs provide a pathway to the development of estate planning recommendations. Figure 16.4 also shows a screenshot of the estate planning estimation procedure using the Financial Planning Analysis Excel™ package that accompanies the book. Potential recommendations are also provided.

Figure 16.4. The Hubbles' Current Estate Planning Situation and Potential Recommendations.

ESTATE TAX PLANNING ANALYSIS		
Assumed Asset & Expense Growth Per Year	4%	
Checking Account	$4,250.00	
Savings Account	$5,000.00	
Money Market Account	$5,000.00	
Other Monetary Assets	$0.00	
EE/I Bonds	$12,500.00	
Mutual Funds	$26,500.00	
Other Investment Assets	$0.00	
Primary Residence	$125,000.00	
Other Housing Assets	$0.00	
Vehicles	$17,750.00	
Personal Property	$40,650.00	
Retirement Assets	$255,000.00	
Other Assets	$0.00	
Life Insurance	$168,467.00	
GROSS ESTATE		**$660,117.00**
Deductions from Gross Estate		
Less Funeral & Burial Expenses	$9,000.00	
Less Estate Fees, Legal Fees, & Executor Fees	$13,500.00	
Less Mortgage, Debts, & Losses	$73,114.00	
ADJUSTED GROSS ESTATE		**$564,503.00**
Taxable Estate (Exclude Marital Deduction)		
Charitable Donation Deduction	$0.00	
TAXABLE ESTATE BEFORE MARITAL DEDUCTION		**$564,503.00**
Tax Assuming No Marital Deduction		
Gross Tax	$179,665.74	
Less Unified Credit	$4,769,800.00	
Less State Death Tax Credit	$0.00	

TAX DUE WITHOUT MARITAL DEDUCTION		−$4,590,134.26
Assets Available For Marital Deduction	$564,503.00	
Spouse's/Co-Client's Gross Estate After Marital Deduction Transfer		
Assumed Asset & Expense Growth Per Year	4%	
Checking Account	$4,250.00	
Savings Account	$5,000.00	
Money Market Account	$5,000.00	
Other Monetary Assets	$0.00	
EE/I Bonds	$12,500.00	
Mutual Funds	$26,500.00	
Other Investment Assets	$0.00	
Primary Residence	$125,000.00	
Other Housing Assets	$0.00	
Vehicles	$17,750.00	
Personal Property	$40,650.00	
Retirement Assets	$224,750.00	
Other Assets	$0.00	
Life Insurance	$230,000.00	
Marital Transfer	$564,503.00	
GROSS ESTATE		**$1,255,903.00**
Deductions from Gross Estate		
Less Funeral & Burial Expenses	$9,000.00	
Less Estate Fees, Legal Fees, & Executor Fees	$13,500.00	
Less Mortgage, Debts, & Losses	$73,114.00	
ADJUSTED GROSS ESTATE		**$1,160,289.00**
Taxable Estate (Exclude Marital Deduction)		
Charitable Donation Deduction		
TAXABLE ESTATE		**$1,160,289.00**
Tax Calculation		
Gross Tax	$409,915	
Less Unified Credit	$4,769,800	
Less State Death Tax Credit		
TAX DUE		**−$4,359,884.80**

When evaluating the data in Figure 16.4, it is important to keep the following points in mind. First, when estimating the estate tax liability, it is the gross value of assets that are included in each person's estate. This means, for example, that only one-half of assets owned as JTWROS are included in each spouse's gross estate; likewise, only one-half of debt associated with assets held as JTWROS is deductible. Second, only the unused exclusion amount is portable, and third, the scenario shown in Figure 16.4 assumes the death of Rachel occurs soon after the death of Chandler (the first-to-die spouse). This assumption may not be realistic in practice. A robust estimate of a household's possible estate tax liability should include a growth factor of assets held by the second to die.

Based on an assessment of the estate planning calculations shown in Figure 16.4, a number of possible recommendations immediately present themselves for possible use to Chandler and Rachel when addressing estate planning shortfalls. Although the Hubble family does not have, nor will they likely ever have, an estate or gift tax liability, an evaluation of the family's estate tax situation shows a need for specific estate planning recommendations. Specifically:

- Chandler and Rachel used a will kit purchased at an office supply store several years ago as a mechanism to draft their wills.

- Neither Chandler nor Rachel have looked at the wills since the documents were drafted.

- In their wills, Rachel's oldest sister, Barbara—who is single and living in Oregon—was named guardian of Phoebe.

- The Hubbles' wills leave all assets to each other.

- Chandler's current will is not adequate at this time: an executor should be named, Rachel should not be the sole beneficiary of all assets, perhaps a different guardian ought to be considered, the will alone does not ensure privacy of financial affairs, and Chandler's estate will be subject to probate.

- Rachel's will situation is identical to that of Chandler.

- Other estate planning documentation is either non-existent or out-of-date.

Based on these observations, the following recommendations are worthy of consideration:
- Consult with an attorney to draft the following documents:

  o New wills, including a provision for managing assets received by Phoebe if she is named as a beneficiary.

  o Advance medical directives.

  o Durable powers of attorney for health care.

  o Durable powers of attorney for finances.

Other recommendations include:
- Consider a living trust to maintain maximum financial privacy.

- Chandler and Rachel should each draft a final letter of instructions detailing their wishes regarding the disposition of specific tangible property, as well as funeral and burial wishes. This letter, which is given to the executor, may contain information regarding the location of important personal documents, safe deposit boxes, outstanding loans, and other personal and financial information that the executor will use to administer the decedent's estate.

- Chandler and Rachel should discuss with their attorney the possibility of setting up a standby trust to be the contingent beneficiary of their life insurance policies unless an irrevocable life insurance trust is established for this purpose. If recommended by the attorney, they should draft the document and notify the insurance companies to add the trust as the contingent beneficiary on their policies.

- Chandler and Rachel should carefully consider who will be named as the guardian for Phoebe.

Step 4: Develop the Financial Planning Recommendation(s)

The number and type of possible estate planning recommendations available to meet client goals is never-ending. Estate planning often calls for specialized work on the part of attorneys and accountants. A best practice calls for financial planners to refer clients with complex estate issues to other professionals or to bring in a competent expert to consult as needed. Another best practice is to always consider basic estate planning strategies before introducing more complex tactics. A financial planner should never assume that a client, regardless of wealth or income, has necessary, basic documents in place, such as a **will**, **power of attorney (POA)**, **living will**, or **advance medical directive** (AMD). This means that although there may be opportunities for a financial planner to develop multifaceted estate planning strategies, recommendations should generally follow what many would classify as fundamental estate planning recommendations.

It is important to remember that financial planners who are not attorneys should proceed carefully when developing and presenting estate planning recommendations. It is improper (and in some states illegal) for non-attorneys to draft legal documents for clients. When in doubt, a financial planner should work collaboratively with the client and an attorney when formalizing estate planning recommendations. This method of planning preserves a financial planner's fiduciary status while limiting liability related to the implementation of an inappropriate recommendation. Collaboration also limits exposure to penalties for the unauthorized practice of law. As with tax planning, financial planner recommendations should include a **disclaimer** in materials presented to clients, such as "Prior to implementing these recommendations, please confirm suggestions, recommendations, and implementation strategies with an attorney."

As noted above, the strategies that evolved from an estate planning analysis can range from basic to extremely complex. The intent of the following discussion is to provide examples of common (fundamental) estate planning strategies. Readers interested in developing more complex strategies and recommendations should consider reading *Principles of Estate Planning 3rd Edition*, published by the National Underwriter Company.

[A] General Considerations

Clients are well served when a financial planner helps the client carefully consider potential family conflicts, **conflicts of interest**, or the qualifications required for those appointed to serve a function within an estate plan (e.g., a guardian for children or the executor of a will). Individuals selected to help manage a client's estate must fully understand and accept the responsibilities inherent in their appointed role. This also extends to medical providers and other family or household members. For example, it is important for a family physician to be fully informed of a client's end-of-life preferences and decisions. That is, copies of a living will, advanced medical directive, and/or medical power of attorney should be distributed among appropriate medical, financial, and legal professionals, as well as a client's spouse, partner, or family.

Emotional distress, and perhaps a loss of **privacy**, is the primary disadvantage associated with this strategy. Although family discussions may be uncomfortable, it is nonetheless important that guardians and executors be informed of choices made by the client. It is also important for named non-clients to be willing to serve. Furthermore, it is important for appointees to understand their financial obligations. Certainly, any preliminary distress will be less traumatic than disclosing this information after the death of a family member or friend, or failing to appoint someone, thus prompting court involvement.

According to a 2011 ABC News poll, only 50 percent of all U.S. adults have a **will**—a document written to direct the distribution of one's property at death—and even fewer—only 42 percent—have a living will, health care proxy, or advance medical directive that can be used to direct end-of-life or health care decisions (i.e., someone a client appoints, such as a family member or friend, to make health care decisions for the client if the client is unable to make their own decision).[1]

A financial planner must evaluate the strategies, products, and/or legal techniques a client is currently using to accumulate, preserve, and distribute assets over time. Although only an attorney should ever draft a legal document for a client (clients may also draft their own legal documents), every financial planner who writes a comprehensive financial plan should help their clients think through the complex issues associated with planning an estate. As part of this review, it is very important that financial planners determine whether a client (and spouse or partner) holds any of the following documents, when they were drafted, and whether they are still applicable:

- **Client will(s)**: A legal document outlining how property will be transferred at death.

- **Letter(s) of last instruction**: A document written to a significant other (usually a spouse or children) to provide directions regarding the execution of a client's will.

- **Codicil**: An attachment or amendment to an existing will.

- **Power of attorney** (medical or financial): A legal document appointing another person to act for the client if the client becomes incapacitated.

- **Living will** or **advance medical directive** (AMD): A directive written for the use of a physician or hospital that outlines a client's wishes regarding medical and end-of-life treatment in the event of the client's incapacitation.

In addition to these legal documents, any prepaid, contracted, or even informal final arrangements should also be discussed, and the location of any contracts determined, if applicable. Finally, it is important to verify and review the following documents to develop a comprehensive profile of the client situation and confirm locations for future use:

- birth certificate(s) for all household members;

- marriage certificate(s) and/or divorce decree(s);

- all in-force insurance policies with beneficiary designations;

- life, health, long-term care, and annuity policies and beneficiary designation form(s) for individual and group policies;

- title(s) to personal property and deed(s) to real property in the state of residence or other states;

- inventory of any special property such as jewelry, fine art, or a collection (e.g., stamps, coins, wine, firearms) including a schedule of beneficiaries;

- brokerage account statements or other evidence of security ownership (e.g., stock certificates);

- business agreements and documentation for any outstanding unpaid debts or unsettled legal claims;

- income tax returns for the previous three years; and

- the location of a safety deposit box, an inventory of contents, the location of key(s), and a determination of whether state law requires that the box be sealed until inventoried by a representative of the court.

After reviewing a client's current estate planning situation, a variety of issues may need to be addressed. Working through methods to address questions and client concerns can be useful when developing recommendations for a client. A client's last will and testament often needs immediate remedial attention. The checklist shown in Figure 16.5 can be used to guide the evaluation of a client's current will and end-of-life documentation to determine whether legal documents should be retained or rewritten.

Figure 16.5. Estate Planning Documentation Checklist.

Estate Planning Documentation Checklist		
Question	Yes	No
1. Is the client's name correct on all documents?		
2. Is the spouse's or partner's name correct on all documents?		
3. Are the children's names and ages (if applicable) correct on all documents?		
4. Is the executor properly named?		
5. Is a guardian for dependent children named?		
6. If named, is the guardian still the appropriate choice?		
7. Are special bequests adequately identified?		
8. Are charitable bequests up to date and adequately identified?		
9. Is the simultaneous death clause appropriate for the state of residence?		
10. Are trust documents referred to in the will?		
11. Does the will refer to a particular trust if a trust exists?		

12. Have trusts, other than testamentary trusts, been funded?		
13. Have special considerations been made for parents?		
14. Have special considerations been made for siblings?		
15. Have special considerations been made for grandchildren?		
16. Are codicils up to date and accurate?		
17. Does the client have a power of attorney in place? If so, what kind and what powers are included?		
18. Has the client written a letter of last instructions?		
19. Depending on the state of residence and need, has the client drafted: (a) a living will?		
(b) an advance medical directive?		
(c) a medical power of attorney?		
(d) a HIPAA authorization?		
20. Does the client share time in different states? If so, are all documents appropriate and in place?		
21. Is there a current list of all financial professionals, including the estate attorney, available for the survivors or the executor?		

[B] Property Titling Techniques

Titling assets properly is one tool a financial planner can use to help a client manage their estate plan. Generally, whenever someone is added to the title of a property, the IRS considers the addition a **taxable gift** the equal to the fair market value of the new ownership position. Understanding when a taxable gift might be triggered can save a client significant gift and estate taxes.

Planning Reminder

When adding someone to an account, if the original owner can make a withdrawal from an asset account without the permission of the new owner, no gift tax will be due until the new owner takes a distribution. For example, no gift tax is due when a joint owner is added to a bank account until the new owner makes a withdrawal. If a security is held in street name, no gift tax is incurred upon joint titling; however, if a security is held JTWROS, a gift tax may be incurred.

The following titling methods can be used for property owned by more than one person:

- **Tenancy in common**: Used by two or more individuals; ownership interests need not be equal; each owner can sell, exchange, or otherwise dispose of their interest without the consent of the other owners; there are no survivorship rights.

- **Joint tenancy with right of survivorship** (JTWROS): Used by two or more individuals; ownership is equal among owners; ownership passes automatically to survivors upon the death of an owner; ownership can be terminated by death, mutual agreement, and divorce.

- **Tenancy by the entirety**: Used only by married couples, primarily for real property; survivorship interest passes automatically to the surviving spouse.

- **Community property**: Used only by married couples living and acquiring property in community property states; survivorship interest does not automatically pass to the surviving spouse.

Planning Reminder

Separate property in a community property state is:
- Property a client owned before marriage;
- Property purchased with separate funds;
- Money a client earns while living in a non-community property state;
- Property received as a gift or inheritance.

Community property is:
- Any property acquired during marriage while living in a community property state if the property was commingled with spouse or purchased with community assets and
- Property client and spouse agreed to convert to community property under state law.

In the case of JTWROS and tenancy in common, creditors can access the value of the co-owner's interest. Only tenancy by the entirety protects a couple's home from creditor or liability claims against one member of the couple. Some states, such as Virginia, also allow married couples to title investment assets as tenants by the entirety. Potential gift taxes can arise with a change in titling.

Ten states provide married couples with an alternative to tenancy by the entirety. Alaska, Arizona, California, Idaho, Louisiana, Nevada, New Mexico, Texas, Washington, and Wisconsin each have a form of community property law. **Community property** refers to all assets obtained while a couple is married. Each spouse legally owns one-half of each asset purchased as community property.

Community property is unique, however, in that any property owned by a spouse prior to marriage remains the sole property of that spouse unless it is commingled with community property assets. Furthermore, if a spouse receives a gift or inheritance while married, those assets remain the separate property of the spouse.

One advantage associated with community property titling is that, upon the death of one spouse, all assets receive a 100 percent step-up in basis. This compares favorably to the 50 percent **step-up in basis** for assets held by spouses as JTWROS (i.e., titling procedure in which ownership of an asset transfers automatically at death to the surviving owners) or as tenancy by the entirety. Few banks, title companies, or other financial service firms automatically title marital assets as community property. A financial planner who fails to guide their community property clientele in the appropriate use of this titling option can cause clients to pay higher taxes in the future because of the lost step-up in basis associated with JTWROS titling.

[C] Gifting

An effective way to decrease a client's gross estate involves taking full advantage of the **gift tax annual exclusion**. Using this strategy, a client can give up to the annual gift tax exclusion amount each year gift tax free to as many individuals (related or not) as the client desires. Married couples can double the value of tax-free gifts. It is possible to reduce an estate substantially over time just by systematically making gifts to one or more persons. The primary disadvantage associated with this strategy is that, once a gift has been made, the transfer is irrevocable. Further, gifts to others cannot be used to generate income for the donor. Gifts of more than the annual exclusion effectively decrease a client's unified credit and subject the donor to gift taxation.

Planning Reminder

- Present gifts greater than the annual exclusion are currently taxable.
- Future interest gifts are currently taxable.
- No gift tax is due on a gift if the current gift plus all lifetime gifts do not exceed the applicable exclusion amount.

[D] Portability

In late December 2010, Congress passed the Tax Relief, Unemployment Insurance Reauthorization, and Job Creation Act of 2010 (Act). This legislation extended estate, gift, and generation-skipping transfer taxes (GSTT). The Act also increased the exemption threshold and lowered the marginal tax rates. The legislation reunified the estate and **gift tax rate**, so that a single lifetime exemption can be used for both lifetime gifts and/or upon-death bequests. In late 2018, Congress enacted the Tax Cuts and Jobs Act. This act effectively removed the threat of gift or estate taxes for all but the wealthiest Americans.

Under current law, the **unified credit** applies to both the gift tax and the estate tax and is subtracted from any gift or estate tax that a client may owe. An estate tax return for a U.S. citizen or resident needs to be filed only if the gross estate exceeds the applicable exclusion amount. Once an estate exceeds the exemption amount, the maximum tax rate applied is 40 percent.

The 2010 Act made **portability** permanent. Portability allows a taxpayer to transfer any unused exemption to a surviving spouse. The **portable estate exemption** allows the unused portion of a spouse's **estate tax exclusion** (i.e., the amount of assets that can be transferred tax free at the death of a spouse) to be shifted to the surviving spouse. This means that even if the first-to-die spouse fails to use their entire exemption, the unused estate exemption can be utilized by the second-to-die spouse. In effect, the portable estate exemption allows almost $25 million for a married couple to be sheltered from taxes. The only requirement is that clients (or the client's executor) file IRS Form 706 to maintain the portable estate exemption, even if the first-to-die's estate is not taxable.

[E] Trust Considerations

Given the size and number of potential gift and estate tax liabilities, it may be advisable to explore the use of trusts in addition to gifting strategies within a client's estate plan. A **trust** is an arrangement that grants a trustee legal title to assets. A trustee is required to act as a fiduciary when managing assets for the benefit of trust beneficiaries. In most cases, the **beneficiary** is the person who holds the beneficial title to trust assets. In general, trust income is passed directly from the trust to the **income beneficiary**, as opposed to the **remainder beneficiary**—the person or entity entitled to receive the assets upon termination of the trust. Often, the income beneficiary and remainder beneficiary are the same person or entity, although it is possible for a trust to have only income beneficiaries.

There are two types of trusts:

- **Testamentary trusts**, funded upon death; and

- **Living trusts**, funded prior to death.

The most common type of testamentary trust is a **standard family trust** (also known as an **A-B trust arrangement**), which is a legal tool established to hold assets and transfer income to a surviving spouse without the surviving spouse actually taking ownership of the assets. Upon the death of the surviving spouse, a trustee then distributes the remaining assets to beneficiaries, often referred to as **remaindermen**.

In addition to the distinction between living and testamentary trusts, living trusts can also be sub-classified as either irrevocable or revocable. **Revocable trusts** are also known as **grantor trusts** because the trust or trust assets can be revoked or modified by the grantor. **Irrevocable trusts**, as the name implies, cannot be modified, amended, or revoked by the grantor; only the trustee has this authority, according to trust document guidelines.

[F] Applying Planning Skills to the Hubble Case

Generally, only modest changes will need to be made to the initial recommendations developed at Step Three of the financial planning process, although it is possible that new client information or data can necessitate the need for a reevaluation. Figure 16.6 provides a summary of the final estate planning recommendations that match the Hubble family's financial goals.

Figure 16.6. Estate Planning Recommendations for Chandler and Rachel.

The final estate planning recommendations developed for the Hubble family match the preliminary recommendations identified at Step Three of the financial planning process. Specifically, Chandler and Rachel should draft:
• New wills, including a provision for managing assets received by Phoebe if she is named as a beneficiary. • Advance medical directives. • Durable powers of attorney for health care. • Durable powers of attorney for finances.
Chandler and Rachel should also do the following:
• Chandler and Rachel should establish a living trust to maintain maximum financial privacy. • Chandler and Rachel should each draft a final letter of instructions detailing their wishes regarding the disposition of specific tangible property, as well as funeral and burial wishes. This letter, which is given to the executor, may contain information regarding the location of important personal documents, safe deposit boxes, outstanding loans, and other personal and financial information that the executor will use to administer the decedent's estate. • Chandler and Rachel should discuss with their attorney the possibility of setting up a standby trust to be the contingent beneficiary of their life insurance policies, unless an irrevocable life insurance trust is established for this purpose. If recommended by the attorney, they should draft the document and notify the insurance companies to add the trust as the contingent beneficiary on their policies. • Chandler and Rachel should carefully consider who will be named as the guardian for Phoebe.
In the context of other financial planning recommendations, including the purchase of new life insurance policies, Chandler and Rachel should be reminded of the following:
• Avoid naming a life insurance policy owner or the owner's estate as the beneficiary because of (1) possible estate tax or state inheritance tax implications; (2) lack of protection of the funds from creditors; and (3) delays with the probate court that will make the funds inaccessible. • Avoid establishing a trust to manage life insurance proceeds while naming an individual as the beneficiary of the policy. The proceeds will go to the beneficiary instead of the trust. • Avoid delays in updating a policy beneficiary after major life events. In a few states, divorce automatically revokes a beneficiary designation naming the ex-spouse. Otherwise, an ex-spouse could receive the policy proceeds years after the divorce. • Avoid naming only one beneficiary, opting instead for a primary and one or more contingent beneficiaries. Should the beneficiary, without a contingent named, pre-decease the insured, the insurance proceeds would then be payable to the estate if a second in-line contingent is not named. • Avoid naming minor children, such as Phoebe, as a beneficiary unless the will names a guardian or trust to manage the funds on behalf of the child. If the court must appoint someone, there will be additional expense—paid from the insurance proceeds.

Step 5: Present the Financial Planning Recommendation(s)

Few aspects associated with the development of a financial plan provide as many opportunities to recommend strategies to meet multiple client goals as the estate planning section of a plan. When viewed holistically, the estate planning process can be seen as a unifying procedure that helps clients better understand the lifetime accumulation, preservation, and ultimate distribution of assets. Because estate planning deals with end-of-life issues, this topic within a financial plan can sometimes meet with resistance by clients. Few clients are prepared to openly discuss illness, incapacitation, and death. As such, great care must be taken when presenting recommendations.

Figure 16.7 highlights some of the important factors to consider when presenting estate planning recommendations to Chandler and Rachel Hubble.

Figure 16.7. Factors to Consider When Presenting Estate Planning Recommendations.

An important consideration when presenting estate planning recommendations to Chandler and Rachel involves communicating that, as a couple, many immediate estate planning needs exist, even though Chandler and Rachel are not subject to the estate tax. Estate planning involves more considerations than just minimizing or avoiding estate taxes. Estate planning is important for anyone who wishes to control their financial legacy. This is true for all individuals and households, not just the ultra-wealthy.

It is also important to communicate urgency in implementation. Based on the fact that Chandler and Rachel did not create wills until Phoebe was two years old, a competent financial planner should anticipate some reluctance on the part of Chandler and Rachel to implement estate planning recommendations. It may take prompting and nudging to move Chandler and Rachel towards recommendation implementation. This can be done by spending time discussing the outcome of the Hubble family's current situation and what might happen if estate planning recommendations are postponed or avoided. It may help Chandler and Rachel to feel more motivated if they understand the deficiencies in their current estate plan and potential consequences, particularly to Phoebe, if action is delayed.

Step 6: Implement the Financial Planning Recommendation(s)

Given the emotional nature that surrounds the presentation and implementation of nearly all estate planning recommendations, coupled with the realization on the part of a client that a new person—an attorney—will be introduced into the financial planning process, clients often need to be nudged toward recommendation implementation. One way to make recommendation implementation easier is to provide a detailed implementation procedure for each recommendation. The presentation of a recommendation needs to match a client's information processing style and preferences. Figure 16.8 shows how one of the recommendations developed for Chandler and Rachel can be presented within a financial plan.

Figure 16.8. Implementing an Estate Recommendation for the Hubble Family.

Recommendation #1: Have new estate planning documents drafted.	
Who:	Chandler and Rachel.
What:	You should have two copies of the following estate planning documents, one each for Chandler and Rachel, drafted by an attorney: • New wills, including a provision for managing assets received by Phoebe if she is named as a beneficiary; • Advance medical directives; • Durable powers of attorney for health care; and • Durable powers of attorney for finances.
When:	Within the next thirty to forty-five days.
Where:	At the office of a reputable, licensed estate attorney.
Why:	To ensure that your wishes are known in the event that either Chandler or Rachel pass away or become incapacitated. Estate planning documents help household assets avoid probate, which can be a lengthy, non-private, and expensive process.
How:	Set up an appointment and meet with a reputable, licensed estate attorney. Our financial planning team can provide a referral to an estate planning attorney. Prior to the meeting, confirm the information summarized in this section of the financial plan, especially in regard to passing property in the event of death, wishes regarding medical and end-of-life treatment in the event of incapacitation, and who should be appointed in the event one or both become incapacitated.
How much:	The cost of this recommendation is included with the drafting of a living trust. Based on similar client situations involving the development of estate planning documents, you can expect to pay approximately $2,000. This can be funded using cash from the savings account.
Effect on cash flow:	Implementation of this recommendation has no impact on cash flow (the fee will be paid from cash assets).

Step 7: Monitor Progress and Update

A client's estate plan is never finished. This is another way of saying that a financial planner must constantly monitor previously implemented recommendations, and in situations where a client has failed to implement a strategy, continue to prompt client action. Given the highly political nature of the gift and estate tax, it is realistic to assume the Congress will continue to alter gift and estate laws. Any change in federal tax policy is enough to warrant a reevaluation of a client's potential tax liability.

Based on the level of the federal estate exclusion, it is unlikely that many clients will trigger an estate or gift tax. It is much more likely that a client will be subject to a state or local estate or gift tax. Financial planners who work with clients who live in states where the estate tax is not tied to or loosely linked with the federal estate tax should perform annual evaluations of potential tax liabilities. Obviously, any state gift or estate tax change should prompt an immediate review of a client's situation. In addition to tax law changes, any number of household level events should also trigger a reevaluation of the viability of a client's estate planning documentation. Client-specific characteristics and/or events to monitor include:

- Change in employment or income status

- Pregnancy or adoption

- Separation

- Divorce

- Receipt of an inheritance

- Receipt of a large gift

- Receipt of life insurance proceeds

- New information related to a client's health situation or insurance coverage

- Disability

- Retirement

- Change in a child's status (e.g., attending school/college, no longer a financial dependent, etc.)

- Purchase of expensive assets

- Payment of large debts

As with other financial planning topics, changes to a client's circumstances should prompt a review and/or reevaluation of previously made recommendations. At a minimum, a client's estate planning situation should be monitored on an annual basis. A client's health, employment status, marital status, preferences, and attitudes can change over time. Changes almost always warrant a review of previously implemented recommendations. Figure 16.9 provides an overview of some of the factors that require ongoing monitoring for Chandler and Rachel Hubble.

Figure 16.9. Issues to Monitor in the Hubble Case.

> **Numerous ongoing monitoring issues are at play in the domain of estate planning. It is important to evaluate each of these issues at least on an annual basis. Some of the most important life events that may impact the Hubble family's estate needs include:**
>
> - Change in employment or promotion for Chandler or Rachel (i.e., change in income).
> - Changes related to Phoebe (i.e., her death, reaching the age of majority, etc.).
> - Inheritance from Chandler's parents.
> - Receipt of large gift.
> - Pregnancy or adoption.
> - Divorce.
> - New, more dangerous hobbies or jobs.
> - Disability of a family member.

16.2 COMPREHENSIVE HUBBLE CASE

Estate planning is an important topic within nearly all comprehensive financial plans. While a financial planner, who is not a licensed attorney, is prohibited from drafting legal documents, it is permissible to conduct a thorough gift and estate planning analysis, as well as a review of estate planning documentation. Ensuring that a client has the necessary and appropriate documents and forms in place prior to death or incapacitation is a meaningful outcome associated with the financial planning and estate planning process. The following narrative is an example of how the estate planning section within a comprehensive financial plan can be written.

Estate

Overview of Estate:

Many clients find it difficult to begin planning for incapacitation or eventual death; however, it is vital to begin making estate planning preparations early in life to ensure that your wishes are known and your loved ones are protected. Estate planning documents should be drafted by a licensed estate attorney. Because this is a specialized field of law, our firm can assist by providing a legal referral. Our staff will work closely with the estate attorney in implementing recommendations. It is important to note that we are not attorneys. As such, our firm's recommendations should be discussed with your attorney prior to drafting any new estate planning documents. As financial planners, our role includes recognizing which estate planning documents are needed and anticipating what estate planning documents may be needed in the future.

Estate Definitions:

The following definitions will be useful as you review the analysis presented in this section:

- *Codicil*: An attachment or amendment to an existing will.

- *Contingent beneficiary*: The person who will receive the benefits of a will, trust, life insurance policy, annuity, or other asset in the event of the owner's death if the primary beneficiary is deceased.

- *Letter(s) of last instruction*: A document written to a significant other (usually a spouse or children) to provide directions regarding the execution of a client's will.

- *Living will or advance medical directive (AMD)*: A directive written for the use of a physician or hospital that outlines a client's wishes regarding medical and end-of-life treatment in the event of the client's incapacitation.

- *Power of attorney (medical or financial)*: A legal document appointing another person to act for the client if the client becomes incapacitated.

- *Primary beneficiary*: The person who will receive the benefits of a will, trust, life insurance policy, annuity, or other asset in the event of the owner's death.

- *Probate*: The legal and public procedure that validates a will and the distribution of assets as described in a will.

- *Trust*: An arrangement that grants a trustee legal title to assets.

- *Will*: A legal document outlining how property will be transferred at death.

Planning Assumptions:

- The assumed appreciation rate on your gross estate, debt, loans, and other financial position items is 4 percent.

- Funeral and administration expenses are assumed to be $9,000 for each person living in the household. These expenses will grow 4 percent annually.

- Executor fees are anticipated to be approximately $13,500 per person living in the household.

Goals:

- To prepare for future events, such as incapacity or death, that can impact your family's financial situation.

- To adequately provide for Phoebe in the event of Chandler and Rachel's death.

- To minimize estate settlement costs, such as probate, inheritance taxes, and estate taxes.

- To avoid probate and maintain privacy of the family's financial affairs.

- To ensure that end-of-life wishes, both to protect your family and your financial situation, are known and planned for to the greatest extent possible.

Your Current Estate Situation:

Chandler and Rachel, you both wrote wills when Phoebe was two years old. These wills were written without advice or assistance from an estate attorney. The wills have not been reviewed since the documents were drafted three years ago. Phoebe is currently a minor. Rachel's older sister, Barbara, was named in both wills as Phoebe's guardian. Barbara is currently single and living in Oregon. Chandler's will leaves all assets to Rachel, and Rachel's will leaves all assets to Chandler.

Chandler and Rachel, your wills do not name executors or contingent inheritors. For these reasons, your wills should be updated as soon as possible. Please note that a will is not sufficient to ensure the privacy of your affairs. Based on the information provided by you during the data gathering stage of the financial planning engagement, you have not created any estate documents other than wills.

Based on our analysis, you will not have an estate tax liability in the event that either Chandler or Rachel was to pass away this year or in the foreseeable future. Based on current law, each partner in a marriage receives an estate exclusion of over $12M. As a couple, you will not incur an estate tax liability unless or until the value of your joint estates exceeds over $24M. A summary of your federal estate tax situation is shown below:

ESTATE TAX PLANNING ANALYSIS		
Assumed Asset & Expense Growth Per Year	4%	
Checking Account	$4,250.00	
Savings Account	$5,000.00	
Money Market Account	$5,000.00	
Other Monetary Assets	$0.00	
EE/I Bonds	$12,500.00	
Mutual Funds	$26,500.00	
Other Investment Assets	$0.00	
Primary Residence	$125,000.00	
Other Housing Assets	$0.00	
Vehicles	$17,750.00	
Personal Property	$40,650.00	
Retirement Assets	$255,000.00	
Other Assets	$0.00	
Life Insurance	$168,467.00	
GROSS ESTATE		**$660,117.00**
Deductions from Gross Estate		
Less Funeral & Burial Expenses	$9,000.00	
Less Estate Fees, Legal Fees, & Executor Fees	$13,500.00	
Less Mortgage, Debts, & Losses	$73,114.00	
ADJUSTED GROSS ESTATE		**$564,503.00**
Taxable Estate (Exclude Marital Deduction)		
Charitable Donation Deduction	$0.00	
TAXABLE ESTATE BEFORE MARITAL DEDUCTION		**$564,503.00**
Tax Assuming No Marital Deduction		
Gross Tax	$179,665.74	
Less Unified Credit	$4,769,800.00	
Less State Death Tax Credit	$0.00	
TAX DUE WITHOUT MARITAL DEDUCTION		**−$4,590,134.26**
Assets Available For Marital Deduction	$564,503.00	
Spouse's/Co-Client's Gross Estate After Marital Deduction Transfer		
Assumed Asset & Expense Growth Per Year	4%	
Checking Account	$4,250.00	

Savings Account	$5,000.00	
Money Market Account	$5,000.00	
Other Monetary Assets	$0.00	
EE/I Bonds	$12,500.00	
Mutual Funds	$26,500.00	
Other Investment Assets	$0.00	
Primary Residence	$125,000.00	
Other Housing Assets	$0.00	
Vehicles	$17,750.00	
Personal Property	$40,650.00	
Retirement Assets	$224,750.00	
Other Assets	$0.00	
Life Insurance	$230,000.00	
Marital Transfer	$564,503.00	
GROSS ESTATE		**$1,255,903.00**
Deductions from Gross Estate		
Less Funeral & Burial Expenses	$9,000.00	
Less Estate Fees, Legal Fees, & Executor Fees	$13,500.00	
Less Mortgage, Debts, & Losses	$73,114.00	
ADJUSTED GROSS ESTATE		**$1,160,289.00**
Taxable Estate (Exclude Marital Deduction)		
Charitable Donation Deduction		
TAXABLE ESTATE		**$1,160,289.00**
Tax Calculation		
Gross Tax	$ 409,915	
Less Unified Credit	$ 4,769,800	
Less State Death Tax Credit		
TAX DUE		**−$4,359,884.80**

Estate Recommendations:

The following tables summarize the recommendations that have been designed to help you reach your estate planning goals. As with all recommendations presented in this financial plan, our firm is available to answer any questions that might arise and to assist with specific implementation procedures.

Recommendation #1: Have new estate planning documents drafted.	
Who:	Chandler and Rachel.
What:	You should have two copies of the following estate planning documents, one each for Chandler and Rachel, drafted by an attorney: • New wills, including a provision for managing assets received by Phoebe if she is named as a beneficiary; • Advanced medical directives; • Durable powers of attorney for health care; and • Durable powers of attorney for finances.
When:	Within the next thirty to forty-five days.
Where:	At the office of a reputable, licensed estate attorney.
Why:	To ensure that your wishes are known in the event that either Chandler or Rachel pass away or become incapacitated. Estate planning documents help household assets avoid probate, which can be a lengthy, non-private, and expensive process.
How:	Set up an appointment and meet with a reputable, licensed estate attorney. Our financial planning team can provide a referral to an estate planning attorney. Prior to the meeting, confirm the information summarized in this section of the financial plan, especially in regard to passing property in the event of death, wishes regarding medical and end-of-life treatment in the event of incapacitation, and who should be appointed in the event one or both become incapacitated.
How much:	The cost of this recommendation is included with the drafting of a living trust. Based on similar client situations involving the development of estate planning documents, you can expect to pay approximately $2,000. This can be funded using cash from the savings account.
Effect on cash flow:	Implementation of this recommendation has no impact on cash flow (the fee will be paid from cash assets).

Recommendation #2: Ensure primary and contingent beneficiaries are named on all assets.	
Who:	Chandler and Rachel.
What:	Based on the information obtained from you, we recommend that Chandler name Rachel as primary beneficiary on his assets. Chandler should also name Phoebe as contingent beneficiary. We recommend that Rachel name Chandler as primary beneficiary of her assets. Phoebe should be named as contingent beneficiary.
When:	Within the next thirty to forty-five days.
Where:	Life insurance: directly with the insurance company. Retirement plan assets: directly with the custodian of plan assets. Bank account assets: directly with the bank. *Note: our staff will assist with locating the appropriate forms as needed.*
Why:	Beneficiary designations allow assets to pass to a stated beneficiary outside the probate process. Generally, beneficiary designations supersede directions made in a will. Should the beneficiary, without a contingent beneficiary being named, predecease the owner of the asset, the proceeds or distribution of the asset will be paid to the owner's estate. For this reason, it is important to name a contingent beneficiary for any titled assets. For life insurance policies, it is important to avoid naming the policy owner or the owner's estate as the beneficiary because of: (1) possible estate tax or state inheritance tax implications; (2) lack of protection of the funds from creditors; and (3) delays with the probate court that will make the funds inaccessible.
How:	For financial assets, you should visit the website of the custodian of the account or other financial asset. Within your account, select the option to change your beneficiary designation. Bear in mind that you may need to provide the birth date or other information about your beneficiary choice. To change or update beneficiaries on insurance policies, contact the insurance company. A representative will lead you through the company's process for updating beneficiaries. As with other implementation issues, our staff is available to assist with these issues.
How much:	There is no cost associated with this recommendation.
Effect on cash flow:	Implementation of this recommendation has no impact on cash flow.

Recommendation #3: Establish a living trust.	
Who:	Chandler and Rachel.
What:	A living trust (also known as a revocable living trust) is funded prior to death. Funding essentially means transferring ownership of all titled assets (e.g., homes, cars, boat, bank accounts, brokerage accounts, etc.) to a trust. A trust has three parties: (1) the grantor or the person(s) who establishes and funds the trust; (2) a trustee or the person(s) who manage trust assets on a day-to-day basis. Chandler and Rachel, you will serve as co-trustees, which provides total freedom to add to the trust or dispose of assets in the trust. As trustees, all income from the trust will flow directly to you; (3) one or more beneficiaries. Chandler and Rachel, you will name yourselves as primary beneficiaries, with Phoebe as a contingent beneficiary.
When:	Within the next thirty to forty-five days.
Where:	At the office of a reputable, licensed estate attorney.
Why:	Establishing a living trust meets your goal to avoid probate and minimize publicity at death. A living trust also maximizes financial management flexibility.
How:	Set up an appointment and meet with a reputable, licensed estate attorney. Our financial planning team can provide a referral to an estate planning attorney. Prior to the meeting, discuss your wishes with each other regarding property transfer desires in the event of death.
How much:	The cost of this recommendation is included with the drafting of a will. Based on similar client situations involving the development of estate planning documents, you can expect to pay approximately $2,000. This can be funded using cash from the savings account.
Effect on cash flow:	Implementation of this recommendation has no impact on cash flow (the fee will be paid from cash assets).

Recommendation #4: Draft a final letter of last instructions.	
Who:	Chandler and Rachel.
What:	A final letter of last instructions details your wishes regarding the disposition of specific tangible property, as well as funeral and burial wishes. This letter is given to your estate's executor in the event of your death. The letter may contain information regarding the location of important personal documents, safe deposit boxes, outstanding loans, and other personal and financial information that the executor will use to administer your estate. The letter can (and should) also provide information about burial/cremation wishes, as well as any memorial desires.
When:	Within the next thirty to forty-five days.
Where:	At home or at the office of a reputable, licensed estate attorney. Our financial planning team can provide a referral to an estate planning attorney.
Why:	To ensure that your executor(s) has the information necessary to fulfill your last wishes and desires.
How:	Set up an appointment and meet with a reputable, licensed estate attorney. Our financial planning team can provide a referral to an estate planning attorney. Consult the attorney about the type of information that should be included in the letter of last instructions. Your attorney should retain a copy of the letter. A copy can also be kept in your files with our firm.
How much:	The cost of drafting the letter is typically included in the cost of a will.
Effect on cash flow:	This recommendation has no impact on cash flow.

Recommendation #5: Discuss who should be named as Phoebe's guardian.	
Who:	Chandler and Rachel.
What:	Currently, Barbara (Rachel's sister) is named as Phoebe's guardian in the event that both of you were to pass away. It is important to discuss whether designating Barbara as Phoebe's guardian still represents your wishes or whether you would like to consider naming a different person. It is worth considering a guardian's proximity to the family, Phoebe's knowledge and familiarity of the person, and the financial stability of the proposed guardian.
When:	Within the next thirty to forty-five days.
Where:	This discussion can take place at home, in our firm's offices, or with your attorney.
Why:	To ensure that Phoebe will be cared for according to your wishes.
How:	Once you have considered who should be Phoebe's guardian, you should inform the guardian of your wishes to confirm that the person is willing and able to take on this responsibility. Assuming the answer is yes, provide him or her with information about the location of your wills and other estate planning documents (most likely to be held by your attorney and/or our firm).
How much:	There is no cost associated with this action.
Effect on cash flow:	Implementation of this recommendation has no impact on cash flow.

Current vs. Recommended Outcome:

Chandler and Rachel, in the event of a death in the family, few of your estate planning goals can be met. If you both passed away prior to updating your wills, nearly all assets owned would be subject to the probate process. The lack of contingent beneficiaries on some legal documents means that Phoebe's financial situation could be marginalized. As a reminder, the probate process, while efficient, provides no privacy protection. Probate can be a lengthy process, and it is possible that money would not be available for Phoebe's care during the probate process period. Since your wills do not name executors for your estates, the court will appoint an executor, which will add significant costs and time to the probate process.

Implementing the recommendations described above will provide you with privacy for your affairs and ensure your wishes are known and followed by those you leave behind in the event of death or incapacity. Although there are initial costs involved in establishing an estate plan, later life expenses will be reduced by minimizing probate and estate administration costs. Additionally, pre-planning will ensure that Phoebe's financial and day-to-day needs are met, and that she will be cared for by a trusted guardian.

Alternative Recommendations and Outcome(s):

In addition to the recommendations described above, you should discuss with your estate attorney the possibility of setting up a standby trust or an irrevocable life insurance trust (ILIT) to be the contingent beneficiary of your cash value life insurance policies. This strategy will allow you to appoint a trustee—a person or institution—to manage the life proceeds on behalf of and for the benefit of the beneficiary, Phoebe. If this strategy is recommended by your estate attorney, the attorney should draft the trust document. Our firm staff can assist in changing the ownership of the policy. Please note that if this strategy is implemented, the life insurance proceeds will transfer directly to the trust at death, thus eliminating the need to name contingent beneficiaries because the trust document will outline the beneficiary status of the trust.

Plan Implementation and Monitoring Procedures:

Although it can sometimes be difficult to feel a sense of urgency regarding estate administration matters, the implementation of the estate planning recommendations provided in this financial plan should begin as soon as possible to minimize estate administration costs, issues with probate, and general administration of your financial affairs at incapacitation or death. The first step to begin implementation involves setting up an appointment with a licensed and reputable attorney that specializes in estate planning matters. We know this can be a difficult task. As such, we do maintain a list of several estate planning attorneys for referral. In any event, you should interview more than one attorney (the first meeting should be fee free). Once you have selected an attorney, you should schedule an appointment to discuss your wishes and confirm with the attorney the recommendations made in this financial plan. Once the estate documents have been drafted and signed, please provide our firm with copies to maintain for our records.

Chandler and Rachel, your estate planning documents should be reviewed annually to determine whether existing estate planning documents still reflect your wishes or whether one or more documents need to be updated. It is important to avoid delays when updating estate planning documents and beneficiary designations. This is particularly true after major life events, as major life events can have serious ramifications on the distribution and management of property at incapacitation or death. For example, in a few states, divorce automatically revokes a beneficiary designation naming an ex-spouse; however, in other states, this is not the case. Please notify our firm if any of the following events or changes occurs, as one or more of these events may indicate a need to update your estate planning documents:

- Change in employment or promotion for Chandler or Rachel (i.e., change in income)

- Changes related to Phoebe (i.e., her death, reaching the age of majority, etc.)

- Inheritance from Chandler's parents

- Receipt of large gift

- Pregnancy or adoption

- Divorce

- New, more dangerous hobbies or jobs

- Disability of a family member

16.3 SELF-TEST

[A] Questions

Self-Test 1

Which of the following are allowable deductions from the adjusted gross estate when estimating a client's taxable estate?

(a) Qualified charitable deduction

(b) Marital deduction

(c) Deduction for taxes paid

(d) All the above

Self-Test 2

A living trust is also known as a(n):

(a) Revocable trust

(b) A-B trust

(c) Irrevocable trust

(d) POA trust

Self-Test 3

Malek and Nelda were married and have lived in Nevada their entire life. Nelda recently passed away. Their home was valued at $500,000 at Nelda's death. The basis in the home was $100,000. What is Malek's new basis in the property?

(a) $50,000

(b) $100,000

(c) $250,000

(d) $500,000

Self-Test 4

Emily and John, who are both U.S. citizens, have been married for thirty years. They currently own all property JTWROS. If John dies before Emily, how much may he leave her estate and gift tax free?

(a) $0

(b) The equivalent of the current gift tax exclusion

(c) An unlimited dollar amount

(d) An amount equal to the current year unified credit

Self-Test 5

A document written to provide directions regarding the execution of a will is known as a:

(a) letter of last instruction

(b) POA

(c) living will

(d) durable power of instruction

[B] Answers

Question 1: d

Question 2: a

Question 3: d

Question 4: c

Question 5: a

CHAPTER RESOURCES

Legal Information Institute, Cornell University Law School, 26 USC § 2518 – Disclaimers. Available at: www.law.cornell.edu/uscode/text/26/2518.

Napoleon. Philatelic Estate Disposition for the Novice, *American Philatelist*. Available at: https://classic.stamps.org/userfiles/file/Estate/PhilatelicEstateDispositionfortheNovice.pdf, p. 159.

IRS Form 706 Instructions: Generation Assignment. Available at http://www.irs.gov/instructions/i706gst/ch01.html.

CHAPTER ENDNOTE

1. Gary Langer, Poll: *Americans Not Planning for the Future.* Available at http://abcnews.go.com/Business/story?id=86992&page=1#.TvpMeZg5tFI.

Index